standard catalog of®
Stocks
&
Bonds

Rainer Stahlberg
with Colin R. Bruce II

Published by

krause publications

700 East State Street • Iola, WI 54990-0001
715/445-2214 • FAX: 715/445-4087 www.krause.com

Please call or write for our free catalog of publications.
Our toll-free number to place an order or obtain a free catalog is 800-258-0929
or please use our regular business telephone, 715-445-2214.

Library of Congress Catalog Number: 2001096280
ISBN: 0-87349-356-7

Printed in the United States of America

Table of Contents

Current Value Catalog of Cancelled U.S. Stocks & Bond Certificates

Countries

Acknowledgments

This work could not have been brought to fruition without the help of many people, in particular, Chet Krause who made his personal collection available and the back files of Krause Publications for inclusion in this work.

George H. LaBarre of LaBarre Galleries, Inc., one of the largest stock and bond certificate dealers in America, was kind enough to assist. Mr. LaBarre, using the knowledge garnered over a 20-year period, helped to place a value on many of the certificates which presented a problem in regards to pricing. However, all errors and omissions are those of the author.

In alphabetical order, I would like to thank Franz Höglinger of Austria for help with material from that country; Mikhail Istomin regarding Russian certificates, Geert Leemeijer of Netherlands for valuable advice on layout and contents; Volker Malik of Historisches Wertpapierhaus A.G. for helping to acquire various certificates; Juri Rudich of Estonia on material from the Baltic States, Robert Salvato for reviewing the first draft of the work-in-progress and making corrections, his advice on valuation of certificates reflecting his many years of experience.

Sven Stau for making his Canadian duplicates available for the book, Ricardo de Leon Tallavas for making available copies of his Mexican certificates and the valuable advice regarding their rarity; Péter Ványai of Hungary for making copies of his large collection available for inclusion and for the patient advice given over a period of time, Elvis Velez of Ecuador for assisting with stock certificates from that country.

To the more than one hundred sellers on eBay who sold me the certificates forming the bulk of the illustrations goes a special thanks. In between lost mail, lost payments, and other problems associated with mail order buying I must express thanks for their assistance and patience.

Introduction

As a child, I found a large bundle of old stock certificates in a bombed office building. For months after that, I was learning how to use large numbers to figure out the largesse I had. I can't quite remember exactly how much, but the number was in several million gold Pengos, Hungarian.

Recently a foray on eBay netted me a $1,250,000 8% bond from Texaco for the price of a bottle of wine. Such is the stuff dreams are made of. In addition to the nice design, the official looking seal, and other attractions, stock and bond certificates do represent money. I don't know about you, but I like the stuff a lot.

Nothing ever removes the romance of buying for a dollar a 1,000 share certificate of an old Western mining company and spending months finding out where it is today, only to discover that the company went out of business 80 years ago. At one time, as a conversation piece, I had an impressive looking stock certificate framed representing some $100,000 in par value, the frame cost $10 and the certificate $2.

The collecting of cancelled stock and bond certificates is said to be the fastest growing hobby in North America. There is even an official name for it, "scripophily." The term is a combination of English Scrip, which denotes ownership and the Greek word philos, which means to love. The name was chosen in 1976 as a result of a contest sponsored by the Financial Times of London. The growth in the hobby is explosive and, in spite of today's electronic trading, the romance of stock certificates is still with us. To illustrate the growth in one year, the daily eBay listings have risen from 1,500 scripophily items to over 2,000.

As with collecting of stamps, coins, or currency, the almost unlimited varieties of certificates can be a daunting task. There are excellent catalogs for stamps, coins, and paper money, but as yet we do not have well-organized catalogues and publications for the beginner collector of stocks and bonds. Neither do we have a reliable catalog of values except for some specialized issues.

Many catalogs of scripophily dealers reflect a more or less wishful desire as to what their merchandise is worth. In order to provide an unbiased picture, we have developed a price guide by following final bid prices on eBay and other auction marts. This enables one to have a good idea of the selling price of the certificates. An attempt was made to provide a large enough compendium of these prices to guide the reader. These prices reflect current values, but were derived from a relatively small sample. They are provided as a guide only.

To give you an idea of price variability, a Baltimore & Ohio Railroad certificate was offered at $20.00 by one seller on eBay, another on the same page offered one at $5.00, and a page over, 10 different certificates including

B&O were offered for $10.00. In the end, it works out at $1.00 per certificate. The only one receiving bids was the 10 certificate lot. Until you are experienced and savy about values stick to the low end of the market.

The value of certificates can range from one dollar through $10,000 for an 1878 Standard Oil Company (Ohio) stock certificate signed by John D. Rockefeller. Many professionals have framed stock certificates on their office walls, while others are treasured mementoes of a business career, business ventures, or failures. Then we have the great frauds from the gold mine stocks of the "Wild West" to the Canadian Javelin Company and the Bre-X Minerals Ltd. scandal. Because of the relatively low price, a great collection can be assembled at low cost.

The value of a stock certificate depends on:
* rarity
* the issuer
* signatures
* quality of engraving
* overall appearance
* condition
* date of issue

Occasionally, we hear about someone striking it rich from an old certificate (most of these anecdotes are connected to mining stocks). Having a worthless certificate turning into a $20,000 windfall does not happen often, and requires plenty of detective work. I followed the history of a small mining venture through four amalgamations only to find that it's still a penny stock. During the process, I learned of the ups and downs of a number of struggling companies and the dreams of the investors. The search was fun and provided hours of entertainment, as well as an interesting history lesson.

There is a great discussion among dealers about survivability, generally it's assumed that only 5% of the certificates, survive to reach collectors. There are some companies who have a policy to destroy cancelled certificates, while those of other companies are available in great numbers and varieties. Prices for rare certificates can greatly drop when a hoard is discovered in some unlikely place.

Scripophily can be as challenging as any other hobby; I hope that the following material is of some help to you to enjoy the wacky world of high finance. This is the first edition of what we hope to be "The Standard Catalog of Stocks and Bonds," as such, it's far from complete. Included are foreign certificates as a primer, in the future, separate volumes will be issued for foreign certificates.

Your comments, suggestions or corrections are welcome to improve the quality and completeness of forthcoming volumes.

Chapter 1

History of Stocks and Bonds

In one form or another, the history of stocks and bonds parallels the history of money and commerce. Stocks usually represent a portion of ownership in an incorporated entity, while bonds represent indebtedness of a government or a business. There are also preferred shares, which can be both. Stocks can be voting or non-voting, with a myriad variations to suit the needs of the issuing entity. Then there are warrants, deferred stocks, stock options and the like.

Prior to paper, there were clay and bronze tablets representing ownership interest in many enterprises. Papyrus and parchment came into use, and existing examples show a wide variety of financial transations. With the introduction of papermaking, we saw a gradual swing toward paper certificates.

One of the premier stock companies, still in existence to this day, is the Hudson's Bay Company. Its story is as follows: England's King Charles II was an impecunious monarch surrounded by hungry courtiers. He was always glad of an opportunity to satisfy them by concessions that cost him nothing. Many of them were adventurers untroubled by scruples and ready to gamble on the chance of lucrative returns. Two Frenchmen, the Sieur de Groseilliers and Pierre Esprit Radisson, won the courtiers interest with tangible evidence of wealth of the fur areas around Hudson's Bay.

A company was formed; the king's cousin, Prince Rupert, was placed at its head, and in 1670, a royal charter was issued giving to "The Governor and Company of Adventurers of England trading into Hudson's Bay" the monopoly of trade in that area, and full ownership of all lands that were reached through Hudson Strait. It was a profitable venture for the original backers. The initial £10,500 of stock increased in value to £104,000 during the next fifty years, and during that period, there were annual dividends as high as 150 percent.

While the French Revolution and the Napoleonic wars were making a bloody and fiery tragedy on the continent of Europe, a change occurred in England, that in the long run has made the siege of the Bastille and the battle of Waterloo seem almost insignificant by comparison. This change was the Industrial Revolution. No other event in modern history has affected the lives of the common men more tremendously, or opened up wider vistas of human progress, or caused keener suffering and discontent.

A revolution does two things—it overthrows an old order, and in its place, sets up or tries to set up a new order. The revolutions of history have been of different kinds; they have taken place in different fields. Some have affected government—political; some have affected the church—religious; some have affected the life and privileges of certain groups of people—social. Many, perhaps most, great revolutions have been attended with much noisy and destructive violence—war, executions, migrations, confiscations. However, some like the Intellectual Revolution have taken place more quietly, but none the less effectively.

The Industrial Revolution was mainly peaceful, because it was mechanical; but it was destructive as well as constructive, and after it got started, it was also very noisy. It was a fundamental change or a series of changes in the methods of producing cloth, iron, steel and other manufactured goods. It was largely the displacing of handwork by machine work.

The history of the Industrial Revolution is reflected through stock and bond certificates in minute detail. These certificates, unlike stamps are printed on durable paper and were treasured. Thus, we have them today to illustrate the modern history of the world. Initially, large enterprises were made possible by forming partnerships. However, as very large projects were taking place, companies were formed, and stock issued to represent the investment made by a person or an entity. In my collection, there are stock certificates ranging from one share to 550,000 shares.

Starting in England, but rapidly spreading to the United States, we saw:

- Machines driven by steam engines or by water power were invented to take the place of human labor in making cloth and other commodities.
- The age of iron, steel, and coal was ushered in by a long series of inventions, which made it possible to produce and use these commodities on a large scale.
- The invention of the steam locomotive and the steamboat revolutionized transportation and commerce.
- Millions and millions of working people, who had previously labored in their own homes with handlooms or simple tools, now left their homes to work in the factories, mines, and mills. This caused the industries to grow by leaps and bounds.
- Capitalism gained immensely in power and importance, because the new factories, mines, and railways were owned and controlled by capitalists. The capitalists were also the employers of the workers.
- The old restrictions upon industry and trade imposed by the guilds and the mercantilist statesmen were taken away to clear the field for free business competition. This, however, was a temporary phase.
- Industry and commerce expanded tremendously, soon overshadowing agriculture by flooding the market with machine-made goods at low prices. This made it possible for common people to have more conveniences.
- Population, increasing at an unheard of rate, was more and more concentrated in the cities. They were the industrial and commercial centers, until the majority of the people were no longer found in the country, but rather, in the cities.

An example of how people took advantage of the Industrial Revolution, is the history of the Pullman Car Company. When long distance railway travel became a reality in the 1850s, passengers had to endure heat and dust or cold depending on the season. Given that most of the trains were short-line affairs, passengers had to disembark and carry their bags to the next railroad. George Mortimer Pullman, a contractor and cabinetmaker, saw an opportunity. He designed a sleeping car that ushered in long-distance passenger comfort.

These cars traveled from one railway to another, and cars were switched to new trains without the passengers having to leave their cars. The cars featured fold-down berths, and the interiors were lavishly decorated with staff to serve the passengers.

When air travel took the passengers away from the ocean liners another major shift in paradigm occurred. These are all detailed on the vignettes of stock and bond certificates, making the certificates themselves a true reflection of history. The large number of bonds from Czarist Russia, Nazi Germany and pre Peoples Republic of China illustrates that not all bonds are made equal. I very much doubt that any of these will ever have any real fiscal value, what they have is collector value, and many times that exceeds the face value. This is small consolation to the original investors.

The vignettes (small pictures) on older certificates provide us with a fascinating glimpse of times past. Looking at the vignette of an older railroad certificate shows two trains in a station with a switching yard in the background. Some others show some of the great locomotives at the century's turn.

Interestingly, many railroad companies issued certificates in the 1950s showing turn-of-the-century scenes. Phelps Dodge Corporation vignette shows the great mining operation with a smelter in the foreground. Some collectors spend hours studying the details. It's a tribute to engravers at the American Bank Note Company and similar companies that when you look through a magnifying glass a whole other level of detail is revealed.

There are many dealers of scripophily. Most will offer their wares on the Internet, and you will find some at most coin and paper money shows. Stamp dealers specializing in revenue stamps were some of the first dealers in this market, as most older certificates will have stock transfer stamps either on them, or attached to, the transfer slip. Most foreign governments also like the idea of generating revenue from these transactions. You will quite often find certificates embossed by British, Dutch, or French revenue agencies, or having revenue stamps affixed to them.

There are an incredible variety of companies issuing scrip ranging from blue chips to cow chips. There is constant change in the mix of companies, amalgamations, takeovers, bankruptcy, you name it. With self-made millionaires, the saying is that the first generation makes it, the second generation keeps it, and the third generation pisses it away. With corporations there is somewhat greater longevity, but William Bernstein, in *The Intelligent Asset Allocator,* noted that every major traded company at the beginning of the Civil War no longer exists.

The discontinuity adds another dimension to the hobby, as we look at successor companies that have taken over. In my collection, I have General Plywood Corporation becoming General Resources Corporation, American Tobacco Company turning into American Brands and American Locomotive Company ending up as Alco Products, Inc. This constant change leads to a greater variety of stock certificates for the collector.

In my modest collection, I have varieties of certificates documenting the ups and downs of several companies. These changes can be observed through changing par values, names, signatures, state of incorporation and other manifestations of corporate efforts to better the company's position in life. This is particularly evident where the founder surrenders control to hired hands, sometimes for the better. We all have heard stories how the stubbornness of the founders has led to economic decline in a company's fortunes.

As you accumulate additional certificates you will observe an evolution in the design and information included on certificates. It may start as anti-counterfeiting designs through changes required by regulatory agencies. From the simple designs of pre-1850 certificates to the complex borders and vignettes of the early 1900s to today's machine-readable designs these are reflected in most collections.

Most English certificates derived from the old £5 banknote, in size and in design. This perhaps explains the lack of vignettes on certificates from that country. London, being one of the premier banking centers in the world, was instrumental in raising the financing for much of the world's industrial undertaking. One will encounter bonds and share certificates financing railways in Venezuela, mines in Russia, utilities in Turkey and various other undertakings issued in London, and denominated in English pounds.

One of the ironies are the stock certificates of labor unions. These were mostly issued to finance union buildings, and the like. We see share certificates issued by Union Labor Temples to finance their buildings. This is where the working class turned into budding capitalists.

The era of stock and bond certificates is passing. With the increased use of computers, which are better-suited to maintaining record of ownership and transfers, we see fewer and fewer certificates being issued. There may come a time when they will be a rarity and none, perhaps, may be printed in the future. Even today, they are phased out by major traders to simplify accounting tasks. This provides an added incentive to obtain them now "while the getting is good." So head for your favorite flea market or cruise the Web for sales or auctions to add to your "riches."

Chapter 2

What is a certificate?

A more detailed history on the evolution of certificates traces back to the old land grants from the feudal days. The major components were:

- name of the issuer
- name of the grantee
- a description of the land, its size and location
- the date of the grant
- a signature and a seal of the grantor

Stock and bond certificates invariably show the name of the issuer, the date, name of the owner (except for bearer certificates), the denomination or number of shares, signature of authorized officers, and the seal of the issuer.

The very early certificates were rather small, the size of a check, and very plain. Most simply stated that a number of shares were owned or the dollar value of indebtness. By the early 1840s, we see a definite change in certificates, they are more elaborate, larger and are printed on high-quality paper. This was done in part to deter counterfeiting, and in part, as a form of corporate advertising.

Generally speaking, the so-called temporary certificates do not have vignettes. They usually contain the words "Temporary Certificate - Exchangeable for Engraved Certificate When Prepared." These are usually the least expensive to purchase, and unless it's from a company whose certificates are desired by collectors, will remain relatively inexpensive regardless of age.

As your collection grows, so will your circle of contacts with other collectors. This is when you will start grading your certificates. Grading depends on the type of certificate, for bonds of the Confederate States of America the following is used:

VG (Very Good): Heavily folded but not damaged.

Fine: The borders may be uneven or trimmed. There may be light staining and aging. No major damage.

VF (Very Fine): The paper is fairly bright and free from noticable aging. The borders are intact all around.

EF (Extremely Fine): Single fold.

The criteria for modern certificates is more stringent:

Poor: Some damage with staining or heavy wear.

Fair: Plenty of folds or wear, staple holes.

Fine: Folds and wear.

Very Fine: Minor trace of wear.

Extremely fine: Slight wear, no folds.

Uncirculated: No folds, no staples, no wear.

The cancellation can be of several types, most often encountered are:

- punch out cancels of small holes, sometimes forming words
- punch out cancels of larger holes
- cut out cancels made with a knife or scissors
- slit cancels made with a knife
- pen cancels
- rubber stamp cancels

In general, most people collect issued certificates which have dates, serial numbers, denominations, and signatures all filled in. Unissued certificates may have dates, number of shares and/or signatures blank. Specimen certificates are used for various purposes, mostly as samples attached to prospectuses of new issues. These certificates usually have 00000 as serial number or no serial numbers at all. From time to time, one may encounter "proof" certificates. These are printed on special India paper or heavy stock and are used by engravers to check their work and by printers for a final approval by the customer.

Many bonds and foreign bearer stock certificates often have coupons attached to them. These can be underneath, on the side, or on the top of the certificate. There is a small market for those collecting coupons only. Many of the coupons have a small vignette making them visually attractive.

The major printers past and present of American certificates are:

ABN: American Bank Note Company
EAW: E.A. Wright & Co.
CBN: Columbian Bank Note Company
CNB: Continental Bank Note Company
FBN: Franklin Bank Note Company
FLB: Franklin Lee Bank Note
HBN: Hamilton Bank Note
HLB: Homer Lee Bank Note
JBN: Jeffries Banknote Company
NBN: National Bank Note Company
NYB: New York Bank Note
RWHE: Rawdon, Wright, Hatch & Edson Bank Note
RBN: Republic Bank Note
SBN: Security Bank Note
SCB: Security Columbian Bank Note
W&S: Waterlow & Sons Bank Note
WBN: Western Bank Note

There are many others who printed certificates, but the most prominent engravers were to be found at the above named companies.

If the certificate was signed or issued to a notable or infamous person the value would be higher.

There are three ways to hold an actual certificate:

1. Having a stock certificate in your name issued which you physically hold.
2. Have your stock certificate held in your broker's office making it immediately available for sale.
3. Have the certificate issued in your broker's name, often called "street name" and your ownership confirmed with your broker's monthly statements.

The third option is the one used by most people and that why so many of the cancelled certificates bear the name of various stock brokers. A subgroup consist of certificates issued to estates of various individuals or minors.

Most stock certificates will contain a par value designation. In the case of bonds, par is the value at redemption date. For example, with a stock certificate if you started out with a $100 par value share and the stock splits two for one, then the new certificates will say par $50. To avoid confusion, many companies designate their shares as having no par value. Just another variety the collector has to watch out for.

The signatures will vary with changes in officers of a given company. I have several certificates of the same company with different signatures over the years. Then there is a practice of adding the signatures in the form of a label as the stocks are issued. Another variety for collectors to consider.

High-quality certificates printed by banknote companies will often contain a watermark to foil counterfeiters, adding another dimension to collectors and providing greater variety to the hobby.

A few words on definitions of terms found on certificates:

ADR or American Depository Receipt.
Foreign corporations sometimes deposit shares in the custody of an American bank or trust company. Shares are then issued to represent ownership that can trade in domestic securities markets. The American issued ADR's are treated as negotiable American certificates.

Bearer security: Ownership is evidenced by possession of the certificate.

Coupon: Small detachable claims on some bond and foreign stock certificates. Usually they are for semi-annual payments of interest or numbered for certain share certificates.

Odd lot: Any certificates for less than 100 shares or more than 100 shares not divisible by 100.

Registered: A specific owner is assigned to each certificate and carried on the books of the corporation or its agent.

Round lot: Stock certificate for 100 shares or multiples of 100 shares.

Chapter 3

How to Begin Collecting

New collectors usually start by buying 50 or 100 different certificates either on eBay or from a dealer. This usually works out to spending a dollar per certificate. It's very much like smoking the first cigarette—for most the die is cast. This is usually followed by visits to area antique shops, flea markets, garage sales, and other potential sources of scripophily items. Others start off by finding a certificate or two up in the attic.

Once you have a couple of hundred certificates you will know which topics are of interest to you. Some people display their collection on their walls—very impressive. However, the certificates will fade and age when exposed to sunlight, and over time, you will find the vivid red turning reddish brown and other signs of deterioration. Most collectors use sheet protectors housed in binders to store their certificates. Very large certificates present another problem—the need to fold them. One collector of note uses map filing cabinets to house his oversize unfolded bonds.

Once you have taken the first step, you will, from time to time, come across "certificate books." These usually contain 250 or so unissued certificates with stubs, very much like collecting "bank packs" of currency. This is the turning point when a collector becomes a part-time dealer, as you may want to keep one and sell the others. This was the initial impetus for a collector to become a dealer in Maine.

Using the Web to trade with other collectors is one of the more satisfying ways of adding to your collection. Some estimate that over one third of the 100,000+ collectors trade on the web. For new collectors, this is a good way to learn about relative values and scarcity of various certificates. A note of caution about buying by mail order, if you paid $1 for the certificate and $3 postage then your actual investment is $4. When bidding on certificates always be sure of the mailing charges. Some small dealers make more on shipping charges than on sales of the certificates. Buyer beware! Sending certificates by priority mail means that the post office is getting richer at your expense.

You will find that most antique dealers will have a few certificates, some framed, at prices starting at $10 and up. If you have an idea of the value of the certificate, it may be worth buying. Generally speaking, I try to trade my duplicates for them or give them a pass as most antique dealers do not know the values and go for the most they can get for them. Flea markets usually have more reasonable prices, and sometimes bundles of the certificates can be had.

Sources of Cancelled Certificates

The ultimate great sources of cancelled certificates are the warehouses of companies and transfer agents looking after transferring, canceling, and issuing stock and bond certificates. There are few big scripophily dealers who actively solicit such large accumulations and resell them in smaller lots to other dealers. These are sources of many of the modern cancelled certificates.

Another source are the liquidators for bankrupt companies. One dealer purchased 700 pounds of cancelled certificates of one publicly traded company. Sometimes when older buildings are demolished, bundles of certificates are discovered. Given their money-like appearance, these will eventually find their way to the marketplace.

Older pre-1920 certificates come to market from individuals, estates, flea markets, small hoards, auctions and the like. Then there is the Internet, the explosive growth in scripophily can be attributed to the World Wide Web. Stock certificates are light, easily mailed, and can be traded internationally.

There are a number of organizations and dealers with Internet sites, some of these are:

International Bond & Share Society
(scripophily.org) a London-based association of those interested in the hobby.

Scripophily.Com (scripophily.com) one of the largest and best dealers on the Web. They also do research on specific certificates you may have (for a fee).

R.M. Smythe (rm-smythe.com) an eminent company selling old certificates and will research old, inactive or unlisted stocks.

Collectible Stocks and Bonds
(oldstocks.com) another large dealer

Goldsheet (goldsheet.simplenet.com) helps to research companies

Many of these Web sites have links to others, and if you bookmark them, a few hours can be spent looking at certificates, making trades, or getting information on a company you are researching. The ease of communicating through e-mail makes collecting a joy.

Topical Collecting

Initially, most collectors buy everything they can afford. Eventually they will specialize. Certificates railroads, automobile makers, steamship lines, mining and oil companies are the most popular topics. Many people collect bond certificates of Imperial Russia, stock certificates from ex-colonial lands and the like.

Those who collect railroad stocks and bonds have the greatest variety available. There were hundreds of companies in the US, and if you collect worldwide, then the number of companies is in the thousands. Add to these the various time periods, along with bond issues, and a serious collector can easily have over 10,000 certificates. Steam locomotives of old railroad certificates are the most romantic and aesthetic, and this contributes their relatively high value, in spite of the large numbers available.

Topical collecting is the way most people will focus as their collection grows. I must admit that in my case, this led me from American mining companies to those of other lands, and eventually to industrial stocks and bonds. More or less what has happened to commercial activities worldwide. Along the way, you learn about the natural resources of many lands, tin from Malaya (later Malaysia) becoming ointment tubes for pharmaceuticals in Switzerland. Nickel from Canada becomes part of stainless steel in the United States and the zircon sands of Australia become zirconium metal containers for the nuclear fuel rods used in the electric power industry worldwide.

Depending on your interests, scripophily lets you explore other lands, the history of your state or the country of your ancestors. For example, if you collect certificates of the entertainment industry, a certificate of Houdini Pictures signed by the magician will set you back $42,000. One collection houses nothing but bonds issued to support bible societies around the world, another contains stocks and bonds issued to support Red Cross activities internationally. Given the huge number of issuers, almost all topics are represented in collections. One phone pioneer has over 200 telephone company-related certificates in his collection.

Small companies do not hold the glamour of large, well-known enterprises. This is why inspite of relative rarity, most never make it out from the low dollar range in price. The exceptions are the share certificates issued to the founders. Once I bought a lot of certificates, most were in the 100-share range. However, two were issued for 740,000 shares each—one to the President and another to his wife.

This catalog has listings in an alphabetical format. The reason is simple: Companies diversify as they grow. For example, the Canadian Pacific Railway company recently split into five companies, they represent the railway, hotels, shipping, airline, and petroleum interests of the company. During World War II, the Singer sewing machine company made guns and other defense-related equipment, so where should we list it? It's far easier to use a strick alphabetical order, rather than to confuse the reader with topical classifications.

When the bubble burst on the dot-com companies (we never know when we are in a bubble until it bursts), these certificates gained an instant collector following. I see these trading between $5 to $50, that is a higher value than what the stock represents! After the September 11, 2001 terrorist attacks defense-related stock certificates are in demand. Collecting mimics the market in many ways.

Chapter 4

Frauds with Old Certificates

Western gold mining areas in the late 1800s were overrun with shady operators, who, with a hole in the ground and a hotel room as head office, incorporated Colorado companies by the hundreds. The Cripple Creek area was the center of many of these scams. All night "pen parties" resulted in hundreds of certificates being signed and then other operators took the trains to the east to sell these to hopeful investors.

Another aspect of frauds has to do with old certificates. As with any other hobby, scams abound. These range from counterfeiting to duping people in buying "gold backed bonds." The Securities and Exchange Commission's Central Regional Office in Denver, CO is actively engaged in prosecuting and placing injunctions on dealers in these materials.

A classic is the one involving bonds of the Chicago, Saginaw and Canada Railroad Company. In 1873, 5,500-$1,000 thirty-year gold backed bearer bonds were issued, the word GOLD was prominently overprinted on the certificates. The creditors of the company forced it into bankruptcy in 1876,

and they received less than 25% of what was owed to them. The bond certificates remained in court archives until they were sold, many went to a museum in Grand Rapids, MI.

The museum sold the bonds with other information about the CS&C railroad for $29.95 each; their only value is that of collectible memorabilia. Then along came the scam artists who sold these to investors at face value, and with the promise that they would be paid in gold. Similar scams using East Alabama & Cincinnati Railroad Co., Mad River and Lake Erie Railroad Co. and Marietta & Northern Georgia Railroad Co. also exist.

Some people buy unissued certificates and fill in their name to use as a conversation piece. Some more enterprising individuals try to use these as collateral and this is the reason why most unissued certificates are cancelled. One person in my past used unissued certificates filled in with his name as collateral in a business venture to secure $100,000 loan from another bank Fortunately, or unfortunately, (depending on which side you are on) it failed and the fraud came to light.

Chapter 5

Collector Resources

There are very few publications dealing with scripophily. Most of these describe the hobby and are mostly topical dealing with one area of collecting only.

Currently the following books are available for collectors of certificates:

American Automotive Stock Certificates. Lawrence Falater,1997, 400pp.

American Railroad Stock Certificates. Anne-Marie Hendy, 1988.

The Art of the Market: Two Centuries of American Business As Seen Through Its Stock Certificates. Bob Tamarkin, et al, 1999.

Collector's Guide to Old U.S. Stocks and Bonds. Andrew C. Hall Sr., 1984.

Comprehensive Catalog and History of Confederate Bonds. Douglas M. Ball, 1997.

Confederate and Southern States Bonds: A Descriptive Listing, Including Rarity and Values. Grover C. Criswell, 1992, 4th edition, 415pp.

Historic Shares of the USA, volume 1. Hans Braun, Verlag Hermann Schmidt, Mainz, 1996.

International Price Guide to Antique Stocks and Bonds, Igor de Saint Hyppolyte, Editions Mayer, 1982, 274pp.

Mirrors of the Economy: Historic Shares of the USA. Hans Braun, 1996, volume 1, 283 pp.

Old Securities. Drumm, Ulrich & Hensler, Alfons W., Dortmund, Harenberg Kommunikation, 1978.

Old Securities: Ottoman Empire and Turkey. Drumm & Henseler, in German 1983.

Old Securities: Russian Railway Bonds. Drumm & Henseler, in German, 1979.

Scripophily: The Art of Finance. Keith Hollender, 1983,160pp, 120 illust.

The Stock & Bond Collectors Price Guide. Bill Yacthman, Greentree Stocks 1984, Sedona Arizona.

Stocks and Bonds of North American Railroads: collectors' guide with values. Terry Cox, BNR Press 1995.

General information on existing companies is available through annual publications like Moodies or Standard and Poor's books on publicly traded companies and utilities. These can be useful for obtaining information on corporate activities and help you to navigate through amalgamations and name changes. Many collectors of certificates also collect annual reports of the companies.

Current Value Catalog of Cancelled U.S. Stocks & Bond Certificates

The numbering system is as follows:
A450-12-2
A=Company name starting with the letter A
450=Identifier assigned to the company
-12=12th certificate listed under the company
-2=Signature or transfer agent variation

The order of listing starts with common shares, followed by preferred shares and bonds. Unless otherwise indicated all listings are for cancelled, common shares.

Abbreviations:
f=fractional certificate
o/p=overprint
s=specimen
t=temporary certificate
v=vignette
w=warrant to purchase
u/u unissued/un-cancelled
u/c unissued/cancelled
i/u issued/un-cancelled
**=item is pictured*

3¢ to 49¢ Stores, Inc. (NY par $10)
50-20-10, 1921, v, 35 sh., brown **$6.00**

A

A & B Automatic Carburetor Corporation
A50-20-10, 1930, v, 50 sh., GOES, green . .**$30.00**

Able Grocery Co., Inc. (TN)

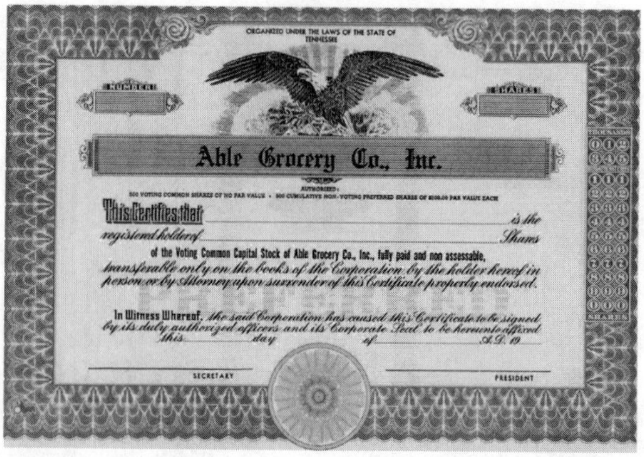

AB80-30-10,* 19xx, v, u/u preferred certificate (par $100), w/o imprint, 11" x 7-1/2" orange $3.00**

The Acacia Gold Mining Company (CO par $1)

*AC70-20-10, 1902, 1,000 sh., grey.......$8.00

Accomack Storage Company, Inc. (VA par $50)

*AC110-20-10, 19xx, v, u/u certificate, orange
.............................$4.00

Ace Liquors, Inc. (AZ no par)

*AC130-20-10, 19xx, v, u/u certificate, w/o
imprint, 11" x 7-3/4", green border.......$3.00

Acme Brick Company (IL par $100)
AC180-20-10, 19xx, v, u/u certificate, grey
.............................$8.00

Acme Missiles & Construction Corporation (DE par 25¢)
AC200-20-10, 1970, 50 class A sh. on a less than
100 sh. certificate, red on pink.........$15.00

The Adams Copper Mining and Refining Company (CO)
AD100-20-10, 1901, v, 100 sh., gold and black
.............................$20.00

Addison Rail Road Company (VT)
AD140-20-10, 1873, v, 1 sh., Hooper, Lewis Co.,
purple $55.00

Admiral Corporation (DE)

*AD180-30-10, 1970, v, 100 sh., ABN, green
.............................$4.00

Adventure Consolidated Copper Company (MI)
AD290-20-10, 1902, v, 100 sh., green.....$15.00

Ahmeek Mining Company
AH100-20-10, 1922, v-beavers, 5 sh., green
.............................$18.00

Air Products and Chemicals Inc. (MI)
AI110-20-10, 1961, v, 1 sh. on a less than 100 sh.
certificate, EAW, green $4.00

Airport Limousine Company (NV par $1)
AI140-20-10, 1946, v, 5,000 sh., orange ...$20.00

**The Akron Odd Fellows Temple Company
(OH par 50¢)**
AK120-20-10, 1917, v, 5 sh., grey $5.00

**Alabama Great Southern Railroad Company
(par $50)**
AL80-20-10, 1895, v, 1 sh., green. $36.00

**The Alabama and Vicksburg Railway
Company (MS 1889, par $100)**
AL120-20-10, 19xx, v, u/c certificate, grey
. . . .$20.00

Alamo Coal Company (CO par $100)

*AL170-20-10, 1940, v, 100 pref. sh., green
. . . .$10.00

**The Alaska and Cape Nome Co.
(CA 1900, par $1)**

*AL200-20-10, 1900, v, 100 sh., green border,
brown $80.00

**Alaska Consolidated Copper Company
(AZ)**
AL230-20-10, 1917, v, $500 first mort. and collateral trust conver. 6% gold bond, green. . .$70.00

Alaska Housing Finance Corporation

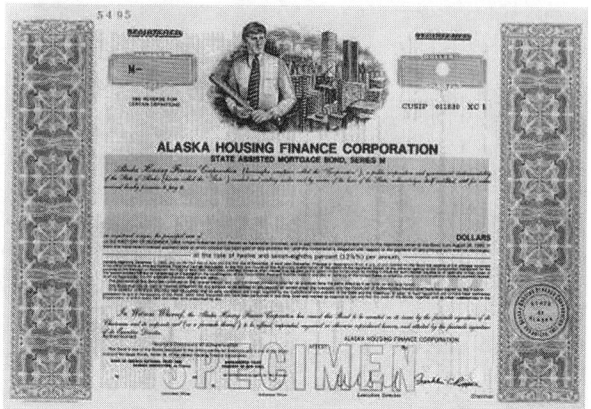

*AL270-20-10, 19xx, v, u/u state assisted mortgage
bond, green. $10.00

Alaska Petroleum and Coal Company (WA)
AL310-20-10, 1917, 766 sh., ...$20.00

Alaska State Bank (AK par $100)
AL350-30-10, 1961, v, 10 sh., grey border
. . . .$12.00

**Alaska Transportation, Trading, Mining &
Manufacturing Co. (WV)**

*AL380-20-10, 19xx, v, u/u certificate, grey
. . . .$14.00

The Alaskan Bonanza Mining, Trading and Transportation Company

AL410-20-10, 1897 $5.00 Profit Sharing Development Bond, green **$36.00**

Albuquerque Hotel Company (NM)

AL450-20-10, 1923, v, 50 sh., 12" x 9", green border **$20.00**

Alcar Instruments Inc. (NJ 1953, par $0.10)

*AL490-20-10, 1967, v, 100 sh., SCB, 11-3/4" x 8-1/2", green **$4.00**

The Alcatraz Company

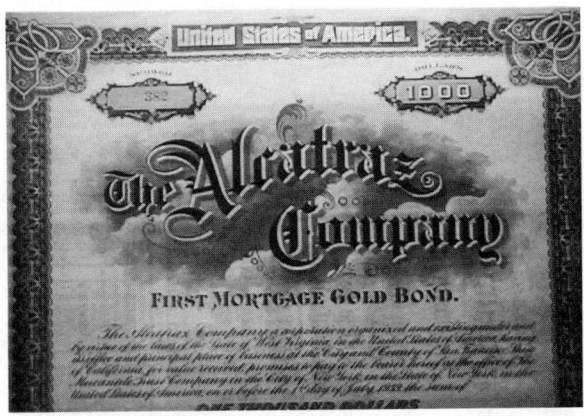

*AL520-40-10, 1899, v, $1,000 1st Mortgage gold bond, green **$21.00**

Alco Products, Incorporated (NY 1901, par $1)

AL550-20-10, 1964, v, 20 sh. on a less than 100 sh. certificate, ABN, 11-3/4" x 8", brown **$5.00**

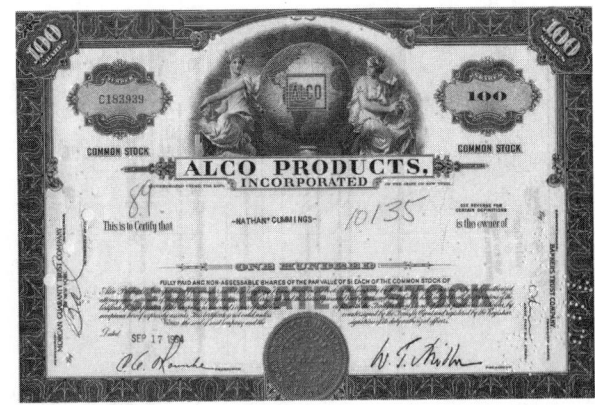

*AL550-30-10, 1964, v, 100 sh., ABN, 12" x 8", green **$4.00**

The Alden Type Setting & Distributing Machine Co. (NY)

AL580-20-10, 18xx, v, unissued certificate, grey **$33.00**

Aldon Industries, Inc. (PA)

A L610-20-10, 1971, v, 10 sh. on a less than 100 sh. certificate, SCB, blue **$4.00**

Allegheny and Bellevue Street Railway Company (PA par $50)

*AL650-20-10, 18xx, v, u/u certificate, Mackenzie Davis & Company, Pittsburgh, brown . . .**$15.00**

Allentown Base Ball Club, Inc. (PA par $10)

AL690-20-10, 1929, v, i/u 1 sh. certificate, grey border **$150.00**

Allied Artists Pictures Corporation (DE)

*AL720-50-10, 1972, w, 900 sh., warrant, void after May 15, 1975; SCB, 12" x 8", blue . .$5.00

Allied Chemical Corporation (NY)

*AL750-30-10, 1965, v, 10 sh. on a less than 100 sh. certificate, 12" x 8", blue. $4.00

*AL750-40-10, 1967, v, 100 sh., green. $5.00
AL750-45-10, 1962, v, 100 sh., ABN, brown
. . . .$5.00

Allied Oil Corporation
AL780-20-10, 1921, 60 sh., blue $5.00

Alma Lincoln Mining Company
AL810-20-10, 1940, v, 1,000 sh., 11" x 7-1/4", orange. $20.00

The Alpha Mining and Milling Company (WI par $1)

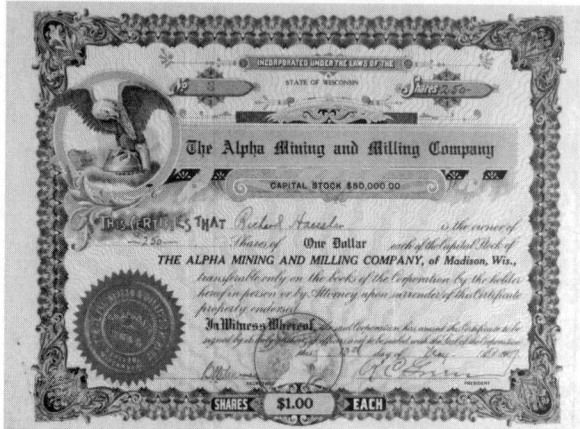

*AL840-20-10, 1907, v, 250 sh., w/o imprint, 11" x 8", grey border $28.00

The Alpine Aqueduct Company (IL $25)

*AL860-20-10, 19xx, v, u/u certificate, brown
. . . .$4.00

Alta Silver Mining Company (par $2)
AL920-20-10, 190x, v, unissued certificate, grey on yellow paper, 10" x 4-1/4" $7.00

Altamina Mining Corporation (UT par $5)

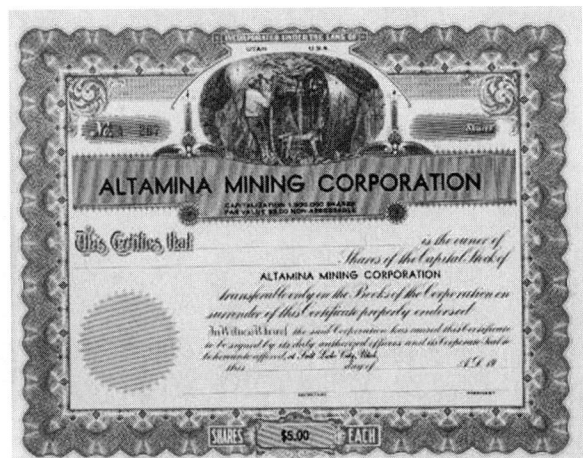

*AL950-20-10, 19xx, v, u/u certificate, brown
. . . .$4.00

Amador Star Mining Company (NV)

AM60-20-10, 1915, 500 sh., revenue stamp, grey
border $20.00

Amalgamated Gold Mines, Company (WY)

*AM100-20-10, 1902, v, 1,000 sh., brown.$100.00

Amalgamated Nevada Mines Company (par $1)

AM150-20-10, 1912, v, 1,000 sh., grey $15.00

Ambergris Mines Company

AM190-20-10, 1916, v-capitol, 100 sh., grey. .$3.00

American Airlines, Inc.

AM260-50-10, 1974, v, $2,000 10% series C due
1989, green. $7.00

*AM260-60-10, 19xx, v, $121,000 4-1/4% subord.
debenture due 1992, convertible prior to 1980,
SCB, 12"x 8", lt. green. $7.00
AM260-70-10, 1978, v, $1,000 4-1/4% subord.
debenture due 1992, orange $13.00
AM260-75-10, 1980, v, $1,000 5-1/4% subord.
debenture due 1998, red. $18.00
AM260-80-10, 1981, v, $1,000 10% series B due
1988, orange. $10.00
AM260-85-10, 1983, v, $3,000 10% series B due
1988, red. $7.00
AM260-90-10, 1984, v, $1,000 10% series C due
1989, olive $7.00

The American Atlantic and Pacific Canal Company

AM300-20-10, 1860, v, 40 sh., grey. $320.00

American Austin Car Company, Inc. (DE no par)

AM330-20-10, 1929, t, 10 sh. on a less than 100 sh.
certificate, orange border $65.00

The American Bag Loaning Co. (Limited) (NY 1883)

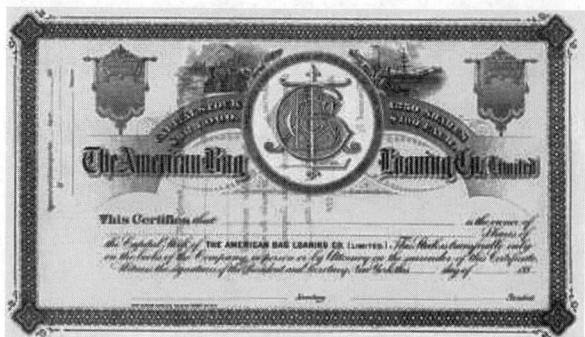

AM370-20-10, 188x, v, unissued certificate, black
....................................$10.00

American Bank Note Corporation (par $10)

AM400-40-10, 1950, v, 10 sh. on a less than 100 sh. certificate, green $7.00

AM400-45-10, 1952, v, 100 sh., orange $7.00

AM400-60-10, 1937, v, 10 sh., 6% pref. on a less than 100 sh. (Par $50) certificate, brown
...............................$12.00

The value of a stock certificate depends on:

- rarity
- the issuer
- signatures
- quality of engraving
- overall appearance
- condition
- date of issue

American Brands, Inc. (NJ par $6.25)

AM480-20-10, 1972, v, 100 sh., ABN, 12" x 8", orange............................$3.00

AM480-20-15, 1977, v, 100 sh., ABN, signature variety, 12" x 8", orange...............$3.00

American By-Products Corporation (WA par $1)

AM500-20-10, 1925, v, 3,600 sh., GOES, 11-3/4" x 9-1/4", green border $4.00

American Cable & Radio Corporation
AM510-30-10, 1959, v, 100 domestic sh., orange
.....................................$8.00

American Can Company (NJ)
*AM560-50-10, 1961 $1,000 30-year 4-1/4% bond
due 1990, l. brown* $5.00
AM460-60-10, 1971 $1,000 30-year bond, red
....$9.00
*AM580-70-10, 198x, v, $100 13-1/4% bond due
1993, red*..........................$5.00

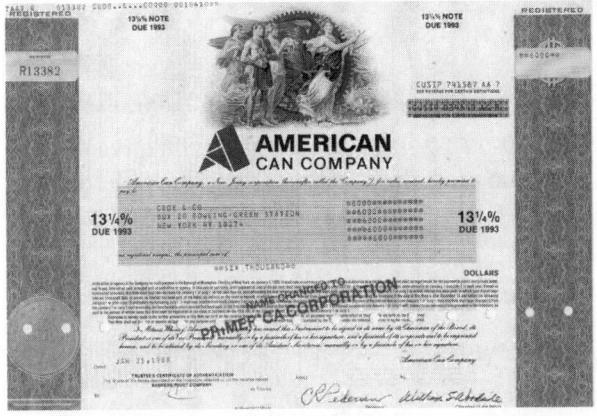

*AM580-75-10, 1988, v, $6,000 13-1/4% note due
1993, o/p name changed to Primerica Corporation, ABN, 12" x 8", red*...............$5.00

American Caramel Company
AM610-30-10, 20 pref. shares, brown $4.00

American Cities Company (NJ)
AM640-20-10, 1917, v, 6 sh., red.........$8.00
AM640-25-10, 1917, v, 6 sh., reddish brown
....$8.00

This catalog has listings in an alphabetical
format. The reason is simple: Companies
diversify as they grow. For example, the
Canadian Pacific Railway company recently
split into five companies. They represent
the railway, hotels, shipping, airline, and
petroleum interests of the company. During
World War II the Singer sewing machine
company made guns and other defense-
related equipment, so where should we list
it? It's far easier to use a strict alphabetical
order, rather than to confuse the reader
with topical classifications.

American Communications and Television, Inc. (DE par $0.001)

*AM680-30-10, 1991, 10,000 sh., SCB, 12" x 8",
red*..............................$4.00

American Compressed Fuel Company (NJ no par)

*AM710-20-10, 19xx, v, u/u certificate, The
Broun-Green Co., 12-1/4" x 9-1/4", green*.$5.00

American Copper Mining Company (MA par $2.50)
*AM750-20-10, 1864, 200 sh., Signed Sylvester
Phelps, black*.....................$175.00

American Crayon Company (OH par $100)

*AM800-30-10, 1951, v, 15 sh., green **$10.00**

American Culm Furnace Company (DE par $10)

*AM840-20-10, 1911, v, 10 sh., brown **$4.00**

American Dredging Company (PA)

*AM900-30-10, 1929, v, 36 sh., brown **$26.00**

American Dual Vest Fund, Incorporated (DE 1966, par $13.00)

AM940-40-10, 1968, v, 100 sh., red **$4.00**

*AM940-60-10, 1967, v, 100 sh. cumulative income pref. sh., to be redeemed in 1979, SCB, 12" x 6", brown **$4.00**

American Export Lines, Inc.

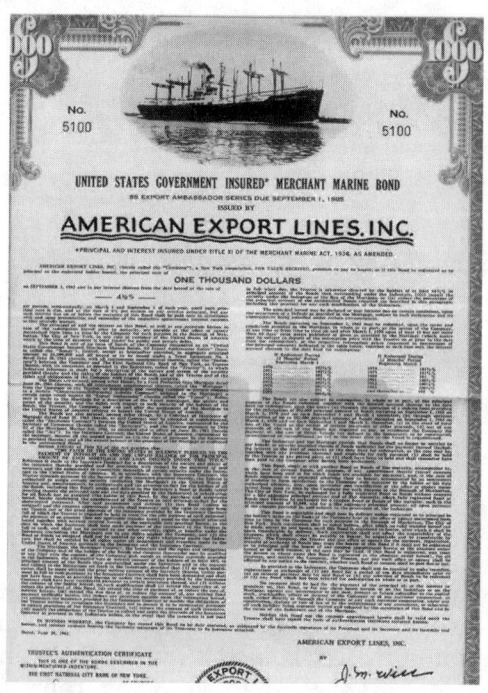

*AM980-50-10, 1961, v, $1,000 United States Government Insured Merchant Marine 4-1/2% Bond, due 1985 w. coupons, SCB, 10" x 14", orange **$15.00**

American Express Company (NY par $0.60)

*AM1020-50-10, 1976, v, 100 sh., ABN, 12" x 8",
red...............................$4.00

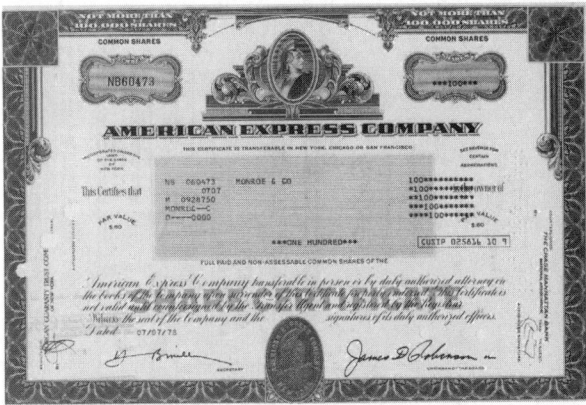

*AM1020-60-10, 1978, v, 100 sh on a blue no more
than 100,000 shares certificate ABN, 12" x 8"
.................................$4.00

American General Corporation (TX)

A successor of the American General Insurance
Company.

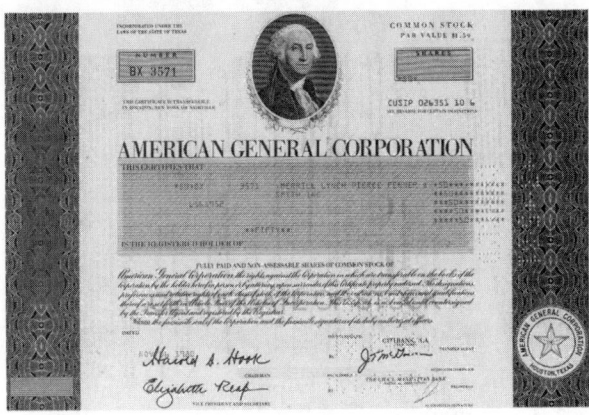

*AM1080-20-10, 1980, v-portrait of Washington,
50 sh. (par $1.50), ABN, 12" x 8", blue ...$5.00

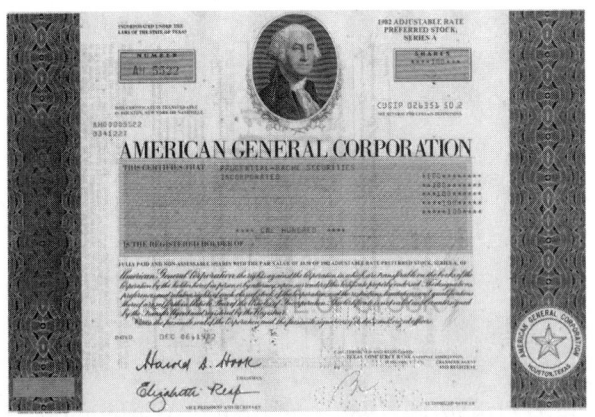

*AM1080-40-10, 1982, v-portrait of Washington,
100 sh., 1982 adjustable rate pref. stock series A,
ABN, 12" x 8", purple $5.00

American General Insurance Company (TX)

*AM1110-40-10, 1964, v-Washington on horse-
back (multicolored), 1 sh. (par $1.50),
blue............................$9.00

*AM1110-60-10, 1971, v-portrait of Washington,
22 sh. on less than 100 sh. certificate (par
$1.50), ABN, 12" x 8", brown $5.00

*AM1110-80-10, 1980, v-portrait of Washington, 94,247 sh. on a not more than 100,000 sh. certificate (par $1.50), ABN, 12" x 8", blue **$5.00**

*AM1110-100-10, 1969, v-portrait of Washington, 16 sh., $1.80 convert. pref. stock, ABN, 12" x 8", orange

. . . . **$5.00**

*AM1110-110-10, 1979, t, v-portrait of Washington, 10 sh., $1.80 convert. pref. stock, o/p note about change in par value, ABN, 12" x 8", aqua
. . . . **$5.00**

AM1110-130-10, 1968, v-Washington on horseback (multicolored), 100 $1.80 conv. pref. sh., green **$9.00**

AM1110-140-10, 1977, v-Washington, 100 sh., $1.80 conv. pref. stock, green **$5.00**

*AM1110-150-10, 1979, v-portrait of Washington, 100 $1.80 pref. sh., o/p note about change in par values, ABN, 12" x 8", green **$5.00**

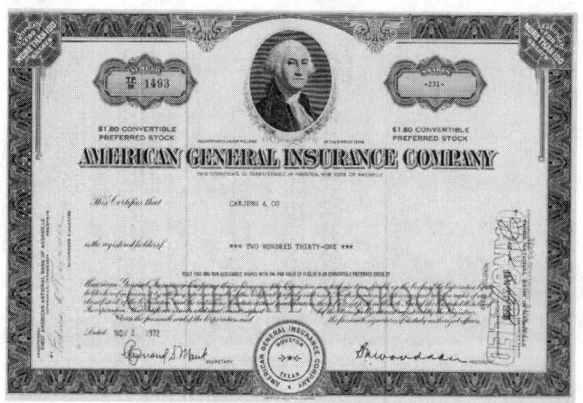

*AM1110-170-10, 1972, v-portrait of Washington, 231 sh., of $1.80 convert. pref. stock on a more than 100 sh. certificate, ABN, 12" x 8", purple
. . . . **$5.00**

*AM1110-180-10, 1977, v-portrait of Washington, 5 sh., of $0.90 convert. pref. stock series 1975 on a less than 100 sh. certificate, ABN, 12" x 8", olive **$5.00**

*AM1110-190-10, 1979, v-portrait of Washington, 100 sh., of $0.90 convert. pref. stock series 1975, ABN, 12" x 8", red **$5.00**

American Gyro Company (CO)

AM1150-10-10, 1933, v, 2,000 class A sh. (Par $0.01), brown **$8.00**

American International Corporation (NY par $100)

AM1200-30-10, 1924, v, 100 sh., ABN, 12" x 8", green **$5.00**

American Israeli Paper Mills Limited (Israel par 1 Israeli Pound)

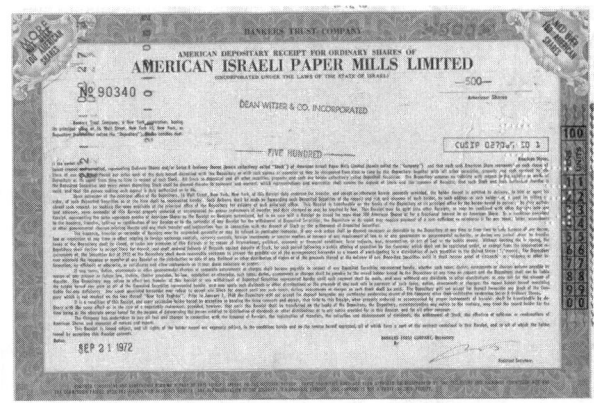

AM1240-20-10, 1972, American Depositary Receipt for 500 sh. on more than 100 sh. certificate (o/p on not over 100 shares), SCB, 12" x 8", orange **$5.00**

American Legato Co. (DE 1991, no par)

AM1300-10-10, 19xx, v, u/u, w/o imprint, 11" x 7-3/4", green **$3.00**

It is generally assumed that only 5% of certificates survive to reach collectors.

American Locomotive Company
(NY 1901, par $1)

AM1360-50-10, 1950, v, 25 sh. on a less than 100
sh. certificate, ABN, 12" x 8", brown.....**$4.00**

AM160-70-10, 1956, v, 100 sh., o/p name changed
to Alco Products Incorporated, orange....**$4.00**

American Machine & Foundry Company

AM1400-40-10, 1961, v, 15 sh. on a less than 100
sh. certificate, orange **$3.00**

AM1400-60-10, 1968, v, 100 sh., ABN, blue
....................................**$4.00**

American Medical International, Inc.

AM1470-30-10, 1986, v, $85,000 9-1/4% subordi-
nated note due 1981, green.............**$9.00**

American Meter Company

AM1500-40-10, 1948, v, 10 sh., green......**$6.00**

AM1500-50-10, 1952, v, 25 sh. on a less than 100
sh. certificate, brown **$4.00**

American Motors Corporation

AM1580-30-10, 1963, v, 50 sh. on less than 100 sh.
certificate, brown **$15.00**

AM1580-40-10, 1960, v, 100 sh., blue....**$60.00**

AM1580-50-10, 1960, v, 1,000 sh., brown
....................................**$22.00**

American National Bank (KY)

AM1620-20-10, 1898, v, 21 sh., brown **$11.00**

American Natural Gas Company (DE)

AM1660-30-10, 1972, v, 50 sh. on a less than 100
sh. certificate, SCB, green **$4.00**

American Oil Company (MT par 10¢)

*AM1700-20-10, 1917, v, 100 sh., dark brown
.................................$10.00

American Petrofina, Incorporated (DE par $1)

AM1800-30-10, 1967, v, 100 sh., class A, blue
................................$5.00

American Railway Equipment Company (NJ)

AM1870-20-10, 189x, v, u/u pref. certificate,
Western Bank Note Company, brown ...$10.00

American Safety Device Co. (NY par $50)

AM1950-20-10, 1932, v, 100 sh., green $10.00

American Safety Equipment Corporation (par $0.25)

*AM1970-30-10, 1959, v, 100 sh., blue.....$4.00

American Solvents & Chemical Corporation

*AM2200-20-10, 1931, v, 20 sh. on a less than 100
sh. certificate, Hamilton Banknote Co., orange
.................................$5.00

American Steamship Company (NY par $100)

*A2280-20-10, 19xx, u/u certificate, GOES,
orange...........................$10.00

American Sugar Company
AM2330-30-10, 1963, v, 100 sh., blue **$10.00**

American Sugar Refining Company (NJ)
AM2350-30-10, 1959, v, 100 sh., ABN, blue
. . . .**$5.00**

American Telephone and Telegraph Company (NY)

*AM2400-40-10, 1954, v, 8 sh. on a less than 100 sh. certificate (par $100), green **$20.00**

*AM2400-60-10, 1970, v-Bell, 10 sh. on a less than 100 sh. certificate, ABN, 12" x 8", green
. . . .**$5.00**
A3400-65-10, 1975, v-Bell, 7 sh. on a less than 100 sh. certificate, green **$5.00**

*AM2400-75-10, 1974, v, 100 sh., ABN, blue
. . . .**$5.00**

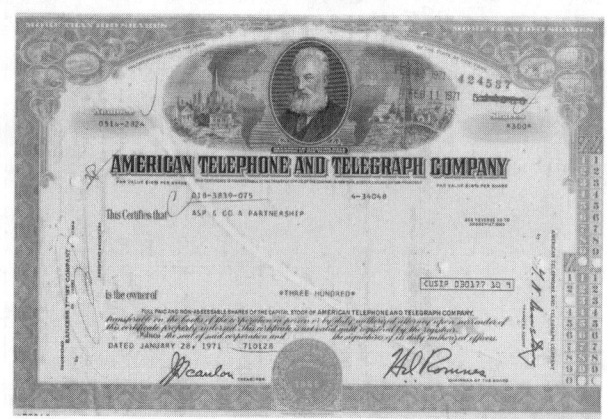

*AM2400-85-10, 1971, v, 300 sh. on a more than 100 sh. certificate, ABN, 12" x 8", orange
. . . .**$6.00**
AM2400-100-10, 1971, v, 1 $4 convert. pref. sh., deep blue and orange **$5.00**

The American Tobacco Company (NJ par $6.25)
AM2470-40-10, 1950, v, 5 sh. on a less than 100 sh. certificate, green **$4.00**
AM2470-50-10, 1960, v, 10 sh. on a less than 100 sh. certificate, Dutch revenue imprint, green
. . . .**$4.00**
AM2470-60-10, 1960, t, 100 sh., orange **$4.00**

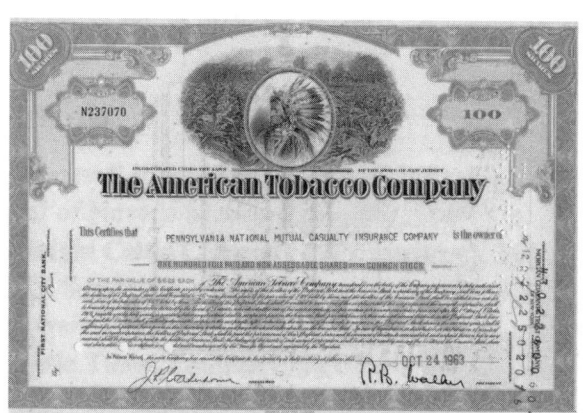

*AM2470-80-10, 1963, v, 100 sh., ABN, 11-3/4" x 8", orange $4.00

The American-Canadian Gold Mining Company (WI par $1)

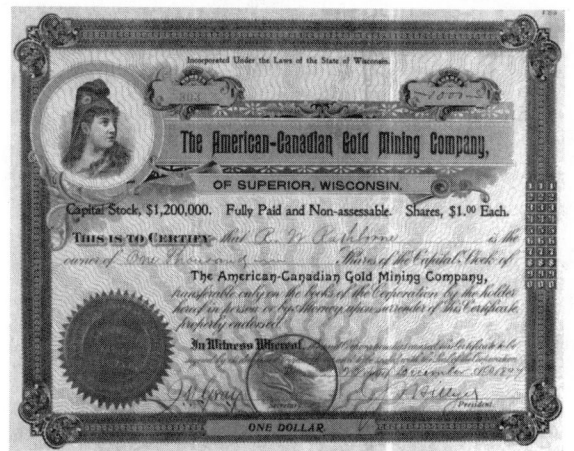

*AM2490-20-10, 1897, v, 1,000 sh., w/o imprint, 11" x 8-1/2", grey border $170.00

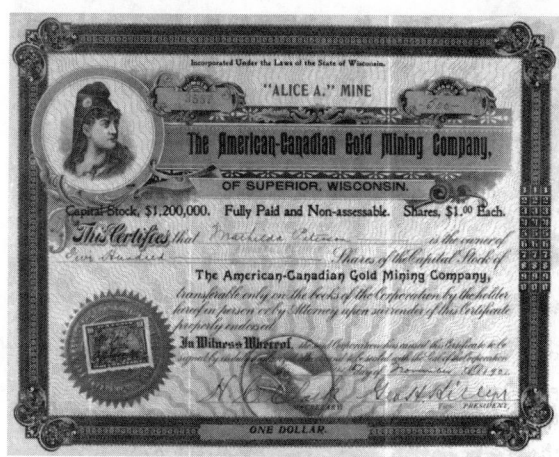

*AM2490-25-10, 1901, v, 500 sh., o/p Alice A. Mine, revenue stamp, w/o imprint, 11" x 8", grey border $150.00

American-Mexico Mining and Developing Company (SD par $1)

*AM2500-20-10, 1904, v, 100 sh., grey border $10.00

Americana Furniture, Inc. (AR)
AM2510-20-10, 1952, v, 100 sh., Northern Bank Note Co., green. $4.00

Amethyst Bullfrog Mining Company (AZ territory)
Mines located in the Bullfrog-Rhyolite mining district of Nevada near Death Valley.
AM2540-20-10, 1909, v, 1,000 sh., green . .$70.00

Ampet Corporation (OK)
AM2670-20-10, 1961, v, 100 sh., green. $4.00

The Anaconda Company (MT no par)

*AN70-20-10, 1966, v, 12 sh. on a less than 100 sh. certificate, blue. $4.00
*AN70-30-10, 1966, v, 100 sh., dark green $4.00

Anaconda Copper Mining Company (MT par $50)

AN90-40-10, 1929, v, 1 sh. on a less than 100 sh. certificate, blue $15.00

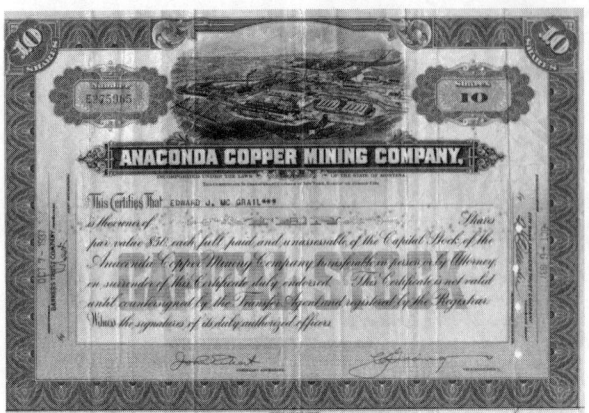

*AN90-50-10, 1937, 10 sh., ABN, 11-3/4" x 8", brown $13.00
AN90-60-10, 1940, 100 sh., green $10.00

Ancorp National Services, Inc. (DE)

AN130-20-10, 1971, v, 5 sh. on a less than 100 sh. certificate, SCB, green $4.00

Andes Petroleum Corporation (DE par $1)

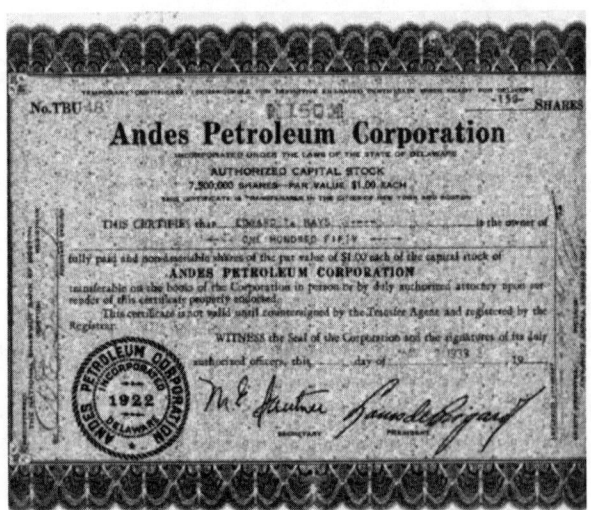

*AN180-30-10, 1933, t, 150 sh., blue. $3.00

R.P. Andrews Paper Co. (DC 1904)

AN230-30-10, 1936, v, 23 sh., orange $6.00

Androscoggin and Kennebec Railroad Co. (ME)

AN260-10-10, 1862, 2 sh., unissued certificate, blue. $35.00

Anglo-American Oil Co. (TX par $1)

*AN280-20-10, 1901, v, 75 sh., 10" x 8", grey
. . . .$36.00

The Anglo California National Bank of San Francisco

*AN300-30-10, 1940, v, 96 sh. on a less than 100 sh. certificate, brown................**$4.00**

Anglo-California Trust Co. (par $100)

*AN330-20-10, 1911, 66 sh., brown........**$7.00**

Anglo-Ecuadorian Oilfields, Limited (par 50 p)

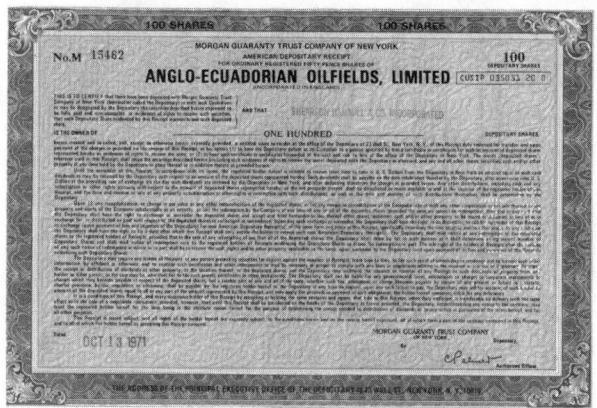

*AN380-20-10, 1971, 100 sh., American depositary receipt, ABN, 12" x 8", green......**$4.00**

The Anglo & London Paris National Bank of San Francisco (par $100)

*AN420-10-10, 1928, 9 sh. on a less than 100 sh. certificate, brown...................**$10.00**

Anglo National Corporation (DE)

*AN450-20-10, 1929, v, 14 sh. on a less than 100 sh. certificate, brown....................**$8.00**

Anheuser-Busch Incorporated (MO)

*AN480-50-10, 1982, v, $17,000 9.90% note due 1986, 12" x 8", brown **$30.00**

The Ann Arbor Railroad Company (par $100)

*AN520-30-10, 19xx, v, 20 pref. sh., voided certificate, green........................**$48.00**

The Ansul Company (WI $1)

*AN540-20-10, ND, t, less than 100 sh., specimen certificate, 12" x 8", green **$5.00**

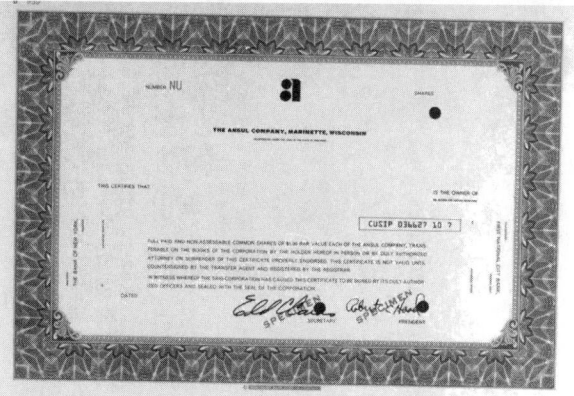

*AN540-22-10, ND, specimen certificate, 12" x 8", green..............................**$5.00**

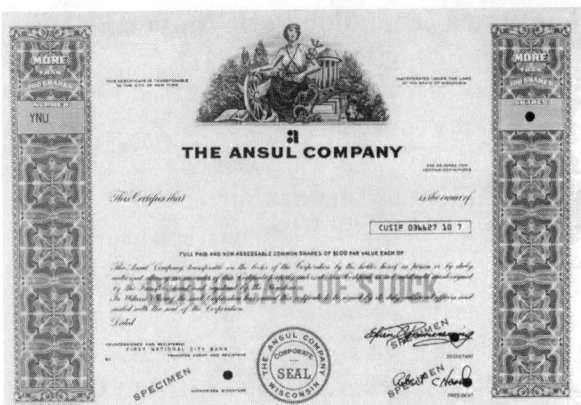

*AN540-25-10, ND, specimen of a more than 100 sh. certificate, 12" x 8", orange.........$5.00

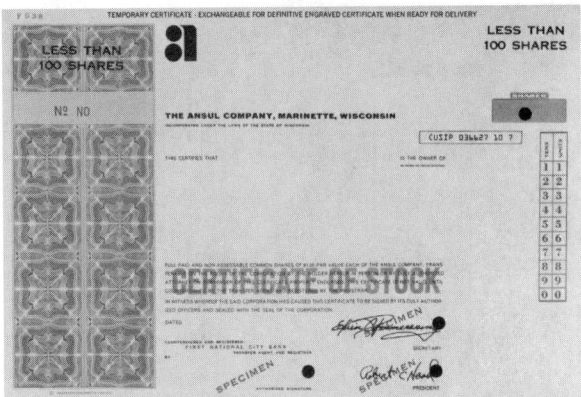

*AN540-30-10, ND, v, less than 100 sh., specimen certificate, 12" x 8", green $5.00

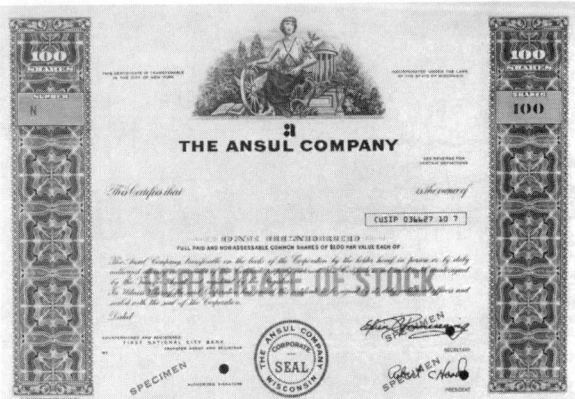

*AN540-35-10, ND, v, 100 sh., specimen, 12" x 8", blue $5.00

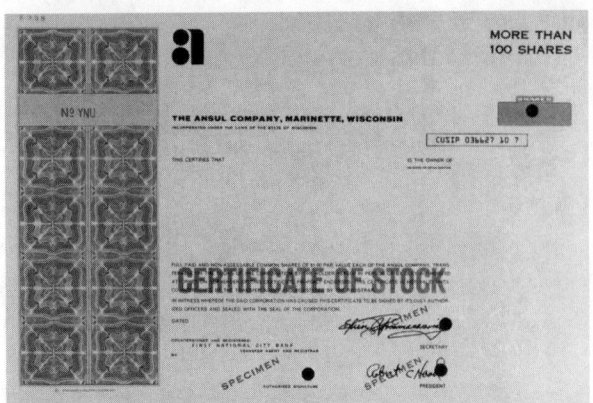

*AN540-40-10, ND, v, specimen on a more than 100 sh. certificate, 12" x 8" $5.00

The Anthracite Beer Company

AN560-20-10, 19xx, v, unissued certificate, green $20.00

Apex Mining Company (ME)

AP60-20-10, 1925, v, 100 sh., brown $10.00

Appalachian Electric Power Company

*AP140-40-10, 1966, v, 100 pref. sh., o/p name changed to Appalachian Power Company, red $5.00

Appalachian Power Company (VA)

AP170-40-10, 1970, v, 10 sh. on a less than 100 sh. certificate, green....................$3.00

*AP170-60-10, 1966, v-eagle, 30 sh., 4-1/2%
cumul. pref. (par $100), ABN, 12" x 8", green
. . . .$4.00

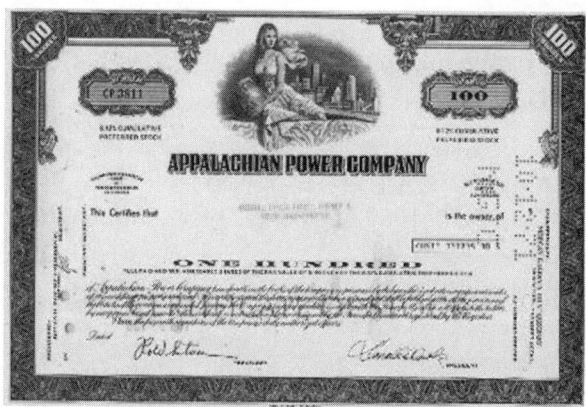

*AP170-80-10, 1971, v, 100 sh., cumulative pref.
stock, blue. $5.00

The Appleton 96th Meridian Oil Co. (WI $1)

*AP180-20-10, 1911, v, 200 sh., 11" x 8", brown
border $50.00

Appleton-Galena Lead and Zinc Company (WI par $1)

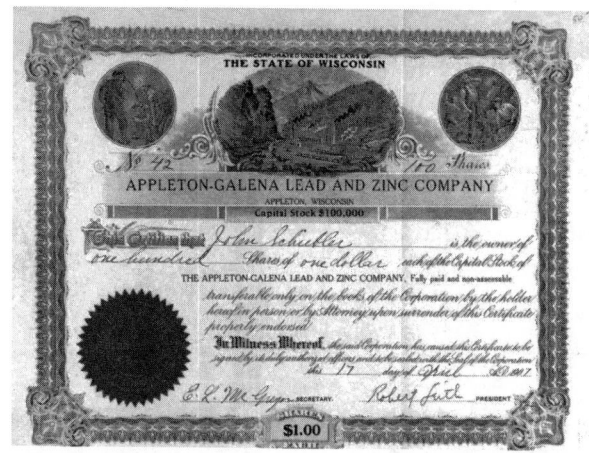

*AP190-20-10, 1907, v, 100 sh., w/o imprint, 11" x
8-1/2", grey border $50.00

Applied Technical Services Company (NY 1964, par $0.01)

AP210-20-10, 19xx, v, unissued 100 sh. certificate,
green. $3.00

A.P.W. Products Company, Inc. (NY par $5)

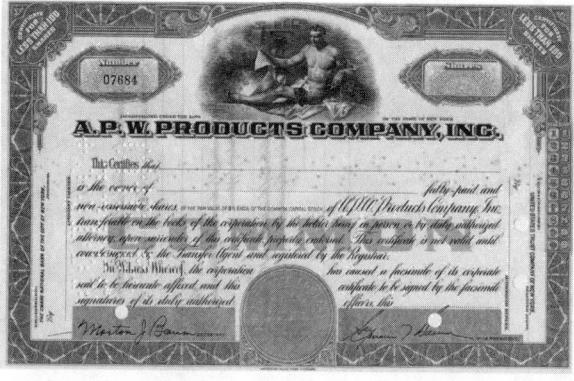

*AP250-30-10, 19xx, v, u/c less than 100 sh. certif-
icate, signature strip, ABN, 11" x 7", red
. . . .$5.00

Argonne Divide Mining Company (NV 2¢)

Mines in the Tonopah gold mountain mining
district of Esmeralda County.

AR100-20-10, 19xx, unissued certificate, brown
. . . .$6.00

Aristar, Inc. (DE par $1)

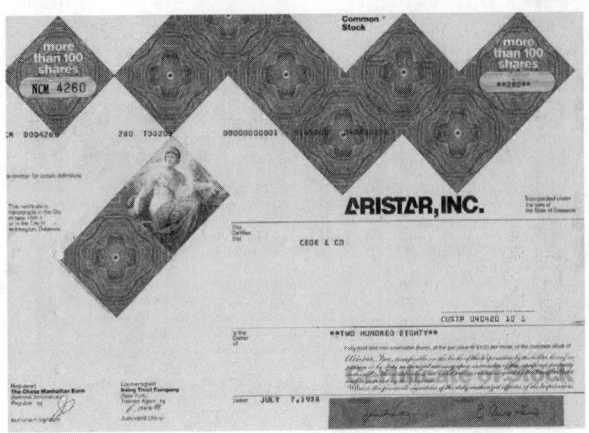

*AR140-20-10, 1978, v, 280 sh. on a more than 100 sh. certificate, signature strip, w/o imprint name, 12" x 8", purple.....................$4.00

Arizona Co-Operative Mercantile Institution (AZ territory par $1)

AR180-20-10, 1892, v, 7 sh., grey $75.00

Arkansas Anthracite Association (AR)

AR240-20-10, 19xx, v, u/u certificate.......$9.00

Arkansas and Arizona Copper Company (AZ)

*AR260-20-10, 1916, 200 sh., blue $10.00

Arkansas Valley Elevator Co. (MO par $100)

AR320-20-10, 18xx, v, u/u certificate, green
.................................$15.00

Armco Steel Corporation

Founded in Ohio in 1900 as the American Rolling Mill Company. Today, it's mostly in stainless steel products.

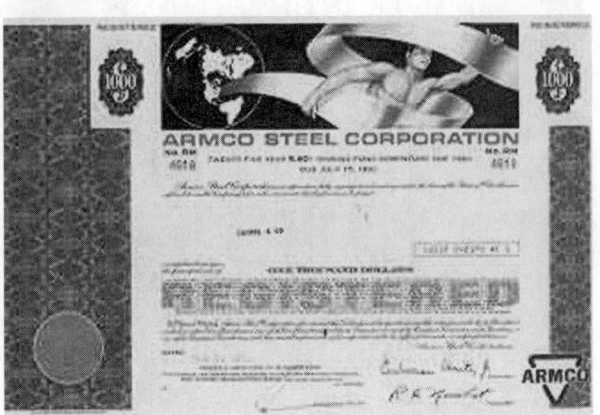

*AR400-40-10, 1973, v, $1,000 bond, brown
.................................$7.00

Armour-Dial Inc. (DE par $1)

AR470-30-10, 1969, v, 100 sh., blue $16.00

The Armstrong Rubber Company (CT)

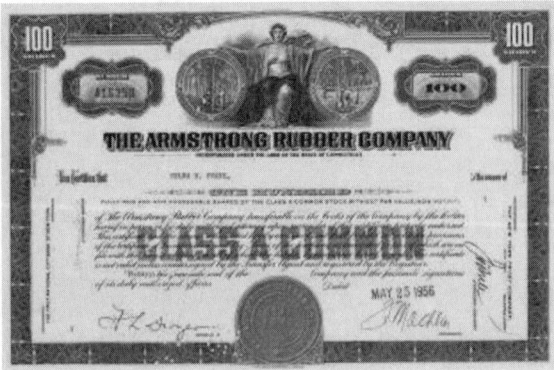

*AR500-40-10, 1956, v, 100 class A sh., CBN, blue
.................................$12.00

Arsenic Producing Corporation (CO)

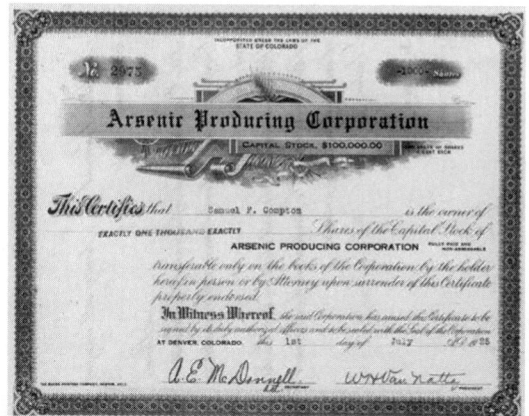

*AR650-20-10, 1925, v, 1,000 sh., grey border
. . . .$10.00

Ashland Home Telephone Company (WI)

*AS80-30-10, ?, v, $100 1st mortgage 20-year 6%
gold bond, orange $50.00

The Ashland National Bank (WI par $100)

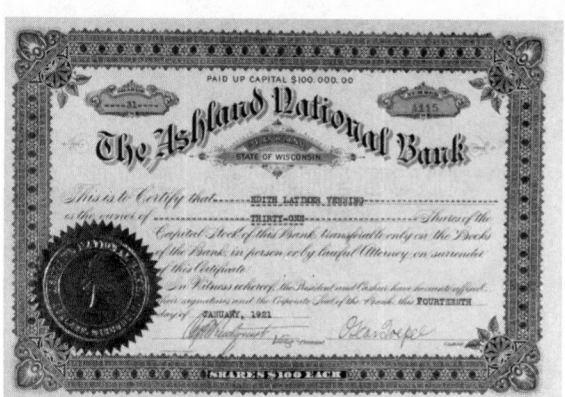

*AS90-20-10, 1921, 31 sh., 10-1/2" x 8", brown
border $28.00

Ashley Valley Oil Company (10¢)

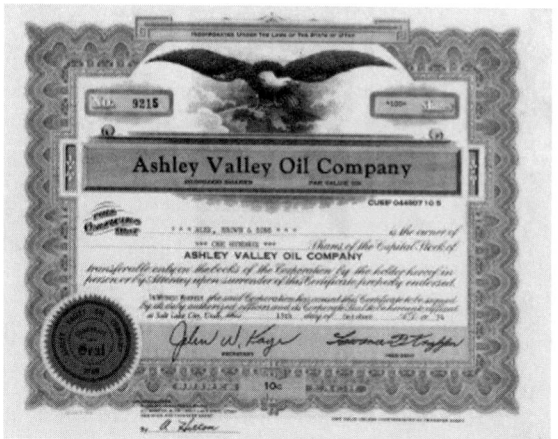

*AS100-20-10, 1974, v, 100 sh., orange . . .$13.00

Associated Beer Depots, Inc. (WI par $100)

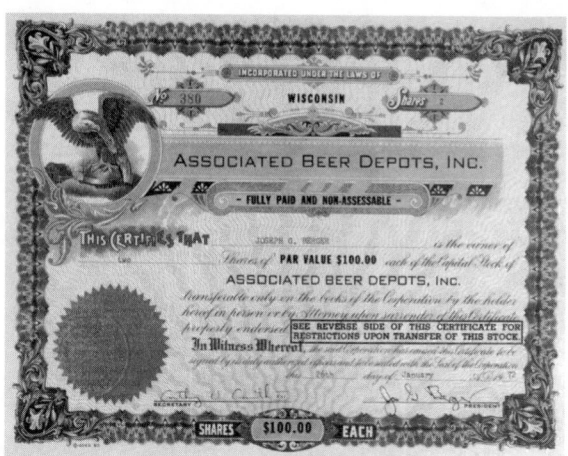

*AS140-20-10, 1972, v, 2 sh., GOES, 11" x 8",
brown border $12.00

Associated Gas and Electric Company
(NY 1906, par $100)

AS160-20-10, 19xx, v, unissued 100 sh. certificate,
green. $6.00
AS160-30-10, 1934, v, 100 class A sh., orange
. . . .$5.00
AS160-50-10, 1927, v, 10 sh., $5 pref., orange
. . . .$6.00

*AS160-60-10, 1930, t, 5 cumul. pref. sh. (no par) on a less than 100 sh. certificate, Dutch revenue imprint, 11-3/4" x 8", blue $4.00

Associated Pharmacists, Inc. (DE)

*AS220-20-10, 1912, v, 200 sh., blue......$11.00

Associated Sales Analysts Inc. (NY 1958, par 5¢)

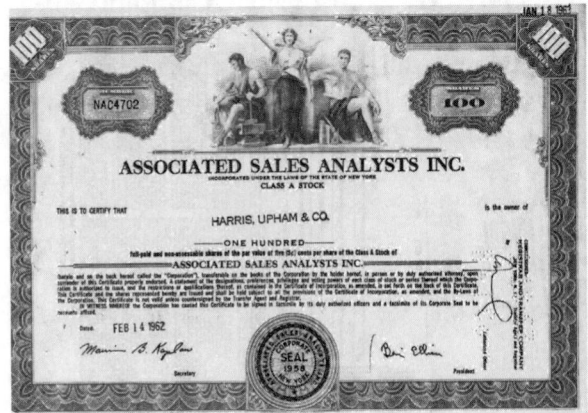

*AS260-20-10, 1962, v, 100 class A sh., SCB, 12-1/4" x 8-1/4", orange...............$3.00

Associated Telephone Company, Ltd. (CA)

Starting with Long Beach and expanding to communities around Los Angeles the company was the parent of General Telephone. In 1988 the company changed its name to GTE California, Inc., then merged with Bell Atlantic to create Verizon.

AS300-50-10, 1946, v, 25 pref. sh. on a less than 100 sh. certificate, red $25.00

Astrosystems International, Inc. (DE 1967, par $1)

*AS340-20-10, 1968, v, i/u 100 sh., SCB, 12" x 8", blue.............................$3.00

Astrotherm Corporation (DE 1960, par 10¢)

*AS350-20-10, 1961, v, 100 sh., blue $3.00

Atari Corporation (NV)

Established in 1972 by Nolan Bushnell in Sunny-
vale, California. In 1976, the company was sold
to Warner Communications. In 1996, it merged
with JTS Corporation, which was purchased by
Hasbro in 1998.

AT50-20-10, 1987, v, 12,500 sh., blue $26.00

AT50-25-10, 1987, v, 21 sh., United States Banknote Corporation, blue $26.00

Atchison & Nebraska Rail Road Company

*AT100-20-10, 1880, v, 5 sh., grey $24.00

Atchison, Topeka and Santa Fe Railroad Company

AT130-40-10, 1889 $50 income gold security bond,
green $14.00

*AT130-45-10, 1894, v, $50 General Mortgage
gold bond, brown $18.00

AT140-30-10, 1970, v, $5,000 bond, brown
. . . .$11.00

The Atlanta and Charlotte Air Line Railway Company (par $100)

AT200-30-10, 1940, v, 6 sh., brown. $14.00

Atlantic City Racing Association

AT240-20-10, 1951, 100 sh., signed by John B.
Kelly, Sr. the father of Grace Kelly, orange
. . . .$25.00

Atlantic City & Shore Railroad Company (NJ par $100)

AT270-30-10, 1906, v, 100 sh., green $60.00

AT270-40-10, 19xx, v, u/u 100 sh. certificate,
green. $50.00

The Atlantic Coast Line Railroad Company

AT300-20-10, 1897, v, 50 sh., brown. $65.00

*AT300-40-10, 1927, v, $10,000 1st consolidated
mortgage gold bond, deep orange $80.00

Atlantic Department Stores, Inc. (NY)

AT330-30-10, 1971, v, 100 sh., SCB, blue . .$4.00

The value of a stock certificate depends on:
- rarity
- the issuer
- signatures
- quality of engraving
- overall appearance
- condition
- date of issue

Atlantic Iron Mining Company (WI par $25)

*AT360-20-10, 1887, v, 100 sh., 13" x 10", grey border $45.00

Atlantic, Mississippi and Ohio Rail Road Company

*AT400-20-10, 1870, 3 sh., grey border on pink $15.00

Atlantic and Pacific Railroad Company

*AT440-30-10, 1887, v, $1,000 4% guaranteed trust gold bond, green $28.00

It is generally assumed that only 5% of certificates survive to reach collectors.

The Atlantic Refining Company (PA par $10)

*AT470-30-10, 1959, v, 100 sh., ABN, 12" x 8", green $4.00
A5570-40-10, 1956, v- ATLANTIC, 100 sh., green $6.00

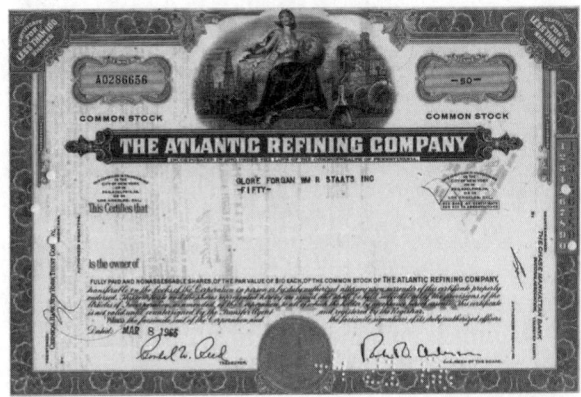

*AT470-50-10, 1966, v-lady, 50 sh. on a less than 100 sh. certificate, ABN, 12" x 8", orange $4.00

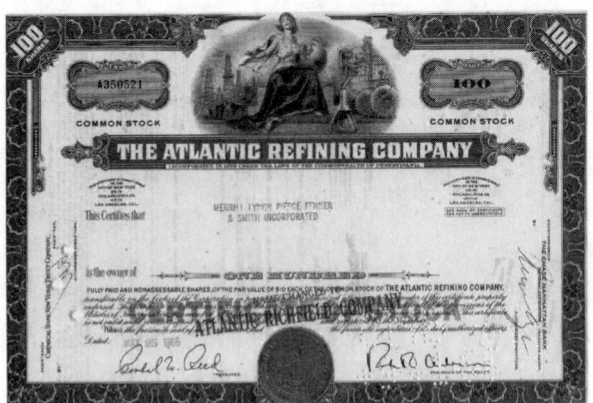

*AT470-60-10, 1966, v-lady, 100 sh. (par $10), o/p name changed to Atlantic Richfield Company, ABN, 12" x 8", green $4.00

AT470-80-10, 1965, v, 10 sh., 3.75% cum. pref. Sh., olive green **$6.00**

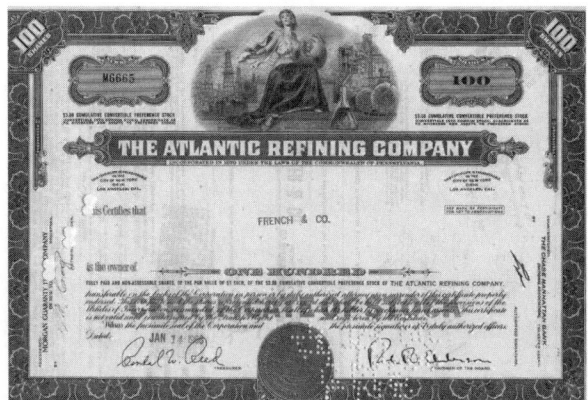

*AT470-90-10, 1966, v, 100 sh., $3.00 cumulative conv. pref., ABN, 12" x 8", purple **$4.00**

Atlantic Richfield Company (PA 1970, par $10)

The company was formed in 1966 by the merger of Atlantic Refining Company with Richfield Oil Corporation. With the acquisition of Sinclair Oil in 1969 the company became ARCO.

*AT500-20-10, 1967, v, 25 sh. on a less than 100 sh. certificate, ABN, 12" x 8", orange **$4.00**

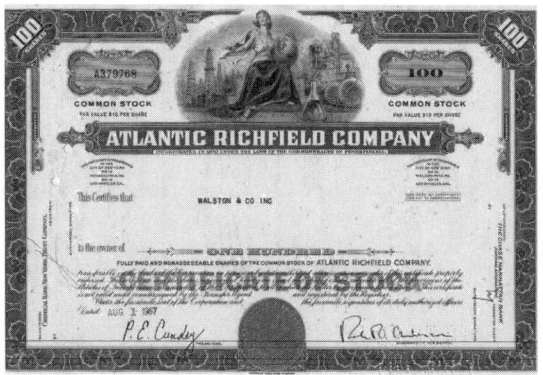

*AT500-30-10, 1967, v, 100 sh., ABN, 12" x 8", green **$4.00**

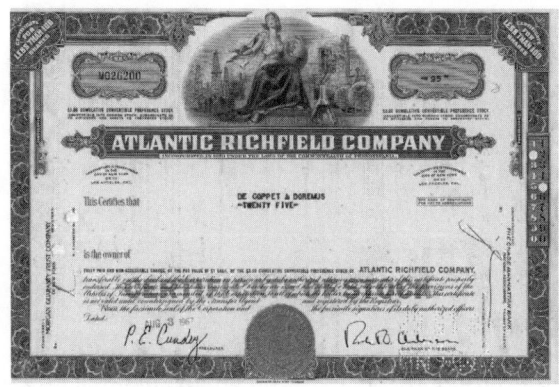

*AT500-60-10, 1967, v, 25 $3.00 cumul. conv. pref. sh. on a less than 100 sh. certificate, ABN, 12" x 8", brown **$4.00**

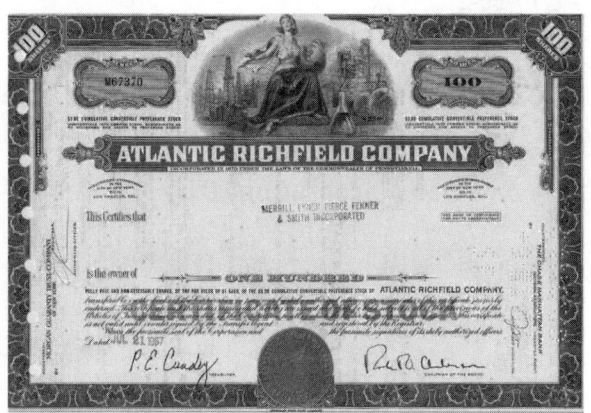

*AT500-70-10, 1967, v, 100 $3.00 cumul. conver. pref. sh., ABN, 12" x 8", purple **$4.00**

*AT500-80-10, 1970, v, 25 $2.80 cumul. convert. pref. sh. on a less than 100 sh. certificate, ABN, 12" x 8", orange $4.00

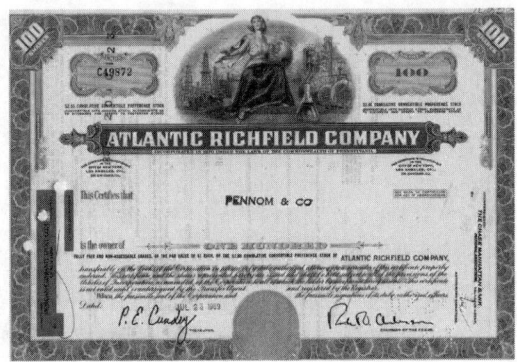

*AT500-90-10, 1969, v, 100 $2.80 cumul. convert. pref. sh., ABN, 12" x 8", light green $4.00

Aurum Mining Company (par $1)
AU70-20-10, 19xx, v, u/u certificate, green
. . . .$7.00

The Automatic Telephone Exchange Co. (WV)
AU110-20-10, 1898, v, 100 sh., l. brown . . .$86.00

The Aviation Corporation (DE)

*AV80-30-10, 1947, v, 40 sh. on a less than 100 sh. certificate, blue-purple $9.00
AV80-40-10, 1946, v, 100 sh. (par $3), brown
. . . .$9.00

Avondale School District

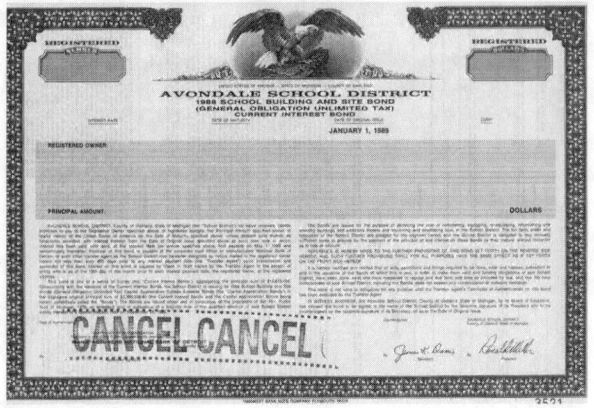

*AV150-30-10, 19xx, v, u/c current interest bond due 1989, Midwest Banknote Co., 12" x 8", blue
. . . .$4.00

Axleton Natural Gas Company (PA par $100)

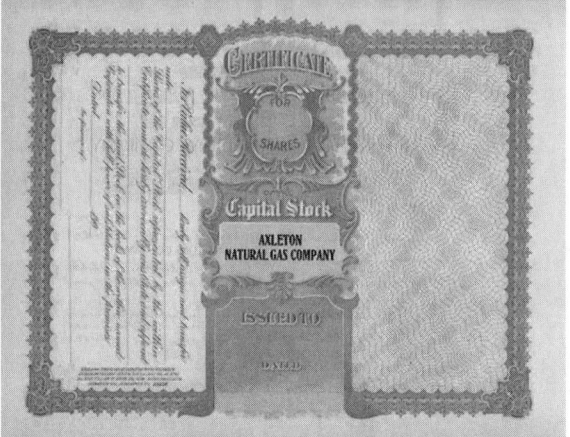

*AX50-20-10, 190x, v, u/u certificate, brown
. . . .$8.00

B

The Babcock & Wilcox Company (NJ)
BA60-30-10, 1956, v, 50 sh. on a less than 100 sh. certificate, ABN, orange $5.00

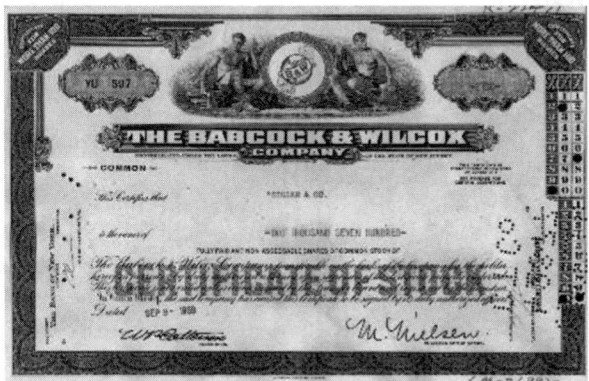

BA60-40-10, 1959, v, 2,700 sh. on a more than 100 sh. certificate $5.00

Bachman Valley Rail Road Company of Maryland (par $50)
BA100-10-10, 18xx, v, u/u certificate, brown $16.00

Baker International Corporation (CA 1913, par $1)
BA170-30-10, 1978, v, 100 sh. on a less than 100,000 sh. certificate, blue $4.00
1979, v, 100 sh., blue $4.00

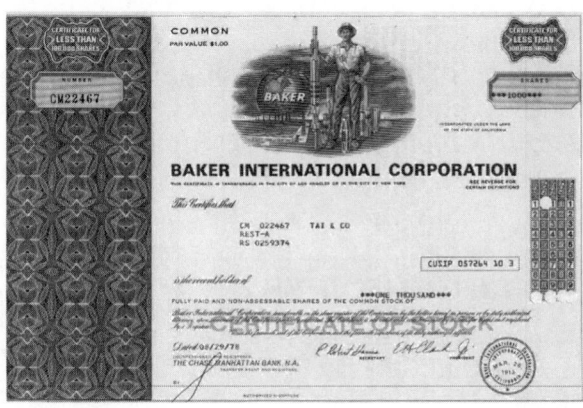

BA170-40-10, 1978, v, i/u 1,000 sh. on a less than 100,000 sh. certificate, Jeffries Banknote Company, 12" x 8", blue $4.00

Baker Motors Inc. (no par)
BA200-20-10, 1925, v, 640 sh., brown $35.00

Baker Oil Tools, Inc. (CO par $1)
BA230-20-10, 1975, v, 100 sh., blue $4.00

Bald Butte Gold Mines (MT par $0.10)
BA300-20-10, 1933, v, 10,000 sh., brown . . . $8.00

The Baldwin Company (OH par $8)

BA350-30-10, 1940, 130 sh., w/o imprint name, 10-1/2" x 8-1/4", yellow $3.00

D.H. Baldwin Company (OH)
Piano maker who by 1923 captured 56% of the player piano market.
BA380-30-10, 1986, v, $1,000 9-3/4% series B debenture due 1989, orange $4.00

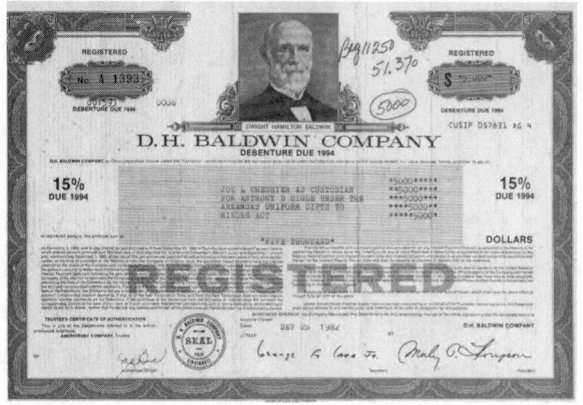

BA380-40-10, 1982, v, $5,000 15% debenture due 1994, ABN, 12" x 8", green $4.00

BA380-45-10, 1982, v, $10,000 13-1/2% debenture
due 1994 . . . .**$8.00**

*BA380-55-10, 1986, v, $10,000 13-1/2% deben-
ture due 1994, green **$4.00**

Baldwin-United Corporation (DE)

*BA400-30-10, 1962, v, 1 sh., green **$3.00**

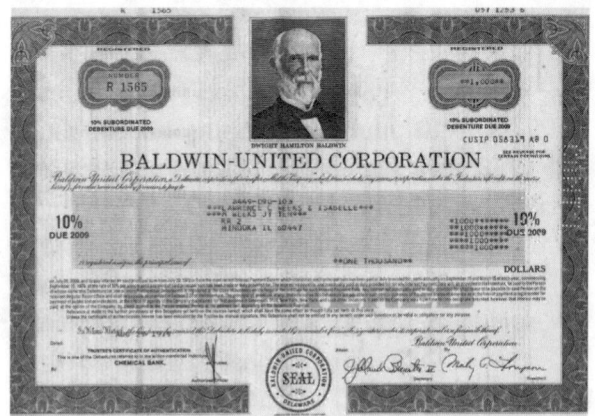

*BA400-40-10, 1979, v, $1,000 10% bond due
2009, ABN, 12" x 8", red **$4.00**

R.B. Ballard & Co.
BA460-20-10, 19xx, v, u/u certificate, brown
. . . .**$3.00**

City of Baltimore
BA550-40-10, 1886, v, $1,000 5% bond, green
. . . .**$35.00**

Baltimore National Bank
BA600-30-10, v, 19xxv, u/u less than 100 sh. certificate, green **$5.00**

The Baltimore and Ohio Railroad Company (MD 1827 par $100)

*BA650-20-10, 1853, v, 1 sh., brown **$43.00**
BA650-30-10, 1858, v, 20 sh., brown-grey .**$36.00**
BA650-40-10, 1858, v, 50 sh., grey **$29.00**
BA650-45-10, 1858, v, 100 sh., brown-grey
. . . .**$33.00**
BA650-50-10, 1876, v, 1 sh., grey **$32.00**
BA650-55-10, 1880, v, 25 sh., grey **$26.00**
BA650-60-10, 18xx, v, unissued Baltimore certifi-
cate, green. **$26.00**
BA650-65-10, 1892, v, 10 sh., New York certifi-
cate, brown **$15.00**
BA650-70-10, 1900, v-topless liberty, 10 sh., blue
. . . .**$15.00**
BA650-75-10, 1901, v-topless liberty, 10 sh. voting
stock trust, blue **$15.00**

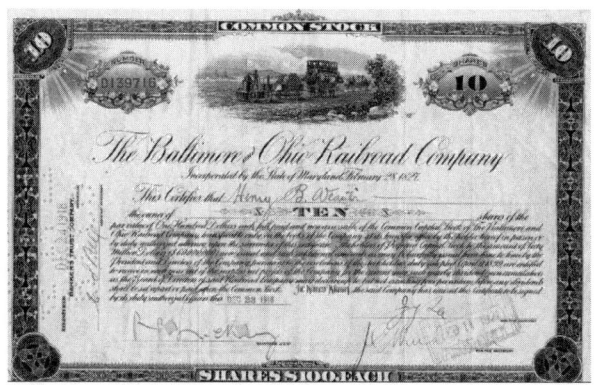

*BA650-80-10, 1918, v-early train, 10 sh., blue
. . . .$15.00

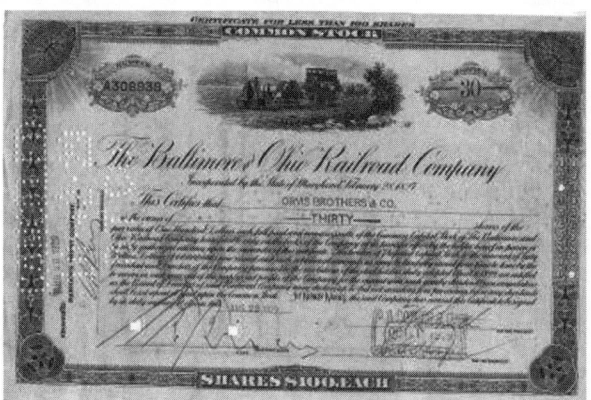

*BA650-85-10, 1929, v, 30 sh. on less than 100 sh.
certificate, green $6.00

*BA650-90-10, 1946, v, 14 sh. on a less than 100
sh. certificate, International Bank Note Co. New
York, 11-1/2" x 7-1/4", olive $6.00
BA650-95-10, 1956, v, 10 sh., blue $6.00
BA650-100-10, 1951, v, 100 sh., brown $6.00

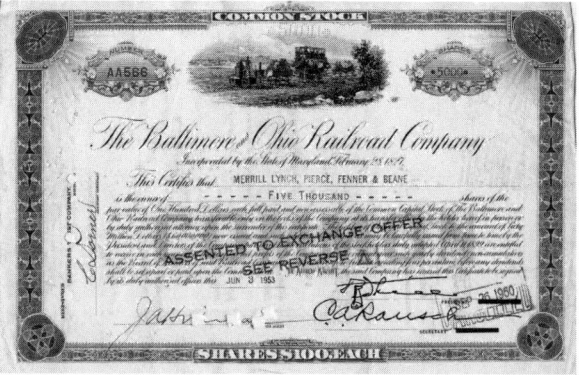

*BA650-105-10, 1953, v, 5,000 sh., o/p Assented to
exchange offer, see reverse side; International
Bank Note Co. New York, 11-1/2" x 7-1/4",
brown $8.00

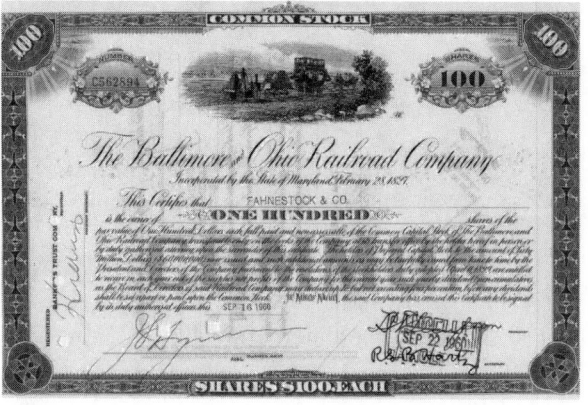

*BA650-110-10, 1960, v, 100 sh., International
Banknote Co., New York; 11-1/2" x 7-1/2",
brown $5.00

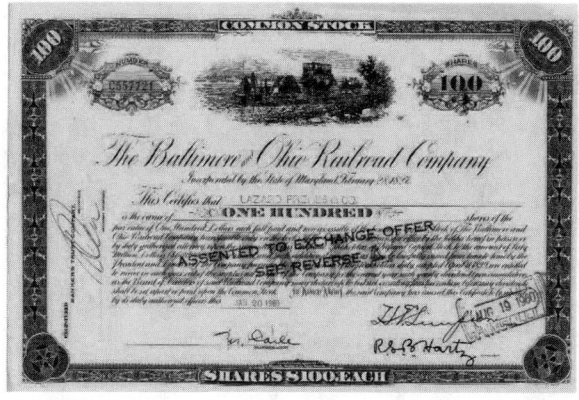

*BA650-115-10, 1960, v, 100 sh., o/p assented to
exchange offer see reverse, International Banknote Co., New York, 11-1/2" x 7-1/2", brown
. . . .$4.00
BA650-130-10, 1899, v, 3 sh., preferred stock trust
certificate, orange $8.00

*BA650-135-10, 1900, v, 10 pref. stock trust sh.,
IBN, orange.........................$10.00

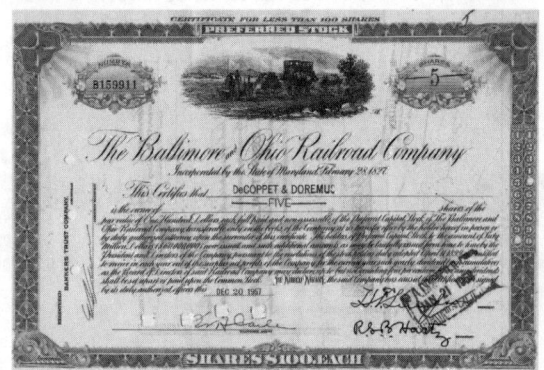

*BA650-150-20, 1957, v, 5 pref. sh. on a less than
100 sh. certificate, International Bank Note Co.,
New York; 11-1/2" x 7-1/2", orange $6.00
BA650-170-10, 1913, v, $5,000 prior lien 3-1/2%
gold bond, olive green $20.00
BA650-195-10, 1960, $2,000 certificate of deposit
5-year 4-1/2% secured notes, blue $5.00

The Baltimore and Ohio Southwestern
Railroad Company (par $100)

BA680-20-10, 1890, v, 4 sh., pref., brown
..................................$15.00

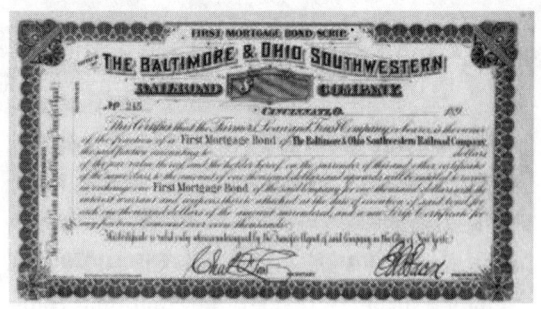

*BA680-40-10, 189x, 1st mortgage bond script,
ABN, black on white $6.00

Baltimore and Philadelphia Steamboat
Company (MD par $20)

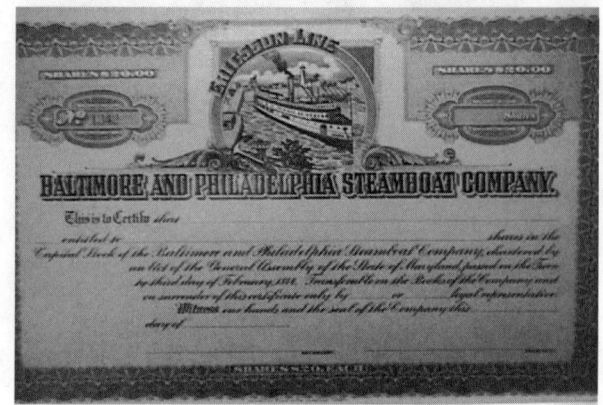

*BA730-20-10, 19xx, v, u/u certificate, green
..................................$26.00

Bammann & Ebel Restaurant, Inc.
(NY par $50)

*BA800-10-10, 19xx, u/u certificate, J. Meyers
Inc., NYC, 10-3/4" x 8-1/2", orange $4.00

Bangor & Aroostook Corporation
(ME 1960)

BA900-30-10, 1963, v, 80 sh. on a less than 100 sh.
certificate, red.....................$10.00

*It is generally assumed that
only 5% of certificates survive
to reach collectors.*

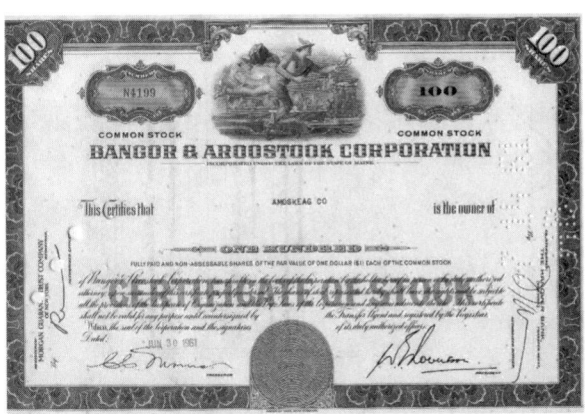

*BA900-40-10, 1961, v, 100 sh. (par $1), ABN, 12" x 8", green $5.00

Bank of America National Association (par $25)

*BA920-20-10, 1930, v, 5 sh. on a less than 100 sh. certificate, ABN, 11" x 7", green border .$12.00

Bank of Cameron (WI par $100)

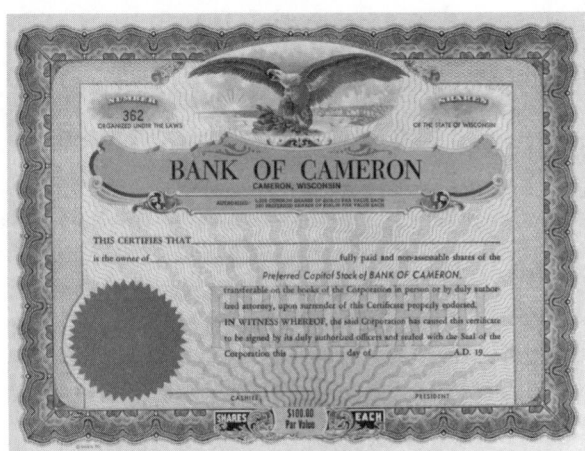

*BA930-20-10, 19xx, v, u/u certificate, GOES, 11" x 8", purple $5.00

Bank of Huntington (NY par $10)

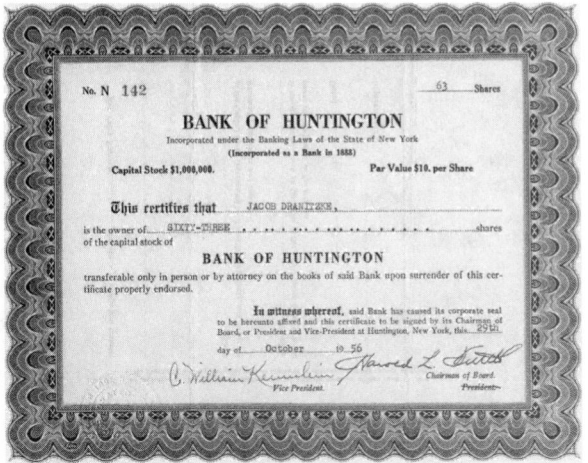

*BA950-20-10, 1956, i/u 63 sh., GOES, 11" x 8-1/2", brown $5.00

Bank of Kentucky (KY par $100)
BA980-20-10, 1860, v, 5 sh., grey $37.00

Bankers Trust New York Corporation (NY 1965)

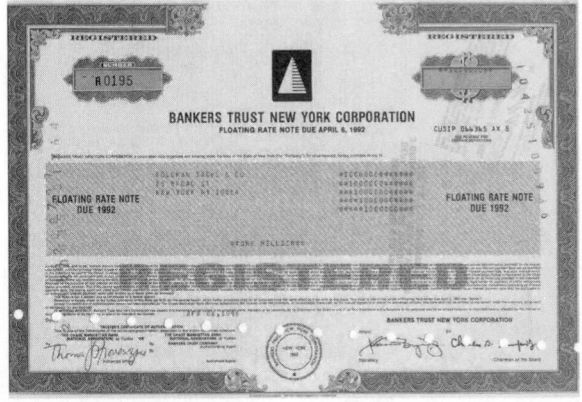

*BA1050-60-10, 1990, v, $1,000,000 floating rate note due 1992, SCB, 12" x 8", maroon border $5.00

The value of a stock certificate depends on:
- rarity
- the issuer
- signatures
- quality of engraving
- overall appearance
- condition
- date of issue

Banner Life Insurance Co. (GA par $2.50)

BA1110-20-10, 1957, v, 10 sh., grey on green
. . . .$13.00

Baruch-Foster Corporation (DE 1924, par $0.50)

BA1200-20-10, 1969, v, 100 sh., SCB, 12" x 8",
green $3.00

Basic Resources Corporation (UT par $0.10)

BA1260-20-10, 1967, 100 sh., green $5.00

UNLISTED TYPES & VARIETIES

Readers are welcome to contact the author
directly at:

Rainer Stahlberg
P.O. Box 1044
Rooseveltown, New York 13683

Batavia & Humboldt Gold & Silver Mining Co.

BA1310-20-10, 1869, v, 100 sh., with revenue
stamp, black on white. $150.00

The Bay Bridge Company (par $50)

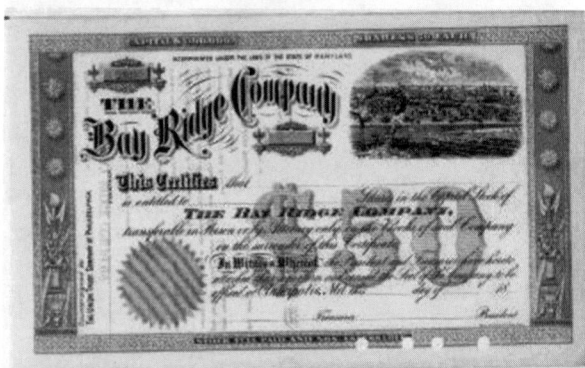

BA1400-20-10, 19xx, u/u certificate, brown
. . . .$44.00

Bay State Gas Company (DE)

BA1450-20-10, 1914, v, 50 sh., orange $6.00

Bayano River Lumber Company (ME par $1)
BA1500-20-10, 1909, v, 10 sh., brown.....**$20.00**

The Bear Valley and Alessandro Development Company (par $100)
"Each share is equal to one share in the Bear Valley Irrigation Co."
BE100-20-10, 1891, v, 50 sh., orange **$150.00**

Beaver Creek Distillery, Inc. (IA par $1)

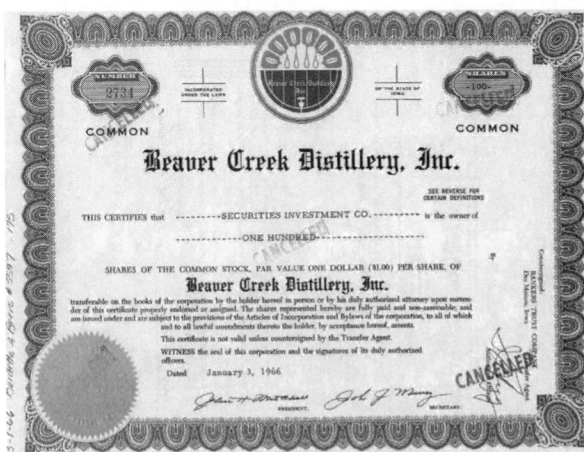

*BE200-20-10, 1966, v, 100 sh., Messenger Pt. Co. Ft. Dodge, IA, 11" x 8-1/2", brown **$4.00**

Beaver Creek Industries, Inc.

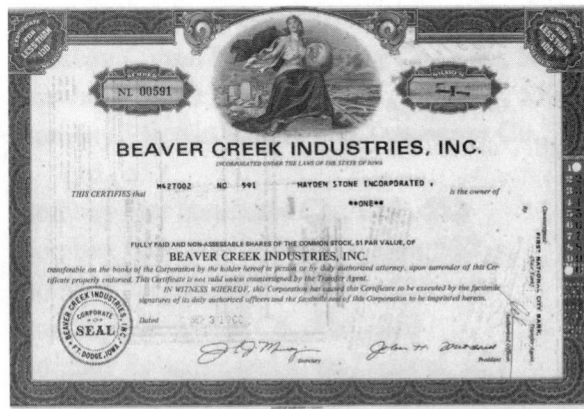

*BE230-20-10, 1968, v, 1 sh. on a less than 100 sh. certificate (IA par $1), ABN, 12" x 8", green
.................**$4.00**

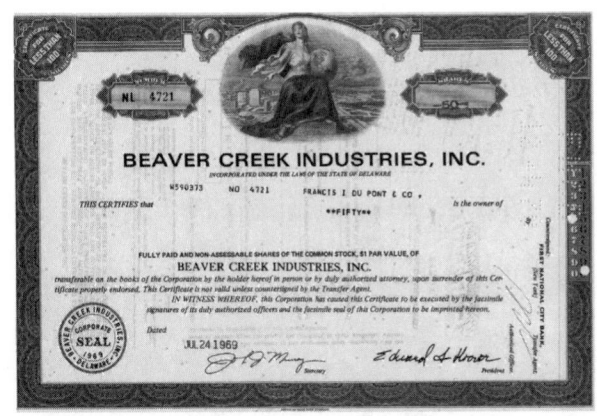

*BE230-20-15, 1969, v, 50 sh. on a less than 100 sh. certificate (DE 1969, par $1), ABN, 12" x 8", green.................**$4.00**

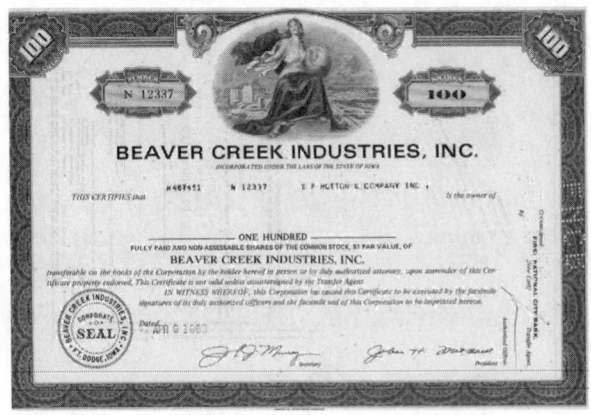

*BE230-30-10, 1969, v, 100 sh. (IA par $1), ABN, 12" x 8", blue.................**$4.00**
BE230-40-10, 1970, v, 100 sh. (DE par $1) blue
.................**$4.00**

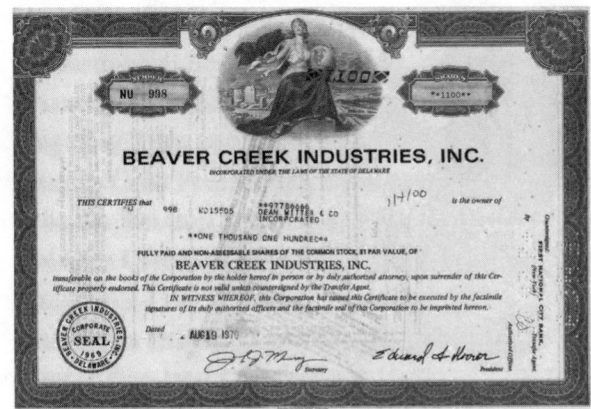

*BE230-50-10, 1970, v, 1,100 sh. (DE 1969, par $1), ABN, 12" x 8", olive green.........**$5.00**

Beaver Dam Gold Mining Co. (par $100)
Mines at Beaver Dam, Nova Scotia.
BE260-20-10, 18xx, v, u/u certificate, brown
. . . .$18.00

Bechaud Brewing Company (WI $100)

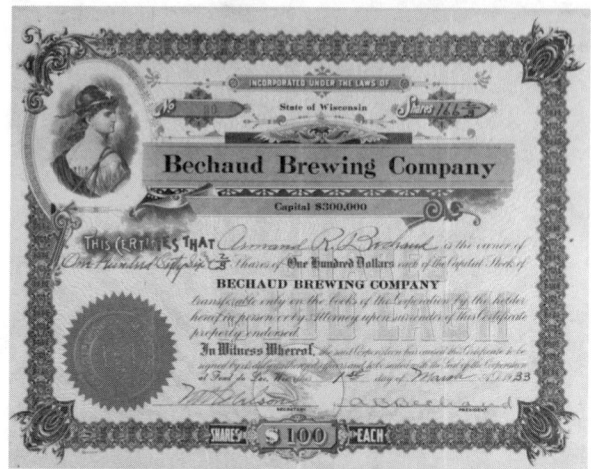

BE280-20-10, 1933, v, 166 sh., GOES, 11" x 8-1/2",
brown border $120.00

Beck Industries, Inc. (DE 1932, par $1)

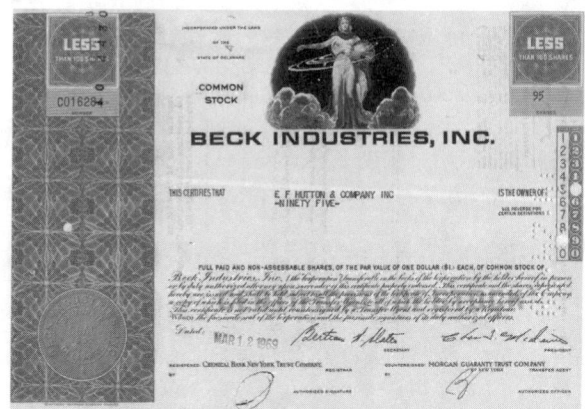

BE300-20-10, 1969, v, 95 sh. on a less than 100
sh. certificate, SCB, 12" x 8", orange $4.00

> ### It is generally assumed that only 5% of certificates survive to reach collectors.

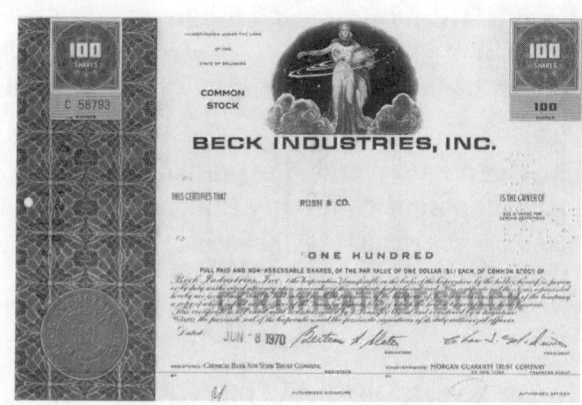

BE300-30-10, 1970, v, 100 sh., SCB, 12" x 8",
green $4.00

Beech Creek Coal and Coke Company (PA)
BE400-20-10, 19xx, v, u/c 100 sh. certificate,
ABN, green. $10.00

BE400-40-10, 19xx, v, u/c less than 100 sh., pref.
sh. certificate, orange $6.00

Beech Creek Railroad Company (PA par $50)

BE460-30-10, 1941, v, 5 sh., brown $7.00
BE460-40-10, 1936, v, 100 sh., brown $10.00

BE460-50-10, 18xx, v, u/c 100 sh. certificate, ABN, green **$11.00**
BE460-60-10, 18xx, 100 sh., unissued pref. certificate, brown **$9.00**

Belco Petroleum Corporation

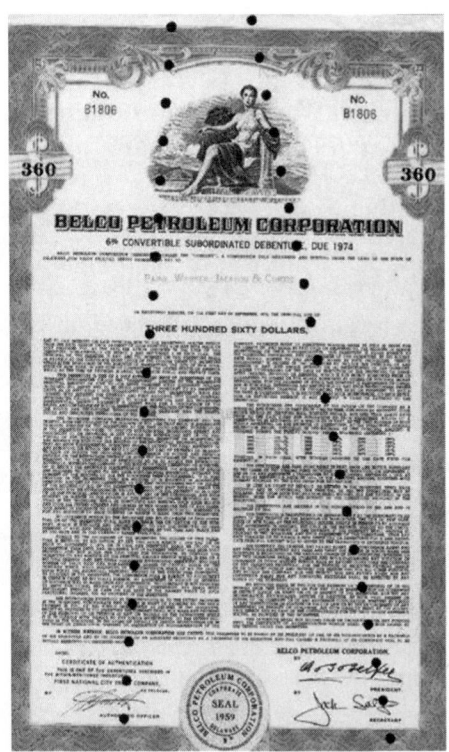

*BE600-40-10, 1974, v, $360 6% convertible subordinated debenture due 1974, orange **$5.00**

*BE460-80-10, 1893, v, $1,000 bond, green .**$8.00**

*BE460-90-10, 19xx, v, u/c $1,000 4% bond, due 1936, orange **$5.00**

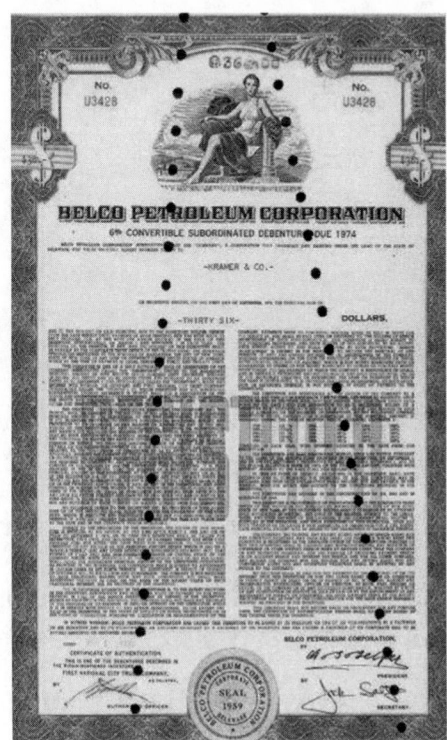

*BE600-50-10, 1974, v, $360 6% convertible subord. debenture due 1974, red **$5.00**

**Belding Hemingway Company, Inc.
(DE 1947)**
BE650-20-10, 1977, v, 100 sh., brown.....$26.00

**Belknap Hardware and Manufacturing
Company (KY 1880, no par)**

*BE700-20-10, 1953, v, 130 sh., FLB, 11-3/4" x
7-3/4", brown **$4.00**
BE700-30-10, 1982, v, 500 sh., one signature strip,
brown $4.00

**The Belleaire, Zanesville and Cincinnati
Railway Company (par $50)**

*BE760-20-10, 189x, v, u/u certificate with o/p,
FBN, grey $40.00

**Bellehelen Mo-We-Na Mining Company
(par 10¢)**
BE810-20-10, 19xx, v, unissued certificate, brown
.................................$21.00

**Belleville and Southern Illinois Railroad
Company (IL)**
BE870-30-10, 1896, v, 100 pref. sh., orange
.................................$32.00

Belmont County (Ohio)

*BE920-30-10, 1871, v, $100 7% road bond, brown
.................................$20.00

The Belmont Iron Works (PA)
BE950-30-10, 1949, v, 100 sh., green $14.00

**Belt Rail Road & Stock Yard Co.
(IN par $50)**
BE990-20-10, 18xx, v, u/u certificate, blue
.................................$10.00

*BE990-30-10, 1914, v, 10 sh., grey $10.00

Berkeley Development Co. (CA par $10)
BE1160-20-10, 189x, unissued certificate, black
.................................$15.00

Bessie Gold Company (WA par $1)
BE1240-20-10, 1903, v, 1,000 sh., brown ..$13.00

Phillip Best Brewing Company (WI par $1,000)

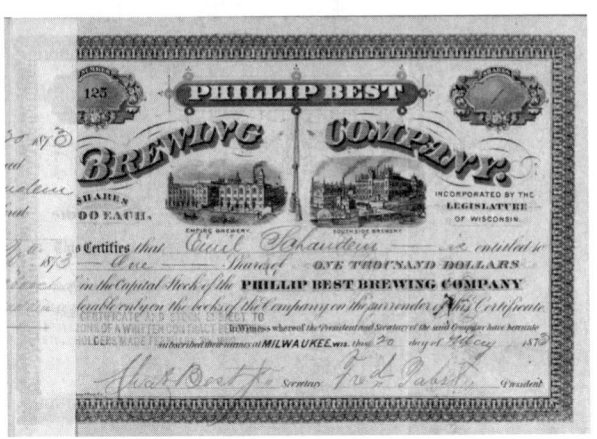

*BE1270-20-10, 1873, v, 1 sh., 10" x 7", brown
. . . .$500.00

Bethlehem Steel Corporation (DE)

BE1400-50-10, 1968, v, 10 sh. on a less than 100
sh. certificate, brown. $13.00
BE1400-60-10, 1963, v, 100 sh., ABN, green
. . . .$6.00

Bewitching Hosiery, Inc. (NY no par)

BE1500-20-10, 19xx, v, u/u certificate, orange
. . . .$9.00

Bickford Mining Company (WI par $1)

*BI100-20-10, 1906, v, 100 sh., 10" x 4-1/2", grey
border $35.00

Big Bend Uranium Company (UT par 5¢)

BI310-20-10, 1956, v, 1,000 sh., green $9.00

Big Blackfoot Railway Company (par $100)

BI340-20-10, 19xx, v, u/u certificate, brown border
. . . .$26.00

The Big Five Mining Company (WY)

BI450-20-10, 1912, v, 67 sh., smallish certificate,
grey. $15.00

*BI450-30-10, 19xx, v, u/u certificate, grey .$5.00

Big Ledge Copper Company (AZ par $5)

*BI570-20-10, 1922, v, 100 sh., orange. . . .$12.00

Big Value Oil & Gas Co. (TX par $10)

BI700-20-10, 1915, v, 2 sh., grey-brown. . .$10.00

The Big Walnut Oil & Gas Company

BI770-20-10, 1916, v, 10 sh., brown $7.00

Blackhawk Mining Company, Ltd. (KY par $100)

BL100-20-10, 19xx, v, u/u certificates, green border. $5.00

Bloomsburg Silk Mill (par $100)

BL200-20-10, 1893, v, 7 sh., grey $12.00

Blyvooruitzicht Gold Mining Company, Limited

*BL300-20-10, 1968, 100 American Depositary sh., ABN, 12" x 8", green $3.00

The Boeing Company (DE)

BO100-30-10, 1972, v, ABN, brown $7.00

Bohn Aluminum & Brass Corporation

BO180-20-10, 1957, v, 100 sh., lilac $4.00

Bond Stores, Incorporated (MD 1937, par $1.00)

A chain of clothing stores.
BO230-20-10, 19xx, u/c less than 100 sh. certificate, cancelled in 1945, red. $4.00

*BO230-30-10, 1953, v, 25 sh. on a less than 100 sh. certificate, ABN, 12" x 8", red $4.00

*BO230-30-15, 1965, v, 30 sh. on a less than 100 sh. certificate, signature variety, ABN, 12" x 8", red. $3.00
BO230-40-10, 1955, v, 100 sh., blue $4.00

*BO230-50-10, 1965, v, 100 sh., blue $3.00

Borough Park Credit Corporation (DE)

*BO280-20-10, 19xx, v, u/u pref. stock certificate (par $100), green $4.00

Boston and Albany Railroad Company (MA par $100)

A consolidation of the Boston and Worcester, The Western, the Albany and West Stockbridge and the Hudson and Boston RR companies.

*BO390-20-10, 1883, v, 1 sh., grey $10.00

*BO390-30-10, 1938, v, 2 sh. on a less than 100 sh. certificate, rubber stamp "not over two shares", ABN, 11-3/4" x 8-1/4", green. $8.00
BO390-40-10, 1939, v, 1 sh. on a less than 100 sh. certificate, brown $8.00
BO390-50-10, 1943, v, 50 sh. on a less than 100 sh. certificate, green $8.00
BO390-60-10, 1950, v, 1 sh. on a less than 100 sh. certificate, green $6.00

*BO390-90-10, 1902, v, $1,000 refunding 3-1/2% bond, ABN, 13" x 9", brown $7.00

*BO390-100-10, 1913, v, $1,000 5% refunding bond, red. $8.00

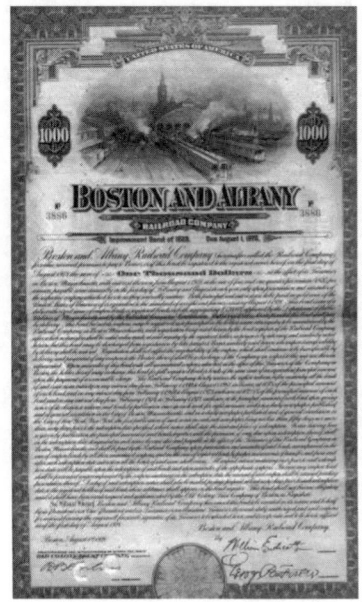

*BO390-110-10, 1928, v, $1,000 4-1/4% Improvement bond, ABN, blue $17.00

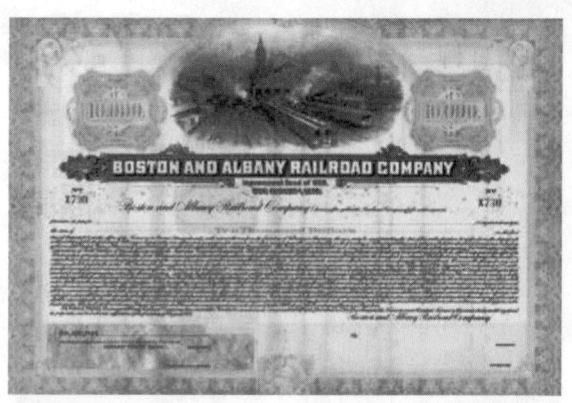

*BO390-120-10, 1928, v, u/u certificate $10,000
Improvement bond, orange **$13.00**

BO390-130-10, 1943, v, $1,000 bond, green
. . . . **$8.00**

Boston Chamber of Commerce Realty Trust

BO440-30-10, 1923, v, 5 first pref. sh., brown
. . . . **$6.00**

The Boston Coal and Fuel Company (CO par $1)

BO470-20-10, 1901, v, 200 sh., green **$9.00**

Boston Edison Company (MA 1886 par $25)

BO520-30-10, 1959, v, 5 sh. on a less than 100 sh.
certificate, blue **$5.00**

*BO520-40-10, 1953, v, 100 sh., ABN, 11-1/2" x
7-1/2", strip signature, orange **$4.00**

BO520-50-10, 1955, v, 100 sh., ABN, 11-1/2" x
7-1/2", orange **$5.00**

Boston Elevated Railway Company (MA par $100)

BO550-20-10, 1906, v, 50 sh., ABN, red
. . . . **$15.00**

*BO550-40-10, 1924, v, 6 pref. sh. (par $100),
green **$16.00**

Boston and Great Falls Electric Light and Power Company

BO590-20-10, 189x, v, green, blank certificate
. . . . **$7.00**

Boston Insulating and Fire Protection Company (ME 1890, par $10)

BO620-20-10, 1891, v, 1,000 sh., green . . . **$35.00**

Boston and Maine Corporation (DE par $1)

BO660-20-10, 1966, v, 20 sh. on a less than 100 sh.
certificate, blue **$13.00**

Boston and Maine Railroad (MA-ME-NH-NY)

*BO680-20-10, 1954, v, 100 sh., green **$10.00**

BO680-30-10, 1956, v, 10 5% pref. sh. on a less
than 100 sh. certificate, red **$10.00**

Boston Mexican Petroleum Trustees, Unincorporated

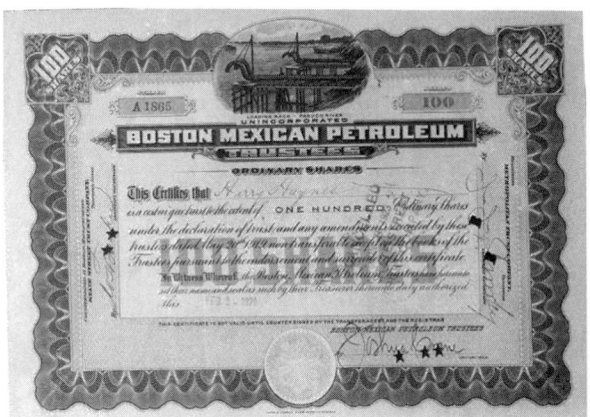

BO720-20-10, 1920, v, 100 sh., John A. Lowell Bank Note Co., Boston; brown and black .**$8.00**

Boston and Montana Mining Company

BO750-20-10, 1922, t, 100 sh., brown **$8.00**

Boston and Nova Scotia Gold Mining Company

BO790-20-10, 1865, v, 200 sh., revenue stamp, grey. **$90.00**

Boston and Providence Railroad Corporation (par $100)

BO830-10-10, 1852, v, 4 sh., Rawdon, Wright & Hatch, brown. **$40.00**

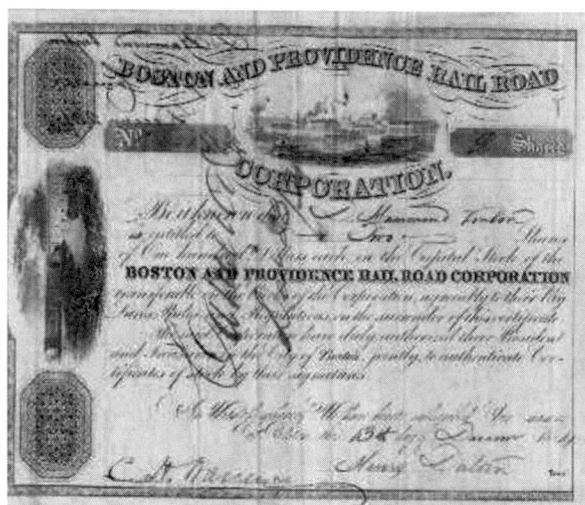

BO830-20-10, 1854, v, 2 sh., brown **$35.00**

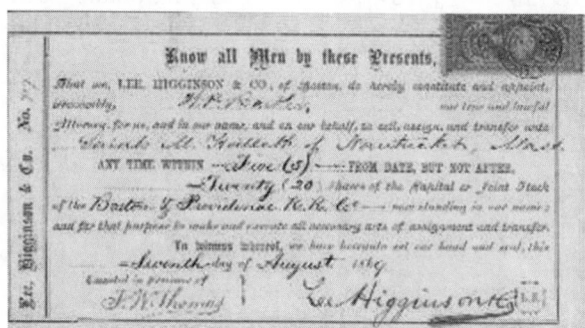

BO830-30-10, 1869, 20 sh., w. revenue stamp, grey. **$25.00**

Boston Railroad Holding Company (1909)

Formed by the New York, New Haven & Hartford to hold shares of the Boston & Maine Railroad.

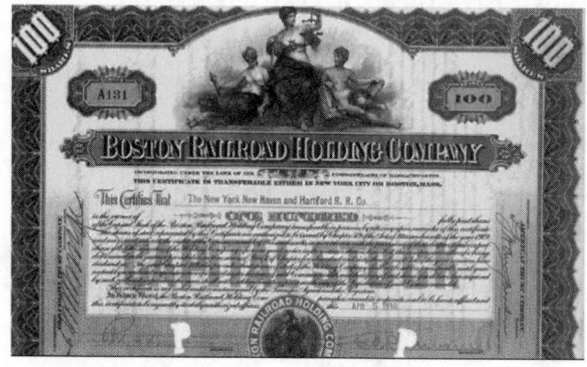

BO870-20-10, 1910, v, 100 sh., green **$5.00**
BO870-40-10, 1912, v, 8 pref. sh. on a less than 100 sh. certificate, brown. **$12.00**

*BO870-50-10, 19xx, v, 100 u/u pref. sh. certificate, green.........................$10.00

The Boston Terminal Company
BO930-30-10, 1897, v, $1,000 50-year bond, green
.................................$20.00

*BO930-40-10, 1897, v, $2,000 3-1/2% registered 50-year bond, green $20.00

Bown Livestock Co. (UT par $100)
BO1000-20-10, 1922, v-cow, 35 sh., green
.................................$18.00

Boyertown Burial Casket Co. (PA par $100)

*BO1050-20-10, 1917, v, 36 sh., grey $25.00

The Bradford Building, Loan and Savings Association
BR100-20-10, 1929, v, 10 sh., l. brown.....$8.00

Brainerd Light and Power Company (MN par $100)

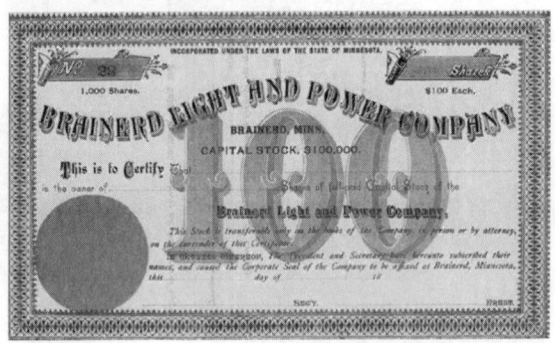

*BR200-20-10, 18xx, v, u/u certificate, brown on yellow...........................$12.00

Branch Mint Mining and Milling Company (SD par $1)

*BR270-20-10, 1911, v, i/u 1,000 sh., GOES, grey
.................................$20.00

Brandywine Raceway Association, Inc. (DE 1952, par $1)
BR300-20-10, 1965, v, 50 sh., blue $5.00

Brandywine Sports Inc. (DE 1977, par $1)

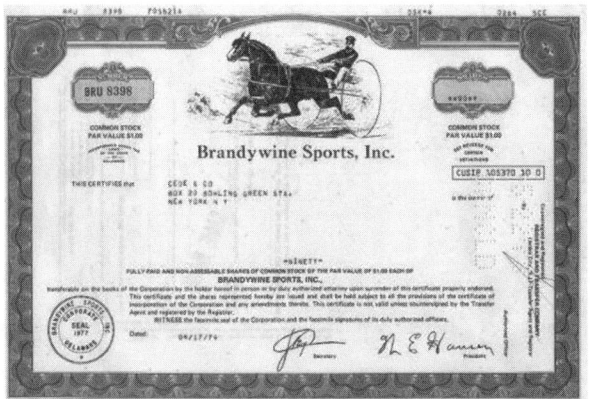

*BR310-20-10, 1979, v, 90 sh., ABN, blue
. . . .$3.00

Braniff Airways, Incorporated (NV)

BR340-30-10, 1972, v, less than 100 sh., brown
. . . .$29.00

The Bridgeport Gas Light Company (CT par $100)

BR400-30-10, 1911, v, 50 sh., purple. $10.00
BR400-40-10, 19xx, v, unissued 100 sh. certificate, orange $10.00

Brillo Manufacturing Company, Inc. (NY no par)

The company's founder Milton B. Loeb made steel wool a commercial reality. The company was merged into Purex in 1962.
BR460-30-10, 1957, 10 sh. on a less than 100 sh. certificate $25.00

Bristol Brass and Clock Company (CT par $25)

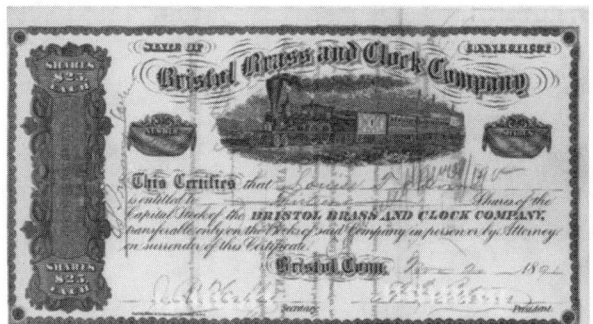

*BR560-20-10, 1891, v, 13 sh., grey $16.00

Bristol Silver Mining Company (par $25)

BR590-20-10, 1881, v, 31 sh., grey $157.00

Bristol-Myers Company (DE)

BR630-30-10, 1976, v, 5 sh. on a less 100 sh. certificate, ABN, purple $4.00

Britannia Mining Company (WI par $1)

*BR660-20-10, 1899, v, 250 sh., 11" x 8-1/2", grey border $195.00

*BR660-20-15, 1900, v, 50 sh., revenue stamp, signature variety, 10" x 8", grey border . . .$175.00

Brocton Fruit Juice Company (NY par $50)

BR700-20-10, 1901, v, 6 sh., revenue stamp on back, grey border $10.00

Brookline Oil Co. (CA par $1)

*BR750-20-10, 1939, v, 100 sh., orange $3.00

Brooklyn and Queens Transit Corporation (NY)

BR790-30-10, 1937, v, 25 pref. sh. on a less than 100 sh. certificate, green..............$8.00

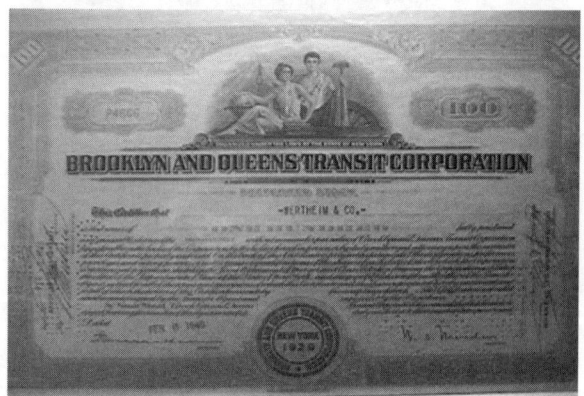

*BR790-40-10, 1945, v, 100 pref. sh., orange $10.00

The value of a stock certificate depends on:

- rarity
- the issuer
- signatures
- quality of engraving
- overall appearance
- condition
- date of issue

County of Brown (WI)

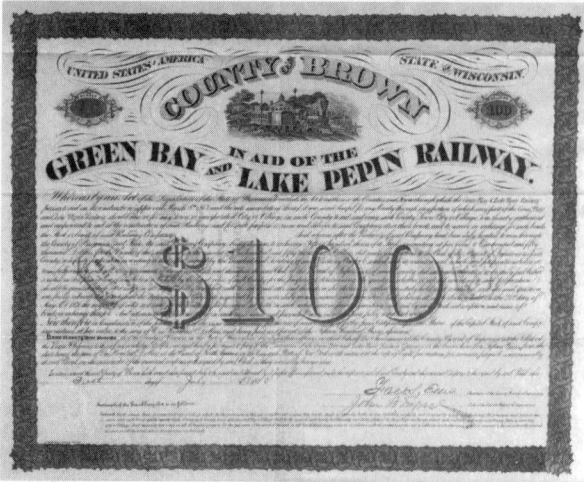

*BR830-20-10, 1867, v, $100 4% bond in aid of the Green Bay and Lake Pepin Railway, 14" x 10", green border $170.00

Browning-Ferris Industries, Inc.

Incorporated in 1967 BFI is one of the largest waste management firms on the continent.

*BR860-30-10, 1981, v, 200 sh. on a more than 100 sh. certificate, orange $12.00

Brush Electric Light and Power Company (MT territory, par $50)

BR930-20-10, 188x, v, unissued certificate, grey $11.00

Bryr Mawr Land and Improvements Company (MN par $100)

*BR960-20-10, 1888, v, 26 sh., ABN, 11" x 9", brown $125.00

Buckingham Slate Company of Virginia (VA par $100)

BU90-10-10, 1869, v, 10 sh., grey $40.00

Bucks County Trust Company (PA 1886, par $100)

BU140-20-10, 1918, 1 sh., grey $10.00

Buena Vista Mining Co. (CA)

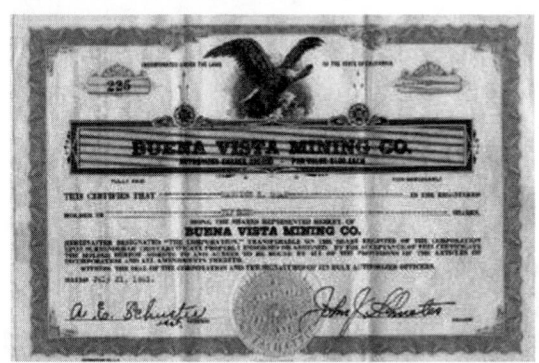

*BU200-20-10, 1941, v, 50 sh., orange $7.00

Buffalo Brewing Company (1888)

BU250-20-10, 19xx, v-buffalo, unissued certificate, grey. $20.00

Buffalo, Niagara and Eastern Power Corporation (NY 1925)

Eventually became the Niagara Power Corporation, known today as Niagara Mohawk.

BU280-20-10, 19xx, unissued, less than 100 sh., blue, v $12.00

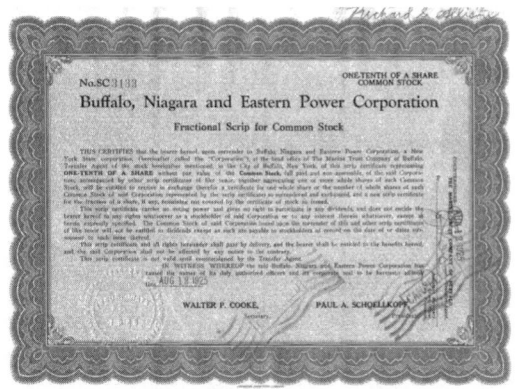

*BU280-30-10, 1925, f, i/u 1/10th of a share fractional scrip, ABN, 10-1/2" x 8", brown . . .$3.00

The Buffalo Placer Mining and Milling Company (CO 1905)

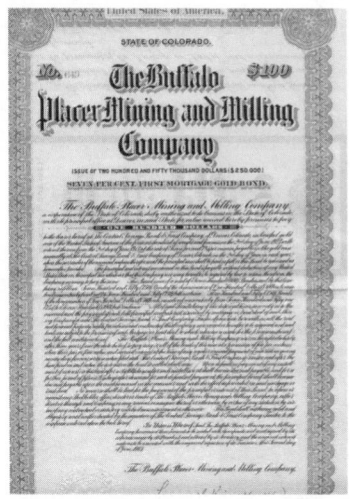

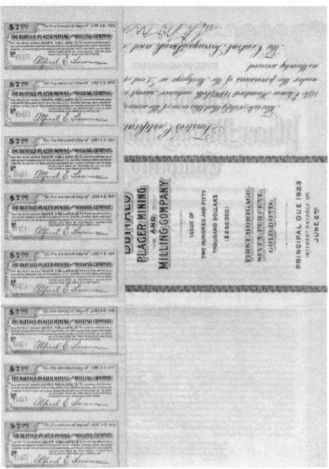

*BU330-30-10, 1913, v, i/u $100 bearer 7% 1st mort. gold bond, Bankers Supply Co., Denver; 9-1/4" x 15", l. brown. $7.00

Buffalo & Susquehanna Railroad Company
BU370-20-10, 1xxx, v, unissued pref. stock on a
less than 100 sh. certificate, brown......**$15.00**

**Builders' & Contractors Association
(MA par $25)**

*BU420-20-10, 19??, v, 1 sh., grey **$10.00**

Building Products, Inc. (DE)

*BU490-20-10, 1932, 15 conv. pref. sh. (par $10),
ABN, 11-1/4" x 7-3/4", purple **$4.00**

Bull & Bear Group Inc. (NY 1959)
BU550-20-10, 1985, 2,000 class A sh., green
...................................**$10.00**

Bull Creek Oil Company
BU580-20-10, 1865, v, 300 sh., blue border
...................................**$65.00**

**The Bullfrog Gold Bullion Mining
Company (AZ territory, par $1)**
BU630-20-10, 1906, v, 300 sh., brown ...**$230.00**

**Bullfrog Keystone Gold Mining Co.
(SD par $1)**
BU650-20-10, 1906, v, 500 sh., brown border
...................................**$80.00**

**Bullfrog North Star Mining Company
(AZ par $1)**

*BU670-20-10, 1907, v, 1,000 sh. on a not over
1,000 sh. certificate, 10" x 8-1/2", black .**$23.00**

**Bunker Hill Consolidated Mining Company
(CA 1889, par $1)**
Mines in Amador County, California.
BU720-20-10, 1921, v, 500 sh., grey border
...................................**$10.00**

**Bureau County Mineral Railway Company
(IL par $100)**
BU770-20-10, 190x, u/u certificate, brown ..**$8.00**

**Burley Tobacco Company of Cynthiana
(KY par $1)**
BU810-20-10, 1919, v, 100 sh., green **$25.00**

**Burlington, Cedar Rapids and Northern
Railway Company of Iowa (IA par $100)**
BU850-20-10, 1878, v, 21 sh., green **$20.00**

*BU850-30-10, 1892, v, 7 sh., green $10.00

*BU850-40-10, 1891, v, 100 sh., brown. $8.00

Burlington County Trust Company (NJ 1890 par $20)

BU880-20-10, 189x, v, unissued certificate, green
. . . .$4.00

BU880-30-10, 192x, v, unissued certificate, black
. . . .$4.00

BU880-40-10, 1932, v, 1 sh., green $5.00

BU880-60-10, 1954, v, 3,000 class D pref. sh. (par
$10), blue $6.00

Burlington Industries, Inc.

*BU940-30-10, 1969, v, $5,000 5% conver. subord.
debenture due 1991, green $6.00

Burlington and Missouri River Railroad Company (IA par $100)

BU980-20-10, 1871, v, 7 sh., green $25.00
BU980-30-10, 1875, v, 50 sh., brown $21.00

Burlington Northern Inc.

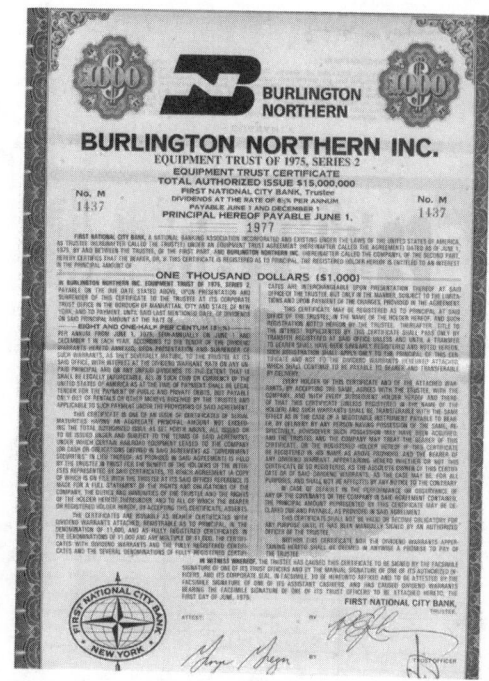

*BU1030-40-10, 1975, v, u/u $1,000 equipment
trust of 1975, series 2, 8-1/2% due 1977, ABN,
9-1/2" x 13-1/2", purple $6.00

The Burlington and Northwestern Railway Company (IA par $100)

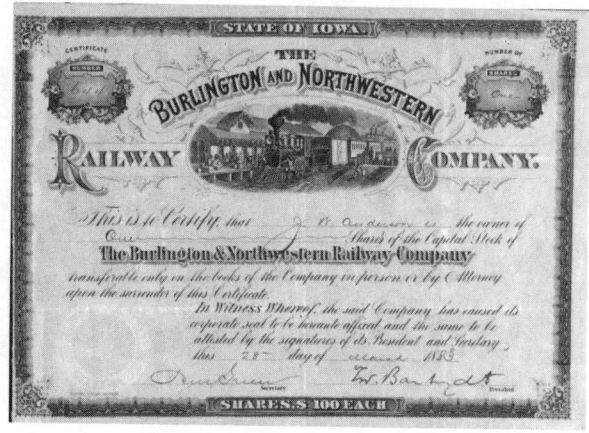

*BU1050-20-10, 1883, v, 1 sh., 10-1/2" x 8", brown
border $30.00

Bush Terminal Company (NY no par)

*BU1100-30-10, 1928, v, 4 sh. on a less than 100 sh. certificate, RBN, 11-1/2" x 8-1/2", reddish $4.00

*BU1100-50-10, 1932, v, 10 sh., 7% debenture stock on a less than 100 sh. certificate, RBN, 11-1/2" x 8-1/2", purple $4.00

Butler Aviation International, Inc. (DE par $1)

*BU1160-20-10, 1974, 100 sh., SCB, 12" x 8", blue................................$6.00

Butte Carriage Works (MT par $1)

BU1200-20-10, 19xx, v, unissued certificate, dark brown $8.00

Butte Gas, Light and Fuel Company (MT par $100)

BU1230-20-10, 1xxx, v, u/u certificate, grey border $22.00

Butterfly Consolidated Mines, Inc.

*BU1270-20-10, 19xx, v, u/u certificate, black $4.00

C

The Cactus Mining Company (UT par $25)

CA100-10-10, 1899, v, 1 bearer sh., green . .**$24.00**

Cadena de Cobre Mining Co. (AZ par $1)

CA150-20-10, 19??, v, 5,000 sh., green **$20.00**

Cairo and Fulton Railroad Company of Arkansas

CA260-20-10, xxxx, v, u/u $100 land trust certificate, pink **$30.00**

Calaveras Water and Mining Company

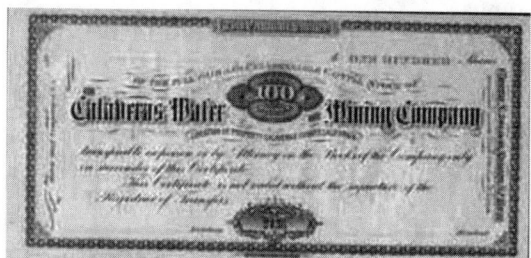

*CA350-20-10, 1xxx, u/u 100 sh. certificate, green
. . . .**$5.00**

California Diamond Oil Company (AZ 1905 par $1)

This San Francisco based company was affiliated with Amalgamated Mines & Oil, Goldfield Somerset Mining, Manhattan Nevada Gold Mines, Murchie Extention Gold Mines, Murchie Leasing & Mining and United Tonopah & Gold Mines.

CA400-20-10, 190x, 25 pref. sh., green **$15.00**

California-Nevada Creamery Company (1892, par $1)

*CA440-20-10, 189x, v, u/u certificate, small certificate, grey **$6.00**

California Street Cable Railroad Co. (par $100)

*CA500-20-10, 1888, v, 100 sh., blue **$150.00**

Caltex Oil Company (NV par $1)

*CA600-20-10, 1919, 50 sh., bearer certificate, British revenue imprint, brown **$5.00**

Calumet and Arizona Mining Company

CA660-20-10, 1922, v, 8 sh. on a less than 100 sh. certificate, blue **$12.00**

Calumet & Hecla, Inc.

CA690-30-10, 1962, v, 50 sh. on a less than 100 sh. certificate, ABN, green **$5.00**

*CA690-40-10, 1955, v, 100 sh., red **$4.00**

Calumet and Hecla Consolidated Copper Company (par $5)

CA700-30-10, 1946, v, 30 sh. on a less than 100 sh. certificate, blue $15.00

The Calumet Mining, Milling and Smelting Company (WY par $1)

CA730-20-10, 1902, v, 500 sh., green $30.00

County of Cambria (PA)

*CA770-20-10, 1880, v, $500 bond, grey . . .$7.00

*CA770-30-10, 1890, v, $500 bond, 10-1/2" x 14-1/2", pink border $8.00

UNLISTED TYPES & VARIETIES

Readers are welcome to contact the author directly at:

**Rainer Stahlberg
P.O. Box 1044
Rooseveltown, New York 13683**

Cambria County Coal Company (PA par $100)

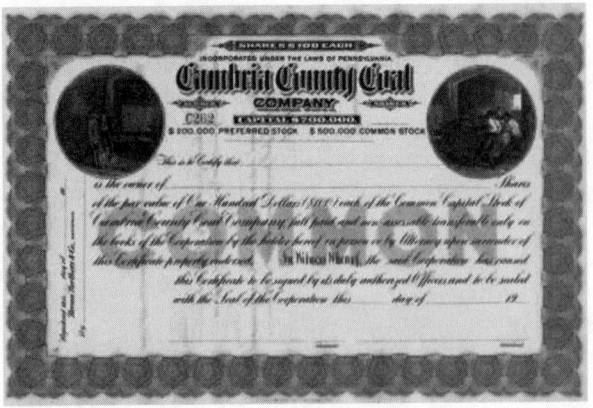

*CA800-20-10, 19xx, v, u/u certificate, reddish orange $6.00

Camden & Philadelphia Steamboat Ferry Company

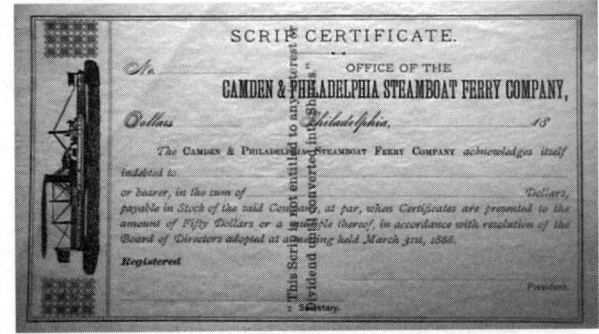

*CA830-20-10, 18xx, v, u/u scrip certificate (par $50), black on light brown $20.00

The Camp Bird Mining, Leasing and Power Company (CO par $1)

CA870-20-10, 1914, v, 1,000 sh., brown . . .$50.00

The Campbell Creek Coal Company (OH par $100)

CA900-20-10, 19xx, v, unissued certificate, green $17.00

CA900-20-10, 1928, v-river boat, 3 sh., green $25.00

The Canada Hill Gold Mining Company (CO 1899)

CA930-20-10, 1899, 1,000 sh., grey border $20.00

Canada Southern Railway Company (NY par $100)

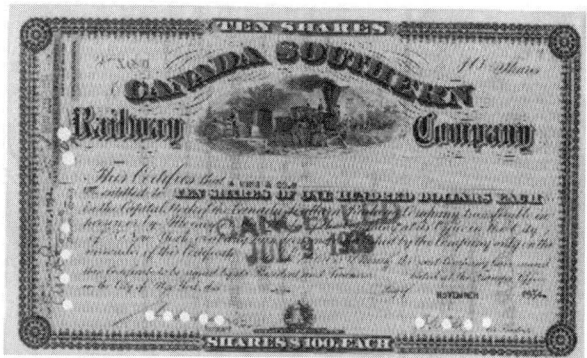

*CA960-30-10, 1934, v, 10 sh., green $6.00

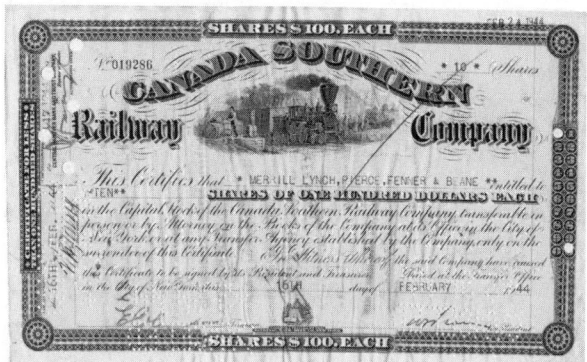

*CA960-40-10, 1944, v, 10 sh. on a less than 100 sh. certificate, NBN, 11-1/4" x 6-3/4", grey on yellow $8.00
1954, v, 10 sh., brown. $7.00

*CA960-60-10, 1880, v, $1,000 2nd Mortgage registered bond, green $18.00

Canadian (County) Mill and Elevator Co. (OK)

CA1000-20-10, 1911, v, 100 sh., grey $15.00

Cane Springs Oil & Minerals Corp. (UT par 5¢)

*CA1070-20-10, 1966, v, 100 sh., SCB, 12" x 8-1/4", brown $3.00

Cape Breton Petroleum Company (MA par $1)

*CA1140-20-10, 1948, v, 525 sh., green . . . $14.00

The Capital City Power and Mining Company (CO)

CA1200-20-10, 1907, v, 2 sh., grey $10.00

The Capital Petroleum Transportation Company

CA1230-20-10, 1920, v, 48 sh., green $25.00

Capital Traction Company (DC par $100)

*CA1260-20-10, 1897, v, 57 sh., ABN, green
. . . .$15.00

Capitol Bank and Trust Company (MA)

CA1320-20-10, 1971, v, 100 sh., blue $5.00

Capitol House Consultants, Ltd. (MI par $10)

*CA1350-20-10, 19xx, v, u/u certificate, w/o
imprint, 11" x 7-1/2", red border $3.00

Capitol Petroleum Company

CA1390-20-10, 1930, v, 8,000 sh., green. . . .$8.00

It is generally assumed that only 5% of certificates survive to reach collectors.

Carbonate Flume Company of Carbonate Mining Camp Dakota (Dakota Territory, par $5)

Located in the Black Hills area.

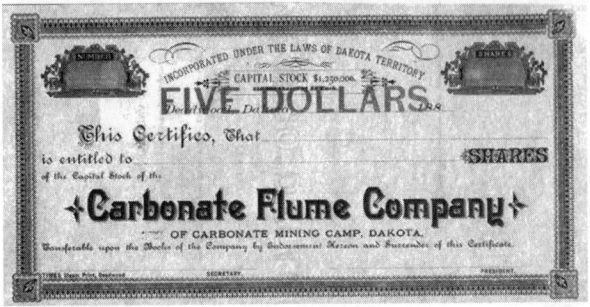

CA1480-20-10, 188x, u/u certificate, Times Print,
Deadwood, grey-brown border $18.00

The Carborundum Company

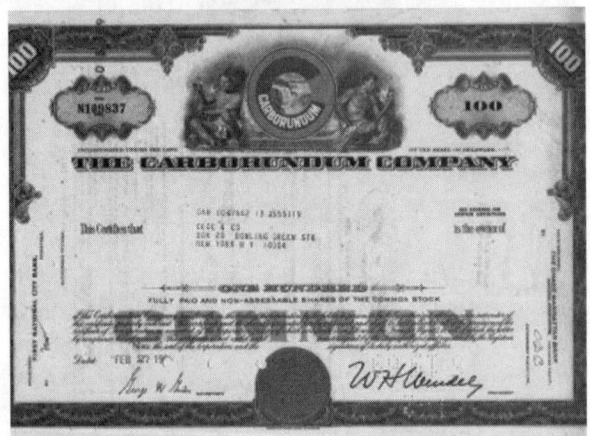

*CA1520-30-10, 1967, v, 100 sh., blue $6.00

The Caribou Silver Mining Company (CO par $1)

CA1550-20-10, 1928, v, 2,160 sh., green. . .$30.00

Carnie Mining Company

CA1590-20-10, 1904, v, 8 sh. (par $25), blue $4.00

The Carolina & Northwestern Railway Company (NC par $50)

CA1660-20-10, 1897, v, 12 sh., brown $70.00

Carolina Power & Light Company (NC 1926)

CA1690-30-10, 1967, v, 100 sh., blue $7.00

Carriers & General Corporation (MD)
CA1740-20-10, 1964, v, 10 sh. on less than 100 sh. certificate, red **$15.00**

Carson Hill Gold Mining Corporation (NV 1931)
The certificate states "Mines at Carson Hill and Melones, California."
CA1800-20-10, 19xx, v, specimen certificate, green **$20.00**

Carte Blanche Corporation (DE 1965)
CA1900-30-10, 1966, v, 1 class A sh. (par $1) on a less than 100 sh. certificate non voting), ABN, blue **$6.00**

J.I. Case Company (WI par $1)
CA1950-40-10, 1968, v, 100 sh., red **$10.00**

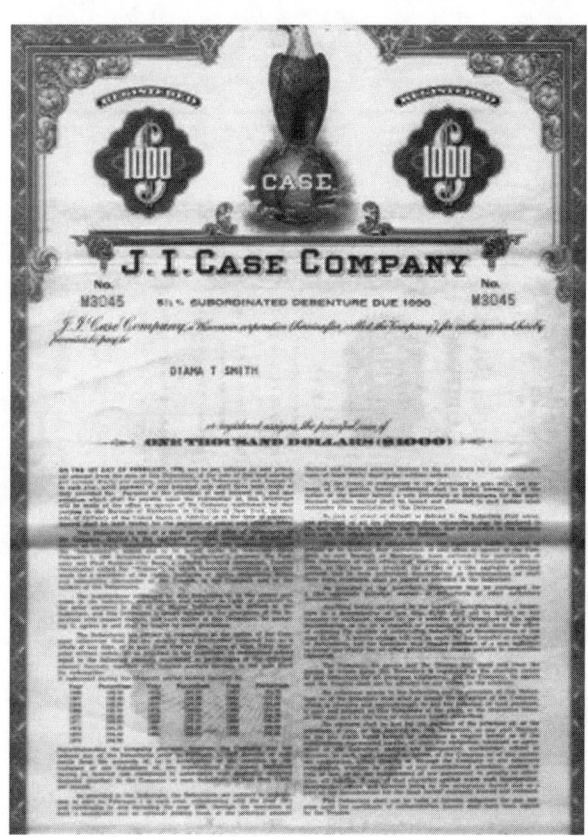

CA1950-70-10, 1965, v, $1,000 bond, blue
. . . .**$13.00**

Cash Boy Consolidated Mining Company (NV par $1)

*CA2000-20-10, 1916, v, 1,000 sh., grey . . .**$7.00**

Catskill Evening Line, Inc.
CA2100-30-10, 19xx, v, $1,000 unissued due 1947 bond, orange **$10.00**

Cedar Falls & Minnesota Rail Road Company (IA par $100)
CE100-20-10, 186x, v, u/u certificate, light green
. . . .**$18.00**

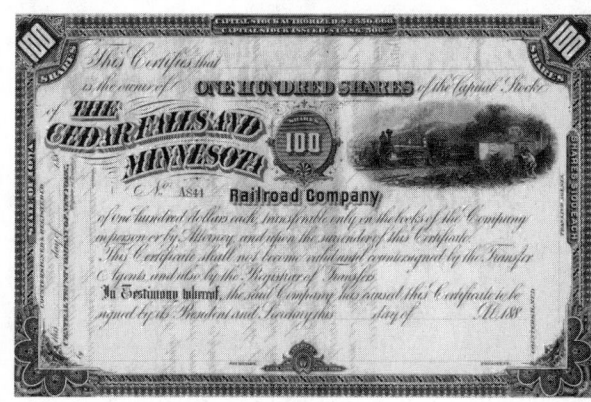

*CE100-25-10, 188x, v, 100 sh., u/u certificate, ABN, 10-1/2" x 7", grey **$15.00**

The value of a stock certificate depends on:
- rarity
- the issuer
- signatures
- quality of engraving
- overall appearance
- condition
- date of issue

Celanese Corporation of America

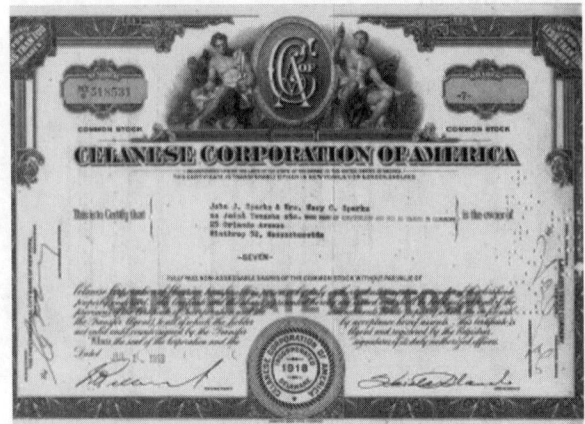

*CE240-30-10, 1959, v, 7 sh. on a less than 100 sh. certificate, brown **$6.00**
CE240-40-10, 1970, v, 100 sh., olive **$5.00**

*CE240-60-10, 1957, v, 40 pref. sh. on a less than 100 sh. certificate, orange **$6.00**

Centennial Mining Company (par $25)

CE360-20-10, 1892, v, 50 sh., grey border
. . . .**$150.00**

Central American Life Insurance Company (TX)

*CE400-20-10, 1957, v, 22 sh., Hester's - Lubbock, 11" x 8-1/2", grey **$3.00**

*CE400-30-10, 1962, v, 100 sh., HFLCO, 10-1/2 x 8-1/4", grey **$3.00**

Central American Naval Stores, Inc. (par $5)

*CE430-20-10, 19xx, v, u/u certificate, green
. . . .**$10.00**

The Central Foundry Company
(ME 1911, par $1.00)

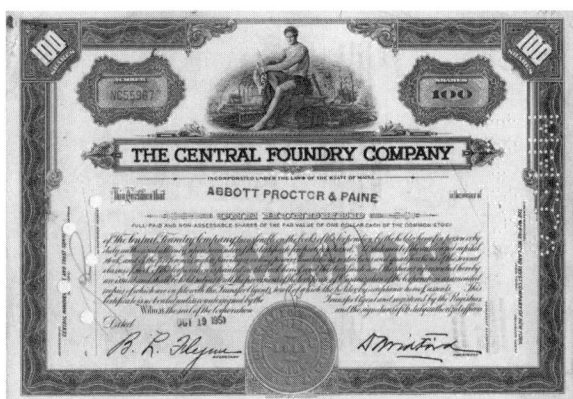

*CE500-30-10, 1951, v, 100 sh., CBN, 11-1/2" x 8", green $5.00

CE500-40-10, 1958, v, 100 sh., issued to Francis I. Dupont & Co., green. $6.00

Central of Georgia Railway Company

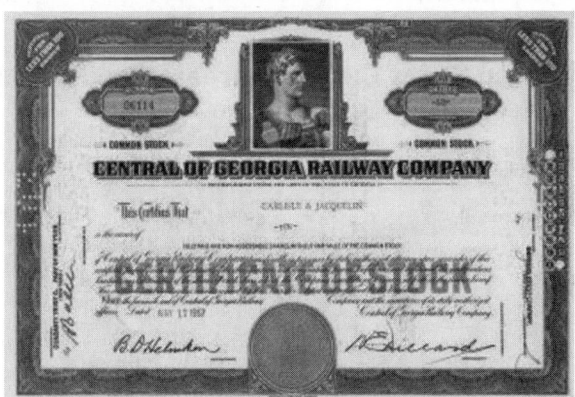

*CE570-20-10, 1957, v, 10 sh. on a less than 100 sh. certificate, brown. $9.00

*CE570-40-10, 1953, v, 100 preferred sh., blue
. . . .$13.00

Central Illinois Light Company (IL 1913)

*CE610-40-10, 1933, v, $100,000 u/c specimen bond, red. $9.00

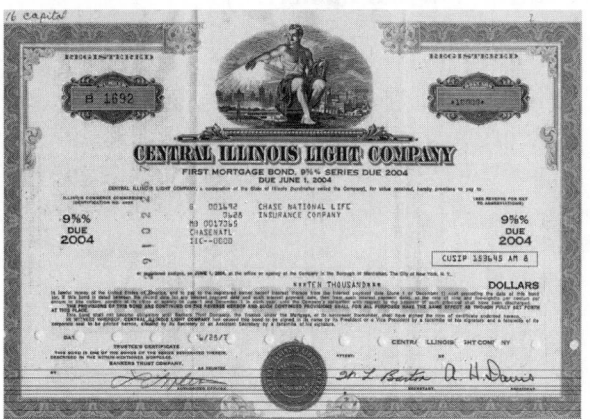

*CE610-60-10, 197?, v, $10,000 9% first mort. bond due 2004, SCB, 12" x 8", brown. . . .$5.00

Central Instrument Corp. (NY par 10¢)

*CE660-20-10, 1952, v, 100 sh., brown $3.00

Central Mexican Oil Company (DE par $100)

*CE710-20-10, 1921, v, 8 sh., green $10.00

Central National Bank (DC)

CE760-20-10, 1905, 5 sh., grey-brown $12.00

Central Ohio Rail Road Company as Reorganized (par $50)

CE800-20-10, 18xx, v, u/u pref. certificate, grey
....$18.00

Central Pacific Railway Company

*CE900-40-10, 1944, v, $1,000 series A 4-1/4%
due 1974, orange....................$7.00

Central Passenger Railway Company

CE950-20-10, 19xx, v, u/u certificate, green
....$20.00

Central Public Utility Corporation (DE)

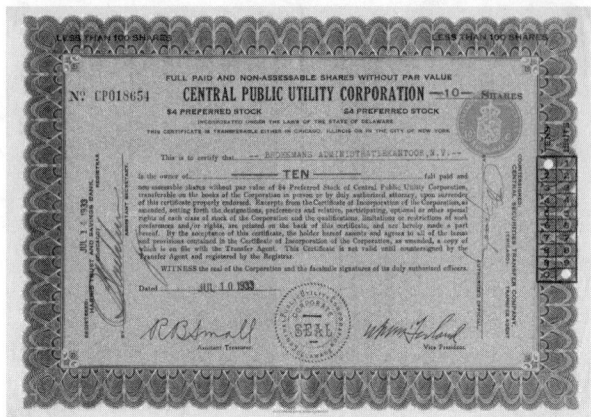

*CE980-25-10, 1933, 10 sh., of $4 Pref. on a less
than 100 sh. certificate, w. Dutch revenue
imprint, CBN, 11" x 8", brown $3.00

Central States Electric Corporation (VA 1912)

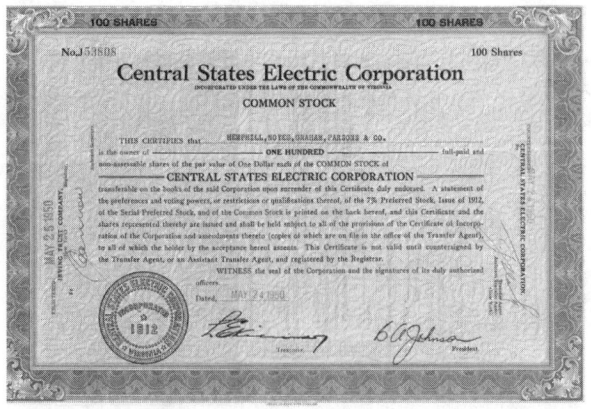

*CE1030-30-10, 1950, 100 sh. (par $1), ABN, 12"
x 8", brown.......................$3.00

It is generally assumed that only 5% of certificates survive to reach collectors.

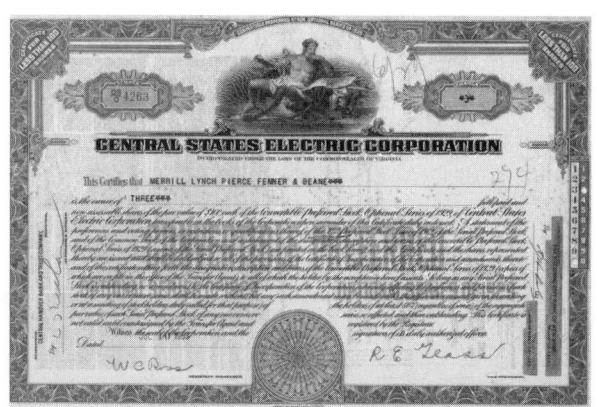

*CE1030-50-10, 1953, v, 3 convertible preferred optional series of 1929 sh. on a less than 100 sh. certificate (par $100), ABN, 12" x 8", brown
. . . .$4.00

CE1030-60-10, 1950, v, 50 sh., conv. pref. on a less than 100 sh. certificate (par $100), brown
. . . .$4.00

Central Wisconsin Electric Cooperative (WI)

*CE1060-30-10, 1997, v, membership of Chester L. Krause, GOES, 11" x 8", brown border
. . . .$5.00

Century Natural Gas & Oil Corporation (DE 1949, par $0.50)

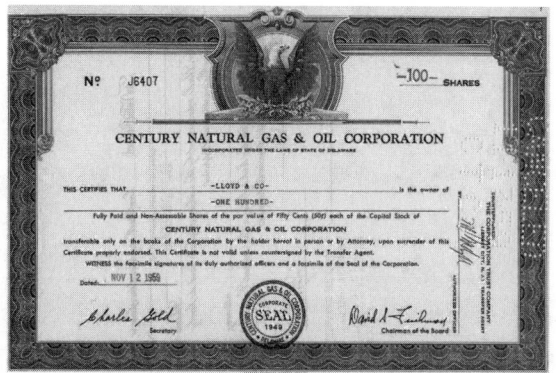

*CE1100-20-10, 1959, v, 100 sh., SCB, 11-3/4" x 7-3/4", green. $3.00

Century Ribbon Mills, Inc. (NY)

*CE1140-20-10, 1946, v, 28 sh. on a less than 100 sh. certificate, orange $3.00

Ceralvo Mexico Mining and Beneficiating Syndicate (par $10)

*CE1220-20-10, 188x, v, u/u certificate . . .$12.00

Chance Vought Aircraft, Incorporated (par $1)

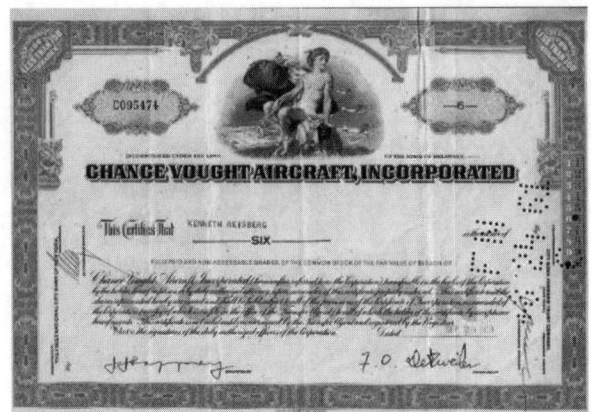

*CH100-20-10, 1959, v, 6 sh. on a less than 100 sh. certificate, orange $8.00

The Charliers Railway Company (PA par $50)

CH170-20-10, 1906, v, 7 sh., green $16.00

The Chase Manhattan Bank (1799)

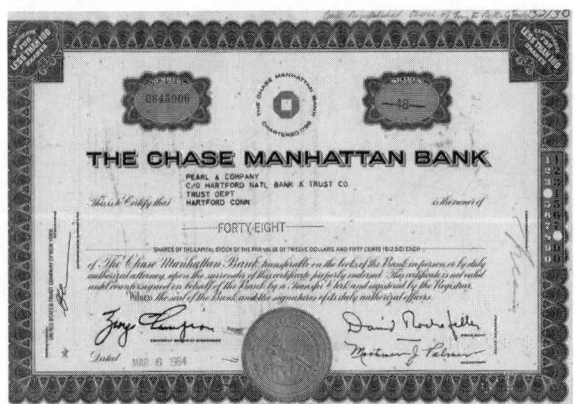

*CH210-30-10, 1964, v, 48 sh. on a less than 100 sh. certificate (par $12.50), ABN, 12" x 8-1/4", green $8.00

The value of a stock certificate depends on:
- rarity
- the issuer
- signatures
- quality of engraving
- overall appearance
- condition
- date of issue

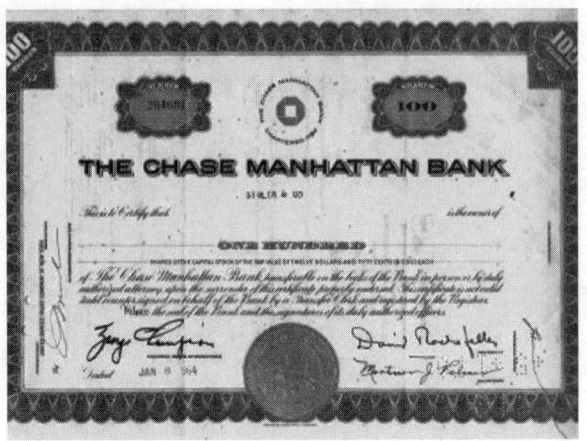

*CH210-40-10, 1964, v, 100 sh., blue $8.00

The Chase National Bank of the City of New York (par $20)

CH240-30-10, 1932, v, 5 sh., red border . . .$15.00

The Chateaugay and Lake Placid Railway Company (NY)

*CH300-25-10, 1922, v, 100 pref. sh., grey . .$15.00

Chattanooga, Rome and Southern Railroad Company

CH360-20-10, 1898, v, 10 sh., l. brown. . . .$40.00

The Chattanooga Union Railway Company (par $100)

CH390-20-10, 18xx, v, unissued certificate, l. brown $18.00

Chelten Corporation

CH420-20-10, 1944, v, 1 sh. on a less than 100 sh.
certificate, blue **$4.00**

Chemsol, Incorporated (NJ 1948, par $0.50)

CH450-20-10, 1965, v, 15 sh., SCB, 12" x 8",
brown **$3.00**

CH450-30-10, 1963, v, 100 sh., SCB, 12" x 8", l.
green **$3.00**

The Chesapeake and Delaware Canal Company (PA-DE-MD)

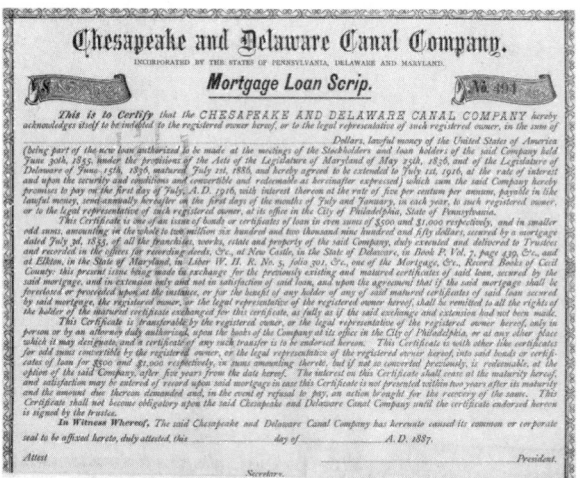

*CH500-30-10, 1887, u/u 5% mortgage loan scrip
certificate, w/o imprint, 10-1/4" x 9", grey
. . . .**$5.00**

The Chesapeake and Ohio Railway Company (VA par $25)

*CH540-30-10, 1970, v, 50 sh. on a less than 100
sh. certificate, blue **$7.00**
CH540-40-10, 1972, v, 100 sh., purple **$9.00**

This catalog has listings in an alphabetical topical format. The reason is simple: Companies diversify as they grow. For example, the Canadian Pacific Railway company recently split into five companies. They represent the railway, hotels, shipping, airline, and petroleum interests of the company. During World War II, the Singer sewing machine company made guns and other defense-related equipment, so where should we list it? It's far easier to use a strict alphabetical order, rather than to confuse the reader with topical classifications.

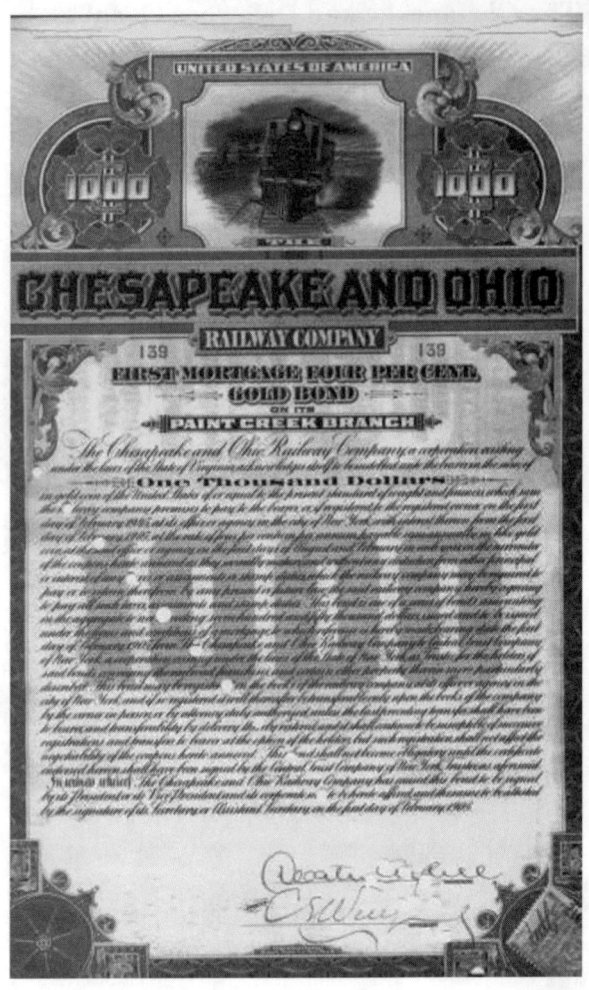

*CH540-60-10, 1905, v, $1,000 1st mortgage bond on the Paint Creek Branch, International Bank Note Company, green $26.00

The Chesapeake, Ohio and Southwestern Railroad Company (par $100)
CH570-20-10, 188x, v, unissued certificate signed by C.P. Huntington, green $42.00

Chesapeake Western Railway (VA)
CH600-50-10, 1951, v, $10,000 bond, brown $11.00

Chessie System, Inc. (par $12.50)
CH640-20-10, 1974, v, 10 sh., orange $20.00

Chester, Darby and Philadelphia Railway Company (PA par $50)

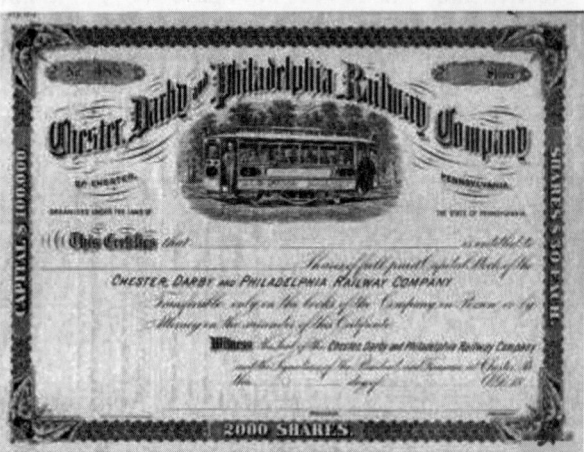

*CH680-20-10, 18xx, v, u/u certificate, brown $14.00

Chester River Steamboat Company (par $100)

*CH700-20-10, 18xx, v, u/u certificate, brown border $40.00

Chestnut Hill & Glenside Rapid Transit Street Railway Co.
CH720-20-10, 19xx, unissued certificate. . . $10.00

It is generally assumed that only 5% of certificates survive to reach collectors.

The Chestnut Hill Rail Road Company (1848, par $50)

CH750-30-10, 1935, v, 6 sh., blue **$10.00**

The Chicago and Alton Railroad Company

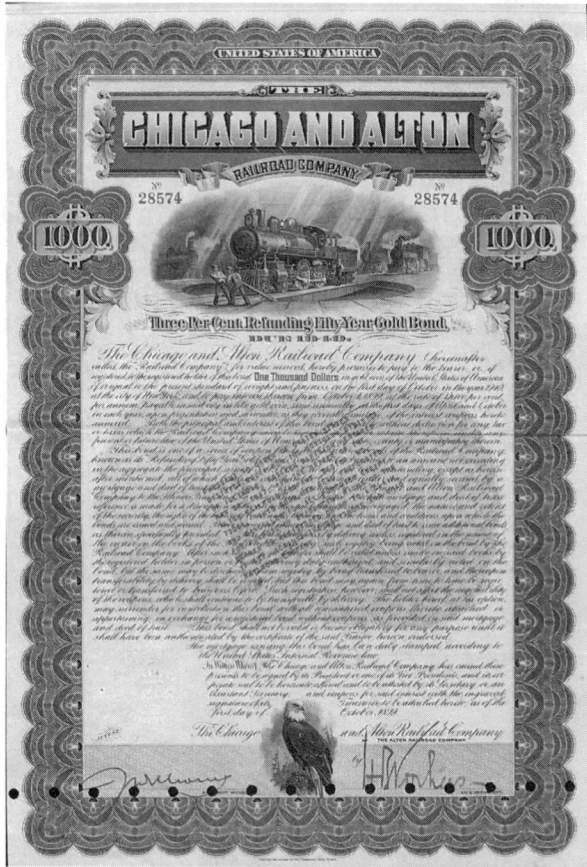

CH800-30-10, 1899, v, $1,000 3% refunding 50-year gold bond, green **$25.00**

Chicago, Aurora and Elgin Corporation

CH830-30-10, 1922, v, $100 3% gold bond, brown **$21.00**

Chicago, Aurora and Elgin Railway Company (IL par $1)

CH840-30-10, 1959, 100 sh., orange **$9.00**

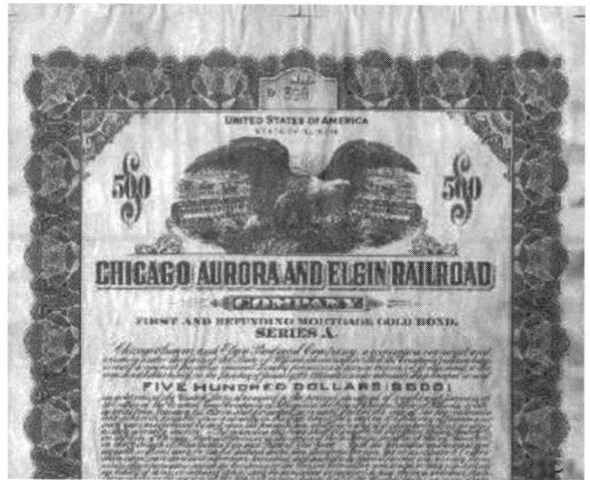

CH840-50-10, 1926, v, $500 series A 6% 1st and refunding mortgage gold bond, due 1951 w. coupons, brown **$12.00**

Chicago, Burlington and Quincy Railroad Company (IL par $100)

*CH870-20-10, 1878, v, i/u 50 sh., black...$15.00

*CH870-30-10, 188x, v, u/c certificate, blue
....$20.00
CH870-40-10, 1881, v, 10 sh., grey......$17.00
CH870-50-10, 1891, v, 5 sh., orange.....$17.00
CH870-60-10, 1884, v, 1 sh., brown.....$17.00
CH870-70-10, 1901, v, 25 sh., orange.....$17.00

Chicago and Canada Southern Railway Company

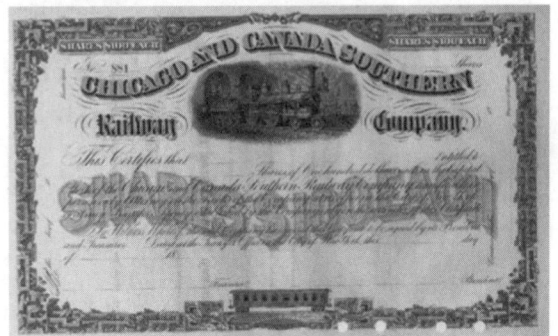

*CH900-20-10, 18xx, v, u/c certificate (par $100),
blue...........................$26.00

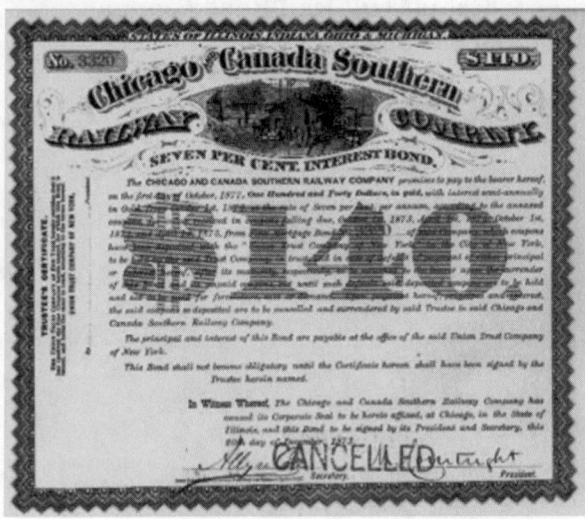

*CH900-40-10, 1873, v, $140 7% bond, brown
.....................................$26.00

Chicago Cotton Manufacturing Co. (par $100)

CH930-20-10, 19xx, v, u/u certificate, grey border
.....................................$15.00

The Chicago & Denver Reduction Company (CO par $100)

CH970-20-10, 1887, 5 sh., brown........$17.00

Chicago and Eastern Illinois Railroad Company (par $100)

CH1000-30-10, 19xx, v, u/c certificate for less than
100 sh., green........................$8.00
CH1000-50-10, 1891, v, 10 sh., Pref. stock, blue
.....................................$20.00

*CH1000-60-10, 18xx, v, u/c 100 pref. sh., brown
.....................................$8.00
CH1000-70-10, 19xx, v, u/u 100 sh. certificate,
orange..............................$15.00

Chicago Great Western Railroad Company (IL)

CH1030-20-10, 1939, v, 100 sh., ABN, brown
......................................$10.00

CH1030-30-10, 1930, v, 100 pref. sh. (par $100), ABN, 12" x 8-1/2", brown $10.00

Chicago Great Western Railway Company (DE par $10)

CH1040-20-10, 1964, v, 100 sh., purple $8.00

Chicago, Lake Geneva & Pacific Railway Co. (WI par $100)

CH1060-20-10, 18xx, v, 12-1/2" x 10-1/2", grey border $35.00

Chicago, Milwaukee and Gary Railway Company (IL par $100)

CH1080-20-10, 1908, v, u/u certificate, Western Bank Note Company, 12" x 8", brown border
................................$20.00

Chicago, Milwaukee and Puget Sound Railway Company (WA par $100)

CH1090-20-10, 1921, v, 1 sh., 10" x 8", grey border.............................$75.00

Chicago-Milwaukee Road and Realty Company (ME)

CH1100-20-10, 1909, v, 10 sh., green border
................................$7.00

Chicago, Milwaukee and St. Paul Railway Company

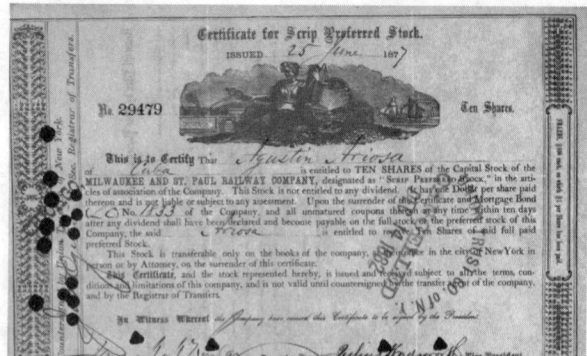

*CH1120-25-10, 1877, v, 10 scrip pref. sh. (par $100 of which $1 has been paid), number on right, 10-1/2" x 6", grey border.........$60.00

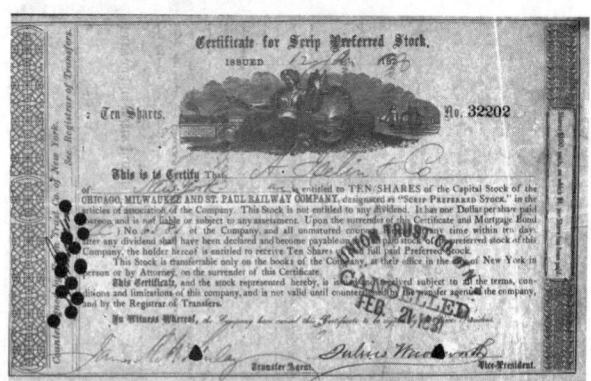

*CH1120-26-10, 1878, v, 10 scrip pref. sh. (par $100 of which $1 has been paid), number on left, 10" x 5-1/2", grey border $60.00

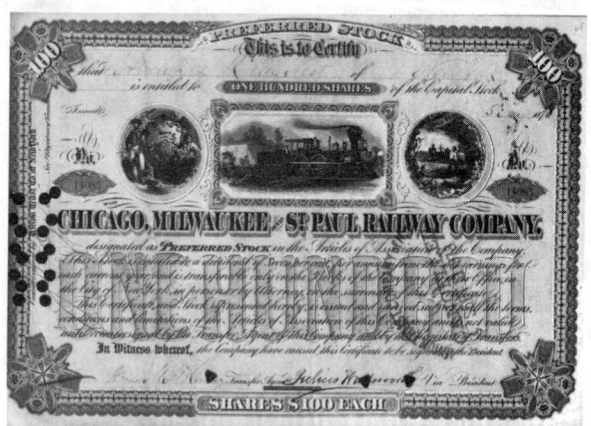

*CH1120-30-10, 1878, v, 100 pref. sh., 11" x 8", brown $60.00

Chicago, Milwaukee & St. Paul Railway Company of Idaho (ID par $100)

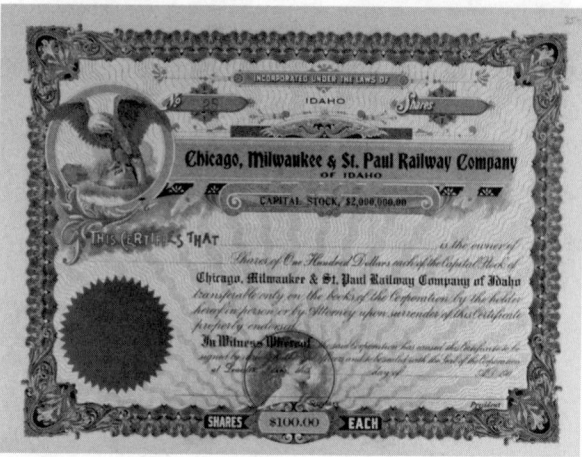

*CH1122-20-10, 190x, v, u/u certificate, 11" x 8-1/2", brown border $35.00

Chicago, Milwaukee & St. Paul Railway Company of South Dakota (SD par $100)

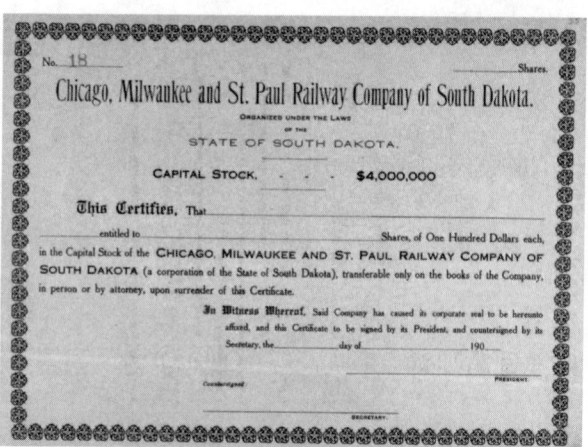

*CH1124-20-10, 190x, u/u certificate, 9" x 7", brown border $35.00

The value of a stock certificate depends on:

- **rarity**
- **the issuer**
- **signatures**
- **quality of engraving**
- **overall appearance**
- **condition**
- **date of issue**

Chicago, Milwaukee & St. Paul Railway Company of Washington (WA par $100)

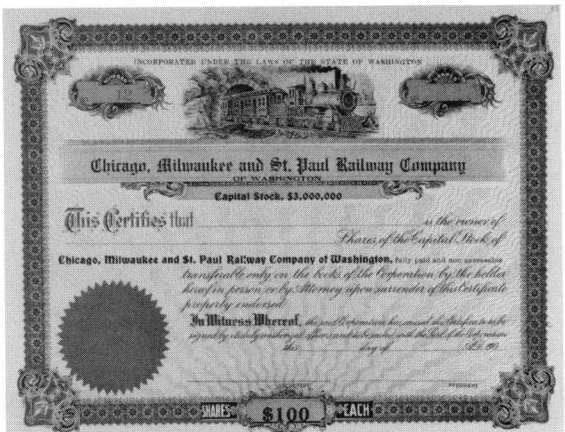

*CH1126-20-10, 190x, v, u/u certificate, 11" x 8-1/2", brown border. $35.00

Chicago, Milwaukee, St. Paul and Pacific Railroad Company (WI)

*CH1130-15-10, 1932, v, 5 sh. on a less than 100 sh. certificate (no par), ABN, 12" x 8", green border $35.00

*CH1130-20-10, 1930, v, 100 sh. (no par), ABN, 12" x 8", maroon. $25.00

CH1130-30-10, 1938, v, 100 pref. sh., orange $35.00

*CH1130-35-10, 1939, v, 90 sh. on a less than 100 sh. certificate (par $100), SBC, 12" x 8", blue border $30.00

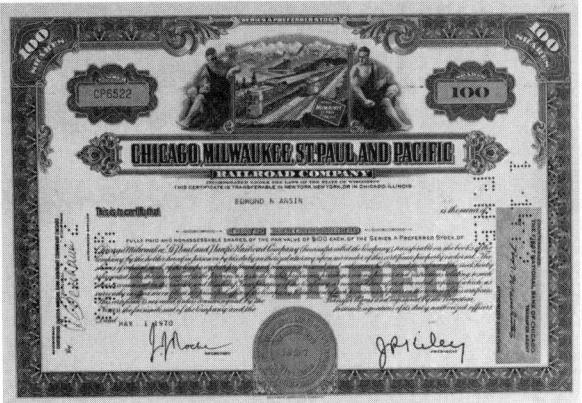

*CH1130-40-10, 1970, v, 100 series A pref. sh. (par $100), 12" x 8", blue border $15.00

*CH1130-60-10, 1928, t, specimen $80 scrip certificate series A, 50-year 5% mort. gold bond, ABN, 11-1/2" x 8", orange. $15.00

Chicago and North Western Railway Company (WI)

*CH1170-20-10, 1952, v, 100 sh. (no par), ABN, 12"x 8", green......................$8.00

*CH1170-30-10, 1947, v, 10 5% series A pref. sh. on a less than 100 sh. certificate (par $100), ABN, 12" x 8", brown $9.00

*CH1170-40-10, 1958, v, 100 pref. series A 5% sh. (par $100), ABN, 12" x 8", blue.........$8.00

*CH1170-60-10, 1959, v, $1,000 2nd mortgage 4-1/2% convertible income bond, series A, 10" x 16", brown border....................$15.00

*CH1170-65-10, 1964, v, $5,000 2nd mort. 4-1/2% convert. income bond, 10" x 16", blue border $15.00

Chicago, Portage and Superior Railway Company (IL, WI)

CH1200-20-10, 18xx, v, u/u certificate, Franklin Banknote Co., 11" x 8", green border....**$30.00**

CH1200-40-10, 1881, v, $1,000 6% 1st mortgage land grant bond, due 1971, 10-1/2" x 12", grey border **$40.00**

Chicago, Rock Island and Pacific Railroad Company (DE)

CH1230-20-10, 1915, v, 10 sh. on a less than 100 sh. certificate(IL), ABN, orange........**$11.00**

CH1230-30-10, 1964, v, 1 sh. on a less than 100 sh. certificate, brown **$7.00**

CH1230-40-10, 1964, v, 100 sh., blue **$7.00**

CH1230-50-10, 1964, v, 1,000 sh., brown ...**$7.00**

CH1230-70-10, 1911, v, $1,000 first mortgage 4% bond, grey........................**$14.00**

CH1230-80-10, 19xx, v, $5,000 bond, brown **$12.00**

Chicago, Rock Island and Pacific Railway Company (IL-IA)

CH1240-20-10, 1959, v, 100 sh., blue.....**$4.00**

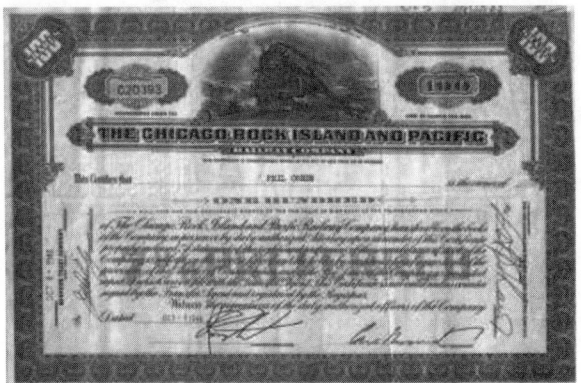

CH1240-40-10, 1946, v, 100 pref. sh., brown **$8.00**

CH1240-60-10, 1887, v, $15,000 1st mortgage bond, 13" x 9", brown **$10.00**

CH1240-70-10, 1891, v, $5,000 first mort. bond, orange..........................**$20.00**

CH1240-80-10, 1911, v, $1,000 1st and refunding mort. 4% gold bond, dark grey **$20.00**

CH1240-90-10, 1988, v, u/c $5,000 general mortgage gold bond, ABN, green **$13.00**

Chicago, St. Louis and Pittsburgh Railroad Company

CH1280-20-10, 1883, v, 50 sh., orange **$15.00**

Chicago South Shore and South Bend Railroad (IN)

*CH1320-40-10, 1929, v, 25 class A pref. 6-1/2% (par $100) on a less than 100 sh. certificate, green **$15.00**

Chicago & South Western Railway Company (par $100)

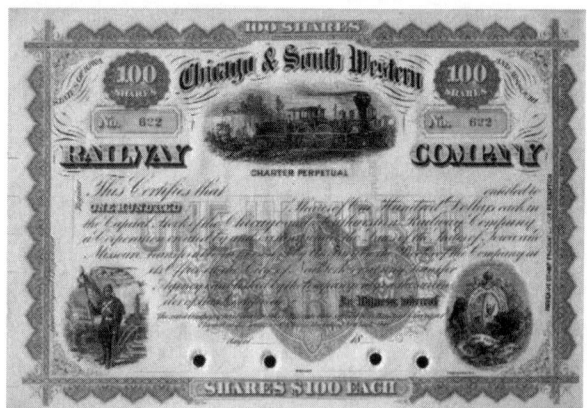

*CH1350-20-10, 18xx, v, u/c 100 sh. certificate, green **$20.00**

Chicago Terminal Transfer Railroad Company (IL par $100)

*CH1380-30-10, 1899, v, 100 pref. sh., revenue stamps on the back, brown **$6.00**

Chicago and Texas Railroad Company

*CH1420-40-10, 189x, v, u/u preferred stock certificate, green **$15.00**

Chicago Union Station Company

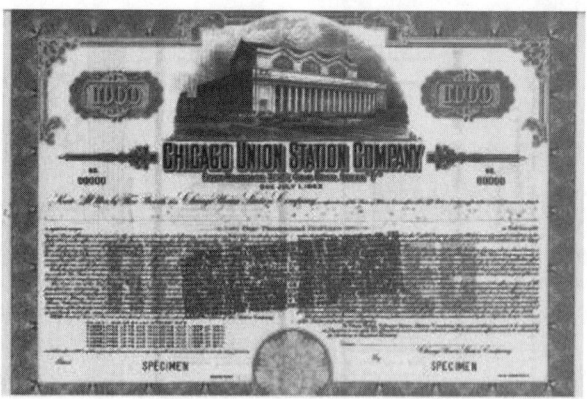

*CH1450-40-10, 19xx, v, u/u specimen certificate $1,000 1st mortgage 3-1/4% gold bond, series F, orange **$16.00**

Chicago and Western Indiana Railroad Company (par $100)

CH1480-20-10, 18xx, v, u/u consolidated stock, FBN, green $8.00

Chicago, Wisconsin and Minnesota Railroad Company

CH1490-30-10, 1895, v, 100 trustees sh., 9-1/2" x 8", brown border. $150.00

Chicago & Wisconsin Valley Street Railways Company (WI)

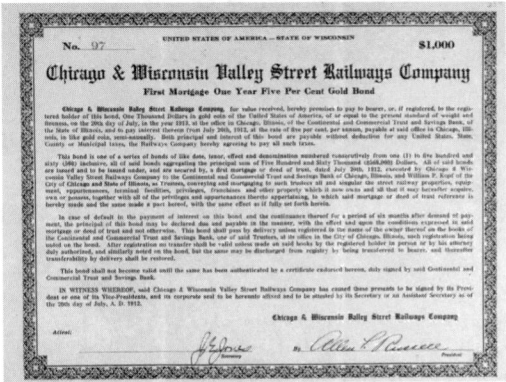

CH1500-30-10, 1912 $1,000 1st mortgage 1-year 5% gold bond, 11" x 8-1/2", brown border $25.00

Chico Gold and Silver Mining Company (1867 par $100)

Jardin District, Humboldt County, Nevada.
CH1520-20-10, 186x, v, unissued certificate, grey $15.00

Childs Company (NY)

A New York restaurant

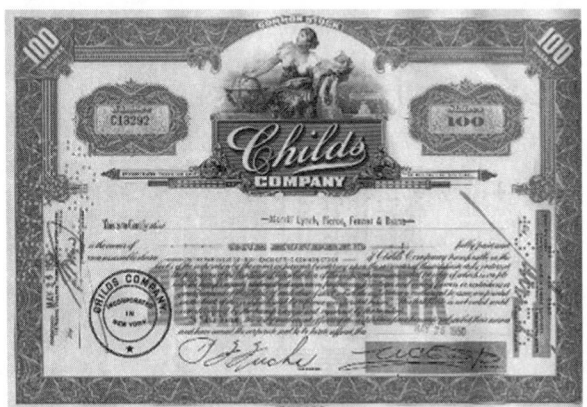

CH1560-20-10, 1950, v, 100 sh., signature strip, red. $5.00

Chimo Copper Company (ME)

CH1580-20-10, 1920, v, 5 sh., ABN, green border $10.00

Chipmunk Timber Company (MT par $1)

CH1600-20-10, 19xx, v, u/u certificate, 11" x 8-1/2", black $6.00

Choctaw, Oklahoma & Gulf Railroad Company (PA par $50)

CH1700-20-10, 1898, v, 50 trust sh., green . .**$9.00**

*CH1700-40-10, 1897, v, 100 sh., preferred stock, FBN, red **$11.00**

*CH1700-50-10, 1897, v, 10 pref. sh., with revenue stamps, green **$5.00**

Chollar Gold and Silver Mining Company (1904, par 50¢)

CH1760-20-10, 1932, v, 500 sh., light brown, small certificate (4-1/4" x 9-1/2"). **$10.00**

Chrysler Corporation

CH1820-40-10, 1967, v, 100 sh., red **$25.00**

UNLISTED TYPES & VARIETIES

Readers are welcome to contact the author directly at:

**Rainer Stahlberg
P.O. Box 1044
Rooseveltown, New York 13683**

Cincinnati and Fort Wayne Railroad

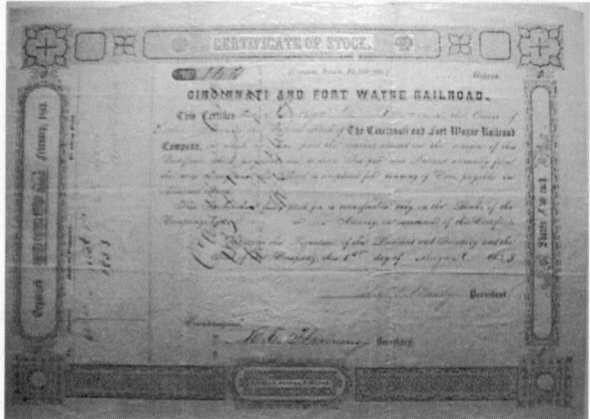

*CI200-10-10, 1853, 5 sh., brown **$35.00**

Cincinnati, Indianapolis, St. Louis & Chicago Railway Company (par $100)

*CI250-20-10,*18xx, v, u/u 100 sh. certificate, brown **$12.00**

Cincinnati, Jackson and Mackinaw Railway Company (OH-MI)

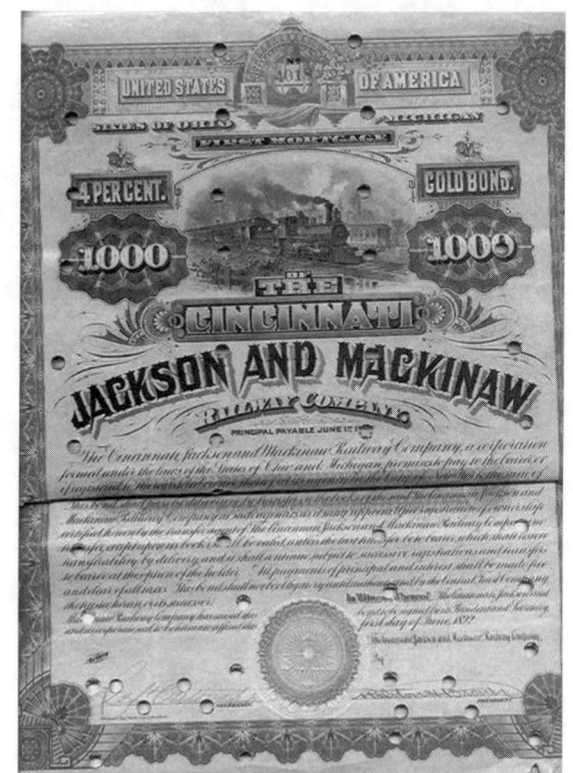

*CI280-40-10, 1892, v, $1,000 4% 1st mort. gold bond, due 1991, green **$45.00**

Cincinnati, Lafayette and Chicago Railroad Company

CI320-40-10, 1871, v, $1,000 7% first mortgage
bond w. coupons, brown green........$40.00

Cincinnati, Sandusky and Cleveland Railroad Company

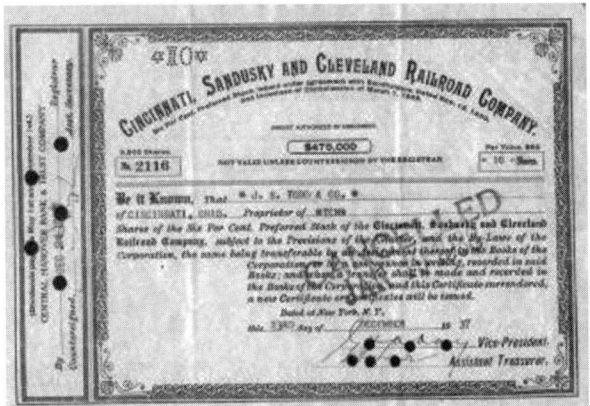

*CI400-20-10, 10 sh., grey..............$8.00

The Cincinnati and Springfield Railway Company (OH)

CI430-40-10, 1871, v, $1,000 first mortgage bond,
green and black....................$45.00

The Cincinnati, Washington and Baltimore Railroad Company (OH par $100)

*CI500-20-10, 1887, v, u/u certificate, ABN,
orange...........................$10.00
CI500-40-10, 1886, v, 10 pref. sh., green...$10.00

*CI500-50-10, 188x, v, u/u pref. certificate
.............................$12.00

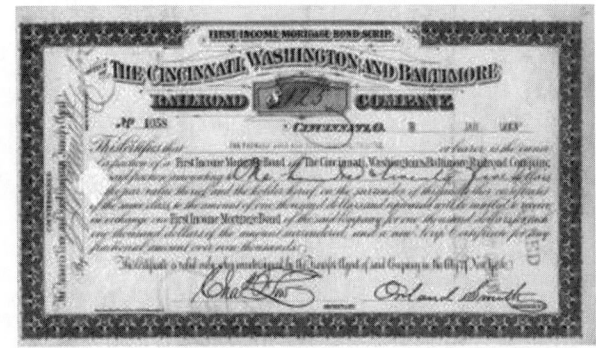

*CI500-70-10, 1887, v, $125 1st Income Mortgage
Bond Scrip, ABN, black on white.......$6.00

Cincinnati, Wilmington & Zanesville Rail Road Company (par $50)

*CI530-10-10, 1857, v, 1 sh., grey.......$53.00

Cinerama, Inc. (NY 1950, par 1¢)

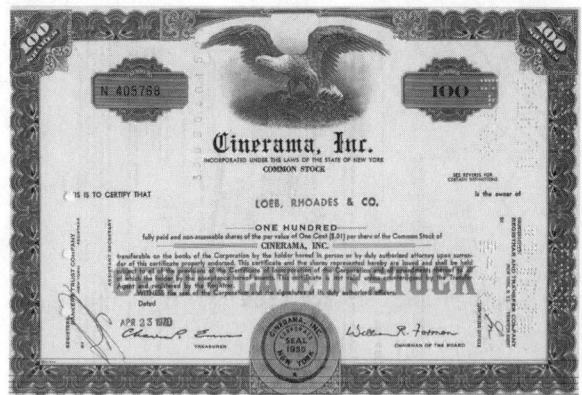

*CI570-20-10, 1969, v, 100 sh., brown **$3.00**

Cities Service Company (DE 1910)

*CI620-30-10, 1982, v, $300 zero coupon guaranteed note due 1989, SCB, 12" x 8", brown
. . . .**$3.00**

*CI620-35-10, 1989, v, $600 zero coupon guaranteed note due 1989, brown, o/p changed to Occi-

dental Petroleum Corporation of California, SCB, 12" x 8", brown **$3.00**

Citizens' Electric Company (MT par $10)

CI660-20-10, 190x, v, u/u certificate, brown border
. . . . **$10.00**

The Citizens National Bank of Dayton, Wash. (par $100)

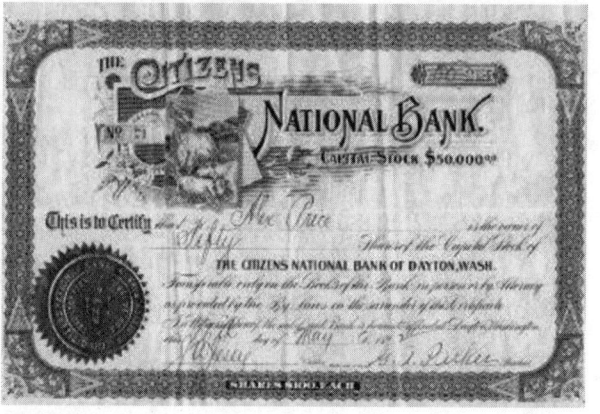

*CI720-20-10, 1892, v, 50 sh., Salt Lake Litho Co., grey **$70.00**

Citizens Securities Company (CA par $100)

*CI740-20-10, 1910, v, 20 sh., Grimes-Stassforth Stationery Co., Los Angeles; 9-1/2" x 8", brown border **$10.00**

City Bank of McKeesport (PA par $100)

CI770-20-10, 19xx, v, u/u certificate, grey . . **$6.00**

The City National Bank of Susquehanna, Pa. (U.S. par $100)

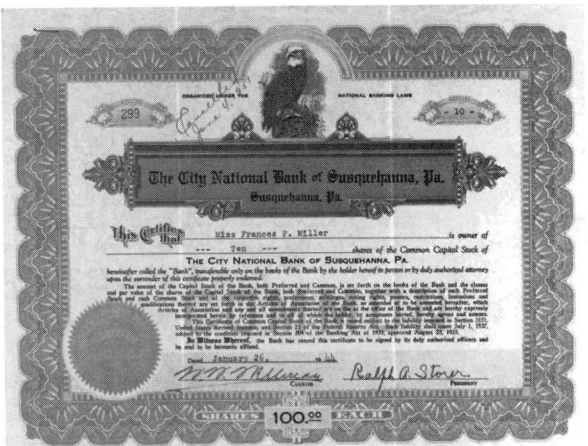

*CI1800-20-10, 1944, v, 10 sh., 12" x 9", orange border $30.00

The City Railway Company (Dayton, Ohio) (OH par $100)

CI830-20-10, 1915, v, 25 sh., orange-brown $10.00

*CI830-40-10, 1941, v, 17 pref. sh. (par $100), green $6.00

Clara-Swansea Mining Company (NV)

Mines in Planet district, hematite containing iron, gold, silver and copper.
CL160-20-10, 1929, v, 25 sh. (par $1), green $11.00
CL60-40-10, 1926, v, 1,500 sh., pref., orange $15.00

Clark Equipment Company

*CL200-20-10, 19xx, v, u/u specimen less than 100 sh. certificate, blue $8.00

Clarkson State Bank (MI par $100)

CL250-20-10, 19xx, v, unissued certificate, brown $5.00
CL250-30-10, 19xx, v, unissued certificate, green $5.00

The Clear Fork Oil Company (OH par $10)

*CL310-20-10, 1901, v, i/u 16 sh., grey, Mount & Co., Cleveland, OH., 10-1/4" x 8-1/4", grey $4.00
CL310-30-10, 190x, v, unissued certificate, grey $5.00

Clearfield Dairy Company, Inc. (PA 1925)

CL370-20-10, 19xx, v, unissued certificate, green $8.00

Cleveland, Cincinnati, Chicago and St. Louis Railway Company (OH-IN)

This company was the result of amalgamation of the Cincinnati, Indianapolis, St. Louis & Chicago RR, the Cleveland, Columbus, Cincinnati & Indianapolis RR and the Indianapolis & St. Louis RR in 1889.

*CL430-30-10, 1954, 10 sh., pref. (par $100), brown $6.00

CL430-50-10, 1890, v, $1,000 bond secured by 1st mortgage on Cairo, Vincennes & Chicago Railroad, ABN, 10" x 13", green. $15.00

*CL430-53-10, 1890, v, $1,000 4% gold bond to fund the Springfield & Columbus RR division, brown $15.00

CL430-55-10, 1890, v, $10,000 4% gold bond, green $13.00

*CL430-60-10, 1891, v, $1,000 4% bond for funding the Cincinnati, Wabash and Michigan Railroad Co., International Bank Note Co., 10" x 15", orange $16.00

*CL430-70-10, 1893, v-reapers, $1,000 4% general mortgage gold bond w. coupons, ABN, brown $23.00

*CL430-75-10, 1893, v, $1,000 4% general mort. gold bond, green **$15.00**

*CL430-90-10, 1927, v, $1,000 series E 4-1/2% refunding and improvement bond, ABN, blue
. . . .$15.00

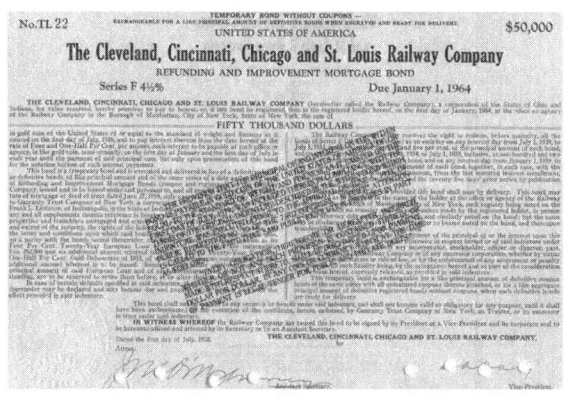

*CL430-100-10, 1938, t, $50,000 refunding and improvement bond, series F, 4-1/2% due 1964, o/p regarding gold bonds, ABN, 13-3/4" x 10", orange **$7.00**

CL430-110-10, 1950, v, $1,000 4% gold bond, FBN, green **$15.00**

*CL430-120-10, 1952, v, $1,000 1st collateral trust mortgage, St. Louis Division, 4% gold bond, FBN, green **$16.00**

Cleveland, Columbus, Cincinnati & Indianapolis Railway Company (par $100)

*CL460-20-10, 1870, v, 10 sh., black **$30.00**

*CL460-40-10, 1884, v, $1,000 gold bond secured by mortgage on building and equipment, 6% 15 year; green $15.00

Cleveland Gas Light and Coke Company
CL500-20-10, 1873, v, 41 sh., grey $20.00

Cleveland and Pittsburgh Rail Road Company (OH 1836, par $50)
CL600-20-10, 18xx, v, u/u certificate, Robertson, Seibert & Shearman, thin paper, grey....$15.00

The Cleveland Short Line Railway Company (OH)

*CL650-30-10, 1911, v, $1,000 1st mortgage 50 year gold bond, ABN, brown $19.00

Cleveland & Toledo Rail Road Co. (par $50)
CL690-20-10, 1862, v, 100 sh., grey $35.00

Clyde Kraut Company (OH Par $100)
CL920-20-10, 1905, v, 9 sh., grey border ..$35.00

C.M. & R. Oil and Gas Company (OH par $100)
CM100-20-10, 19xx, v, u/u certificate, grey .$4.00

Coal River Railway Company
CO60-30-10, 1905 $1,000 first mortgage 4% gold bond, olive green $8.00

Coastal States Gas Producing Company (DE 1955, par $5.33a)
CO110-20-10, 1976, v, 10 sh. on a less than 100 sh. certificate, green....................$4.00

*CO110-30-10, 1970, v, 100 sh., brown $4.00
CO110-40-10, 1975, v, 100 sh., blue.......$4.00

This catalog has listings in an alphabetical format. The reason is simple: Companies diversify as they grow. For example, the Canadian Pacific Railway company recently split into five companies. They represent the railway, hotels, shipping, airline, and petroleum interests of the company. During World War II, the Singer sewing machine company made guns and other defense-related equipment, so where should we list it? It's far easier to use a strict alphabetical order, rather than to confuse the reader with topical classifications.

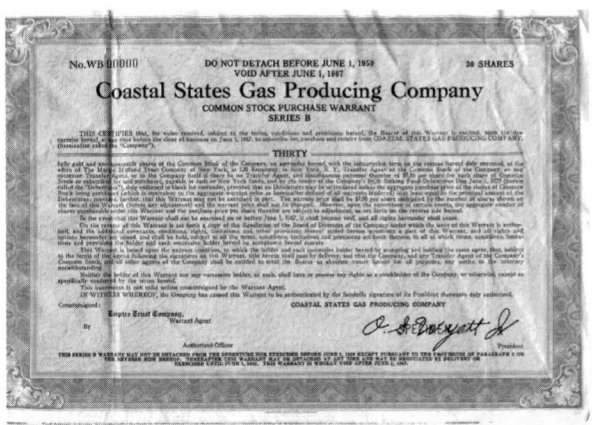

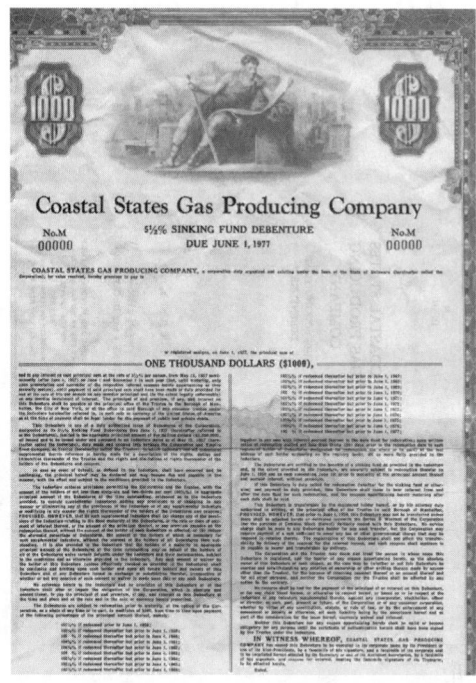

*CO110-90-10, 1958, v, s, $1,000 5-1/2% sinking fund debenture due 1977. Attached common stock purchase warrant for 30 sh., ABN, 10-1/4" x 15-1/4", orange $9.00

Cobalt Central Mines Company (ME par $1)

*CO140-20-10, 1911, v, 100 sh., green $10.00

*CO110-45-10, 1959, s, 30 sh., warrant void after 1967, series B, orange. $3.00
CO110-60-10, 1972, v, 5 $1.19 series A pref. sh. on a less than 100 sh. certificate, purple $4.00
CO110-70-10, 1974, v, 1,000 series B pref. sh. on a more than 100 sh. certificate, orange $5.00

It is generally assumed that only 5% of certificates survive to reach collectors.

The C.O.D. Gold Mining Company (CO par $1)

*CO200-20-10, 19xx, v, u/u certificate, grey on green $5.00

Cody Sanidary (sic) (WY par $100)

CO250-20-10, 19xx, v, unissued 6% pref. stock certificate, grey and gold $4.00

Coeur d'Alene Mining & Smelting Co. Ltd. (ID par $1)

CO300-20-10, 1915, v, 1,000 sh., grey $10.00

Coin Phones Inc. (NY)

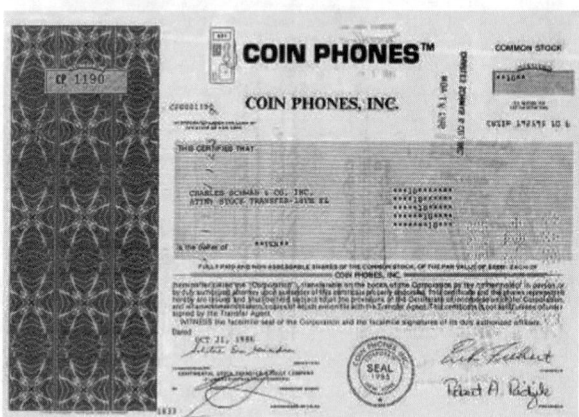

*CO390-10-10, 1986, v, 10 sh., SCB, blue . .$3.00

Cole Motor Car Company (IN par $100)

*CO430-20-10, 1916, v, 10 sh. (par $100) on a less than 100 sh. certificate, orange. $100.00
CO430-30-10, 19xx, t, u/c certificate, green
. . . .$35.00

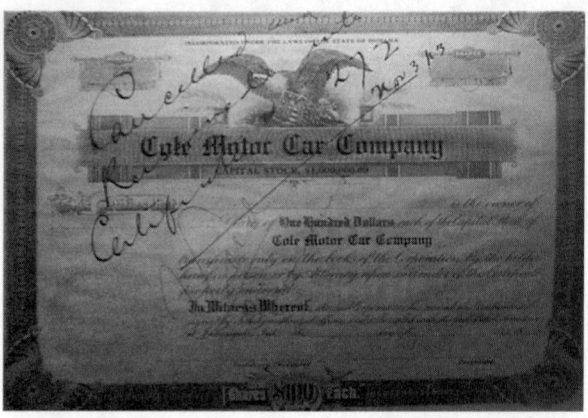

*CO430-40-10, 19xx, v, u/c certificate, brown
. . . .$25.00
CO430-50-10, 19xx, v, u/u 100 sh. certificate, green. $43.00

The value of a stock certificate depends on:

- **rarity**
- **the issuer**
- **signatures**
- **quality of engraving**
- **overall appearance**
- **condition**
- **date of issue**

Collins Radio Company (IA)

First incorporated in 1937 as a Delaware corporation. Built the communications equipment (except receivers) for the Byrd Antarctic expedition in 1934. Merged into Rockwell International Corp. in 1973.

*CO470-20-10, 1969, v, 100 sh. (par $1), blue
..................................$6.00

Colonial Aircraft Corporation (NY)

*CO530-20-10, 1968, v, 20 sh., blue $24.00

Colonial Cranberry Company (par $50)
CO570-20-10, 189x, v, u/u certificate, brown $6.00

The Colonial Dairy Company (IL par $50)
CO600-20-10, 1940, v, 9 sh., green $10.00

Colonial Steel Company
CO660-20-10, 1926, v, 1 sh., brown $8.00

Colorado Interstate Gas Company (DE par $5)

*CO730-20-10, 1963, v, 100 sh., orange....$4.00

Colorado Midland Railway Company

*CO770-40-10, 1897, v, $1,000 1st Mortgage 4% 50 year gold bond, brown.............$20.00

The Colorado Milling and Elevator Company (CO par $100)
CO800-20-10, 1913, v, 10 sh., brown $7.00

The Colorado Mining, Land and Investment Company (CO par $1)

*CO830-20-10, 19xx, v, u/u certificate, brown
. . . .$10.00

The Colorado, Texas and Mexico Railroad Company of Oklahoma (OK par $100)

*CO900-20-10, 19xx, v, u/u certificate, green
. . . .$15.00

The value of a stock certificate depends on:
- rarity
- the issuer
- signatures
- quality of engraving
- overall appearance
- condition
- date of issue

*CO900-30-10, 19xx, v, u/u preferred stock certificate, orange. $15.00

Colt's Manufacturing Company (CT)

*CO970-50-10, 1954, v, 100 sh. (par $10), brown
. . . .$60.00

Columbia Airlines, Incorporated (MD)

*CO1030-20-10, 19xx, v, u/u certificate, green
. . . .$40.00

Columbia Broadcasting System, Inc.
CO1070-20-10, 1958, v, i/u 1 class B sh., blue
............................$30.00

The Columbia Gas System, Inc.
CO1110-20-10, 1970, v, 100 sh., orange $4.00

Columbia Graphophone Manufacturing Company

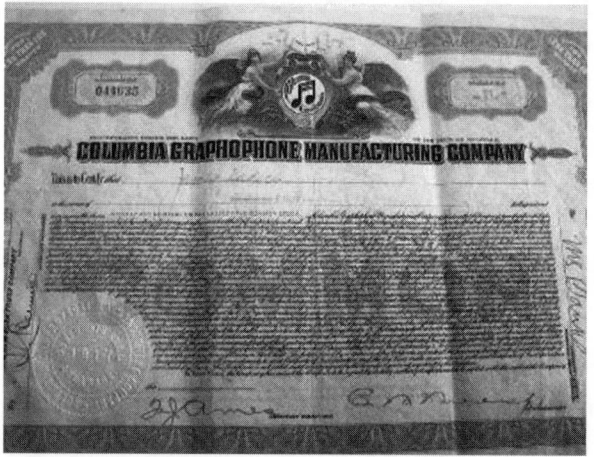

*CO1140-20-10, 1921, v, 10 sh., orange ...$20.00

Columbia Pictures Industries, Inc. (DE 1969)

*CO1200-30-10, 1970, v, 50 sh. on a less than 100 sh. certificate, blue $10.00

Columbia Technical Corporation (NY 1950)
In 1977 the name was changed to Columbia Chase Corp., which was reincorporated in MA as Chase Corp. in 1988.

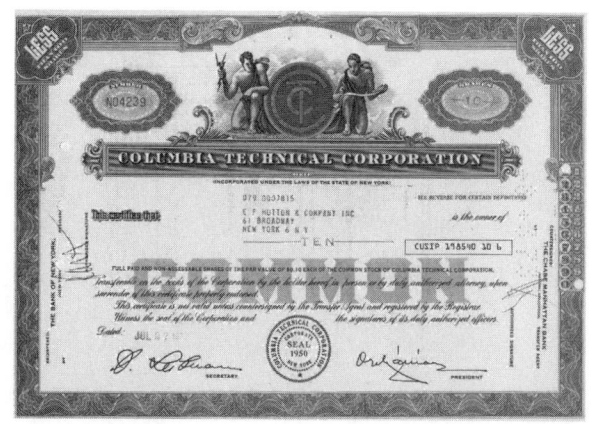

*CO1260-20-10, 1973, v, 10 sh. on a less than 100 sh. certificate (par $0.10), CBN, 11-3/4" x 8-1/4", brown $4.00

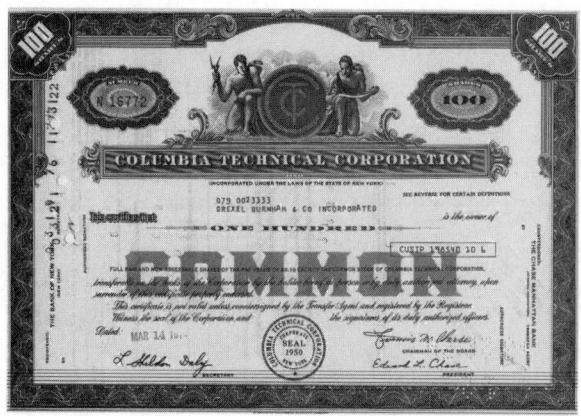

*CO1260-30-10, 1974, v, 100 sh. (par $0.10), SCB, 12" x 8-1/4", blue...................$4.00

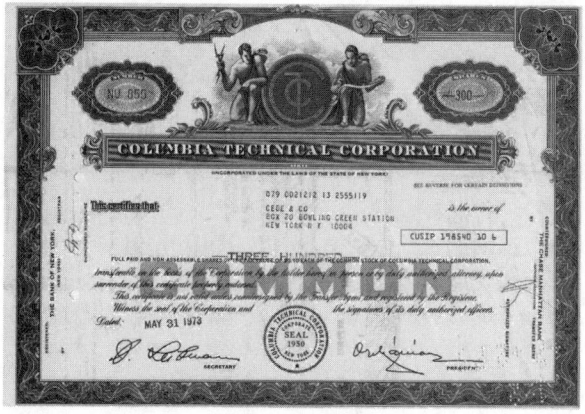

*CO1260-40-10, 1973, v, 300 sh. (par $0.10), CBN, 11-3/4" x 8", green..............$4.00

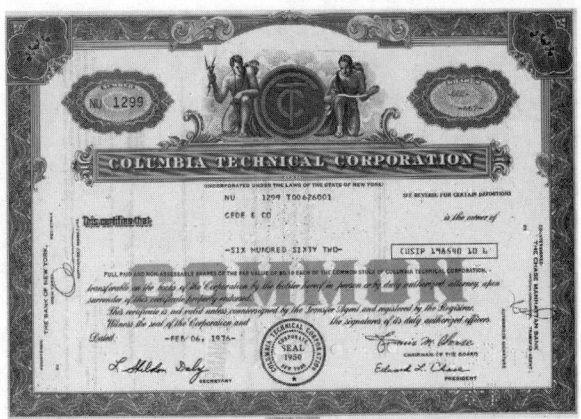

*CO1260-45-10, 1976, v, 662 sh. (par $0.10), three signature, CBN, 11-3/4" x 8", green......$4.00

Columbia-Sterling Publishing Company (DE par $1)

CO1310-20-10, 1911, 101 sh., green.......$7.00

Columbus, Chicago and Indiana Central Railway Company (par $100)

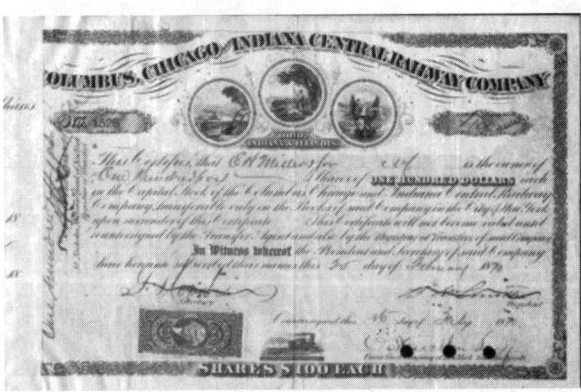

*CO1390-20-10, 1880, v, 100 sh., with U.S. revenue stamp, grey on beige $25.00

Columbus & Indianapolis Railroad Company (OH par $50)

CO1430-10-10, 1864, v, 9 sh., blue.......$20.00

Columbus & Maysville Railway Co. (OH 1877)

CO1470-30-10, 19xx, v, u/u $500 7% first mortgage bond, grey....................$40.00

The Columbus and Ninth Avenue Railroad Company (NY)

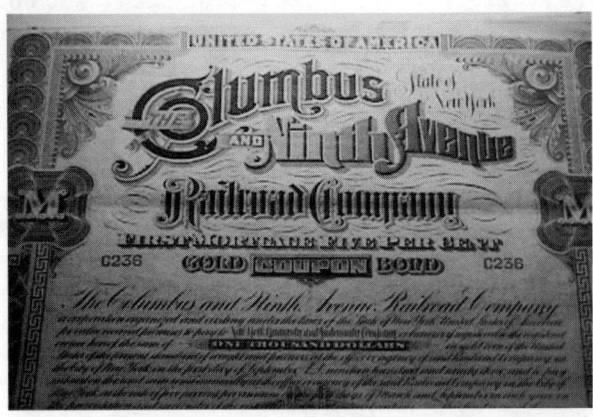

*CO1500-30-10, 1893, v, $1,000 1st Mortgage 5% gold bond, brown $15.00

Columbus Piqua and Indiana Rail Road Company (OH par $50)

CO1530-10-10, 1852, v, 1 sh., grey, thin paper $20.00

The Columbus Southern Railway Company (par $100)

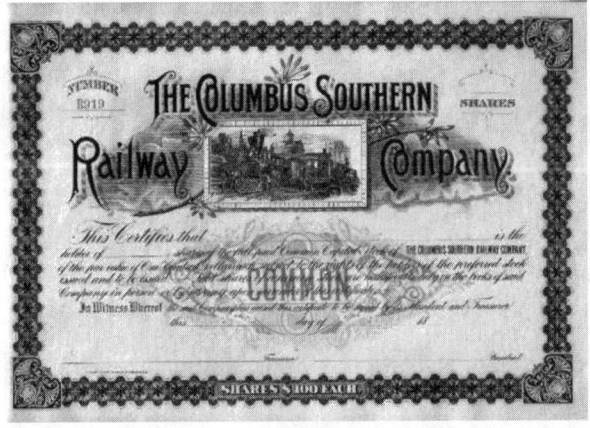

*CO1570-20-10, 18xx, v, u/u certificate, grey $9.00

CO1570-30-10, 18xx, v, u/u 100 sh. certificate, brown $15.00

CO1570-40-10, 18xx, v, u/u preferred stock certificate, green.........................$15.00

Columbus & Xenia Rail Road Company (OH)

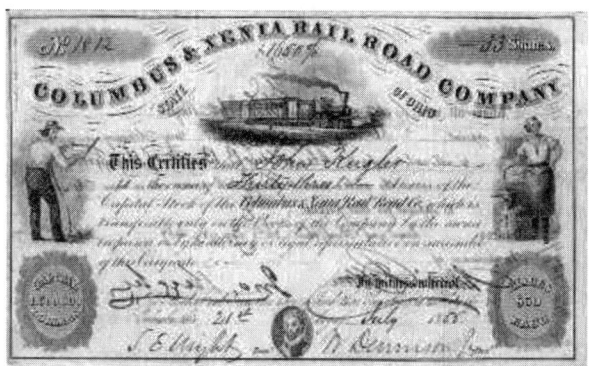

*CO1610-10-10, 1855, v, 33 sh. (par $50), light brown $25.00

CO1610-30-10, 1921, v, 100 sh. (par $50), dark brown $18.00

Combined Mining and Leasing Company of Goldfield, Nevada (SD par $1)

CO1650-20-10, 1908, v, 1,000 sh., brown ..$41.00

Combined Oil Land Company (1901, par $1)

CO1700-20-10, 1904, v, 55 sh., green border $15.00

Comet Automobile Company (DE 1916, par $10)

CO1740-20-10, 1919, v, 8 sh., grey border $65.00

Comet Mining Company of Utah, U.S.A.

In French it states Mines de Cuivre Argentifére Comet et Morrison, a silver bearing copper mine.

CO1770-20-10, 1883, v, 500 French Franc bearer share w. coupons, grey $48.00

The Commercial Cable Company

CO1820-30-10, 1897, v, u/u interim 4% gold bond certificate, brown $12.00

Commercial Credit Company (DE 1912)

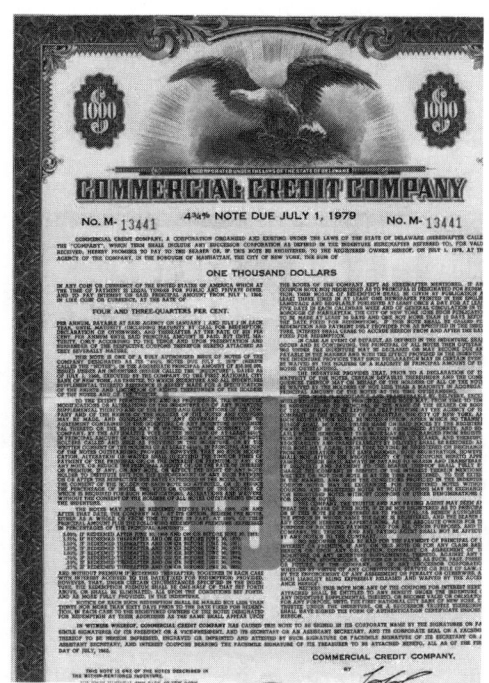

*CO1850-30-10, 1960 $1,000 4-3/4% note due 1979 no coupons, SCB, 10" x 14", red....$4.00

The Commercial Real Estate, Loan and Improvement Company (SC par $100)

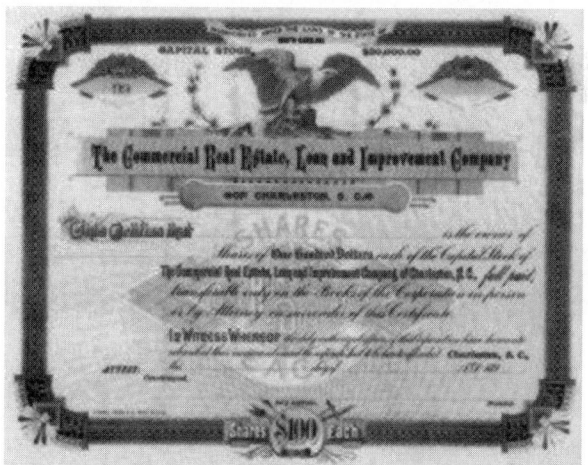

*CO1910-20-10, 189x, v, u/u certificate, grey $6.00

The Common Stock Fund (DE)

A class of the capital stock of Group Securities Inc.

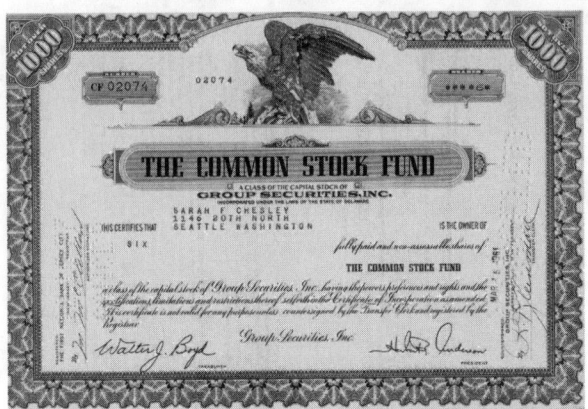

*CO1960-20-10, 1961, 6 sh. on a not over 1,000 sh. certificate, printer group securities inc., 12" x 8", l. blue..........................$3.00

Commonwealth Telephone Company (PA)

CO2010-20-10, 1965, v, 5 sh. on a less tan 100 sh. certificate, orange....................$5.00

Como Mines Company (NV)

CO2040-20-10, 1935, 100 sh., green......$10.00

Computer Applications Incorporated (DE par 10¢)

CO2080-20-10, 1970, v, 30 sh. on a less than 100 sh. certificate, SCB, l. blue............$17.00

Comstock-Keystone Mining Co. (NV)

CO2120-20-10, 1955, v, 1,000 sh., orange..$15.00

Con-Virginia Mining Company (NV 1904, par $10)

CO2170-20-10, 1910, v, 100 sh., small certificate like a check, grey $10.00

UNLISTED TYPES & VARIETIES

Readers are welcome to contact the author directly at:

Rainer Stahlberg
P.O. Box 1044
Roosevelttown, New York 13683

Connecticut Fire Insurance Company (CT par $100)

*CO2230-20-10, 1877, v, 40 sh., green.....$9.00

*CO2230-30-10, 1906, v, 15 sh., reddish ...$8.00

The Connecting Railway Company

*CO2270-30-10, 1951, v, $1,000 8-1/4% 1st mortgage series A bond, 10" x 15", red......$24.00

Consolidated Chollar, Gould and Savage Mining Company (CA 1933)

CO2340-20-10, 1939, 100 sh., blue $8.00

Consolidated Edison Company of New York, Inc. (NY 1884)

*CO2400-40-10, 1974, v, $1,000 1st and refunding 7.9% series GG bond, green $4.00

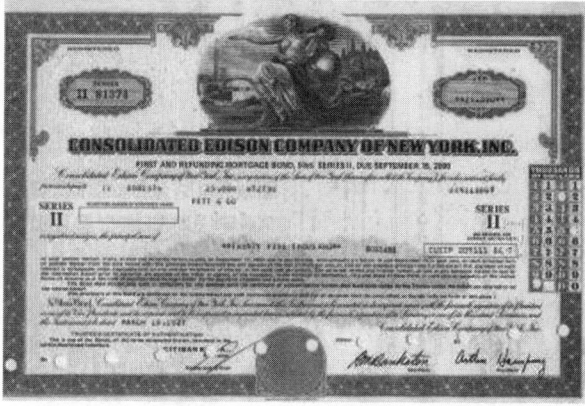

*CO2400-50-10, 19??, v, $25,000 1st and refunding mort. bond, series II, due 2000; green
. . . .$4.00

> **It is generally assumed that only 5% of certificates survive to reach collectors.**

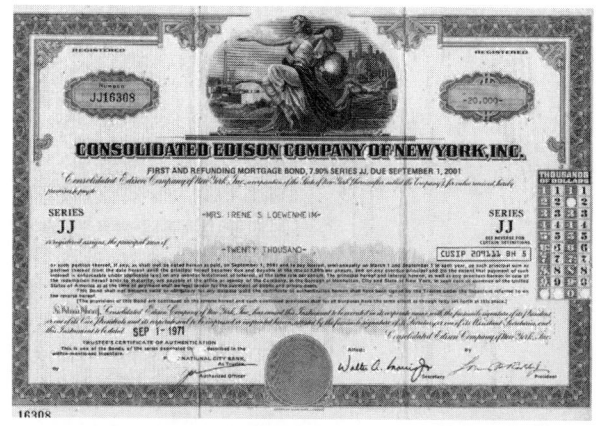

*CO2400-60-10, 1971, v, $20,000 1st and refunding mortg. bond, 7.90% series JJ due 2001, ABN, 12" x 8", green $4.00

Consolidated Esperanza Mining Company - La Compañia Minera Consolidada de la Esperanza Pachuca Mexico

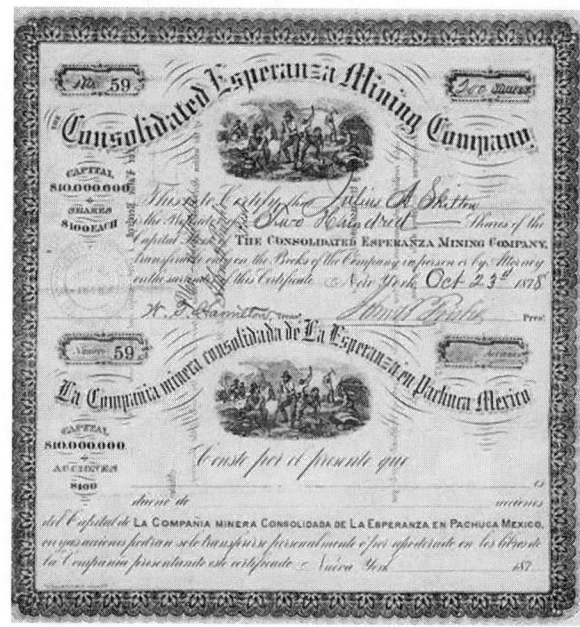

*CO2430-20-10, 1878, v, 200 sh., text in English and Spanish., brown frame $12.00

Consolidated Flagstaff Mines Company (WI par $5)

*CO2450-20-10, 1907, v, 100 sh., w/o imprint, 10-1/2" x 8", brown border............$12.00

Consolidated Gas Company of the City of Pittsburgh (PA)

*CO2470-20-10, 189x, v, u/u 500 sh. certificate (par $50), brown.....................$6.00

Consolidated Investment Trust (1933, par $1)

*CO2520-20-10, 1966, v, 100 sh., FLB, 12" x 8", orange..........................$4.00

Consolidated Kansas City Smelting and Refining Company

CO2560-30-10, 189x, v, unissued 100 pref. sh. certificate, brown.....................$6.00

Consolidated Metals, Inc. (CO 1926)

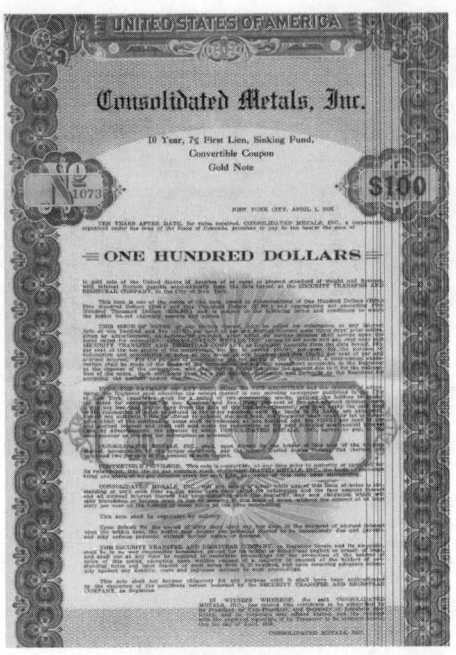

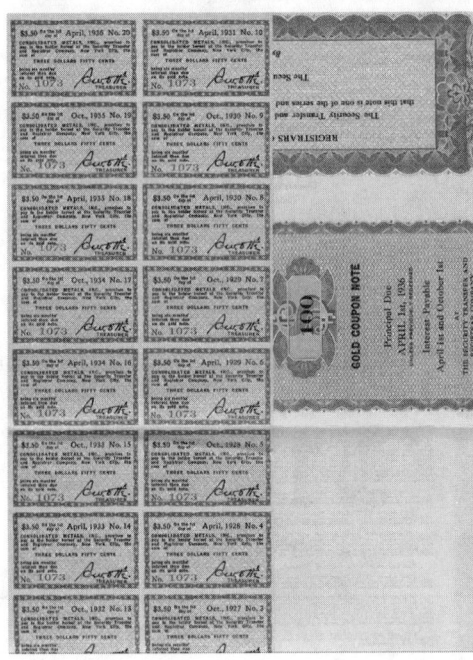

*CO2610-30-10, 1926, u/u $100 gold note, 10 year 7% first lien, sinking fund, convertible coupon, H.K. Brewer & Co. Inc., 9-3/4" x 15-1/4", green $4.00

Consolidated Natural Gas Company

CO2660-40-10, 1963, v, $1,000 4-1/2 debenture, green **$8.00**

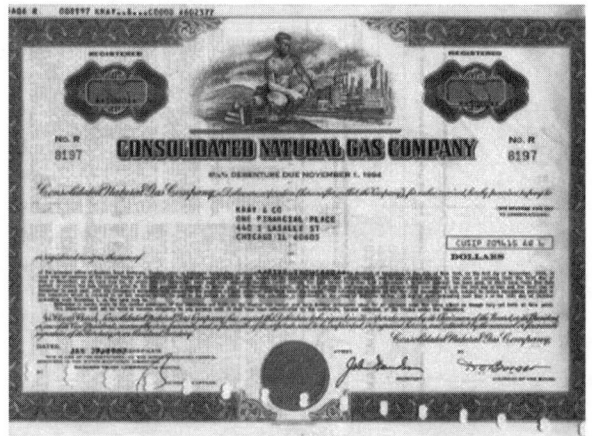

*CO2660-50-10, 1987, v, $5,000 bond, brown **$8.00**

Consolidated Oil Corporation

CO2720-20-10, 1935, v, 5 sh. on a less than 100 sh. certificate, red **$4.00**

The Consolidated Railway Company (CT)

CO2800-40-10, 1905, v, u/u $10,000 debenture, ABN, purple **$25.00**

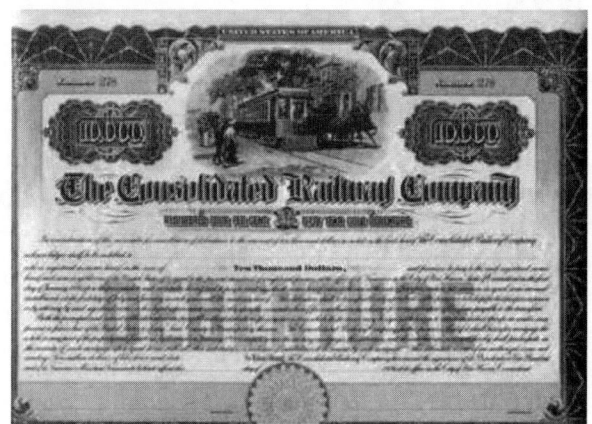

*CO2800-45-10, 1906, v, u/u $10,000 debenture, green **$16.00**
CO2800-50-10, 1915, v, $10,000 unissued debenture, brown **$17.00**

The Consolidated Realty and Investment Co. (CO 1909, par $1)

*CO2830-20-10, 1914, v, 100 sh., w/o imprint, 11" x 8-1/2", gold border and grey v. **$4.00**

Consolidated Steamship Lines (ME par $100)

CO2900-20-10, 1907, v, 100 sh., green **$21.00**

Consolidated Traction Company (PA par $50)

*CO2960-20-10, 19xx, v, u/c 100 sh. certificate, brown **$10.00**
CO2960-30-10, 189x, v, u/c 500 sh., pref. certificate, orange. **$10.00**

Consolidated Uranium Mines, Inc.
(NV par 7-1/2¢)

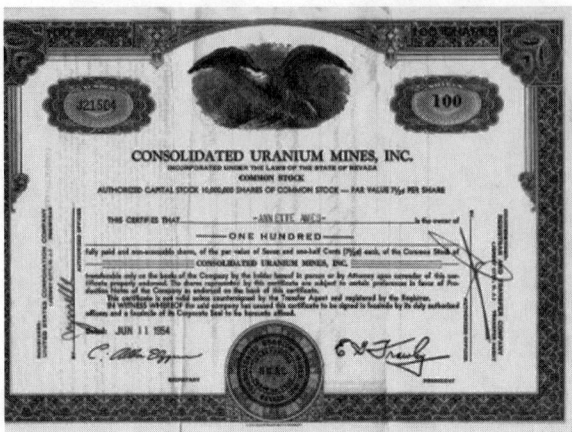

*CO3000-20-10, 1954, v, i/u 100 sh., green
......................................$12.00

Consolidated Virginia & Andes
Corporation (NV 1932, par $1)

CO3060-20-10, 1935, t, 1,000 sh., green $6.00

*CO3060-35-10, 1935, v, 1,000 sh., GOES, 10" x
5-3/4", grey........................$6.00

Consolidated Virginia Mining Company
(par $1)

CO3090-20-10, 1949, v, 2,000 sh., yellow, small
certificate $7.00

UNLISTED TYPES & VARIETIES

Readers are welcome to contact the author
directly at:

Rainer Stahlberg
P.O. Box 1044
Rooseveltown, New York 13683

Consumer Cooperative of Walworth County
(WI par $10)

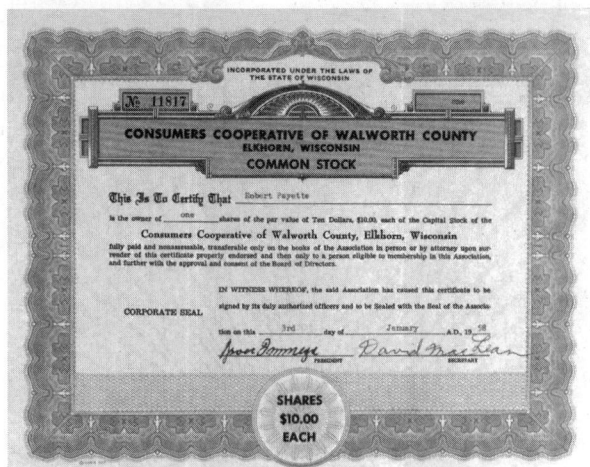

*CO3160-20-10, 1958, 1 sh., GOES, 11" x 8",
orange border $4.00

Consumers Power Company (MI)

CO3190-35-10, 1973, v, $1,000 8-1/4% 1st mort-
gage bond, due 1976, blue $6.00

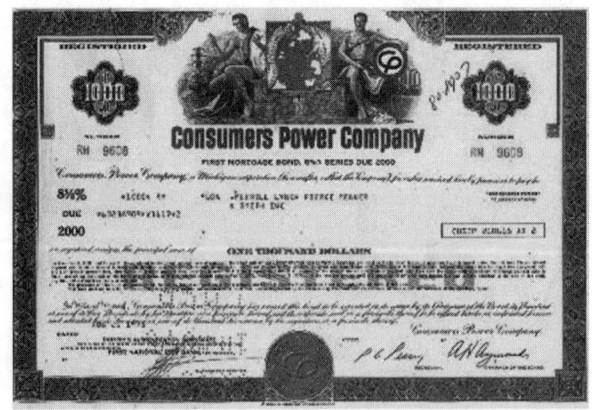

*CO3190-40-10, 1975, v, $1,000 8-5/8% 1st mort-
gage bond, due 2000, purple $6.00

Continental Air Lines, Inc.

CO3300-30-10, 1971, v, $1,000 bond, red
..................................$12.00

The Continental Consolidated Mines Co. (WY par $1)

*CO3350-20-10, 1907, 100 sh., 10" x 6-3/4", brown $10.00

The Continental Gold Mining and Milling Company (CO par $1)

CO3400-20-10, 190x, v, u/u certificate, rubber stamp "Treasury Stock", grey $20.00

Continental Materials Corporation (DE)

CO3470-20-10, 1968, 100 sh., green $3.00

Continental Passenger Railway Company of Pennsylvania (PA)

*CO35200-20-10, 1891, v, 20 sh., ABN, brown
. . . .$10.00

Continental Steel Corporation

CO3600-20-10, 1972, v, 50 sh. on a less than 100 sh. certificate, green $7.00

Contra Estaca Consolidated Mexico Mining Co. (CA)

CO3680-20-10, 1889, v, 10,000 sh., signed by D.M. Burns, Col. Burns was a CA Senator, grey, small certificate $7.00

Controls Company of America (DE par $5)

*CO3800-20-10, 1963, v, 1 sh. on a less than 100 sh. certificate, ABN, 12" x 8", green $4.00

The Co-Operative Pure Milk Association, Inc. (OH 1923)

CO3900-20-10, 19xx, v, u/u certificate (par $3), green $4.00

Copper Crown Mining Company (WA par 5¢)

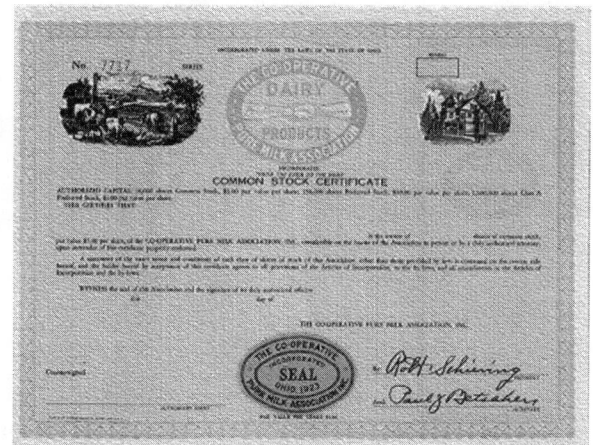

*CO3970-20-10, 1899, v, 500 sh., with revenue stamps, grey $15.00

Copper Hill Mining Company (par $100)
Mine in Soledad district, Los Angeles County.
CO4010-20-10, 1863, v, 100 sh., grey on green
.................................$375.00

**Copper King Mines Corporation
(AZ par $1)**
CO4070-20-10, 1909, v, 250 sh., grey $11.00
CO4070-30-10, 1910, v, 25 pref. sh., brown
....................................$8.00

Copper King Mining and Smelting Co. (ID)
CO4090-20-10, 19xx, v, unissued certificate, green
....................................$7.00

**Cornell-Dubilier Electric Corporation
(DE 1938)**
CO4150-20-10, 1939, 25 sh., light brown ...$4.00
CO4150-30-10, 1937, 100 sh., green $4.00

Coronino Cattle Company (AZ par $100)
CO4210-20-10, 1920, v, 100 sh., orange ...$30.00

Corporate Securities Co. of Chicago

CO4250-20-10, 1930, v, i/u 10 sh. on a less than
100 sh. certificate, RBN, olive green $12.00

**Corroon & Black Corporation
(DE 1928, par 25¢)**

CO4300-20-10, 1978, v, 100 sh. on a not more
than 100,000 sh. certificate, SCB, 12" x 8",
brown $4.00

Coty Inc. (DE)

CO4400-20-10, 1937, v, 19 sh. on a less than 100
sh. certificate, ABN, brown $20.00
CO4400-30-10, 1945, v, 100 sh., red......$17.00

County Bank & Trust Co. of Somerset (NJ)
CO4500-20-10, 1968, v, 20 sh., brown $5.00

This catalog has listings in an alphabetical format. The reason is simple: Companies diversify as they grow. For example, the Canadian Pacific Railway company recently split into five companies. They represent the railway, hotels, shipping, airline, and petroleum interests of the company. During World War II, the Singer sewing machine company made guns and other defense-related equipment, so where should we list it? It's far easier to use a strict alphabetical order, rather than to confuse the reader with topical classifications.

Covington Improvement Company (VA par $100)

*CO4600-20-10, 189x, v, u/u certificate, brown
.................................$10.00

Crader Oil Company (TX par $1)

CR110-20-10, 1946, v, 10 sh., red $16.00

Crary Farmers Elevator Company (SD par $25)

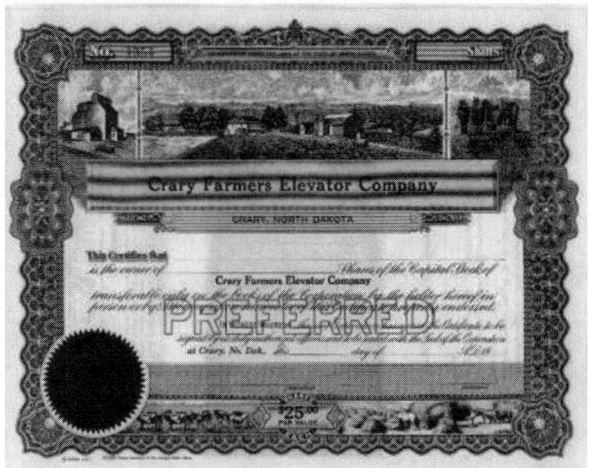

*CR210-30-10, 19xx, v, u/u preferred certificate,
green $4.00

Creole Petroleum Corporation (DE)

CR300-20-10, 1930, w, 33 sh., warrant expiring in
1930, olive $3.00

Crescent Consolidated Mining Company (WI par $1)

*CR330-20-10, 1910, v, 1 sh., w/o imprint, 11" x
8", brown $9.00

Crescent Silver Company of Cincinnati (OH)

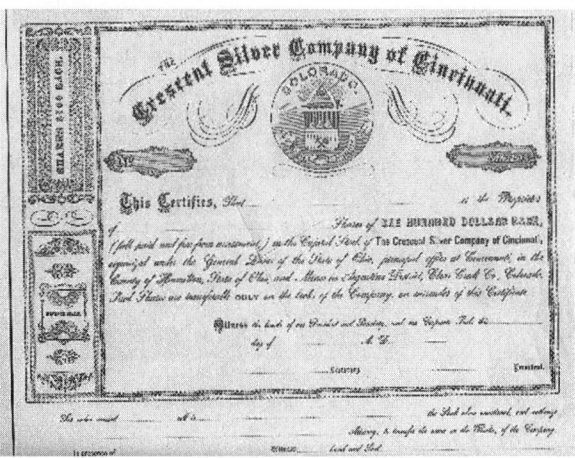

*CR350-20-10, 18xx, v, u/c certificate, brown on
white............................$12.00

Crescent Tool & Manufacturing Co. (MO par $100)

CR390-20-10, 19xx, v, u/u certificate, grey..$7.00

Crescenthill Gold Mines Company of California

CR470-20-10, 19xx, u/u certificate, brown ..$4.00

The Cresson Consolidated Gold Mining and Milling Company

*CR530-20-10, 1916, v, 100 sh., green $11.00

The Cripple Creek Gold Milling Company (CO)

CR600-20-10, 189x, v, u/u certificate, brown
.... $40.00

Crompton & Knowles Loom Works

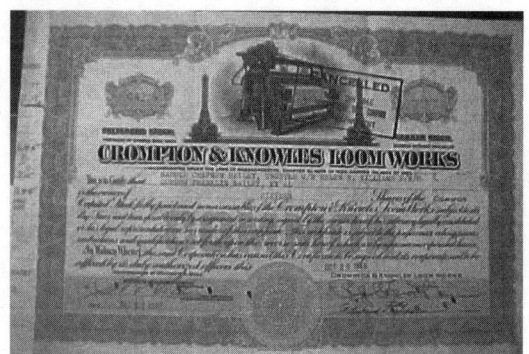

*CR700-20-10, 1946, v, 16 sh., orange $6.00

Crown-Zellerbach Corporation

*CR760-20-10, 1953, v, 100 sh., English revenue imprint, orange $12.00

Crusader Oil and Uranium Company (par 1¢)

CR840-20-10, 1958, v, 10,000 sh., orange.. $10.00

Crystal Lead Mines Company (ID par 10¢)

CR900-20-10, 19xx, v, u/u certificate, brown
.... $8.00

The Cuba Company (NJ)

*CU40-20-10, 1933, v, 100 sh., ABN, brown
.... $7.00

The Cuba Railroad Company (NJ par $100)

*CU100-30-10, 1911, v, 10 pref. sh., ABN, brown
.... $15.00

Cuban Cane Products Co., Inc.

CU130-20-10, 1931, v, 100 sh., green..... $25.00

Cuban Electric Company (FL)

*CU180-20-10, 1961, v, 1,000 sh., text in English and Spanish, green $25.00

Curtice Manufacturing Company, Inc. (CO no par)

*CU250-20-10, 19xx, v, u/c punch "SAMPLE", GOES, 10-3/4" x 8-1/2", gold border.....$3.00

Curtiss-Wright Corporation (NJ 1923, par $1)

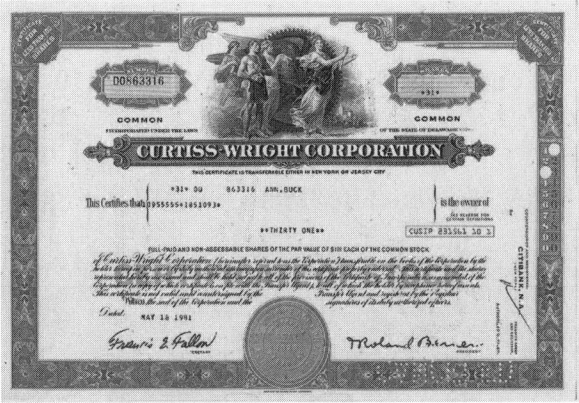

*CU290-20-10, 1981, v, 31 sh. on a less than 100 sh. certificate, red...................$10.00

Curtline of America, Inc. (NY 1965, par $1)

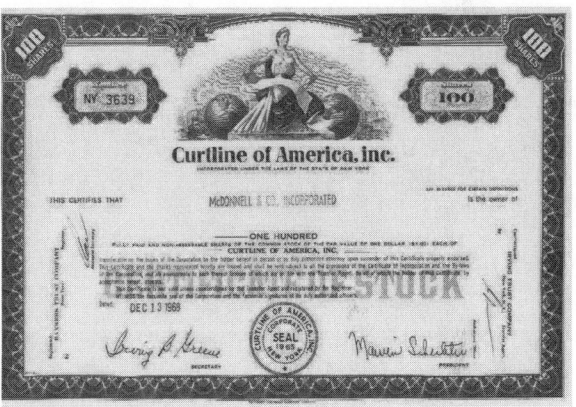

*CU330-20-10, 1968, v, 100 sh., brown $3.00

Custer Channel Wing Corporation (MD 1939, par 5¢)

CU400-40-10, 1968, v, 100 class B sh., 12" x 8", green...........................$10.00

Cutting Block Lumber Corporation (NY par $100)

CU460-20-10, 19xx, v, u/u certificate, grey border $4.00

D

Dakoming Oil Company (WY par $0.10)
DA100-20-10, 1920, v, 100 sh., grey **$7.00**

Daley Molybdenite Company (WI par $1)

DA130-20-10, 1921, v, 200 sh., GOES, 11" x 8",
brown border. **$11.00**

The Dallas Manufacturing Company (AL)

DA150-20-10, 19xx, v, specimen certificate, brown
. . . .**$7.00**

> ***It is generally assumed that
> only 5% of certificates survive
> to reach collectors.***

Dalto Electronics Corporation
(DE 1958, par $0.50)

*DA200-20-10, 1963, v, 100 sh., SCB, 11-3/4" x
8-1/4", blue. **$4.00**
DA200-30-10, 1967, v, 100 sh., green **$4.00**

Danbury and Norwalk Railroad Company
(CT)
DA260-30-10, 1905, v, unissued $5,000 50-year
bond, green. **$20.00**

The Dante Gold Mining Company (CO)

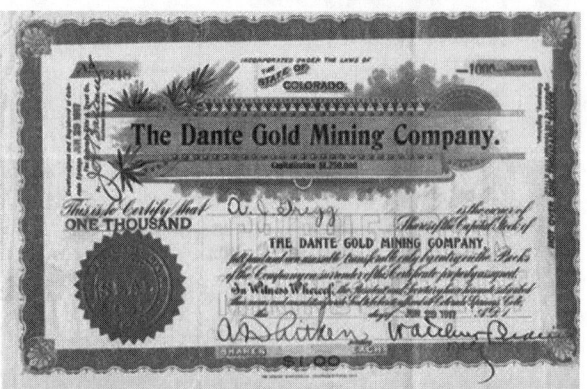

*DA310-20-10, 1917, v, i/u 1,000 sh., brown
. . . .**$30.00**

Danville, Mocksville & Southwestern
Railroad Company (NC par $100)
DA340-20-10, 18xx, v, unissued certificate, brown
. . . .**$150.00**

Daryl Industries, Inc. (FL 1952, par $0.50)

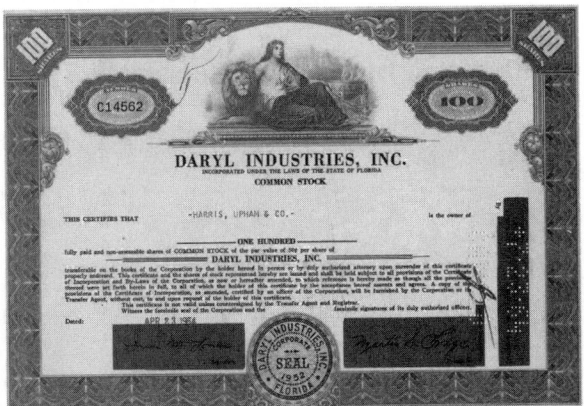

*DA440-20-10, 1964, v, 100 sh., CBN, 11-3/4" x 8", scrip sign., red $4.00

Davega Stores Corporation (NY par $2)

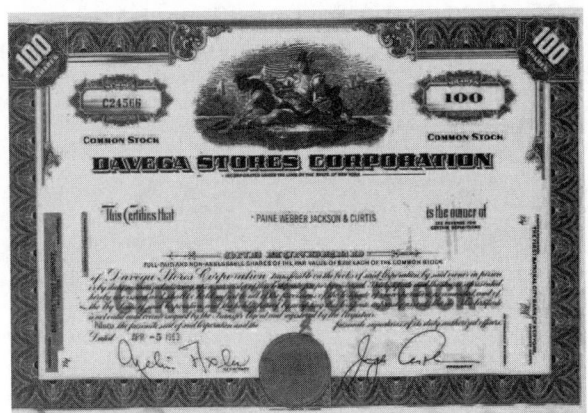

*DA580-20-10, 1963, v, 100 sh., red $3.00

Davenport, Clinton & Eastern Railway Company (IA par $100)

DA620-20-10, 1xxx, v, u/u certificate, brown
. . . .$10.00

Davenport Consolidated Gold Mining Company (par $1)

DA650-20-10, 19xx, v, u/u certificate, brown
. . . .$10.00

Davenport, Rock Island and Northwestern Railway Company (IL)

DA680-20-10, 1xxx, v, unissued certificate, grey
. . . .$13.00

De Beers Consolidated Mines Limited

The company's Central Selling Organization (the diamond cartel) controls 70% of the world's diamond production by having interests in 18 African diamond mines. Controlled by Anglo American Corporation, and thus, the Oppenheimer family.

*DE60-20-10, 1970, 100 American Depositary Receipt shares, purple $25.00

De Pere & New York Iron Company (WI par $25.00)

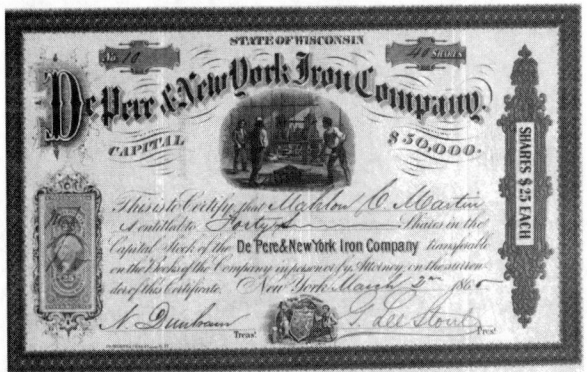

*DE90-20-10, 1860, v, 40 sh., revenue stamp, 10" x 7", grey border. $150.00

Death Valley-Arcalvada Consolidated Mines Company (WY)

DE120-20-10, 1911, v, 100 sh., orange $56.00

The Decatur Land Improvement & Furnace Company (AL 1887, par $100)

*DE210-20-10, 1888, v, 5 sh., 11" x 9-3/4", blue border $40.00

The Decatur Water Company (AL 1887)

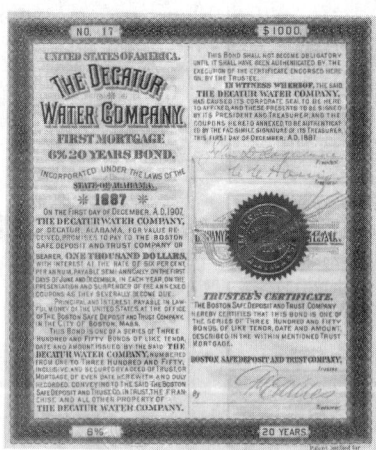

*DE240-30-10, 1887, v, u/u $1,000 first mort. 6% 20 year bond due 1907, black, tied together w. coupons, no printer named, 8" x 9-1/4" . . .$6.00

Deer Lodge Livery Company (MT)
*DE350-20-10, 190x, v, u/u certificate, blue. . $7.00

Deinhardt & Brandestein, Inc. (NY no par)

*DE520-20-10, 19xx, u/u certificate, J. Meyers Inc., NYC, 11" x 8-1/4", blue. $3.00

Del Monte Irrigation Co.

*DE600-20-10, 1892, v, 50 sh., revenue stamp on the back, grey $20.00

Delaware and Hudson Railway Company (DE)
DE650-30-10, 19xx, u/u 1st and general mort. 9-1/2% series B due 1983 bond, black. . .$12.00

Delaware, Lackawanna and Western Railroad Company (PA par $50)

DE700-20-10, 1960, v, 50 sh. on a less than 100 sh. certificate, blue $7.00

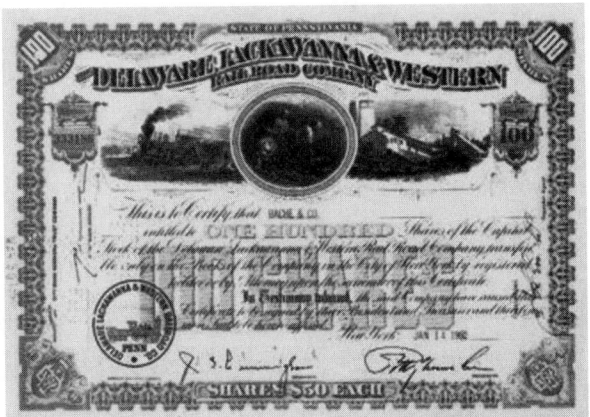

DE700-30-10, 1959, v, 100 sh., l. brown . . .$7.00

DE700-40-10, 1957, v, 1,000 sh. on a more than 100 sh. certificate, green. $14.00

DE700-70-10, 1942, v, $1,000 Morris and Essex Division Collateral Trust Bond, ABN, green $10.00

The Delaware Railroad Company (DE par $25)

DE760-20-10, 1927, v, 100 sh., green $7.00

Delaware and Schuylkill Canal Company

DE790-10-10, 1836, 175 sh., brown. $155.00

Delaware Shore Rail Road Company (NJ par $50)

DE820-20-10, 187x, v, unissued certificate $15.00

Delaware Water Gap Slate Company (NJ 1860, par $50)

DE850-20-10, 1869, v, 100 sh., grey $48.00

UNLISTED TYPES & VARIETIES

Readers are welcome to contact the author directly at:

Rainer Stahlberg
P.O. Box 1044
Rooseveltown, New York 13683

Delaware Water Improvement Company (DE)

DE880-20-10, 1911, v, 9 sh., brown $5.00

Dennos Food Company of Portland (par $10)

DE940-20-10, 1914, v, i/u 1 sh., grey and brown $5.00

The Denver and Rio Grande Railroad Company (CO-UT par $100)

DE970-20-10, 1912, v, 100 sh., dark brown $60.00

The Denver & Salt Lake Railway Tunnel Company

*DE1000-20-10, 190x, v, u/u certificate, green
....................................$10.00

Depere Company (WI 1854, par $10)

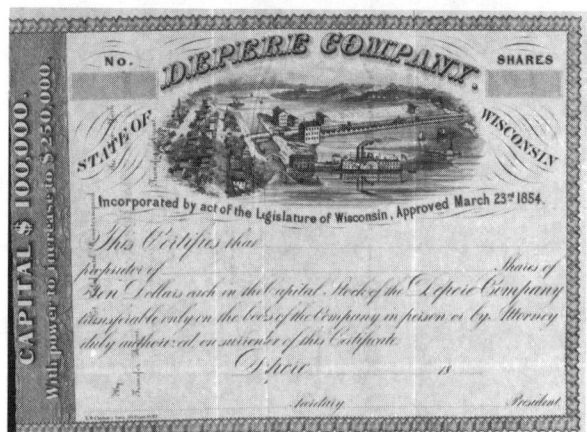

*DE1060-20-10, 18xx, v, u/u certificate, E.B.
Clayton & Sons, N.Y.; 8-1/2" x 6-1/2", brown
border $60.00

Desert View Development Company (NV par 10¢)

DE1130-20-10, 1926, v, 25,000 sh., brown
....................................$11.00

Detroit Citizens Street Railway Company

DE1260-20-10, 1895, 10 sh., light brown ..$18.00

Detroit and Cleveland Navigation Company (par $10)

DE1290-20-10, 1925, v, 100 sh., orange ...$15.00

Detroit, Hillsdale & South-Western Railroad Company (MI par $100)

DE1340-30-10, 1942, v, 6 sh., ABN, grey border
....................................$10.00

Detroit Steel Corporation

DE1400-20-10, 1960, v, 100 sh., blue......$6.00

Detroit, Toledo and Milwaukee Railroad Company (MI)

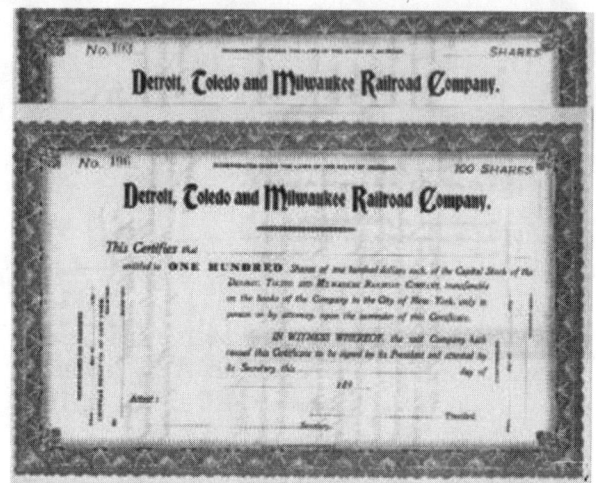

*DE1430-20-10, 189x, u/u certificate, brown
....................................$5.00
*DE1430-25-10, 189x, u/u 100 sh. certificate,
brown $6.00
DE1430-35-10, 1967, 1 sh., brown $8.00

Developers Small Business Investment Company (NJ 1961, par 1¢)

*DE1520-20-10, 1965, v, 100 sh., Broun-Green
Co. N.Y.; 11-1/2" x 8", green border.....$3.00

Dewey and Almy Chemical Company (MA 1919, par $1)

*DE1600-20-10, 1952, v, 53 sh. on a less than 100 sh. certificate ABN, 12" x 8", blue **$4.00**

Dewey Portland Cement Company (DE)

*DE1630-20-10, 1957, 14 class A sh. (par $7.50), GOES Litho, 11" x 8-1/2", orange **$3.00**

The Diamond Coal and Coke Company (WY par $10)

DI90-20-10, 189x, v, u/u certificate, grey . .**$15.00**

The value of a stock certificate depends on:
- rarity
- the issuer
- signatures
- quality of engraving
- overall appearance
- condition
- date of issue

Diamond International Corporation (DE)

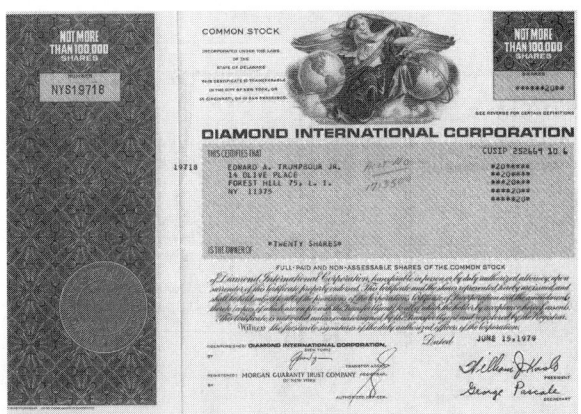

*DI120-20-10, 1979, v, 20 sh. on a not more than 100,000 sh. certificate, SCB, 12" x 8", brown and green **$4.00**

The Diamond Match Company (par $1)

DI160-20-10, 1955, v, 100 sh., red **$13.00**

Diamond Oil Company (CO par $0.01)

DI190-20-10, 1917, v, 1,000 sh., grey **$10.00**

Dictator Consolidated Mining Co. (NV 1886, par $100)

*DI230-10-10, 1886, v, 500 sh., signed by Hume Yerington, early pioneer and rancher; grey border. **$40.00**

Differential Wheel Corporation (DE par $100)

DI300-20-10, 1950, v, 100 sh., orange **$16.00**

Dile Motor Car Company (PA par $50)

DI410-20-10, 19xx, v, u/u certificate, green
. . . .**$55.00**

DI410-30-10, 19xx, v, u/u pref. stock certificate, brown **$55.00**

Dillsburg Copper, Lead & Iron Company (par $50)

DI440-20-10, 18xx, v, u/u certificate, grey . .**$7.00**

directomat, Inc. (DE 1957, par $0.01)

*DI550-20-10, 1968, v, 100 sh., SCB, 12" x 8-1/4", blue **$3.00**

Walt Disney Productions

*DI600-20-10, 19xx, v, u/c not more than 100,000 certificate, lilac **$35.00**

Dollar Oil Co. (CA par $1)

DO200-20-10, 1911, v, i/u 50 sh., green . . .**$14.00**

Dolores Creek Mining Co. (par $1)

DO250-20-10, 19xx, v, u/u certificate, 10" x 8", grey **$7.00**

Domenico, Inc. (IL par $10)

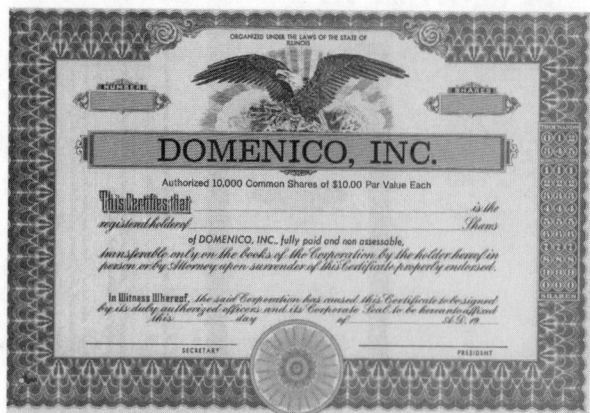

*DO310-20-10, 19xx, v, u/u certificate, w/o imprint, 11" x 7-1/2", red border **$3.00**

Dominguez Oil Fields Company (DE)

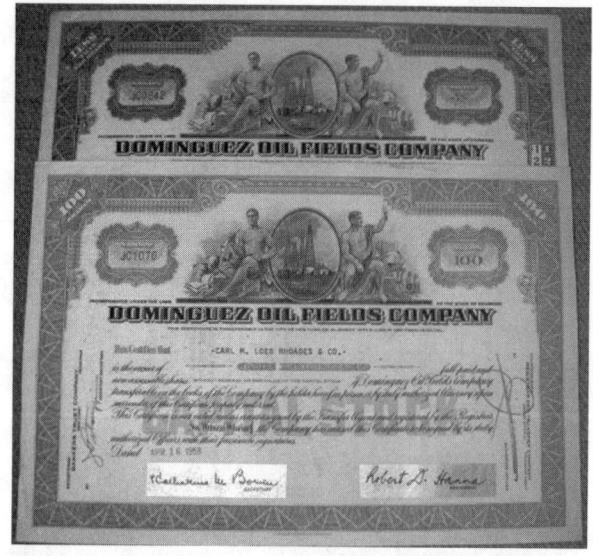

*DO340-20-10, 1958, v, 10 sh. on a less than 100 sh. certificate, green **$4.00**
*DO340-30-10, 1958, v, 100 sh., orange **$4.00**

Dorchester Manufacturing Company (NY)

DO390-20-10, 1857, v, 10 sh., grey **$25.00**

The Dow Chemical Company

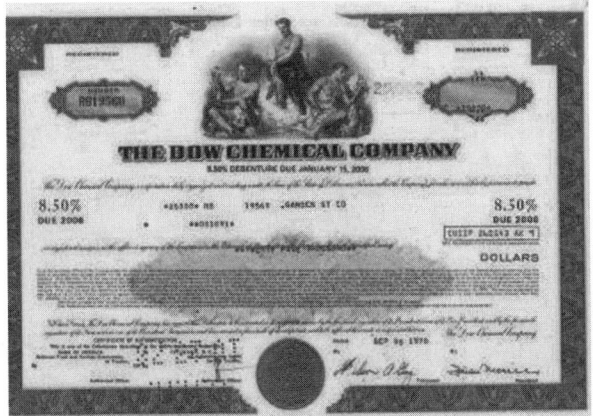

*DO460-45-10, 1978, v, $25,000 8.50% debenture due 2008, green....................$10.00

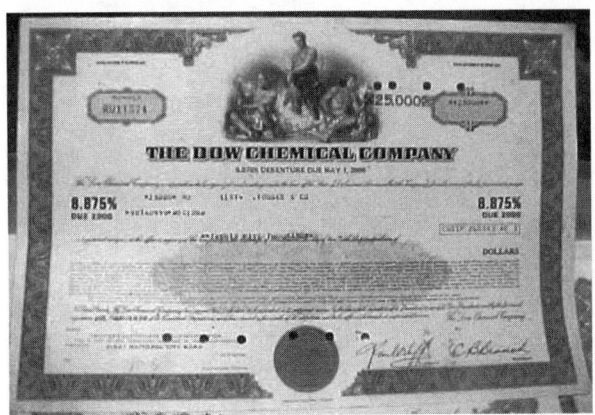

*DO460-50-10, 19??, v, $25,000 8.875% debenture due 2008, purple $10.00

Draper Corporation (ME no par)

*DR50-20-10, 1965, v, 100 sh., 11-1/2" x 8", green
....$15.00

Dry Ice Corporation of California (CA par $10)

*DR180-20-10, 19xx, v, u/u certificate, brown
....$5.00

Duke Drugs, Inc. (no par)

*DU100-20-10, 19xx, v, u/u certificate, GOES, 11" x 8-1/2", green border $2.00

Duke Power Company (NC)

DU190-50-10, 1975, v, $1,000 6.85% note due 1978, blue border $5.00

Dunedin Isles, Inc.

*DU240-20-10, 192?, 1,500 class A sh., blue
....$4.00

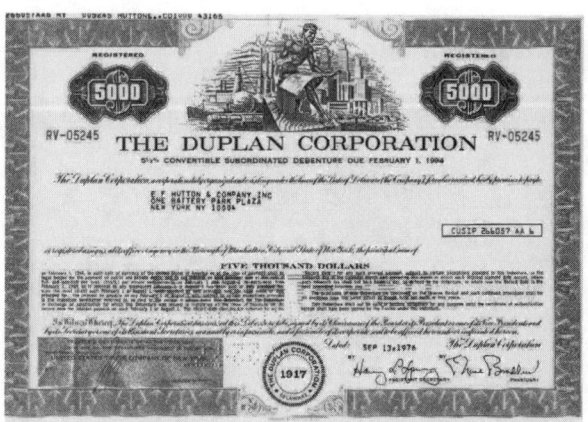

*DU240-30-10, 192?, 1,150 class B sh., green
...................................**$4.00**

Dunleith & Dubuque Bridge Co. (IA par $100)

DU280-20-10, 1868, 50 sh., grey........**$45.00**

DU280-30-10, 1884, v, 291 sh., grey.....**$25.00**

DU280-35-10, 18xx, v, u/u certificate, grey
...................................**$10.00**

DU280-50-10, 1868, v, $1,000 8% bond due 1893, black and red.....................**$44.00**

The Duplan Corporation (DE 1917)

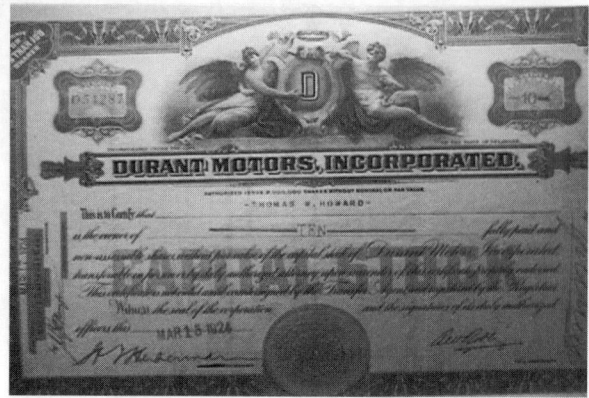

DU350-40-10, 1976, v, $5,000 5-1/2% subordinated debenture due 1994, orange **$4.00**

Durant Motors, Incorporated (1930, no par)

DU400-10-10, 1924, v, 10 sh. on a less than 100 sh. certificate, brown **$40.00**

DU400-20-10, 1930, v, 100 sh., olive green
...................................**$50.00**

DU400-30-10, 1929, v, 10 pref. sh., green
...................................**$65.00**

E

Eagle Lock Co. (CT 1854)
EA80-20-10, 1926, v, 50 sh., black........**$20.00**

**The East Colorado Springs Land Company
(CO 1896, par $1)**
EA150-20-10, 1915, v, 20,000 sh., grey....**$16.00**

The East Harrisburg Passenger Railway Co.

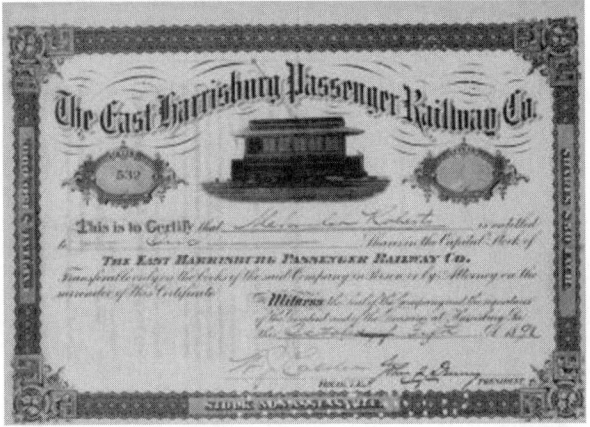

EA220-20-10, 1891, v, 1 sh., grey **$62.00**

**East Mahanoy Rail Road Company
(PA par $50)**

EA290-20-10, 1941, v, 3 sh., grey **$20.00**

EA290-30-10, 1942, v, 77 sh., signature variety,
grey...........................**$20.00**

**East St. Louis-New Athens Brewing
Company (IL)**

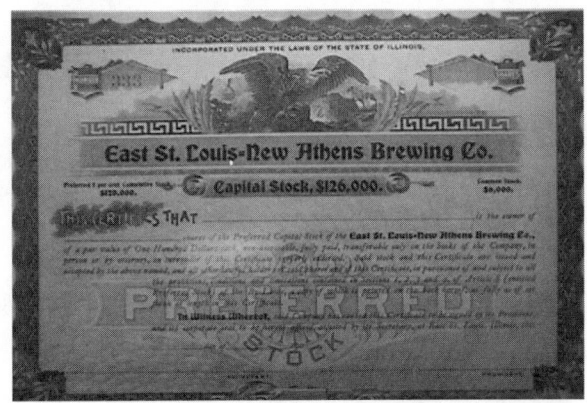

EA360-20-10, 190x, v, u/u certificate pref. stock
(par $100), blue-grey **$12.00**

**East Texas Petroleum Corporation
(TX par $50)**
EA430-20-10, 1930, v, 1 sh., green **$10.00**

**The value of a stock certificate
depends on:**

- **rarity**
- **the issuer**
- **signatures**
- **quality of engraving**
- **overall appearance**
- **condition**
- **date of issue**

Eastern Air Lines, Inc. (DE 1938)

The story of this company reflects the evolution of air transportation. The company's early start was by carrying mail. In order to bid on airmail shipments the company had to separate itself from its parent, North American Aviation.

EA510-20-10, 1938, t, 100 sh. (par $1), signed by Eddie Rickenbacker, EAW, green $40.00

The Eastern Company

EA550-20-10, 1954, v, 10 sh., blue $4.00

EA550-20-15, 1968, v, 5 sh., signature variety, blue $4.00

Eastern Fisheries Company (ME par $10)

EA620-20-10, 19xx, v, u/u preferred stock certificate, GOES, 10-3/4" x 8-1/2", green $3.00

Eastern Gas and Fuel Associates (MA 1929)

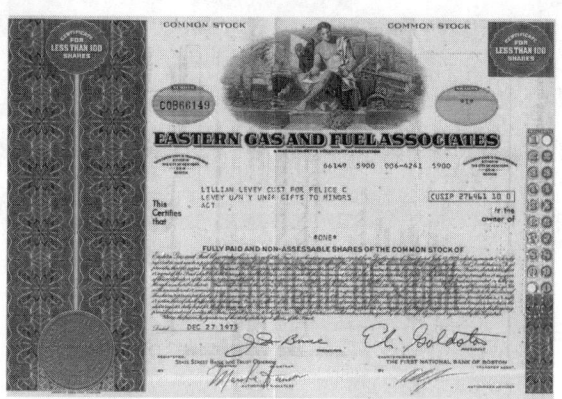

EA660-20-10, 1973, v - man w. ships, 1 sh. on a less than 100 sh. certificate, ABN, 12" x 8", olive green $4.00

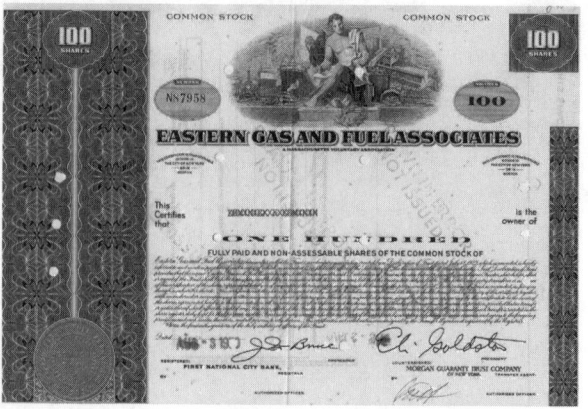

EA660-30-10, 1970, v - man w. ships, 100 sh., ABN, 12" x 8", brown $4.00

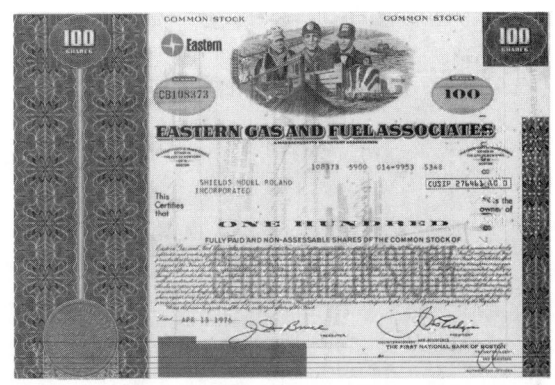

*EA660-40-10, 1976, v - 3 workmen, 100 sh., ABN, 12" x 8", brown $4.00

Eastern Idaho Mining and Water Company (ID territory, par $10)

EA720-20-10, 188x, v, unissued certificate, grey $21.00

The Eastern Malleable Iron Company (CT 1912, par $25)

*EA760-20-10, 1957, v, 1 sh., EAW, 11-1/2" x 8-1/2", blue $4.00

*EA760-30-10, 1958, v, 10 sh., green $4.00

Eastern Steamship Lines, Inc. (ME no par)

EA820-20-10, 1923, t, 50 sh., cum. pref., green $7.00

Eastman Kodak Company

*EA900-50-10, 1982, v, $100,000 8-1/4% conver. subord. debenture due 2007, orange $20.00

Eaton & Howard Balanced Fund

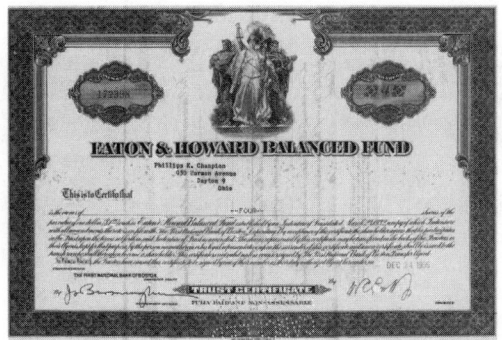

*EA960-20-10, 1955, v, 4 sh., trust certificate (par $1), ABN, 12" x 8", green border $4.00

Eau Claire Grocer Company (WI par $100)

*EA1000-20-10, 1931, v, 65 sh., GOES, 11" x 8", brown border $25.00

Eco Electrical Manufacturing Corporation (FL 1960, par 1¢)

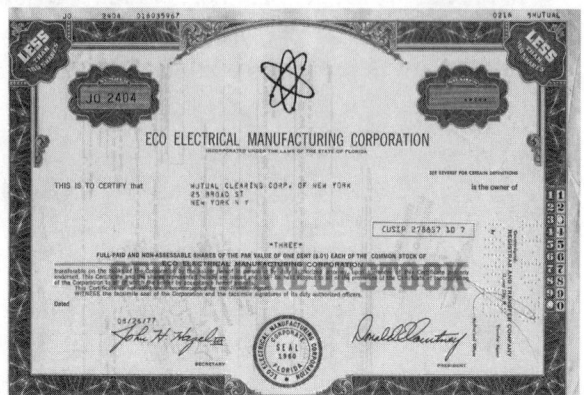

*EC100-20-10, 1977, v, 3 sh. on a less than 100 sh. certificate, SCB, 12" x 8", blue.........$4.00

Ediphone Service Incorporated (NJ 1928, par $100)

Only ten shares were issued.

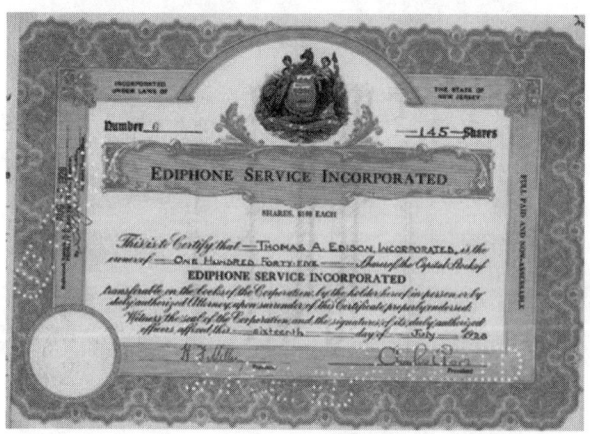

*ED100-10-10, 1928, v, 145 sh., signed by Charles Edison, orange, with Ediphone booklet
..............................$150.00

Edison Kinetophone Company (NJ)
ED140-10-10, 19xx, v, 100 unissued shares, brown
..............................$31.00

Edison Phonographs, Ltd. (NJ par $100)

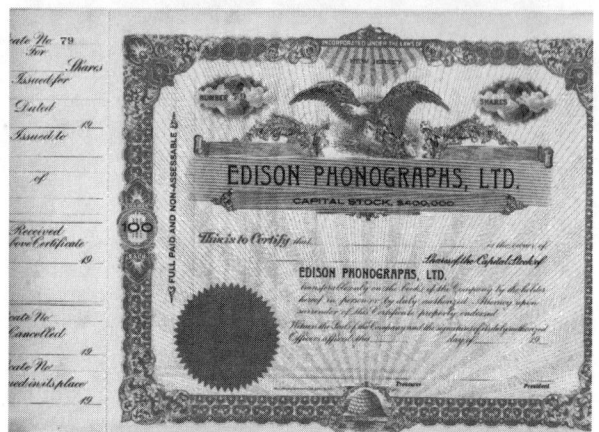

*ED170-20-10, 19xx, u/u certificate, Broun-Green NY, brown $140.00

Edison Storage Battery Company (NJ par $100)

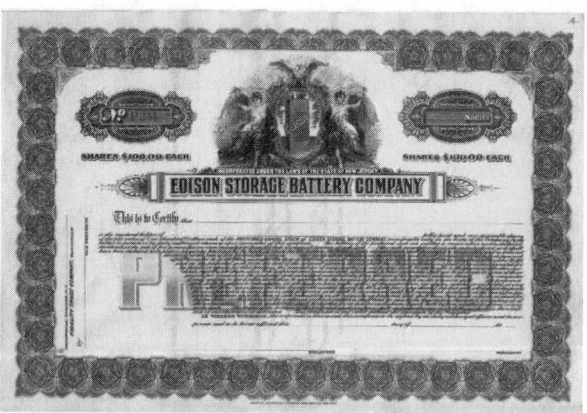

*ED200-20-10, 191x, v, unissued pref. sh. certificate, green.........................$15.00

Educational Film and Supply Company (DE par $100)
ED280-20-10, 1930, v, 3 sh., brown $4.00

El Canada Mines Inc. (DE 1929)
EL100-20-10, 1929, 100 sh., orange $5.00

UNLISTED TYPES & VARIETIES

Readers are welcome to contact the author directly at:

**Rainer Stahlberg
P.O. Box 1044
Rooseveltown, New York 13683**

*EL100-30-10,1934, 20 sh. (par $1), Broun-Green Co. NY, 11-1/4" x 8", orange...........**$4.00**

Elberta Oil Association (TX par $10)

*EL115-20-10, 1919, v, 10 sh., green border
.................................**$4.00**

Elder-Beerman Stores Corp. (OH no par)
EL150-20-10, 1968, v, 100 sh., brown......**$3.00**

The Electric Storage Battery Company

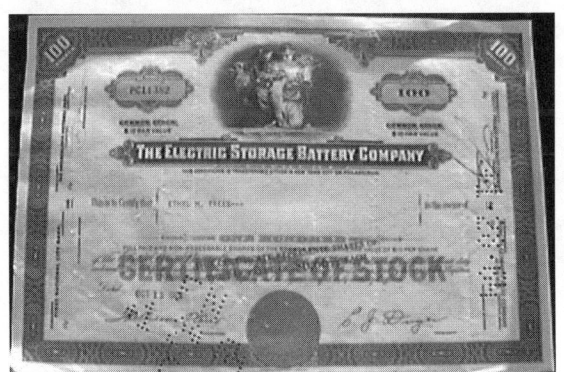

*EL210-20-10, 1963, v, 100 sh., red **$5.00**

Elgin National Watch Company (IL)
EL280-20-10, 1950, v, 30 sh. on a less than 100 sh. certificate, green.....................**$22.00**
EL280-30-10, 1951, v, 100 sh., blue **$43.00**

The Elizabeth Gold Mines Company (AZ par $1)
EL360-20-10, 1904, v, 1,000 sh., green.....**$9.00**

Elk Horn Coal Corporation (WV)

*EL430-20-10, 1924, v, 100 sh., RBN, orange
.................................**$12.00**
EL430-40-10, 1925, v, $1,000 6-year 7% debenture due 1931, green **$12.00**

Ellington Farmers Telephone Company (WI par $10)

*EL440-20-10, 1909, v, 5 sh., 11" x 8", brown border **$60.00**

The Elm Grove Mining Company (WI par $1)

*EL450-20-10, 1907, v, 500 sh., 10-1/2" x 8", brown border......................$12.00

Elmira and Williamsport Railroad Company

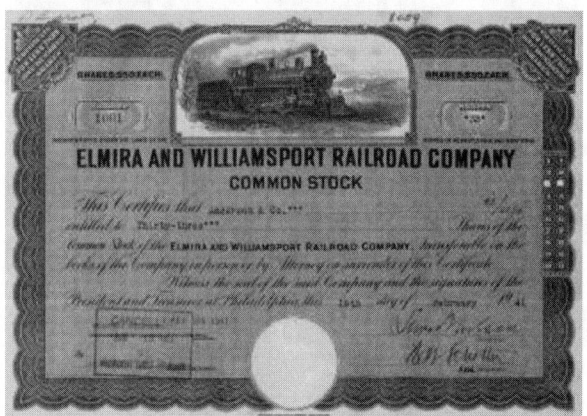

*EL460-20-10, 1957, v, u/c less than 100 sh. certificate, ABN, brown $16.00

EL460-40-10, 1863, v, $500 bearer bond, guaranteed by the Pennsylvania Railroad Company, blue..............................$15.00

> *It is generally assumed that only 5% of certificates survive to reach collectors.*

Ely Consolidated Copper Company (UT)

*EL510-20-10, 1917, v, 100 sh., brown....$11.00

Emma Silver Mines Company (UT par $1)

*EM100-20-10, 19??, v, 100 sh., brown $6.00

The Empire Lee Mining Company (CO par 5¢)

*EM230-20-10, 1951, v, 2,450 sh., brown ...$10.00

Empire Mines Company (ID par $1)

EM260-20-10, 19xx, v, unissued certificate, brown
..................................$9.00

Empire Public Service Corporation

EM300-20-10, 1932, v, 2 sh., orange **$15.00**

Equity Funding Corporation of America

This company's fraud forced revising the Securities
and Exchange Commission and audit procedures
used by CPAs.

EQ80-30-10, 1971, v, $5,000 5-1/2% conv. subord.
debenture due 1991, green **$24.00**

Erie Mining Company (WI par $1)

ER220-20-10, 1908, v, 100 sh., 11" x 8-1/2", grey
border **$65.00**

Erie & Ohio Railroad

ER250-20-10, 18xx, v, unissued certificate, brown
. . . . **$14.00**

Erie Railroad Company (NY no par)

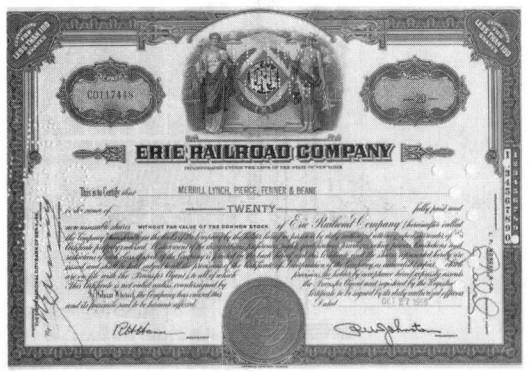

ER280-20-20, 1955, v, 20 sh. on a less than 100
sh. certificate, ABN, 12" x 8", green **$4.00**

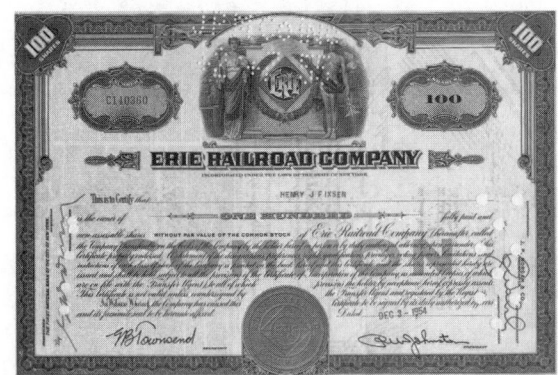

ER280-30-10, 1954, v, 100 sh., ABN, 12" x 8",
blue **$4.00**
ER280-40-10, 1958, v, 10 pref. series A sh., blue
. . . . **$4.00**

Erie-Lackawanna Railroad Company (NY no par)

ER320-20-10, 1964, v, 2 sh. on a less than 100 sh.
certificate, brown **$4.00**

ER320-30-10, 1962, v, 100 sh., ABN, 12" x 8",
red. **$4.00**

*ER320-30-15, 1964, v, 100 sh., signature variety, ABN, 12" x 8", red $4.00

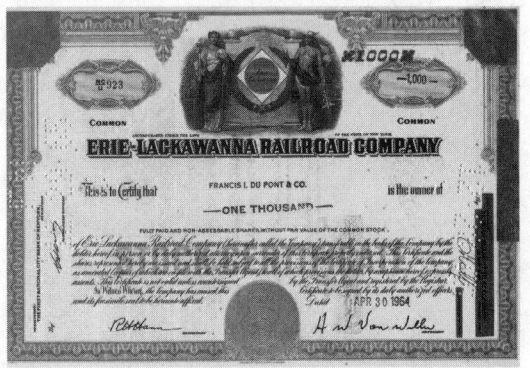

*ER320-40-10, 1964, v, 1,000 sh., ABN, 12" x 8", orange $4.00

Esperance Gold, Silver and Copper Mining Co. (1863, par $100)

ES290-20-10, 186x, v, unissued certificate, green $12.00

The Espiritu Mexican Mining Company (AZ 1910, par $1)

*ES370-20-10, ND, v, 5 bearer shares w. coupons, text in English and French $8.00

The Essex County Building and Loan Association (NJ 1885)

ES410-20-10, 1909, v, 15 sh., green $8.00

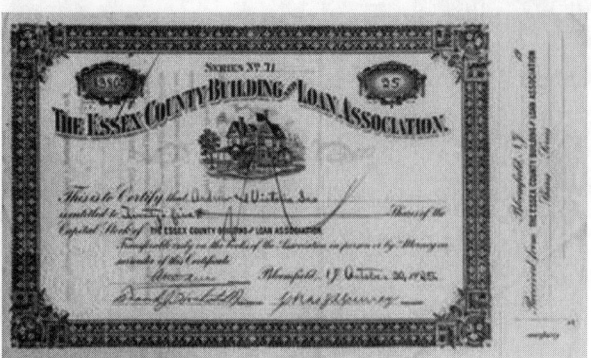

*ES410-30-10, 1925, v, 25 sh., grey $5.00

Estella Mining Co. (WI par $25)

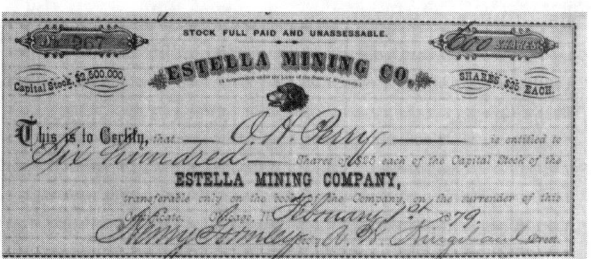

*ES450-20-10, 1879, v, 600 sh., 8" x 3-1/2", grey
. . . .$150.00

Eureka Smelting Company (NV par $1)

EU100-20-10, 1929, v, 100 sh., green $5.00

Eurofund, Inc. (MD 1959, par $1)

*EU190-20-10, 1962, v - map, 11 sh. on a less than 100 sh. certificate, SCB, 12" x 8", blue . . .$4.00
EU190-30-10, 1966, v, 65 sh. on a less than 100 share certificate, green $4.00

EU190-40-10, 1965, v, 100 sh., orange **$4.00**

EU190-50-10, 1966, v, 100 sh., De la Rue Banknote Company, 12" x 8", red **$4.00**

Evansville and Terre Haute Rail Road Company (IN par $50)

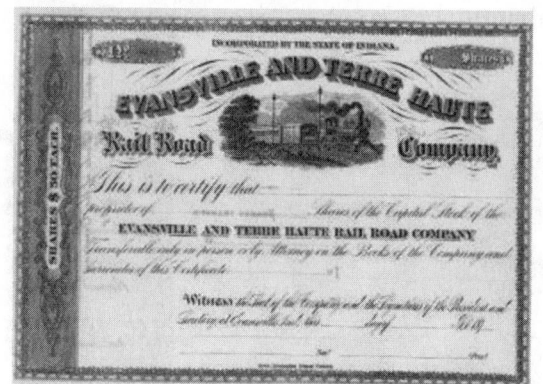

EV100-20-10, 187x, v, u/u certificate, grey
..............................**$12.00**

Everett Resort, Inc. (WI)

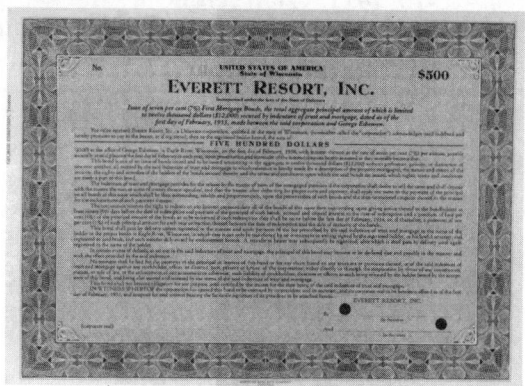

EV150-30-10, 1933, $500 1ˢᵗ mort. 7% bond, Northern Bank Note Co., 11" x 8", blue...**$9.00**

Eversharp, Inc. (DE par $1)
Razor manufacturer.

EV170-20-10, 1967, v, 3 sh. on a less than 100 sh. certificate, red.......................**$6.00**

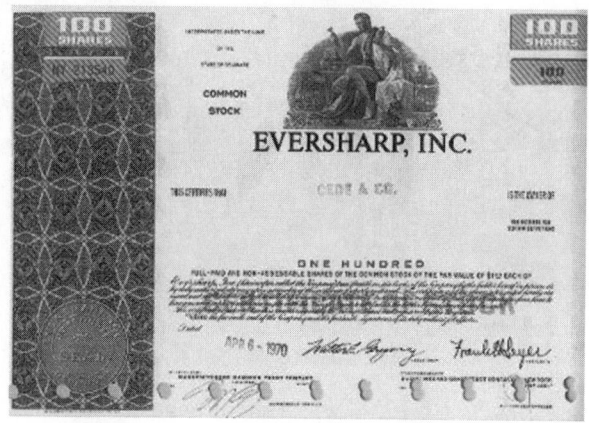

EV170-30-10, 1970, v, 100 sh., purple **$5.00**

Excelsior-Henderson Motorcycle Manufacturing Company (MN)
EX100-10-10, 2000, v, 1 sh., green **$60.00**

Exchequer Gold and Silver Mining Company
EX170-20-10, 19xx, v, u/u certificate, grey, 10" x 4-1/4" **$5.00**

F

Faberge, Incorporated

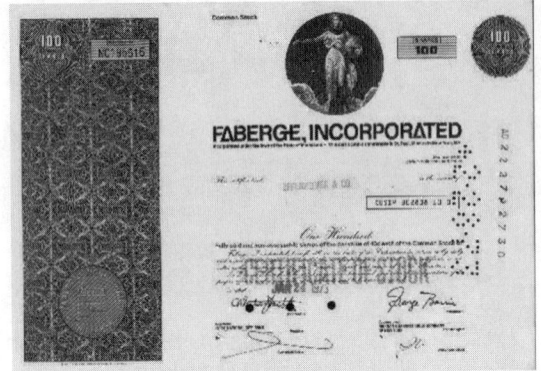

FA60-20-10, 1973, v, 100 sh., green **$4.00**

Fabbrica Automobili Isotta Fraschini

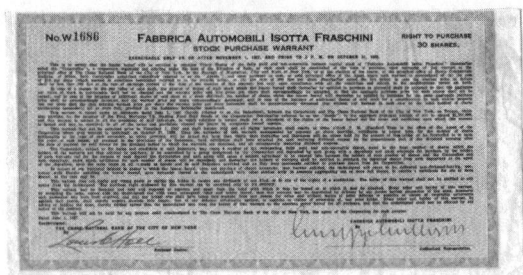

FA150-20-10, 1926, w, 30 sh., orange-red
.................................**$35.00**

Factory Equipment Company
(WI par $100)

FA200-20-10, 19xx, v, u/u certificate, 11" x 8",
green border **$6.00**

Fair Oaks Transit Co. (CA 1912, par $1)

FA370-20-10, 19xx, v, u/u certificate, grey
.................................**$4.00**

Fair Trading Company (VA par $100)
FA400-20-10, 1919, v, 10 sh., brown **$5.00**

Fairbanks Financial Corporation (TX)

FA440-20-10, 19xx, v, u/u certificate, grey
.................................**$4.00**

> **The value of a stock certificate depends on:**
>
> - **rarity**
> - **the issuer**
> - **signatures**
> - **quality of engraving**
> - **overall appearance**
> - **condition**
> - **date of issue**

The Fairmont, Morgantown, and Pittsburgh Railroad Company (PA-WV)

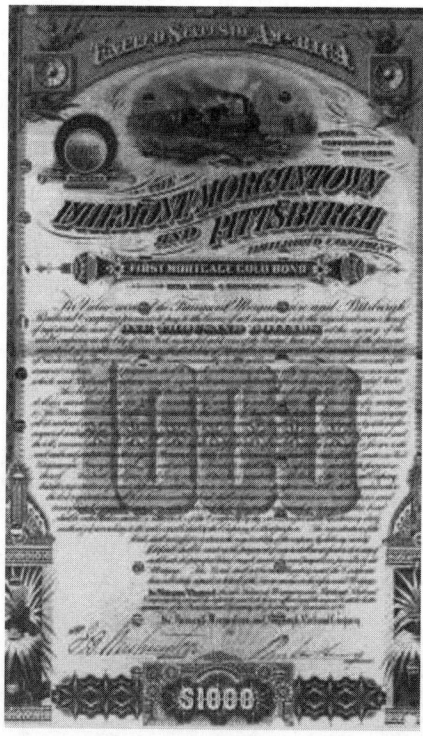

FA500-30-10, 1893, v, $1,000 first mortgage gold bond, Homer Lee Company, brown **$15.00**

Falls Creek Copper Mining Company, Ltd. (par $1)
FA610-20-10, 1907, v, 1,000 sh., brown border
..................................**$12.00**

Falstaff Brewing Corporation

FA660-20-10, 1967, v, 30 sh. on a less than 100 sh. certificate, CBN, blue **$5.00**

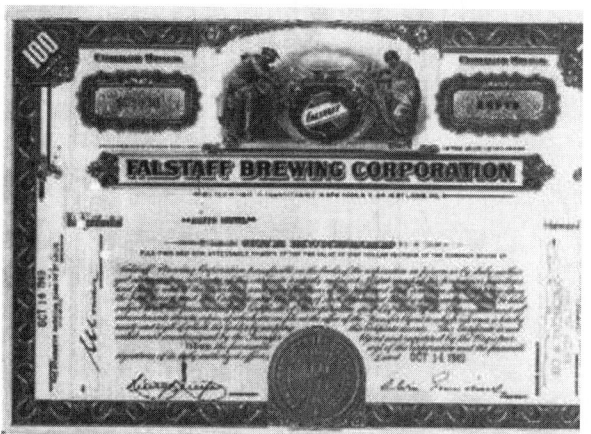

FA660-30-10, 1949, v, 100 sh., CBN, brown
..................................**$5.00**

FA660-30-15, 1970, v, 100 sh., signature variety, brown **$7.00**

FA660-40-10, 1967, v, 1,000 sh., SCB, red
..................................**$5.00**

The Famise Corporation (DE)
FA710-30-10, 1951, v, 200 sh., orange **$4.00**

Farmers Bank of Virginia

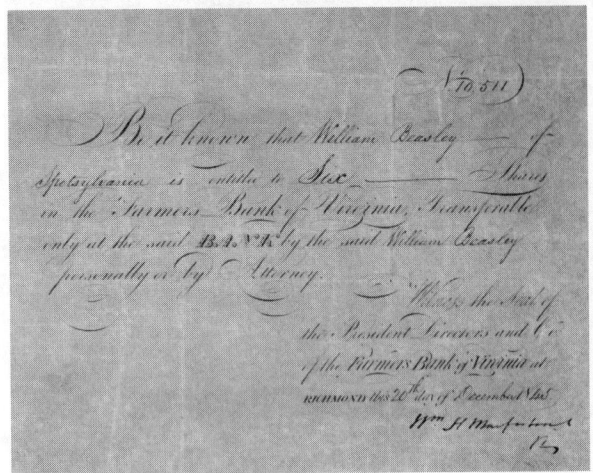

*FA800-10-10, 1845, 6 sh., 8" x 6", brown
. . . .$150.00

Farmer's Co-Operative Elevator Company of Belvidere (IL par $100)

FA810-20-10, 1952, v, 1 sh., green $5.00

Farmers Deposit National Bank (par $100)

Part of the Mellon Bank.

FA840-20-10, 19xx, v - dog, unissued certificate, green $11.00

*FA840-25-10, 1906, v, 100 sh., green $35.00

Farmers Equity Elevator Company (ND par $100)

FA870-20-10, 1919, v, 1 sh., orange-brown
. . . .$6.00

Farmers Feed Company of New York (NY 1905, par $100)

FA900-10-10, 19xx, unissued certificate, black
. . . .$4.00

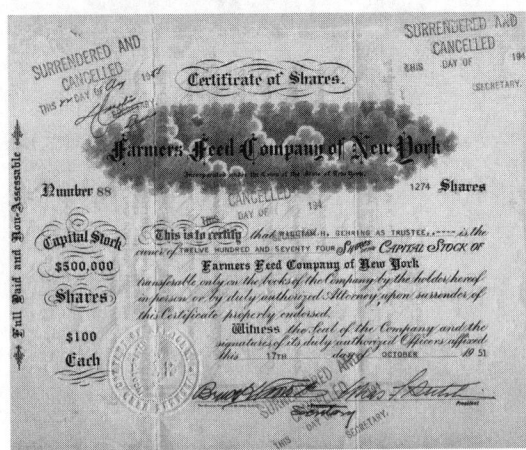

*FA900-20-10, 1951, 1,274 sh., Brown-Green Co., 11-1/4" x 9", black $6.00

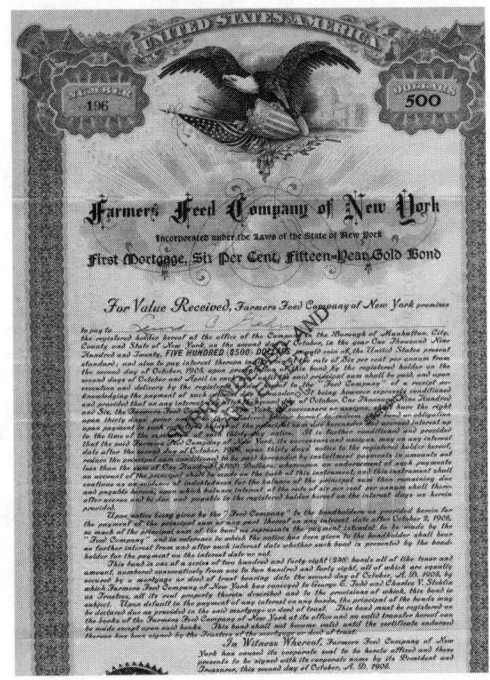

*FA900-40-10, 1905, v, $500 first mort. 6% 15-year gold bond, Brown-Green Co., 9-1/2" x 15", brown $6.00

Farmers National Mortgage Institute

FA1020-30-10, 1928, v, $1,000 7% Hungarian Land and Mortgage sinking fund, gold bond w. coupons, green $10.00

The Farmers' Union of San Jose, California (par $100)

FA1200-20-10, 1877, v, 1 sh., grey $12.00

FA1200-25-10, 187x, v, u/u certificate, grey
..................................$6.00

Father De Smet Consolidated Gold Mining Company (1878, par $100)

Mine was located in the Black Hills, Lawrence County, Dakota. Eventually became part of Homestake Mining.

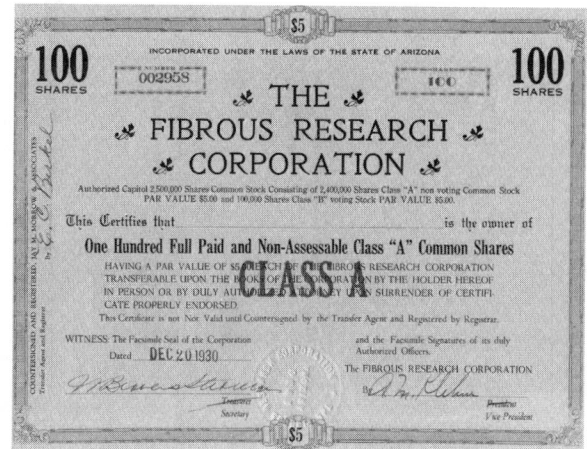

FA1330-20-10, 1880, v, 100 sh., orange ..$37.00

The Favorite Gold Mining Company

FA1430-20-10, 1895, 9,000 sh., grey on green paper, small certificate $13.00

Federal Bond & Share Company (DE)

FE140-20-10, 1931, v, 5 sh., blue $5.00

Federal Pacific Electric Company

FE270-20-10, 1963, v, 1 sh. on a less than 100 sh. certificate, orange $8.00

Federal Power & Light Company (ME)

FE310-20-10, 1917, v, 992 sh., green $7.00

Federal Street and Pleasant Valley Passenger Railway Company (PA)

FE440-20-10, 1896, v, 10 sh., New York Bank Note Company, green................$12.00

The Fibrous Research Corporation (AZ par $5)

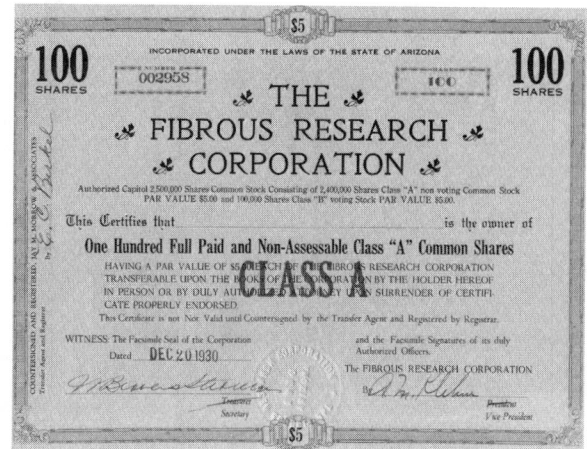

FI60-20-10, 1930, i/u 100 class A sh., w/o imprint, 10-3/4" x 8-1/4", green.........$4.00

Fieldcrest Mills, Inc. (DE 1953, no par)

FI300-20-10, 1964, v, 100 sh., green.......$9.00

The Findley Gold Mining Company (CO par $1)

Mines located at Cripple Creek, El Paso County, CO.

FI350-20-10, 1896, v, 3,000 sh., brown....$12.00

Finnish-American Mining Company (MN par $1)

FI380-20-10, 1909, v, 50 sh., w/o imprint, 11" x 8-1/4", orange.....................$15.00

First Charter Financial Corporation (CA)

*FI500-20-10, 1975, v, 100 sh., JBN, blue
. . . .$10.00

First City Properties Inc. (DE 1979)

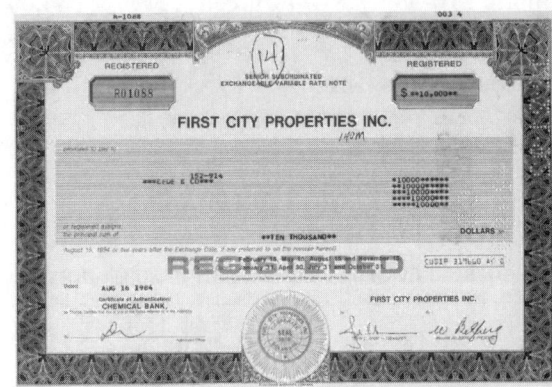

*FI540-40-10, 1984, $10,000 senior subord.
exchangeable variable rate note, Jeffries Banknote Company, 12" x 8", blue. $4.00

First Financial Bancorp, Inc., Belvidere, Illinois (DE 1983, Par $0.10)

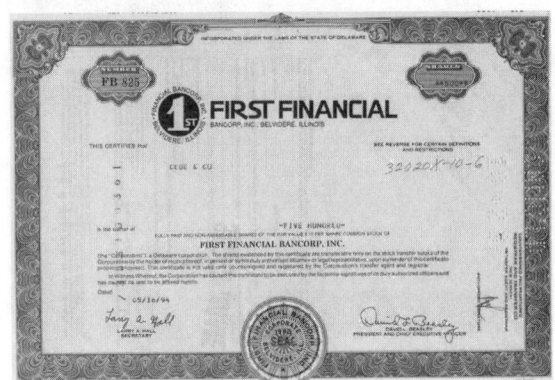

*FI690-20-10, 1994, v, 500 sh., GOES, 12" x 8",
green $4.00

The First National Bank of Carbondale (PA par $10)

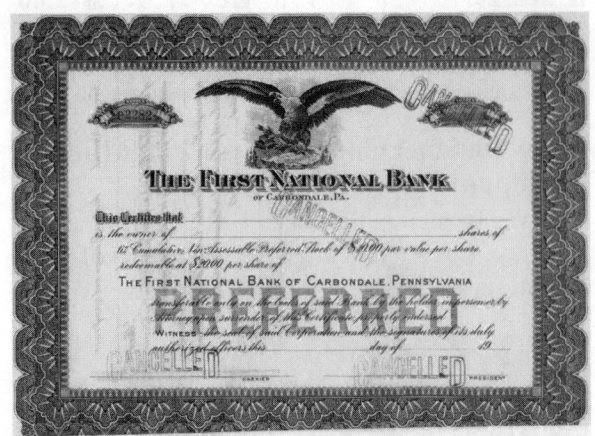

*FI810-20-10, 19xx, v - eagle, u/c certificate, w/o
imprint, 11-3/4" x 8-3/4", brown $4.00

The First National Bank of Chicago, Illinois (IL par $100)

*FI820-20-10, 1865, v, 25 sh., revenue stamp,
11" x 8", brown border. $70.00

The First National Bank of Frederick, Md. (MD)

FI840-20-10, 1897, v, 1 sh., Cushings & Bailey,
9-1/2" x 6-1/2", brown $18.00

First National Bank of Woodbury (NJ)

FI880-20-10, 1875, v, 10 sh., brown $6.00
FI880-30-10, 1907, v, 2 sh., brown $6.00

FI880-35-10, 1913, v, 5 sh. (par $50), brown
. . . .$6.00

FI880-40-10, 1914, v, 20 sh. (par $50), brown
. . . .$13.00

First National Bank in Yonkers (NY)
FI920-20-10, 1961, v, 17 sh., 11" x 8-1/2", blue
border $3.00

First United, Inc. (DE par $1)

FI1060-20-10, 1980, v, 2 sh., ABN, 12" x 8",
green $4.00

First United Life Insurance Company (IN par $1)

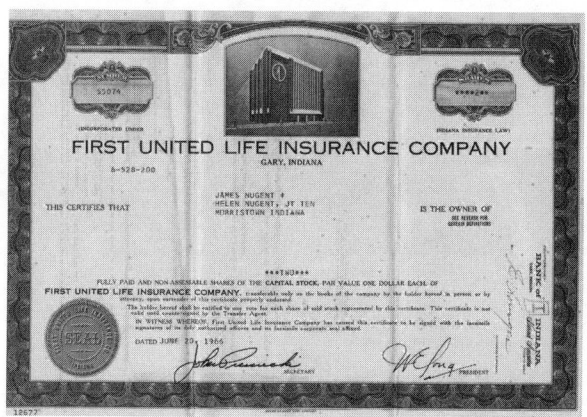

FI1090-20-10, 1966, v, 2 sh., ABN, 12" x 8",
green $4.00

The Fisherbody Ohio Company
FI1300-20-10, 1922, v, 20 pref. sh. on a less than
100 sh. certificate, green. $125.00

The Fisk Rubber Company
Fisk was taken over by U.S. Rubber, which eventually became Uniroyal.

FI1340-20-10, 1929, v, 20 sh., orange. . . .$22.00

Fitchburg & Worchester Rail Road Co.
FI1400-30-10, 1869, v, $100 bond w. coupons.,
ABN, grey $65.00

FI1340-30-10, 1930, v, 100 sh., brown . . .$14.00

Five Mile Oil Company (SD par $1)
FI1480-20-10, 1919, v, i/u 125 sh., brown . .$9.00

Flint Creek Mining Company (MT par $5)
FL140-20-10, 189x, unissued certificate . . .**$15.00**

Flint and Pere Marquette Railroad Company (MI par $100)

*FL210-20-10, 1880, v, 40 sh., grey **$26.00**
FL210-30-10, 1883, v, 50 sh., orange. **$28.00**

*FL210-40-10, 19xx, v, u/u certificate for common capital stock, blue **$11.00**

*FL210-50-10, 1880, v, 13 pref. shares, brown
. . . .**$13.00**

FL210-55-10, 1880, v, 100 sh., pref., brown
. . . .**$25.00**
FL210-60-10, 1885, v, 50 sh., pref., brown
. . . .**$18.00**

Florence County Cooperative (WI)

*FL330-20-10, 1947, 1 sh. (par $500), 11" x 8-1/2", brown border **$10.00**

Florence Stove Company

*FL350-20-10, 1939, v, 50 sh. on a less than 100 sh. certificate, blue **$3.00**

State of Florida
FL400-40-10, 1972, v, $5,000 University System Improvement revenue bond, green. **$9.00**

Florida East Coast Railway Company (FL par $25)

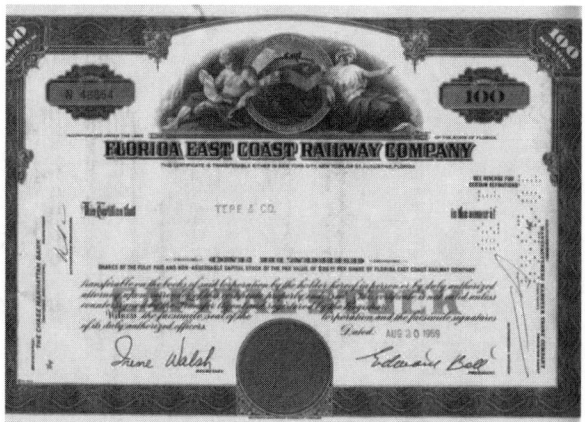

*FL450-20-10, 1969, v, 100 sh., green. $30.00

Florida Power & Light Company (FL 1925)

*FL540-40-10, 1988, v, $,5000 1st mortgage,
8-1/2% due 2004, ABN, 12" x 8", l. brown **$5.00**
FL540-50-10, 1990, v, $2,000 first mortgage
7-3/4% bond due 2001, green **$6.00**

UNLISTED TYPES & VARIETIES

Readers are welcome to contact the author directly at:

Rainer Stahlberg
P.O. Box 1044
Rooseveltown, New York 13683

Florida West Airlines, Inc. (DE 1968, par 10¢)

*FL610-20-10, 19xx, u/u Specimen certificate,
Columbia Financial Printing Company, red
. . . . $10.00

The Flowery Mines Company (DE par $1)

FL690-20-10, 1924, v, 20,000 sh., green . . . **$10.00**

Follansbee Steel Corporation

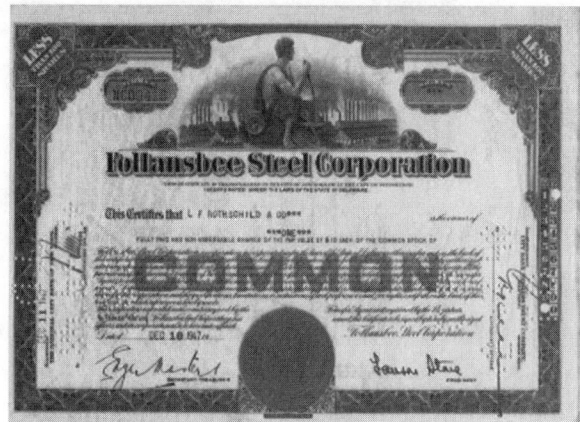

*FO130-20-10, 1948, v, 1 sh. on a less than 100 sh.
certificate, green $16.00

It is generally assumed that only 5% of certificates survive to reach collectors.

The Fond du Lac Water Company (WI par $100)

*FO210-20-10, 1xxx, v, u/u certificate, GOES, 10" x 8", grey border. $30.00

Food Fair Stores, Inc.

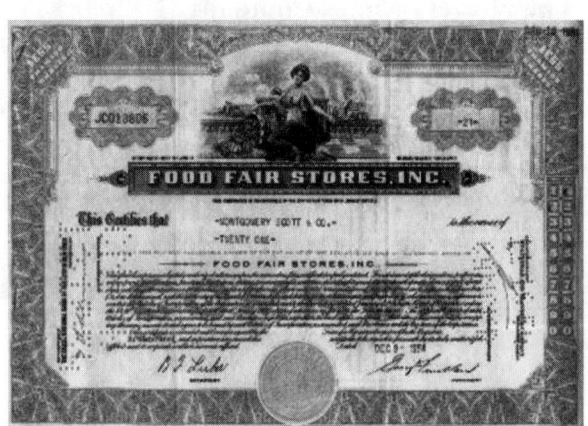

*FO320-20-10, 1954, v, 21 sh. on a less than 100 sh. certificate, yellow brown. $4.00

Foote, Cone & Belding Communications, Inc. (DE)
FO390-20-10, 1973, v, 100 sh., green $10.00

Ford International Capital Corporation
FO440-30-10, 1968, v, $1,000 bond, blue border
. . . .$11.00

Foremost Dairies, Inc.

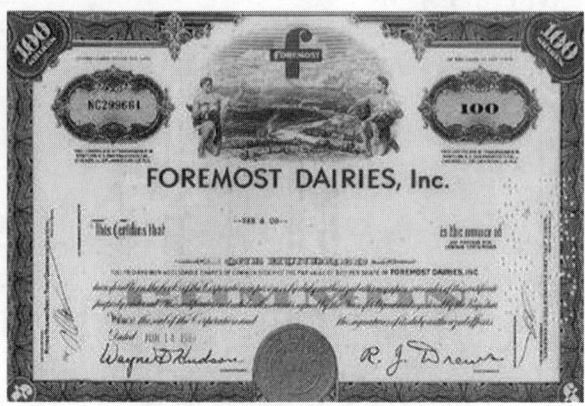

*FO460-30-10, 1967, v, 100 sh., blue border
. . . .$4.00

The Forest City Railway Company (OH par $100)
FO490-20-10, 1905, v, 40 sh., brown $12.00

Fort Howard Paper Company (DE)
FO570-20-10, 1975, v, 100 sh., green $4.00

The Fort Pitt Traction Company (PA par $50)

*FO610-20-10, 18xx, v, u/u 100 sh. certificate, green. $15.00

Fort Street and Elmwood Railway Co.
FO650-20-10, 186x, v, u/u certificate, 12-1/4" x 6-3/4", blue. $45.00

Fort Wayne & Jackson Railroad Company (par $100)

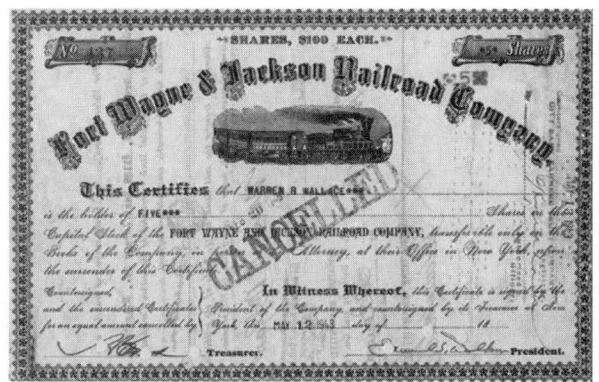

FO710-20-10, 1943, v, 5 sh., grey $4.00

Fostoria Glass Company (par $10)

FO760-20-10, 19xx, v, unissued certificate, green
. . . .$15.00

The Four Wheel Drive Auto Company (WI)

FO820-15-10, 1917, v, 5 sh. (par $100), GOES,
11" x 8-1/2", brown border. $30.00

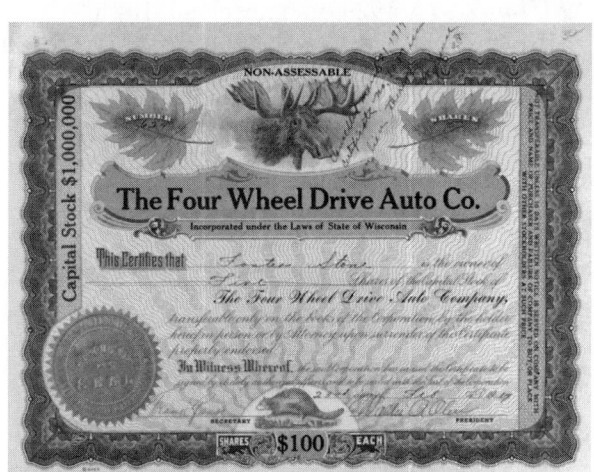

FO820-20-10, 1929, v, 1 sh. (par $100), revenue
stamp, GOES, 11" x 8-1/2", brown border
. . . .$25.00

FO820-30-10, 1953, v, 1 sh. (par $10) on a less
than 100 sh. certificate, ABN, 12" x 8", green
border $15.00

FO820-35-10, 1958, v, 100 sh., ABN, 12" x 8",
blue. $15.00

Fowler Farm Oil Corporation (OK par $1)

FO910-20-10, 1951, v, 25 sh., grey $6.00

Fox Head Brewing Company (WI par $1.25)

FO970-20-10, 1961, v, 100 sh., 12" x 8", black
..................................$7.00

The Foxboro Company (MA par $1)

FO1000-20-10, 1970, v, 8 sh. on a less than 100 sh.
certificate, green $8.00

Frankford & Southwark Passenger Railroad Company, Philadelphia City (PA)

FR130-20-10, 1910, v, 15 sh., green $12.00

Franklin Trust Company

FR170-20-10, 1929, v, 100 sh...........$38.00

Fravel-Paymaster Mining Company (ME)

FR230-20-10, 1919, 100 sh., green border
..................................$5.00

Fruehauf Trailer Company (par $1)

FR510-20-10, 1955, v, 1 sh. on a less than 100 sh.
certificate, purple $10.00

FSI Corporation (NY par 10¢)

FS110-20-10, 1971, 1 sh., red $4.00

The Fulton County National Bank of Gloversville (NY par $100)

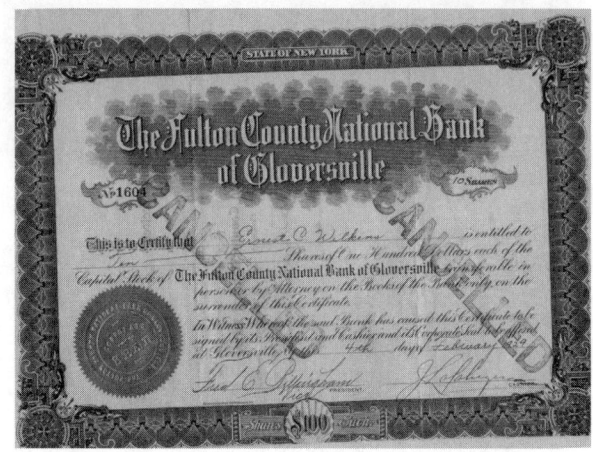

FU140-20-10, 1929, v - grey cloud, 10 sh.,
Brown, Lent & Pett. NY, 12" x 9", grey ..$4.00

The Fulton County National Bank and Trust Company of Gloversville (NY)

FU170-20-10, 19xx, v, unissued certificate, green
..................................$4.00

Fulton Motors Corporation

FU240-20-10, 1921, v, 11 sh., orange $33.00

Fuqua Industries, Inc.

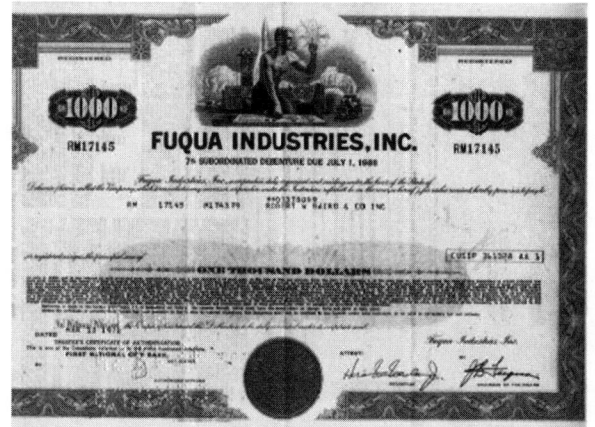

*FU310-30-10, 1972, v, $1,000 7% subord. debenture due 1988, blue.................$12.00

FWD Corporation (WI par $10)

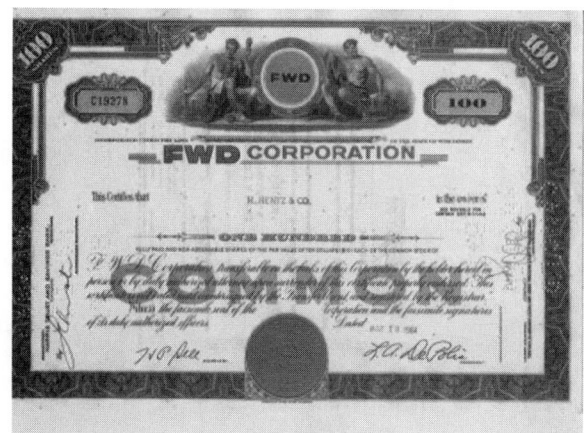

*FW50-20-10, 1964, v, 100 sh., blue......$12.00

G

Galco Leasing System (NJ)
GA140-20-10, 1973, v, 1,000 sh., orange....**$5.00**

Gallatin Valley Electric Railway (MT 1908, par $100)

*GA200-10-10, 1909, 12 sh., grey **$25.00**

Gardner-Denver Company (DE 1927, no par)

*GA340-20-10, 1946, v, 50 sh. on a less than 100 sh. certificate, CBN, 11-1/2" x 8", orange .**$5.00**
GA340-30-10, 1964, v, 10 sh. on a less than 100 sh. certificate, red......................**$4.00**

*GA340-40-10, 1959, v, 100 sh., CBN, 11-3/4" x 8", blue..........................**$4.00**

The Gavilan Mining & Milling Company

*GA400-20-10, 189x, v, u/u certificate, grey on yellow..........................**$5.00**

General American Investors Company, Inc. (DE 1928, par $1)

GE100-20-10, 1976, v, 764 sh. on a more than 100 sh. certificate, ABN, 12" x 8", red **$4.00**

*GE100-30-10, 1983, v - man w. wheel, 150 sh.,
ABN, 12" x 8", blue $4.00

General American Transportation Corporation

GE160-40-10, 1983, v, $10,000 6.6% equipment
trust certificate due 1991, grey and brown
..............................$7.00

General Box Company (DE par $1)

GE240-20-10, 1954, v, 100 sh., green $3.00

*GE240-25-10, 1964, v, 100 sh., SCB, 12" x 8",
green $3.00

General Development Corporation (DE 1928)

*G320-30-10, 1990, v, $20,000 bond, olive green
..............................$6.00

General Electric Company (par $5)

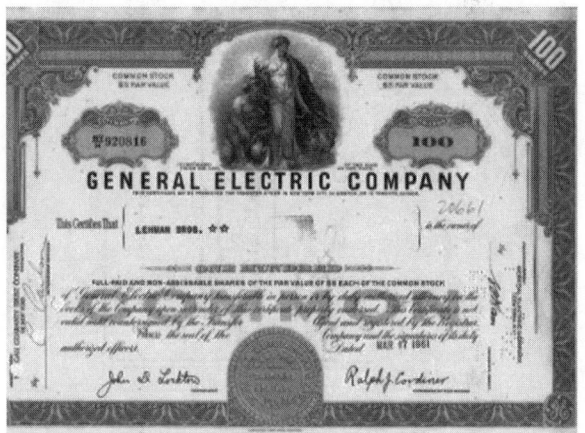

*GE400-20-10, 1961, v, 100 sh., red......$30.00

This catalog has listings in an alphabetical format. The reason is simple: Companies diversify as they grow. For example, the Canadian Pacific Railway company recently split into five companies. They represent the railway, hotels, shipping, airline, and petroleum interests of the company. During World War II, the Singer sewing machine company made guns and other defense-related equipment, so where should we list it? It's far easier to use a strict alphabetical order, rather than to confuse the reader with topical classifications.

General Electric Overseas Capital Corporation

*GE440-30-10, 1965, v, $1,000 4-1/4% guar. bond due 1985 w. coupons, ABN, 10-1/4" x 15", green
....$6.00

General Foods Corporation (DE 1922 no par)

*GE520-20-10, 1966, v, 5 sh. on a less than 100 sh. certificate, ABN, 12" x 8", brown $4.00

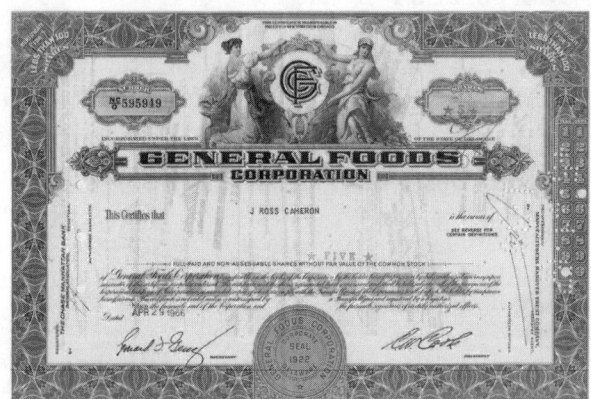

*GE520-30-10, 1971, 100 sh., ABN, 12" x 8", green $4.00

GE520-40-10, 1971, 500 sh. on a more than 100 sh. certificate, orange $4.00

General Investors Trust (MA par $1)

*GE620-20-10, 1965, v, 100 sh., green $3.00

General Motors Corporation (DE par $1.2/3)

GE760-20-10, 1951, v, 25 sh. on a less than 100 sh. certificate, red **$7.00**

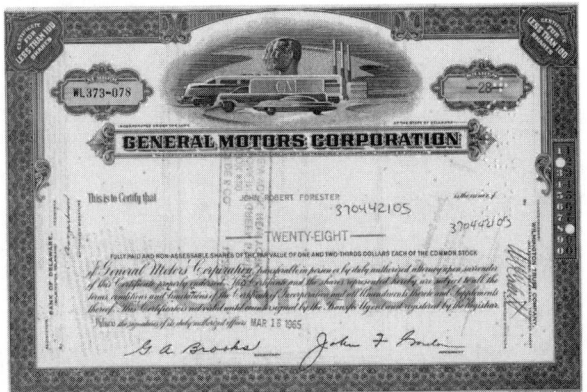

GE760-30-10, 1965, v, 28 sh. on a less than 100 sh. certificate, ABN, 12" x 8", green **$5.00**

GE760-30-15, 1974, v, 12 sh. on a less than 100 sh. certificate, ABN, 11-1/4" x 8", green . .**$4.00**

GE760-40-10, 1955, v, 100 sh., ABN, 12" x 8", orange **$5.00**

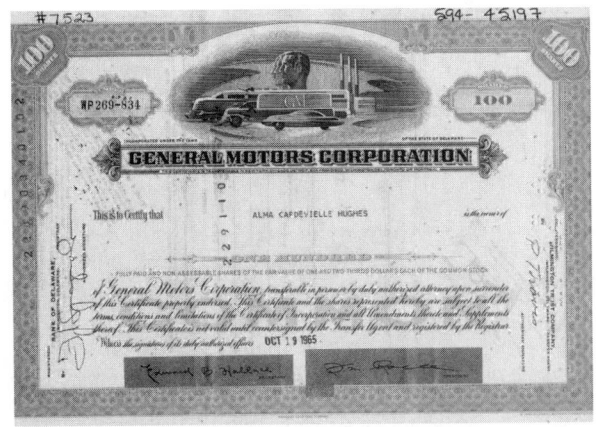

GE760-40-15, 1965, v, 100 sh., ABN, signature variety and strips, ABN, 12" x 8", orange .**$5.00**

GE760-50-10, 1977, v, 1 sh. on a less than 10,000 sh. certificate, ABN, 12" x 8", aquamarine **$4.00**

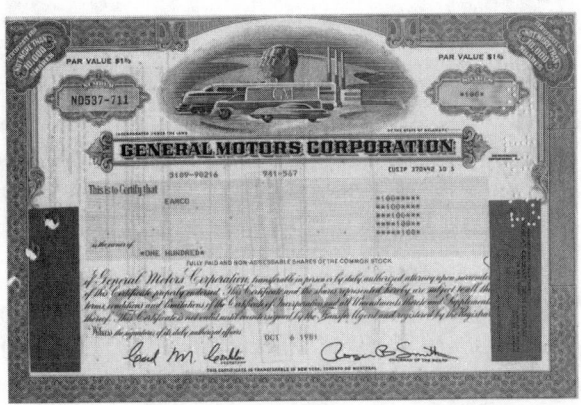

GE760-50-15, 1981, v, 100 sh. on a less than 10,000 sh. certificate, Morgan Guaranty and Chase Manhattan as registrars; ABN, 12" x 8", aquamarine **$5.00**

GE760-55-10, 1981, v, 44 sh. on a less than 100 sh. certificate, blue. **$4.00**

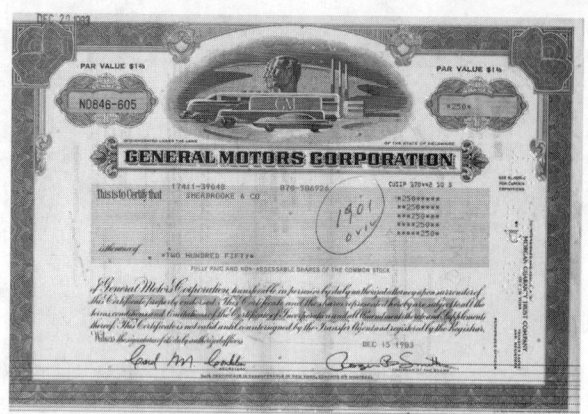

GE760-60-10, 1983, v, 250 sh., SCB, 12" x 8",
aquamarine **$4.00**

General Motors Acceptance Corporation

GE800-20-10, 1972, v, $25,000 3-5/8% debenture
due 1975, purple **$8.00**

General Oil and Refining Company

GE850-20-10, 1920, 26 sh., l. green **$10.00**

General Plywood Corporation
(KY par $0.50)

GE920-20-10, 1961, v, 25 sh. on a less than 100
sh. certificate, CBN, 11-3/4" x 8", brown. .**$4.00**
GE920-30-10, 1969, v, 100 sh., blue **$4.00**

***It is generally assumed that
only 5% of certificates survive
to reach collectors.***

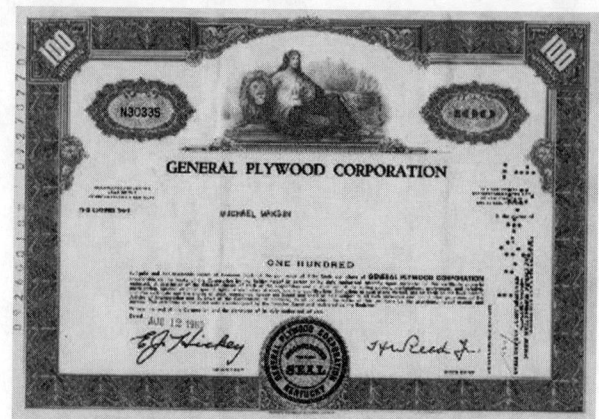

GE920-35-10, 1969, v, 100 sh., SCB, 11-3/4" x
8", red **$4.00**

GE920-40-10, 1973, v, 100 sh., o/p name changed
to General Resources Corporation, SCB, 11-3/4"
x 8", red **$4.00**

General Resources Corporation
(DE 1972, par $0.50)

GE970-20-10, 1978, v, 100 sh., SCB, 11-3/4" x
8", red **$4.00**

General Stores Corporation
(NY 1916, par $1)

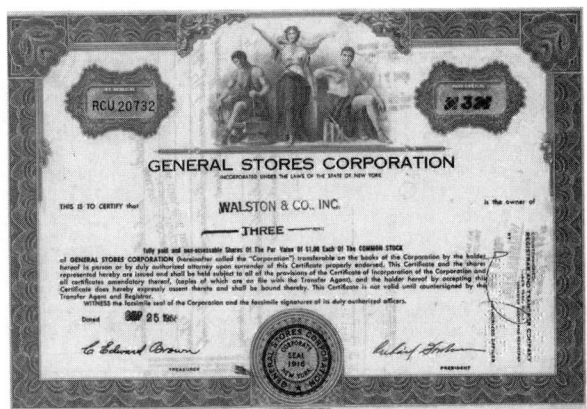

*GE1020-20-10, 1968, v, 3 sh., SCB, 12" x 8", orange $3.00

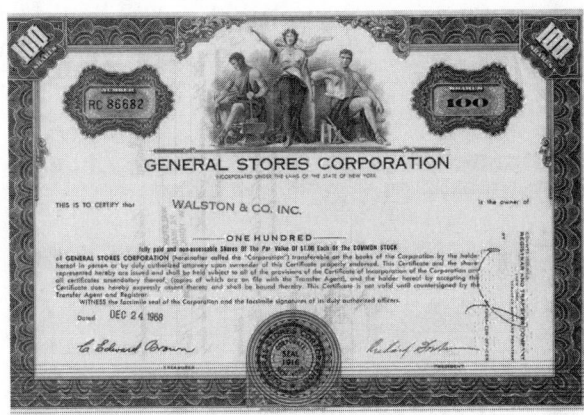

*GE1020-30-10, 1968, v, 100 sh., SCB, 12" x 8", blue $3.00

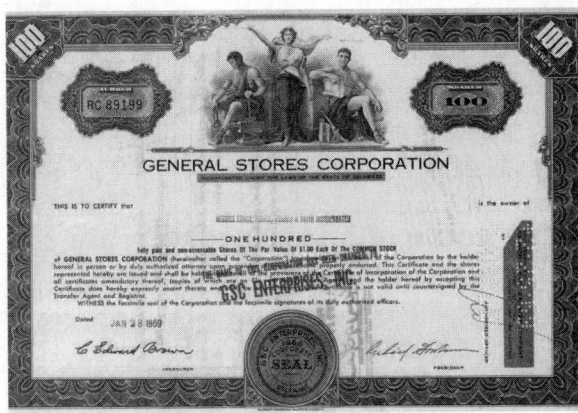

*GE1020-35-10, 1969, v, 100 sh., blue, o/p name changed to GSC Enterprises, Inc., SCB, 12" x 8", blue $3.00

General Telephone & Electronics Corporation

GE1080-30-10, 1971, v, $1,000 6-1/4% sinking fund debenture due 1991, red. $6.00

GE1080-40-10, 1975, v, $100,000 6-1/4% Sinking fund debenture due 1991, aqua $8.00

General Theatres Equipment, Inc.

GE1150-20-10, 1931, t, 10 voting $8 preferred sh. on a less than 100 sh. certificate, red $3.00

General Tin Investments Ltd.

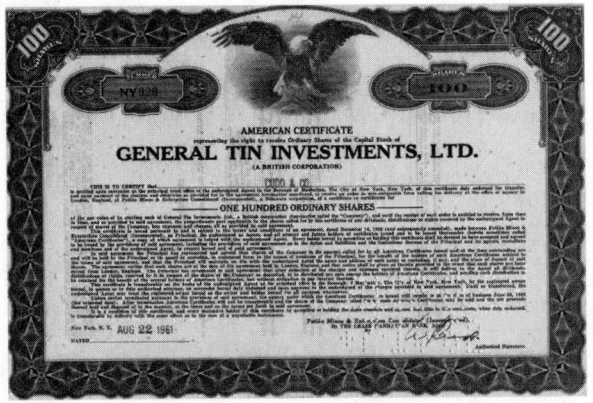

*GE1200-20-10, 1961, 100 sh., American Certificate (par 5 shillings), ABN-LOW, 12" x 8", green. $3.00

Genesee County Telephone Company (MI)

GE1250-40-10, 1908, v, $100 1st mortgage 6% gold bond w. coupons, grey border $100.00

Geneva, Corning and Southern Railroad Company (NY)

GE1320-20-10, 19xx, v, u/c 100 sh. certificate, brown $10.00

Georgetown National Bank (U.S. par $100)

*GE1340-20-10, 190x, v, 10 sh., 10-1/2" x 8",
brown border.......................$25.00

Georgia & Florida Railroad
*GE1360-20-10, 1929, i/u 100 sh. certificate, blue
...............................$22.00

Georgia Midland Terminal Company (par $100)
GE1410-20-10, 18xx, v, unissued certificate,
brown $9.00

Georgia-Pacific Corporation
Founded in 1927 as the Georgia Hardwood Lumber Company.
GE1500-40-10, 1976, 1976, v, $5,000 6-1/4% convertible subord. debenture due 2000, red
...............................$5.00
GE1500-45-10, 1977, v, $25,000 5-1/4% due in 1996 bond........................$8.00

Georgia Power Company (GA)
GE1560-30-10, 1960, v, $1,000 first mortgage 4?% bond due 1990, red..............$6.00

Georgia Southern and Florida Railway Company (par $100)
GE1610-20-10, 1944, 15 sh., first pref., green
...............................$8.00

The Gerlach-Barklow Company (DE no par)

*GE1660-20-10, 1929, t, 20 sh. on a less than 100 sh. certificate, ABN, 10-3/4" x 7-3/4", brown
...............................$3.00
GE1660-30-10, 1929, v, 100 conv. pref. sh., brown
...............................$4.00

German-American Fire Insurance Co. of Baltimore City (MD par $25)

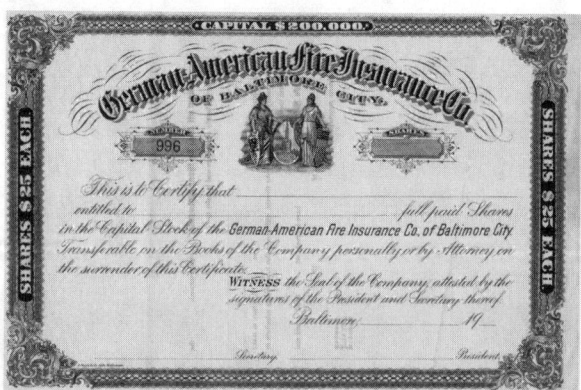

*GE1690-20-10, 19xx, v, u/u certificate, A. Hoen & Co. Lith. Baltimore, 11" x 8", grey $3.00

The value of a stock certificate depends on:

- rarity
- the issuer
- signatures
- quality of engraving
- overall appearance
- condition
- date of issue

German-American Title Insurance, Trust and Safe Deposit Company (PA)

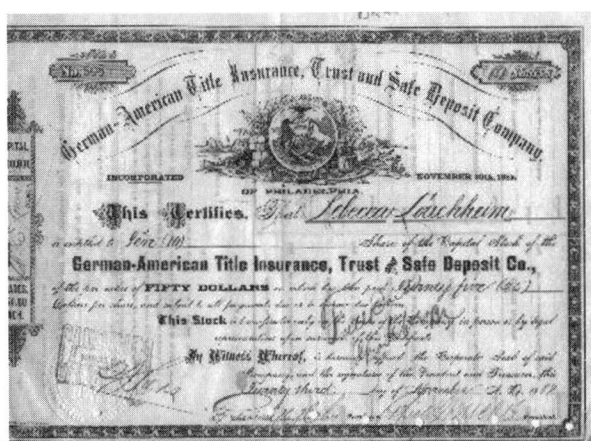

*GE1720-20-10, 1887, v, 10 sh. (par $50), grey
................................$20.00

Village of Germantown (WI)

*GE1740-40-10, 1956, v, $1,000 Sewage Disposal Bond, brown $7.00

Germantown Passenger Rail Way Company (PA par $50)

GE1750-20-10, 1928, v, 99 sh., greyish brown
................................$14.00

Geuder, Paeschke & Frey Co. (WI)

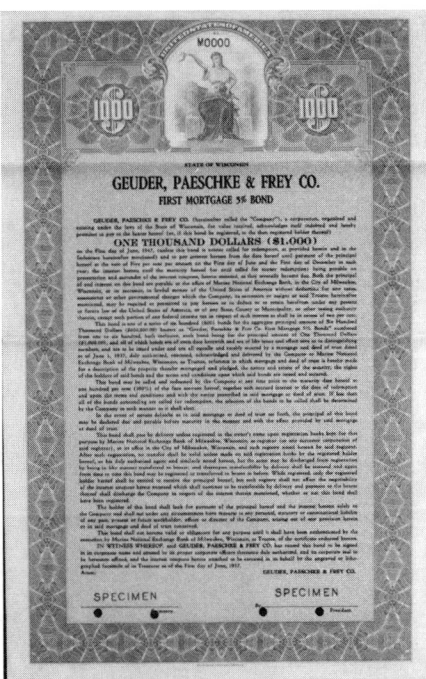

*GE1790-40-10, 1932, v, $1,000 1st mortgage 5% bond, 10-1/2" x 11-1/2", orange border ..$15.00

The Gibbs & Ball Plow Company (OH par $100)

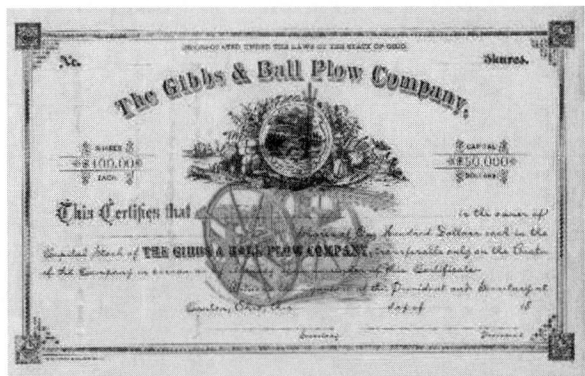

*GI60-20-10, 18xx, v, u/u certificate, black and red
................................$20.00

Gibraltar Oil Company (CO)

GI170-20-10, 1917, v, 500 sh., unissued certificate, multicolored $20.00

Gilbert Desert Gold Mining Company (NV par $0.10)

GI240-20-10, 1926, v, 1,000 sh., orange ...**$13.00**

Gilbert-Eureka Mining & Milling Company (par $1)

The company was founded in 1925 with mines located in Gilbert, Nevada. Today it's a ghost town.

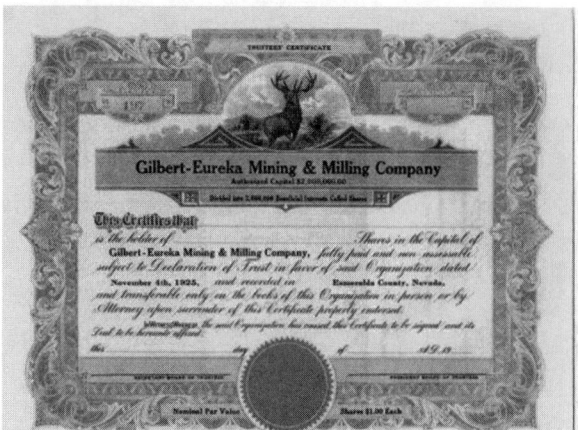

*GI270-20-10, 19xx, v, u/u trustees certificate, orange **$6.00**

Gillette Rubber Company (WI par $10)

*GI320-20-10, 1921, v, 10 sh., 11-1/2" x 9", orange **$25.00**

The Gilpin Mining Company (CO)

GI410-20-10, 1911, v, i/u 6 sh., brown border **$40.00**

The Gilpin-Orion Gold Mining Company (CO)

GI430-20-10, 1919, v, i/u 1,000 sh., green border **$18.00**

Glen Alden Coal Company (PA)

GL100-30-10, 1936, v, 100 sh., blue **$20.00**

Glen Alden Corporation (DE 1966)

Coal mining.

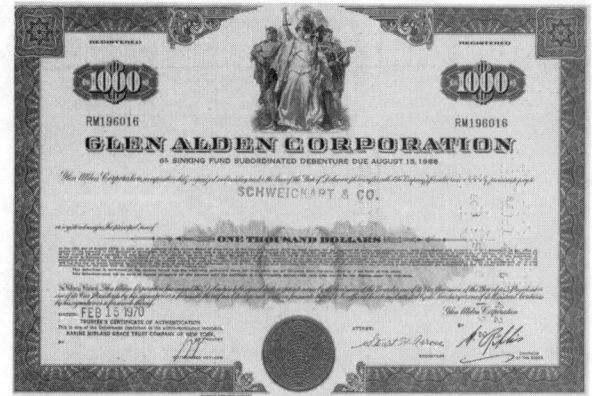

*GL130-30-10, 1969, v, $1,000 6% sinking fund subord. debenture due 1988, ABN, 12" x 8", green **$4.00**

Glenborough Realty Trust Incorporated

GL180-20-10, 1996, v, 1 sh., ABN, green ..**$10.00**

Glendale Homes, Inc. (NY par $100)

*GL210-20-10, 19xx, v, u/u certificate, w/o imprint, 11" x 8-1/4", green **$4.00**

**The Globe Crude Oil Company
(CO par 1 mil)**
GL380-20-10, 1919, v, 1,000 sh., grey.....**$10.00**

Gogebic Iron Syndicate (WI par $25)

*GO80-20-10, 1887, v, 100 sh., 11-1/2" x 9", w/o
imprint, green border **$100.00**

**Gold Circle Queen Mining Company
(NV par $1)**
GO160-20-10, 19xx, v, unissued certificate, green
..................................**$7.00**

Gold Hill Mines Inc. (DE)
GO210-20-10, 19xx, v, unissued certificate, orange
..................................**$10.00**

**The Gold Leaf Consolidated Mines Co.
(AZ territory, par $1)**

*GO250-20-10, 1906, v, 1,000 sh., 10" x 6-3/4",
blue............................**$10.00**

**Gold Pioneer Mining Company
(NM territory, par $10)**

*GO320-20-10, 1907, v, 250 sh., 11" x 8", brown
border..........................**$11.00**

**Gold Reef Consolidated Gold & Silver
Mining Company (NV 1905, par $1)**
GO350-20-10, 19xx, v, u/u certificate, grey border
..................................**$10.00**

**The Gold Valley Placer Mining Company
(par $1)**
GO410-20-10, 189x, v, unissued certificate, brown
..................................**$19.00**

Goldak Corporation (DE no par)

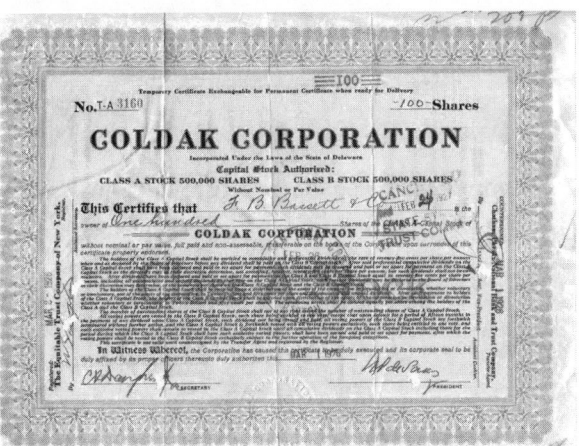

*GO490-20-10, 1926, t, 100 class A sh., w/o
imprint, 12" x 9", orange.............**$6.00**

The Golden Cycle Mining and Reduction Company (WV par $1.00)

The certificate states "The largest cyanide mill in the United States - daily capacity 1200 tons."
GO560-20-10, 1915, v, 500 sh., brown $19.00
GO560-25-10, 1918, v, 200 sh., brown $15.00

Golden Gate Bridge and Highway District

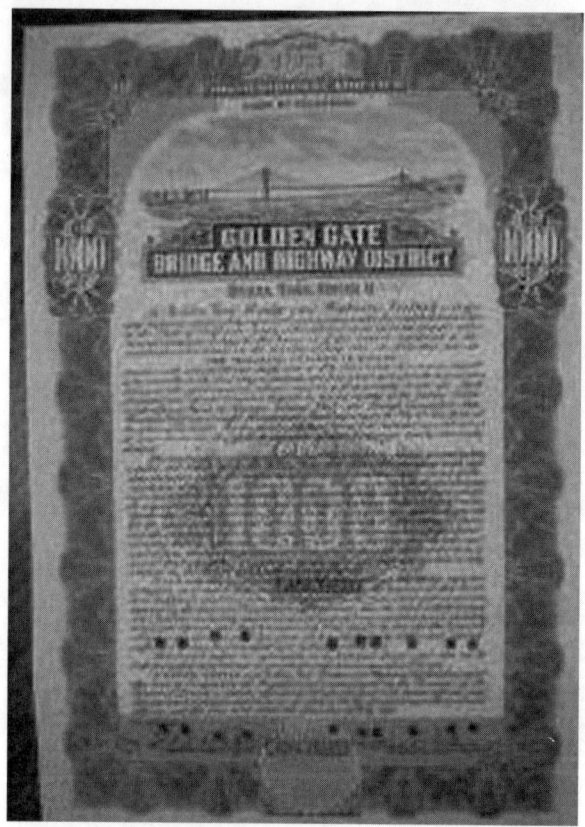

GO610-20-10, 1933, v, $1,000 bridge bond series 8, green $85.00

Golden Gate Divide Mining Co. (par 10¢)

GO640-20-10, 1918, 1,000 sh., grey $8.00

Goldfield Annex Mining Company (DE par $1)

GO710-20-10, 1909, v, 500 sh., brown . . . $20.00

The Goldfield Consolidated Mines Company (WY 1906)

GO750-20-10, 1937, t, 100 sh., green $9.00

Goldfield Daisy Mining Syndicate (AZ territory)

GO790-20-10, 1907, v, 100 sh., brown . . . $15.00

It is generally assumed that only 5% of certificates survive to reach collectors.

Goldfield Deep Mines Company (par 5¢)

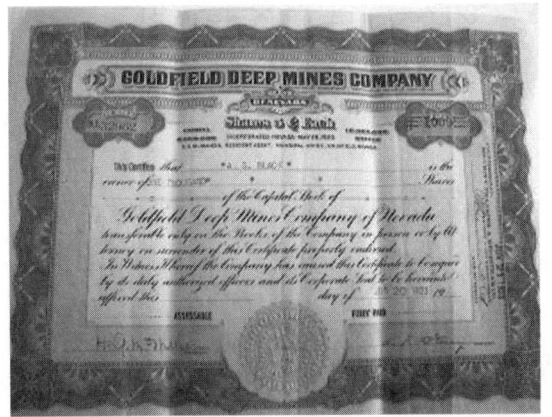

GO830-20-10, 1923, v, 1,000 sh., green . .$10.00

Goldfield Great Bend Mining Company, Re-Inc. (NV 1915, par $1)

GO890-20-10, 1917, v, 500 sh., GOES, light brown $20.00

Goldfield Merger Mines Company (WA par $100)

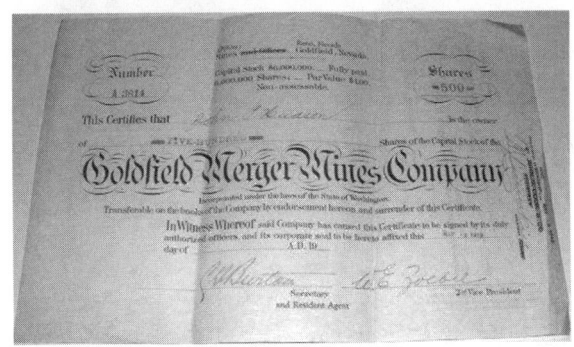

GO980-20-10, 1919, i/u 500 sh., black on white $20.00

The Goodwin Company (WV par $100)

GO1100-20-10, 19xx, v, u/u certificate, w/o imprint, 11" x 7-1/2", red border $3.00

Gordon Jewelry Corporation (DE)

GO1200-20-10, 1969, v, 1 class A sh. on a less than 100 sh. certificate, blue $4.00

GO1200-25-10, 1969, v, 100 class A sh., (par $1), green $4.00

GO1200-30-10, 1969, v, 1,000 class A sh. on a more than 100 sh. certificate, red $5.00

W.R. Grace & Co. (CT 1899)

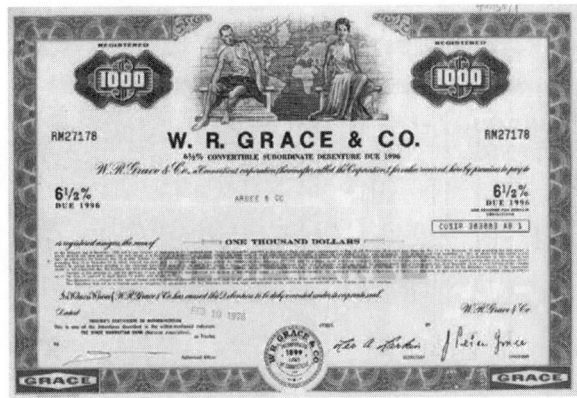

GR70-80-10, 1976, v, $1,000 6-1/2% convertible subord. dcbenture due 1996, 12" x 8", green border $20.00

The Grafton Consolidated Mining Company (par $10)

Mine located at Leadville, Lake County, CO.

GR100-20-10, 1901, v, i/u 1 sh., l. brown border $40.00

John W. Graham & Co. (WA 1896, par $100)

This company sold paper products and office supplies. They were printers of stationery and post
cards. In 1973 the downtown Seattle store was
closed and in 1987 it became J.K. Gill.
GR120-20-10, 1xxx, v, u/u certificate, GOES,
green border **$4.00**

Grain Elevator Warehouse Company (DE 10¢)

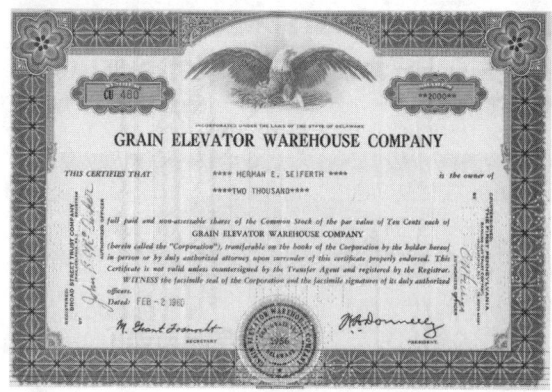

GR170-20-10, 1960, v, 2,000 sh., SBC, 12" x
8-1/4", green **$4.00**

Grand Oil & Development Company, Inc. (no par)

GR230-20-10, 1922, v, 1 sh., orange and black
...................................**$25.00**

Grand Rapids and Indiana Rail Road Company (IN-MI par $100)

GR270-20-10, 1858, v, 3 sh., brown.......**$53.00**

The Grand Union Company (DE 1928, par $5)

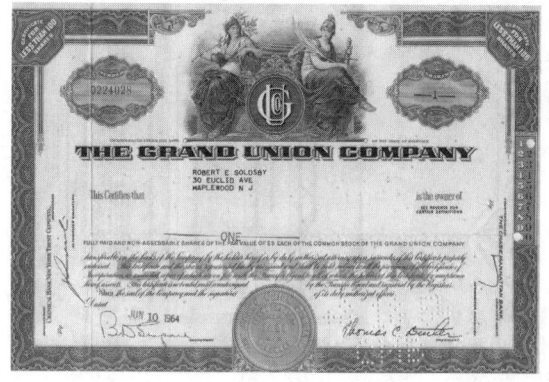

GR330-20-10, 1964, v, 1 sh. on a less than 100 sh.
certificate, ABN, 12" x 8", green **$4.00**
GR330-30-10, 1928, v, 100 sh., purple.....**$10.00**

GR330-40-10, 1965, v, 100 sh., ABN, 12" x 8",
blue.............................**$4.00**

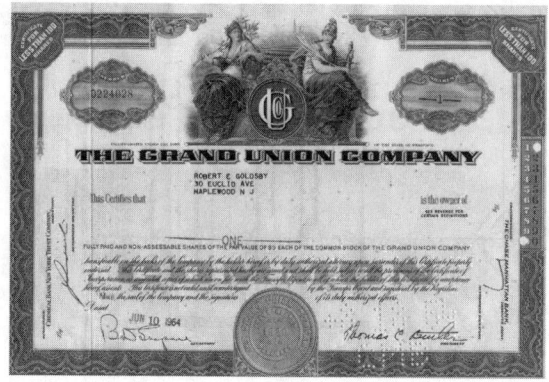

GR330-40-15, 1970, v, 100 sh., ABN, 12" x 8",
signatures variety, blue................**$4.00**

Granite City Steel Company (DE par $5)

GR410-20-10, 1960, v, 15 sh. on a less than 100 sh.
certificate, blue......................**$8.00**
GR410-30-10, 1970, v, 100 sh., orange **$9.00**

The Gray Manufacturing Company (CT par $5)

GR610-20-10, 1969, v, 1 sh. on a less than 100 sh.
certificate, FBN, brown **$5.00**

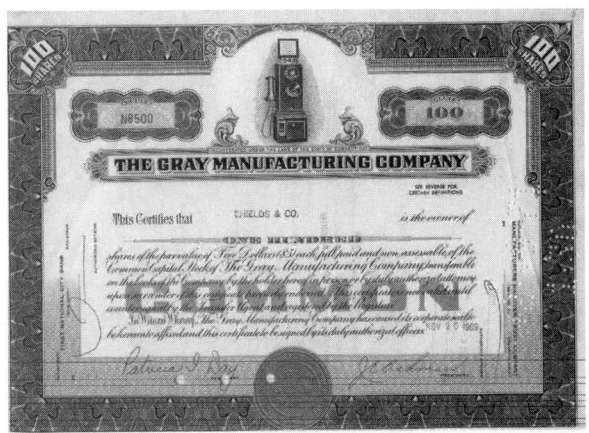

*GR610-30-10, 1969, v, 100 sh., Federated Banknote Printing Co., 12" x 8-3/4", blue .**$5.00**

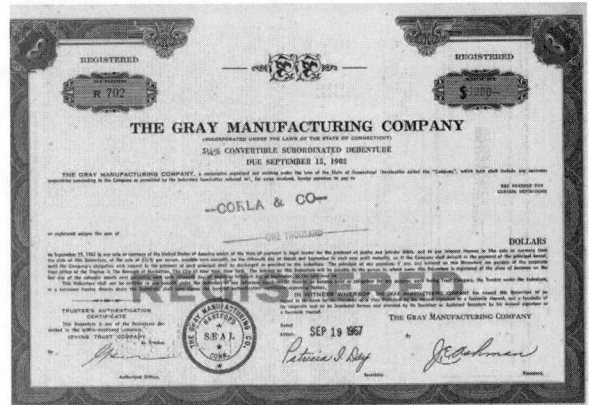

*GR610-60-10, 1967, v, $1,000 5-1/4% convertible subord. debenture due 1982, ABN, 12" x 8", blue **$5.00**

The Great Atlantic & Pacific Tea Company (MD 1925, par $1)

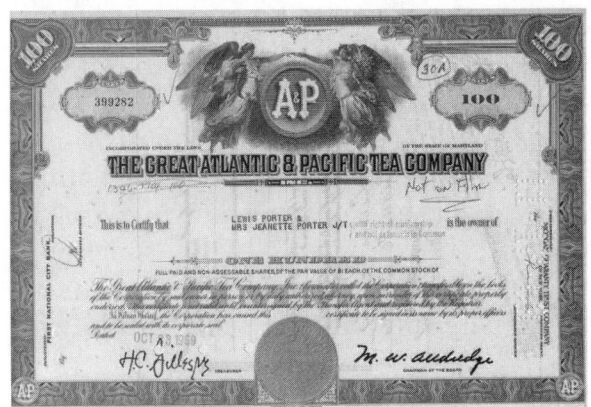

*GR710-20-10, 1969, v, 100 sh., ABN, 12" x 8", olive green **$4.00**

*GR710-20-15, 1969, v, 100 sh., ABN, signature strip, 12" x 8", olive green **$4.00**

The Great Divide Oil Company (CO par $0.50)

GR770-20-10, 19xx, v, unissued certificate, green **$4.00**

Great Falls, Montana

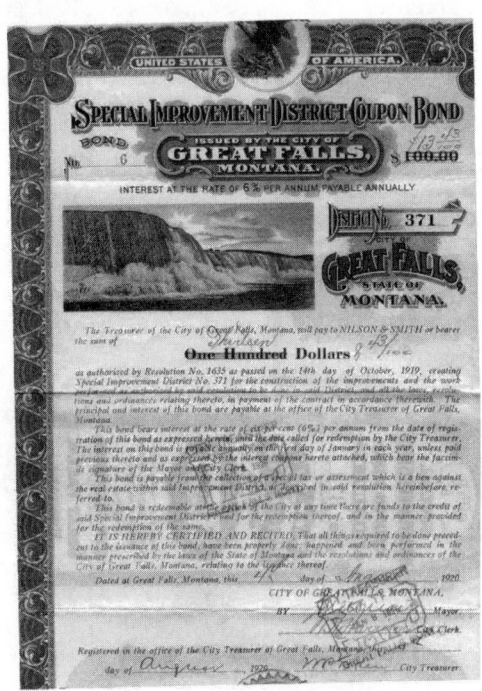

*GR840-20-10, 1913, v, $500 special improvement district bond, 11" x 16", green **$7.00**

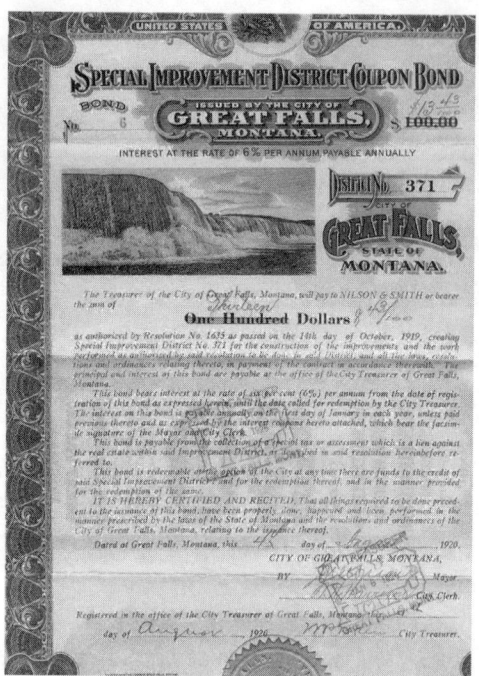

GR840-30-10, 1920, v, $13.43 on a $100 special improvement district 6% coupon bond, Tribune Printing Company, Great Falls, Montana; 11" x 15", green **$6.00**

GR840-40-10, 1924, v, $200 special improvement district 6% coupon bond, green **$6.00**

Great Falls Gold Mining Company (DE par $1)

GR870-20-10, 189x, v, unissued certificate, brown **$7.00**

Great Northern Nekoosa Corporation (ME par $5)

GR1020-20-10, 1976, v, 100 sh., ABN, 12" x 8", blue **$4.00**

GR1020-30-10, 1977, v, 500 sh., brown. **$4.00**

Great Northern Railway Company (MN no par)

GR1100-20-10, 1962, v, 10 sh., orange . . .**$15.00**

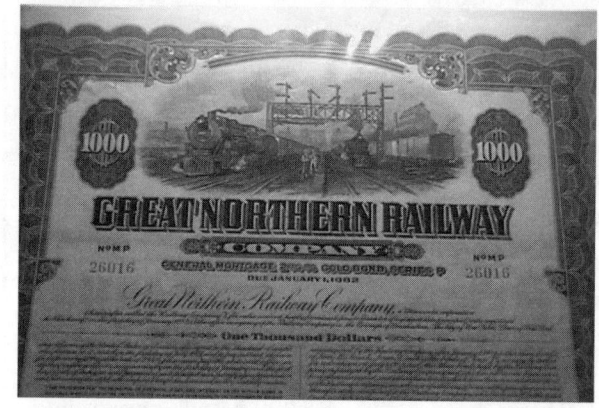

GR1100-30-10, 1946, v, $1,000 2-3/4% series P general mortgage gold bond, due 1982, green **$12.00**

This catalog has listings in an alphabetical format. The reason is simple: Companies diversify as they grow. For example, the Canadian Pacific Railway company recently split into five companies. They represent the railway, hotels, shipping, airline, and petroleum interests of the company. During World War II, the Singer sewing machine company made guns and other defense-related equipment, so where should we list it? It's far easier to use a strict alphabetical order, rather than to confuse the reader with topical classifications.

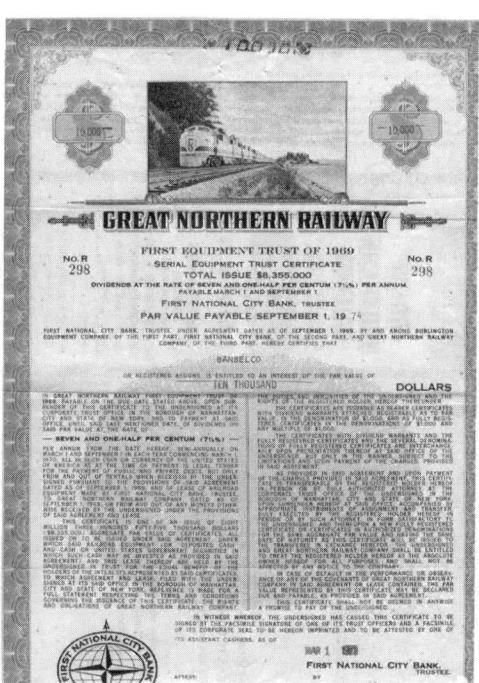

GR1100-60-10, 1973, v, $10,000 first equipment trust of 1969, 7-1/2%, ABN, 9-1/4" x 13-1/4", orange **$7.00**

Great Plains Railway Company (NE par $1)

GR1200-20-10, 19xx, v, u/u certificate, grey **$8.00**

> ***It is generally assumed that only 5% of certificates survive to reach collectors.***

Great Western Sugar Company (NJ no par)

Headquarters in Loveland, CO. The company had several sugar beet plants and a railroad.

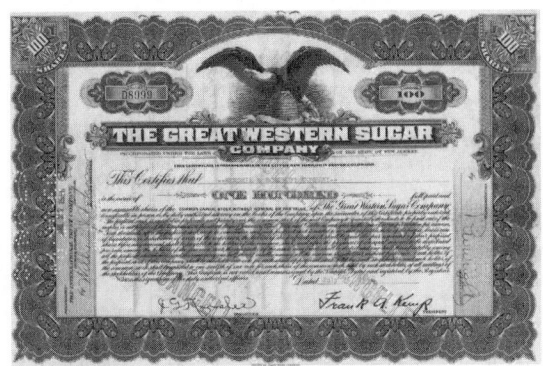

GR1470-20-10, 1956, v, 100 sh., ABN, 11-1/2" x 7-1/2", green **$4.00**

GR1470-30-10, 1921, v, 5 pref. sh. on a less than 100 sh. certificate, olive **$20.00**

Green Bay Iron Company (WI)

GR1570-40-10, 1878, v, $500 8% 1st mortgage bond w. coupons, 14" x 13", brown border **$150.00**

Green Bay & Lake Pepin Railway Company (par $100)

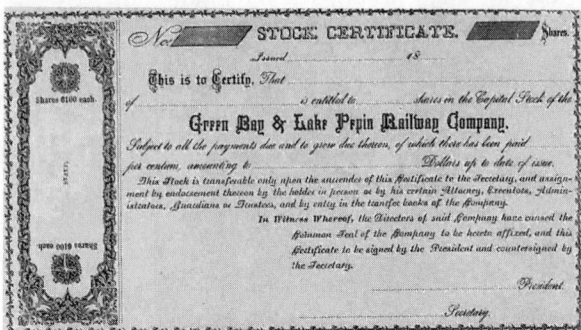

*GR1600-10-10, 18xx, u/u certificate, green
. . . . **$10.00**

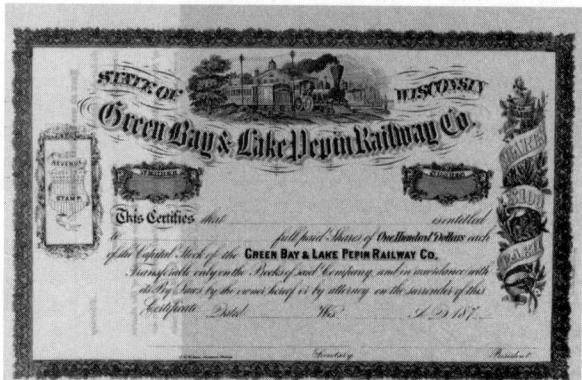

*GR1600-20-10, 187x, v, u/u certificate, 11" x 6-1/2", brown border. **$55.00**

Green Bay & Minnesota Rail Road Co. (WI par $100)

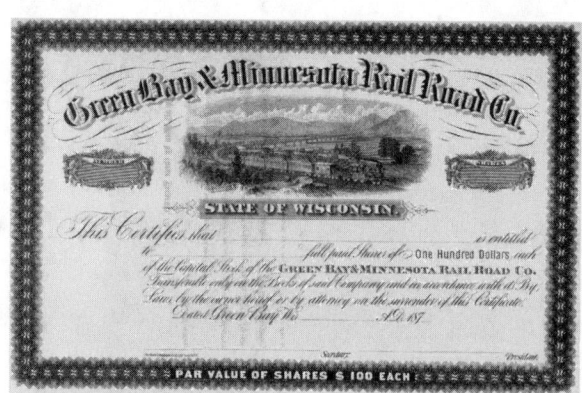

*GR1620-20-10, 187x, v, u/u certificate, The Hatch Lithographic Co., N.Y., 11" x 7-1/4", grey
. . . . **$35.00**

Green Bay, Winona and St. Paul Railroad Company (WI)

*GR1650-40-10, 1895, v, $1,000 7% 2nd mortgage income bond, 10" x 12", orange border . **$110.00**

Green Bay and Western Railroad Company (par $100)

GR1680-20-10, 1926, v, 10 sh., brown **$15.00**

*GR1680-30-10, 1917, v, 100 sh., green . . . **$10.00**

*GR1680-40-10, 1952, v, 8 sh. on a less than 100
sh. certificate, 10-1/2" x 7", brown border
..................................$15.00

Greenbrier Smokeless Coal Co.
(WV par $100)
GR1760-20-10, 19xx, unissued certificate, brown
.....................................$25.00

Greene Consolidated Gold Company (WV)

*GR1810-20-10, 1905, v, i/u 100 sh., brown
.....................................$10.00

Greenville and Whitewright Northern
Traction Company (TX par $100)
GR1920-20-10, 1913, v, 1 sh., 8% pref., brown
.....................................$28.00

Greenwater Consolidated Mining Company
(AZ par $1)

*GR2010-20-10, 1908, v, 2,625 sh., 10" x 8-1/2",
brown $75.00

Greenwater Copper Mining and Smelter
Company (DE)
The Greenwater district of Death Valley never pro-
duced as expected and the rush lasted only about
a year.
GR2040-20-10, 1907, 500 sh., grey border on
green..............................$14.00

Greenwich & Johnsonville Rail Road
Company (NY par $100)
GR2110-20-10, 1869, v, 2 sh., grey.......$20.00

Griffiths Oil Company, a trust estate
(par $1)
GR2280-20-10, 1922, v, i/u 45 sh., brown
.....................................$20.00

The Grover Gas and Oil Company
(CO par 1¢)
GR2420-20-10, 1919, v, 1,000 sh., green ..$10.00

Gruss Mining Company (CA)
GR2520-20-10, 1920, v, 100 sh., orange $5.00
GR2520-25-10, 1921, v, 500 sh., orange $4.00
GR2520-30-10, 1941, v, 5,000 sh., orange ..$5.00

Guanajuato Consolidated Mining & Milling Company (WV par $5)

*GU100-20-10, 1905, v, 100 sh., ABN, grey-blue
............................$8.00

*GU100-20-15, 1907, v, 100 sh., signature variety, ABN, grey-blue......................$7.00

*GU100-20-20, 1921, v, 100 sh., signature variety, ABN, grey-blue......................$7.00

Guaranty Oil Company (CA par $1)

*GU190-20-10, 1921, v, 450 sh., green border
............................$10.00

Guelph Mining and Milling Co., Ltd. (par $1)

The company became the Ambergris Consolidated Mining Company.

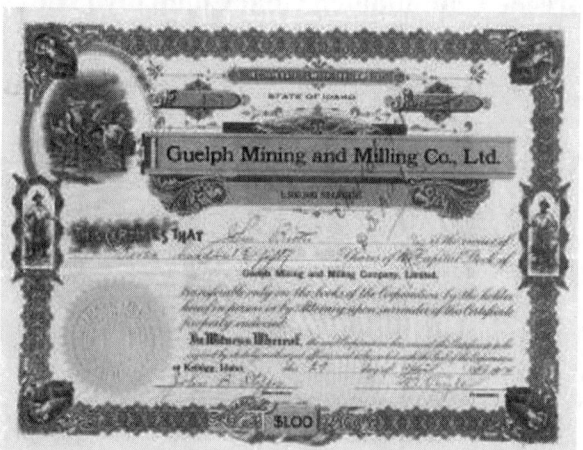

*GU290-20-10, 1914, v, 750 sh., grey on green
............................$18.00

The value of a stock certificate depends on:
- rarity
- the issuer
- signatures
- quality of engraving
- overall appearance
- condition
- date of issue

Guerrero Mines Company (ME par $5)

*GU350-20-10, 1911, v, 100 sh., New York Bank Note Co., orange and black..........$13.00

Gulf, Mobile and Northern Railroad Company (par $100)

GU410-20-10, 1936, v, 15 sh. on less than 100 sh. certificate, ABN, blue.................$7.00
GU410-25-10, 1932, v, 100 sh., brown $15.00
GU410-30-10, 1938, v, 25 pref. sh. on a less than 100 sh. certificate, orange..............$8.00
GU410-35-10, 1937, v, 100 pref. sh., ABN, green $5.00

Gulf, Mobile and Ohio Railroad Company (MS no par)

*GU440-20-10, 1940, v, 50 sh. on a less than 100 sh. certificate, brown.................$6.00

GU440-25-10, 1957, v, 50 sh. on less than 100 sh. certificate, brown $7.00
GU440-35-10, 1940, v, 100 sh., blue.......$7.00
GU440-40-10, 1968, v, 100 sh., blue.......$5.00
GU440-45-10, 1971, v, 10 sh., $5 pref. orange $5.00
GU440-50-10, 1954, v, 100 $5 pref. sh., green $5.00

Gulf Republic Financial Corp. (TX par $0.50)

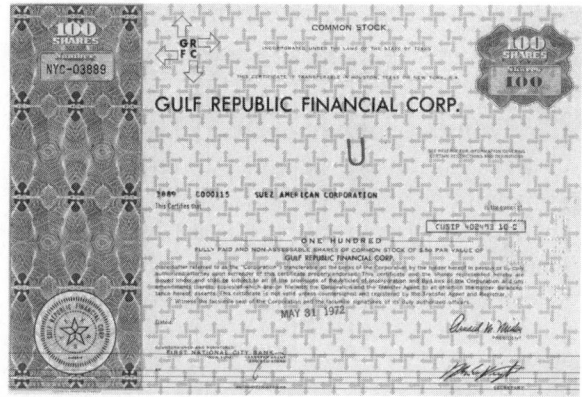

*GU510-20-10, 1972, v, 100 sh., Federated Banknote Co., 12" x 8", green $4.00

Gulf and Ship Island Railroad Company (MS par $100)

GU590-20-10, 1925, v, 1 sh., brown $22.00

H

Halifax Tonopah Mining Company (UT par $1)

Mines in Tonopah, NV.

HA210-20-10, 1922, v, 1,000 shs., brown, 8-1/2" x 11".....................................$32.00

Joseph R. Hammel, Inc.

HA260-20-10, 19xx, v, u/u certificate, grey border $3.00

M.A. Hanna Company (DE 1923)

Started out as mining, shipping, warehousing and shipbuilding company. In the 1980s, the company ceased iron ore activities and branched out into specialty polymers business. Merged with Geon in 2000 and ceased to be Hanna.

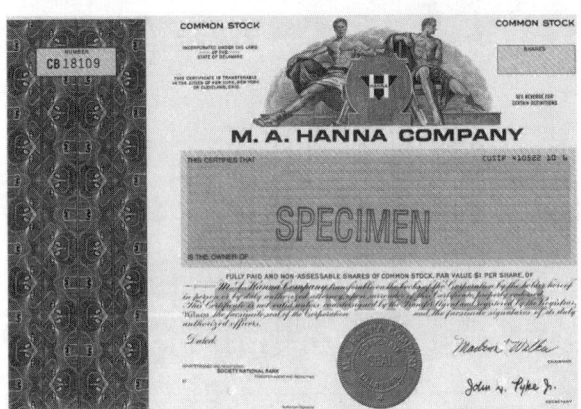

*HA340-30-10, 19xx, v, specimen cert., SBN. 12" x 8"..$5.00

The Hanna Mining and Milling Company (CO)

HA370-20-10, 1905, v, 1,000 shs., grey....$15.00

UNLISTED TYPES & VARIETIES

Readers are welcome to contact the author directly at:

**Rainer Stahlberg
P.O. Box 1044
Rooseveltown, New York 13683**

Hannibal, Missouri Bottling Company (GA no par)

*HA410-30-10, 19xx, v, u/u $1.25 pref. stock certificate, GOES Litho, 11-3/4" x 8", brown. **$4.00**

Hannibal Union Depot Company (MO par $100)

HA450-20-10, 188x, v, u/u certificate, black on white..$30.00

Hanover Bessemer Iron and Copper Company (DE par $1)

HA510-20-10, 1918, v, 2,364 shs., green...**$22.00**

Hanover and York Rail Road Company

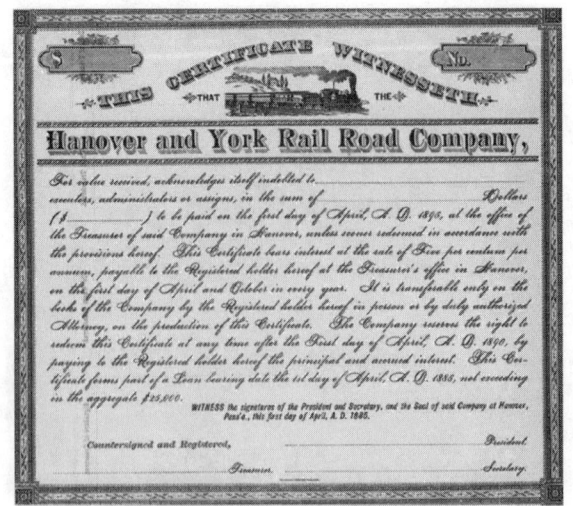

*HA550-30-10, 1885, v, u/u loan certificate, 5% due in 1898, grey $8.00

Harcourt Brace Jovanovich, Inc.

HA670-30-10, 19??, v - angels, 14-3/4% bond, due 2002 ....$8.00

Harmony Pacific Oil Co., Inc.

*HA710-20-10, 19xx, v, u/u certificate, brown
.................................$5.00

Harnischfeger Corporation (WI par $10)

*HA730-30-10, 1966, v, 100 shs., 12" x 8", green
.................................$6.00

Harris-Stanley Coal and Land Company (KY par $100)

HA745-20-10, 1925, v, 1 shs., grey border...$7.00

Harrisburg Railways Company (PA)

*HA760-20-10, 1915, v, 50 sh. on less than 100 sh.
certificate (par $50), green $5.00

*HA760-30-10, 1920, v, 100 shs., brown ...$5.00
HA760-35-10, 1920, v, 100 sh., orange.....$9.00

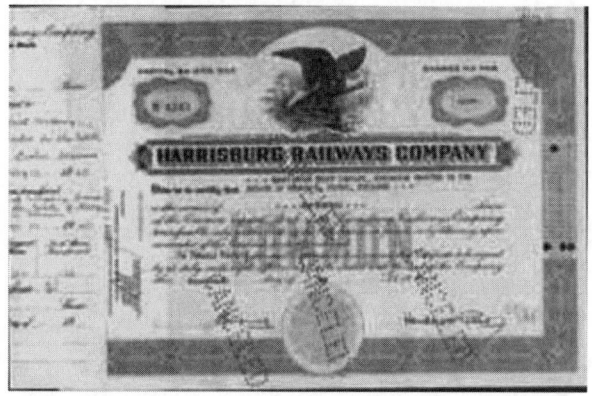

*HA760-40-10, 1943, v, 100 shs., orange ...$5.00

The Hartford Steam Boiler Inspection and Insurance Company (CT)

HA820-20-10, 1934, v, 50 sh. (par $10), orange
.................................$5.00
HA820-30-10, 1969, v, 100 sh. (par $5), orange
.................................$8.00

Havre Electric Company (MT par $100)

HA920-20-10, 190x, v, u/u certificate, 10" x 8",
grey.............................$12.00

State of Hawaii

HA1000-20-10, 1975, v, $5,000 6.30% general
obligation bond series AE, due 1988, blue
.................................$8.00
HA1000-25-10, 1975, v, $5,000 general obligation
bond, series AL, due 1988, blue.........$8.00

*HA1000-35-10, 1985, v, $50,000 7.3% general
obligation bond, series BC, due 1986, SCB,
12" x 8"............................$8.00

Hawaiian Natural Water Company, Inc.
HA1040-20-10, 19xx, v, u/u certificate, blue border
...................................$33.00

The Hawley Prospecting and Mining Co.
(WI par $1)

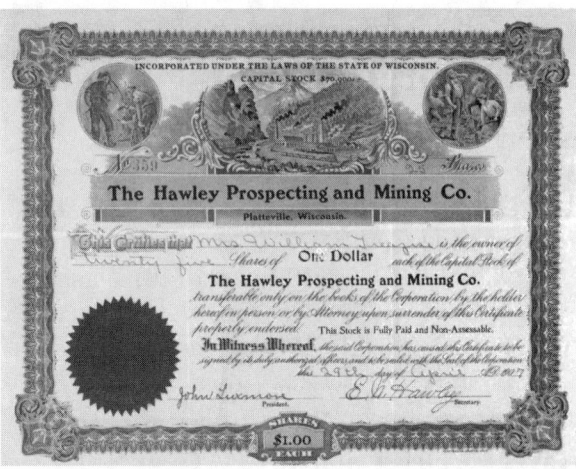

*HA1100-20-10, 1907, v, 25 shs., 11" x 8-1/2",
green border $80.00

Hawthorne Mines Incorporated
(NV par $1)
HA1130-20-10, 1927, v, 27 shs., green $24.00

The Hazel Green Mining Company
(WI par $1)

*HA1200-20-10, 1903, v, 500 shs., 11" x 8-1/2",
green border $80.00

Hebrew National Foods, Inc.
HE90-20-10, 1963, 10 shs., orange border ..$3.00
HE90-30-10, 1963, 100 shs., blue border ...$3.00

The Hecla Co-Operative Granite Co.
(CO par $50)
HE140-20-10, 1911, v, 1 shs., orange $16.00

H.J. Heinz Company
H360-30-10, 1966, v, 100 shs., green $18.00

The Helena Electric Railway Company
(MT par $100)

*H380-20-10, 189x, v, u/u certificate, Western
Bank Note Company, green...........$20.00

Heli-Coil Corporation (DE no par)

*H410-20-10, 1970, v, 100 shs., blue......$7.00

The W. E. Hendricks Corporation (CO)

*HE400-20-10, 19xx, v, u/u 2-1/2% Royalty units
certificate, orange $50.00

Herkimer and Mohawk Street Railroad Co.
HE470-20-10, 18xx, v, u/u certificate, grey
..................................$25.00

The value of a stock certificate depends on:
- rarity
- the issuer
- signatures
- quality of engraving
- overall appearance
- condition
- date of issue

High Point Financial Corp. (NJ 1982, no par)

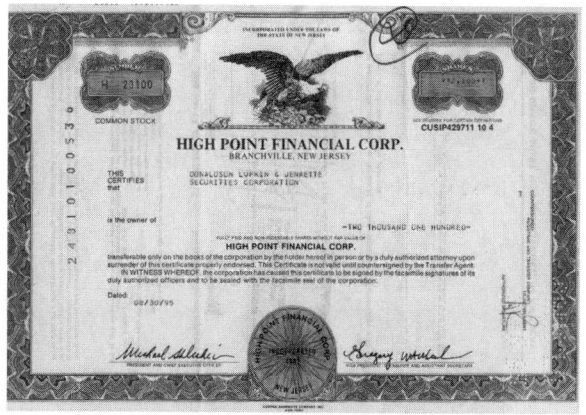

*HI100-20-10, 1995, v - eagle, 2,100 shs., Corpex
Banknote Co. Inc., NY, 12" x 8-1/4", green
..................................$4.00

Hill-Pierce Oil & Refining Co. (DE par $10)
HI230-20-10, 1923, v, 20 sh., green $14.00

Hipke Drug Co. (WI par $100)

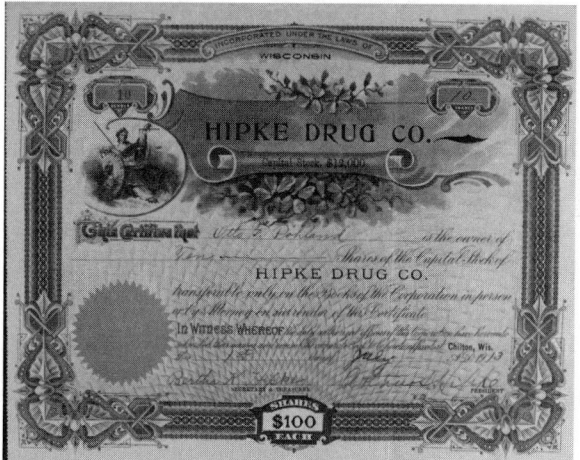

*HI320-20-10, 1913, v, 10 shs., 10-1/2" x 8",
brown border $15.00

City of Hoboken (NJ)
HO170-20-10, 19xx, v, $1,000 School bond, green
..................................$16.00

The Hodag Oil Company (WI par $1)

HO200-20-10, 1906, v, 110 shs., 10-1/2" x 8",
brown border.....................$100.00

Holman Locomotive Speeding-Truck Company (par $100)

HO250-20-10, 1899, v, 10 sh., green, small certificate $48.00

Holmes Mining and Milling Company (WI par 25¢)

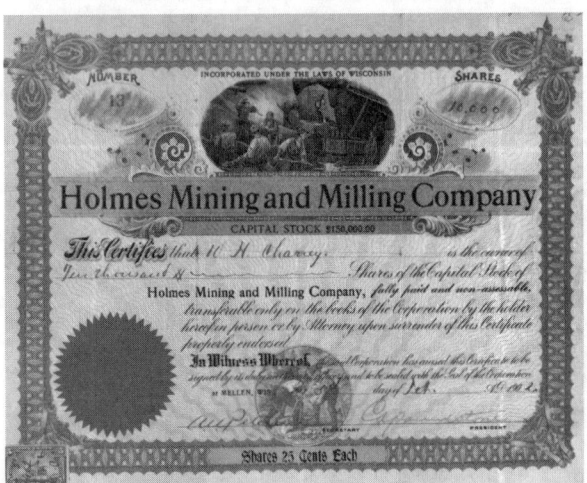

HO280-20-10, 1902, v, 10,000 shs., revenue
stamp, 10" x 7-1/2", orange $100.00

It is generally assumed that only 5% of certificates survive to reach collectors.

The Holstein & Friesian Association of America (NY)

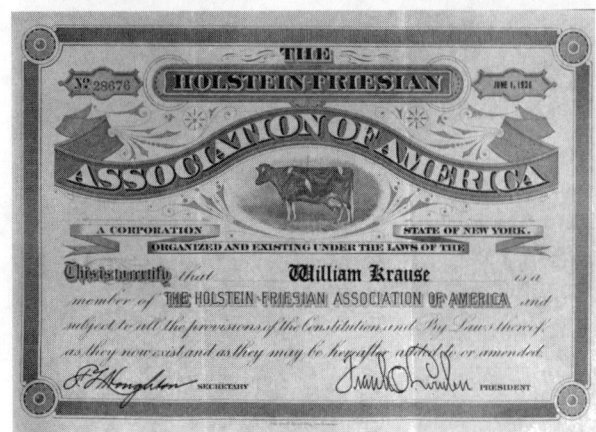

HO290-20-10, 1926, v, membership of William
Krause, 11-1/2" x 8", brown border.....$12.00

The Home Building and Development Company (OH par $4)

HO310-20-10, 1928, v, 25 shs., brown $6.00

The Home Insurance Company

HO370-20-10, 1963, v, 100 shs., grey.....$4.00

Homestake Mining Company

In operation since 1877 is one of the most historically significant gold mines in the US.
HO450-20-10, 1886, v, 100 sh. (par $100), blue
...............................$30.00

HO450-30-10, 1906, v, 25 sh. (par $100), grey border, light blue $10.00

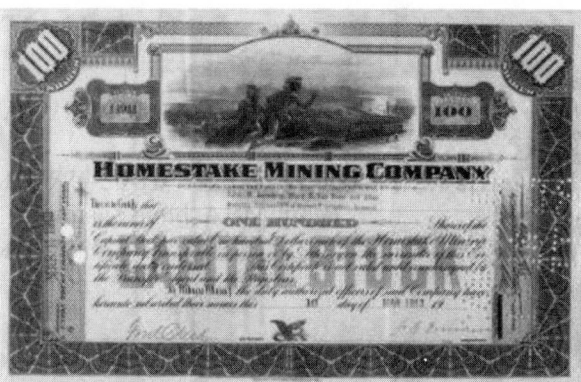

HO450-40-10, 1913, v, 100 shs., blue $10.00

HO450-50-10, 1940, v, 10 sh. on a less than 100 sh. certificate, green $10.00

HO450-60-10, 1937, v, 100 shs., orange . . .$9.00

The Homestead Iron Mining Company (WI par $25)

HO480-20-10, 1892, v, 100 shs., Bankers Stationery Supply Co., Chicago; 10-1/2" x 8-1/2", grey border $125.00

Honest Gold and Silver Mining Company (par $100)

HO570-20-10, 186x, v, u/u certificate, grey $30.00

Hope Hose and Steam Fire Engine Company No. 2

HO670-20-10, 18xx, v, u/u certificate, brown
. . . .$40.00

Hornsilver Mining and Milling Co. (ID 1901, par 10¢)

The company operated mines in the Coeur d'Alene mining district near Wallace, Idaho.

HO820-20-10, 1907, v, 2,500 sh. $21.00

Hospital Corporation of America (par $100)

The corporation runs 330 hospitals with 60,000 beds.

HO940-20-10, 1972, 5 sh. on a less than 100 sh. certificate, blue $9.00

HO940-30-10, 1971, v, 100 shs., green $8.00

The Houston & Great Northern Railroad Co. of Texas

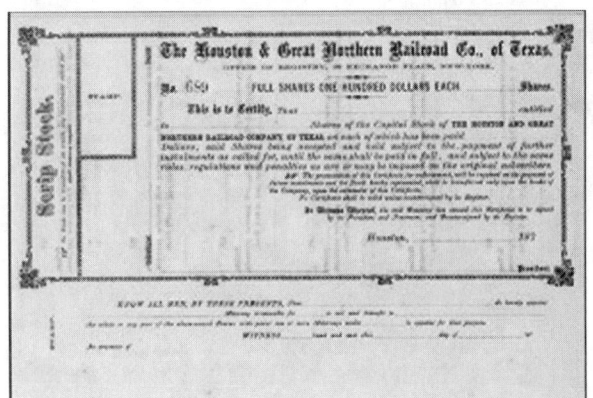

HO1000-20-10, 187x, u/u stock script, brown on yellow $19.00

Houston Oil Company of Texas (TX)

*HO1070-20-10, 1942, v, 10 sh. on a less than 100 sh., voting trust certificate, brown $9.00

HO1070-30-10, 1930, v, 100 sh., voting trust, green. $15.00

HO1070-40-10, 1940, v, 100 sh., voting trust, blue
. . . .$15.00

Houston, Tap and Brazoria Railway Company (TX par $100)

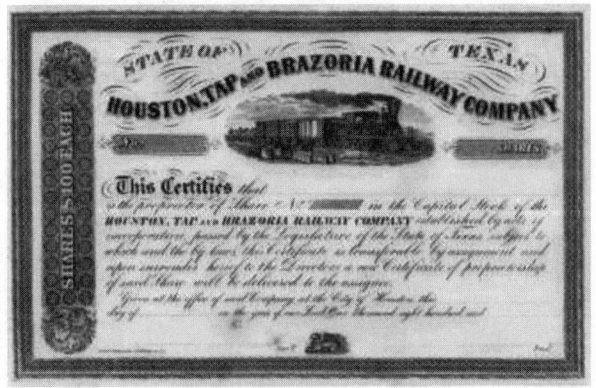

*HO1180-20-10, 18xx, v, u/u certificate, brown
. . . .$10.00

Hovermarine Corporation (PA par 1¢)

HO1310-20-10, 1974, v, 100 shs., green $3.00

Howard Johnson Company
(MD 1961, par $1)

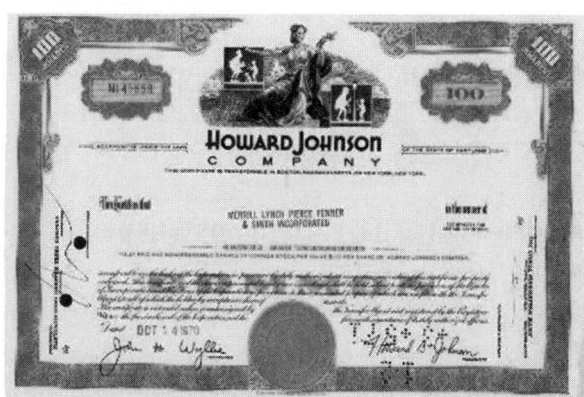

*HO1420-20-10, 1970, v, 100 sh., orange . . .$3.00
HO1420-30-10, 1961, v, 2,000 shs., blue. . . .$4.00

The Hudson Avenue Rail Road Company of Brooklyn (NY par $100)

HU130-20-10, 186x, v, u/u certificate, grey
. . . .$51.00

Hudson Car Company (NJ par $100)

HU170-20-10, 18xx, v, u/u certificate, brown
. . . .$25.00

Hudson Coal Company (PA)

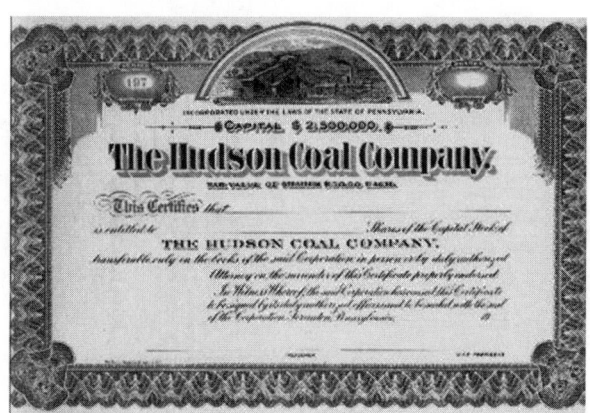

*HU200-20-10, 19xx, v, u/u certificate, brown
border $8.00

Hudson & Manhattan Railroad Company

This company formed in later years PATH (Port Authority Trans Hudson).
HU250-20-10, 1929, v, 100 shs., red $40.00

*HU250-30-10, 19xx, v, u/u 100 sh. certificate, red
. . . .$7.00

*HU250-40-10, 1xxx, v, u/u 100 pref. sh. certificate, blue. $5.00

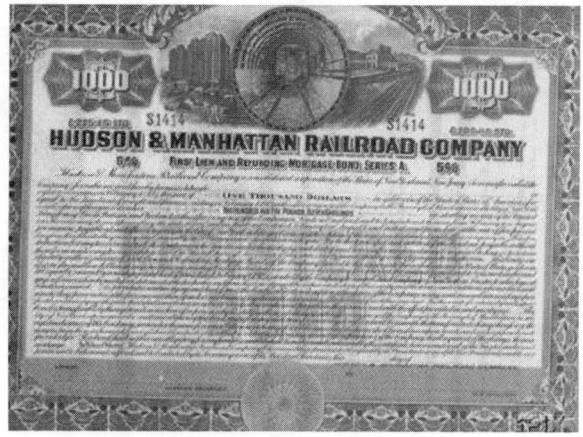

*HU250-50-10, 1913, v, $1,000 5% 1st lien refunding mort. bond series A, green $8.00

Hudson Motor Car Company (MI)
HU280-20-10, 1959, v, 1 sh. on a less than 100 sh. certificate, orange **$40.00**

Hugo's Cleaning Service Inc.
HU370-10-10, 19xx, u/u certificate, green. . .**$3.00**

**Huntington Products Company
(DE par $10)**
HU500-20-10, 1921, v, 40 sh., olive green ..**$5.00**

Hydraulic Press Brick Company
HY100-30-10, 1946, v, 50 pref. shs., brown border
. . . .**$4.00**

The Hydraulic Steel Company
HY140-20-10, 1921, v, 3 sh. on a less than 100 sh. certificate, ABN, green. **$14.00**

Hydro-United Tire Company (no par)
HU210-20-10, 1921, 1 shs., green **$10.00**

I

Idaho Gas Filter Corporation
ID60-20-10, 19xx, v, unissued certificate, green
. . . .$4.00

Idaho & Washington Northern Railroad (ID par $100)
ID140-20-10, 19xx, v, u/u certificate, brown
. . . .$13.00

Illinois Central Rail Road Company
IL110-20-10, 188x, v, u/u certificate, brown
. . . .$36.00

Illinois Central Railroad Company (IL no par)

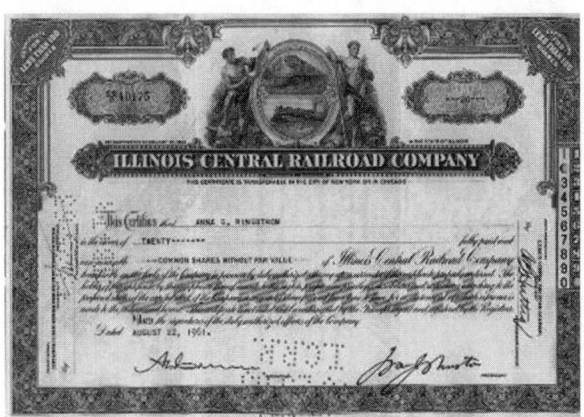

IL120-20-10, 1961, v, 20 sh. on a less than 100 sh. certificate, brown $5.00

IL120-30-10, 1956, v, 100 sh., ABN, orange
. . . .$6.00

IL120-40-10, 1852, Provisional certificate for 1 Construction bond of $500=£104/3/4, grey
. . . .$18.00

Illinois Power and Light Corporation (IL 1923)

The company was formed to acquire the Illinois Traction Company and Southern Illinois Light and Power. Later it owned several railroads such as the St. Louis Electric Terminal Railway, Cairo and St. Louis Railway and Illinois Belt Railway.

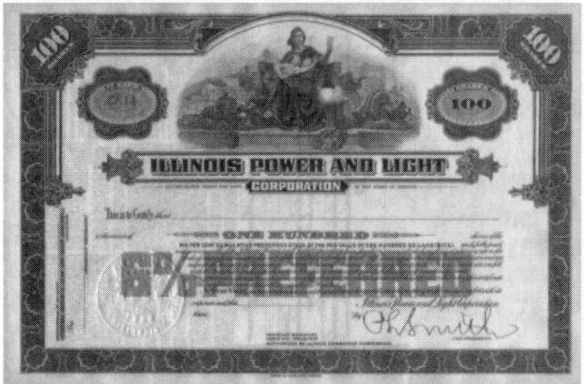

IL240-40-10, 19xx, v, u/u 100 sh., 6% pref. certificate, gray $8.00

The Illinois Pure Aluminum Company (IL 1893)

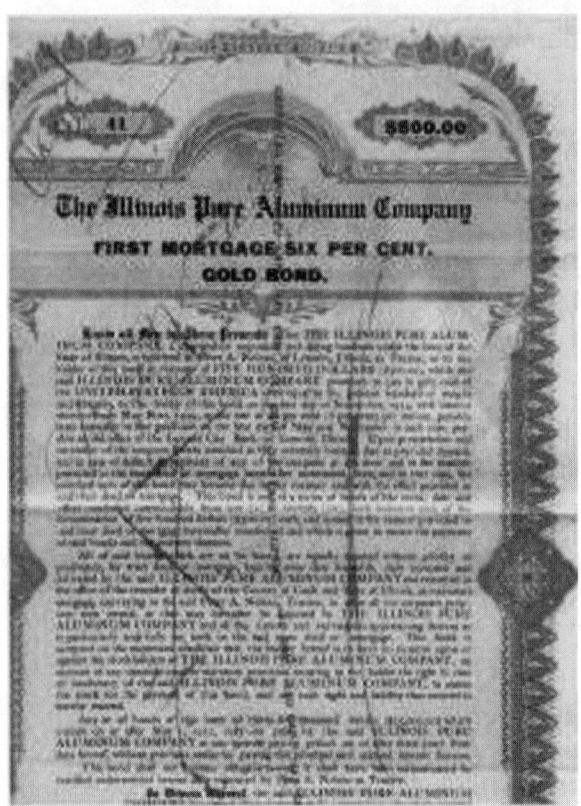

IL270-30-10, 1909, v, $500 1st mortgage 6% gold bond, green **$5.00**

Illinois Traction Company (ME 1904)

Operated regional rail lines and was acquired by Illinois Light and Power in 1923

IL310-20-10, 19xx, 25 sh., v, orange, blank certificate **$7.00**

IL310-30-10, 1911, 10 pref. sh. on a less than 100 sh. certificate, green **$7.00**

The Illinois Vapor Fuel Company (IL)

IL400-20-10, 1884, v, 125 sh., grey **$13.00**

Ilseng Gasoline Corporation (DE par $100)

IL520-20-10, 1926, v, 50 sh., green **$31.00**

Imex Corp. (DE 1968, par 10¢)

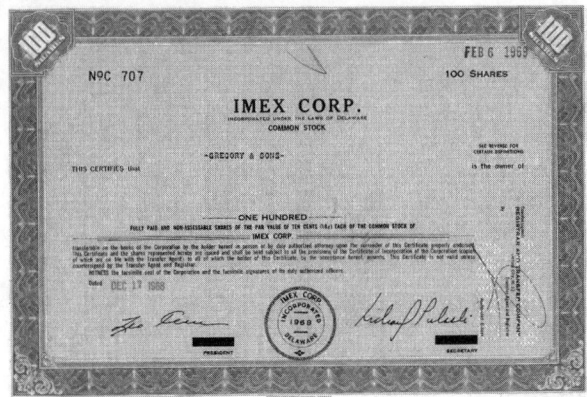

IM70-20-10, 1968, 100 sh., SCB, 12" x 8", orange **$4.00**

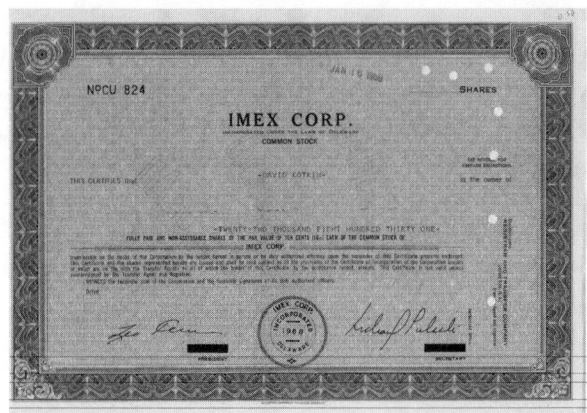

IM70-25-10, 1969, 22,831 sh., SCB, 12" x 8", blue **$4.00**

Imperial Paper Company (OH par $1)

IM200-20-10, 1971, v, 100 sh. certificate, The Judson-Brooks Company, Cleveland, Ohio; 12" x 8-1/4", l. blue **$4.00**

The Independent Torpedo Company (OH par $100)

IN130-20-10, 1911, v - eagle, 2 sh., dark brown
. . . .$11.00

IN130-25-10, 1920, v - oil derricks, 2 sh., brown
. . . .$10.00

Indiahoma Refining Company

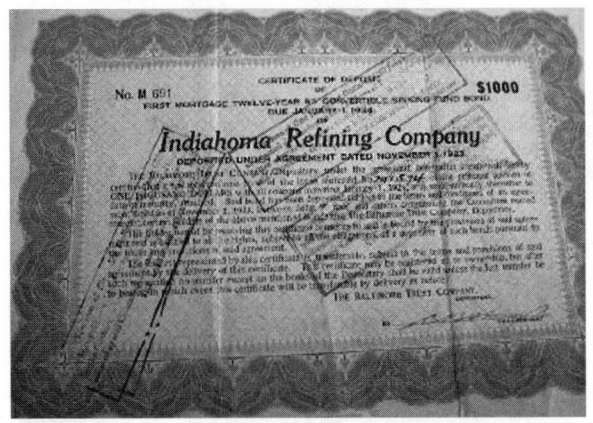

*IN200-30-10, 1923, $1,000 1st mortgage 8% conver. sinking fund bond, due 1934, orange
. . . .$4.00

Indiana Bell Telephone Company, Incorporated

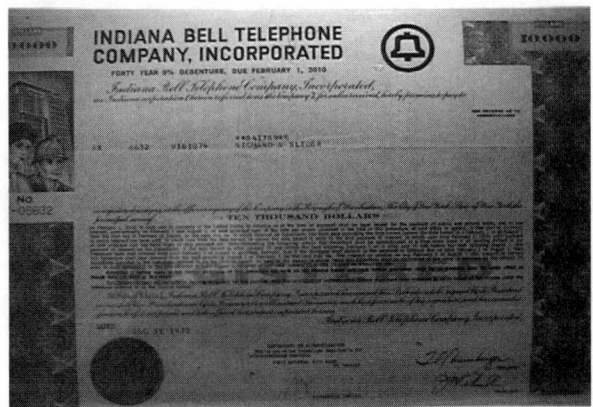

*IN250-40-10, 1973, v, $10,000 40-year 9% debenture due 2010, blue $7.00

Indiana Coal and Railway Company

IN280-20-10, 1881, v, $500=£100 first mortgage bond w. coupons, grey $45.00

The Indiana Consolidated Oil and Asphaltum Co. (AZ territory, par $1)

*IN300-20-10, 1903, v, 800 sh., 11" x 8-1/2", brown border $25.00

Indiana Harbor Belt Railroad Company (IN)

In 1907 this company took over portions of the Chicago Junction Railway.

IN320-40-10, 1924, v, $5,000 50-year bond, ABN, red border $12.00

Indiana, Illinois & Iowa Railroad Company

*IN330-30-10, 1906, v, $1,000 4% bond, brown
. . . .$12.00

Indianapolis & Greenfield Rapid Transit Co. (IN par $50)

*IN410-20-10, 19xx, v, u/u certificate, grey
. . . .$10.00

Indianapolis and Louisville Traction Railway Company (IN par $100)

IN460-20-10, 19xx, v, u/u certificate, brown
. . . .$13.00

Indianapolis & St. Louis Railway Company (IN par $100)

IN520-20-10, 18xx, v, u/u certificate, grey .$12.00

Industrial Trust Company (PA par $5)

*IN610-20-10, 19xx, v, u/u certificate, EAW, 11" x 8", green $4.00

Insull Utility Investments, Inc.

*IN840-20-10, 1931, v, i/u 100 sh., brown
. . . .$13.00

Inter-State Mining Company of Helena, Montana (MT)

*IN920-20-10, 189x, v, u/u certificate, 10" x 9",
grey. $10.00

Intercontinent Petroleum Corporation (DE)

IN970-20-10, 1931, 100 sh., brown $8.00

The value of a stock certificate depends on:
- rarity
- the issuer
- signatures
- quality of engraving
- overall appearance
- condition
- date of issue

Intermountain Architects-Engineers, Inc. (CO par $1)

*IN1030-10-10, 19xx, v, u/c certificate pinhole SAMPLE, GOES, 11" x 8-1/2", gold border
....................................$3.00

International Aeroproducts, Inc. (DE 1969, par $1)

*IN1110-20-10, 1971, v, 100 sh., SCB, 12" x 8", olive green $4.00

International Business Machines Corporation (NY)

IN1200-20-10, 1950, v, 50 sh. on a less than 100 sh. certificate, ABN, brown $20.00

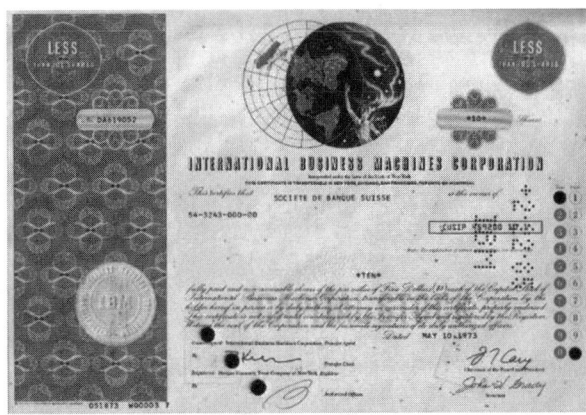

*IN1200-30-10, 1973, v, 10 sh. on a less than 100 sh. certificate, 11-3/4" x 8", brown $20.00

International Combustion Engineering Corporation (DE)

IN1290-30-10, 1933, v, i/u 100 sh., ABN, orange
....................................$10.00

International & Great Northern Railroad Co. (TX par $100)

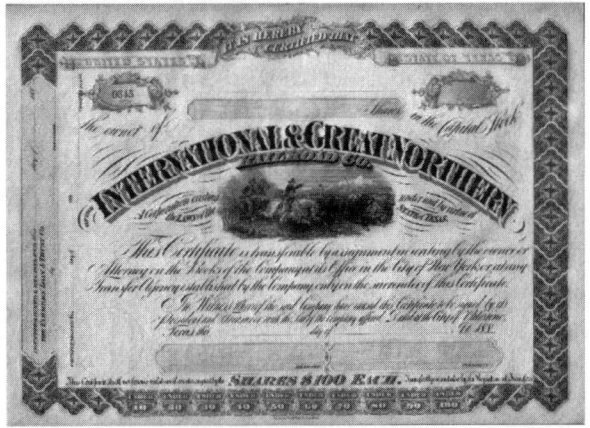

*IN1410-20-10, 188x, v, u/u certificate, blue
....................................$14.00

International Mercantile Marine Company (NJ no par)

A J.P. Morgan company.

*IN1500-20-10, 1915, t, 25 sh. (par $100), ABN, 10-3/4" x 7-3/4", green $5.00

*IN1500-30-10, 1929, t, 2 sh. on a less than 100 sh. certificate (no par), blue $5.00
IN1500-35-10, 1921, v, 20 sh., brown $20.00
IN1500-40-10, 1929, v, 100 sh., green $20.00

*IN1500-50-10, 1941, v, 100 sh., green $20.00

*IN1500-45-10, 1937, v, 100 sh., orange. . .$20.00
IN1500-60-10, 1929, v, 15,788 sh., brown
. . . .$20.00

*IN1500-70-10, 1919, v (5) 6% cum. pref. sh. on a less than 100 sh. certificate (par $100), purple
. . . .$20.00
IN1500-75-10, 1918, v, 100 pref. sh., green
. . . .$20.00

International Minerals & Chemical Corporation (NY 1909, par $5)

*IN1540-30-10, 1971, v, 20 sh. on a less than 100 sh. certificate, brown $4.00

*IN1540-40-10, 1971, v, 100 sh., ABN, 12" x 8", red.................................$4.00

International Nickel Company (NJ par $25)

*IN1600-20-10, 1919, v, 100 sh., brown $4.00

International Pulp Company (NY)

*IN1700-30-10, 189x, v, u/u 100 sh. certificate, ABN, orange.......................$10.00

International Security Management Company (DE)

*IN1800-20-10, 1929, t, 50 sh., brown $3.00
*IN1800-20-10, 1929, t, 100 class A sh., orange
.................................$4.00

The International Silver Company (CT 1946)

*IN1840-40-10, 1973, v, $1,000 5% convertible subord. debenture, red $5.00

International Standard Electric Corporation (DE 1918)

*IN1900-40-10, 1967, v, $1,000 6% sinking fund debenture due 1987 w. coupons; ABN, 10" x 15-1/4", orange.....................$6.00

*IN1900-50-10, 1971, v, $1,000 8-1/4% sinking
fund debenture due 1986 w. coupons, ABN,
10" x 15", purple....................**$6.00**

International Stock Food Company
(ME par $100)
*IN1960-20-10, 1918, v, 1 pref. sh., green....**$4.00**

The International Telephone and
Telegraph Corporation (DE 1920, par $1)
*IN2010-20-10, 1957, v, 100 sh. (no par), blue
................................**$7.00**

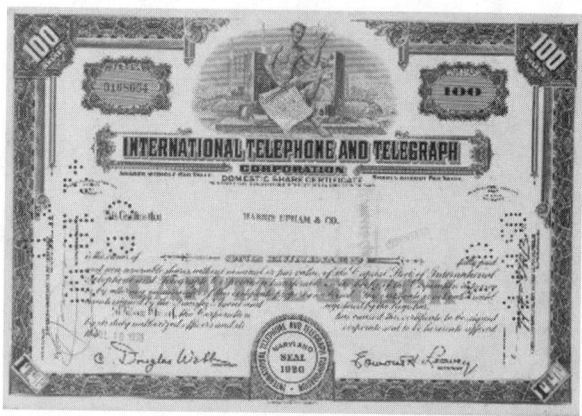

*IN2010-30-10, 1967, v, 100 sh., domestic certifi-
cate (MD 1920 no par), blue............**$4.00**

*IN2010-40-10, 1976, v, 100 domestic sh., ABN,
12" x 8", blue......................**$4.00**

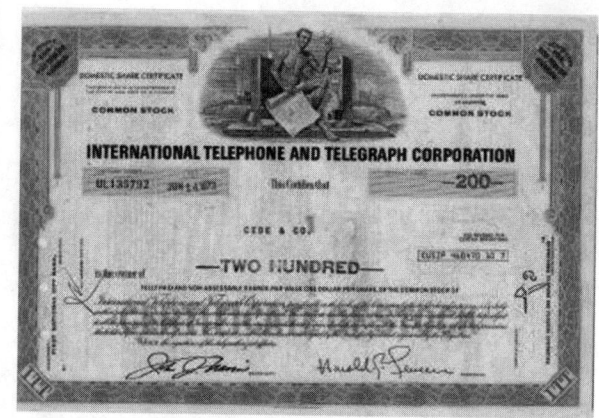

*IN2010-50-10, 1973, v, 200 domestic sh. on a not
more than 1000 sh. certificate, orange....**$4.00**
*IN2010-60-10, 1973, v, 100 sh., domestic cumul.
pref. $2.25 convert., series N, purple.....**$5.00**

The International Telepost Company, Inc.

*IN2050-20-10, 1930, v, 1 sh., orange.....**$10.00**

Interstate Gasoline Company (DE par $1)

*IN2200-20-10, 1922, v, 25 sh., brown $12.00

The Interstate Stock Yard Company (OH par $100)

IN2270-20-10, 1932, v, 10 sh., yellow-orange
. . . .$20.00

Investment Resources & Properties Corporation (UT 1911, par $1)

IN2320-30-10, 1961, v, 62 sh., brown border
. . . .$3.00

Investment Technology Group, Inc. (DE 1983, par $0.01)

*IN2350-10-10, 19xx, v, u/u specimen certificate,
orange and blue. $15.00

Iola Co-operative Mercantile Company (WI par $100)

*IO50-20-10, 1915, v, i/u 1 sh., issued to Carl
Krause, 11" x 8", grey border. $30.00

Iola Farm Produce Company (WI par $10)

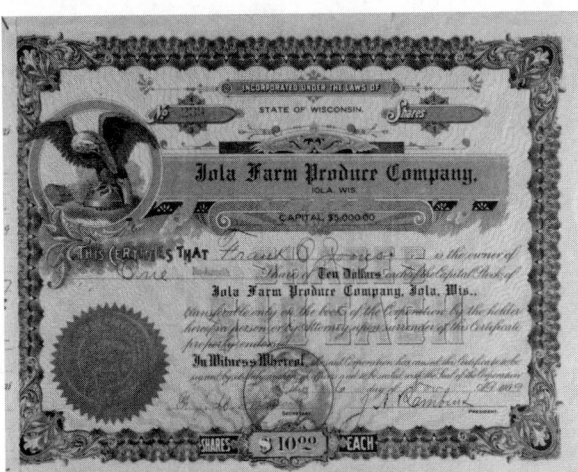

*IO70-20-10, 1909, v, i/u 1 sh., w/o imprint,
11-1/2" x 8", grey border $15.00

The Iola Hospital and Nursing Home (WI)

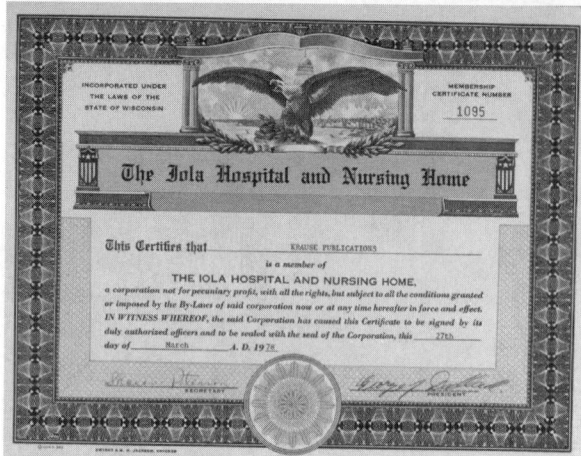

*IO90-20-10, 1978, v, membership, GOES, 11" x 8", blue border $16.00

Ionia and Lansing Railroad Company (MI)

IO120-30-10, 1869, v, $1,000 due 1889, grey $100.00

Iowa Resources Inc. (IA)

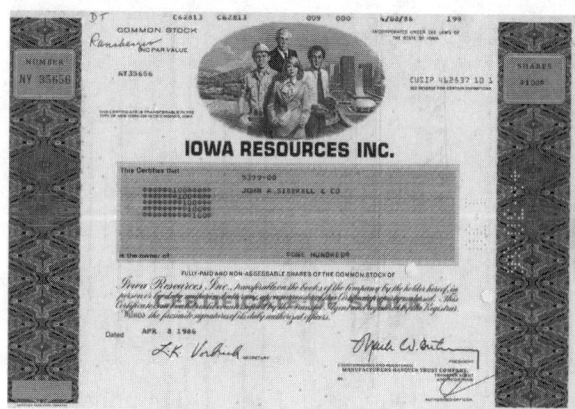

*IO100-20-10, 1986, v - people, 100 sh., ABN, 12" x 8", blue $4.00

It is generally assumed that only 5% of certificates survive to reach collectors.

Iron Mountain Incorporated (DE 1969, par $0.50)

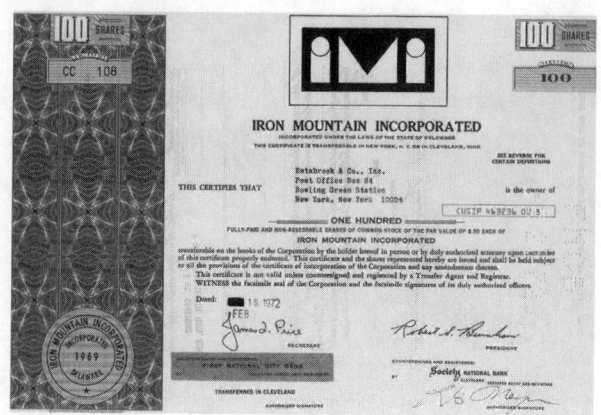

*IR170-20-10, 1972, v, 100 sh., SCB, 12" x 8", green $4.00

Irving Trust Company (NR par $10)

*IR240-20-10, 1949, v, 100 sh., 11" x 7", ABN, orange border $8.00

The Isabella Gold Mining Company (par $1) Cripple Creek district

IS100-20-10, 1896, v, 100 sh., orange $10.00
IS100-30-10, 1895, v, 500 sh., reddish $12.00
IS100-40-10, 19xx, v, unissued certificate, orange $7.00

The Italian Fraternal Building Society (MO)

IT100-10-10, 1925 . . . . $6.00

ITT Financial Corporation

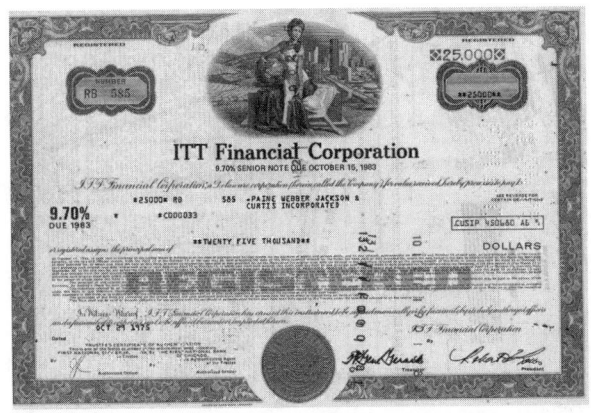

IT310-30-10, 1975, v, $5,000 9.70% senior note due 1983, ABN, 12" x 8", brown **$4.00**

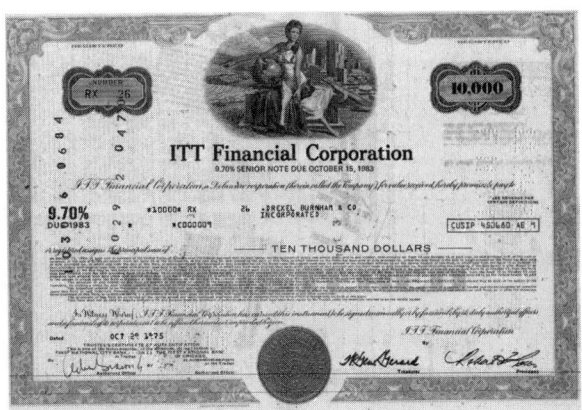

IT310-35-10, 1975, v, $10,000 9.70% senior note due 1983, ABN, 12" x 8", orange. **$4.00**

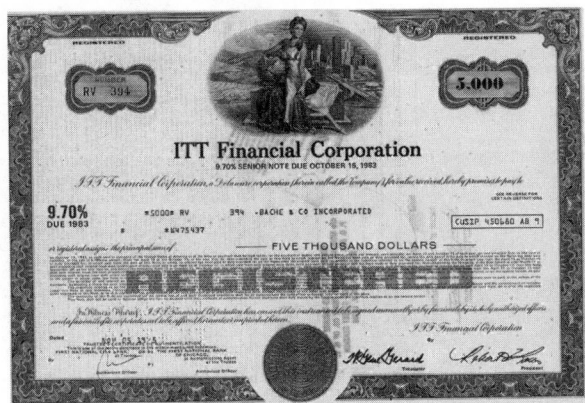

IT310-40-10, 1975, v, $25,000 9.70% senior note due 1983, ABN, 12" x 8", red **$4.00**

J

Byron Jackson Co.

JA100-20-10, 1936, v, 50 sh. on a less than 100 sh. certificate, orange $3.00

Jacksonville Terminal Company (FL)

JA150-30-10, 1948, v, $1,000 1ˢᵗ mort. 3-3/4% bond, series A due 1977, brown $12.00

Jamestown, Franklin and Clearfield Railroad Company

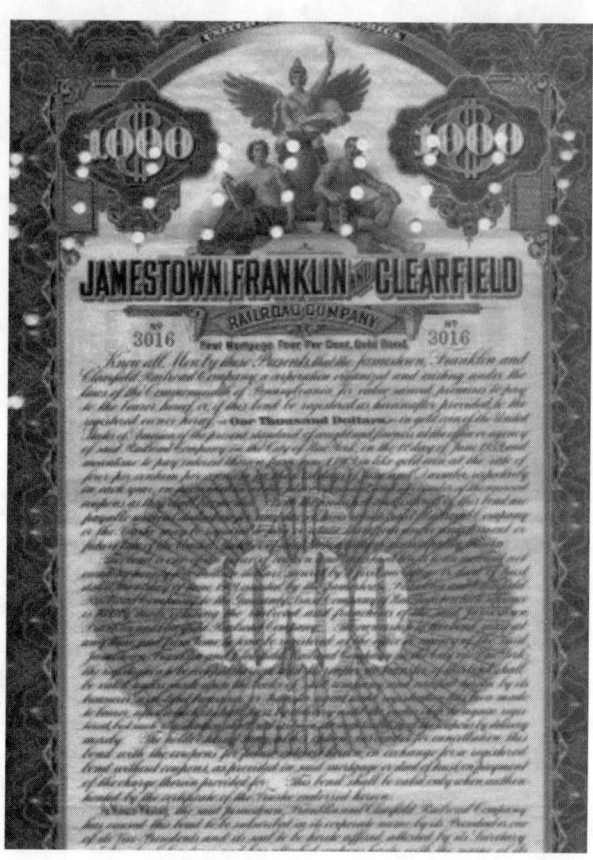

JA240-40-10, 1909, v, $1,000 1ˢᵗ mort. 4% bond, blue.............................$15.00

Jamestown, Westfield and Northwestern Railroad Company (NY par $100)

JA280-20-10, 19xx, v, u/u certificate, SBN, green
..................................$15.00

Jantzen, Inc.

JA330-20-10, 1962, v, 50 sh. on a less than 100 sh. certificate, green...................$7.00

Jefferson Coal Company (WV par $100)

JE110-20-10, 189x, v, u/u certificate, green
..................................$9.00

Jefferson Stores, Inc. (DE 1961, par $1)

JE150-20-10, 1969, v, 100 sh., SCB, green..$4.00

*JE150-25-10, 1969, v, 200 sh., SCB, 12" x 8",
   blue $4.00

Jefferson & Teton Mining Company (MT par 25¢)

JE180-20-10, 19xx, v, u/u certificate, green .$6.00

Jefferson-Travis Radio Mfg. Corporation (NY)

*JE210-20-10, 19xx, v, u/u certificate, green
   . . . .$4.00

Jeffersonville City Railway Company (IN par $100)

JE240-20-10, 189x, v, u/u certificate, Falls City
   Litho. Co., brown $8.00

City of Jersey City, County of Hudson NJ

JE320-20-10, 1902, v, $1,000 7% bond, green
   . . . .$18.00
JE320-25-10, 1911, v, $1,000 4-1/2% water gold
   bond, 10" x 15", red $8.00
JE320-30-10, 1920, v, $1,000 5-1/2% water bond,
   Hamilton Bank Note Co., blue $12.00

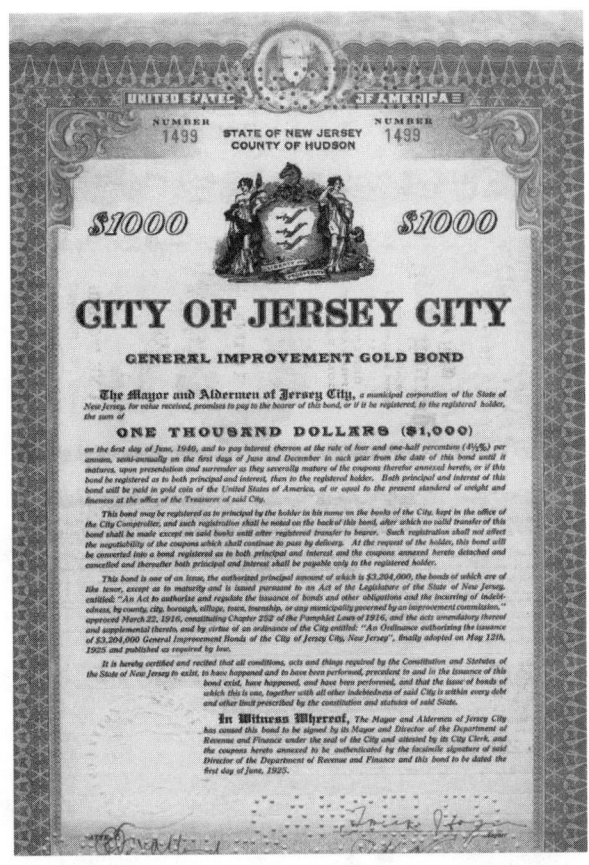

*JE320-40-10, 1925, v, $1,000 4-1/2% General
   Improvement Gold Bond, due 1940, signed by
   Frank Hague the infamous boss of politics,
   brown $11.00
JE320-50-10, 1925, v, $1,000 water gold bond,
   green. $17.00

Jersey Central Power & Light Company (NJ)

JE350-30-10, 1965, v, $1,000 4-7/8% 1st mortgage
   bond, SCB, orange $9.00
JE350-40-10, 1970, v, $1,000 10% 1st mortgage
   bond, SCB, orange $7.00

The Jersey Shore, Pine Creek & Buffalo Railway Company (par $50)

JE380-20-10, 18xx, v, u/u certificate, ABN, black
   . . . .$15.00

Johnstown Coal & Coke Company (WV par $100)

*JO100-20-10, 19xx, u/u certificate, orange
. . . .$12.00

Joliet and Chicago Railroad Company (IL par $100)

JO150-20-10, 1924, v, 10 sh., black. $40.00

Jolliffe Importers, Inc. (CO par $1)

*JO180-20-10, 19xx, v, u/c certificate, pin imprint SAMPLE, GOES, 11-1/4" x 8-1/2", green
. . . .$3.00

Josephine Gold and Copper Mining Company (UT par 1¢)

JO240-20-10, 1902, v, 100 sh., brown. $9.00

Julian Oil & Royalty Company (AZ no par)

JU90-20-10, 1935, v, 13 sh., green. $50.00

Julie Research Laboratories

JU120-20-10, 1964, v, 2 sh., red $3.00
JU120-30-10, 1989, v, 100 sh., blue. $3.00

Jumbo Junior Mining Company (NV)

*JU150-20-10, 1917, v, i/u 2,000 sh., grey
. . . .$15.00

The Jumbo Wonder Mining Company (AZ par $1)

*JU180-20-10, 1918, v, 200 sh., orange . . .$20.00

Junction Bit & Tool Co. (CO par $1)

*JU220-20-10, 19xx, v, u/c certificate, pin imprint SAMPLE, GOES, 11" x 8-1/2", gold border
. . . .$3.00

The Justice Hill Mining Co. (CO)

JU290-20-10, 1935, v, 280 sh., brown. $30.00

K

Kaiser-Frazer Corporation
KA150-20-10, 1946, t, 100 sh., brown **$5.00**

Kakagon Iron Company (WI par $25)

KA200-20-10, 1888, v, 50 sh., 13" x 11", grey
border **$120.00**

Kalamazoo, Allegan & Grand Rapids Rail Road Company (par $100)

KA190-20-10, 1971, v, 50 sh., grey **$15.00**

Kanawha & Michigan Railway Company (OH-WV)
KA270-30-10, 1890, v, $1,000 first mort. 4% 100-
year gold bond, brown **$40.00**

Kankakee & Seneca Railroad Company (IL)
KA320-30-10, 1881, v, $1,000 1st mort. 40-year 8%
bond, brown **$29.00**

Kansas City Baseball Club, Inc. (MO no par)

KA350-20-10, 19xx, u/u certificate, 11-1/2" x 8",
brown border **$200.00**

Kansas City, Mexico & Orient Railway Company
KA370-30-10, 1912, cert. of deposit $1,000
50-year first mort. 4% gold bond, black. . .**$7.00**

Kansas City, St. Louis and Chicago Railroad Company (par $100)

KA400-30-10, 1945, v, 5 pref. sh., ABN, green
. . . .**$15.00**

Kansas City Terminal Company
KA430-20-10, ND, $500,000 series B non-negotia-
ble receipt, 1st mortgage 2-7/8% bond, pink
. . . .**$15.00**

Kansas City Terminal Railway Company

*KA440-30-10, 19xx, v, s/c $10,000 1st mortgage serial bond, due 19xx, brown $15.00

Karth Furniture and Undertaking Co. (WI par $100)

*KA480-20-10, 1918, v, 5 sh., GOES, 11" x 8", grey. $50.00

Kaskaskia Tool and Machine, Inc. (IL no par)

*KA520-20-10, 19xx, v, u/u certificate, w/o imprint, 11" x 7-1/2", red border $3.00

Kavanaugh-Owsley, Inc. (CO no par)

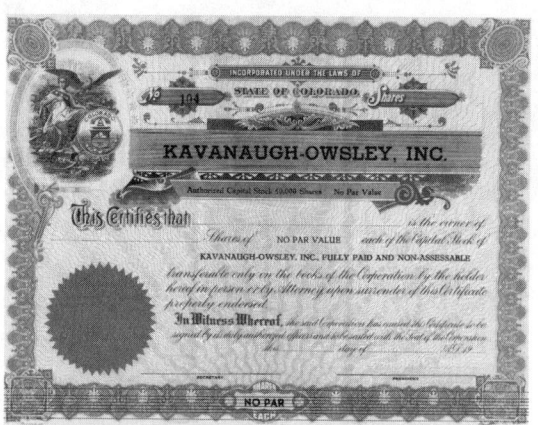

*KA640-10-10, 19xx, v, u/c certificate with pin perforation "SAMPLE," GOES, 10-3/4" x 8-1/2", gold border $3.00

Kelsey Motor Car Company (PA)

*KE120-20-10, 19xx, v, u/u certificate, brown $35.00

Kelwin Realty Corporation (NY par $100)

KE220-20-10, 19xx, v, u/u certificate, J. Meyers Inc., NYC, 10-3/4" x 8-1/2", brown **$4.00**

Kennecott Copper Corporation

KE310-20-10, 1928, v, 50 sh. on a less than 100 sh. certificate, orange **$24.00**

KE310-30-10, 1934, v, 100 sh., green **$19.00**

Kensington National Bank (PA)

KE390-20-10, 1926, v, 5 sh., brown **$17.00**

Kentucky and Great Eastern Railway Company

KE450-30-10,1872, v, $1,000 7% gold bearer bond, green. **$55.00**

The Kentucky Western Railway Co. (KY par $100)

KE490-20-10, 19xx, v, u/u certificate, black **$6.00**

Kenyon & Eckhart, Incorporated (par $1)

KE530-20-10, 1950, v, 250 sh., red **$4.00**

Keokuk and Des Moines Railway Company

*KE630-20-10,*19xx, v, u/u pref. sh. certificate, CNB, grey on pink **$7.00**

Keta Gas & Oil Corporation (DE 1941)

KE740-20-10, 1953, v, 50 sh. on a less than 100 sh. certificate, orange **$4.00**

Keystone Chemical Company (SD par $1)

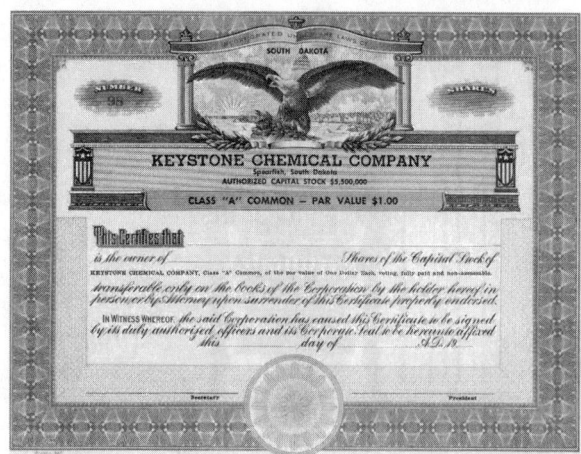

KE840-20-10, 19xx, v, u/u certificate, GOES Litho, 11" x 8-1/2", orange **$5.00**

Keystone Consolidated Mining Company (WI 1881, par $10)

KE870-19-10, 1882, 10 sh., 9" x 4½", grey border
. . . .**$150.00**

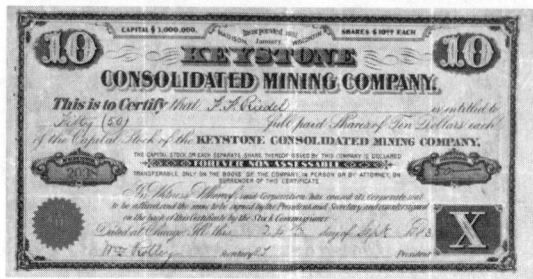

KE870-20-10, 1883, 50 sh., signature variety, 9" x 3-1/2", grey border **$120.00**

Kidder Participations Incorporated No. 3 (MA no par)

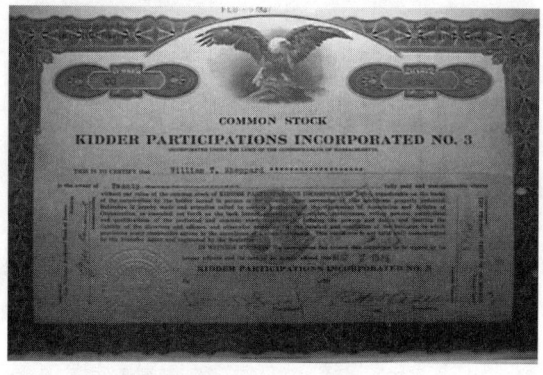

KI140-20-10, 1937, v, 20 sh., blue **$5.00**

Kim Mutual Telephone Association (not for profit) (CO par $300)

KI210-20-10, 19xx, v, u/c certificate with pin hole SAMPLE, GOES, 11" x 8-1/2", gold border
. . . .**$3.00**

Kineo Company (ME par $100)
KI240-20-10, 189x, v, u/u certificate, brown
. . . .**$26.00**

King Mining Company (ID par $0.10)
KI270-20-10, 19xx, v, unissued certificate, grey
. . . .$6.00

King Mining Company (MA par $10)
KI280-20-10, 190x, v, unissued certificate, green
. . . .$10.00

Kings County Elevated Railroad Co. (NY)

*KI310-20-10, 1xxx, v, u/u certificate, ABN,
Orange. $28.00

**Kleckner Dry Goods Co. Mahanoy City, Pa.
(PA par $100)**
KL100-20-10, 19xx, v, unissued certificate, brown
. . . .$100.00

**Knickerbocker Trust Company for the
Brooklyn Ferry Company of New York**

*KN160-30-10, 1906, v, $1,000 certificate of
deposit on 1st consol. mort. 5% gold bond due
1945, green $25.00

Knox Divide Mining Company (NV)
KN260-20-10, 1919, v - miners, 100 sh., blue
. . . .$10.00
KN290-25-10, 1920, v, 100 sh., green $10.00

Knox and Lincoln Railroad Company
KN310-20-10, 187x, v, unissued certificate, grey
. . . .$10.00

The Knox Tire & Rubber Company (OH)

*KN400-20-10, 1920, v, i/u 25 sh., brown. . .$3.00

*KN400-30-10, 1920, v, i/u 5 pref. sh. (par $100),
GOES, 10-1/2" x 8-1/4", green $4.00

*It is generally assumed that
only 5% of certificates survive
to reach collectors.*

Knoxville & Ohio Railroad Company (par $100)

*KN450-20-10, 1877, 20 sh., grey $38.00

Kohinoor Blende Mining Co. (WI par $1)

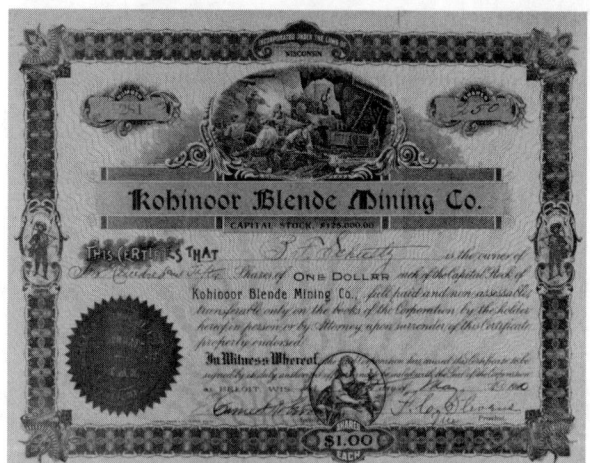

*KO200-20-10, 1910, v, 250 sh., 11" x 8-1/2",
  brown border. $125.00

Kropp Forge Company (IL par $100)

KR100-20-10, 1941, v, 75 sh., grey $12.00

The Kruger and Blind Company (PA par $50)

KR180-20-10, 19xx, v, unissued certificate, brown
  . . . .$4.00

K-Squared Enterprises Inc.

KS80-20-10, 19xx, v, unissued certificate green
  . . . .$4.00

Kwal Paints, Inc. (CO par $10)

*KW80-20-10, 19xx, v, u/c pref. stock certificate,
  with pin hole SAMPLE, GOES, 11" x 8-1/2",
  grey on gold $3.00

L

La Crosse & Milwaukee Rail Road Company (WI par $100)

LA50-10-10, 18??, v, 20 sh., 10-1/2" x 8-1/2", brown border.....................$60.00

*LA50-40-10, 1857, v, $1,000 7% bond, 12" x 9-1/2", brown border...............$450.00

*LA50-45-10, 1858, v, $1,000 5% Land Grant bond, 11" x 7", brown..............$275.00

UNLISTED TYPES & VARIETIES

Readers are welcome to contact the author directly at:

Rainer Stahlberg
P.O. Box 1044
Rooseveltown, New York 13683

La Guardia East Sire Plan Hotel, Inc. (NY)

*LA80-20-10, 19xx, v, u/u specimen pref. sh. certificate, green $5.00

La Rose National Bank (U.S. par $100)

*LA110-20-10, 1918, 10 sh., revenue stamp, 11" x 8", grey border $50.00

La Tula Mining Company (NY par $10)

LA140-20-10, 1910, v, 100 sh., grey $15.00

Lackawanna Securities Company (DE no par)

LA200-20-10, 19xx, v, unissued 100 sh. certificate, orange............................$6.00

The Laclede Gas Light Company (MO)

It was one of the original 12 companies chosen by Charles Dow from the Dow Jones Industrial Average in 1896.

LA260-20-10, 18xx, v, blue, pref. sh blank certificate $10.00

LA260-30-10, 1903, v, 100 sh., green $9.00

Lake Copper Company (MI par $5)

LA350-20-10, 1919, v, 50 sh., signed by W.A, Paine one of the founders of Paine, Webber & Co., green $150.00

Lake Shore and Michigan Southern Railway Company (IL)

LA410-20-10, 1897, v, $1,000 gold bond, green $13.00
LA410-30-10, 1903, v, $1,000 4% bond, green $18.00
LA410-40-10, 1938, v, $1,000 bond $12.00
LA410-50-10, 1945, v, $1,000 3-1/2% gold bond, grey $15.00
LA410-70-10, 1973, v, $50,000 3-1/2% gold bond, ABN, green border $17.00

The Lake Sub-Marine Company (NJ par $100)

LA480-20-10, 1899, v, 2 sh., brown $30.00

Lake Superior Mining Company (WI par $10)

*LA500-20-10, 1907, v, 25 sh., Castle-Pierce Press, Oshkosh, Wis., 11" x 8-1/4", brown border $75.00

Lake Superior Southern Railway Company (MI-WI)

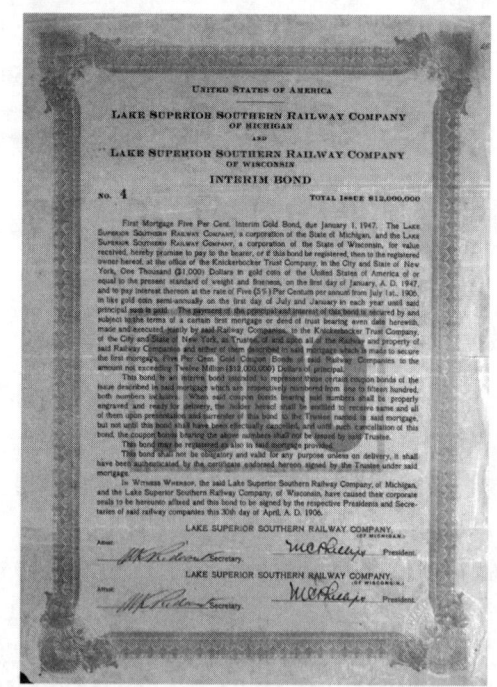

*LA505-40-10, 1906, $1,000 1st mortgage 5% interim gold bond, due 1947, 10" x 14", green border $65.00

The Lake Superior & Southwestern Railway Company (WI par $100)

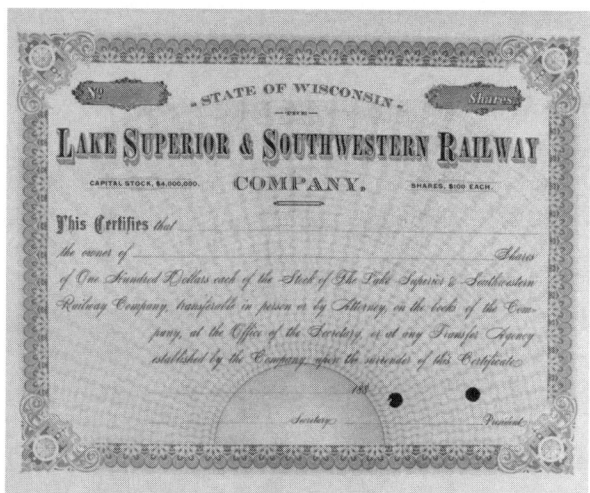

LA510-20-10, 188x, u/c certificate, 10-1/2" x 8-1/2", l. brown border $10.00

The Lake Torpedo Boat Company (ME par $10)

LA530-10-10, 1913, v, 1 sh., brown and grey $38.00

LA530-15-10, 19xx, v, blank certificate, brown & grey $9.00

Lancaster Drug Company (DE par $50)

LA620-20-10, 1905, v, 50 sh., grey $12.00

Landsing Pacific Fund, Inc. (MD 1993, par $0.001)

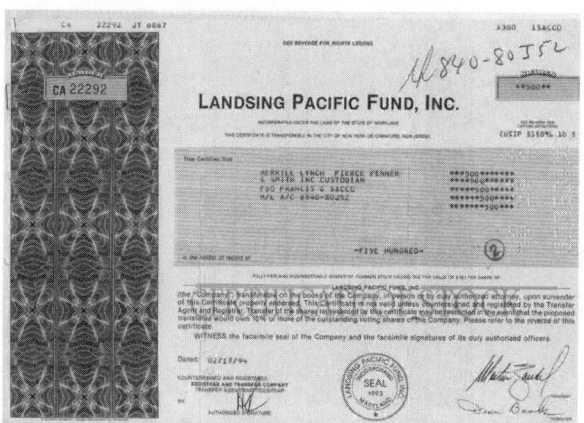

LA670-20-10, 1994, 500 sh., SCB, 12" x 8", blue $4.00

Langcliffe Collieries, Inc. (PA)

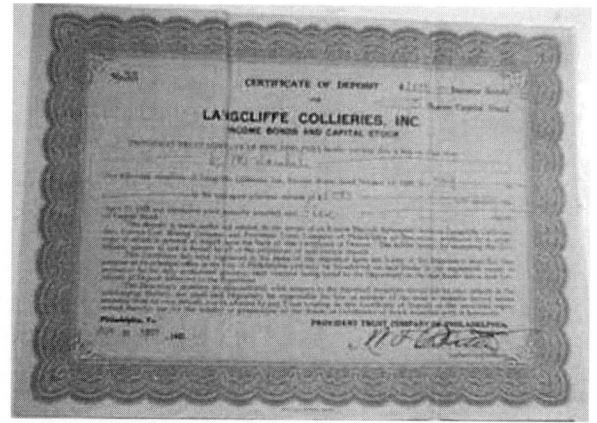

LA720-20-10, 1931, 5 sh. certificate of deposit, 10-3/4" x 7-1/2", orange $3.00

Lansing Transit Railway (MI)

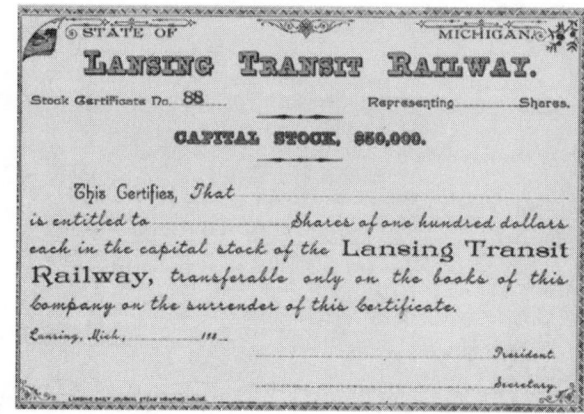

LA810-20-10, 188x, u/u certificate, black . .$4.00

Last Chance Copper Mining Company (MT par $1)

Mines located at Saltese, Montana.

LA1040-20-10, 1911, v, 1,000 sh., McKee Printing Co., Butte, brown $17.00

The value of a stock certificate depends on:
- rarity
- the issuer
- signatures
- quality of engraving
- overall appearance
- condition
- date of issue

J A Law & Associates, Inc. (IL no par)

*LA1100-20-10, 19xx, v, u/u certificate, w/o imprint, 11" x 7-1/2", green border $3.00

Lawson Airplane Company (WI par $10)

*LA1130-20-10, 1921, v, 100 sh., GOES, 11" x 8-1/2", grey border $150.00

Lawyers Mortgage Company (NY par $20)

*LA1170-20-10, 1929, 100 sh., blue $14.00

Julius J. Lax, Inc.

LA1240-25-10, 19xx, v, $1,000 8% 1st mortgage gold bond w. coupons, due 1933, 9-1/2" x 15", brown $6.00

Leadville & Gunnison Gold & Silver Mining Company (IL par $100)

Mines in Colorado.

LE50-20-10, 1880, v, 300 sh., grey border
. . . . $170.00

Leasco Corporation

Saul Steinberg took over the company to control Reliance Insurance. It was one of the first companies leasing computers.

LE100-20-10, 1973, v, 332 sh., green $36.00

The LeClair Mines Company (CO)

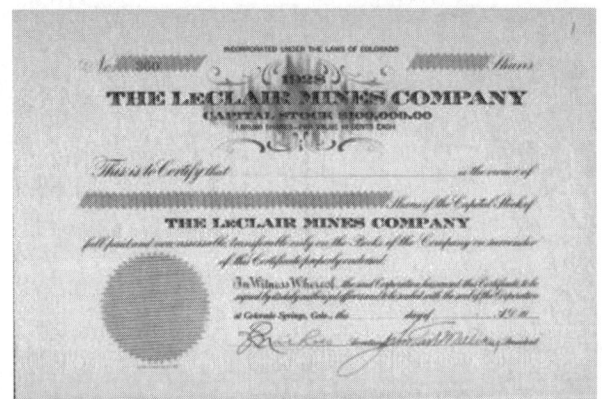

LE170-20-10, 19xx, u/u certificate, grey . . . $3.00

Leeds and Lippincott Company (NJ 1903)

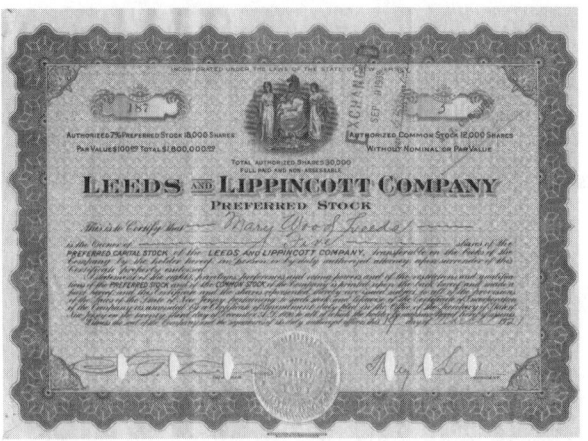

LE240-20-10, 1921, v, 5, 7% pref. sh. (par $100), NBN, 12" x 8-1/2", green $4.00

Leeds & Northrup Company (PA 25¢)

LE270-20-10, 1976, v, 100 sh., green. **$6.00**

The Lehigh Coal and Navigation Company (PA no par)

LE330-20-10, 1938, v, 50 sh. on a less than 100 sh. certificate, brown **$4.00**
LE330-30-10, 1932, v, 100 sh., green. **$4.00**

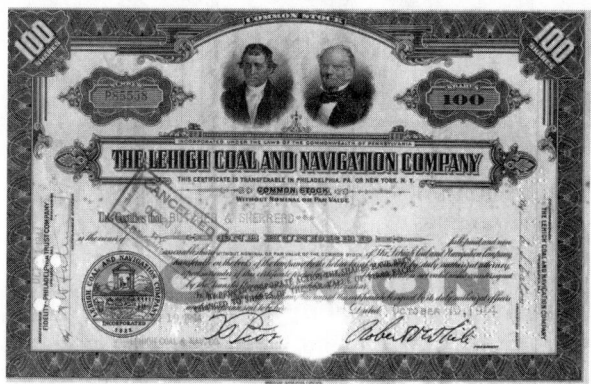

*LE330-25-10, 1939, v, 100 sh., ABN, 11" x 7", green **$4.00**

*LE330-30-10, 1944, v, 100 sh, o/p shares have been changed to par $20, ABN, 11" x 7", green **$4.00**

Lehigh Navigation Company (PA)

LE390-10-10, 1800, 1 sh., fair condition . .**$750.00**

Lehigh Valley Railroad Company (PA par $50)

LE430-20-10, 1893, v, 8 sh., green. **$20.00**
LE430-25-10, 1901, v, 5 sh., green. **$20.00**
LE430-30-10, 1901, v, 30 sh., beige and black **$20.00**
LE430-40-10, 1901, v, 100 sh., NYB, orange **$20.00**

LE430-50-10, 1957, v, 75 sh. on a less than 100 sh. certificate, brown **$6.00**
LE430-60-10, 1932, v, $1,000 General Cons. gold bond, green. **$7.00**
LE430-70-10, 1944, v, $5,000 General Cons. gold bond, green. **$12.00**

*LE430-75-10, 1949, v, $1,000 General Consolidated Mortgage bond, 4% series A w. coupons, ABN, 10" x 15", brown **$7.00**
LE430-80-10, 1972, v, $1,000 bond, purple .**$6.00**

The Lehigh Valley Rail Way Company (PA 1890)

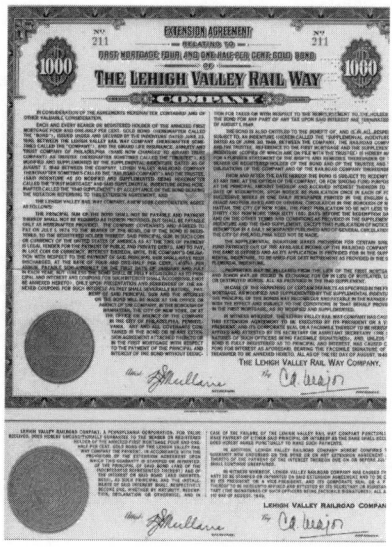

*LE440-40-10, 1949, v, $1,000 extension 1st mortgage 4-1/2% gold bond, ABN, 9-3/4" x 11-3/4", green. **$4.00**

Lehigh Valley Terminal Railway Company
LE470-25-10, 1949, $1,000 Extension agreement first mort. 5% gold bond, brown.........**$5.00**

Lehigh Valley Transit Company (PA par $50)

LE500-20-10, 1915, v - PA coat of arms, 100 sh., EAW, 11-3/4" x 8-1/2", green **$5.00**

Lemmon Oil Basin Company (SD par 10¢)
LE600-20-10, 1920, v, 1,000 sh., grey.....**$4.00**

Leonard Oil Development Company (DE)

LE690-20-10, 1933, v, i/u 266 sh., green ..**$10.00**

Lescarden Inc. (NY par 1¢)
LE850-20-10, 1983, v, 100 sh., green.......**$4.00**

Lexan Realty Corporation (NY)
LE960-10-10, 19xx, v, unissued certificate, green
....................................**$4.00**

Fred T. Ley & Co. (DE 192x no par)
New York based construction company that went out of business in the late 1970s.
LE1000-10-10, 1936, v, 5 sh. on a less than 100 sh. certificate, orange...................**$4.00**

Liberty Bell Racing Association (PA)

LI100-30-10, 1960, v, u/u 3-6% unsecured debentures, GOES, 10" x 15-1/2", blue........**$6.00**

Liberty Logging Company (WA par $100)
LI130-20-10, 1918, v, i/u 1 sh. certificate, grey
..................................**$15.00**

Liggett Group Inc.
LI280-20-10, 1977, v, 10 sh., blue........**$5.00**

Liggett & Myers Incorporated (DE)

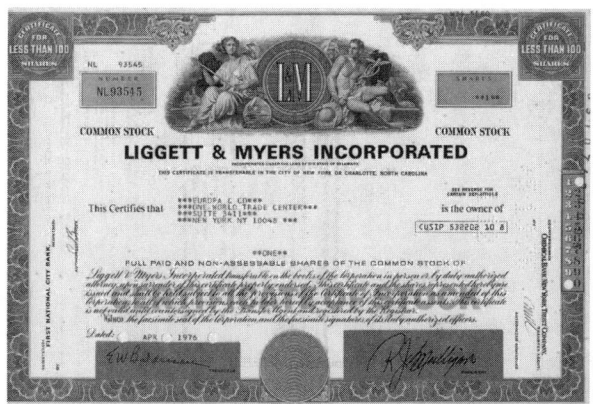

LI290-20-10, 1976, v, 1 sh. on a less than 100 sh. certificate, signature strip, ABN, 12" x 8", red $4.00

LI290-25-10, 1976, v, 1 sh. on a less than 100 sh. certificate, o/p name changed to Liggett Group, red................................$4.00

The Lima Cord Sole and Heel Company
LI380-20-10, 1928, t, 25 sh., orange........$4.00

Lincoln Financial Bancorp, Inc. (DE 1994, par $0.01)

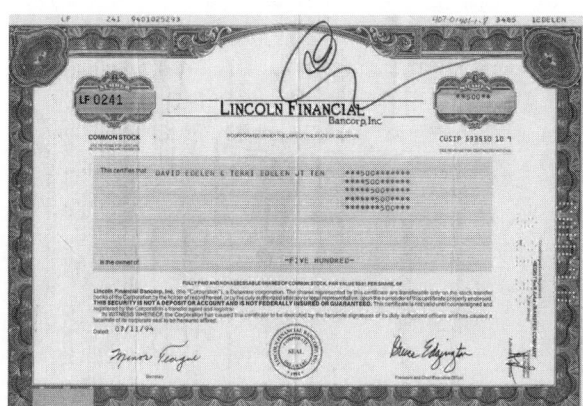

LI450-20-10, 1994, 500 sh., ABN, 11-3/4" x 8", brown $3.00

Lincoln Motor Company
LI480-20-10, 1920, t, 6 sh. on a less than 100 sh. certificate, orange $36.00

LI480-30-10, 1920, t, 100 sh., signed by W.I. Eland and W. Nash, green..................$45.00

Lincoln Stock Farms Co. (WA par $100)

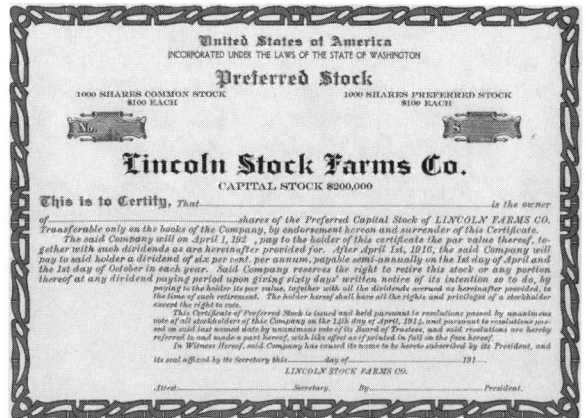

LI520-20-10, 191x, u/u pref. stock certificate, w/o imprint, 11" x 8-1/2", green........$4.00

The Lionel Corporation
Maker of toy trains.

LI570-20-10, 1963, v, 10 sh. on a less than 100 sh. certificate, blue....................$10.00

LI570-30-10, 1963, v, 100 sh., orange....$10.00

Lisbon Valley Uranium Company (CO par 1¢)
LI690-20-10, 19xx, v, u/u 500 share certificate, GOES Litho., brown..................$6.00

Little Evelyn Mining Company (ME par $5)

*LI780-20-10, 1909, v, 40 sh., grey $15.00

Little King Mines, Incorporated (CO par $1)

*LI820-20-10, 19xx, v, u/u certificate, grey. .$6.00

Little Miami Rail Road Company (OH)
LI860-20-10, 185x, v, u/u certificate, grey. .$10.00

> ### It is generally assumed that only 5% of certificates survive to reach collectors.

Little Miami Railroad Company (OH par $50)

*LI870-20-10, 1870, v, 38 sh., grey $11.00

*LI870-25-10, 1870 $40 Stock Scrip (par $50),
 revenue stamp. $11.00

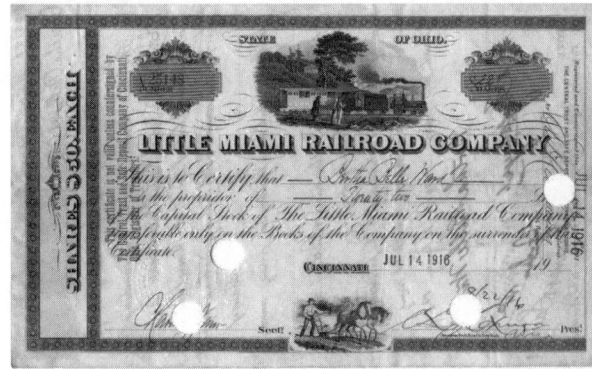

*LI870-35-10, 1916, v, 22 sh., revenue stamps on
 the back side, ABN, 9-1/4" x 5-3/4", grey
 . . . .$8.00
LI870-45-10, 1940, v, 10 sh., grey. $5.00
LI870-50-10, 1948, v, 8 sh., grey. $4.00
LI870-60-10, 1960, v, 100 sh., grey. $4.00

Little Pittsburg Consolidated Mining Company
LI910-20-10, 1880, v, 50 sh., brown, signed by Jerome Chaffee **$350.00**

Local Loan & Finance Co.
LO210-20-10, 19xx, u/u certificate, blue **$4.00**

Loew's Boston Theatres Co.

LO310-20-10, 1928, v, 100 sh. (par $25), brown
. . . .**$18.00**

The Loma Vista Petroleum Company (CA par $1)
LO410-10-10, 1900, v, 100 sh., U.S. revenue stamps, grey border. **$16.00**

The Lomax Company (ME)

LO440-20-10, 1917, v, 4 sh., 12-1/4" x 8-3/4", orange **$4.00**

Lomax Investment Company (DE)

LO460-20-10, 1915, v, 2 sh., U.S. revenue stamp, grey. **$8.00**

London Mining Company (NY)
LO520-20-10, 1882, $500 bond, brown. . . .**$32.00**

Lone Pine Surprise Consolidated Mining Co. (par $1)
LO550-20-10, 1xxx, v, u/u certificate, brown
. . . .**$9.00**

Lone Star Cement Corporation
LO580-30-10, 1978, v, $3,000 5-1/2% conv. subord. debenture due 1993, orange **$6.00**

The Long Horn Oil Company (CO par 1¢)

LO620-20-10, 1920, v, 100 sh., orange . . .**$22.00**

Long Island Lighting Company

*LO650-30-10, 1953, v, $1,000 1st mort. 3-1/2%
bond due 1989, orange $8.00

Longfellow Water Supply Company
(PA par $100)
LO690-20-10, 1905, v, 50 sh., brown. $11.00

City of Los Angeles

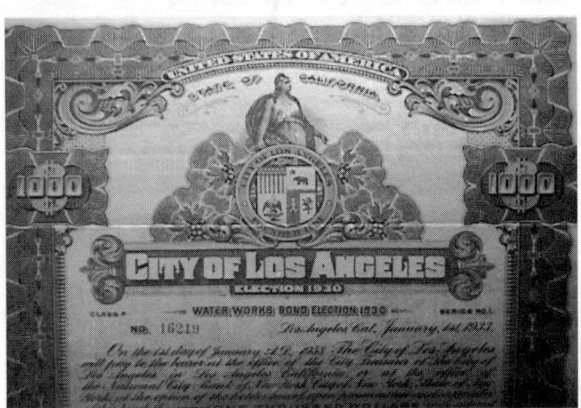

*LO710-30-10, 1929, v, $1,000 Class F Water
Works bond Election 1930, purple $8.00

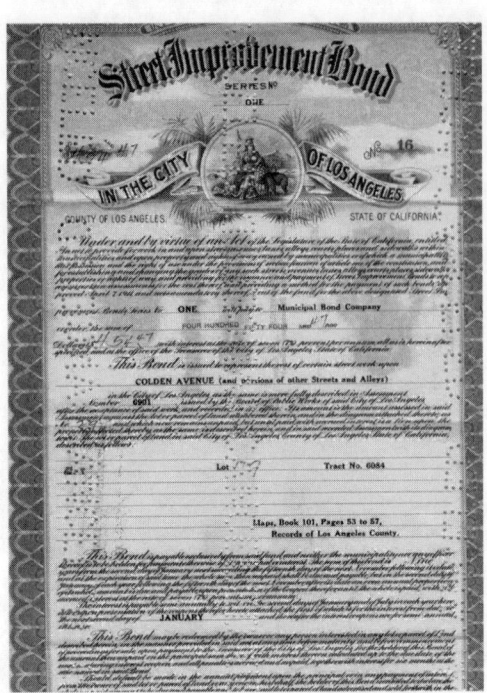

*LO710-40-10, 1930, v, $454.47 Street Improve-
ment bond w. coupons, Colden Avenue, Neuner
Corporation Litho. Los Angeles; 9-1/2" x
15-1/2", orange. $6.00

*LO710-50-10, 1950, v, $30 Street Improvement
Bond, Denny Avenue, w. coupons, Jeffries Banknote Co., 9-1/4" x 16-1/4", yellow $4.00

UNLISTED TYPES & VARIETIES
Readers are welcome to contact the author
directly at:

Rainer Stahlberg
P.O. Box 1044
Rooseveltown, New York 13683

Los Angeles Metropolitan Airport (CA)

LO740-20-10, 19xx, v, u/u certificate, orange
. . . .$25.00

State of Louisiana

LO830-20-10, 1874, v - child $5 bond, payable
7-1/2¢ every six months $20.00
LO830-30-10, 1892, v, $500 new consol. bond,
orange $20.00

The Louisiana Land and Exploration Company

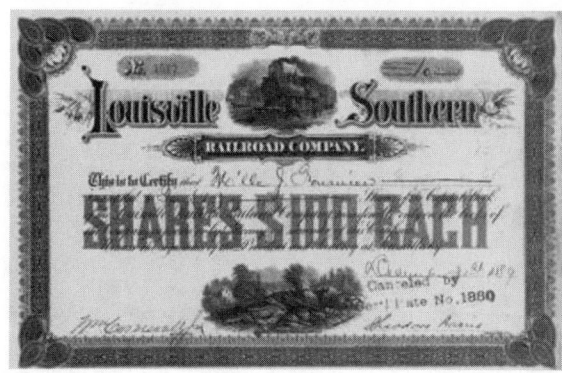

LO870-20-10, 1967, v, 100 sh., blue $10.00

Louisiana and Missouri River Railroad Company

LO900-20-10, 1871, v, 15 sh., pref., red . . .$60.00

Louisville Bridge Company (KY par $100)

LO950-20-10, 1895, v, 12 sh., grey $10.00

Louisville and Nashville Railroad Company (KY par $50)

LO990-20-10, 19xx, t, less than 100 sh., specimen
certificate, green $8.00

Louisville Railway Company (KY par $100)

LO1020-20-10, 1895, v - trolley, 10 sh., orange
. . . .$8.00

*LO1020-25-10, 18xx, v, u/u certificate., brown
. . . .$8.00

Louisville Southern Railroad Co. (KY par $100)

*LO1050-20-10, 1889, v, 10 sh., ABN, brown
. . . .$35.00
LO1050-30-10, 1890, v, 100 sh., brown . . .$50.00
LO1050-35-10, 18xx, v, u/u certificate, grey
. . . .$30.00

Lovle Products, Inc. (FL 1962, par 1¢)

*LO1120-20-10, 1970, v, 100 sh., SCB, 12" x 8",
blue. $4.00

L & S Electronics Inc. (NY 1962, par 10¢)

*LS100-20-10, 1969, v, 100 sh., GOES, 12" x 8", green $4.00

The L-T Building Company

*LT60-20-10, 1925, v, 1 sh., brown $3.00

Lucky Discovery Gold Inc. (CO par 1¢)
LU160-20-10, 1933, v, 1,000 sh., green $15.00

The value of a stock certificate depends on:

- rarity
- the issuer
- signatures
- quality of engraving
- overall appearance
- condition
- date of issue

Lumber Products, Inc. (CO par $1)

*LU270-20-10, 19xx, v, u/c with pin hole SAM-PLE, GOES, 11" x 8-1/2", grey on gold . .$3.00

Lundelius & Eccleston Motors Corporation (DE par $10)
LU310-20-10, 1926, v, 300 sh., grey $64.00

Lusk Moorcroft Oil Company (WY par $1)
LU410-20-10, 19xx, v, unissued certificate, brown $4.00

Lycoming Coal Company (PA 1878, par $50)

*LY80-20-10, 18xx, v, u/u certificate, grey . $12.00

The Lyght Mining Company (WI par $1)

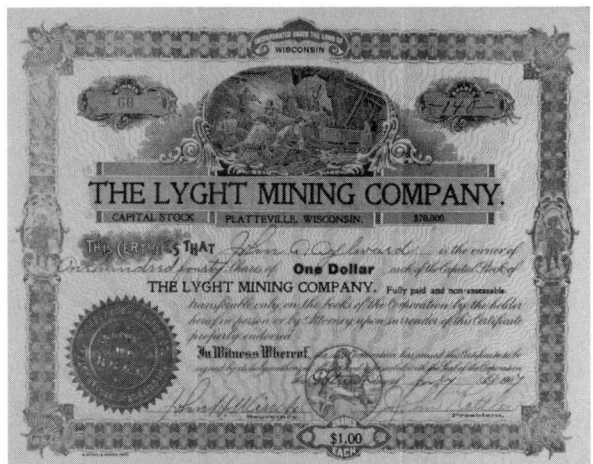

*LY120-20-10, 1907, v, 140 sh., 11-1/2" x 8-1/2", brown border. $60.00

Lynnhaven Oyster Company, Incorporated (VA par $100)

LY180-20-10, 191x, unissued certificate, orange
. . . .$8.00

UNLISTED TYPES & VARIETIES

Readers are welcome to contact the author directly at:

Rainer Stahlberg
P.O. Box 1044
Rooseveltown, New York 13683

Lyons Petroleum Company (DE par $1)

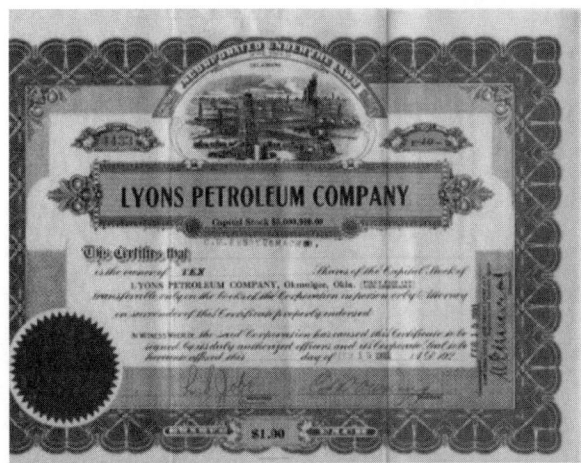

*LY210-20-10, 1921, v, 10 sh., green $15.00

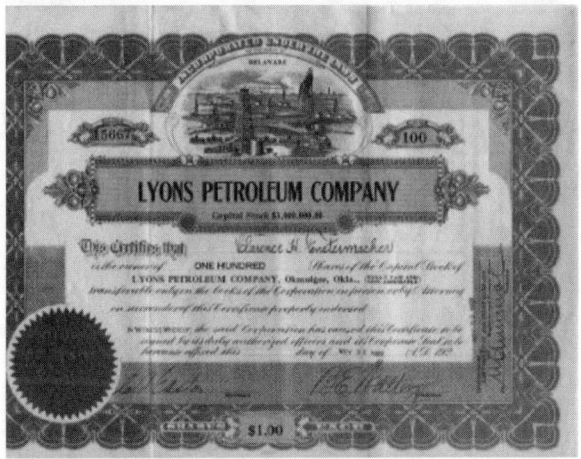

*LY210-25-10, 1922, v, 100 sh., brown. . . .$20.00

M

Maddox Coffee Company, Atlanta, Georgia (par $100)

MA120-20-10, 19xx, v, u/u certificate, brown
. . . .$9.00

Madison Square Garden Corporation

MA190-20-10, 1973, v, 5 (new) sh., on a less than 100 sh., certificate, brown. $11.00

Maggie Creek Mining Company, Ltd.
MA240-20-10, 1956, v, u/u certificate, grey. .$6.00

The Maginnis Mining Company (MT par $5)
MA300-20-10, 18xx, u/u certificate, grey border on green $5.00

Magma Copper Company (ME 1910, no par)

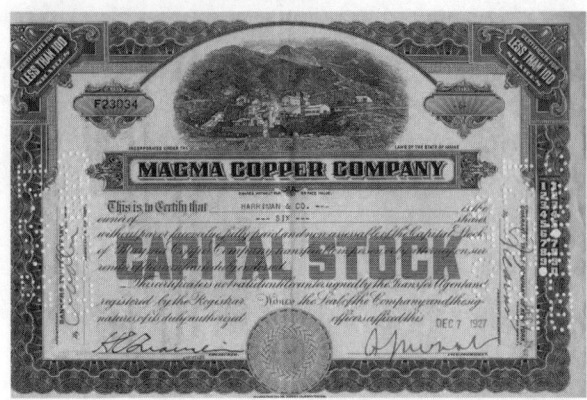

MA370-20-10, 1927, v, 6 sh., on a less than100 sh., certificate, HBN, 12" x 8", blue. $4.00

MA370-30-10, 1936, v, 5 sh., on a less than 100 sh., certificate, brown. $4.00

MA370-30-15, 1961, v, 1 sh., on a less than 100 sh., certificate, signature variety, brown . .$4.00

*MA370-40-10, 1951, v, 100 sh., green **$4.00**

I. Magnin & Co. (DE no par)
California Fashion house.

*MA410-20-10, 19xx, v, u/u less than 100 sh., certificate, brown **$5.00**

*MA410-30-10, 19xx, v, u/u 100 sh., certificate, blue **$7.00**
MA410-35-10, 1941, v, 100 sh., blue **$6.00**

MA410-45-10, 1930, v, 10 sh., pref. on a less than 100 sh., certificate, green **$6.00**
MA410-50-10, 1928, v, 100 sh., pref., orange
. . . .**$6.00**

Magnolia Cemetery (SC)

*MA460-10-10, 18xx, u/u certificate, grey . .**$8.00**

Magnum Communications Corp. (DE)
MA480-20-10, 1970, v, 100 sh., blue border
. . . .**$3.00**

Mahala Oil and Gas Co. (par $1)

*MA510-20-10, 1920, v, 100 sh., orange **$4.00**

It is generally assumed that only 5% of certificates survive to reach collectors.

The Mahoning Coal Railroad Company
(OH par $50)

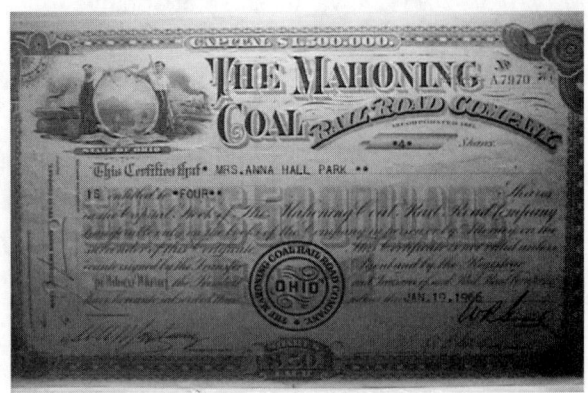

MA570-20-10, 1966, v, 4 sh., brown **$8.00**

MA570-20-15, 1972, v, 10 sh., signature strip, brown **$8.00**

Maine Central Railroad Company
(ME 1862, par $100)

MA640-20-10, 1912, v, 10 sh., green **$18.00**

MA640-25-10, 19xx, v, u/u certificate for less than 100 sh., olive green **$12.00**

MA640-35-10, 19xx, v, u/u 100 sh., certificate, brown **$15.00**

MA640-40-10, 1925, v, 100 sh., ABN, brown **$18.00**

UNLISTED TYPES & VARIETIES

Readers are welcome to contact the author directly at:

Rainer Stahlberg
P.O. Box 1044
Rooseveltown, New York 13683

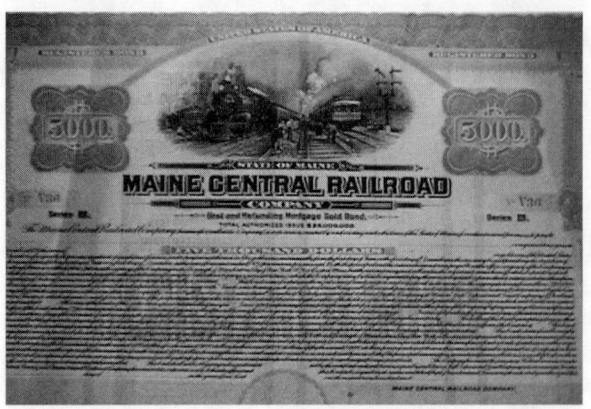

MA640-45-10, 19xx, v, $5,000 u/u 6% bond, orange **$12.00**

MA640-50-10, 19xx, v, u/u 7% bond, green **$15.00**

MA640-60-10, 1955, v, u/u $500 5% 1st mortgage and collateral bond, due 1980, ABN, green **$9.00**

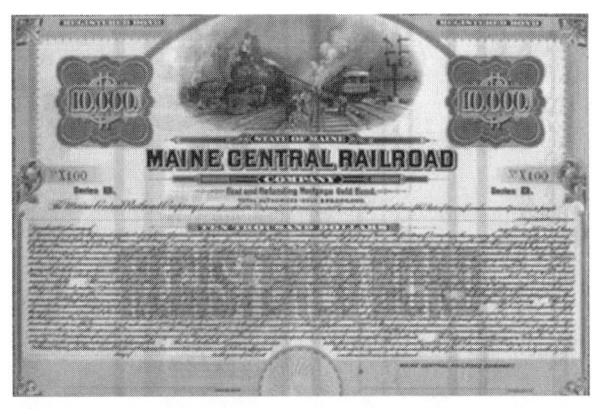

*MA640-70-10, 19xx, v, $10,000 printer's
specimen bond, ABN, brown $9.00

Majestic Mining Company (ME par $10)
MA700-20-10, 1904, v, 2 sh., brown $11.00

**The Malapai Mining Company
(AZ territory par $1)**
MA810-20-10, 1911, v, 500 sh., grey $22.00

**Manhattan Giant Mining Company
(SD par $1)**
MA930-20-10, 190x, u/u certificate, grey. . . .$7.00

**Manhattan Isabella Mining Company
(NV par $1)**
MA960-20-10, 19xx, v, u/u certificate, grey
. . . .$7.00

**Manhattan-Main Gold Mining Company
(AZ par $1)**

*MA990-20-10, 1906, v, 1,000 sh., 10" x 8-1/2",
brown $26.00

**The Manufactured Rubber Company
(par $10)**
MA1050-20-10, 19xx, v, unissued certificate, green
. . . .$10.00

Manufacturers Fuel Company
MA1080-20-10, 1904, v, 10 sh., green. $6.00

**Maracaibo Oil Exploration Corporation
(DE)**

*MA1140-20-10, 1952, v, 100 sh., blue. . . .$13.00

**Marathon Auto Products Corporation
(NY par $100)**

*MA1180-20-10, 1922, v, 5 sh., grey. $26.00

March Gold, Inc. (DE par $1)

*MA1210-20-10, 1927, v, 25 sh., GOES, 10-3/4" x 8-1/2", grey border $8.00

Marco Communications Corporations (AZ no par)

*MA1250-20-10, 19xx, v, u/u certificate, w/o imprint, 11" x 7-1/2", green border. $3.00

Marconi Wireless Telegraph Company of America

MA1280-20-10, 1913, v, 25 sh., on a less than 100 sh., certificate, blue. $25.00

MA1280-25-10, 1920, v, 50 sh, brown $17.00

Maricopa Mica Mining Company (IL par $10)

*MA1360-20-10, 189x, v, u/u certificate, grey
. . . .$11.00

Marietta & Cincinnati Rail Road Company (par $50)

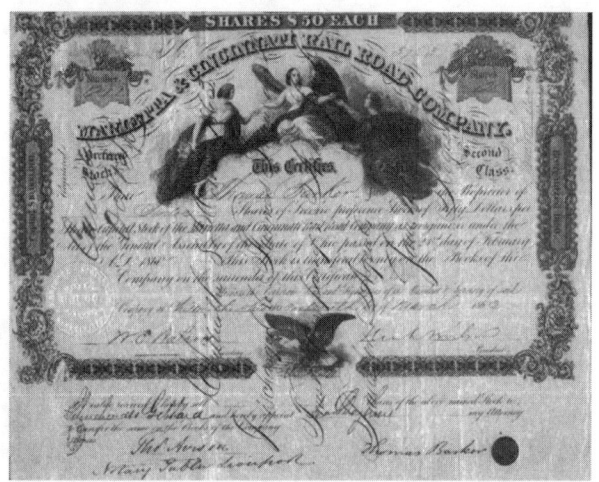

*MA1390-20-10, 1863, v, 12 2nd class pref. sh., black $25.00

Market Street Railway Company (CA)

MA1510-20-10, 19xx, v, u/c prior preference sh., certificate, RBN, green. $8.00

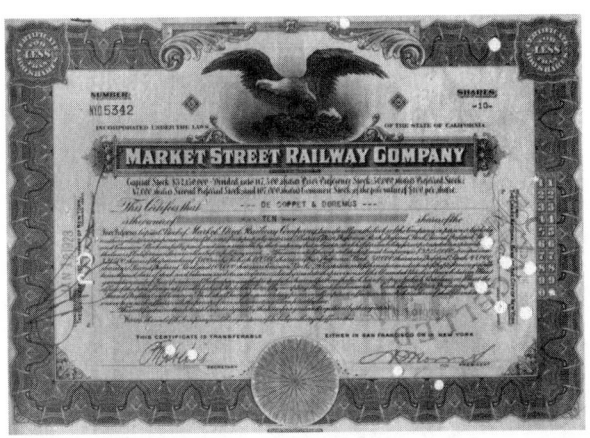

*MA1510-25-10, 1928, v, 10 prior preference sh.,
on a less than 100 sh., certificate, green . . . **$8.00**

The Marmaton Gold Mining, Milling and Investment Company (par $1)

Mines at Cripple Creek.
*MA1580-20-10, 1905, v, 4,000 sh., orange
. . . . **$45.00**

Marquette and Adams County Telephone Co. (WI par $20)

*MA1620-20-10, 1905, v, 1 sh., 11" x 8", brown
border **$35.00**

*MA1620-2015, 1945, v, 1 sh., signature variety,
GOES, 11" x 8", brown border. **$28.00**

Marsh Mines Consolidated (WA par 25¢)

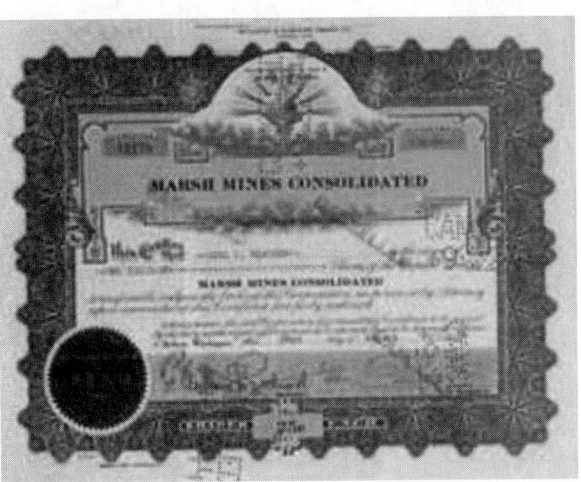

*MA1710-20-10, 1938, v, 1,000 sh., blue . . . **$7.00**

Marshall Field & Company (DE)

Large department store chain.
*MA1740-20-10, 1974, v, 10 sh., on a less than 100
sh., certificate, ABN, red **$10.00**

This catalog has listings in an alphabetical format. The reason is simple: Companies diversify as they grow. For example, the Canadian Pacific Railway company recently split into five companies. They represent the railway, hotels, shipping, airline, and petroleum interests of the company. During World War II, the Singer sewing machine company made guns and other defense-related equipment, so where should we list it? It's far easier to use a strict alphabetical order, rather than to confuse the reader with topical classifications.

Chester A. Martin, Inc. (OK par $1)

MA1770-20-10, 1944, v, 3 sh., w/o imprint,
10-1/4" x 8", purple $4.00

Martinez Bay Point Stage Company (CA)

MA1810-20-10, 19xx, u/u certificate, brown
...................................$9.00

Marvin Holding Corp. (no par)
MA1850-20-10, 19xx, v, unissued certificate, green
...................................$4.00

Maryland Trust Company (par $100)

MA1900-20-10, 1901, v, 1 sh., ABN, brown
...................................$18.00

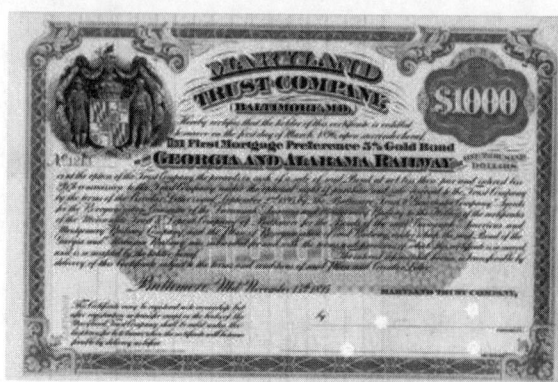

MA1900-30-10, 1895, v, u/c $1,000 1st mortgage
5% preference bond of the Georgia and Alabama
Railway Company, light brown $18.00

The Mason Tire and Rubber Company (OH no par)

MA2000-20-10, 1920, 7 series B shares, orange
...................................$11.00

Massachusetts Investors Trust

MA2080-20-10, 1949, 10 sh., of beneficial interest on a less than 100 sh., certificate, green
...................................$11.00

Massachusetts and New Mexico Mining Company (par $25)

MA2110-20-10, 1879, v, 25 sh., brown . . .**$13.00**

Massachusetts-New Mexico Consolidated Mining Company (ME par $100)

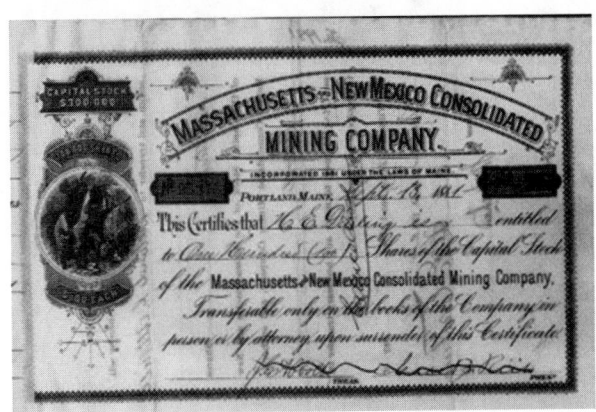

MA2120-20-10, 1881, v, 100 sh., black **$9.00**

Matheson Beet Harvester Corporation (WY par $10)

MA2200-20-10, 19xx, v, u/u certificate, brown
. . . .**$8.00**

The Mathieson Alkali Works

MA2230-20-10, 1929, v, 100 sh., green **$5.00**

The May Department Stores Company (NY)

MA2310-20-10, 1929, v, 3 sh. (par $25), ABN,
green **$10.00**
MA2310-30-10, 1949, v, 1 sh., on a less than 100
sh. certificate, red **$4.00**

Mayflower Hotel Company (DE)

MA2340-20-10, 1928, v, 5 pref. sh. (par $100),
green **$10.00**

Mayflower Investors, Inc. (DE)

MA2370-20-10, 1971, v, 100 sh., blue **$5.00**
MA2370-20-15, 1973, v, 500 sh., blue, signature
variety **$5.00**

The Maysville & Lexington Rail Road Co. (Northern Division) (KY par $50)

MA2410-20-10, 1872, v, 1 sh., grey **$66.00**

McCormick Oil & Gas Partnership

MC100-20-10, 1988, v, $300, blue **$8.00**

McDonald's Corporation (no par)

MC130-20-10, 1968, v, 100 sh., orange, stained
. . . .**$35.00**

McKee Door Corporation

*MC180-20-10, 1930, v, 500 sh., orange $3.00

*MC180-25-10, 1957, v, 200 sh., green $3.00

*MC180-35-10, 1952, v, 500 pref. sh., w. revenue stamps, orange $3.00

McKee Illinois Door Sales, Inc. (IL no par)

*MC210-10-10, 1966, v, 5 sh., brown $3.00

McKesson & Robbins Incorporated (MD par $9)

*MC240-20-10, 1963, v, 50 sh., on a less than 100 sh., certificate, blue $4.00

McKinley Gold Mining Company, Ltd. (ID par $1)
MC270-20-10, 1931?, v, 4,335 sh., grey $6.00

McLouth Steel Corporation (MI par $2)
MC300-20-10, 19xx, v, 1,000 sh., green $6.00

UNLISTED TYPES & VARIETIES
Readers are welcome to contact the author directly at:

Rainer Stahlberg
P.O. Box 1044
Rooseveltown, New York 13683

The Meadow Brook National Bank (NY)

ME100-20-10, 1957, v, 1 sh., blue **$4.00**
ME100-30-10, 1962, v, 100 sh., red **$7.00**

Mecca Tire Company (DE par $1)
ME160-20-10, 1915, 200 sh., green **$48.00**

Mechanics Bank (NJ)
ME190-20-10, 1884, v, 20 sh., grey **$20.00**

Mechanics National Bank of Burlington (NJ)

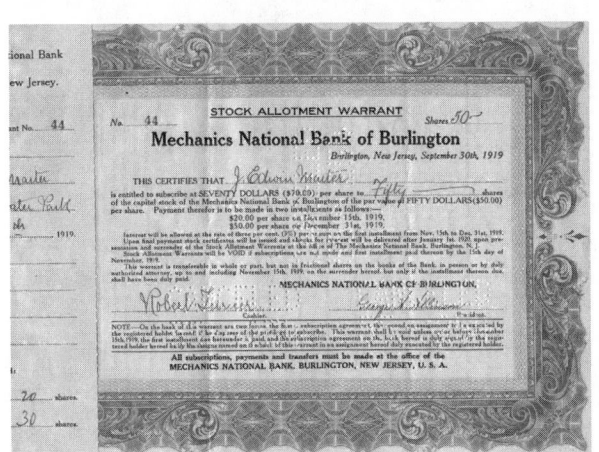

ME220-20-10, 1919, w, 50 sh., at $70, 10-3/4" x
8-1/4", brown **$3.00**

Medcom Inc. (MA 1966, par 10¢)
ME320-20-10, 1975, v, 17 sh., olive **$4.00**

ME320-30-10, 1972, v, 100 sh., ABN, 12" x 8",
green **$4.00**

Medcom Inc. (DE)
ME325-20-10, 1972, v, 100 sh., blue **$4.00**

Medical Communications, Inc.
(MA 1966, par 10¢)

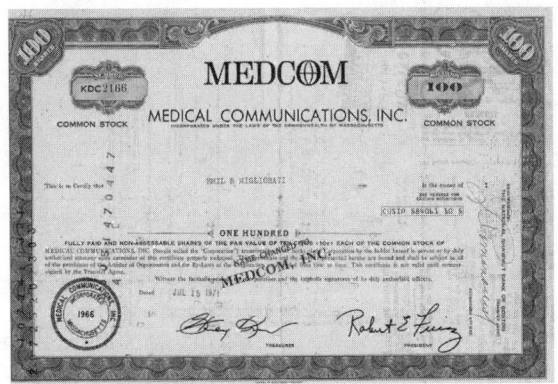

ME370-20-10, 1971, v, 100 sh., o/p name
changed to Medcom Inc., ABN, 12" x 8", green
. . . .**$4.00**

*It is generally assumed that
only 5% of certificates survive
to reach collectors.*

MEI Corporation (DE)

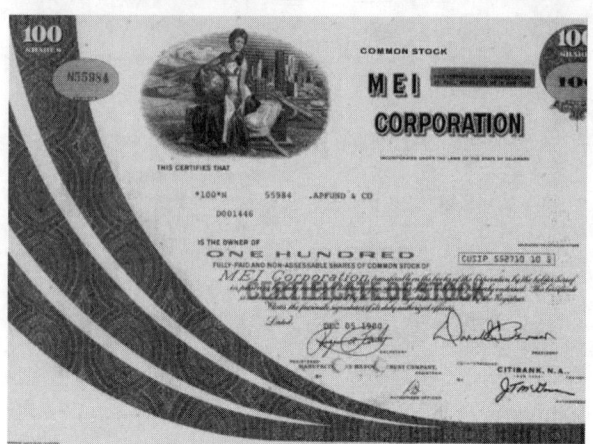

ME430-20-10, 1980, v, 100 sh., green **$4.00**

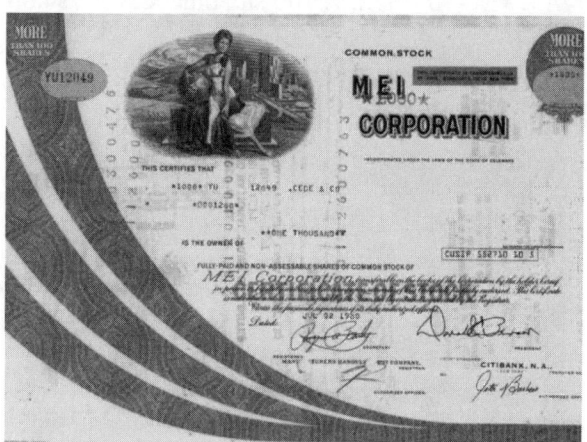

ME430-30-10, 1980, v, 1,000 sh., on a more than 100 sh., certificate, red **$4.00**

Menasco Manufacturing Company (CA par $100)

ME530-20-10, 1971, v, 1 sh., on a less than 100 sh., certificate, green **$6.00**

ME530-30-10, 1971, v, 3,000 sh., blue border **$10.00**

The value of a stock certificate depends on:
- rarity
- the issuer
- signatures
- quality of engraving
- overall appearance
- condition
- date of issue

Menominee Motor Truck Company (WI par $100)

ME560-20-10, 1929, v, 4 sh., GOES, 11" x 8-1/2", brown border. **$25.00**

Merchants Insurance Company (RI par $50)

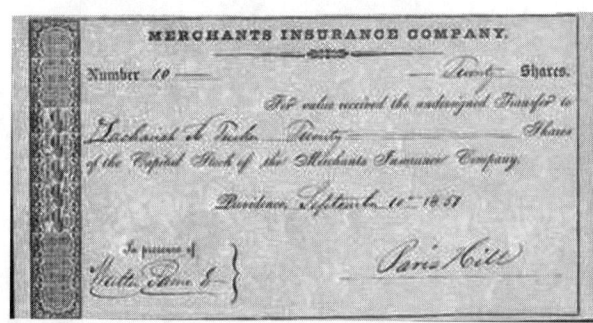

ME700-10-10, 1857, 20 sh., black on blue paper **$8.00**

1863, 1 share certificate, 8" x 4", black on blue paper **$10.00**

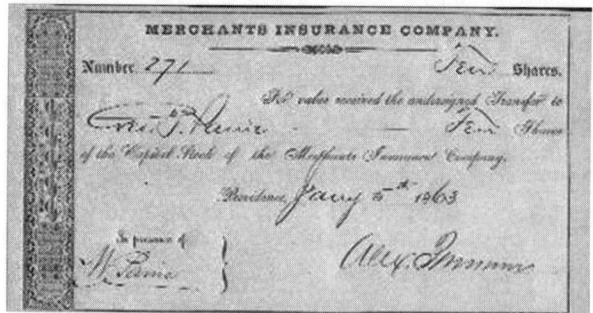

ME700-10-15, 1863, 10 sh., signature variety, black on blue **$8.00**

Merchants and Miners Transportation Company (MD par $100)

ME740-20-10, 1918, 3 sh., orange $6.00

The Merchants National Bank (IL par $100)

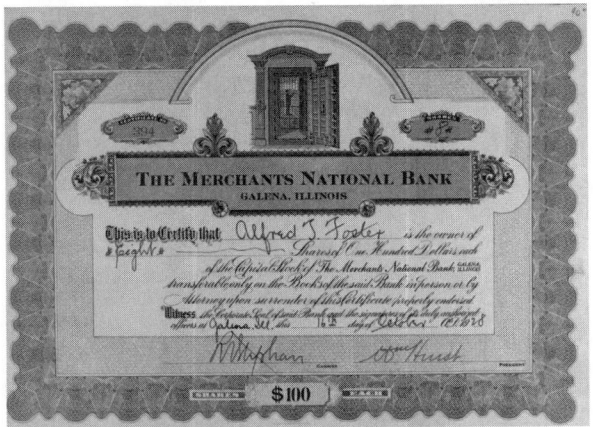

ME750-20-10, 1928, v, 8 sh., 11-1/2" x 8", orange border $40.00

Merchants Warehouse Company (MA par $100)

ME770-20-10, 1937, 21 sh., grey $5.00

Mergenthaler-Horton Basket Machine Company (ME par $1)

ME810-20-10, 1905, v, 100 sh., red-brown border $40.00

Merida-Yucatan Water Company (NJ)

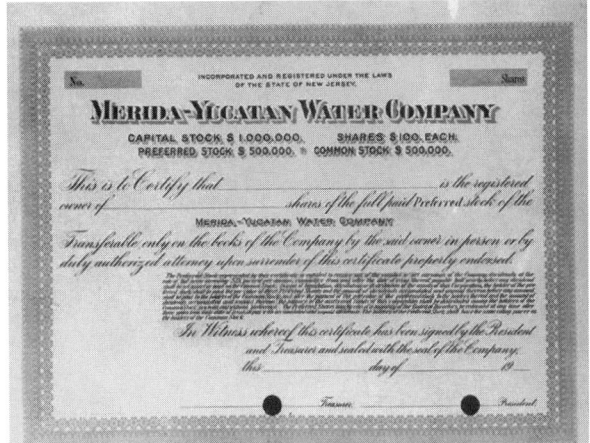

ME840-20-10, 19xx, u/c 6% pref. stock certificate $7.00

Meridian Co. (SD par $100)

Around 1925 a group of Yankton, SD businessmen formed the company to build a bridge across the Missouri River.

ME870-20-10, 19xx, v, u/u certificate, grey $21.00

Merrill Lynch, Pierce, Penner & Smith Incorporated (DE)

ME920-20-10, 1973, v, 100 sh., par $133-1/3), o/p name changed to Merrill Lynch & Co., Inc., 12" x 8", green $25.00
ME920-25-10, 1971, v, 1,000 sh., red $46.00

Messenger Mining Company (WA par $1)
ME970-20-10, 19xx, u/u certificate, grey. . . .$5.00

Metal Extraction and Refining Company (WI par $1)

ME990-20-10, 1911 March, v, 100 sh., 10" x 8", brown border. $25.00

ME990-25-10, 1911 June, v, 100 sh., 10-1/2" x 8-1/2", w/o imprint, grey border $40.00

Methow Mining and Smelting Co. (WA par $1)
ME1010-20-10, 1926, v, 200 sh., multicolored
. . . .$15.00

The Mexican Plantation Company of Wisconsin (WI par $100)

ME1080-30-10, 1903, v, 1 pref. sh., McGill-Warner Co., St. Paul, Minn.; 10" x 8", l. brown border $45.00

The Mexican Telephone Company (NY par $10)

*ME1100-20-10, 1899, 25 sh., black $3.00

Mexico Consolidated Mining & Smelting Company (par $10)

ME1160-20-10, 19xx, v, u/u certificate, brown
. . . .$6.00

Miami Consolidated Mines Company (AZ par $1)

MI100-20-10, 1906, v, 100 sh., 10-3/4" x 8-1/2",
green $13.00

Michigan Air Line Railroad Company (MI-IN par $50)

MI200-20-10, 18xx, v, u/u certificate, brown
. . . .$12.00

This catalog has listings in an alphabetical format. The reason is simple: Companies diversify as they grow. For example, the Canadian Pacific Railway company recently split into five companies. They represent the railway, hotels, shipping, airline, and petroleum interests of the company. During World War II, the Singer sewing machine company made guns and other defense-related equipment, so where should we list it? It's far easier to use a strict alphabetical order, rather than to confuse the reader with topical classifications.

Michigan Central Railroad Company (MI)

Chartered in 1846.

*MI270-40-10, 1901, v, $1,000 1st mortgage gold bond secured by the assets of Jackson, Lansing & Saginaw RR, ABN, green $15.00
MI270-45-10, 1902, v, $1,000 3-1/2% gold first mort. on the main line of road, ABN, green
. . . .$15.00

*MI270-50-10, 1912, v, $1,000 3-1/2% gold bond, blue-green. $15.00

*MI270-55-10, 1934, v, $1,000 4% registered
bond, ABN, green....................**$15.00**

*MI270-60-10, 1935, v, $5,000 4% registered
bond, brown **$15.00**

Michigan Sugar Company (MI)

MI370-20-10, 19xx, v, u/u 100 sh., pref. (par $4)
certificate, red.....................**$16.00**

Michigan Wisconsin Pipe Line Company (DE)

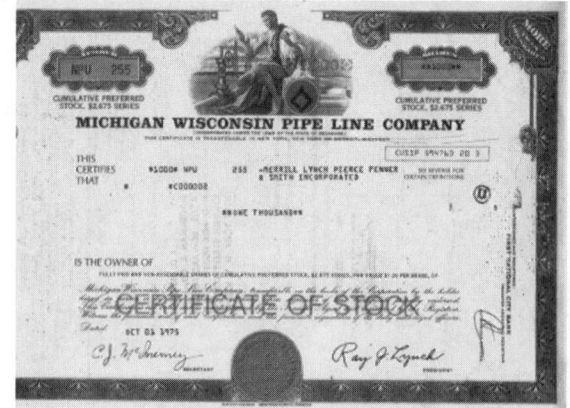

*MI420-30-10, 1975, v, $1,000 $2.475 cumul.
pref. sh., on a more than 100 sh., certificate,
green **$10.00**

*MI420-50-10, 1963, v, $1,000 1st mortgage
4-7/8% 20-year bond, due 1983, brown..**$12.00**

Micro Copper Corporation (DE)

*MI480-20-10, 1958, v, 1,000 sh., green....**$5.00**

Microdot Inc. (CA 1950, no par)

*MI510-20-10, 1960, v, 100 sh., Jeffries Banknote
Company, 12" x 8", green **$3.00**

Mid-Eastern Electronics, Inc. (NJ 1957)

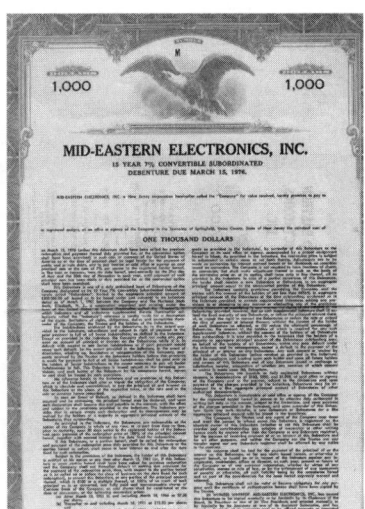

MI580-30-10, 19xx, v, u/c $1,000 15-year 7% conver. subord. debenture due 1976, CBN, 10" x 15-1/4", orange **$4.00**

Middlecreek Valley Prospecting Co. (PA par $100)

MI1610-29-10, 1951, v, 1 sh., 11" x 8-1/2", green border **$4.00**

Middlesex Electric Light Company (ME par $10)

MI630-20-10, 1883, 5 sh., grey border **$9.00**

Middlesex and Somerset Traction Company (NJ par $100)

MI660-20-10, 19xx, v, u/u certificate, brown **$10.00**

The Middletown Street Railway Company (par $25)

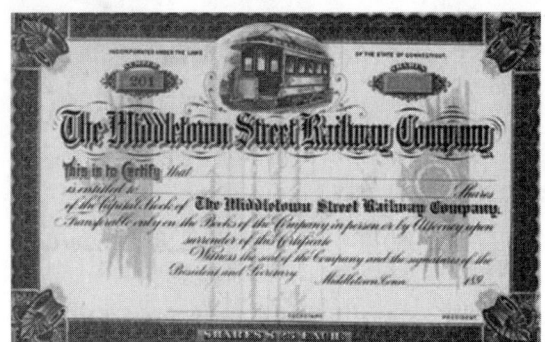

MI700-20-10, 189x, v, u/u certificate, grey **$11.00**

Midland Oil Company (par $1)

MI740-20-10, 1906, v, 100 sh., brown **$5.00**

Mike Henry Consolidated, Inc. (par $5)

MI860-20-10, 1920, v, 100 sh., green **$12.00**

Mildred Lloyd-Star Gold Mines Consolidated (NV 1929, par 10¢)

MI960-20-10, 19xx, v, u/u certificate, grey **$7.00**

Milgo Electronic Corporation (FL 1955, par $1)

MI1010-20-10, 1976, v, 26 sh., on a less than 100 sh., certificate, Federated Banknote Co., 12" x 8", green **$4.00**

Mill Creek Coal and Coke Company (WV par $100)

MI1050-20-10, 1905, v, 1,588 sh., greenish **$35.00**

The value of a stock certificate depends on:

- **rarity**
- **the issuer**
- **signatures**
- **quality of engraving**
- **overall appearance**
- **condition**
- **date of issue**

Mill Creek and Mine Hill Navigation and Railroad (par $25)

PA Narrow gauge railroad.

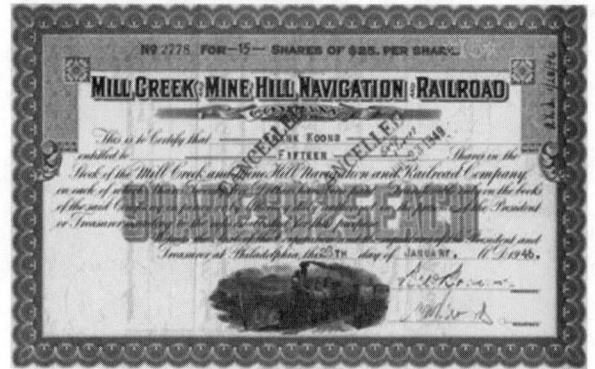

MI1080-20-10, 1946, v, 15 sh., green **$16.00**

Miller Mining Company (SD par $1)

MI1120-20-10, 1926, v, 25 sh., green **$20.00**

Morris Miller (WI)

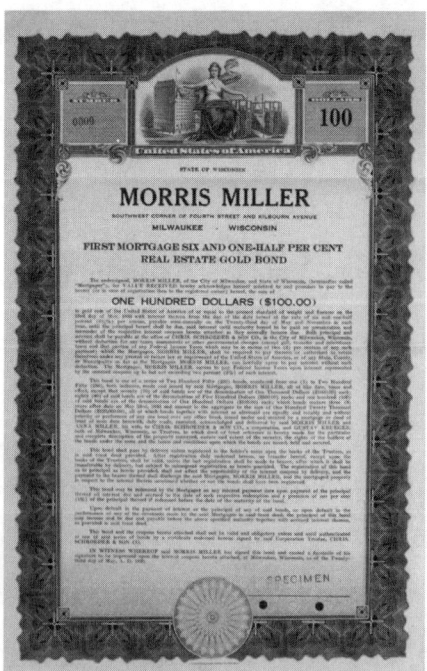

MI1140-30-10, 1930, v, specimen $100 6-1/2% 1st mortgage on southwest corner of Fourth Street and Kilbourn Ave, Milwaukee, 9" x 11", blue border **$7.00**

The Millerstown Iron Company (PA par $30)

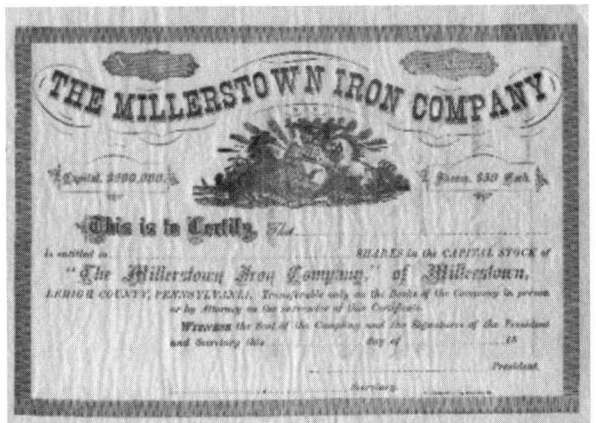

*MI1170-20-10, 18xx, v, u/u certificate, grey
.................................$9.00

Millville Creamery Company

MI1220-20-10, 1913, v, 4 sh., brown......$6.00

Milwaukee Advertising and Novelty Company (WI no par)

*MI1280-20-10, 1928, 10 sh., 11" x 8", green border............................$8.00

It is generally assumed that only 5% of certificates survive to reach collectors.

Milwaukee Lake Shore and Western Rail Road Company (WI $100)

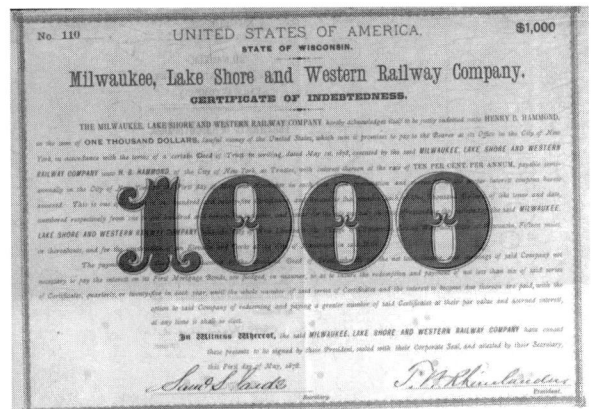

*MI1340-20-10, 18xx, v, u/u certificate, 10-1/2" x 7", brown border....................$25.00

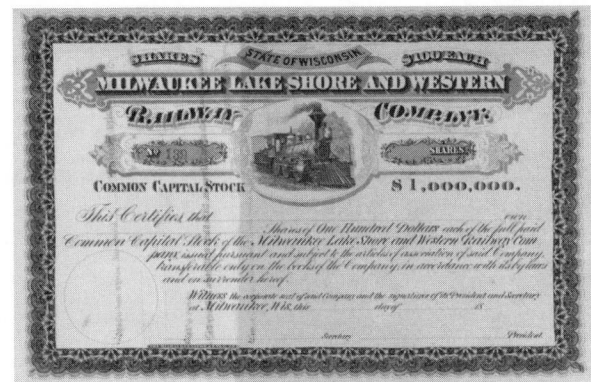

*MI1340-25-10, 18xx, v, u/u certificate, capital $1,000,000, 10-1/2" x 7", brown border..$25.00

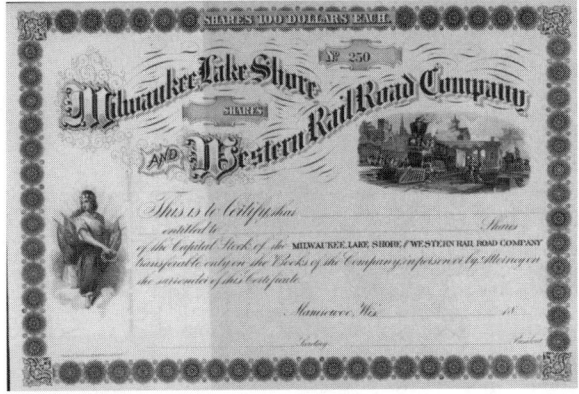

*MI1340-45-10,1878, $1,000 10% certificate of indebtness, 11" x 9", red border.......$150.00

Milwaukee Mining Co. (ID terr., par $1)
Property situated on Canyon Creek, Shoshone Co., Idaho.

MI1380-20-10, 18xx, v, u/u certificate, 11-1/2" x 7-1/2", brown border. $18.00

Milwaukee Mining & Milling Co. (NM)
MI1390-20-10, 1xxx, v, u/u certificate, grey
. . . .$6.00

Milwaukee and Minnesota Rail Road Company (par $100)

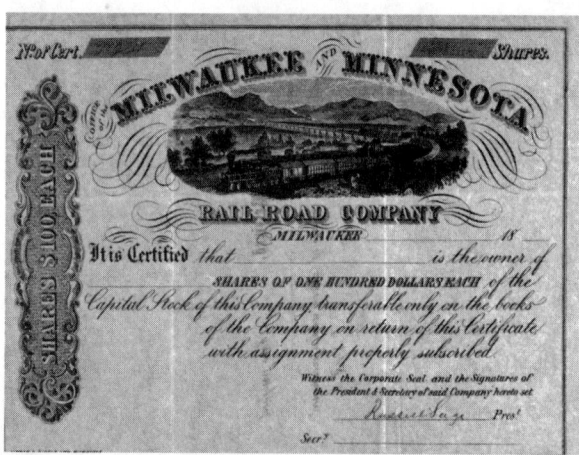

MI1410-20-10, 18xx, v, u/u certificate, Lipman & Riddle Lith. Milwaukee, 9" x 6-1/2", brown border $25.00

Milwaukee and Mississippi Rail Road Company (par $100)

MI1430-8-10, 1856, v, 78 sh., 9-1/2" x 5-1/2", brown border $40.00

MI1430-10-10, 1858, v, 50 sh., 10" x 8", grey border $35.00

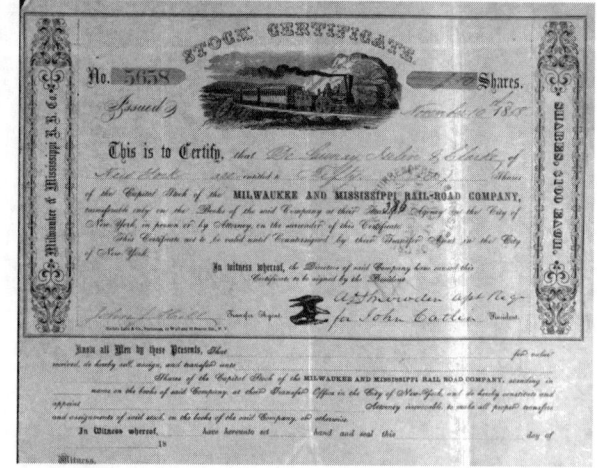

MI1430-15-10, 1861, v, 5 sh., 11" x 6", brown border $35.00

Milwaukee Mutual Mining Company (WI par $1)

MI1470-20-10, 1905, v, 300 sh., James G. Brazell Printer, Milwaukee; 11" x 8", grey border
......................................$20.00

Milwaukee and Northwestern Railway Co. (WI par $100)

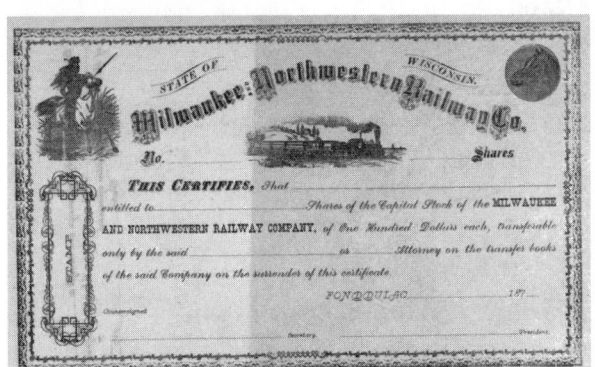

MI1500-20-10, 1872, v, 5 sh., 11" x 6-1/2", brown border......................$75.00

MI1500-21-10, 187x, v, u/u certificate, 11-1/2" x 7", brown border....................$75.00

Milwaukee and Prairie du Chien Railway Company (par $100)

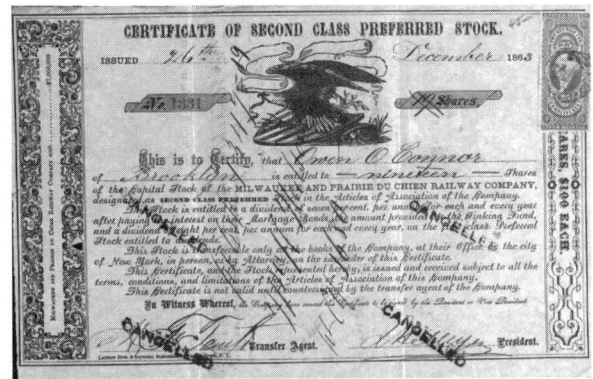

MI1570-20-10, 1865, v, 100 sh., revenue stamp, C.O. Jones Stationer, N.Y.; 10" x 6", light brown
..............................$30.00

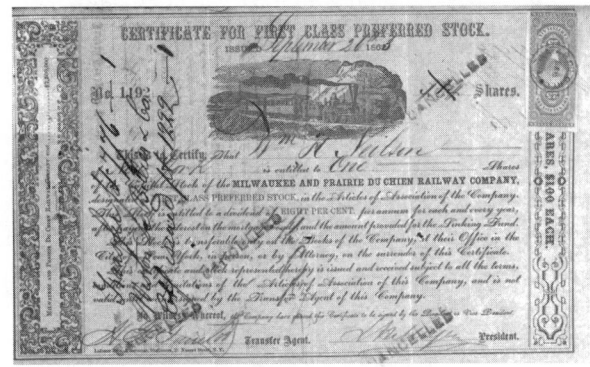

MI1570-30-10, 1863, v, 1 sh., 8% first class pref. stock, revenue stamp, Latimer Bros & Seymour, Stationers, N.Y.; 10" x 6", orange border
..............................$30.00

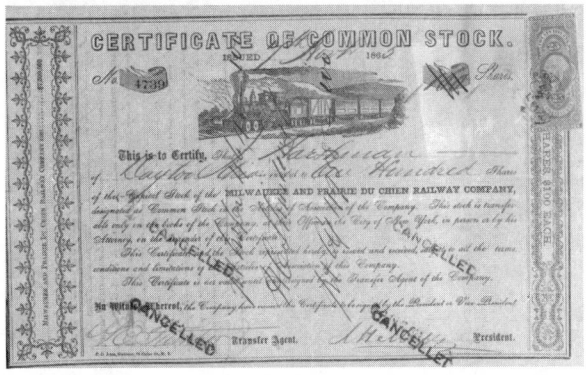

MI1570-35-10, 1863, v, 19 sh., 7% second class pref. stock, revenue stamp, Latimer Bros. & Seymour, Stationers, N.Y.; 9-1/2" x 6", grey border..........................$35.00

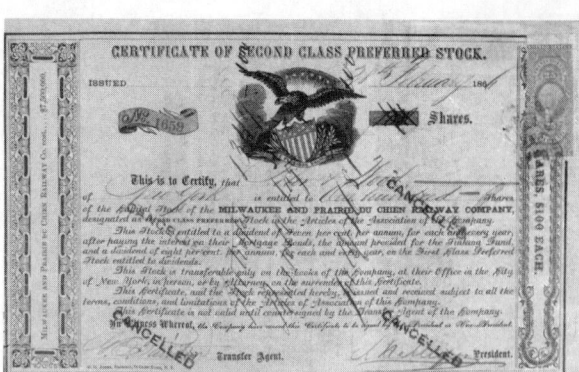

*MI1570-36-10, 1866, v, 100 sh., 7% second class
   pref. stock, revenue stamp, C.O. Jones Stationer,
   N.Y.; 10" x 6", blue-grey border $35.00

Milwaukee and St. Paul Railway Company
MI1640-20-10, 1873, v, 10 sh., "scrip preferred
   stock" par $100 on which $1 has been paid,
   signed by Russell Sage (famous financier), green
   ....$25.00
MI1640-25-10, 1878, v, 10 sh., "Scrip Preferred
   Stock," par $100 on which $1 has been paid,
   green $25.00
MI1640-30-10, 1879, v, 10 sh., "Scrip Preferred
   Stock," par $100 on which $1 has been paid,
   green $25.00

Milwaukee Street Railway Company
   (NJ par $100)

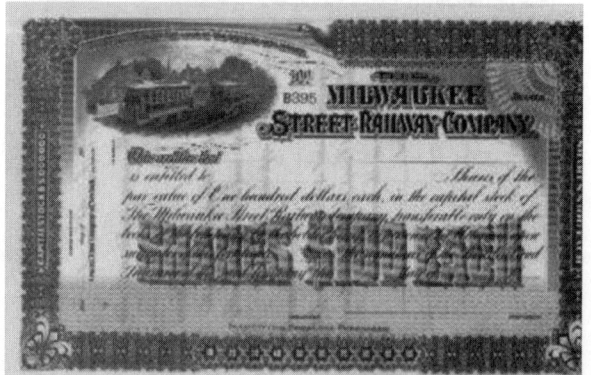

*MI1700-20-10, 18xx, v, u/u odd share certificate,
   w/o imprint, green...................$12.00

Milwaukee-Vermillion Iron &
   Land Company (WI par $2.50)

*MI1790-20-10, 1887, v, 50 sh., 11" x 8", brown
   border $100.00

Mina Gold Mines Company (NV par 10¢)
Mines in Bell mining district, Mineral county,
   Nevada.
MI1840-20-10, 1919, v, 1,000 sh., brown
   ....$22.00

The Minneapolis & St. Louis Railroad
   Company (par $100)
MI1910-20-10, 19xx, v, u/u certificate, blue
   ....$15.00

Mission Development Company
Became part of the J. Paul Getty empire after the
   stock market crash, a former Rockefeller holding
   company.

*MI2170-20-10, 1951, v, 100 sh. (par $5), blue
   ....$12.00

Mississippi and Missouri Railroad Company (IA par $100)

*MI2280-20-10, 185x, u/u certificate, blue .$13.00
MI2280-25-10, 18xx, v, u/u certificate, brown
. . . .$8.00

Mississippi River Fuel Corporation (DE 1928, par $10)

MI2330-20-10, 1960, v, 100 sh., orange.....$4.00

*MI2330-20-15, 1961, v, 100 sh., signature variety, orange. $4.00

Mississippi Valley Corporation (NJ par $100)

MI2390-20-10, 1907, 43 sh., black. $10.00

UNLISTED TYPES & VARIETIES

Readers are welcome to contact the author directly at:

Rainer Stahlberg
P.O. Box 1044
Rooseveltown, New York 13683

State of Missouri

*MI2490-30-10, 1932, v, $1,000 Road Bond, series T 4½% due 1954, RBN, brown . . .$20.00

Missouri, Kansas and Texas Extension Railway Company

MI2570-20-10, 1880, v, 1 sh., brown. $40.00

Missouri, Kansas and Texas Railway Company (par $100)

*MI2580-20-10, 1886, v, 10 sh., ABN, brown
. . . .$23.00

MI2580-30-10, 1887, v, 10 sh. (MO), ABN, signed by George Gould, purple **$15.00**

MI2580-35-10, 1908, v, 10 sh., brown **$15.00**

*MI2580-40-10, 19xx, v, u/c certificate, brown
. . . .**$8.00**

*MI2580-50-10, 1882, v, 100 sh., green. . . . **$12.00**

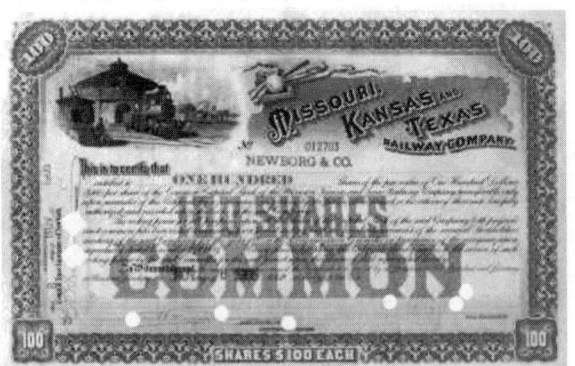

*MI2580-55-10, 1905, v, 100 sh. (NY), FBN,
green **$12.00**

MI2580-65-10, 1899, v, 20 sh., pref., blue
. . . .**$15.00**

MI2580-70-10, 1907, v, 10 pref. sh., orange
. . . .**$15.00**

MI2580-80-10, 1929, v, 30 pref. sh., on a less than
100 sh., certificate (MO), ABN, brown . .**$15.00**

Missouri Pacific Railroad Company (MO)

*MI2640-20-10, 1956, v, 100 sh., brown. . .**$10.00**

MI2640-30-10, 1981, v, 500 sh., on a less than
10,000 sh., certificate, green **$10.00**

*MI2640-30-10, 1955, v, 100 sh., pref., SBN,
orange. **$10.00**

Mitchell County Agricultural Society (IA par $10)

*MI2740-20-10, 1916, v, 1 sh., light green . .**$7.00**

Mitchell Iron & Land Company (WI par $25)

*MI2770-20-10, 1887, v, 3,000 sh., 12-1/2" x 10", orange border $90.00

Mizpah-Montana Mining Company (CA 20¢)

MI2840-20-10, 19xx, v, u/u certificate, grey
. . . .$6.00

Mobile and Birmingham Railroad Company

MO120-20-10, 1960, v, 17 pref. sh., on a less than 100 sh., certificate, brown. $16.00

Mobile and Montgomery Rail-Way Company (AL par $100)

MO180-20-10, 187x, v, u/u certificate, brown
. . . .$10.00

Mobile and Northwestern Railroad Co.

MO220-20-10, 1887, v, u/u receiver's certificate for 500, S.C. Toof & Company, green . . .$15.00

Mobile and Ohio Car Trust

MO250-20-10, 1890, v, $1,000 bond, grey
. . . .$45.00

Mobile and Ohio Railroad Co. (AL par $100)

*MO280-20-10, 1874, v, 40 sh., ABN, orange
. . . .$15.00

The Mohawk and Malone Railway Company (NY)

Herkimer, Newport & Poland Extension RR and the St. Lawrence & Adirondack RR consolidated in 1892 to form the new company.

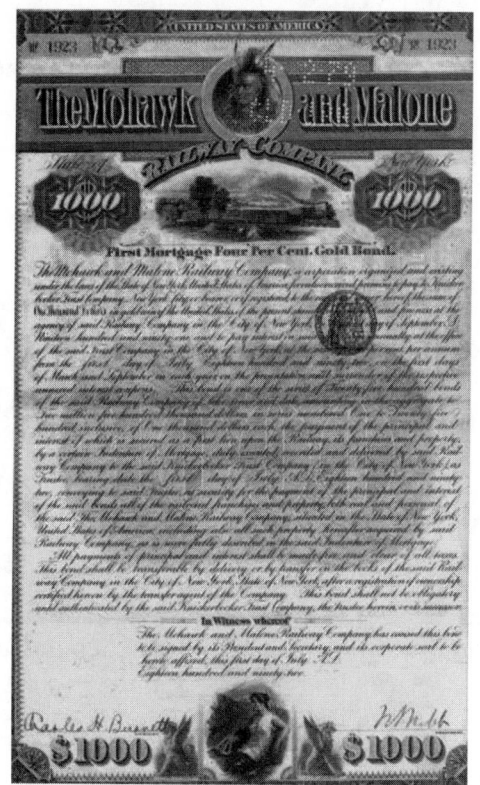

*MO450-30-10, 1892, v, $1,000 first mortgage 4% gold bond, French revenue imprint, ABN, 10" x 14-1/2", green. $20.00

MO450-35-10, 1902, v, $1,000 3-1/2% consol.
  gold mort. bond., green. **$20.00**

*MO450-45-10, 1948, v, $1,000 3-1/2% consoli-
  dated gold mortgage bond, ABN, green . .**$6.00**
MO450-50-10, 1948, v, $5,000 3-1/2% consol.
  mort. gold bond, brown **$6.00**
MO450-55-10, 1948, v, $10,000 3-1/2% consol.
  mort. gold bond, grey **$7.00**

Mojave River Land and Water Company
  (CA par $10)
MO490-20-10, 1912, v, 150 sh., grey border
  . . . .**$30.00**

Mojave Tungsten Company
MO510-20-10, 1918, v, i/u 100 sh., green
  . . . .**$15.00**

The Monarch Mining Company
  (CT par $25)
MO640-20-10, 18xx, v, u/u certificate, black
  . . . .**$9.00**

Monarch Smokeless Coal Co.
  (WV par $100)
MO670-20-10, 1926, v, 3 sh., grey border . . .**$8.00**

The value of a stock certificate depends on:
  • rarity
  • the issuer
  • signatures
  • quality of engraving
  • overall appearance
  • condition
  • date of issue

Monfort of Colorado, Inc. (DE par $1)

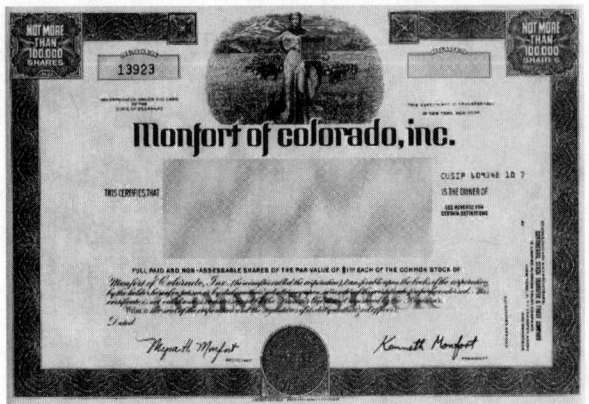

*MO730-20-10, 19xx, v, u/u on a not more than
  100,000 sh., certificate, SCB, green. **$4.00**

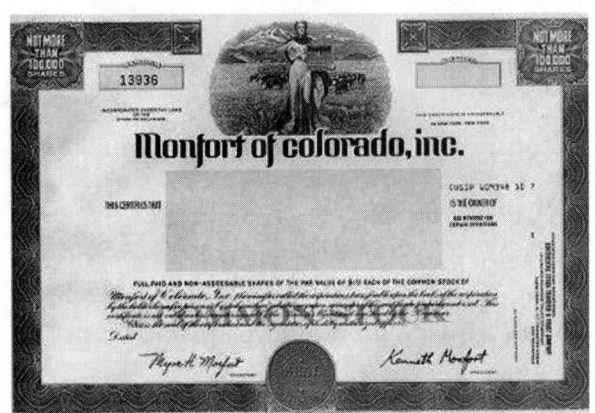

*MO730-25-10, 1980, v, 50 sh., on a not more than
  100,000 sh., certificate, green **$3.00**

The Monitor Gold Mining Company (MT)
MO760-20-10, 1894, v, 1,000 sh., brown . .**$75.00**

The Monitor Mining Company
  (Dakota Terr., par $10)

*MO790-20-10, 1886, v, 500 sh., black. . . .**$25.00**

Monitor Mining Company (ID)

*MO800-20-10, 19xx, v, u/u certificate, grey
...................................$5.00

Monmouth Co-operative Creamery (OR)

MO920-20-10, 1931, v, 1 sh., green.......$4.00

Monmouth Park Jockey Club

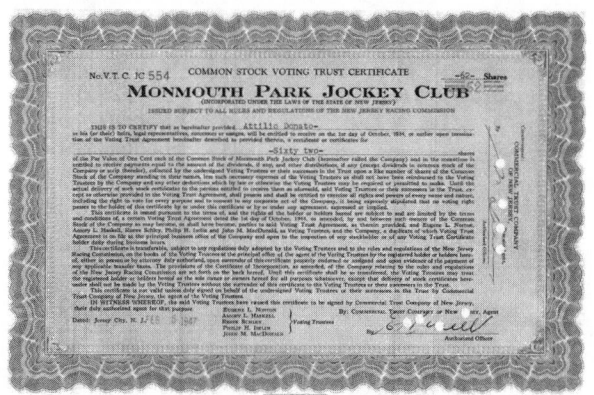

*MO950-20-10, 1947, 62 voting sh. (par 1¢),
Hamilton Bank Note, NY, 12" x 8", orange
...................................$4.00

MO950-30-10, 1964, v, 50 voting sh., blue
...................................$8.00

MO950-35-10, 19xx, v, u/u voting trust certificate,
brown $7.00

MO950-40-10, 1963, v, 100 sh., voting stock,
brown $14.00

MO950-45-10, 19xx, 100 voting sh., orange
...................................$4.00

The Monongahela Railway Company

*MO990-40-10, 1935, v, u/u $1,000 1st mortgage
series B 3-3/4% bond, ABN, red $10.00

Monsanto Company

This company's main activities are crop protection,
biotechnology, NutraSweet, food ingredients
and pharmaceuticals.

*MO1200-40-10, 1978, v, $10,000 9-1/8% sinking
fund debenture due 2000, SCB, 12" x 8", orange
...............................$10.00

Monsanto International Finance Company

MO1210-30-10, 1965, v, $1,000 4-1/2% Guaran-
teed Sinking Fund Debenture due 1985 w. coupons, blue $15.00

Montana, Territory of
MO1280-20-10, 1868, v, $100 bond w. coupon, blue border $60.00

Montana Auto Finance Corporation
MO1320-20-10, 1922, v, 1 sh., green $35.00

Montana Consolidated Coal and Coke Company
MO1350-20-10, 1908, t, 100 sh., green border $6.00

Monte Cristo Gold & Copper Company (UT par 25¢)
MO1375-20-10, 1903, v, i/u 1,000 sh., grey border $15.00

Montgomery Shoshone Consolidated Mining Company (SC par $5)
MO1400-20-10, 1907, v, 100 sh., green $15.00

The Monument Valley Feed and Fuel Company (CO par $1)
MO1480-20-10, 1918, v, 1 sh., grey $15.00

Moon Motor Car Company (DE 1917, no par)
MO1520-20-10, 1930, v, 100 sh., brown $140.00

Moonlight Mining Co. (WI par $1)

MO1550-20-10, 1904, v, 1 sh., 10" x 8", grey border $7.00

The Moraine Mining Company (IL par $10)

MO1640-20-10, 19xx, v, u/u certificate, grey border $6.00

Morning Glory Mines, Inc. (par $1)

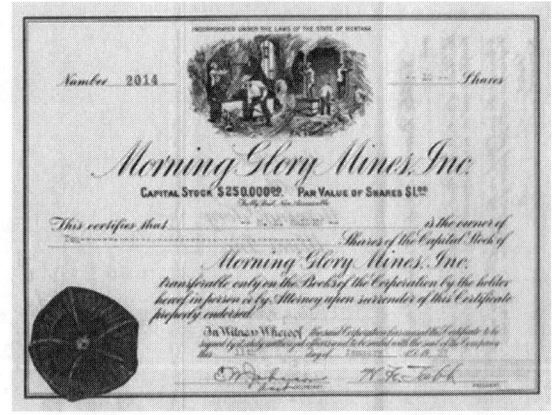

MO1690-20-10, 1937, v, 10 sh., black . . .$51.00

Morris Canal and Banking Company of 1844

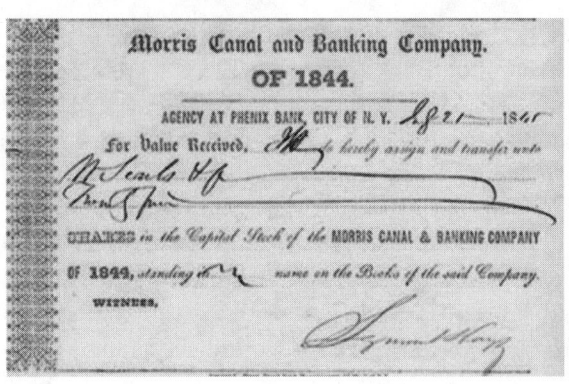

MO1740-20-10, 1865, stock transfer certificate, 7-1/4" x 4-3/4", brown $27.00

The Morris and Essex Railroad Company (NJ)

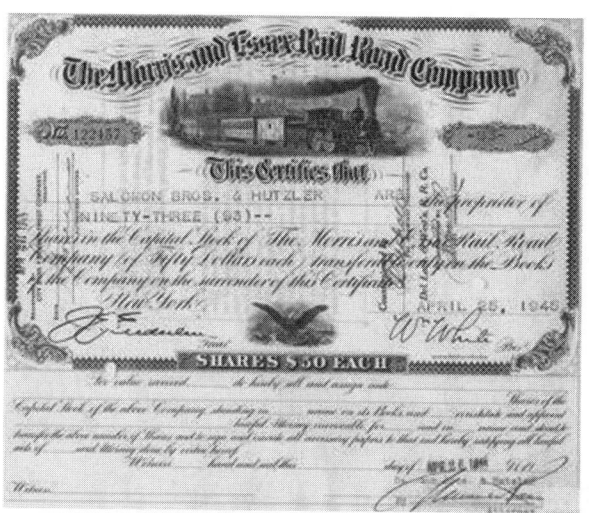

MO1770-20-10, 1945, v, 93 sh. (par $50), grey
. . . .$9.00

MO1770-30-10, 1925, v, $1,000 4-1/2% series C mortgage bond, ABN, green. $10.00

MO1770-35-10, 19xx, v, $1,000 unissued bond, brown $14.00

Philip Morris Incorporated (VA)

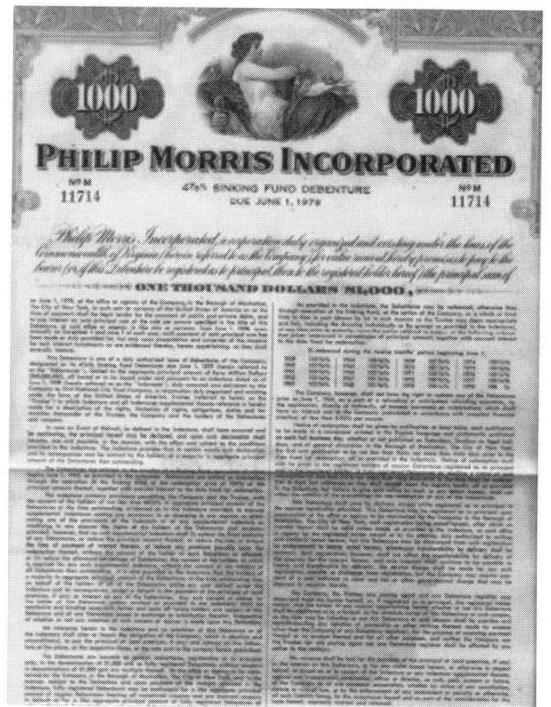

MO1800-40-10, 1959, v, $1,000 4-7/8% sinking fund debenture, ABN, orange. $15.00

The Mortgage Finance Company of Baltimore

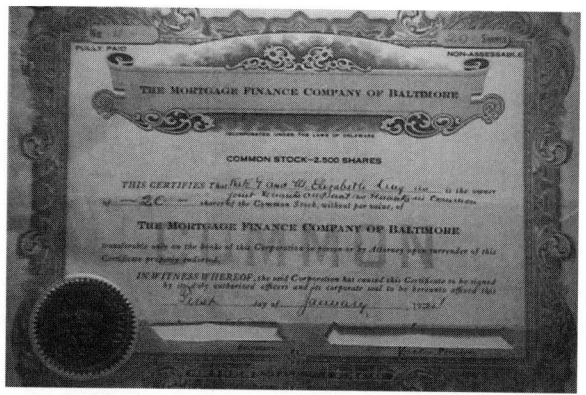

MO1860-20-10, 1924, v, 20 sh., green $5.00

Moulton Mining Company (MT territory par $5)

MO1930-20-10, 188x, v, u/u 100 sh., certificate, blue. $17.00

Mount Olive Coal Company (IL par $100)

MO1970-20-10, 1889, v, 100 sh., 11" x 7-1/2", brown $80.00

Mount Olive Consolidated Coal-Coke Co. (IL, par $100)

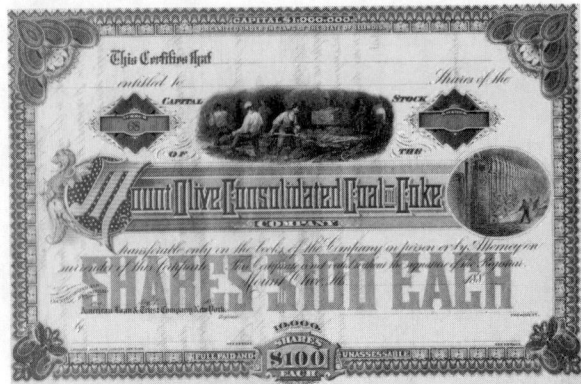

*MO1980-20-10, 188x, v, u/u certificate, ABN, 10-3/4" x 7", light brown $15.00

Mount Whipple Gold Mining Company (AZ Territory)

MO2020-20-10, 19xx, v, u/u certificate, green
. . . .$20.00

Mountain City Copper Company (UT)

Mines were located in Mountain City, Nevada.
MO2060-20-10, 1939, v, 100 sh., green $50.00

Mull Distributing Corporation (NY par $100)

*MU150-10-10, 19xx, v, u/u certificate, GOES o/p Blumgold & Co. NY, 11" x 8-1/2", brown
. . . .$4.00

Murray Creek Mining Company, Re-organized (CA 1896)

MU550-20-10, 189x, u/u certificate, grey border on beige $6.00

N

Napa and Sonoma Wine Company (1872 par $100)

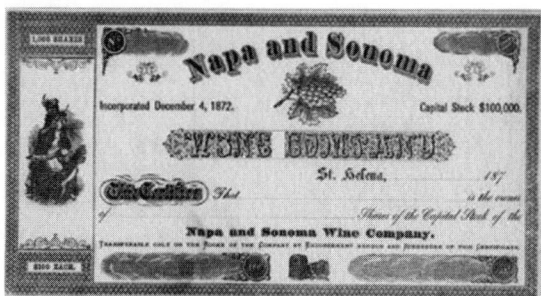

*NA480-20-10, 187x, v, u/u certificate, 10" x 5-1/2", brown..............................$22.00

Narragansett Pier Railroad Company

NA610-20-10, 1879, v, 5 sh., blue........$135.00

The Nash Motors Company (MD no par)

NA710-20-10, 1928, v, 5 sh. on a less than 100 sh. certificate, green....................$40.00

Nashua Corporation (DE par $1)

NA810-20-10, 1972, v, 100 sh., blue.......$13.00

Nashville, Chattanooga and St. Louis Railway Company (par $25)

NA910-20-10, 18xx, v, u/u certificate, ABN, black $15.00

Nashville Electronics, Inc. (TN par $0.10)

*NA970-20-10, 1965, 100 sh., Hasbrouck, Thistle & Co., 11-3/4" x 8-1/4", orange $4.00

The Nassau Electric Railroad Company (NY par $100)

NA1070-20-10, 189x, v, u/u 100 sh. certificate, orange $12.00
NA1070-25-10, 189x, v, u/u 100 sh. certificate, ABN, green........................$20.00

Natal Day Mining and Milling Company, Ltd. (ID par $1)

*NA1120-20-10, 1904, v, 500 sh., green border $13.00

National Airlines, Incorporated (FL)

The company began in 1934 with a 142-mile air-mail route between St. Petersburg-Tampa-Daytona Beach-Lakeland-Orlando. National was the first US airline to operate jets. In 1980, Pan American World Airways acquired National Airlines.

NA1160-20-10, 1969, v, 1 sh. on a less than 100 sh. certificate (par $1), l. blue.............$20.00

*NA1160-25-10, 1974, v, 100 sh. (par 25¢), orange $8.00

National Alfalfa Dehydrating & Milling Co.
(DE 1946, par $3)

NA1190-20-10, 1968, v, 1 sh. on a less than 100 sh. certificate, SCB, 11-3/4" x 8-1/4", green **$4.00**

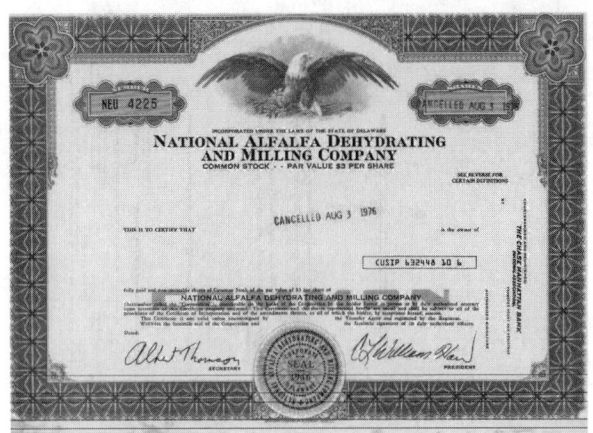

NA1190-25-10, 19xx, v, u/c certificate, SCB, 12" x 8", orange........................**$3.00**

NA1190-30-10, 1963, v, 100 sh., signature strip, SCB, 11-3/4" x 8-1/4", olive **$4.00**

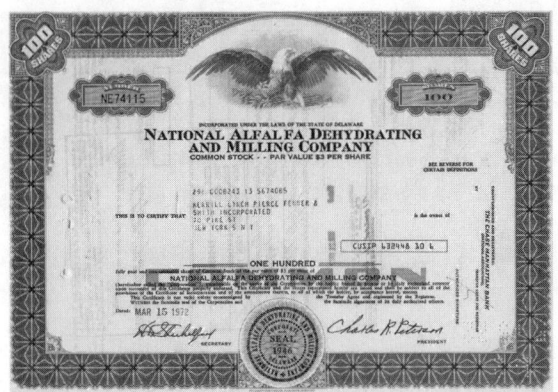

NA1190-35-10, 1972, v - eagle, 100 sh., SCB, 11-3/4" x 8-1/4", olive **$4.00**

National Aviation Corporation

NA1230-20-10, 19xx, v, u/c less than 100 sh. certificate, brown **$18.00**

The National Bank of Huntsville
(AL par $100)

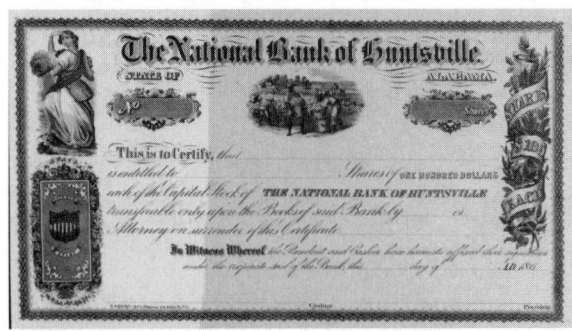

NA1250-20-10, 186x, v, u/u certificate, 11" x 6", brown border **$25.00**

The National Bank of Wilmington and
Brandywine
NA1300-20-10, 1866, v, 15 sh., grey **$15.00**

The National Company (PA par $50)
NA1350-20-10, 1888, v, 100 sh., the National Company's Railway held in trust, brown
.....................................$28.00

National Consolidated Wire and Cable Company (ME par $100)
NA1380-20-10, 1906, v, 10 sh., pref., green..$6.00

National Copper Company (ID par $1)
NA1430-20-10, 1907, v, 500 sh., grey $12.00

National Copper Mining Co. Ltd. (ID par $1)

NA1460-20-10, 19xx, v, u/u certificate, green
.....................................$6.00

National Fuel Gas Company (NJ)

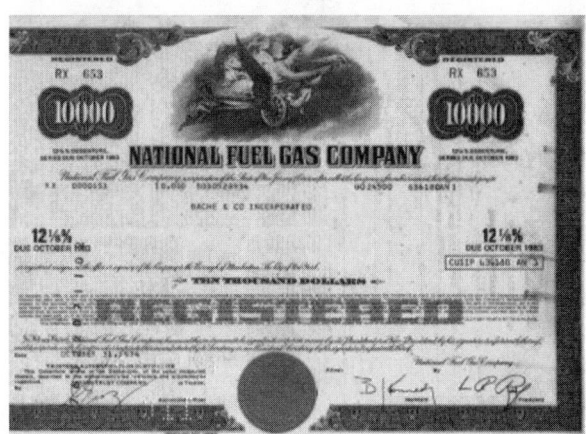

NA1520-40-10, 1974, v, $10,000 12-1/8% bond due 1983, green $7.00

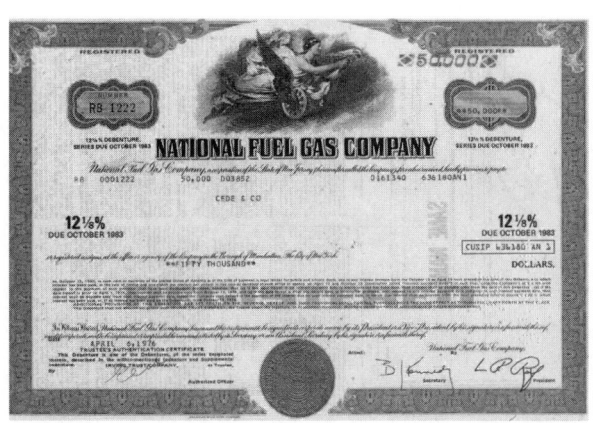

NA1520-50-10, 1976, v, $50,000 12-1/8% debenture due 1983, ABN, 12" x 8", orange $6.00

National Liberty Insurance Company of America (NY par $2)

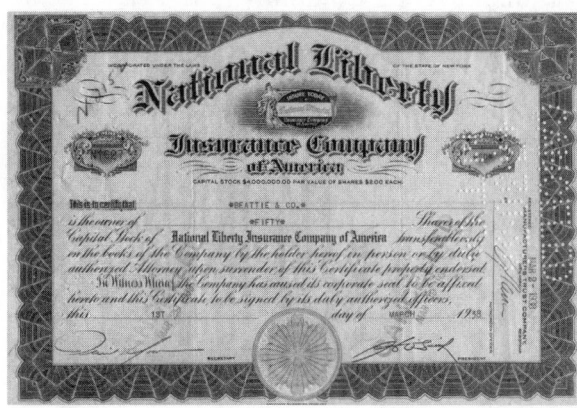

NA1600-20-10, 1938, v, 50 sh., SBN, 11-3/4" x 8", green $4.00

The National Marine Bank of Baltimore (par $30)
NA1740-20-10, 1912, 10 sh., grey $15.00

National Match Company

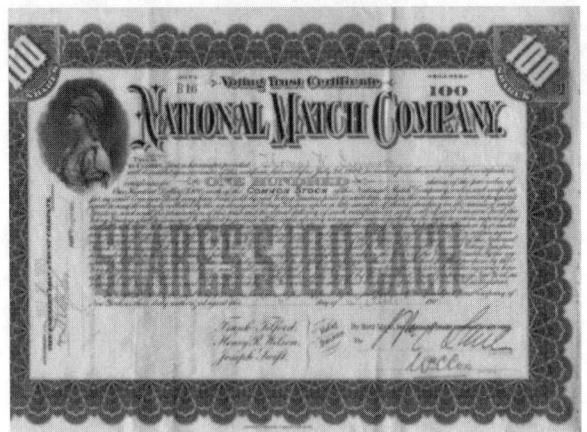

NA1770-20-10, 1901, v, 100 voting trust shares, green **$40.00**

National Metals Company (par $1)

NA1800-20-10, 1915, v, 900 sh., blue. **$10.00**

National Mining Company

NA1830-20-10, 19xx, v, u/u less than 100 sh. certificate, red. **$25.00**

The National Oil Refining and Manufacturing Company (AZ territory)

NA1880-20-10, 1904, v, 550 sh., grey **$10.00**

The National Onyx Mining, Milling and Improvement Company of Mexico (NJ par $500)

NA1920-20-10, 189x, v, u/c certificate. . . .**$10.00**

National Steel Corporation (DE 1929)

NA2010-30-10, 1971, v, 100 sh. (par $5), green **$6.00**

NA2010-40-10, 1959, v, $1,000 first mortgage bond, 4-5/8% due 1969, orange **$6.00**

NA2010-50-10, 1976, v, $25,000 1st mort. bond 8-3/8% series due 2006, SCB, 12" x 8", blue **$6.00**

It is generally assumed that only 5% of certificates survive to reach collectors.

*NA2010-55-10, 1975, v, $25,000 1ˢᵗ mortgage 8%
bond, due 1995, SCB, 12" x 8", l. green...**$6.00**

National Tea Co. (IL no par)

*NA2060-20-10, 1939, v, 100 sh., ABN, 11-1/4" x
7-1/2", brown **$5.00**

National Tunnel & Mines Company
NA2090--20-10, 1938, v, 100 sh. (ME no par),
green **$5.00**
NA2090-25-10, 1946, v, 100 sh. (NY par $1),
brown **$8.00**

The value of a stock certificate depends on:

- rarity
- the issuer
- signatures
- quality of engraving
- overall appearance
- condition
- date of issue

National Union Bank of Boston (MA 1865, par $100)

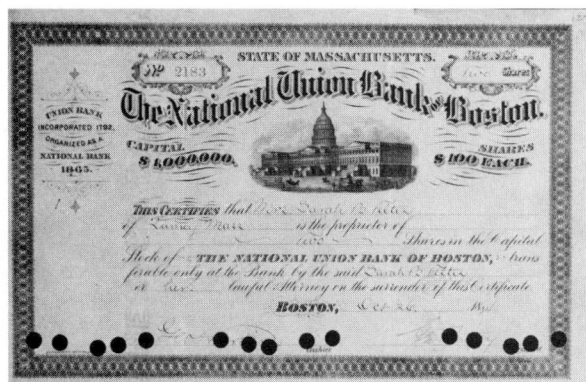

*NA2130-20-10, 1894, v, 2 sh., 11-1/2" x 7", grey
border **$15.00**

The National Water Works Company of New York (NY par $100)
NA2170-20-10, 1890, v, 14 sh., brown.....**$32.00**

Needham, Harper & Steers, Inc.

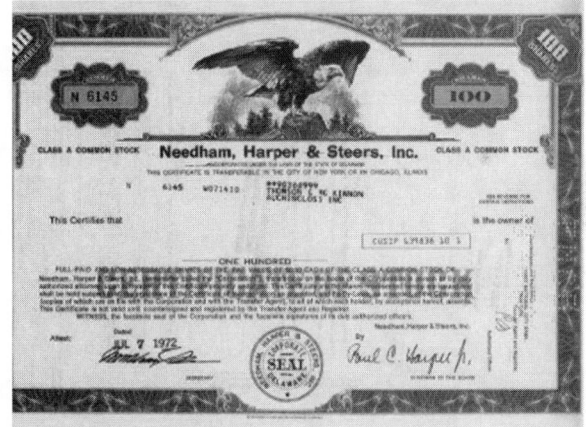

*NE200-20-10, 1972, v, 100 sh., blue **$8.00**

Needham Piano and Organ Company
NE230-30-10, 1906, v, $1,000 6% extended mort-
gage bond, grey-green **$25.00**

The Neighborhood Corporation (MD 1919, par $50)

*NE270-20-10, 1932, v, 1 sh., grey $5.00

Nekoosa-Edwards Paper Company (WI)

*NE360-20-10, 1969, v, 12 class B sh. on a less than 100 sh. certificate, SCB, green $4.00

The Nellie Mining Company (AZ par $1)
NE470-20-10, 1922, v, i/u 300 sh., green...$16.00

The Nelson Mining Company (MT par 10¢)
NE590-20-10, 19xx, v, u/u certificate, green
..................................$12.00

Nevada Belmont Copper Mines Company (NV 1909, par $1)
NE810-20-10, 19xx, v, unissued certificate, brown
..................................$20.00

Nevada Goldfield Reduction Company of Nevada (NV)
NE840-20-10, 1910, bearer trust certificate for 10, in English and French, lilac............$20.00

Nevada and Mountain Lakes Ice Co.
NE870-20-10, 187x, v, u/u certificate, grey..$6.00

Nevada Power Company (NV par $1)

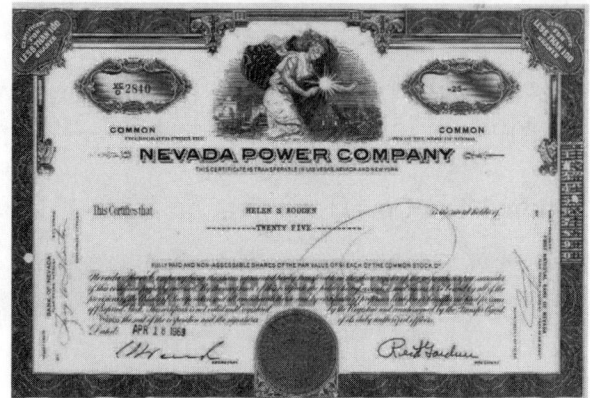

*NE910-20-10, 1969, v, 25 sh. on a less than 100 sh. certificate, green..................$4.00

Nevada Quicksilver Mines, Incorporated (NV 1927 par $1)
Offices in Lovelock, NV.

*NE940-20-10, 1929, v, 500 sh., grey $15.00

New Bedford Acceptance Corporation of New Bedford, Massachusetts (MA)

*NE1020-20-10, 1940, v, 20 pref. sh. (par $6), green $5.00

New Bedford, Martha's Vineyard and Nantucket Steamboat Company

NE1070-20-10, 188x, v, u/u certificate, black $210.00

City of New Britain, CT

NE1100-40-10, 1924, $1,000 4-1/4% School Bond 18th series, green. $40.00

The New Burlingame Telegraphing Typewriter Company (par $10)

NE1130-20-10, 1912, v, 10 sh., grey border $55.00

New Castle & Beaver Valley Railroad Company (PA par $50)

NE1160-20-10, 1863, v, 3 sh., black. $30.00

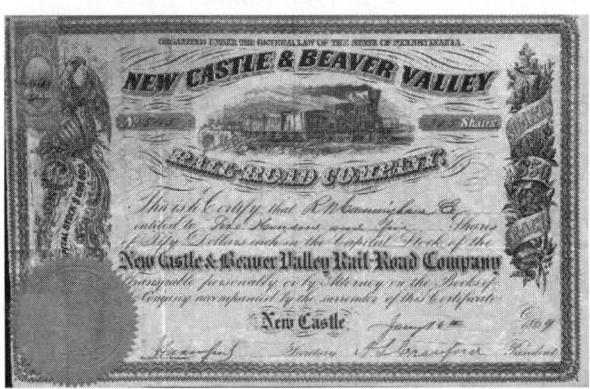

*NE1160-30-10, 1869, v, 205 sh., grey $25.00

New Cornelia Copper Company (DE)

NE1200-20-10, 1915, v, 100 sh., grey $8.00

*NE1200-30-10, 1926, v, 3 sh. on a less than 100 sh. certificate, green $10.00

New Dominion Copper Company (AZ)

NE1260-20-10, 1928, v, 100 sh., orange $8.00

New England and Clifton Copper Company of Arizona (ME)

*NE1300-20-10, 1907, v, u/u certificate 4 sh. (par $5), blue on green. $9.00

New England Gas and Electric Association (MA 1926)

NE1340-20-10, 1941, v, 5 sh. of $5.50 pref. .$6.00

New England Merchants Company, Inc. (MA 1971)

NE1380-20-10, 1975, v, 100 sh., ABN, 12" x 8", blue **$4.00**

New England Mining Company (MA 1857, par $10)

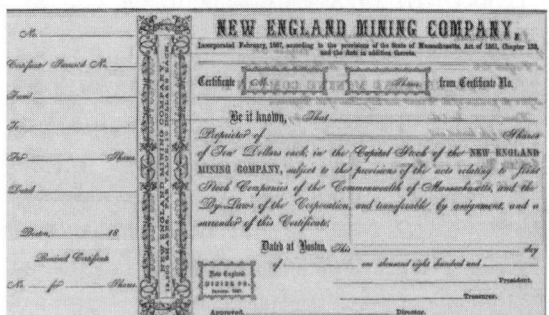

NE1410-10-10, 185x, u/u certificate, 11-1/2" x 6-1/2", pink. **$8.00**

New England Telephone and Telegraph Company

This company became part of NYNEX.

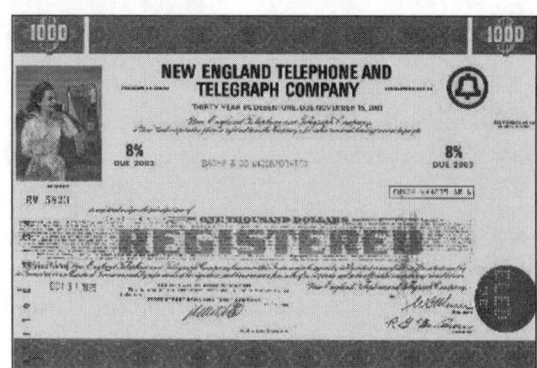

NE1500-40-10, 1975, v, $1,000 8% 30-year debenture due 2003, brown **$6.00**

The New Jersey and New York Railroad Company (NJ-NY par $100)

NE1660-20-10, 1929, v, 2 sh., ABN, green **$15.00**

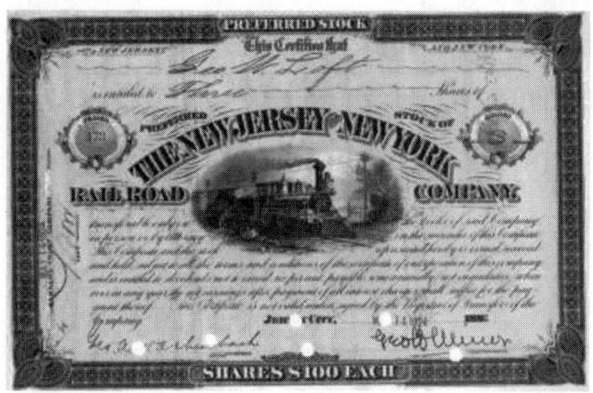

NE1660-30-10, 1924, v, 3 pref. sh., ABN, brown on rose. **$20.00**

New Lisbon Farm Telephone Company (NY par $10)

NE1740-20-10, 1905, v, 2 sh., brown **$15.00**

New Mutual Mining Company (SD)

NE1820-20-10, 191x, v, 100 sh.,. **$5.00**

UNLISTED TYPES & VARIETIES

Readers are welcome to contact the author directly at:

Rainer Stahlberg
P.O. Box 1044
Rooseveltown, New York 13683

New Orleans Great Northern Railway Company

*NE1900-30-10, 1933, v, $1,000 5% Income Debenture due 2032, blue $20.00

New Orleans Lighting Company (NJ par $100)

*NE1930-20-10, 19xx, u/u certificate, orange $4.00

New Orleans & North Eastern Railroad Co. (LA)

NE1960-20-10, 1873, v, 5 sh., brown......$50.00
NE1960-30-10, 1913, 167 sh., grey $35.00

The New Paltz Water Works Company (NY)

NE2010-20-10, 189x, v, unissued certificate, Korff Bros. & Co., green $9.00

The New Process Gold Company, Inc. (NY)

*NE2050-20-10, 19xx, v, u/u certificate, green $4.00

City of New York

*NE2110-40-10, 1971, v, $5,000 7% serial bond for construction of schools, due 1983....$38.00

State of New York

NE2130-20-10, 1868, v, Comptroller's Office $800 New York State Stock, grey $20.00
NE2130-50-10, 1935, v, $1,000 Canal Improvement Bond, Erie, Oswego & Champlain, brown $7.00

New York Auto-Telegraph Co. (NY par $100)

NE2170-20-10, 1885, v, 50 sh., signed by Alonzo B. Cornell, green $195.00

The New York and Boston Silver Lead Company (NY par $10)

NE2200-20-10, 1864, 100 sh., brown......$20.00

It is generally assumed that only 5% of certificates survive to reach collectors.

The New York Central and Hudson River Railroad Company (par $100)

Formed by the consolidation of the New York Central & Hudson River RR of 1869, the Rome, Watertown & Ogdensburg RR, the Oswego & Rome RR and four other railroad corporations.

*NE2240-20-10, 1906, v, 1 sh. on a less than 100 sh. certificate, ABN, 11-3/4" x 8-1/4", grey on yellow $4.00

*NE2240-40-10, 1890, v, $1,000 3-1/2% Michigan Central collateral bond w. coupons, orange
. . . .$15.00
NE2240-50-10, 1897, v, $1,000 3-1/2% coupon gold bond, blue $13.00

*NE2240-55-10, 1898, v, $1,000 3-1/2% Lake Shore collateral gold bond w. coupons, green
. . . .$20.00
NE2240-65-10, 1909, v, $1,000 gold bond secured by First Mortgage on the Spuyten Duyvil & Port Morris Railroad, olive green $15.00
NE2240-70-10, 1912, v, $1,000 30 year 4%, blue
. . . .$12.00

*NE2240-80-10, 1915, v, $10,000 gold bond, olive green $25.00

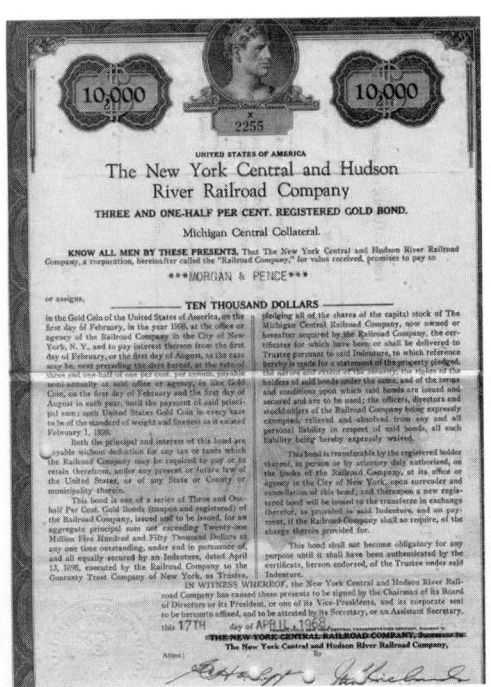

*NE2240-100-10, 1968, $10,000 3-1/2% gold bond, Michigan Central Collateral, ABN, 9-1/2" x 13-1/2", green $4.00

The New York Central Rail Road Company

*NE2270-30-10, 1853, v, $1,000 6% 30-year bond, signed by Erasmus Corning, 12" x 10", grey $31.00

The New York Central Railroad Company
(NY-PA-OH-IN-IL-MI 1914, no par)

*NE2280-20-10, 1934, v, 9 sh. on a less than 100 sh. certificate, ABN, 12" x 8-1/4", brown .$4.00

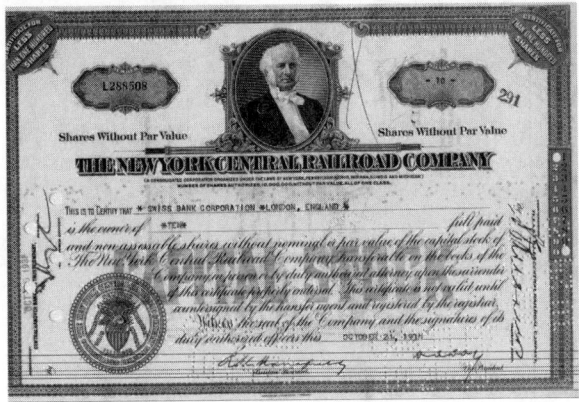

*NE2280-20-15, 1938, v, 10 sh. on a less than 100 sh. certificate, signature variety, ABN, 12" x 8-1/4", brown $4.00

*NE2280-20-20, 1945, v, 50 sh. on a less than 100 sh. certificate, signature variety, ABN, 12" x 8-1/4", brown $4.00

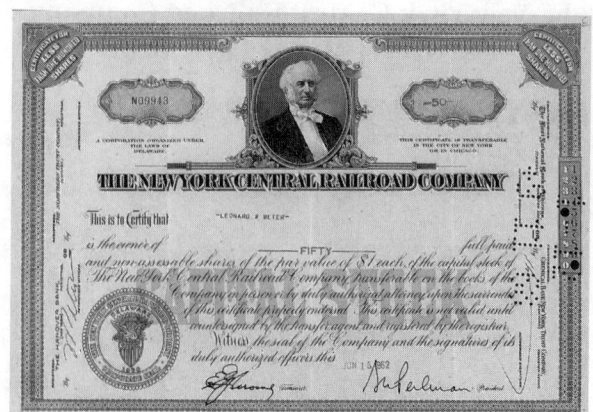

NE2280-20-30, 1962, v, 50 sh. on a less than 100
sh. certificate, signature variety, brown ...**$4.00**

NE22840-30-10, 1944, v, 100 sh., blue **$4.00**

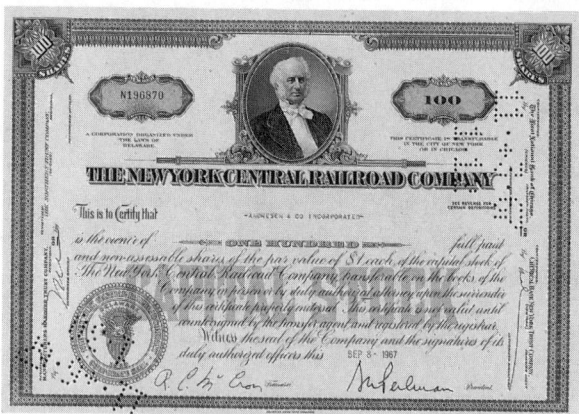

NE2280-40-10, 1967, v, 100 sh. (DE par $1),
ABN, 12-1/4" x 8-1/2", blue **$4.00**

NE2280-45-15, 1964, v, 100 sh. (DE par $1), made
out to Victor Kiam, blue **$9.00**

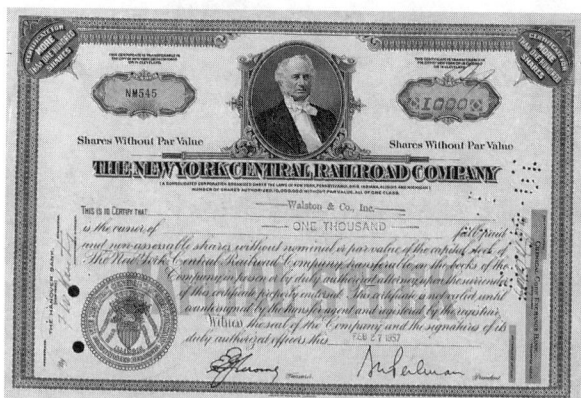

NE2280-55-10, 1957, v, 1,000 sh. on a more than
100 sh. certificate, purple..............**$8.00**

NE2280-75-10, 19xx, v, $1,000 unissued 4% series
A cons. mort. gold bond, green........**$10.00**

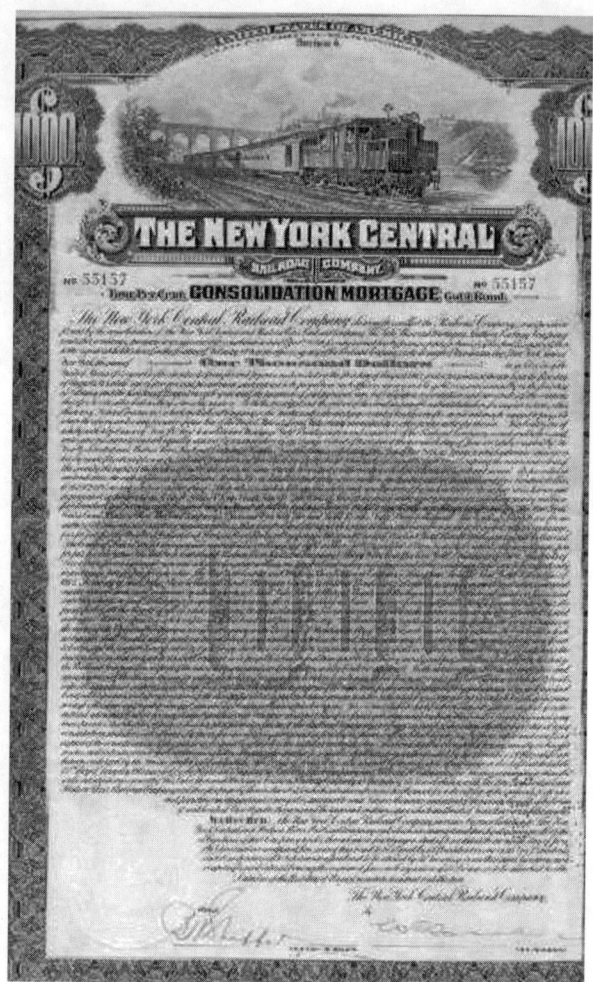

NE2280-80-10, 1913, v, $1,000 4% consol. mort.
bond w. coupons, green...............**$10.00**

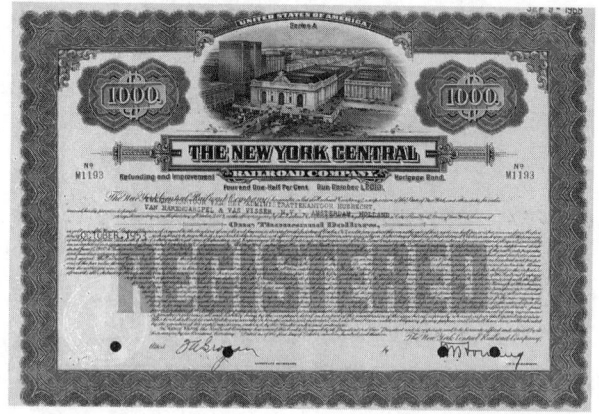

NE2280-100-10, 1953, v, $1,000 series A 4-1/2%
refunding and improvement mort. bond, due
2010, green **$12.00**

NE2280-120-10, 1968, v, $10,000 5% Refunding
and Improvement Mortgage, series C, purple
...................................**$10.00**

The New York, Chicago and St. Louis Railroad Company (1923, par $5)

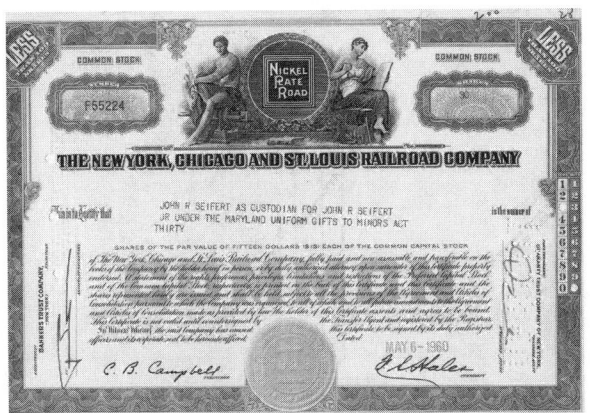

NE2310-30-10, 1960, v, 30 sh. on a less than 100 sh. certificate (par $5), CBN, 12" x 8", l. brown $4.00

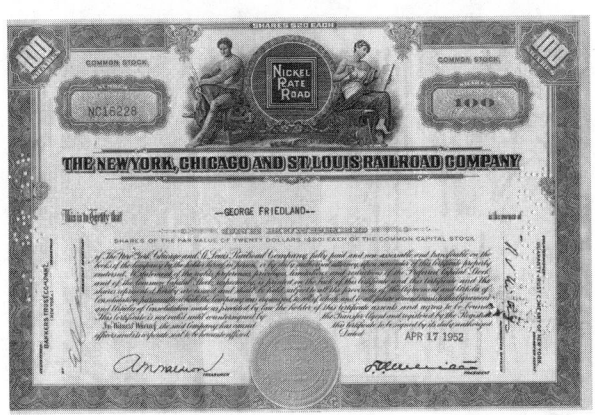

NE2310-40-10, 1952, v, 100 sh. (par $20), CBN, 12" x 8", olive green....................$4.00

NE2310-45-10, 1961, v, 100 sh., olive green $4.00

NE2310-60-10, 1952, v, 100 series A pref. sh., (par $100), red $7.00

New York and Coney Island Railroad Company (par $100)

NE2340-20-10, 18xx, v, unissued certificate, 9" x 12", grey $45.00

The New York Connecting Railroad Company

NE2370-20-10, 191x, v, unissued certificate, red brown $10.00

New York & De Pere Flax Company (WI par $100)

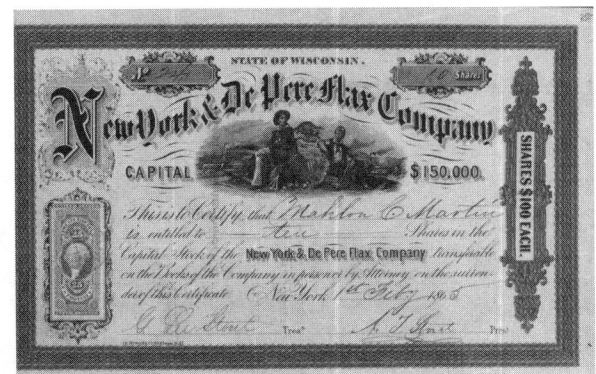

NE2390-20-10, 1865, v, 10 sh., revenue stamp, 10" x 6", brown border..............$350.00

The New York and Harlem Rail Road Company (NY par $50)

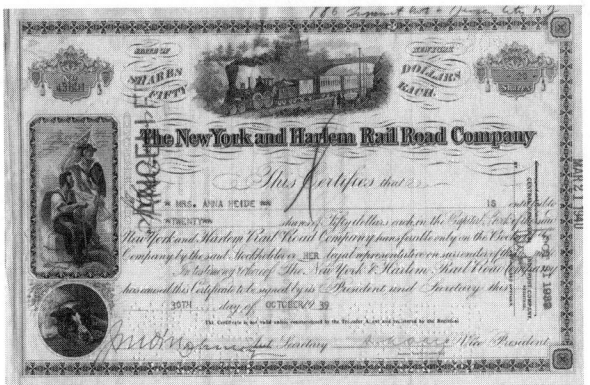

NE2420-20-10, 1939, v, 20 sh., ABN, 10-3/4" x 7", grey $9.00

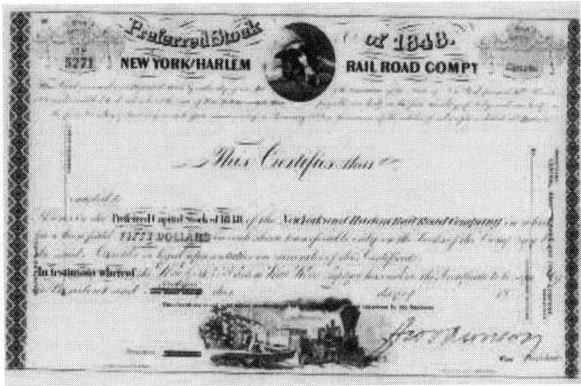

NE2420-30-10, 1848, v, u/c preferred stock certificate, Bald & Cousland, New York, brown $10.00

The New York and Harlem Railroad Company

NE2430-50-10, 1897, v, $5,000 u/c 3-1/2% gold
bond, due 2000, ABN, 12-3/4" x 9-1/2", orange
.....................................**$15.00**

New York, New Haven and Hartford Railroad Company (CT)

NE2520-30-10, 1968, v, 100 sh., conv. 5% series A
pref., brown.........................**$10.00**

NE2520-50-10, 1910, v, $10,000 4% bond, blue
.....................................**$14.00**
NE2520-70-10, 1926, v, $10,000 6% conv. deben-
ture, orange.........................**$26.00**
NE2520-100-10, 1953, v, $1,000 bond, CBN, green
.....................................**$12.00**

**The value of a stock certificate
depends on:**

- **rarity**
- **the issuer**
- **signatures**
- **quality of engraving**
- **overall appearance**
- **condition**
- **date of issue**

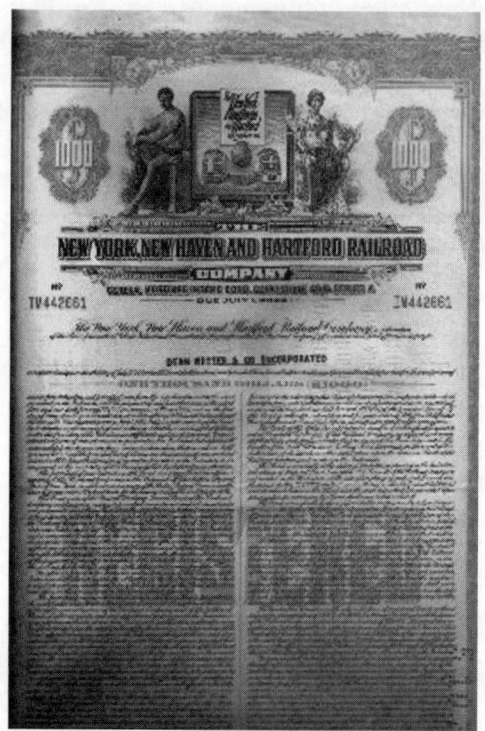

NE2520-110-10, 1957, v, $1,000 bond, orange
.....................................**$7.00**

New York and Ontario Land Company (PA par $50)

NE2600-20-10, 1890, v, 100 sh., brown...**$21.00**

New York, Ontario and Western Railway Company

NE2630-20-10, 1923, v, 10 sh. (par $100), brown
.....................................**$10.00**
NE2630-40-10, 1924, v, $5,000 4% refunding
mortgage bond, green.................**$10.00**

New York, Pittsburgh and Chicago Railway Company (PA-OH par $50)

NE2670-20-10, 18xx, v, u/u certificate, Jordan Stationery Co., grey **$10.00**

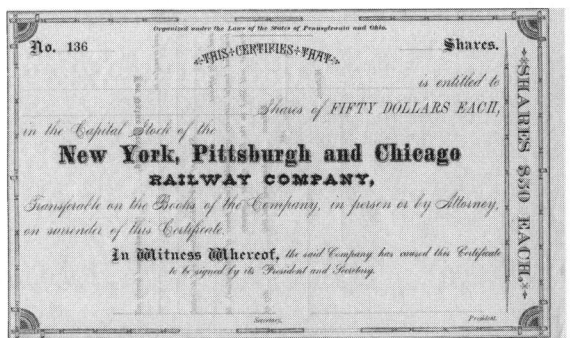

*NE2670-25-10, 188x, u/u certificate, w/o imprint, 11-1/4" x 6-3/4", grey **$4.00**

New York, Providence and Boston Railroad Company (par $100)

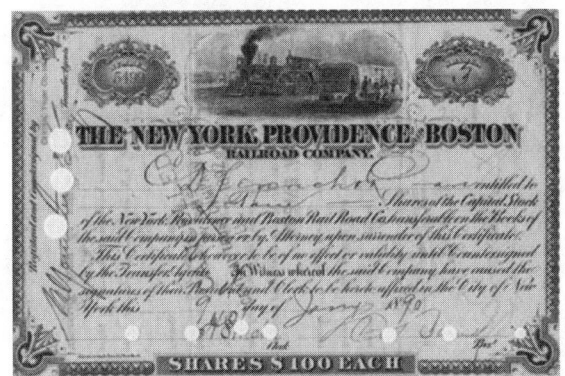

*NE2740-20-10, 1890, v, 3 sh., brown **$18.00**

New York Telephone Company

*NE2810-40-10, 1960, v, $1,000 refunding mort. 4-5/8% bond, series L, due 1997, red **$10.00**

New York Title and Mortgage Company (NY 1927)

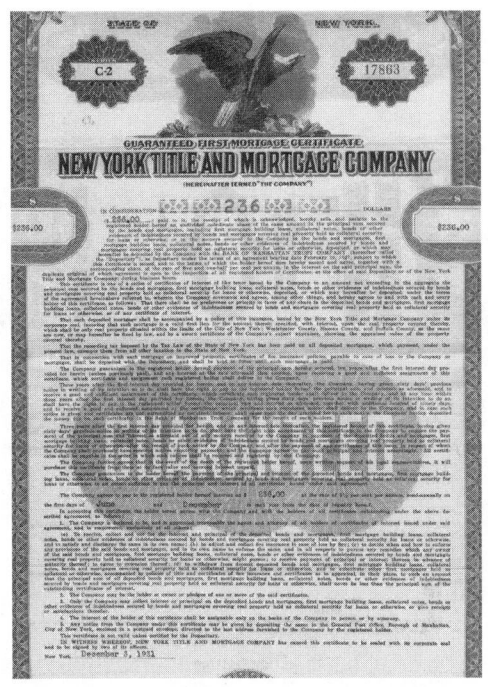

*NE2840-30-10, 1931, v, $236 guaranteed 1st mort. 5-1/2% certificate, ABN, 10-1/4" x 15-1/4", pale green **$5.00**

New York, West Shore and Buffalo Railway Company (par $100)

*NE2970-20-10, 188x, v, u/u 50 sh. certificate, brown **$16.00**

Newmont Mining Corporation

NE3010-20-10, 1969, v, 100 sh., green **$4.00**

Newport & Cincinnati Bridge Company (KY-OH, consolidated 1868, par $100)

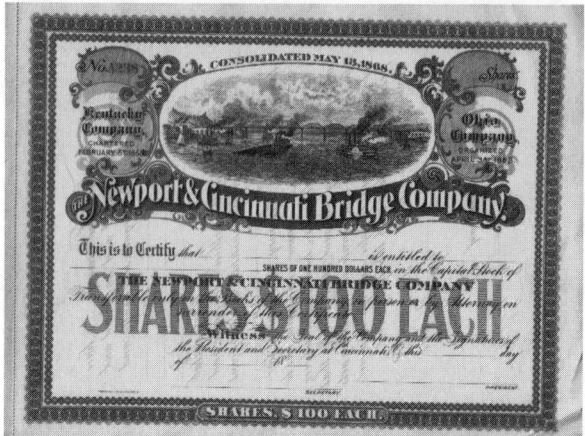

*NE3160-20-10, 18xx, v, u/u certificate, red-brown
................................$12.00

Newport Manufacturing Company

NE3190-10-10, 18xx, v, u/u $1,000 capital stock
certificate, Charles Toppan, Philadelphia, grey
................................$40.00

Nez Perce County Abstract Company (ID)

*NE3240-20-10, 19xx, u/u certificate, brown
................................$5.00

Niagara Mining and Smelting Company (par $10)

NI120-30-10, 1891, v, 50 pref. sh., green...$70.00

Niagara Silver Mining and Smelting Co. of Colorado (par $10)

NI180-20-10, 1882, 100 sh., grey $40.00
NI180-25-10, 18xx, v, u/u certificate, grey..$30.00

Nicaragua Mining Company (DE)

NI230-20-10, 1920, v, i/u 2,000 sh., orange border
................................$11.00

The Nimikon Iron Mining Company (WI par $25)

*NI390-20-10, 1886, v, 25 sh., 11" x 9", grey
border $80.00

NLT Corporation (DE par $5)

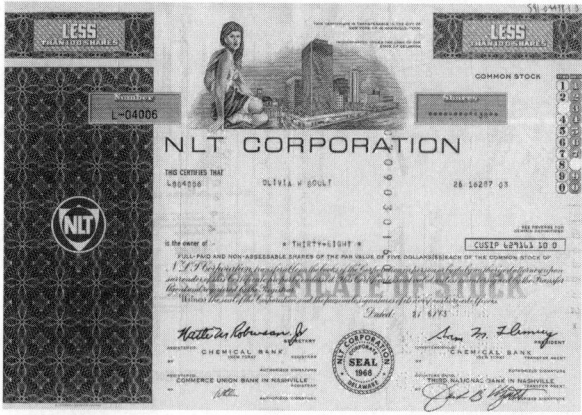

*NL100-20-10, 1973, v, 38 sh. on less than 100 sh.
certificate, Federated Bank Note Company, 12"
x 8", green.........................$3.00

It is generally assumed that only 5% of certificates survive to reach collectors.

*NL100-20-15, 1973, v, 10 sh. on a less than 100 sh. certificate, signature variety, Federated Banknote Company, 12" x 8", green **$3.00**

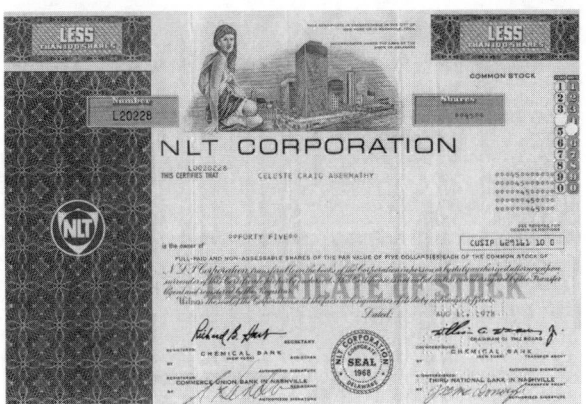

*NL100-20-20, 1978, v, 45 sh. on a less than 100 sh. certificate, signature variety, Federated Banknote Company, 12" x 8", green **$3.00**

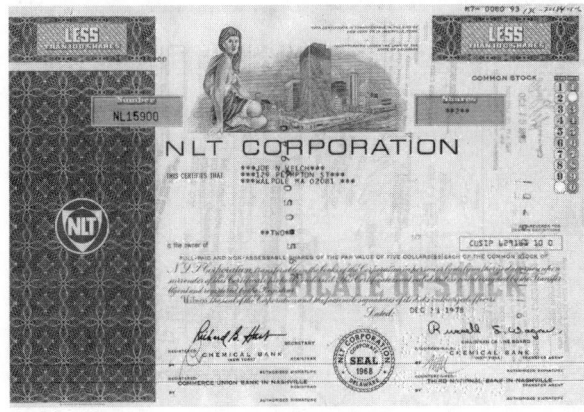

*NL100-20-25, 1978, v, 2 sh. on a less than 100 sh. certificate, signature variety, Federated Banknote Company, 12" x 8", green **$3.00**

*NL100-30-10, 1973, v, 870 sh. on a more than 100 sh. certificate, red **$3.00**

NLT Corporation (TN par $5)

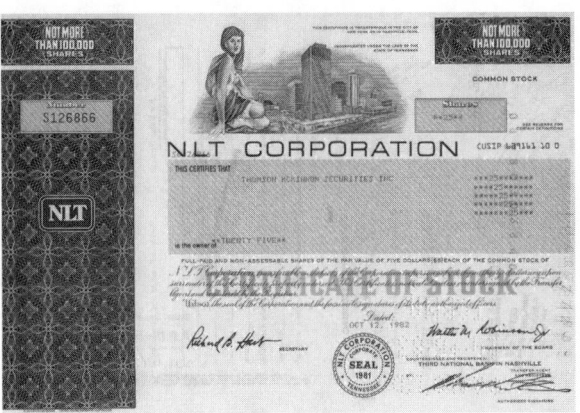

*NL101-20-10, 1982, v, 25 sh. on a not more than 100,00 sh. certificate, SCB, 12" x 8", blue.**$3.00**

Nome and Sinook Company (par $5)

NO470-20-10, 1908, v, 3,000 sh., brown border
. . . .**$50.00**

This catalog has listings in an alphabetical format. The reason is simple: Companies diversify as they grow. For example, the Canadian Pacific Railway company recently split into five companies. They represent the railway, hotels, shipping, airline, and petroleum interests of the company. During World War II, the Singer sewing machine company made guns and other defense-related equipment, so where should we list it? It's far easier to use a strict alphabetical order, rather than to confuse the reader with topical classifications.

Noramco, Inc. (WI par $1.25)

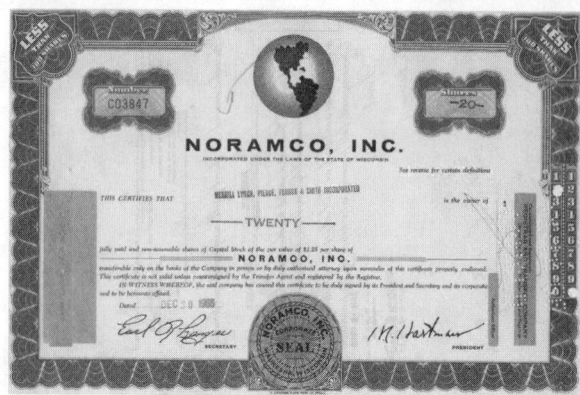

*NO610-20-10, 1965, v, 20 sh. on a less than 100 sh. certificate, EAW, 11-3/4" x 7-3/4", green $4.00

*NO610-30-10, 1965, v, 100 sh., SCB, 12" x 8", blue $4.00

Norfolk and Western Railroad Company

*NO690-20-10, 1887, v, 100 sh. (par $100), green $20.00
NO690-30-10, 1886, 100 preferred sh. (par $100), green $6.00

NO690-50-10, 1933, v, $1,000 1st consol. mort. 4% bond, HLB, brown $14.00

Norfolk and Western Railway Company
NO720-20-10, 1968, v, 100 sh. (par $25), brown $7.00
NO720-30-10, 1895, 4 pref. sh., green $7.00

*NO720-40-10, 1929, v, $5,000 gold bond, green $12.00

Norman Oil Corporation (DE)
NO770-20-10, 1921, v, $1,000 8% 10-year gold bond, green $17.00

North American Aviation, Inc. (DE 1928)
The company had the first airmail route between Newark, NJ and Atlanta GA in 1928. After selling its Eastern Air Line division the company became a designer and manufacturer of military airplanes in 1938.

*NO920-20-10, 1962, v, 25 sh. on a less than 100 sh. certificate, Jeffries Banknote Co., blue $10.00
N2000-30-10, 1964, v, 100 sh., green $7.00

The North American Company
(NJ par $100)

Formed in 1890 to consolidate the Oregon, Trans-continental and other railroads. Later became a holding company for electric light and power companies. One of the original 12 companies that in 1896 formed the first Dow Jones Industrial Index.

NO960-20-10, 1890, v, 100 sh., green **$25.00**

NO960-25-10, 189x, v, 100 sh., green, blank certificate.............................**$15.00**

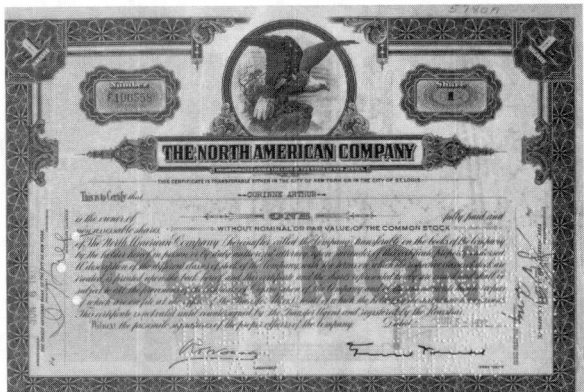

*NO960-35-10, 1933, v, 1 sh. on a 1 sh. certificate (no par), ABN, 12" x 8", brown **$4.00**

*NO960-40-10, 1925, v, 1 sh. on a less than 100 sh. certificate (no par), ABN, 12" x 8", orange **$4.00**

*NO960-45-10, 1934, v, 10 sh. on a less than 100 sh. certificate (no par), ABN, 12" x 8", green **$4.00**

*NO960-55-10, 1943, v, 94 sh. on a less than 100 sh. certificate (par $10), ABN, 12" x 8", brown **$4.00**

*NO960-65-10, 1932, v, 100 sh. (no par), ABN, 12" x 8", red **$4.00**

*NO960-70-10, 1940, v, 100 sh. (par $10), ABN,
12" x 8", blue $4.00

North American Edison Company
(DE no par)

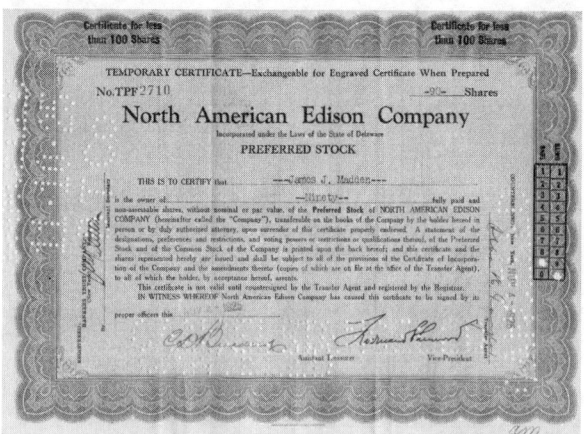

*NO1020-20-10, 1925, t, 90 sh. on a less than 100
sh. certificate, ABN, 10-3/4" x 7-3/4", green
. . . .$5.00
NO1020-30-10, 1929, t, 20 pref. sh. on a less than
100 sh. certificate, green $5.00
NO1020-40-10, 1935, v, 5 pref. sh. on a less than
100 sh. certificate, green $5.00
NO1020-50-10, 1930, v, 100 sh., Pref. stock,
orange $5.00

UNLISTED TYPES & VARIETIES

Readers are welcome to contact the author
directly at:

Rainer Stahlberg
P.O. Box 1044
Rooseveltown, New York 13683

North American Light and Power Company
(DE no par)

Successor of the The North American Co.

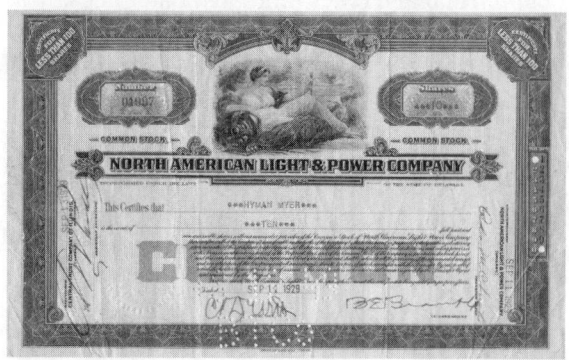

*NO1070-20-10, 1929, v, 10 sh. on a less than 100
sh. certificate, ABN, 11" x 7", grey $6.00

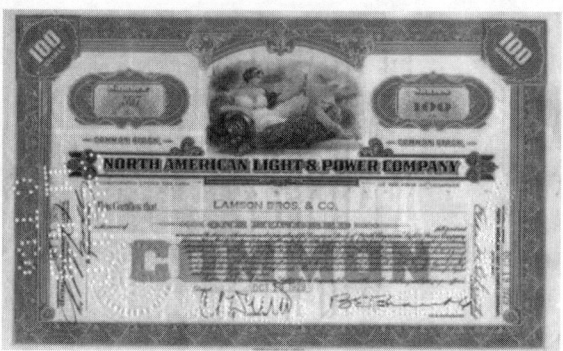

*NO1070-30-10, 1929, v, 100 sh., red $7.00
NO1070-35-10, 1943, v, 100 sh., red $4.00
NO1070-45-10, 1922, 1 pref. sh., 12" x 8", brown
border $4.00

The North American Mining Co.
(CO par $1)

*NO1100-20-10, 19xx, v, u/u certificate, grey
. . . .$4.00

*NO1100-25-10, 1925, v, 217 sh., green border on
light green...........................$5.00

North American Rockwell Corporation
(DE 1928, par $1)

*NO1210-20-10, 1968, v, 16 sh. on a less than 100
sh. certificate, Jeffries Banknote Co., 12" x 8",
green $4.00

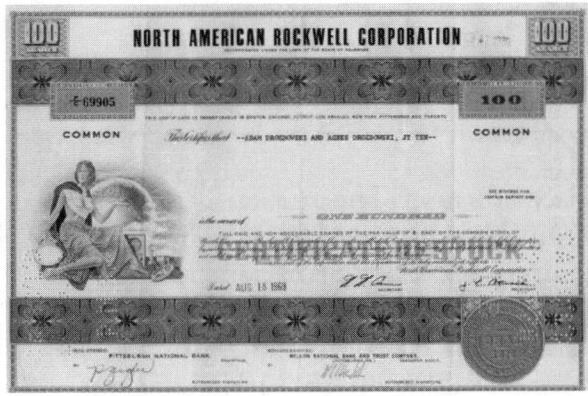

*NO1210-30-10, 1967, v, 100 sh., green $5.00

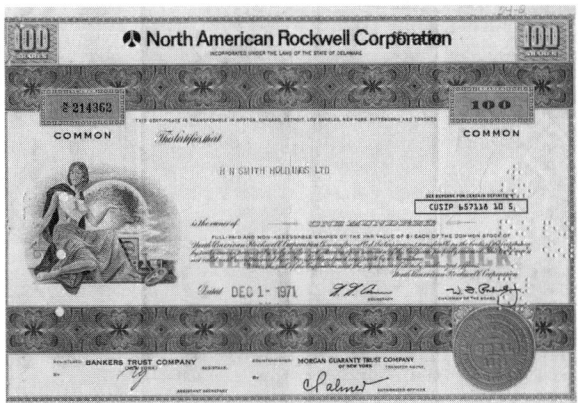

*NO1210-40-10, 1971, v, 100 sh., Jeffries Ban-
knote Company, 12" x 8", olive green $5.00

Township of North Bergen,
in the County of Hudson (NJ)

NO1240-20-10, 1959, v, $1,000 4.7% School bond
due 1967, brown....................$10.00

North Butte Mining Company
(MN par $15)

*NO1320-20-10, 1906, v, 50 sh., green $6.00
NO1320-30-10, 1925, v, 10 sh. on a less than 100
sh. certificate, green.................$8.00
NO1320-35-10, 1929, v, 30 sh. on a less than 100
sh. certificate, blue..................$5.00

The value of a stock certificate depends on:
- rarity
- the issuer
- signatures
- quality of engraving
- overall appearance
- condition
- date of issue

*NO1320-40-10, 1905, v, 100 sh., red $5.00
NO1320-50-10, 1930, v, 100 sh., red $8.00
NO1320-55-10, 19xx, v, less than 100 sh., green
....................................$6.00

North Central Airlines Inc.

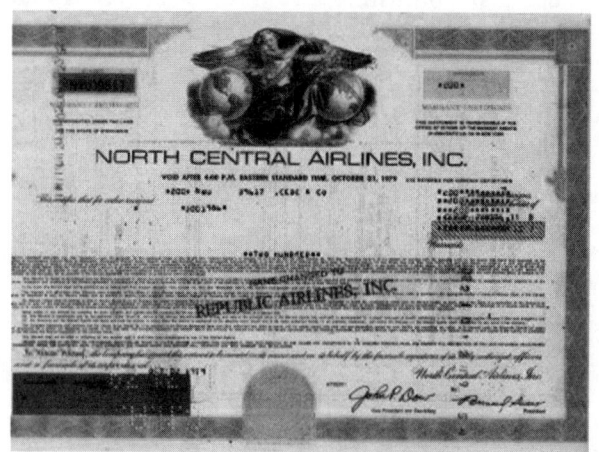

*NO1380-20-10, 1979, w, 200 sh., warrant, o/p
name changed to Republic Airlines Inc., orange
................................$15.00
NO1380-30-10, 1979, v, 32 sh., o/p name changed
Republic Airlines, Inc., yellow $11.00

North European Oil Royalty Trust

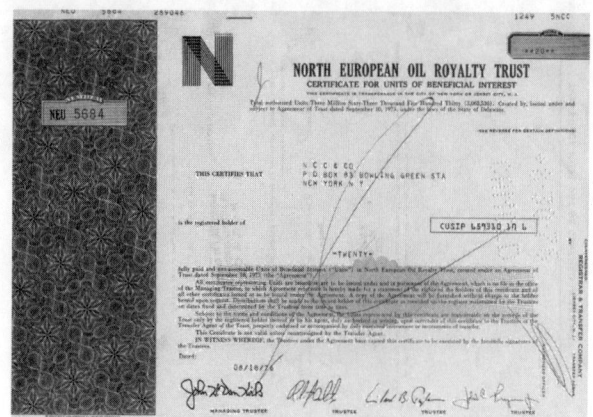

*NO1520-20-10, 1976, v, 20 units (par $1), SCB,
12" x 8", green $4.00

North Utah Mining Company of Bingham (ME $5)

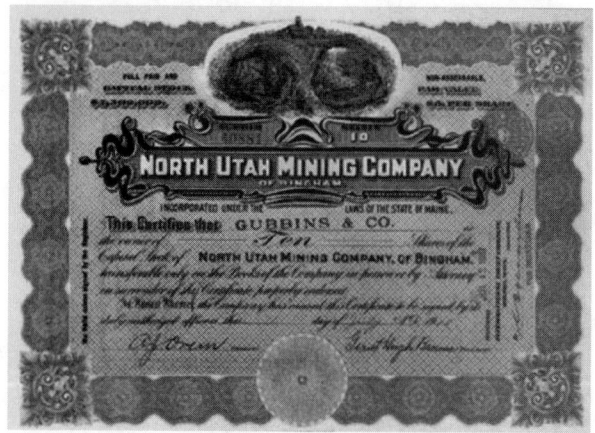

*NO1650-20-10, 1906, v, 10 sh., brown $6.00

This catalog has listings in an alphabetical format. The reason is simple: Companies diversify as they grow. For example, the Canadian Pacific Railway company recently split into five companies. They represent the railway, hotels, shipping, airline, and petroleum interests of the company. During World War II, the Singer sewing machine company made guns and other defense-related equipment, so where should we list it? It's far easier to use a strict alphabetical order, rather than to confuse the reader with topical classifications.

Northern Alabama Coal, Iron and Railway Company

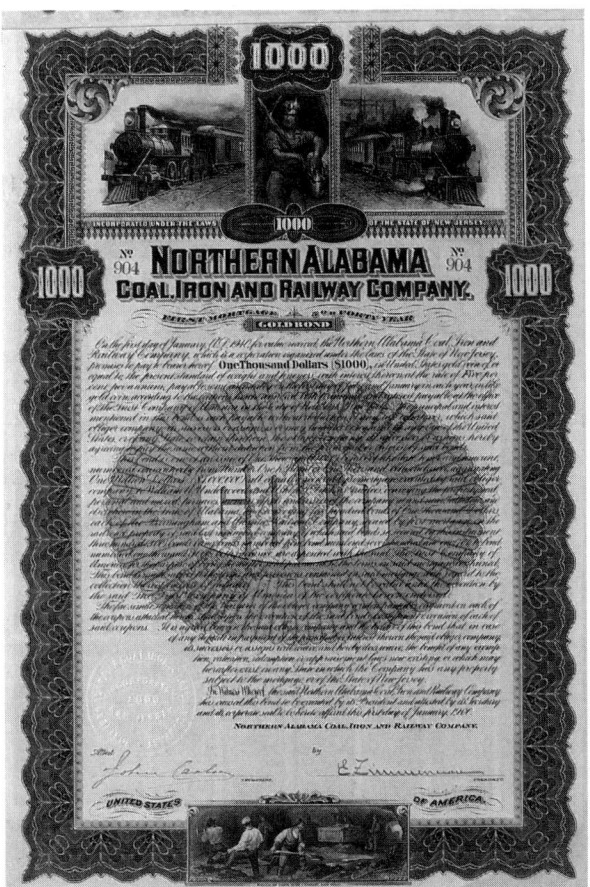

*NO1720-30-10, 1900, v, $1,000 3% 1st mortgage gold bond, green....................$20.00

Northern Alabama Railway Company

NO1750-20-10, 19xx, v, unissued certificate, green $15.00

The Northern Central Railway Company (PA-MD par $50)

In 1854, a consolidation of Baltimore & Susquehanna RR, the York and Maryland RR, the York and York and Cumberland RR and the Susquehanna RR formed this company.

NO1820-20-10, 1923, v, 2 sh., blue-purple ..$8.00

NO1820-30-10, 1952, v, 1 sh., blue-purple ..$6.00

NO1820-40-10, 1924, v, $1,000 general and refunding 5% gold bond w. coupons, ABN, orange $12.00

Northern Liberties Gas Company (PA)

NO1850-10-10, 1854, 1 sh., light brown ...$15.00

Northern National Bank, Ashland, Wis. (WI par $100)

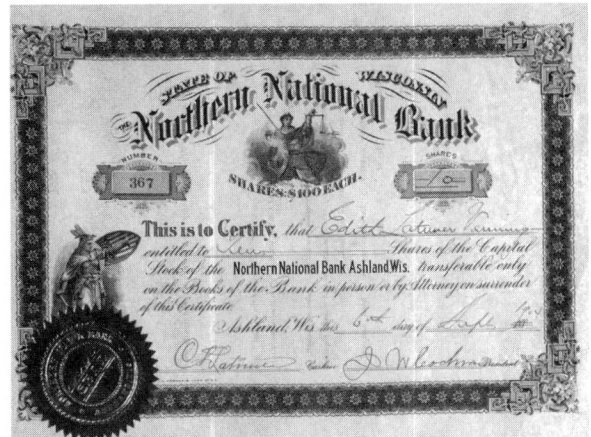

*NO1880-20-10, 1904, v, 10 sh., 11" x 8", grey border $60.00

Northern Pacific Railway Company (WI)

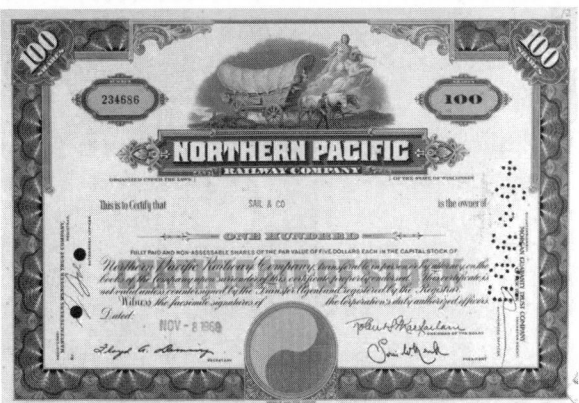

*NO2000-20-10, 1968, v, 100 sh. (par $5), ABN, 12" x 8", brown border.................$15.00

It is generally assumed that only 5% of certificates survive to reach collectors.

*NO2000-40-10, 1896, v, $1,000 General Lien Railway and Land Grant gold bond, brown
. . . .$75.00

NO2000-60-10, 19xx, v - covered wagon, $1,000 4% collateral bond due 1984, brown $10.00

Northern Refrigerator Car Company (WI par $100)

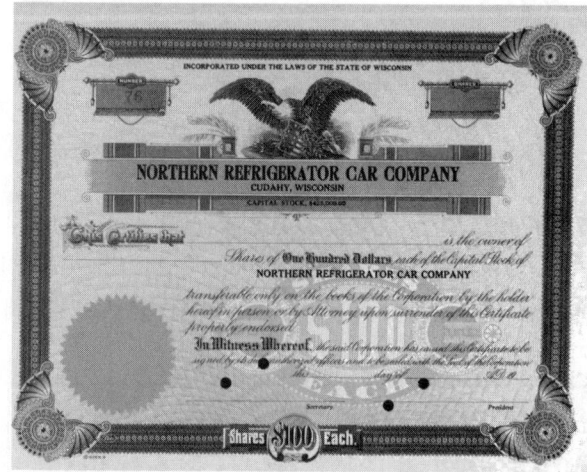

*NO2050-20-10, 19xx, v, u/c certificate, GOES, 10-1/2" x 8", brown border $18.00

Northern Virginia Bankshares, Incorporated (VA par $1)

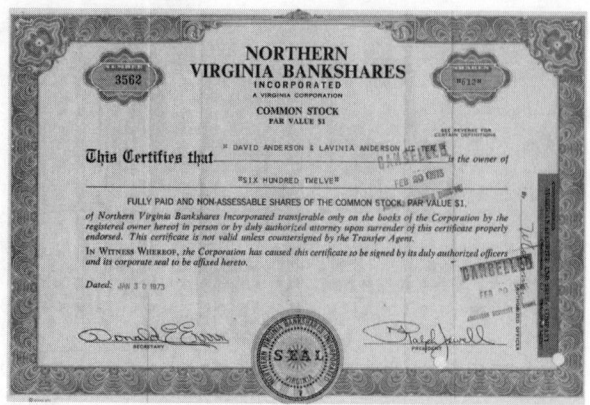

*NO2100-20-10, 1973, v, 612 sh., w/o imprint, 12" x 8", orange. $4.00

Northfork Finance Corporation (WV 1924)

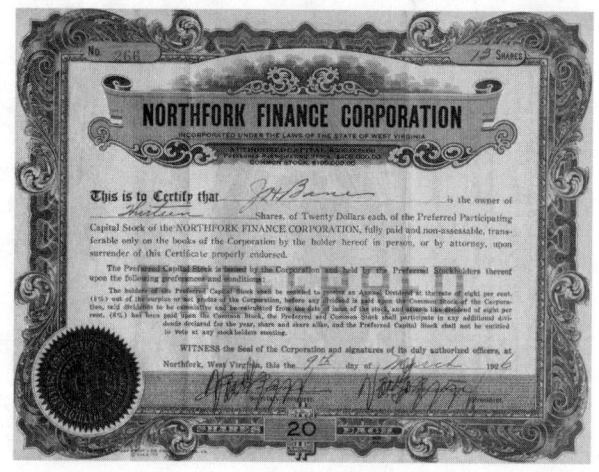

*NO2160-20-10, 1926, 13 8% pref. sh. (par $20), GOES, 11" x 8-1/4", brown. $4.00

The value of a stock certificate depends on:

- rarity
- the issuer
- signatures
- quality of engraving
- overall appearance
- condition
- date of issue

Northwestern Mutual Life Mortgage and Realty Investors

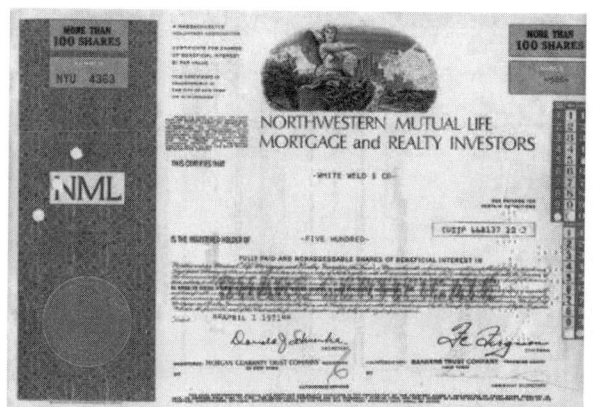

NO2340-20-10, 1971, v, 500 sh., red **$5.00**

Norwegian Consolidated Mining Company (CA par $1)

NO2440-20-10, 1908, v, 1,000 sh., GOES, 11" x 8-1/2", brown border **$8.00**

Norwich & New York Transportation Co. (CT par $25)

NO2470-20-10, 19xx, v, unissued certificate, grey **$15.00**

Norwich & Worcester Railroad Company

NO2500-30-10, 1897, v, $1,000 bearer bond, green **$100.00**

Nuclear-Chicago Corporation (DE 1957)

NU120-20-10, 1964, v, 5 sh., blue **$6.00**

Nuclear Research Associates, Inc. (DE 1960, par $0.10)

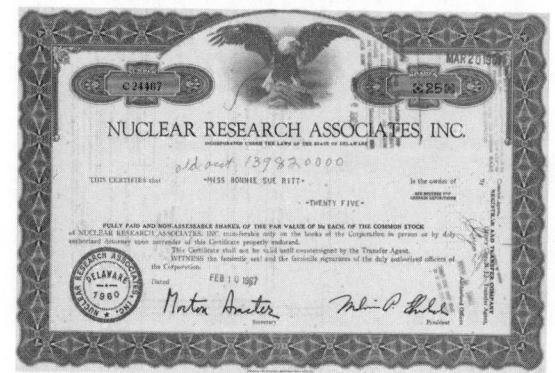

NU250-20-10, 1967, 25 sh., FLB, 11-3/4" x 8", green **$4.00**

The Nuernberg Importing Company (OR 1912, par $100)

NU370-20-10, 1912, v, i/u 12 sh., w/o imprint, 11" x 8-1/2", grey border...............**$3.00**

O

Oakite Products Inc. (NY par $100)

OA70-20-10, 1968, v, 87 sh. on a less than 100 sh. certificate, brown $4.00

Official Films Inc. (DE 1945)

OF110-20-10, 1958, v, 1,000 sh., brown $4.00

OO110-30-10, 1972, v, 100 sh., o/p name changed to Official Industries Inc., green $10.00

The Offshore Company (DE par $0.25)

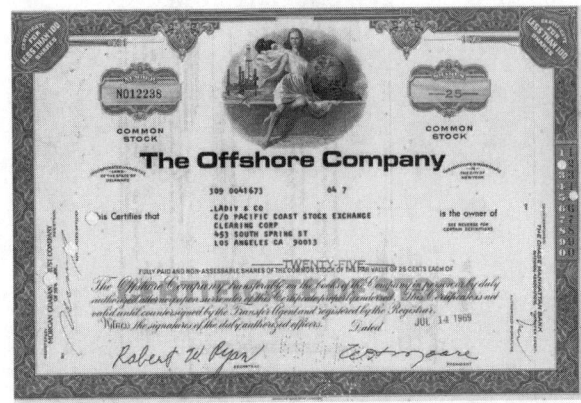

OF190-20-10, 1969, v, 25 sh. on a less than 100 sh. certificate, ABN, 12" x 8", brown $4.00

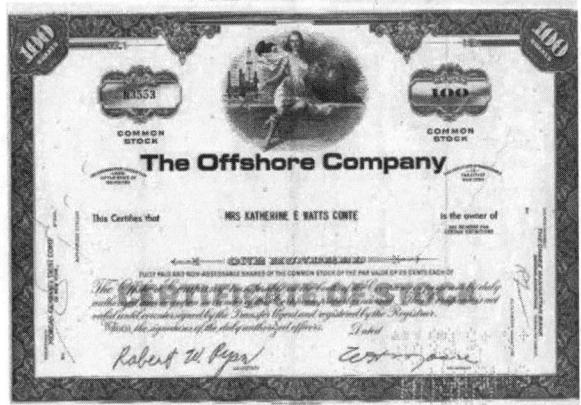

OF190-30-10, 1970, v, 100 sh., blue $4.00

Ohio Edison Company

OH110-40-10, 1989, v, $5,000 9-1/2% 1st mortgage bond, due 2006, red $26.00

Ohio and Little Kanawha Railroad Company

OH180-20-10, 19xx, v, u/u certificate, brown
. . . .$15.00

Ohio & Mississippi Railway Company, Reorganized & Consolidated 1867 (par $100)

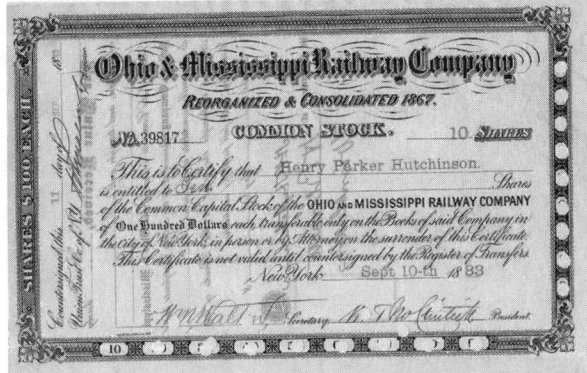

OH230-20-10, 1883, 10 sh., grey-brown border
. . . .$11.00

OH230-25-10, 1888, 10 sh., green $20.00

The value of a stock certificate depends on:

- **rarity**
- **the issuer**
- **signatures**
- **quality of engraving**
- **overall appearance**
- **condition**
- **date of issue**

Ohio & Pennsylvania Railroad Company (par $50)

*OH310-20-10, 1855, v, 50 sh., grey $27.00

Ohio Power Company (OH 1907)

OH340-20-10, 1971, v, 100 sh., blue $4.00
OH340-30-10, 1941, v, 100 sh., 4-1/2% cumul. pref. stock, o/p name changed to Ohio Power Company, blue $6.00

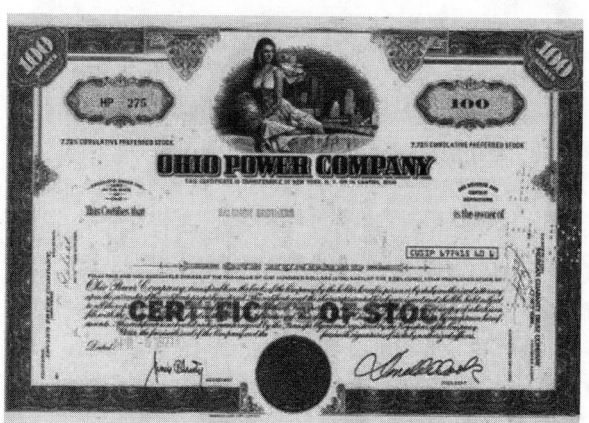

*OH340-30-10, 1971, v, 100 7.25% cumul. pref. sh. (par $100), brown $4.00

Ohio Valley Railway Company (OH par $100)

*OH410-20-10, 188x, v, u/u certificate, ABN, brown $15.00

Oil Desulphurizing Corporation

*OI120-20-10, 192x, v, u/u preferred stock certificate, orange. $5.00

O.K. Silver Mining and Milling Company (UT par 10¢)

OK180-20-10, 1916, v, 200 sh., green border
. . . .$15.00

Old Colony Rail Road Company (MA)

Became part of New England Navigation Co.
OL200-20-10, 1874, v, $1,000 bond, brown
. . . .$40.00

*OL200-25-10, 1881, v, $1,000 bond, grey
......................................$100.00

Old Line Life Insurance Company of America (WI par $10)

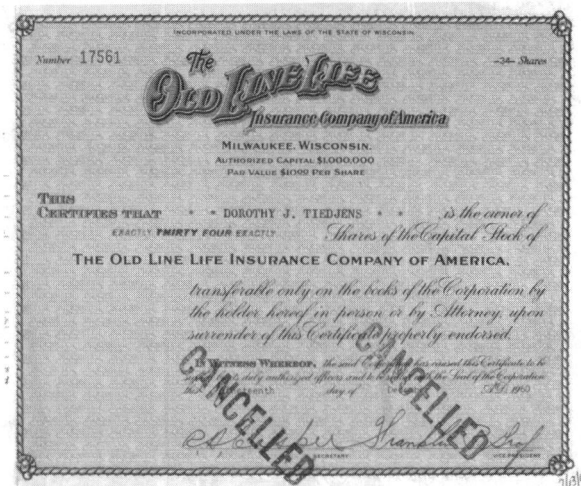

*OL280-20-10, 1960, v, 34 sh., 9" x 7", grey border
......................................$5.00

The Old National Bank of New Brighton (PA)

OL340-20-10, 19xx, v, u/u certificate, grey
......................................$8.00

> **It is generally assumed that only 5% of certificates survive to reach collectors.**

Old Town Corporation (NY 1917, par $1)

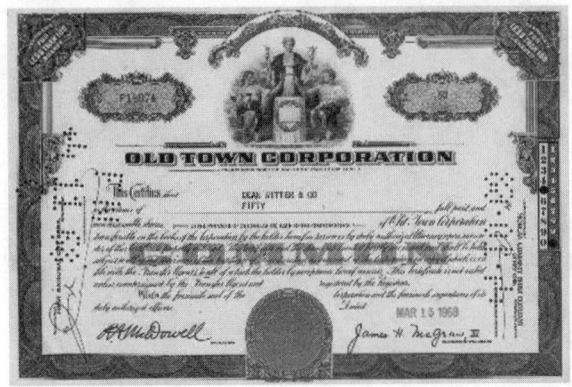

*OL420-20-10, 1968, v, 50 sh. on a less than 100 sh. certificate, blue $4.00

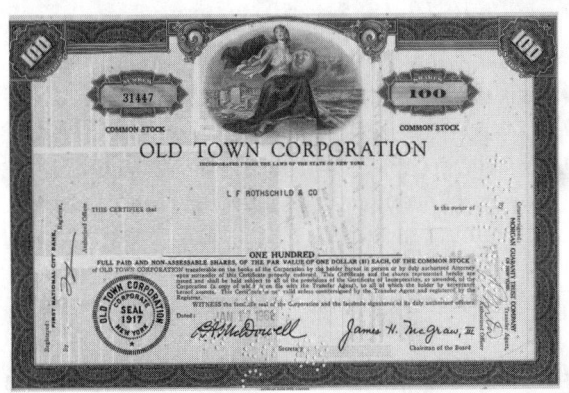

*OL420-30-10, 1968, v, 100 sh., ABN, 12" x 8", green............................$4.00

Olompali Silver Mining Company (1877)

OL540-10-10, 1878, v, 50 sh., blue $85.00

Olympic Building (CA)

*OL650-20-10, 1927, $1,000 1st mort. 6-1/2% gold bond, orange........................$5.00

Omaha Bridge and Terminal Company (NE par $100)

OM110-20-10, 189x, v, unissued certificate, ABN, green $15.00

Omaha and Council Bluffs Street Railway Company (NE par $100)

OM180-20-10, 1938, 14 sh., voting trust certificate, green $6.00

OM180-30-10, 1961, v, 10 sh. on a less than 100 sh. certificate, green $12.00

Omaha Oil and Mining Company

OM300-30-10, 1887, v, 100 sh., grey. $8.00

Oneida Electric Truck Company (WI)

ON170-10-10, 1920, v, 3 sh. (no par), GOES, 11" x 8", brown border $40.00

ON170-20-10, 1920, v, 4 pref. sh. (par $100), GOES, 11" x 8-1/2", brown border. $40.00

Onondaga Copper Company (MI)

ON320-20-10, 1916, v, 100 sh., brown $4.00

O'Okiep Copper Company Limited

OO40-20-10, 19xx, v, 25 American sh. on a less than 100 sh. certificate, brown $4.00

Ophir Extension Consolidated Gold & Silver Mining Company

OP270-20-10, 19xx, v, unissued certificate, brown $9.00

Option Mining Company (ID par 10¢)

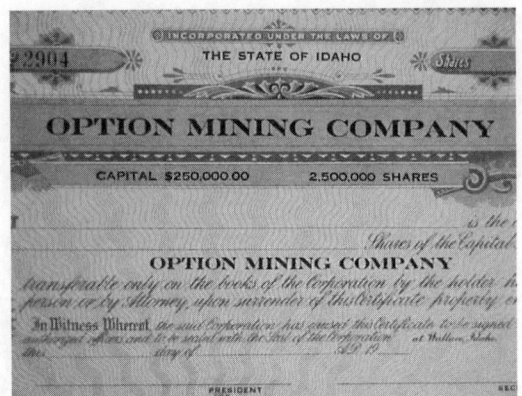

OP400-20-10, 1927, v, 5,000 sh., brown **$8.00**

*OP400-25-10, 19xx, v, u/u certificate, brown
. . . .**$4.00**

O'Quinn Abstract and Title Co. (AZ par $100)

*OQ100-20-10, 1923, v, 50 sh., purple **$5.00**

Orange and Rockland Utilities, Inc. (NY par $10)

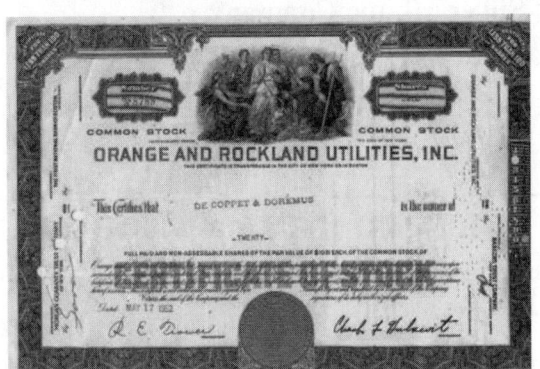

*OR160-20-10, 1962, v, 20 sh. on a less than 100
sh. certificate, green **$5.00**

Orbital Sciences Corporation

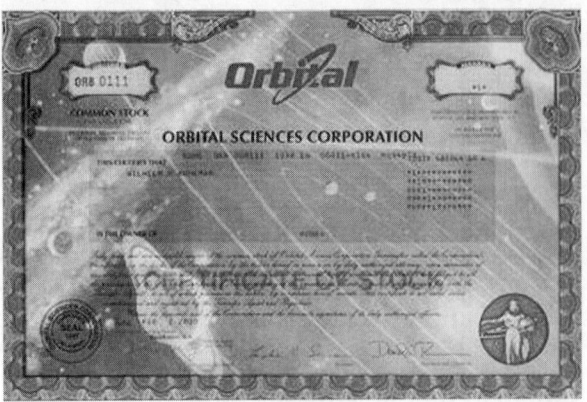

*OR220-20-10, 19??, v, 1 sh., blue **$40.00**

Orcutt Automatic Train Control Company (par $10)

*OR280-20-10, 19xx, v, u/u certificate, brown
. . . .**$15.00**

Oregon Orchard Association (par $100)

*OR360-20-10, 1893, v, 25 sh., Lewis & Dryder
Litho. Co., Portland; brown **$20.00**

Oregon Pacific and Eastern Railway Company

OR390-20-10, 19xx, v, u/u preferred stock, brown
....................................$12.00

Oregon Smelting & Refining Co.

OR440-20-10, 1928, v, 7-1/2 sh. (par $100), grey
....................................$5.00

Oregon and Southeastern Railroad Company

OR470-20-10, 19xx, v, u/u certificate, green
....................................$10.00
OR470-30-10, 19xx, v, u/u preferred stock, brown
....................................$12.00

Oregon and Transcontinental Company (par $100)

OR500-20-10, 1883, v, 100 sh., green $15.00

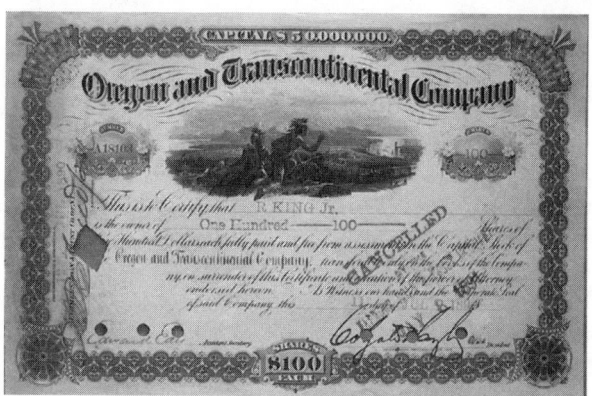

OR500-25-10, 1890, v, 100 sh., grey $8.00
OR500-35-10, 1882, v, $1,000 bond, grey
....................................$15.00

Oro Hondo Mining Company (SD 1902, par $1)

Mines at Lead City.
OR700-20-10, 1902, v, 100 sh., brown border
....................................$15.00

The Orphan Bell Mining and Milling Co. (CO)

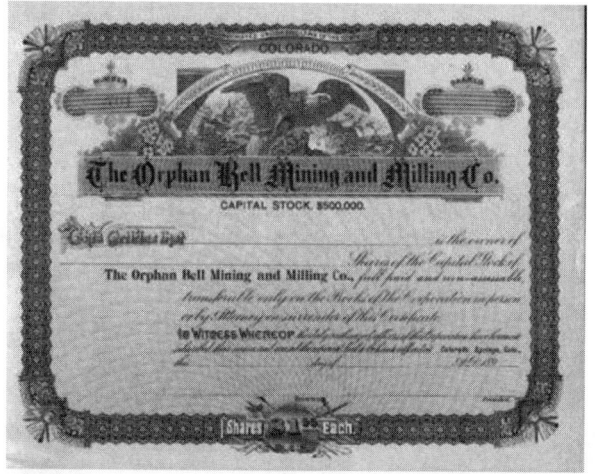

OR760-20-10, 19xx, v, u/u certificate, grey on green....................................$4.00

Oshkosh Consolidated Mining Company (ME 1880)

OS160-20-10, 1880, v, 50 sh., 10-1/2" x 6", grey border....................................$60.00

It is generally assumed that only 5% of certificates survive to reach collectors.

Oshkosh Seed Company (WI par $100)

*OS230-20-10, 1921, v, 20 sh., GOES, 11" x 8-1/2", green $60.00

O'Sullivan Corporation

*OS300-20-10, 19??, v, 50 sh., purple $4.00

Otis Elevator Company (NJ)

OT170-20-10, 1968, v, 50 sh. on a less than 100 sh. certificate, red $18.00

*OT170-40-10, 1972, v, $1,000 6-1/2% conver. subord. due 1995, red $18.00

The Ouray Mining and Reduction Company (CO par 1 mil)

OU200-20-10, 1919, v, 10,500 sh., grey . . .$30.00

The Ouray Smelting and Refining Company (CO)

OU220-20-10, 1916, v, i/u 40 sh., grey border on brown $40.00

Outboard Marine Corporation

OU410-50-10, 1977, v, $10,000 7-3/4% sinking fund debenture due 1996, brown $4.00

Owens-Corning Fiberglass Corporation

The company's parents were Corning Glass Works and Owens-Illinois Glass Co.
OW230-30-10, 1977, v, $50,000 9.5% bond $5.00

Owl Realty Company (WI par $10)

*OW320-20-10, 1924, v, 2 sh., GOES, 10-1/2" x 8", brown border. $11.00

Ozark Mining & Milling Co. (ID par $1)

*OZ80-20-10, 1907, v, 100 sh., green $15.00

P

Pabst Brewing Company (WI par $1,000)

*PA100-20-10, 1908, v, 50 sh., issued to Gustav
  Pabst, 12" x 11", green border **$200.00**

Pacific American Fisheries, Inc.
PA200-30-10, 1936, v, 100 sh., blue **$30.00**

Pacific Northwest Bell Telephone Company (WA)
PA230-40-10, 1977, v, $10,000 7% 7-year note,
  ABN, green **$7.00**

The Pacific Telephone and Telegraph Company (CA 1907, par $14 2/7)

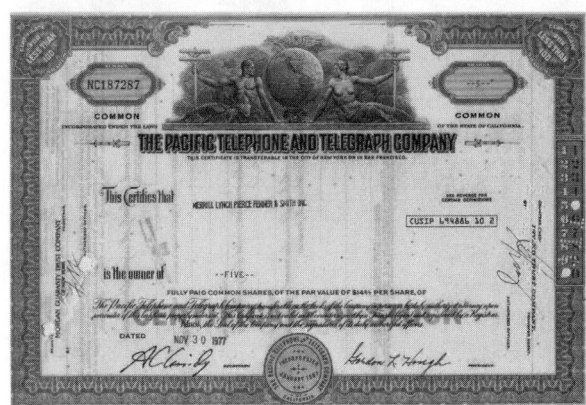

*PA300-20-10, 1977, v, 5 sh. on a less than 100 sh.
  certificate, ABN, 12" x 8-1/4", orange **$4.00**

*PA300-30-10, 1969, v, 100 sh., ABN, 12" x
  8-1/4", purple **$4.00**

*PA300-35-10, 1977, v, 200 sh. on a more than 100
  sh. certificate, ABN, 12" x 8-1/4", blue . . .**$4.00**

Packard Motor Car Company (no par)
PA400-20-10, 1935, v, 50 sh. on a less than 100 sh.
  certificate, orange **$10.00**
PA400-25-10, 1954, v, 67 sh. on a less than 100 sh.
  certificate, orange **$8.00**
PA400-30-10, 1945, v, 100 sh., green **$8.00**
PA400-35-10, 1952, v, 100 sh., deep blue . . .**$8.00**
PA400-40-10, 1954, v, 100 sh., green **$8.00**

Pacolet Manufacturing Company (SC par $100)

PA460-20-10, 1889, v - horse, 2 sh., black
. . . .$20.00

Paducah & Illinois Railroad Company (KY par $100)

PA500-20-10, 1916, v, 3 sh., grey border
. . . .$30.00

Page & Shaw Incorporated

Candy maker.
PA700-20-10, 1929, v, 1 class A sh., brown
. . . .$5.00

Paiute Oil and Mining Corporation (UT)

PA760-20-10, 1971, v, 100 sh., grey $6.00

Palmer Mattress Company, Inc. (FL par $1)

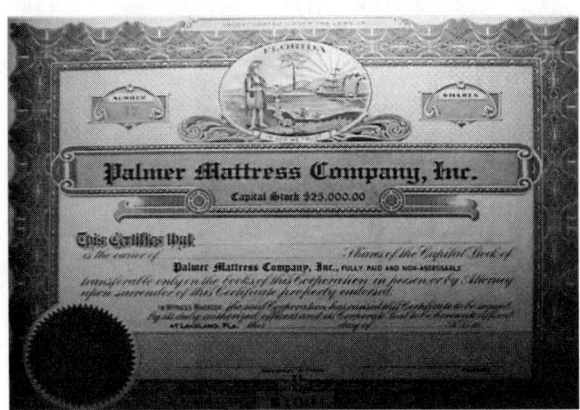

PA820-20-10, 19xx, v, u/u certificate, green
. . . .$7.00

Palmer Union Oil Company (CA par $1)

PA850-20-10, 1928, 500 sh., grey-purple . . .$6.00

PA850-30-10, 1917, 1,000 pref. sh., The Union
Litho Co., 12" x 9", blue $8.00

Paloma Gold and Silver Mining Company (UT)

PA870-20-10, 1919, v, i/u 1,000 sh., brown border
. . . .$13.00

Pamlico, Oriental and Western Railroad Co. (NC par $100)

PA920-20-10, 18xx, v, unissued certificate, brown
. . . .$80.00

Pan Am Corporation (DE 1984)

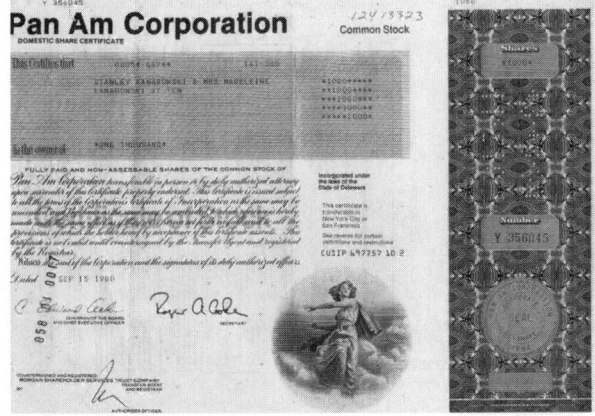

P960-20-10, 1988, v, 1,000 domestic sh., ABN,
12" x 8", blue $4.00

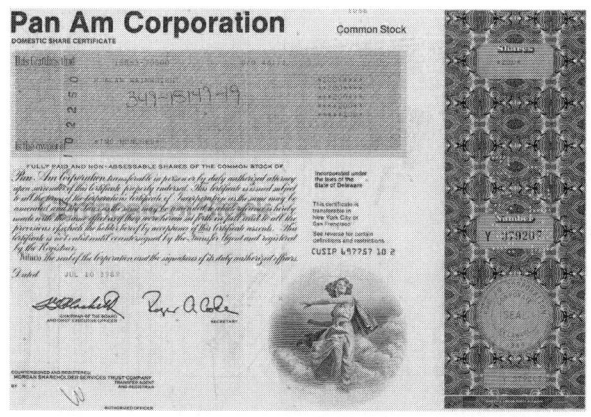

*PA960-20-15, 1989, v, 200 domestic sh., signature variety, ABN, 12" x 8", blue...........$4.00

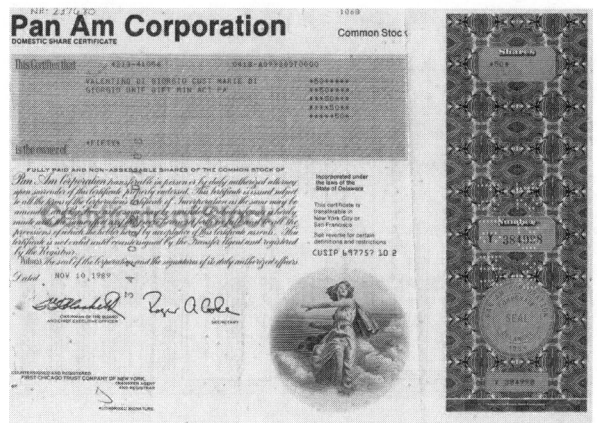

*PA960-20-20, 1989, v, 50 sh., registrar First Chicago Co., ABN, 12" x 8", blue $4.00

Pan American Sulphur Company (DE 1947, par $0.70)

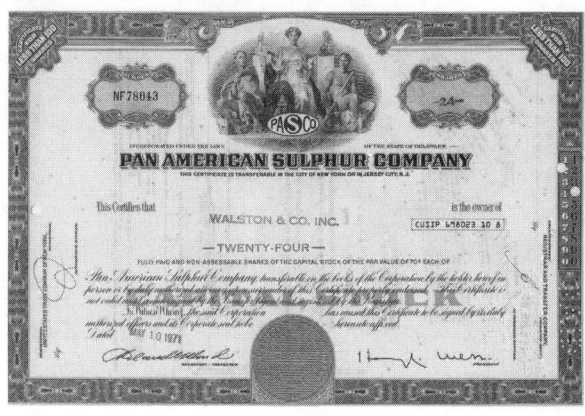

*PA990-20-10, 1971, v, 24 sh. on a less than 100 sh. certificate, ABN, 12" x 8", brown.....$4.00

*PA990-30-10, 1953, v, 100 sh., signature strip, FLB, 12" x 8", green $4.00

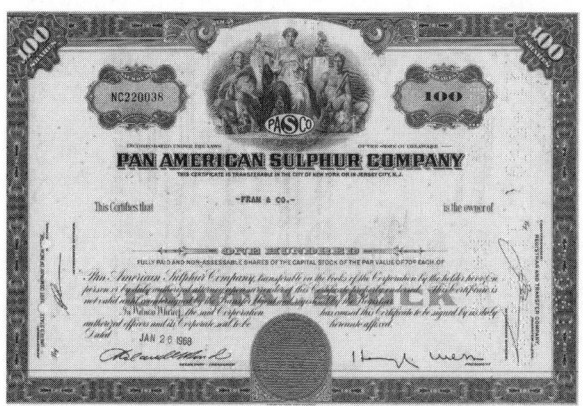

*PA990-35-10, 1968, v, 100 sh., ABN, 12" x 8", green.............................$4.00

*PA990-40-10, 1973, v, 100 sh., green, o/p changed to PASCO, Inc., ABN, 12" x 8".........$4.00

Pan American World Airways, Inc.
(NY 1927)

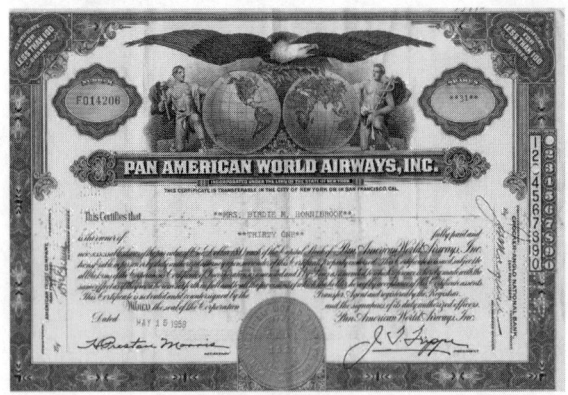

*PA1020-20-10, 1958, v, 31 sh. on a less than 100 sh. certificate, facsimile signature Trippe, ABN, 12" x 8", brown......................$4.00

*PA1020-25-10, 19xx, v, 37 sh. on less than 100 sh., voided certificate, signature strip, ABN, 12" x 8", brown.......................$4.00

PA1020-30-10, 1961, v, 10 sh. on a less than 100 sh. certificate, brown..................$4.00

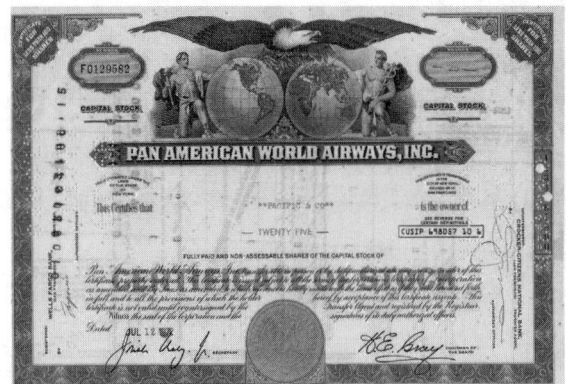

*PA1020-30-15, 1972, v, 25 sh. on less than 100 sh. certificate, signature variety, ABN, 12" x 8", brown $4.00

*PA1020-40-10, 1960, v, 100 sh., ABN, 12" x 8", red................................$4.00

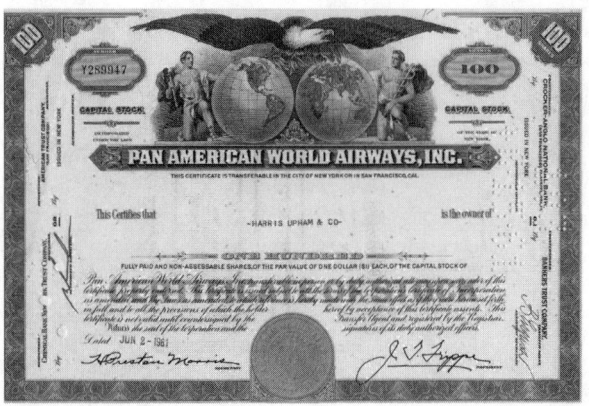

*PA1020-40-15, 1961, v, 100 sh., registrar Chemical Bank, ABN, 12" x 8", red...........$4.00

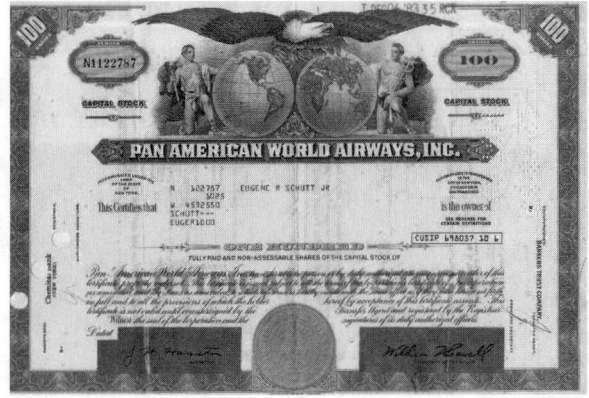

*PA1020-40-20, 1973, v, 100 sh., signature strip, ABN, 12" x 8", red....................$4.00

PA1020-50-10, 1971, v, 1,000 sh., blue.....$5.00

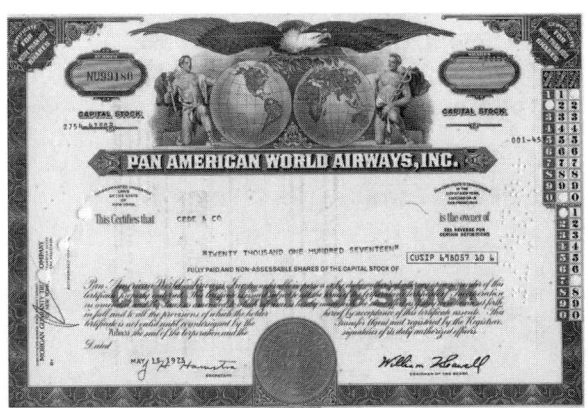

*PA1020-55-10, 1975, v, 20,117 sh. on a more than
100 sh. certificate, ABN, 12" x 8", blue **$5.00**

*PA1020-60-10, 1981, v, 500 sh., ABN, 12" x 8",
aquamarine **$4.00**
PA1020-80-10, 1959, v, $100 4-1/2% conver.
subord. debenture w. coupons, 9" x 13-1/2",
brown border. **$7.00**

Pan State Gas Company

*PA1100-20-10, 1902, v, 100 sh., New York Certif-
icate, green **$4.00**

Papago Chief Consolidated Mining Company (IA par $20)

PA1190-20-10, 1880, v, 100 sh., brown . . **$160.00**

Paramount Pictures Corporation (par $1)

*PA1240-20-10, 1965, v, 100 sh., green . . . **$20.00**

Parke, Davis & Company (MI 1875, no par)

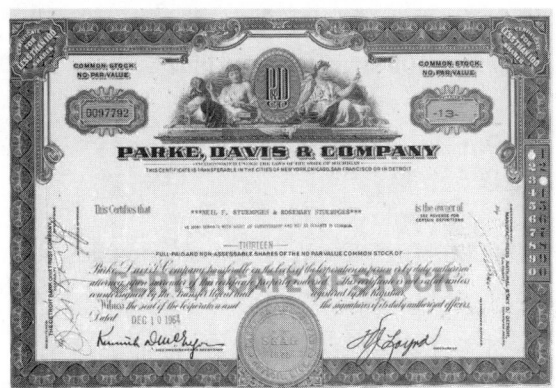

*PA1310-20-10, 1964, v, 13 sh. on a less than 100
sh. certificate, ABN, 12" x 8", green **$4.00**

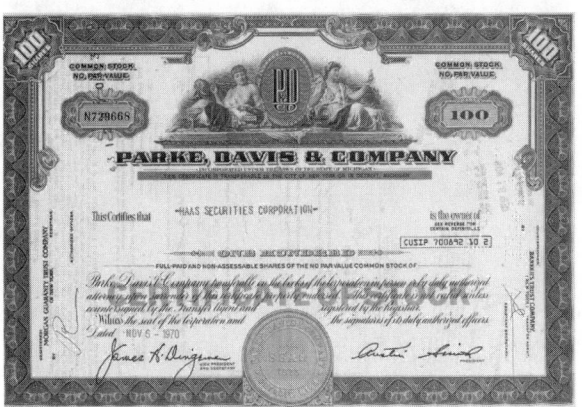

*PA1310-30-10, 1970, v, 100 sh., ABN, 12" x 8",
brown **$4.00**

The Parrot Silver and Copper Company (MT par $10)

PA1420-20-10, 1909, v, 15 sh. on a less than 100 sh. certificate, green $12.00

PA1420-30-10, 19xx, v, u/u 100 sh. certificate, brown $7.00

Patino Mines & Enterprises Consolidated, Incorporated (DE par $5)

*PA1520-20-10, 1954, v, 50 American shares on a less than 100 sh. certificate, blue $5.00

The Pauline Gold Mining Company (CO par $1)

Mines at Cripple Creek.

PA1600-20-10, 1900, v, 10,000 sh., orange $60.00

Pawling Savings Bank (NY par $1)

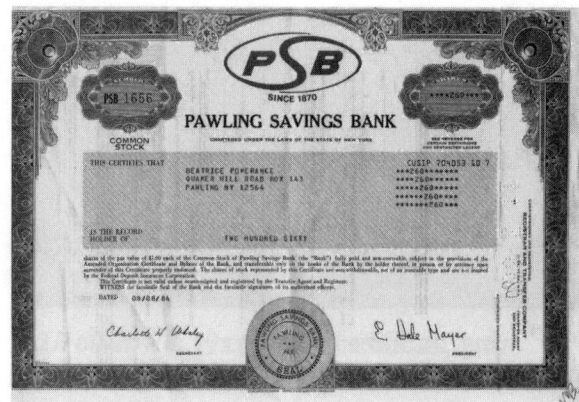

*PA1700-20-10, 1984, v, 100 sh., SCB, 12" x 8", green $4.00

payforview.com corp. (NV 1988, par $0.0001)

PA1790-20-10, 1988, v, specimen certificate $8.00

The Peak Technologies Group, Inc. (DE par 1¢)

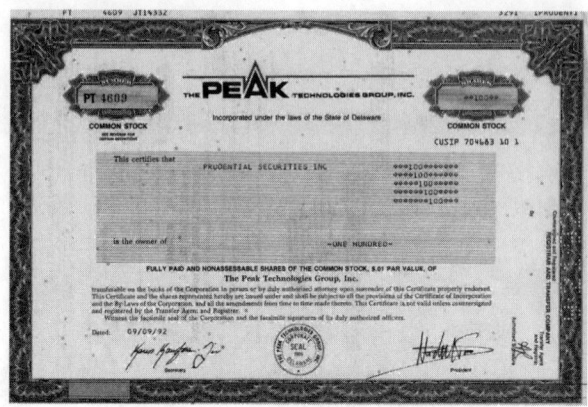

*PE60-20-10, 1992, v, 100 sh., Banknote Corporation of America, 12" x 8", blue $4.00

Peekskill Financial Corporation (DE 1995, par 1¢)

*PE160-20-10, 1996, v - eagle, 2,000 sh., SCB, 12" x 8", blue $5.00

Peerless Mining Company (MT par $1)

PE190-20-10, 19xx, u/u certificate $9.00

Pekin, Lincoln and Decatur Railway Co.

PE290-20-10, 18xx, v, u/u certificate $10.00

Pelham Terrace Apartments

*PE410-30-10, 1924, v, $500 1st mort. 7% gold bond, on 6733 Emlen St., Philadelphia, PA, blue $7.00

Pence Iron Mining Company (WI par $25)

*PE640-20-10, 1887, v, 50 sh., 10-1/2" x 8-1/2", grey border $65.00

The Pence & Snider Iron Development Company (WI par $25)

*PE645-20-10, 1887, v, 150 sh., w/o imprint, 10" x 8", brown border...................$65.00

Penn Central Company (no par)

Formed in 1968 by the merger of the New York Central and the Pennsylvania Railroad.

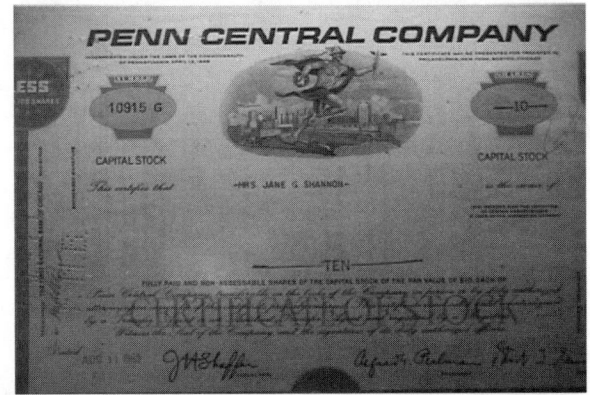

*PE670-20-10, 1969, v, 10 sh. on a less than 100 sh. certificate, brown $8.00
PE670-30-10, 1970, v, 100 sh., red $10.00

This catalog has listings in an alphabetical format. The reason is simple: Companies diversify as they grow. For example, the Canadian Pacific Railway company recently split into five companies. They represent the railway, hotels, shipping, airline, and petroleum interests of the company. During World War II, the Singer sewing machine company made guns and other defense-related equipment, so where should we list it? It's far easier to use a strict alphabetical order, rather than to confuse the reader with topical classifications.

Penn. Commercial Corporation of America (NY)

*PE700-20-10, 1922, v, 3 class A sh. (no par), blue
.....................................$5.00

Penn.-Harris Bond and Mortgage Company (DE 1924)

*PE730-20-10, 1925, v, 11 sh., green $5.00

J.C. Penney Company, Inc.

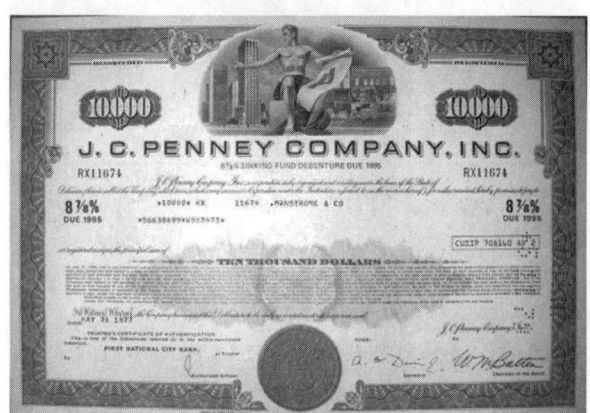

*PE760-40-10, 1977, v, $10,000 8-7/8% sinking
fund deb. due 1995, purple............$20.00

Pennmont Consolidated Mining Company (DC par $1)

*PE810-20-10, 190x, v, u/u certificate, grey-brown
..................................$8.00

Pennock Underground Conduit & Surface Telegraph Company of New Jersey (par $1)

*PE850-20-10, 1887, v, 500 sh., grey $15.00

Pennsalt Chemicals Corporation (PA 1850)

*PE940-20-10, 1963, v, 5 sh. on a less than 100 sh. certificate (par $3), SBC, 11-1/4" x 8-1/2", brown $4.00

*PE940-25-10, 1959, v, 6 sh. on a less than 100 sh. certificate, o/p this stock has been changed to $3 per share, SBN, 12" x 8", brown. $4.00

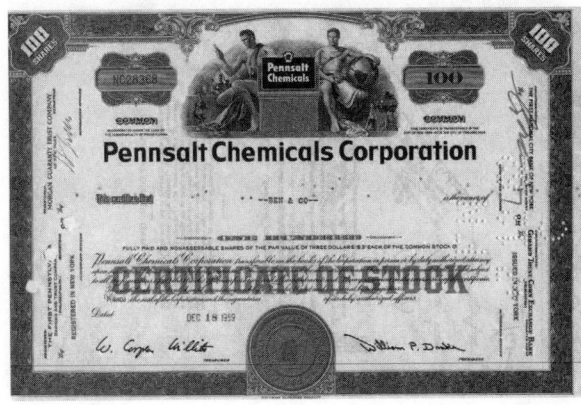

*PE940-35-10, 1959, v, 100 sh. (par $3.00), SBN, 12" x 8", green $4.00

Pennsylvania New York Central Transportation Company

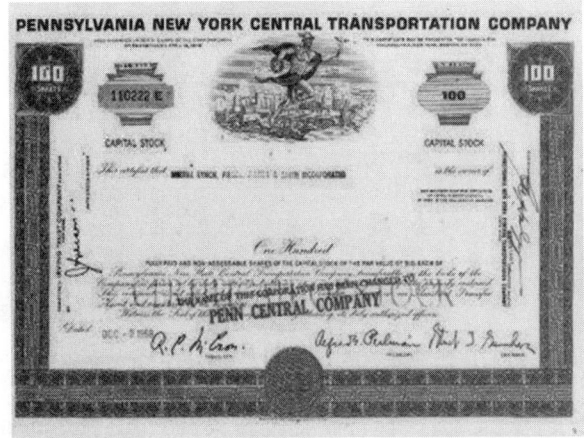

*PE1020-20-10, 1968, v, 100 sh., o/p name changed to Penn Central Company, blue . .$5.00

The Pennsylvania-Ohio Electric Company (par $100)

PE1090-20-10, 19xx, v, 100 sh., pref. sh., green $9.00

PE1090-30-10, 19xx, v, unissued pref. stock certificate, orange $9.00

Pennsylvania & Ohio Oil Company (PA)

PE1120-20-10, 1865, many folds $80.00

The Pennsylvania Railroad Company (PA 1848, par $50)

PE1350-30-10, 1929, v, 10 sh., orange $10.00

*PE1350-35-10, 1950, v, 50 sh., ABN, 11-3/4" x 8", orange $4.00

PE1350-35-15, 1957, v - PA coat of arms, 20 sh.,
signature variety, ABN, 11-3/4" x 8", orange
. . . .$4.00

PE1350-50-10, 1967, v - horseshoe curve, 50 sh.
on a less than 100 sh. certificate (par $10),
orange $4.00
PE1350-60-10, 1941, v, 100 sh., green $4.00

PE1350-65-10, 1953, v - PA coat of arms, 100
sh., ABN, 11-3/4" x 8", green. $4.00

PE1350-65-15, 1955, v - PA coat of arms, 100
sh., signature variety, ABN, 11-3/4" x 8", green
. . . .$4.00

PE1350-75-10, 1967, v - horseshoe curve, 100 sh.
(par $10), green $4.00

The Pennsylvania Salt
Manufacturing Company (PA par $10)

PE1390-20-10, 1939, v, 30 sh. on a less than 100
sh. certificate (par $50), green $4.00
PE1390-30-10, 1960, v, 9 sh. on a less than 100 sh.
certificate, red. $4.00

*PE1390-40-10, 1958, v, 100 sh., o/p name changed Pennsalt Chemicals Corporation, ABN, 12" x 8", blue $4.00

Pennzoil United, Inc. (DE)

*PE1500-40-10, 1976, v, $10,000 5-1/4% conver. subord. debenture due 1996, o/p name changed to Pennzoil Company, ABN, 12" x 8", purple $5.00

Penobscot & Kennebec Railroad Company (ME)

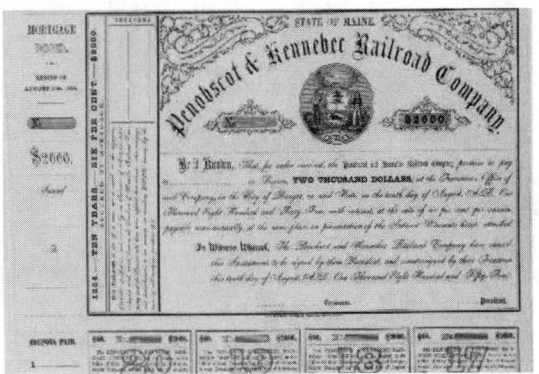

*PE1540-20-10, 1855, ledger page w. three certificates, grey $15.00

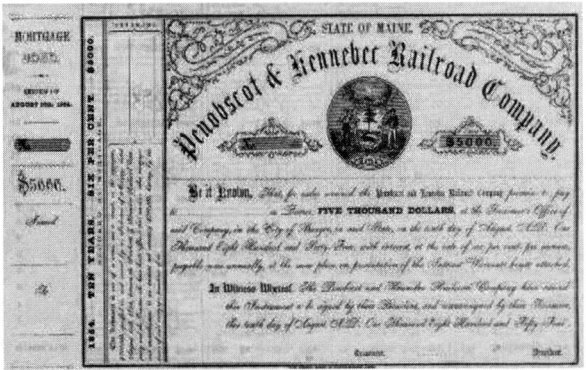

*PE1540-30-10, 1854, v, u/u $2,000 6% ten year bond w. coupons, brown $15.00

*PE1540-35-10, 1854, v, u/u $5,000 bond w. coupons, brown $15.00

Peoples Ice Company (par $100)
PE1610-20-10, 1877, v, 17-1/2 sh., grey, small certificate $50.00

Peoples Savings Bank of McKeesport (PA)
PE1650-20-10, 18xx, v, unissued certificate, grey $4.00

Peoples State Bank (CA 1907, par $100)
PE1680-20-10, 1907, v, 5 sh., grey $5.00

Peoples State Bank (OK par $100)

*PE1690-20-10, 1923, v, 5 sh., brown.....$30.00

Peoples Traction Company of Philadelphia (PA)

PE1720-20-10, 1894, v, 25 sh., green $10.00

The Peoples-First National Bank of Hoosick Falls (NY)

PE1760-20-10, 1925, v, 32 sh. (par $25), grey
................................$12.00

Peora Coal Company (WV par $100)

PE1790-30-10, 1927, v, 74 sh., green $10.00

Peoria, Decatur & Evansville Railway Company (par $100)

PE1820-20-10, 1884, v, 20 sh., 8" x 10-3/4", brown
................................$25.00
PE1820-30-10, 1887, v, 100 sh., green $16.00

The value of a stock certificate depends on:

- rarity
- the issuer
- signatures
- quality of engraving
- overall appearance
- condition
- date of issue

*PE1820-35-10, 18xx, v, u/u 100 sh. certificate,
brown..........................$15.00

Peoria, Decatur and Mattoon Railroad Company (IL $100)

PE1840-20-10, 190x, v, u/u certificate, ABN,
green.............................$6.00

The Peoria and Eastern Railway Company (par $100)

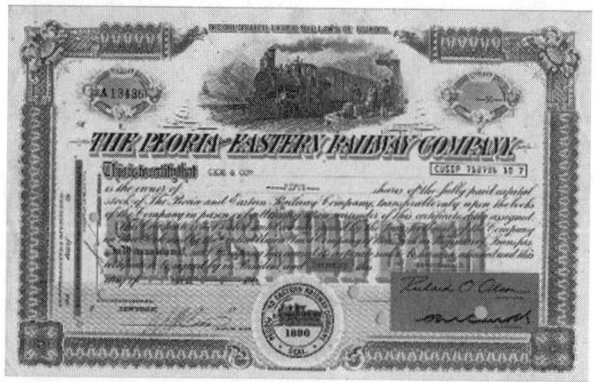

*PE1860-20-10, 1973, v, 50 sh., brown $6.00

*PE1860-30-10, 1973, v, 100 sh., green ...$15.00

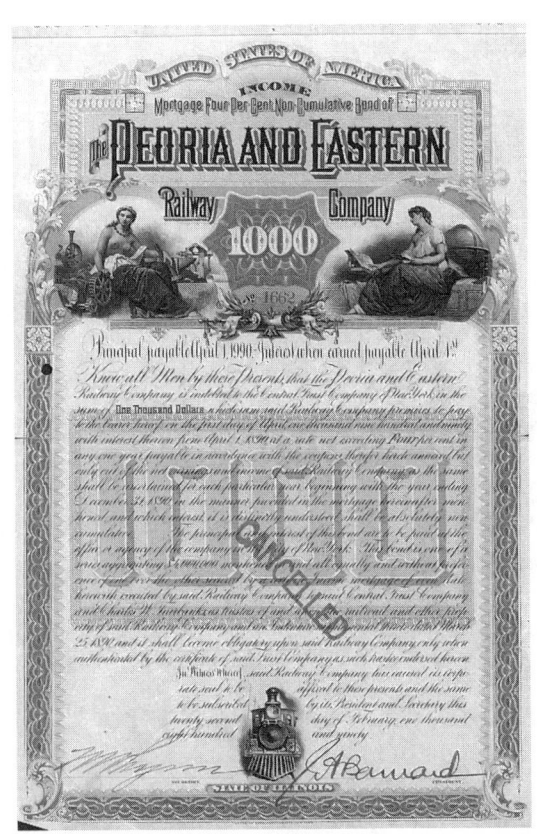

*PE1860-40-10, 1890, v, $1,000 4% Income mort. non-cumulative bond, orange **$22.00**

Peoria and Pekin Terminal Railway (IL par $100)

PE1890-20-10, 19xx, v, unissued certificate, green
. . . . **$20.00**

Pepi Inc. (MD par $5)

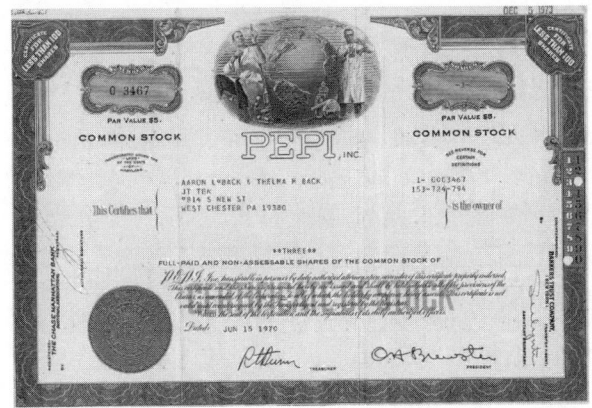

*PE1930-20-10, 1970, v, 3 sh. on a less than 100 sh. certificate, ABN, 12" x 8", purple **$4.00**
PE1930-30-10, 1970, v, 100 sh., green **$4.00**

Pepsi-Cola United Bottlers, Inc. (NY 1928, par $1)

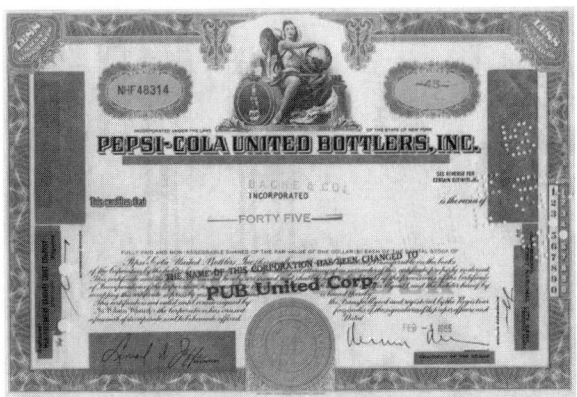

*PE1970-20-10, 1965, v, 45 sh. on a less than 100 sh. certificate, o/p the name of this corporation has been changed to PUB United Corp., SCB, orange **$7.00**
PE1970-30-10, 1960, v, 100 sh., green **$9.00**

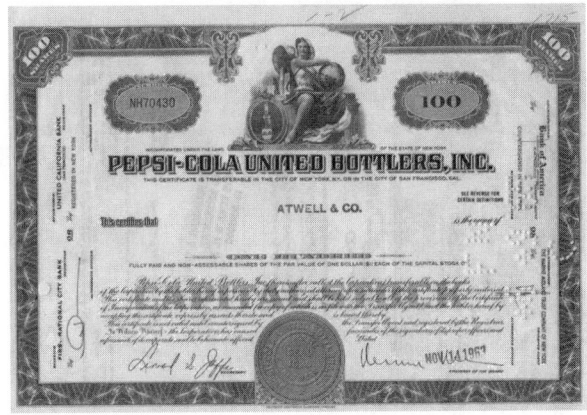

*PE1970-30-15, 1963, v, 100 sh., signature variety, SCB, green **$9.00**

Perfect Film & Chemical Corporation (DE 1937)

PE2000-20-10, 1967, v, 22 sh. on a less than 100 sh. certificate, green **$4.00**

It is generally assumed that only 5% of certificates survive to reach collectors.

*PE2000-30-10, 1968, v, 100 sh. (par $1.20), Federated Banknote Co., 12" x 8", green $4.00

Permaneer Corporation (DE 1968, par $0.50)

*PE2040-20-10, 1969, v, 100 sh., SCB, 12" x 8", blue $4.00

Perry Drug Stores, Inc. (MI)

PE2070-20-10, 1980, v, 500 sh., brown $4.00

Petaluma Oil & Burner Co. (CA 1934, par $100)

*PE2180-20-10, 19xx, v, u/u certificate, green $11.00

Petroleum Corporation of America (DE no par)

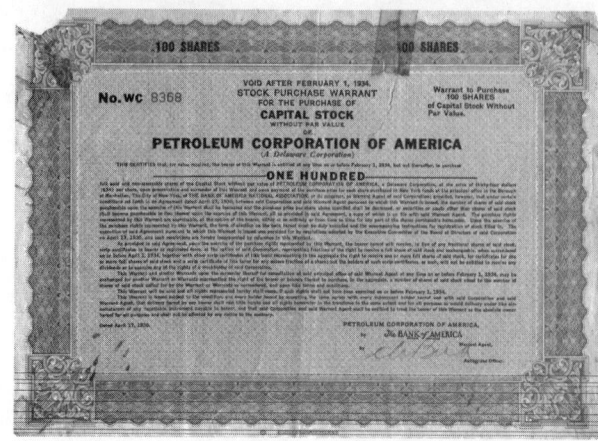

*PE2250-20-10, 1930, w, 100 sh. warrant void after 1934, Quayle & Son, Albany N.Y., 11-1/4" x 8", red $4.00

Petroleum Grubstakes Inc. (CO par 1¢)

PE2280-20-10, 1939, v, 25,000 sh., green $15.00

Petron Corporation (OK par 1¢)

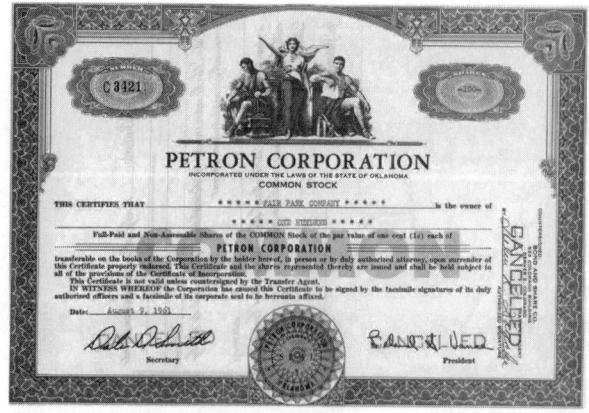

*PE2350-20-10, 1961, v, 100 sh., w/o imprint name, 11" x 8", green $4.00

The Pharmacist Gold Mining Company

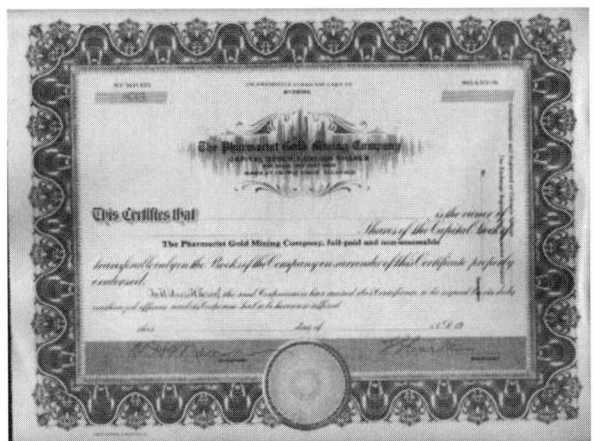

PH150-20-10, 19xx, v, u/u certificate, grey
.................................**$6.00**

Phelps Dodge Corporation
(NY 1885, par $12.50)

Founded as a trading company in 1834, it branched
out into copper mining.

PH250-30-10, 1954, v, 50 sh. on a less than 100 sh.
certificate, green **$6.00**

PH250-40-10, 1949, v, 100 sh., orange **$4.00**

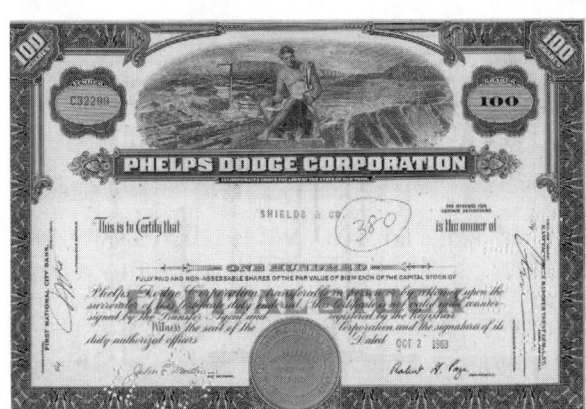

PH250-45-10, 1963, v, 100 sh., ABN, 12" x 8",
blue **$5.00**

PH250-55-10, 19xx, interim receipt, 100 sh.,
orange **$4.00**

City of Philadelphia PA

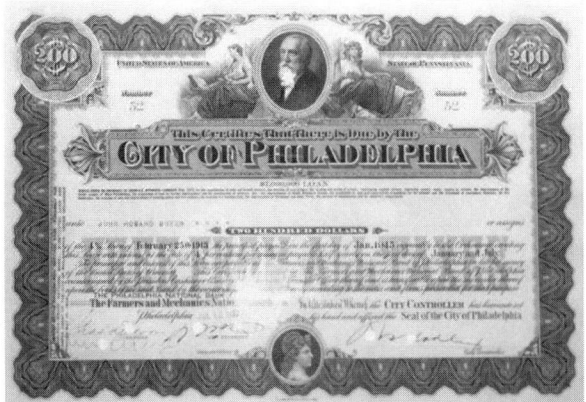

PH320-20-10, 1854, v, $800 6% loan due 1889,
grey..............................**$21.00**

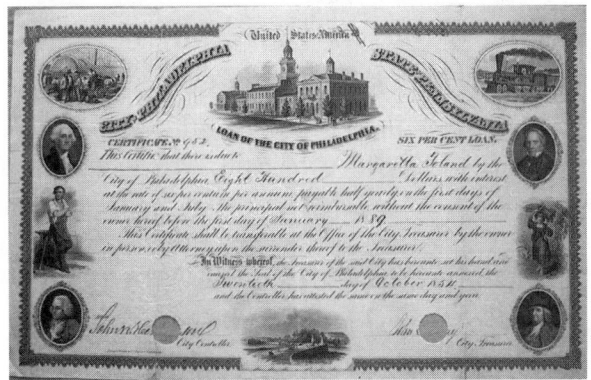

PH320-50-10, 1913, v, $200 7-1/2% bond due
1945, free from all taxes, EAW, 14" x 9-1/2",
grey..............................**$20.00**

Philadelphia Bourse (par $50)

PH350-20-10, 18??, v, 4 sh., green **$11.00**

The Philadelphia City Passenger Railway Company

PH380-30-10, 1938, v, $1,000 5% coupon bond, 9-1/2" x 14", green $22.00

Philadelphia Company (PA 1884)

*PH410-30-10, 19xx, v, u/s 2-5/8% collateral trust note, due 1943, Republic Banknote Co. Pittsburgh, Pa.,13-1/2" x 9", green $6.00

Philadelphia Electric Company (PA 1929)

PH470-20-10, 1960, v, 100 sh., purple. $15.00

Philadelphia Rapid Transit Company (PA)

PH570-30-10, 1938, v, 100 7% cumul. pref. sh., blue $15.00

Philadelphia and Reading Railroad Company

*PH610-40-10, 1893, v, $1,000 6% bond, grey $11.00

Philadelphia Traction Company (PA 1883, par $50)

PH680-15-10, 1886, v, 5 sh., ABN, grey border $13.00

*PH680-20-10, 1899, v, 10 sh., red $12.00

Philadelphia & West Chester Turnpike Road Co.

PH750-20-10, 1853, v, 4 sh., 11" x 5-1/2", brown on thin blue paper. $24.00
PH750-25-10, 18xx, unissued stock certificate, brown $20.00
PH750-40-10, 1868, $10 bond. $30.00

Philadelphia, Wilmington and Baltimore Railroad Company

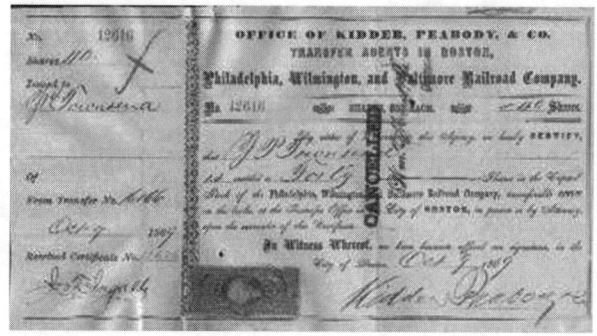

*PH780-20-10, 1868, v, 40 sh., dark blue on light blue. $11.00

Philco Corporation

PH830-30-10, 1959, v, 10 sh., 3-3/4% pref. on a
less than 100 sh. certificate, red **$16.00**

Phillips Petroleum Company (DE)

PH910-40-10, 1974, v, $5,000 7-1/8% bond due
2001, blue **$5.00**

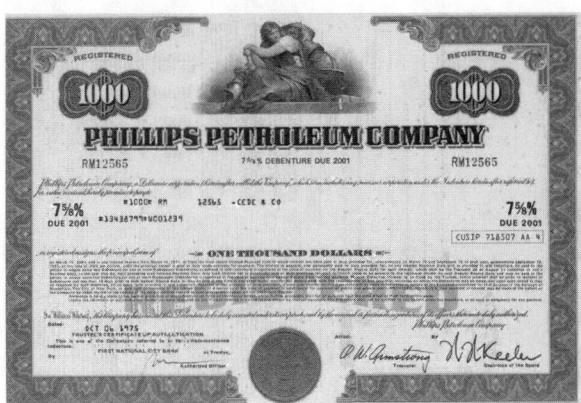

PH910-45-10, 1975, v, $1,000 7-5/8% debenture
due 2001, ABN, 12" x 8", red..........**$4.00**

PH910-50-10, 1976, v, $25,000 7-5/8% debenture
due 2001, ABN, 12" x 8", blue.........**$5.00**

PHL Corp. (PA 1987)

Primarily a railroad car leasing company.

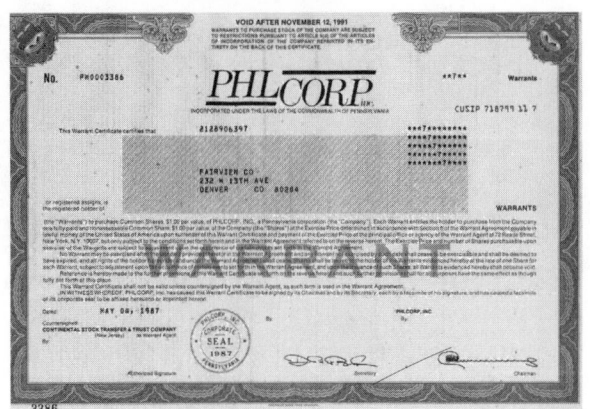

PH960-20-10, 1987, w, expiry 1991, 7 sh., ABN,
12" x 8", brown **$4.00**

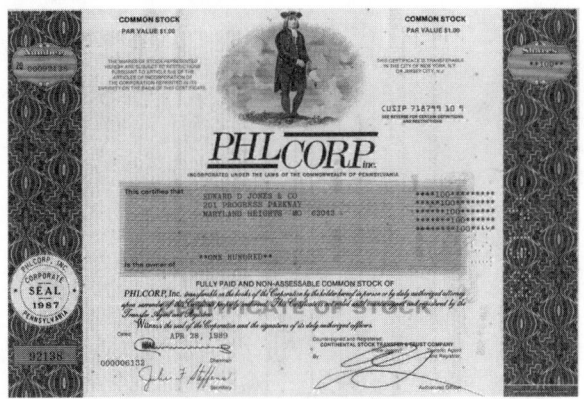

PH960-30-10, 1989, v, 100 sh. (par $1), ABN,
12" x 8", blue **$4.00**

Phoenix Insurance Company (CT)

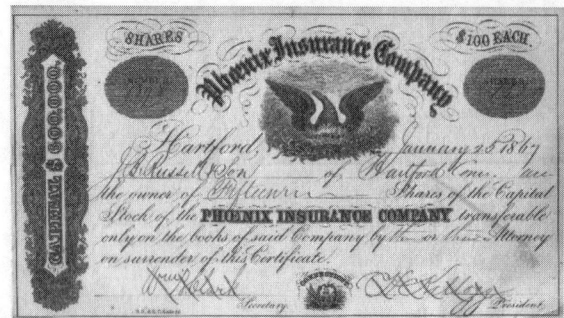

PH1090-20-10, 1867, v, 15 sh. (par $100), E.B. & E.C. Kellogg, grey $13.00

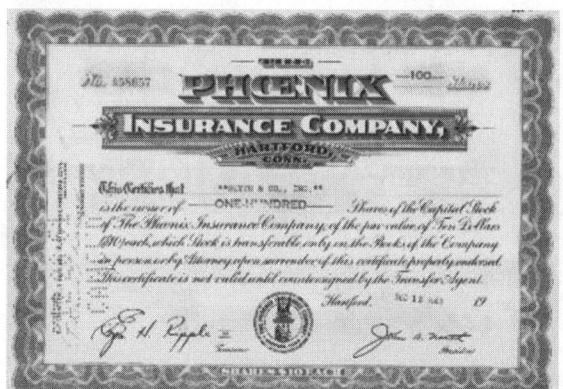

PH1090-40-10, 1967, v, 100 sh. (par $10), brown $4.00

The Phoenix Mining Company (ID par $1)

PH1120-20-10, 190x, v, u/u certificate, 10-3/4" x 8-1/4", brown $5.00

The Pickwick Corporation

PI190-20-10, 1928, v, 20 sh., lilac $4.00

PI190-30-10, 1927, v, 15 8% pref. sh., l. blue $4.00

Pierce Oil Corporation (VA par $100)

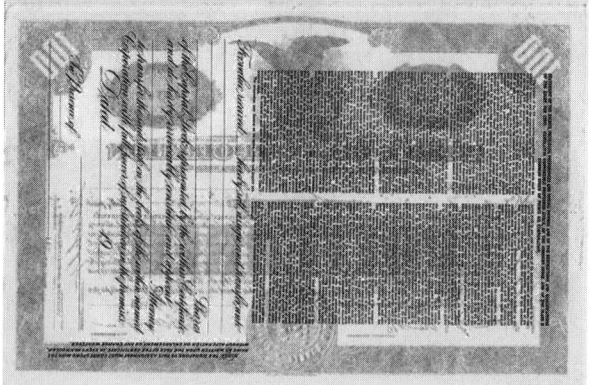

PI290-30-10, 1925, v, 100 sh., 8% preferred stock, blue..........................$9.00

County of Pike (OH)

PI420-20-10, 1910, $500 4% Bridge Repair Bond, grey..................................$7.00

The Pikes Peak Cottage City Corporation (CO)

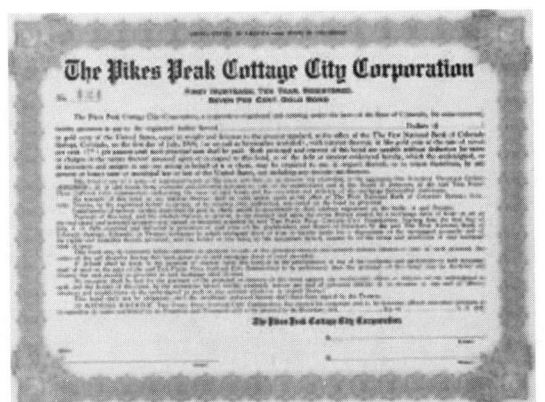

*PI450-20-10, 1920, u/u bond, orange......$4.00

Village of Pilger, Nebraska

*PI520-20-10, 1928, v, $500 sewer bond, orange
.................................$5.00

Pilgrim Mortgage Corporation (NY)

*PI550-20-10, 19xx, v, u/u certificate, green
.................................$5.00

The Pillsbury Company (DE no par)
PI580-20-10, 1971, v, 100 sh., orange......$5.00

Pioche Consolidated Mining and Reduction Co. (UT territory par $10)
PI660-20-10, 1891, 136 sh., brown......$100.00

Pioneer Plastics Corporation (NJ)

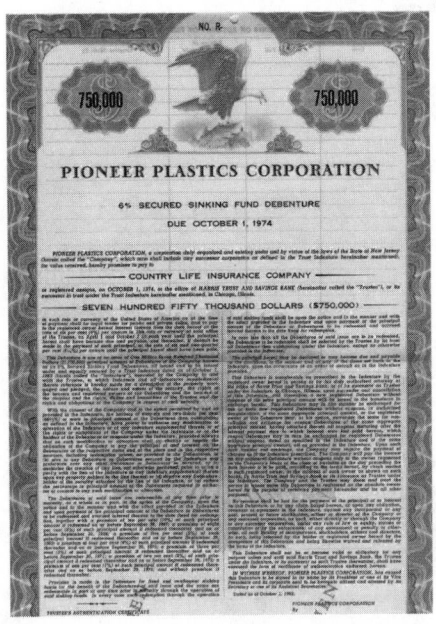

*PI710-30-10, 1962, v, u/s/c $750,000 6% secured sinking fund debenture due 1974, Northern Banknote Co. Chicago, 9-3/4" x 15", orange
.................................$10.00

Pioneer Suspender Company (PA par $1)
PI740-20-10, 1943, v, 100 sh., green.......$4.00

Pittsburg Consolidated Mining, Milling and Tunnel Company (CO)

*PI850-20-10, 1906, v, 10,000 sh., brown
.................................$23.00

The Pittsburg Lead & Zinc Co. (WI par $1)

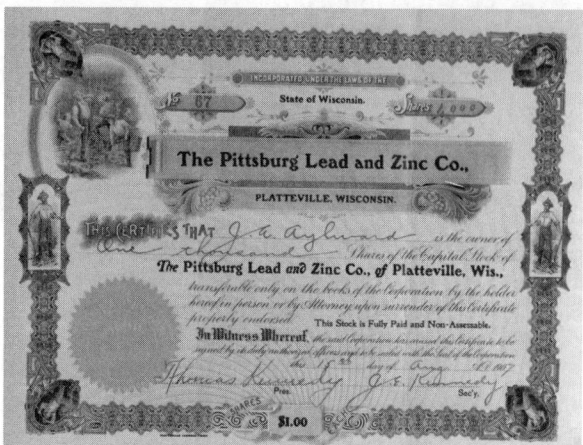

*PI1860-20-10, 1907, v, 1,000 sh., 11-1/2" x 8", brown border......................$50.00

City of Pittsburgh

PI880-30-10, 1951, v, unissued General Public Improvement Bond, series A, green.....$10.00
PI880-40-10, 1958, v, unissued General Public Improvement Bond, series B, blue.......$9.00

The Pittsburgh, Allegheny and Manchester Traction Company (PA)

*PI910-20-10, 1893, v, 100 sh., ABN, green
..................................$15.00

Pittsburgh, Cincinnati, Chicago and St. Louis Railroad Company (PA-OH-WV-IN-IL)

*PI940-40-10, 1920, v, $1,000 gen. mortgage 5% gold bond, series A due 1970, blue-grey ..$9.00
PI940-50-10, 1972, v, $10,000 bond, red-orange
..................................$10.00

The Pittsburgh, Cincinnati, Chicago and St. Louis Railway Company

*PI950-30-10, 1890, v, 10 pref. shares (par $100), ABN, brown........................$10.00
PI950-40-10, 1920, v, $1,000 general mortgage 5% gold bond, series A, due 1970, blue......$5.00

It is generally assumed that only 5% of certificates survive to reach collectors.

The Pittsburgh, Cincinnati and St. Louis Rail Way Company (1868)

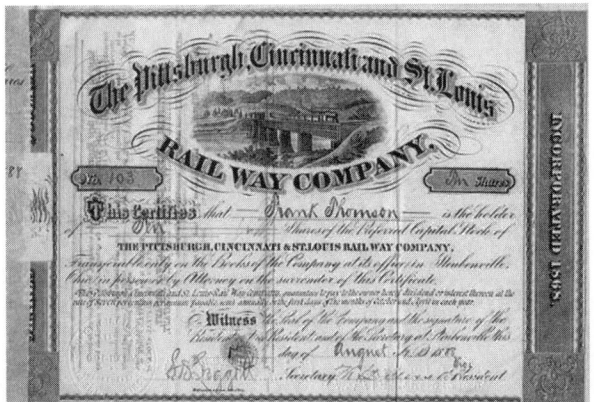

*PI955-20-10, 1888, v, 1 pref. sh., grey border
. . . .$35.00

Pittsburgh, Fort Wayne and Chicago Rail Road Company

*PI980-10-10, 1861, v, 1 sh., dark blue on light blue $45.00

*PI980-30-10, 1869, v, $75 guaranteed stock scrip (par $100), grey $26.00
PI980-60-10, 1958, v, 30 sh. on a less than 100 pref. sh. certificate, green $7.00

Pittsburgh Industrial Iron Works (PA par $100)

*PI1010-20-10, 1906, v, 650 sh., grey. $24.00

Pittsburgh-Jerome Copper Company (AZ par $1)

*PI1040-20-10, 1917, v, 50 sh., 11" x 8", green
. . . .$10.00

This catalog has listings in an alphabetical format. The reason is simple: Companies diversify as they grow. For example, the Canadian Pacific Railway company recently split into five companies. They represent the railway, hotels, shipping, airline, and petroleum interests of the company. During World War II, the Singer sewing machine company made guns and other defense-related equipment, so where should we list it? It's far easier to use a strict alphabetical order, rather than to confuse the reader with topical classifications.

Pittsburgh and Lake Erie Railroad Co. (par $50)

PI1070-20-10, 1936, v, 10 sh., green **$6.00**
PI1070-25-10, 1951, v, 10 sh., green **$4.00**

Pittsburgh, Lisbon & Western Railroad Company (par $100)

Main line operated from New Galilee, PA to
Lisbon, OH. In 1945 became part of the
Youngstown and Southern RR.
PI1100-20-10, 1905, v, 100 sh., brown **$50.00**

The Pittsburgh, McKeesport and Youghiogheny Railroad Company

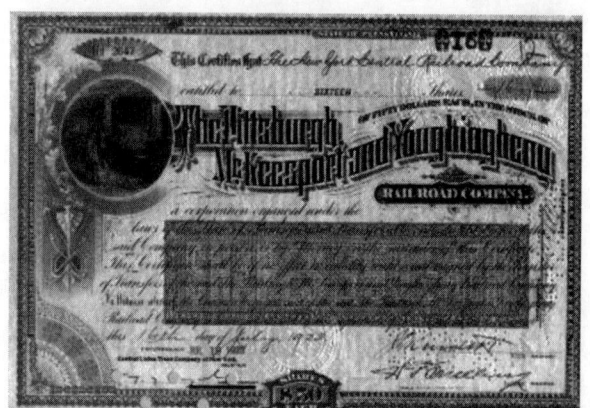

PI1130-20-10, 1923, v, 16 sh., green **$15.00**

Pittsburgh & Mt. Shasta Corporation

Successor to the Pittsburgh & Mt. Shasta Mining
and Manufacturing Company.
PI1145-20-10, 1927, v, i/u 100 sh., brown border
. . . . **$35.00**

Pittsburgh Plate Glass Company (PA par $10)

PI1160-20-10, 1968, v, 100 sh., green **$5.00**

Pittsburgh Screw and Bolt Corporation (par $100)

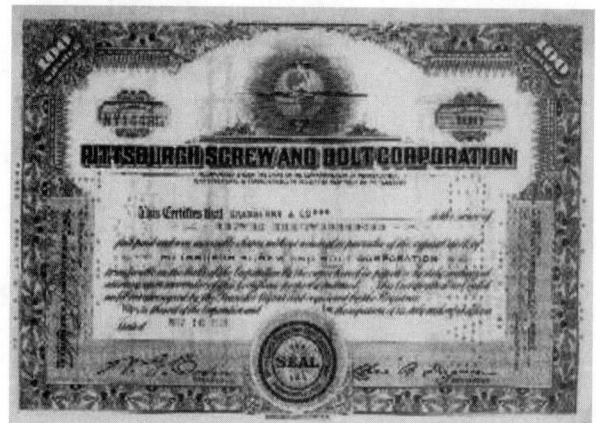

PI1200-20-10, 1929, v, 100 sh., green **$12.00**

Pittsburgh Traction Company (par $50)

PI1250-20-10, 1890, v, 100 sh., green **$8.00**

Pittsburgh & West End Passenger Railway Company (par $50)

PI1320-20-10, 188x, v, u/u certificate, green on blue $15.00

The Pittsburgh, Youngstown and Ashtabula Railroad Company

*PI1360-20-10, 1889, v, 25 sh. (par $50), brown $20.00

The Pittsburgh, Youngstown and Ashtabula Railway Company (PA-OH par $100)

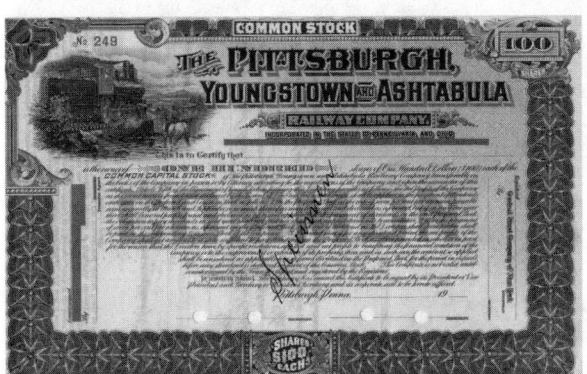

*PI1370-20-10, 19xx, v, u/c 100 sh. certificate, marked in ink as Specimen, ABN, 11" x 7-1/4", purple $8.00
PI1370-30-10, 18xx, v, u/u pref. sh. certificate (par $50), green. $10.00
PI1370-35-10, 18xx, v, u/c 100 pref. sh. certificate, brown $12.00

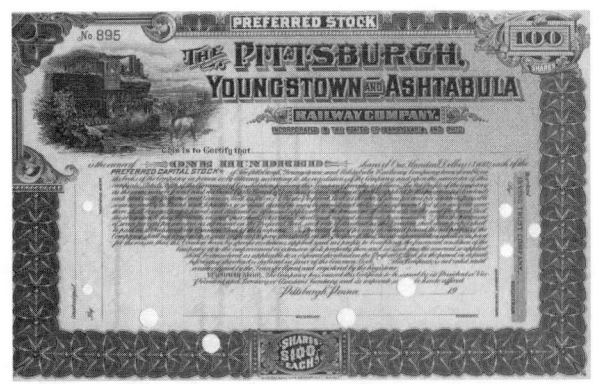

*PI1370-40-10, 19xx, v, u/c 100 pref. sh. certificate, brown $8.00
PI1370-45-10, 1924, v, 25 sh., pref. on a less than 100 sh. certificate, brown $20.00
PI1370-50-10, 1971, v, 40 sh., pref. on a less than 100 sh. certificate, brown $10.00

The Planters Loan and Savings Bank (GA par $10)

PL120-20-10, 19xx, v, unissued certificate, black $24.00

Playboy Enterprises, Inc.

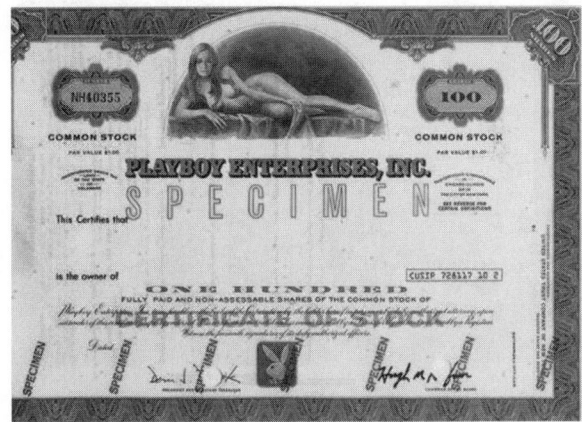

*PL210-20-10, 19xx, v - nude, 100 sh. (par $1), Specimen cert., signed by Hugh Heffner, olive green. $155.00
PL210-25-10, 1990, v - striding woman, 1 sh., blue $42.00

County of Pleasants, WV

PL300-40-10, 1935, v, $1,000 Washington Magisterial District Refunding Bond, light brown $7.00

The Plymouth Rock Mining Co. (1879 par $25)

PL500-20-10, 1880, v, 5 sh., brown $38.00

PL500-25-10, 18xx, v, unissued certificate, grey
. . . . $20.00

Pocahontas Consolidated Collieries Company, Incorporated (VA par $100)

PO160-20-10, 1907, 100 sh., green $15.00

Pocahontas Fuel Company

PO190-20-10, 19xx, v, u/u certificate, brown
. . . . $6.00

Polaris Development & Mining Company (ID par 5¢)

PO270-20-10, 19xx, v, u/u certificate, grey
. . . . $6.00

Polysonics Inc. (NY 1960, par 1¢)

PO350-20-10, 1961, v, 100 sh., SCB, 11-3/4" x 8", blue $4.00

Pony Mercantile Association

This group operated in Pony, Montana in the high Tobacco Root Mountains.

PO420-20-10, 19xx, v, u/u certificate $8.00

UNLISTED TYPES & VARIETIES

Readers are welcome to contact the author directly at:

Rainer Stahlberg
P.O. Box 1044
Rooseveltown, New York 13683

The Poole Engineering and Machine Company (MD no par)

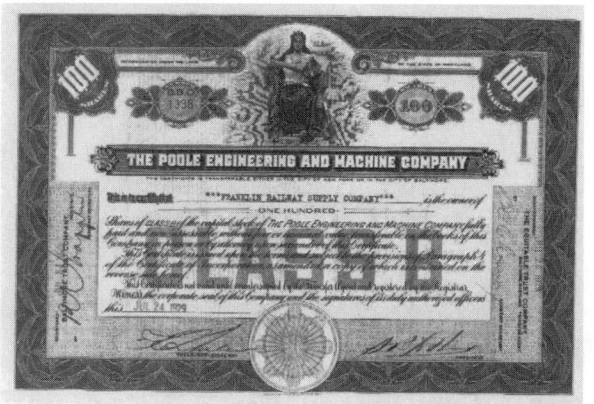

*PO520-20-10, 1929, v, 100 class B sh., brown
. . . .$4.00

The Porcupine Gold Mines Company (DE)

PO620-20-10, 1914, v, 100 sh., green $7.00

Porcupine United Gold Mines, Inc.

PO650-20-10, 1929, v, escrow shares for March
Gold Inc., brown border $6.00

The Port of New York Authority

*PO740-20-10, 19xx, v, $1,000 general and
refunding bond, 1-1/2% 9th series due 1985,
ABN, brown $10.00
PO740-25-10, 19xx, v, $5,000 state guaranteed
commuter car bond, green $12.00

H.K. Porter Company, Inc. (DE 1956, par $5)

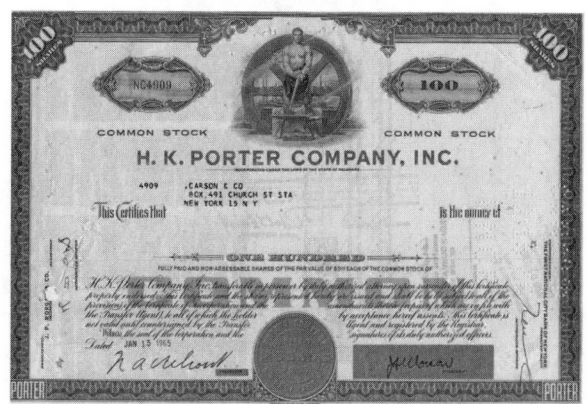

*PO770-20-10, 1965, v, 100 sh., ABN, 12" x 8",
blue $4.00

Portland General Electric Company (OR)

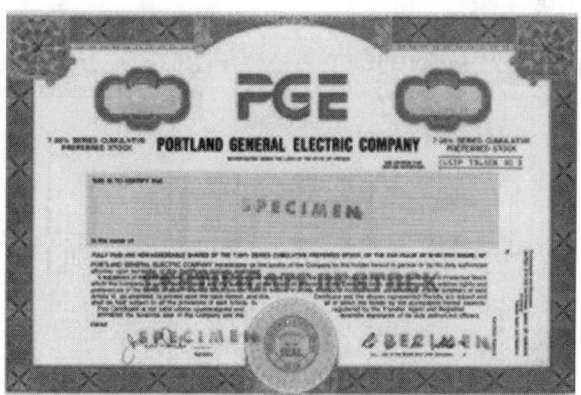

*PO820-20-10, 19xx, v, u/s pref. stock certificate,
red. $6.00

Portland Mining Company (ID 1940, par 10¢)

PO850-20-10, 19xx, v, u/u certificate, grey. .$6.00

Portland and Ogdensburg Railway

PO880-20-10, 1940, v, 2 sh., orange $7.00

Portland Terminal Company (ME 1911)

PO910-40-10, 19xx, v, u/u $5,000 1st mort. gold
bond, grey. $12.00

*PO910-50-10, 1981, v, $50,000 1st mortgage bond 6-1/4% due 1986, ABN, blue $9.00

Porto Rico Telephone Company (DE 1914, par $20)

*PO960-20-10, 1961, v, 100 sh. certificate, o/p name changed to Puerto Rico Telephone Company, red $15.00

Portsmouth Coal Mining Company (ME)
PO1000-20-10, 1912, i/u 2,000 sh., blue ...$10.00

Poughkeepsie, Hartford and Boston Railroad Company (NY)
PO1100-30-10, 1875, v, $1,000 second mort. convertible bond, brown.............$125.00

Power Authority of the State of New York

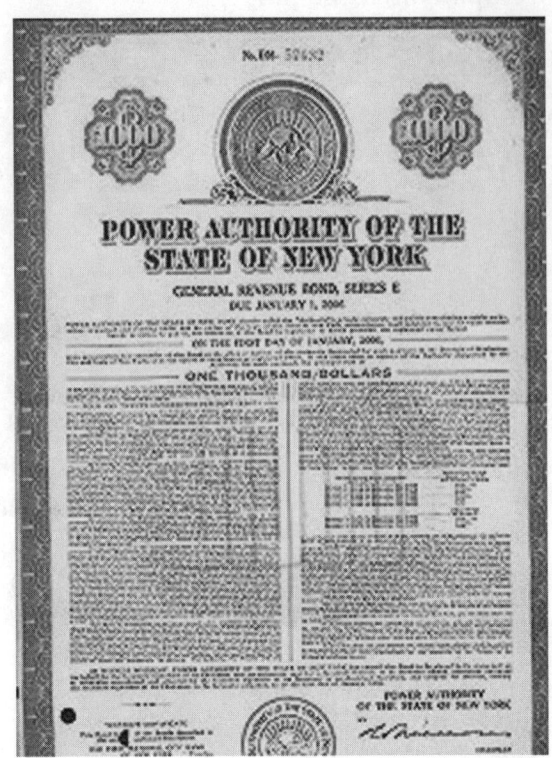

*PO1200-30-10, 1959, v, $1,000 6% General Revenue Bond, series E due 2004, 9-1/2" x 13-1/2", brown $6.00

Poynter Motors Inc. (KS par $100)
PO1300-20-10, 19xx, v, 265 sh., green $22.00

PPG Industries, Inc.
Founded in 1883 as the Pittsburgh Plate Glass Company.

*PP50-20-10, 1969, v, 20 sh. on a less than 100 sh. certificate, green.....................$4.00

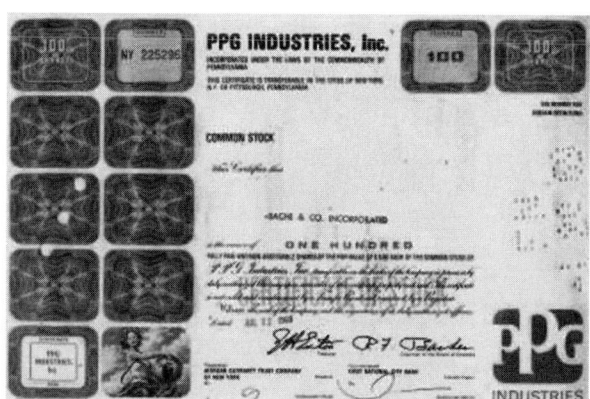

PP50-30-10, 1968, v, 100 sh., blue $5.00

The Prairie Pipe Line Company (KS par $25)

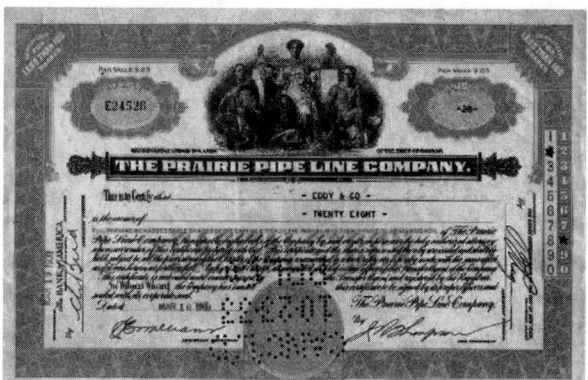

PR100-20-10, 1930, v, 28 sh. on a less than 100 sh. certificate, orange $4.00

PR100-30-10, 1929, v, 100 sh., blue $10.00

Precision Polymers, Inc. (DE 1968, par 5¢)

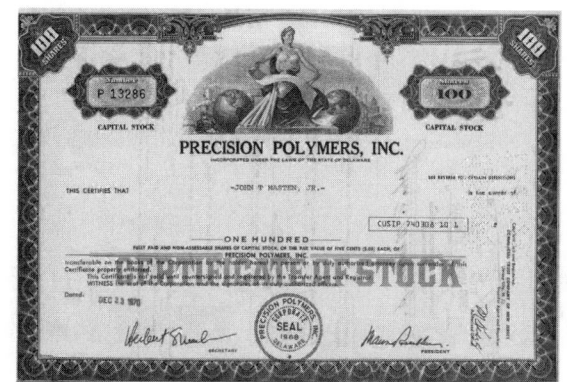

PR180-20-10, 1970, v, 100 sh., SCB, 12" x 8", blue.............................$4.00

The Premier Mining Co. (WI par $1)

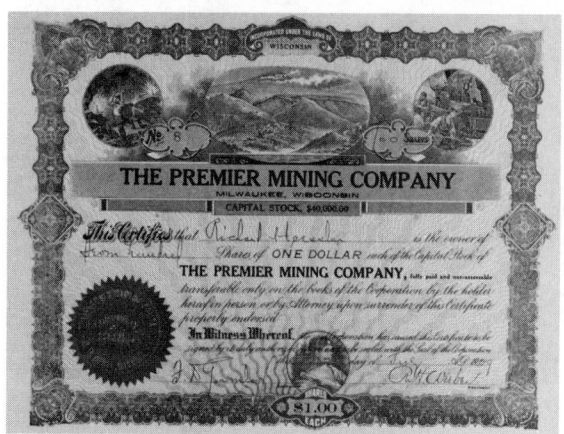

PR270-20-10, 1909, v, 100 sh., brown border
...............................$45.00

The Premix Corporation (DE 1970, par 10¢)

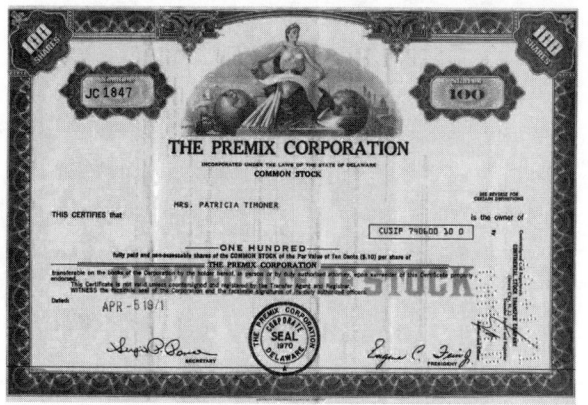

PR310-20-10, 1971, v, 100 sh., SCB, 12" x 8", orange..............................$4.00

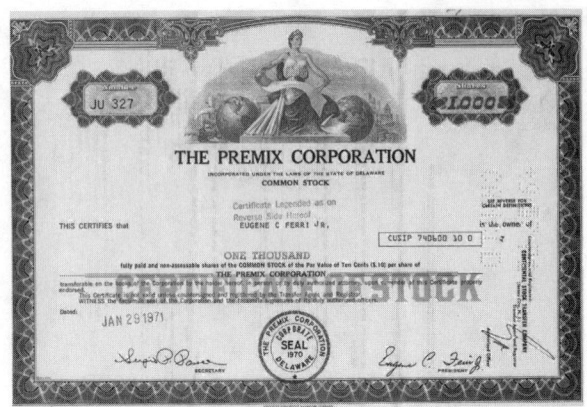

*PR310-30-10, 1971, v, 1,000 sh., SCB, 12" x 8",
blue **$4.00**

Premix Products, Inc. (FL 1956, par 10¢)

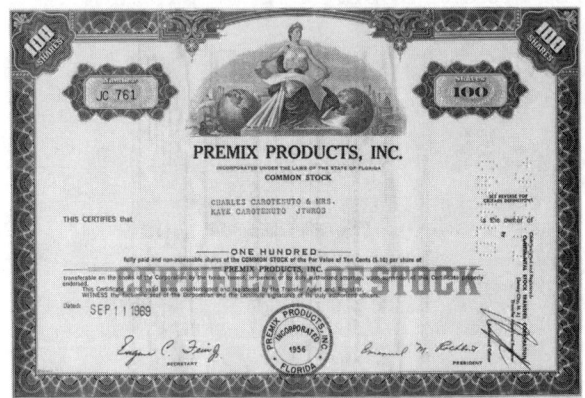

*PR340-20-10, 1969, v, 100 sh., SCB, 12" x 8",
blue **$4.00**

Primary Minerals Corporation
(NV 1955, par $.0.01)

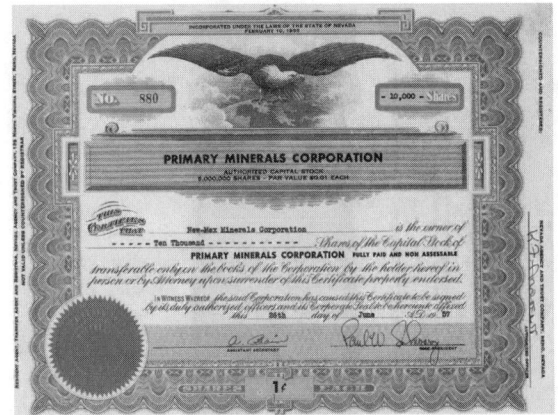

*PR510-20-10, 1955, v, 30,000 sh., GOES, 11" x
8-1/2", green **$4.00**

*PR510-25-10, 1957, v, 10,000 sh., GOES, 11" x
8-1/2", orange **$4.00**

The Primrose Consolidated Gold Mines Co.
(par $1)

Mines at Cripple Creek.
PR580-20-10, 1899, v, 2,500 sh., brown . . .**$30.00**

Producers Oil and Gas Company
(MT par 10¢)

*PR610-20-10, 1920, v, 3,200 sh., 11" x 8-1/2",
orange border **$5.00**

> *It is generally assumed that only 5% of certificates survive to reach collectors.*

Profile Metals Company (ID 1919, par 1¢)

The company had a group of promising gold, silver, lead, copper and zinc properties located in Profile Valley County, Idaho.

*PR650-20-10, 19xx, v, u/u certificate, green
. . . .$6.00

Programming and Systems, Inc.
(NY 1959, par $0.08)

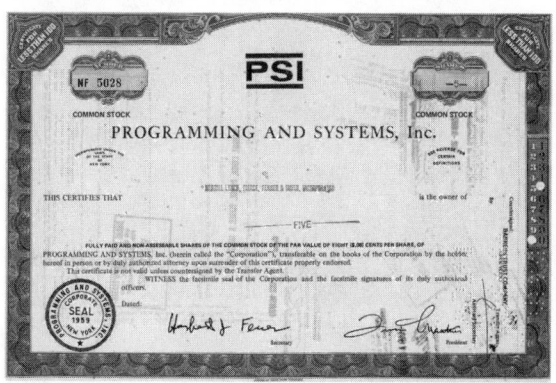

*PR680-20-10, 1970, v, 5 sh. on a less than 100 sh. certificate, Bankers Trust Co., ABN, 12" x 8", brown $4.00

The value of a stock certificate depends on:
- rarity
- the issuer
- signatures
- quality of engraving
- overall appearance
- condition
- date of issue

*PR680-20-15, 1972, v, 25 sh. on a less than 100 sh. certificate, changed to Registrar and Transfer Co., ABN, 12" x 8", brown $4.00

City of Providence (RI)

PR770-20-10, 1949, v, $1,000 bond, brown
. . . .$6.00

The Providence Securities Company

Owned by The New York, New Haven & Hartford Railway Company to control The Rhode Island Co., United Traction & Electric Co., and Rhode Island Suburban Railway.

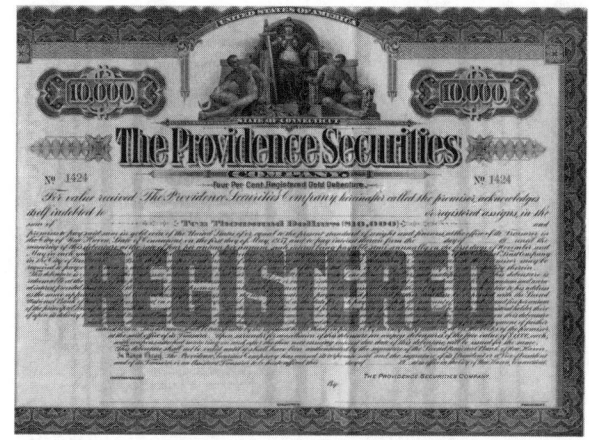

*PR830-20-10, 19xx, v, u/u $10,000 4% gold bond, ABN, 13-1/2" x 9-1/2", purple $7.00

*PR830-25-10, 19xx, v, u/u $10,000 4% gold bond, ABN, 13-1/2" x 9-1/2", brown **$7.00**

Providence and Worcester Railroad Company (RI par $100)

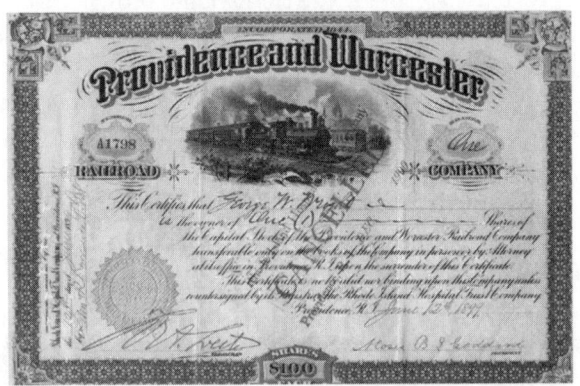

*PR860-20-10, 1899, v, 1 sh., green **$15.00**
PR860-25-10, 19xx, v, unissued share certificate
. . . .**$20.00**

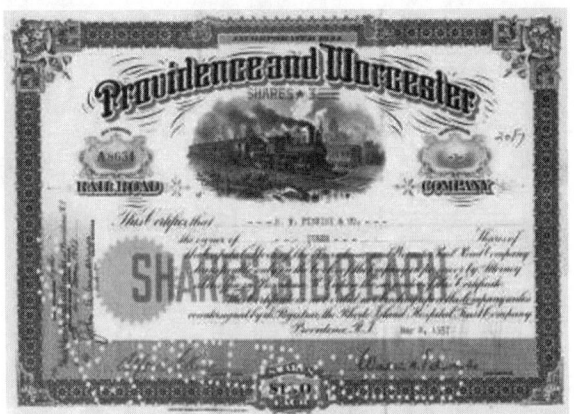

*PR860-30-10, 1936, v, 4 sh., green **$10.00**

*PR860-35-10, 1929, v, 3 sh., ABN, green
. . . .**$16.00**

Prudential Oil and Refining Company (IL par $1)

PR980-20-10, 1918, v, 10 sh., green **$10.00**

Public Finance Service, Inc. (DE)

*PU100-30-10, 1936, v, u/c $500 20-year 6% sinking fund debenture, due 1956, Elco, Philadelphia, 10-1/2" x 15-3/4", red. **$6.00**

*PU100-35-10, 1936, v, u/c $1,000 20-year 6%
sinking fund debenture, due 1956, Elco, Philadelphia, 10-1/2" x 15-3/4", brown **$6.00**

Pueblo International, Inc. (DE 1969, par $1)

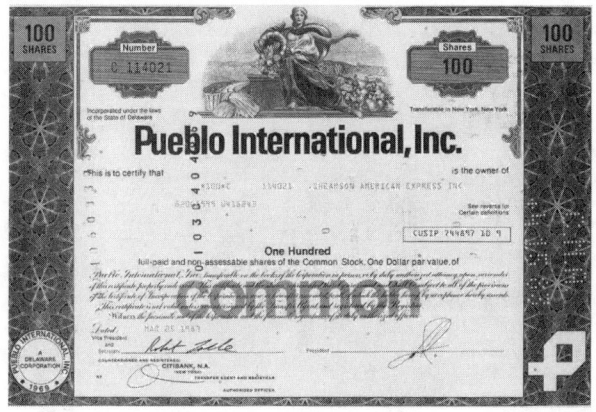

*PU190-20-10, 1983, v, 100 sh., SCB, 12" x 8",
blue **$4.00**

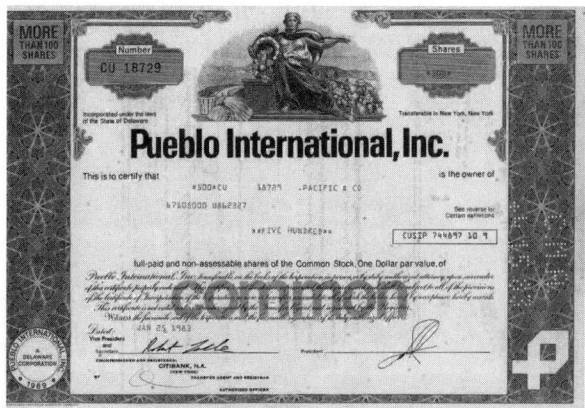

*PU190-30-10, 1983, v, 500 sh. on a more than
100 share certificate, SCB, 12" x 8", red . .**$4.00**

The Pullman Company (IL 1867 par $100)

PU340-20-10, 1918, v, 58 sh. on a less than 100 sh.
certificate, orange. **$10.00**

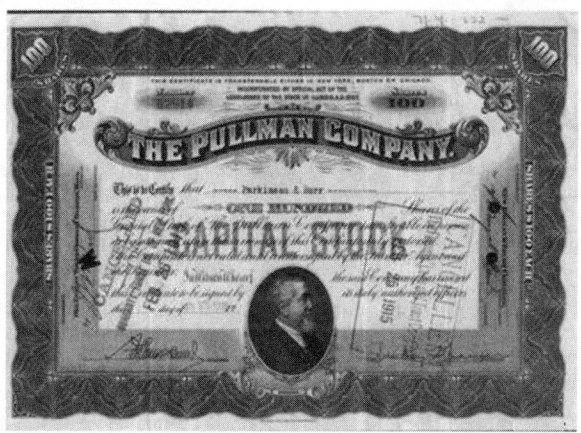

*PU340-30-10, 1915, 100 sh., RBN, blue . . .**$7.00**

This catalog has listings in an alphabetical format. The reason is simple: Companies diversify as they grow. For
example, the Canadian Pacific Railway
company recently split into five companies. They represent the railway, hotels,
shipping, airline, and petroleum interests of the company. During World War
II, the Singer sewing machine company
made guns and other defense-related
equipment, so where should we list it?
It's far easier to use a strict alphabetical
order, rather than to confuse the reader
with topical classifications.

Pullman's Palace Car Company (par $100)

Horace Porter (1837-1921) graduated from West Point and won the Medal of Honor at Chickamauga. Became Grant's aide-de-camp and later became a RR businessman.

*PU350-20-10, 1893, v, 3 sh., signed by Horace Porter, grey $50.00

Pull-More Motor Truck Company (DE, par $10)

PU380-20-10, 1917, t, 500 8% cum. pref. sh., green $80.00

The Puncheon Coal Company (OH par $100)

PU500-20-10, 1921, v, 20 sh., green $5.00

Punta Alegre Sugar Company

PU570-20-10, 1932, v, 100 sh., green $27.00

Purex Corporation Ltd. (CA)

*PU650-20-10, 1974, v, 100 series 1 pref. sh., o/p name changed to Purex Corporation, orange $10.00

Puritan Mining Company, Ltd. (ID par $1)

*PU690-20-10, 19xx, v - Lincoln, u/u certificate, grey. $3.00
*PU690-25-10, 1906, v, 100 sh., grey $3.00

Pyramid Oil Company (CA par $1)

*PY100-20-10, 1910, v, 50 sh., grey $5.00

It is generally assumed that only 5% of certificates survive to reach collectors.

Q

The Quadrangle Oil Company (KS par $1)

*QU80-20-10, 1919, v, i/u 1,000 sh., GOES, 10-3/4" x 8-1/4", grey $5.00

Quaker City Industries, Inc. (NY 1945, par 1¢)

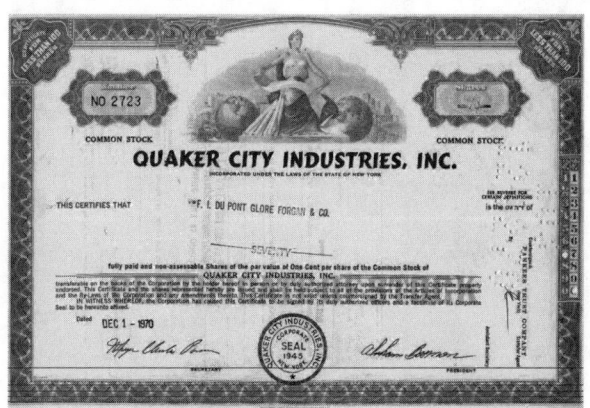

*QU160-20-10, 1970, v, 70 sh. on a less than 100 sh. certificate, SCB, 12" x 8", orange $4.00

Quebrada Grande Mining and Development Company (IL par $5)

*QU230-20-10, 1921, v, 1,000 sh., GOES, 10-1/2" x 8", orange $6.00

Quinby Oil Corporation (DE)
QU380-20-10, 1927, 100 sh., red $9.00

Quincy Mining Company (MI par $25)
QU410-20-10, 1929, v, 1 sh., brown $9.00

Quincy Turn-Verein (par $10)

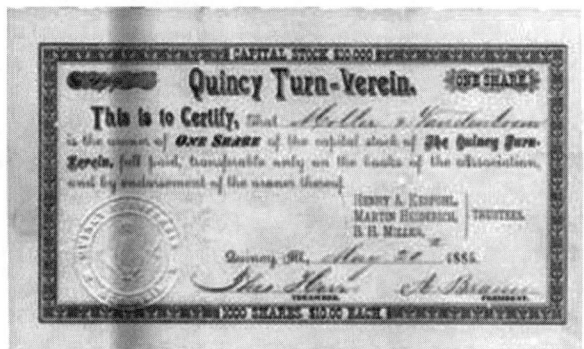

*QU440-20-10, 1885, v, 1 share, 8-3/4" x 5", black $4.00

R

Racine Hardware Manufacturing Company (WI par $100)

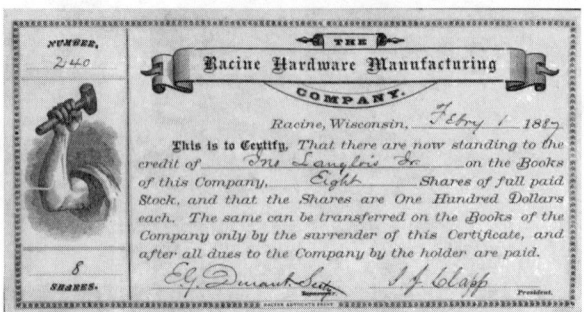

*RA70-20-10, 1887, v, 8 sh., 8-1/2" x 4-1/2",
brown $45.00

Radio Corporation of America (no par)

RA100-20-10, 1933, 1/6 sh., fractional certificate,
purple $11.00

Radium Mothene Manufacturing Company (WA par $1)

RA130-20-10, 19xx, v, u/u certificate, grey . .$8.00

Railroad Electric Safety Appliance Company (ME par $25)

RA210-20-10, 1897, 2 sh., brown $25.00

The Ramie Company of America (par $50)

*RA280-20-10, 1889, 4 sh., blue $10.00

Range States Oil Company, Inc. (NE par $0.10)

RA360-20-10, 1954, v, 1,000 sh., green $4.00

Raritan River Railroad Company

*RA440-20-10, 18xx, v, u/u 100 sh. certificate,
New York Banknote Co., green $17.00
RA440-40-10, 189x, u/u certificate of debt, grey
. . . .$9.00

The Rawhide Box Company (DE par $1)

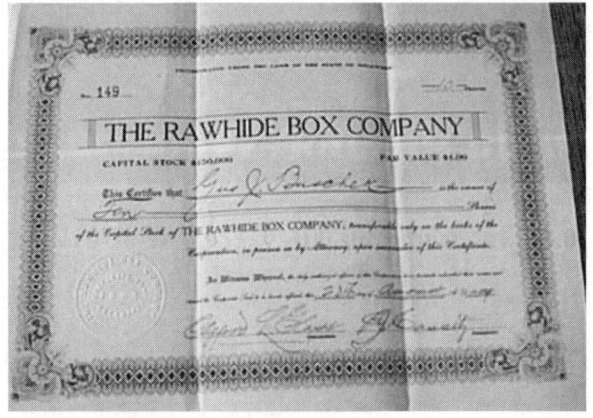

*RA620-20-10, 1909, 10 sh., red border $6.00

The value of a stock certificate depends on:
- rarity
- the issuer
- signatures
- quality of engraving
- overall appearance
- condition
- date of issue

Rawhide Coalition Mines Company (par $1)

*RA650-20-10, 1910, v, 100 sh., dark green
...................................$30.00

The Raycraft Realty Company (NV)

*RA690-20-10, 19xx, v, u/u certificate, brown
...................................$7.00

Reading Company (PA no par)

*RE60-30-10, 1966, v, 25 sh. on a less than 100 sh.
certificate (par $50), ABN, 12" x 8-1/4", green
...................................$4.00

*RE60-40-10, 1965, v, 100 sh., red border ..$4.00
RE60-45-10, 196x, v, 100 sh., unissued certificate,
red.................................$4.00
RE60-50-10, 1968, v, 100 sh., red $4.00

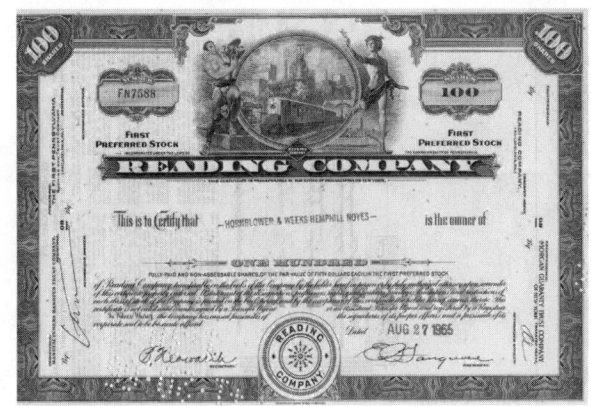

*RE60-60-10, 1965, v, 100 sh., first pref. stock
(par $50), ABN, 12" x 8", brown.........$4.00

*RE60-60-15, 1969, v, 100 first pref. sh. (par $50),
signature variety, ABN, 12" x 8-1/4", brown
...................................$4.00
RE60-70-10, 1958, v, 10 sh., second prefer., grey
...................................$6.00

RE60-75-10, 19xx, v, u/c second pref. certificate, grey **$5.00**

RE60-80-10, 1969, v, 50 sh., second pref. on a less than 100 sh. certificate, brown **$6.00**

RE60-85-10, 1966, v, 100 second pref. sh. (par $50), ABN, 12" x 8-1/4", orange. **$4.00**

RE60-95-10, 1945, v, $1,000 first and refunding 3-1/2% bond, series D, due 1995, w. coupons, orange **$8.00**

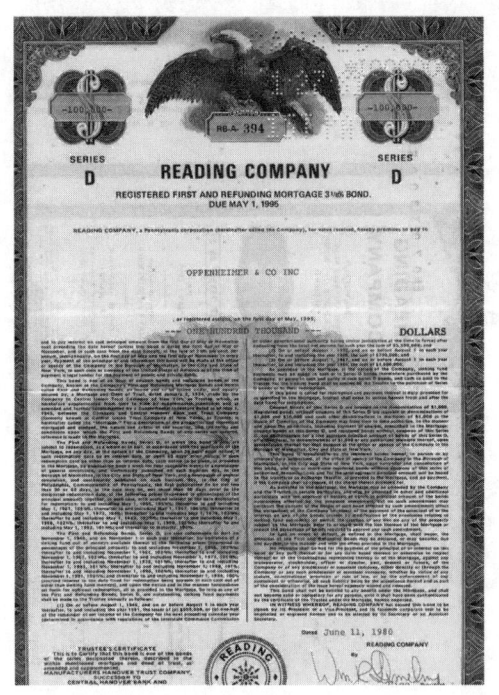

RE60-105-10, 1980, v, $100,000 series D registered 1st and refunding mort. 3-1/8% bond, due 1995, ABN, 9-1/2" x 13-1/2", blue. **$6.00**

Reading Fair Company

RE110-20-10, 1915, v, 1 sh., green **$6.00**

Red Bird Mining Company (WA 1924, par $0.10)

RE280-20-10, 1934, v, 1,000 sh., GOES, 10-3/4" x 8-1/4", grey-gold **$6.00**

Red Hill Florence Mining Company (NV 1916, par $0.10)

RE400-20-10, 1925, 100 sh., brown **$10.00**

Red Hill Mining Company (AZ par $1)

RE430-20-10, 19??, v, 100 sh., greenish grey **$9.00**

The Red Hook Building Company (NY par $1)

RE460-20-10, 1838, v, 1 sh., brown **$80.00**

The Red Mountain Railroad, Mining & Smelting Co. (AZ par $1)

Mines located at Red Mountain, Ouray District.

RE500-30-10, 1904, v, 100 sh., green **$40.00**

RE500-50-10, 1904, v, 100 pref. sh., brown **$40.00**

It is generally assumed that only 5% of certificates survive to reach collectors.

Reiter-Foster Oil Corporation
(DE 1924, par $0.50)

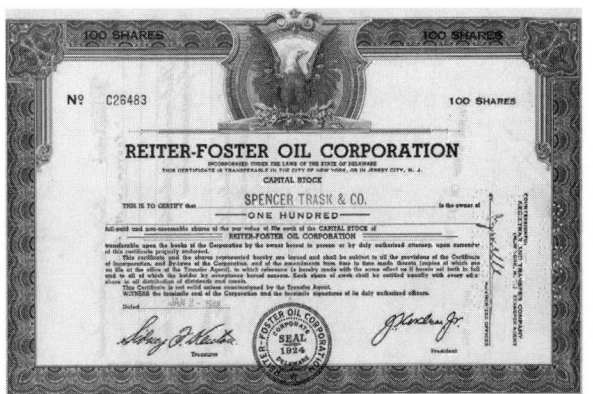

RE610-30-10, 1948, v, 100 sh., CBN, 11-1/2" x
7-1/4", brown $4.00

The Reliable Mining Co. (WI par $1)

RE650-20-10, 1906, v, 100 sh., M.D. Rider & Co.,
Stationers, Chicago, 10" x 8", brown on green
. . . .$45.00

UNLISTED TYPES & VARIETIES

Readers are welcome to contact the author
directly at:

Rainer Stahlberg
P.O. Box 1044
Rooseveltown, New York 13683

The Reliance Electric and Engineering
Company (OH)

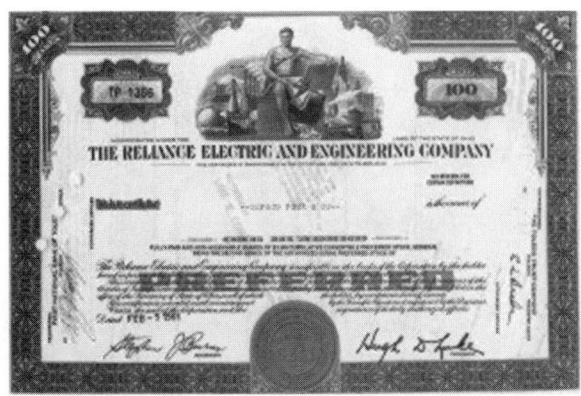

RE670-40-10, 1968, v, 100 preferred sh., green
. . . .$4.00

Remington Rand Corporation
RE780-30-10, 195x, void, green $34.00

Remington Rand Inc. (DE par $1)

RE790-30-10, 1947, v, 100 sh., ABN, 10-3/4" x
7", orange $5.00

Remsen Realty Company (NY par $100)
RE830-20-10, 190x, v, u/u certificate, green
. . . .$10.00

The Renhan Realty Corp. (no par)
RE900-20-10, 19xx, v, u/u certificate, green . $3.00

Reo Motor Car Company (MI par $10)
RE980-20-10, 1916, v, 5 sh. on a less than 100 sh.
certificate $55.00

Reorganized Kewanas Mining Company (NV)
RE1050-20-10, 1915, 100 sh., blue $6.00

Reorganized Pioneer Mines Company (NV 10¢)

*RE1080-20-10, 19xx, v, unissued certificate, green $5.00

Republic Bank (PA 1987, par $5)

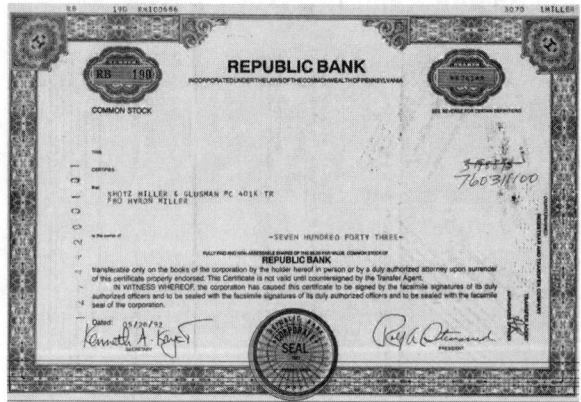

*RE1170-30-10, 1992, 743 sh., Corpex Banknote Co., New York, 11-3/4" x 8", light blue. . .$3.00

Republic Golden Gate Mining Company (WA par 5¢)

RE1210-20-10, 1899, v, 2,000 sh., owner's name not filled in, revenue stamp, grey border
. . . .$18.00

Republic Insurance Company of Chicago

RE1240-20-10, 1870, v, 10 sh., green $75.00

Republican Valley & Kansas Railroad Company (NE)

RE1370-20-10, 188x, unissued certificate, black
. . . .$13.00

Research Investing Corporation (NJ 1959, par $1)

*RE1450-20-10, 1964, v, 25 sh., SCB, 12" x 8", brown $3.00

Retzloff Chemical Company (par $10)

RE1540-20-10, 1958, v, 65 sh., green $4.00

The Revine Gold Mining Company (CO par $1)

RE1630-20-10, 190x, v, u/u certificate, brown
. . . .$12.00

Rheolite Company (WI par $25.00)

*RH150-20-10, 1909, v, 30 sh., Northern Bank & Office Supplies Co., Milwaukee; 11-1/2" x 8", brown border $50.00

The Rhinelander Iron Mining Company (par $25)

A company seeking a lease in Michigan.

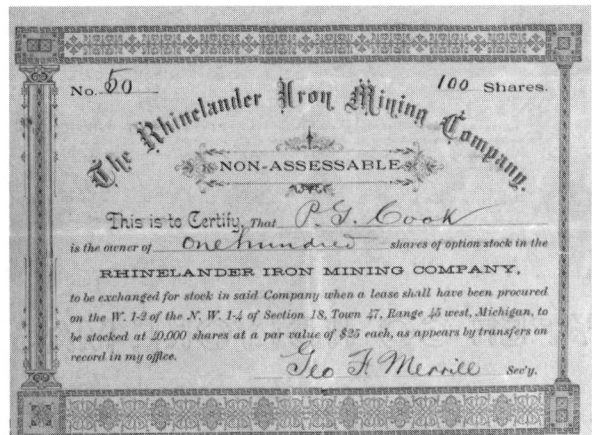

*RH250-20-10, ND, 100 share option, 8" x 6", brown border. **$25.00**

Richfield Oil Corporation (DE)

*RI160-30-10, 1961, v, 4 sh. on a less than 100 sh. certificate, orange **$6.00**

RI160-40-10, 1952, v, 100 sh., blue **$4.00**

Richmond and Danville Railroad Company

RI220-20-10, 188x, v, unissued certificate for less than 50, brown **$15.00**

RI220-30-10, 188x, v, unissued 100 sh. certificate, green **$15.00**

The Rico Mining Company (CO par $10)

RI260-20-10, 1913, 151 sh., brown **$12.00**

Rifle Development Co. (CO par $500)

*RI330-20-10, 19xx, v, u/c certificate with "SAMPLE" pinholes, GOES, 11" x 8-1/2", grey-gold border **$5.00**

Ringling Bros.-Barnum & Bailey Combined Shows, Inc.

*RI660-20-10, 19xx, v, u/s certificate (specimen marked on the back of the certificate), multicolored **$175.00**

RI660-21-10, 1971, v, 50 sh. on a less than 100 sh. certificate, ABN, 12" x 8", red border on multicolored **$230.00**

The value of a stock certificate depends on:
- rarity
- the issuer
- signatures
- quality of engraving
- overall appearance
- condition
- date of issue

Rio Grande Auto Sales (CO par $100)

*RI740-20-10, 19xx, v, u/c with pinhole "SAM-
PLE," GOES, 11" x 8-1/2", gold border...$3.00

Rio Grande Valley Gas Company (TX 1946, par $1)

RI770-30-10, 1967, v, 100 sh., green......$60.00

River Brand Rice Mills, Inc. (DE par $3.50)

RI930-20-10, 1961, v, 27 sh. on a less than 100 sh.
certificate, brown $4.00
RI930-25-10, 1964, v, 82 sh. on a less than 100 sh.
certificate, blue......................$4.00
RI930-30-10, 1961, v, 100 sh., green......$4.00

The River-City Press, Inc.

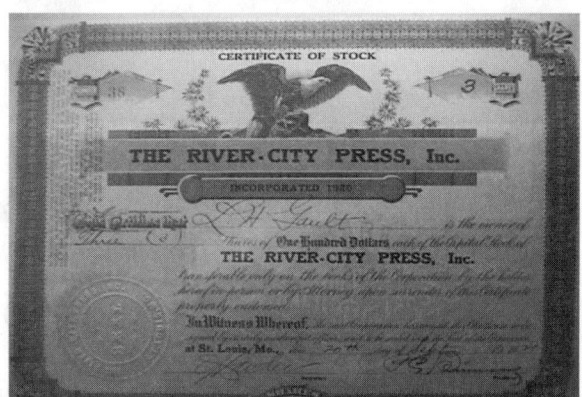

*RI960-20-10, 1921, v, 3 sh. (par $100), grey
.................................$10.00

The Riverside Iron and Coal Company of Scranton (PA par $50)

RI100-20-10, 18xx, v, unissued certificate, 11-1/2"
x 8", black and red $14.00

Riviana Foods Inc. (DE par $3.50)

RI1030-20-10, 1972, v, 50 sh. on a less than 100 sh.
certificate, blue......................$4.00
RI1030-30-10, 1969, v, 100 sh., green......$4.00
RI1030-35-10, 1973, v, 500 sh., brown $4.00

RJR Holdings Corp. (DE 1988)

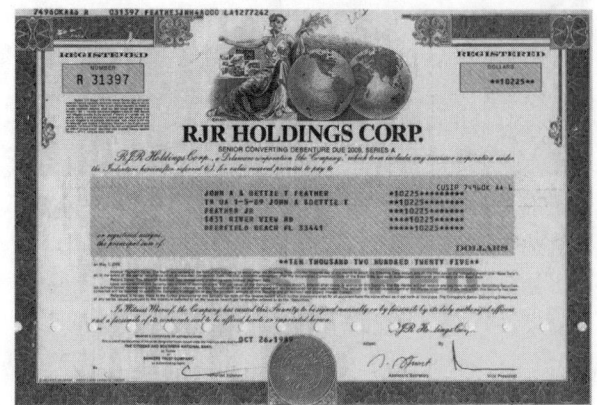

*RJ40-30-10, 1989, v, $775 sen. converting deben-
ture due 2009, series A, SCB, 12" x 8", blue
.................................$4.00

Road-Runner Auto Company

RO110-20-10, 19xx, v, unissued certificate, green
.................................$45.00

Roan Antelope Copper Mines Limited

A copper mining company in Southern Rhodesia.

*RO180-30-10, 1950, v, 100 ADR sh. (American
Depositary Receipt), blue..............$6.00

Roanoke Mining Company (ID)

*RO210-20-10, 19xx, v, u/u certificate, orange
.....................................$9.00

Roberts Development Company (MO)

RO240-20-10, 19xx, v, unissued certificate, grey
....................................$4.00

Rochester City and Brighton Railroad Company (par $100)

RO380-20-10, 1863, v, 10 sh., U.S. revenue stamp, grey.............................$80.00

Rochester Gas and Electric Corporation (NY 1904)

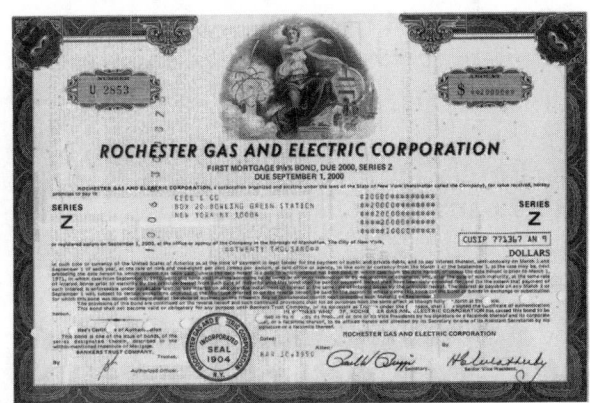

*RO410-40-10, 1990, v, $20,000 first mortgage 9-1/8% bond, due 2000, series Z, ABN, 12" x 8", blue..............................$4.00

Rochester and Genesee Valley Railroad (NY 1854 par $100)

RO440-20-10, 1951, v, 96 sh., grey.......$15.00

The Rock Island Company (par $100)

*RO500-20-10, 1914, v, 10 sh. on a less than 100 sh. certificate, brown $10.00

Rock Island and Peoria Railway Company

RO530-30-10, 1885, v, $1,000 6% bond due 1925 w. coupons, green....................$20.00

Rocket Jet Engineering Corp. (CA 1951)

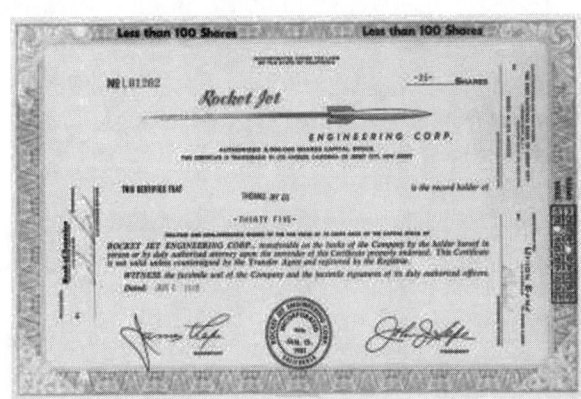

*RO560-20-10, 1962, v, 35 sh. on a less than 100 sh. certificate, Jeffries Bank Note Co., orange
....................................$10.00

> *It is generally assumed that only 5% of certificates survive to reach collectors.*

Rockwell-Poor Company (NY par $100)

*RO600-20-10, 19xx, v, u/u certificate, grey
. . . .$3.00

Rockwell-Standard Corporation

RO630-20-10, 1967, v, 10 sh. on a less than 100 sh.
certificate, green $4.00

Rollins International, Inc.

RO730-30-10, 1972, w, 1,000 sh., prior to 1976,
reddish. $4.00

Rome, Watertown and Ogdensburgh Rail Road Company (NY)

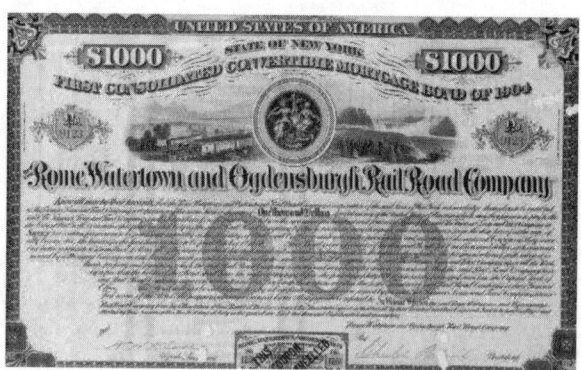

*RO810-40-10, 1874, v, $1,000 1st consolidated
convertible mortgage bond due 1904, ABN,
black on white. $24.00

The Roosevelt Gold Mines Company (DE)

RO910-20-10, 19xx, v, unissued certificate, grey
. . . .$7.00

Rosex Contractors Inc. (NY par $200)

*RO1050-20-10, 19xx, v, u/u certificate, w/o
imprint, 11" x 8-1/4", green $3.00

The Roswell Railroad Company (GA par $100)

RO1160-30-10, 1903, 175 sh., brown $45.00

The Roswell Wool and Hide Company (NM)

RO1190-20-10, 19xx, u/u printer's proof, Clarke
and Courts, Galveston, TX. $23.00

Rothsay Elevator Company (MN par $50)

RO1250-20-10, 1899, v, 1 sh., grey. $12.00

Roundup-Cooke Mining and Milling Company (MT par $1)

RO1360-20-10, 19xx, v, unissued certificate, green
. . . .$12.00

The Royal Zinc Mining Company (WI par $1)

*RO1410-20-10, 1907, v, 200 sh., 10-1/2" x 5-1/2",
brown border $65.00

The Ruby Hill Oil and Gas Company

RU160-30-10, 1931, v, 1,000 sh., 11" x 8-1/2",
  brown $15.00

Ruby Mountain Mining Company of Austin (NV 1920, par 50¢)

*RU190-20-10, 19xx, u/u certificate, GOES, 9-3/
  4" x 5-1/2", grey $4.00

Rumford Falls and Rangeley Lakes Railroad Company (ME 1894, par $100)

*RU370-20-10, 18xx, u/c certificate, Loring, Short
  & Harmon, Portland, Me., 9-1/2" x 7", grey
  . . . .$5.00

Rutland and Burlington Rail-Road Company (VT par $100)

RU570-20-10, 1848, v, 10 sh., black on blue paper,
  small certificate $30.00

Ryder System, Inc.

RY80-30-10, 1976, v, 100 sh., green $5.00

S

Sabre-Pinon Corporation (DE 1954)

*SA70-20-10, 1956, v, 100 sh. (par 20¢), SBN, 12" x 8", brown $4.00

Safety Nitro Powder Company

SA260-20-10, 1883, v, 100 sh., grey.......$66.00

St. Croix Consolidated Copper Company (WI par $1)

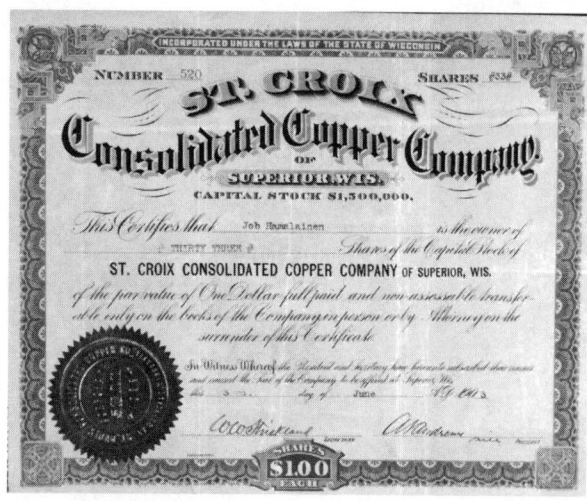

*SA280-20-10, 1903, 33 sh., 10" x 8", green border $70.00

St. Croix Manufacturing & Improvement Co. (WI par $100)

*SA300-10-10, 1863, v, 2 sh., revenue stamp, 10" x 7-1/2", grey border $150.00

St. Helens Gold Mining Co. (WI $1)

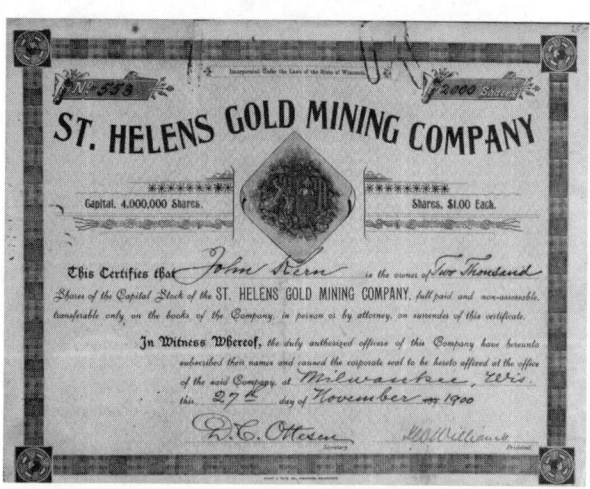

*SA360-20-10, 1900, v, 2,000 sh., Swaun & Tate Co. Printers, Milwaukee, 10-1/2" x 8", brown border $25.00

St. Joe Minerals Corporation (NY 1864, par $10)

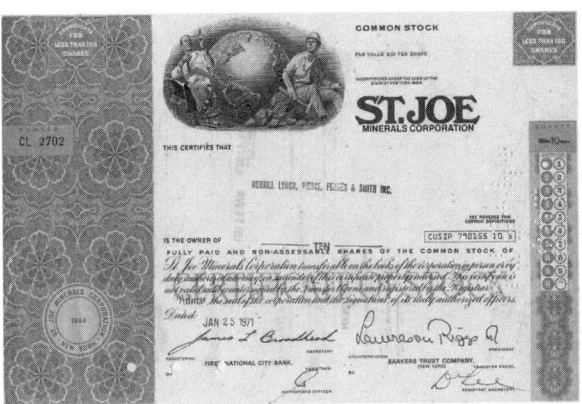

*SA380-40-10, 1971, v, 10 sh. on a less than 100 sh. certificate, ABN, 12" x 8", orange $4.00

St. Joseph Lead Company (NY par $10)

SA410-30-10, 1957, v, 100 sh., green......$6.00

St. Joseph, South Bend & Southern Railroad Company (IN par $100)

SA470-20-10, 19xx, unissued certificate, brown
....$10.00

*SA470-25-10, 1925, v, 25 sh., brown $25.00

It is generally assumed that only 5% of certificates survive to reach collectors.

St. Lawrence and Adirondack Railway Company (NY-CAN par $100)

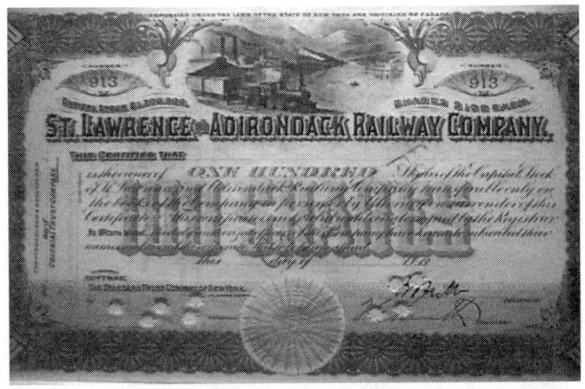

*SA540-20-10, 19xx, 100 sh., u/c certificate, green
....$14.00

St. Louis, Alton and Terre Haute Railroad Company (IL-IN par $100)

*SA610-40-10, 1863, v, 50 sh., 7% preferred stock, red...............................$20.00
SA610-45-10, 1865, 100 sh., 7% pref. stock, red
....$30.00
SA610-50-10, 1878, 100 sh., 7% pref. stock, red
....$24.00
SA610-55-10, 1890, 50 sh., 7% pref. stock, brown
....$40.00

St. Louis, Indianapolis and Eastern Railroad Company (NY par $100)

SA640-30-10, 189x, v, u/u 100 sh. certificate, New York Bank Note Company, orange $15.00

St. Louis, Kansas City and Colorado Railroad Company (par $100)

SA670-20-10, 188x, v, u/u 50 sh. certificate, orange
....$21.00

St. Louis-San Francisco Railway Company
SA720-40-10, 1948, v, $1,000 second mortgage
  bond, orange **$9.00**

SA720-50-10, 1959, v, $1,000 4-1/2% bond,
  orange **$6.00**

St. Nicholas Zinc Extension Company (to be incorporated, par $1)
SA790-20-10, 1917, v, i/u 75 sh., grey **$6.00**

St. Paul and Dunn County Mining Company (MN par $25)

SA820-20-10, 1887, v, 50 sh., 10-1/2" x 8-1/2",
  brown border. **$35.00**

St. Rose Mining Company (WI par $100)

SA840-20-10, 1905, v, 5 sh., 11" x 8", brown
  border **$80.00**

Salyer Consolidated Mines Company (DE par $1)
SA870-20-10, 1930, v, 50 sh. on a less than 100 sh.
  certificate, orange **$9.00**

San Benito Asbestos Company (CA 1918, par $5)
SA920-20-10, 19xx, v, u/u certificate, green
  . . . .**$31.00**

San Francisco Textile Mills Inc.
SA960-30-10, 19xx, v, u/u pref. certificate, orange
  . . . .**$10.00**

Santa Ana Mining Company (AZ territory 1898, par $100)

SA1010-20-10, 1898, v - flags, 1 founders sh.,
  multicolored **$60.00**

The Santa Paula Walnut Association (CA par $5)

SA1070-20-10, 1921, v, 10 sh., brown......$7.00

Santa Rosa Metals Corporation

SA1100-20-10, 1965, v, 100 sh., brown.....$7.00

Santa Rosalia Mining Company (AZ)

*SA1130-20-10, 1911, 22 sh., brown.....$15.00

Sara Lee Corporation (MD 1941)

*SA1300-50-10, 1987, v, New Zealand $100,000 19% note due 1988, SCB, 12" x 8", orange $9.00

Saratoga and Schenectady Rail-Road Company (par $100)

SA1360-20-10, 1860, 5 sh., 7-1/4" x 4", grey $15.00

Saturn Electronics & Engineering, Inc.

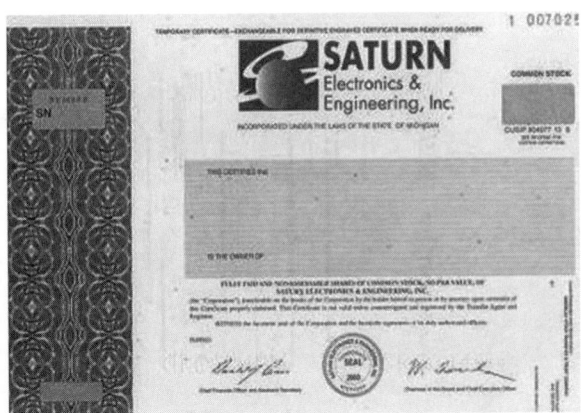

*SA1420-20-10, 19xx, v, u/u certificate, blue $10.00

Savage Gold & Silver Mining Company (CA 1904, par $1)

SA1480-20-10, 1921, 500 sh., grey, small certificate.............................$14.00

The Saw Pit Gold Mining and Milling Co. (WI par $1)

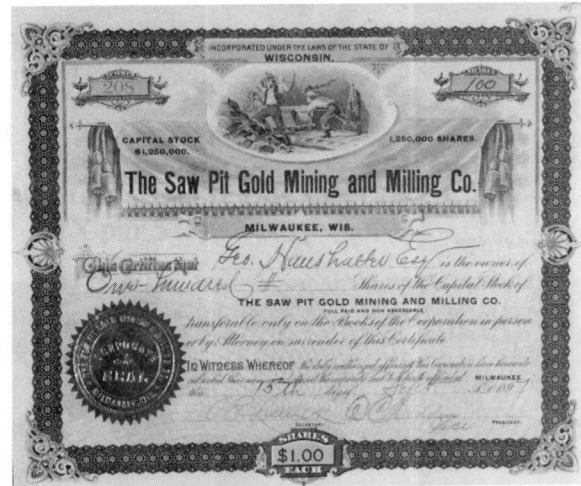

*SA1520-20-10, 1897, v, 100 sh., 10" x 8", brown border.........................$145.00

The value of a stock certificate depends on:
- rarity
- the issuer
- signatures
- quality of engraving
- overall appearance
- condition
- date of issue

Scandinavia Community Hall Corporation (WI par $25)

*SC40-20-10, 1928, 1 sh., GOES, 10-1/2" x 8",
brown $15.00

The F.&M. Schaefer Corporation (NY $10)
SC110-30-10, 1971, v, 100 sh., green......$12.00

Scandinavian Realty Company, Inc. (MI par $50)
SC190-20-10, 19xx, v, unissued certificate, grey
.................................$4.00

Edward Scharnikow Company (MT)
SC250-20-10, 19xx, v, u/u certificate, black border
.................................$6.00

Schering Corporation (NJ 1935)
SC350-30-10, 1969, v, 100 sh., red $7.00

Schering-Plough Corporation (NJ)
SC380-40-10, 1971, v, 100 sh., green......$11.00

Schimmel Production Company (TX par $1)
Oil production company.
SC420-20-10, 1928, v, 100 sh., 11" x 8-1/2", brown
border $15.00

Schine Chain Theatres, Inc. (NY)
SC450-20-10, 19xx, t, unissued certificate, blue
.................................$4.00

*SC450-30-10, 19xx, t, u/c 100 sh. certificate,
Hamilton Banknote Co. N.Y., 12" x 8", brown
.................................$4.00

The Schleswig Telephone Company (WI par $5)

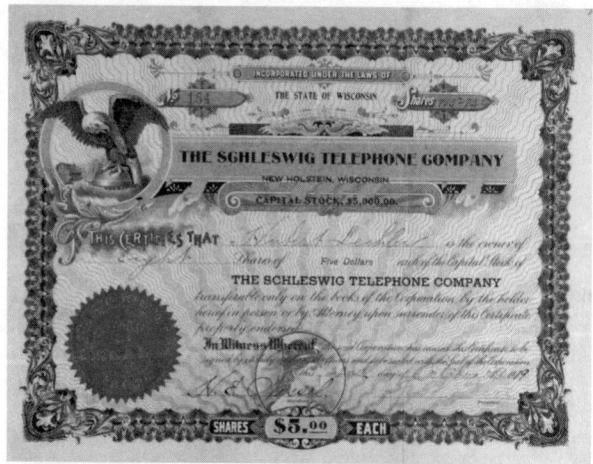

*SC500-20-10, 1919, v, 8 sh., w/o imprint, 11" x
8", brown border...................$60.00

Schuylkill Haven and Lehigh River Rail Road Co. (par $50)
SC670-20-10, 1863, v, 45 sh., U.S. first issue revenue stamp (Scott #R36a), brown $72.00

The Scioto Valley and New England Railroad Company (OH par $100)

*SC730-30-10, 18xx, v, u/u 100 sh. certificate, FBN, green $13.00

SC730-50-10, 18xx, v, $1,000 first mortgage 4% gold bond due 1909, w. coupons, green . .$15.00

Scott Paper Company

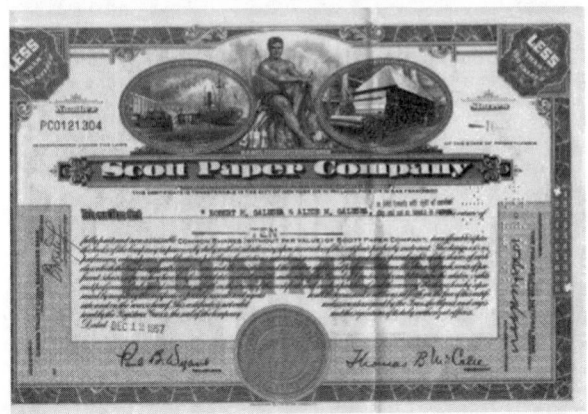

*SC860-20-10, 1957, v, 10 sh. on a less than 100 sh. certificate, green $15.00

Scranton Electric Company (PA)

SC960-20-10, 1932, v, 10 sh., green. $37.00

Scranton National Bank (PA)

*SC990-20-10, 19xx, v, u/c certificate, grey $10.00

Sea Galley Stores Inc. (DE)

*SE110-30-10, 1994, v, 5,000 sh., blue $3.00

The Sea Insurance Company

SE140-20-10, 1836, v, 20 sh., grey $210.00

This catalog has listings in an alphabetical format. The reason is simple: Companies diversify as they grow. For example, the Canadian Pacific Railway company recently split into five companies. They represent the railway, hotels, shipping, airline, and petroleum interests of the company. During World War II, the Singer sewing machine company made guns and other defense-related equipment, so where should we list it? It's far easier to use a strict alphabetical order, rather than to confuse the reader with topical classifications.

Seaboard Air Line Railway Company

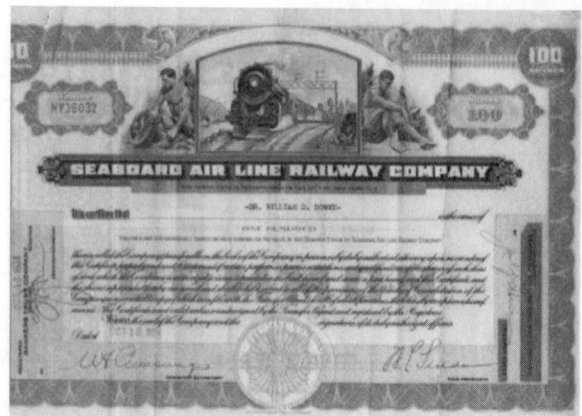

*SE210-30-10, 1934, v, 100 sh., orange....$22.00

Seaboard Coast Line Railroad Equipment Trust

SE240-40-10, 1969, v, $1,000 equipment trust certificate, blue $15.00

Seaboard, Pennsylvania and Western Railroad Company (par $50)

*SE270-20-10, 188x, v, u/u certificate, green
.....................................$19.00

Seacoast Railroad Company (par $50)

SE310-30-10, 1898, unissued pref. sh. certificate, grey................................$8.00

Seal of Nevada Mining Company

SE380-20-10, 188x, v, unissued certificate, grey, small like a check $30.00

Searight Cattle Company (WY territory)

SE460-20-10, 188x, v, u/u certificate, grey
.....................................$28.00

G.D. Searle & Co.

SE490-40-10, 1977, v, $5,000 7-1/2% note due 1980, brown $6.00

Seatrain Lines, Inc. (DE)

*SE650-30-10, 1945, v, 100 class A stock (no par), FLB, 12" x 8", orange $4.00

*SE650-30-15, 1946, v, 100 class A stock (no par), FLB, 12" x 8", orange, signature variety ..$4.00
SE650-40-10, 1949, v, 100 sh. (par $4), blue
.....................................$4.00
SE650-45-10, 1973, v, 100 sh. (par $1), blue
.....................................$4.00

It is generally assumed that only 5% of certificates survive to reach collectors.

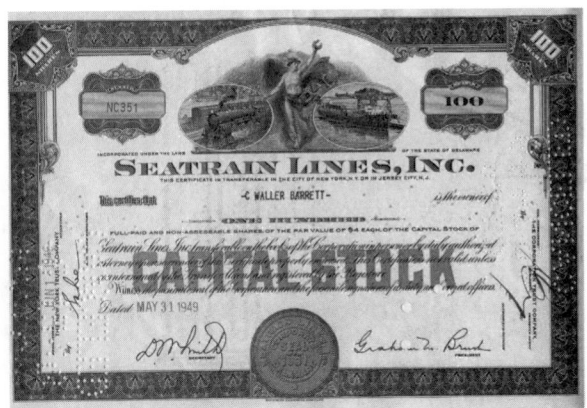

*SE650-50-10, 1949, v, 100 sh. (par $4), SBC, 12"
x 8", blue..........................$4.00

SE650-55-10, 1971, v, 1,000 sh. on a more than
100 sh. certificate, crimson.............$4.00

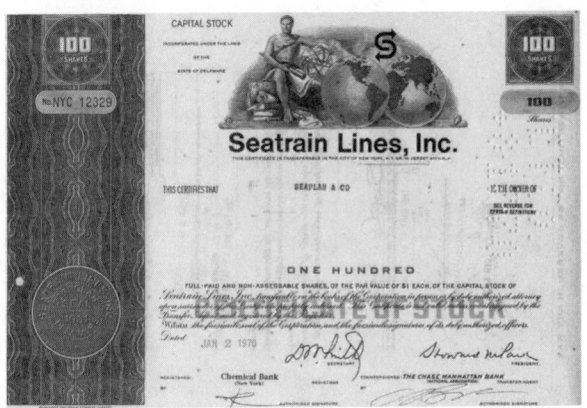

*SE650-60-10, 1970, v, 100 sh. (par $1), SCB, 12"
x 8", blue..........................$4.00

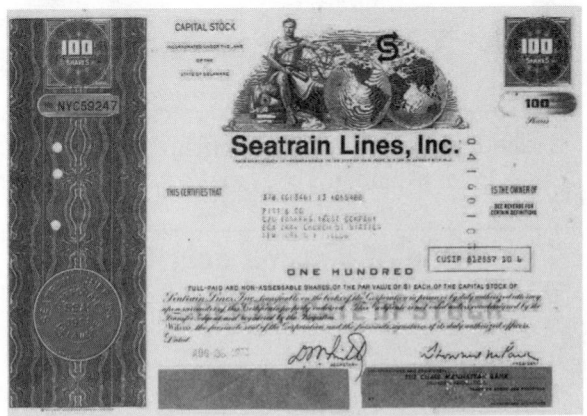

*SE650-70-15, 1972, v, 100 sh. (par $1), 12" x 8",
change in registrar, blue $4.00

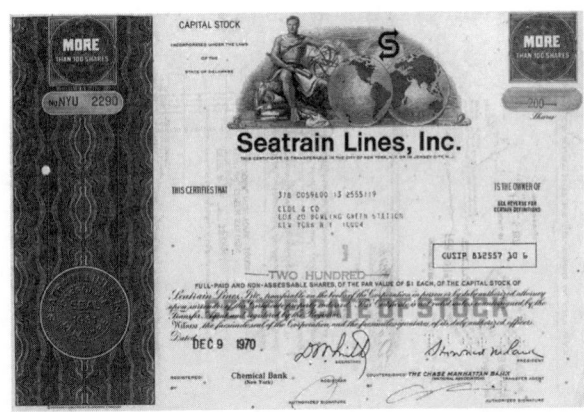

*SE650-80-10, 1970, v, 200 sh. on a more than 100
sh. certificate (par $1), SCB, 12" x 8", red
...................................$4.00

Seattle Times Company

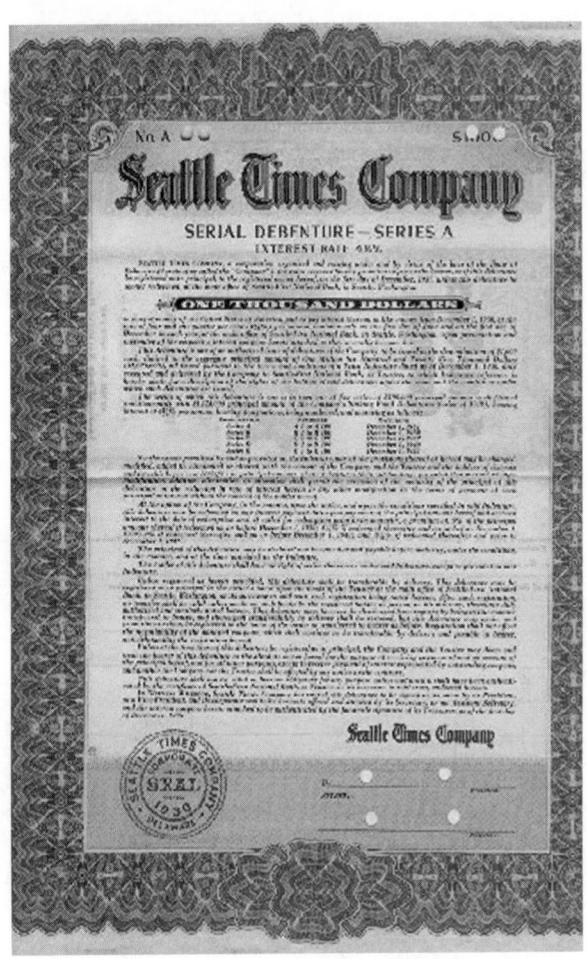

*SE690-40-10, 1936, v, u/c $1,000 serial deben-
ture, 4-1/4% series A, brown $22.00

The Second National Bank of Boston (par $40)

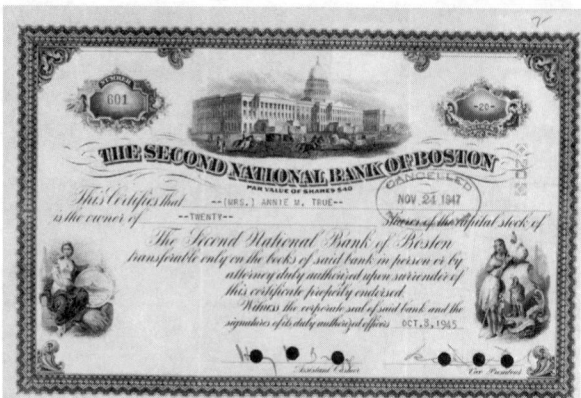

*SE730-20-10, 1945, v, 20 sh., ABN, 11" x 7", grey border $10.00

Second National Bank of Cooperstown (NY par $100)

SE750-20-10, 1888, v, 10 sh., brown $26.00

Second National Bank of New Haven (CT par $12.50)

*SE760-20-10, 1955, v, 50 sh., 11" x 7", brown border $9.00

Second & Third Street Passenger Railway Co. of Philadelphia (PA par $50)

SE790-20-10, 1911, v, 10 sh., grey $12.00

The Security Oil Trust (CO)

*SE840-20-10, 1929, v, 5 sh., brown $5.00

Security Pacific Corporation (DE 1973)

SE870-55-10, 1989, v, $100,000 floating rate extendible note, due 1993, Jeffries Banknote Company, 12" x 8", brown $5.00

*SE870-60-10, 1990, v, $100,000 floating rate extendible note, due 1994, Jeffries Banknote Co., 12" x 8", green $5.00

The value of a stock certificate depends on:

- **rarity**
- **the issuer**
- **signatures**
- **quality of engraving**
- **overall appearance**
- **condition**
- **date of issue**

Security Producing and Refining Company (DE par $1)

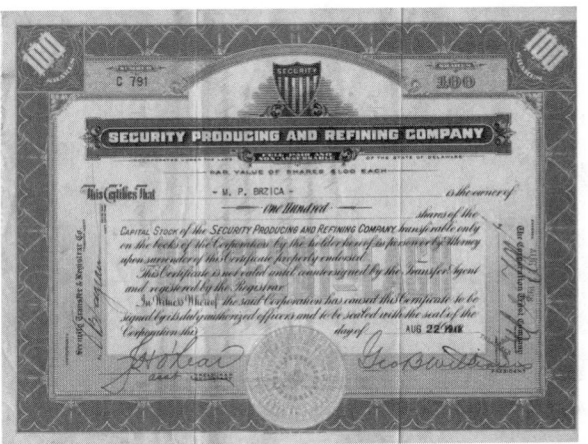

*SE900-30-10, 1918, v, i/u 100 sh., SBN, 11-1/2" x 8-1/2", orange $5.00

Seneca Falls Machine Company (MA par $1)

*SE1180-20-10, 1942, v, 100 sh., FLB, 12-1/4" x 7-3/4", green $4.00

This catalog has listings in an alphabetical format. The reason is simple: Companies diversify as they grow. For example, the Canadian Pacific Railway company recently split into five companies. They represent the railway, hotels, shipping, airline, and petroleum interests of the company. During World War II, the Singer sewing machine company made guns and other defense-related equipment, so where should we list it? It's far easier to use a strict alphabetical order, rather than to confuse the reader with topical classifications.

Sentinel Life Insurance Company (CA 1961, par $1)

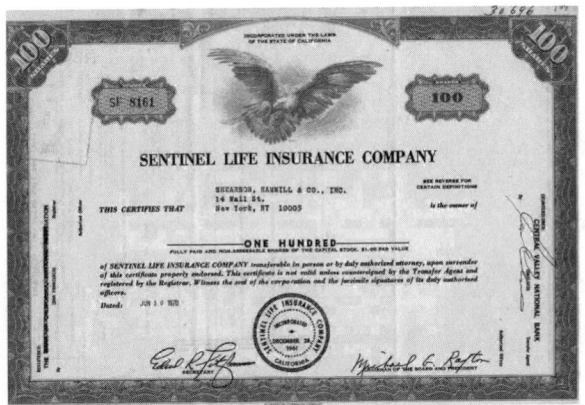

*SE1260-30-10, 1970, v, i/u 100 sh., Jeffries Banknote Co., 12" x 8", orange $4.00

The Sentinel Publishing Co. (MT par $5)

SE1290-20-10, 190x, u/u certificate, 11" x 7", blue $12.00

Sentinel Radio Corporation (IL par $1)

*SE1320-20-10, 19xx, v, u/c less than 100 sh. certificate, Columbian Bank Note Company, 11-3/4" x 7-3/4" brown. $4.00

The Sequatchie Coal & Iron Company (TN par $100)

SE1460-20-10, 18xx, v, u/u certificate, grey $6.00

Shackelford Drilling Company (AZ par $10)

SH70-20-10, 1935, v, 1 sh., orange $10.00

Shaklee Corporation (no par)

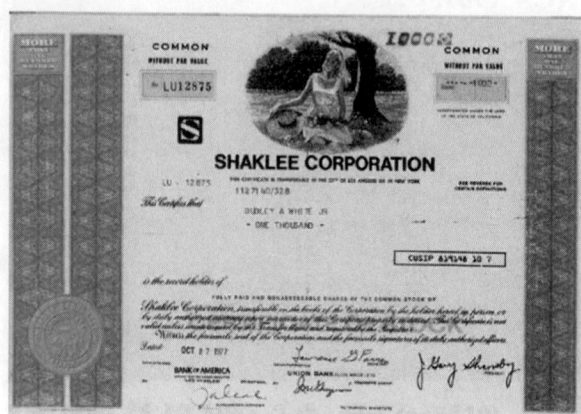

*SH160-30-10, 1977, v, 1,000 sh. on a more than 100 sh. certificate, orange............$10.00

The Sharon Railway Company (PA par $50)

*SH270-20-10, 1940, v, 40 sh., ABN, green
...................................$22.00

Sheffield Furnace Company (AL 1886)
SH450-20-10, 1887, v, 1 sh., green $10.00

Shelby Northwestern Railway Company (MO)
SH580-40-10, 1913 $100 first mort. 5% bond, orange.............................$35.00

> *It is generally assumed that only 5% of certificates survive to reach collectors.*

Shell Oil Company (DE par $1)

*SH660-30-10, 1967, v, 100 sh., green.....$4.00

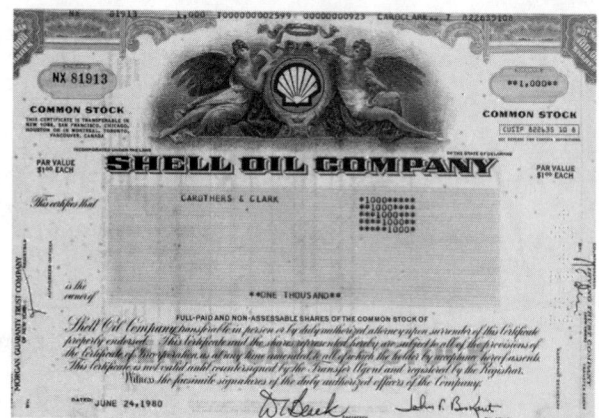

*SH660-40-10, 1980, v, 1,000 sh. on a not more than 100,000 sh. certificate, ABN, 12" x 8", orange..............................$6.00

*SH660-60-10, 1976, v, $1,000 8-1/2% debenture due 2000, green $10.00

W. M. Sheridan & Company
(AZ 1908, par $1)

*SH830-20-10, 1914, v, i/u 60 sh., GOES, 10-3/4"
x 8-1/2", grey $4.00

The Sheridan-Adams Royalty Syndicate
(AZ 1912, par $1)

*SH860-30-10, 1912, v, i/u 800 sh., GOES, 10-3/4"
x 8-1/2", brown $5.00

UNLISTED TYPES & VARIETIES

Readers are welcome to contact the author
directly at:

**Rainer Stahlberg
P.O. Box 1044
Rooseveltown, New York 13683**

*SH860-30-15, 1913, v, i/u 5,000 sh., signature
variety, GOES, 10-3/4" x 8-1/2", brown . .$5.00

Shot-Lite Corporation of America
(CO par $50)
SH1040-20-10, 19xx, v, u/u certificate, light brown
. . . .$40.00

City of Shreveport (LA)
SH1300-20-10, proof on card of Municipal Loan,
grey. $50.00

Shulton, Inc. (NJ 1934, par $0.50)
Makers of Old Spice.

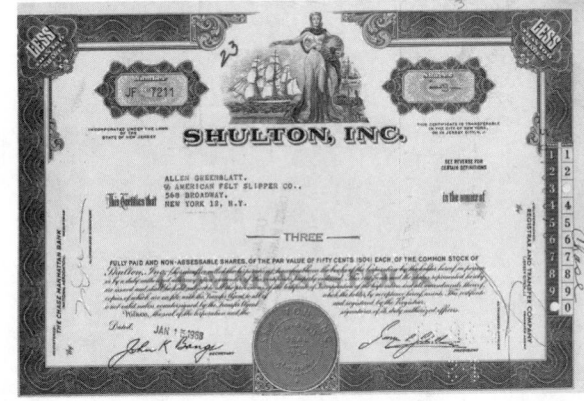

*SH1460-20-10, 1968, v, 3 sh. on a less than 100
sh. certificate, SCB, 12" x 8", green. $4.00

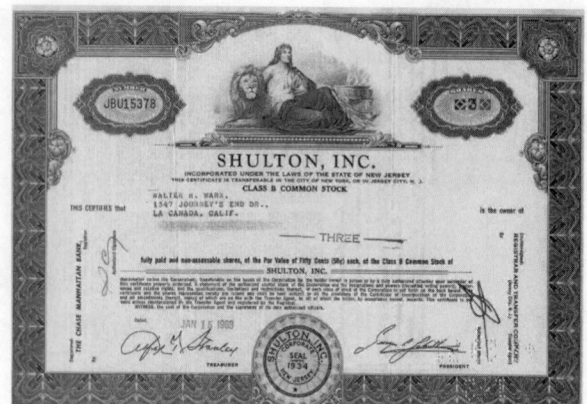

*SH1460-25-10, 1963, v, 3 sh., class B common stock, CBN, 11-3/4" x 8-1/4", blue......$4.00

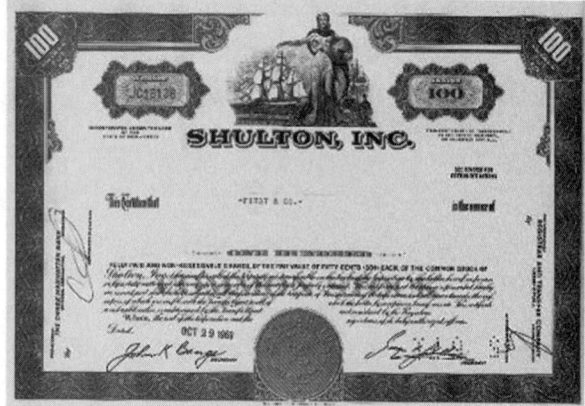

*SH1460-30-10, 1968, v, 100 sh., red $4.00

Sierra Consolidated Mining Company (CA par 25¢)

*SI140-30-10, 1929, v, 2,000 sh., Knight, Counihan Co., 11-3/4" x 8-3/4", green.........$6.00

Sierra Madre and Antelope Valley Toll Road Co. (CA)

SI210-20-10, 1xxx, v, u/u certificate, brown $51.00

Signal Commercial Company (AZ Terr. 1908, par $1)

*SI310-30-10, 1917, v, i/u 7,000 sh., GOES, 12" x 5-3/4", grey........................$7.00

Silver Bell Mines Co. (CO)

*SI370-30-10, 1964, v, 100 sh., green $3.00

Silver Chieftain Company (ID)
SI400-30-10, 1942, v, 100 sh., grey.......$10.00

The Silver Mountain Mining Company
SI440-30-10, 1920, v, 1,100 sh., green $10.00

Silver Rock Cobalt Mines Company (AZ par $1)
SI480-20-10, 1909, 10 sh., treasury stock, black on white..............................$9.00

Silver Star-Queens Mines, Inc. (ID 1929)

*SI510-20-10, 1968, v, i/u 1 sh., GOES Litho, grey
.....................................$6.00

Silverhorn Lead Mining and Smelting Co. (WI par $100)

*SI540-20-10, 1867, v, 10 sh., revenue stamp, 10" x 8-1/2", brown border $550.00

Silvis Mining Company (IL par $100)
SI570-20-10, 190x, v, unissued certificate, brown
....................................$15.00

Simmons Company
Mattress makers.

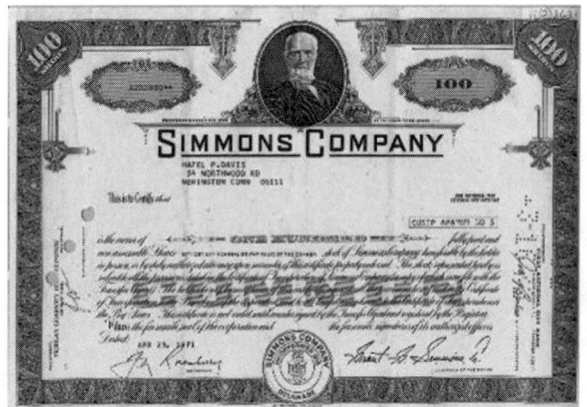

*SI670-30-10, 1971, v, 100 sh., green $4.00

J. Simpson & Co. Inc. (NY)
SI720-20-10, 19xx, v, u/u certificate, orange
.................................$10.00

Sinclair Oil Corporation (NY par $5)
Founded in 1916 by Henry F. Sinclair. In 1969 the company merged with Atlantic Richfield Company, later in 2000 ARCO merged with BP Amoco.

*SI810-20-10, 1967, 77 sh. on a less than 100 sh. certificate, green.....................$4.00

This catalog has listings in an alphabetical format. The reason is simple: Companies diversify as they grow. For example, the Canadian Pacific Railway company recently split into five companies. They represent the railway, hotels, shipping, airline, and petroleum interests of the company. During World War II, the Singer sewing machine company made guns and other defense-related equipment, so where should we list it? It's far easier to use a strict alphabetical order, rather than to confuse the reader with topical classifications.

*SI810-30-10, 1968, v, 100 sh., orange **$4.00**

SI810-40-10, 1969, v, 1,000 sh. on a more than 100
  sh. certificate, blue **$6.00**

Sinclair Venezuelan Oil Company
   (DE 1922, par $1)

*SI840-20-10, 1963, v, 10 sh. on a less than 100 sh.
  certificate, SCB, 11-3/4" x 8-1/4", green . . **$4.00**

Sioux City, Iowa

SI910-30-10, 1921, $500 6% Street Improvement
  bond, blue **$10.00**

The value of a stock certificate depends on:

- rarity
- the issuer
- signatures
- quality of engraving
- overall appearance
- condition
- date of issue

Sioux City and Western Railway Company
   (NE par $100)

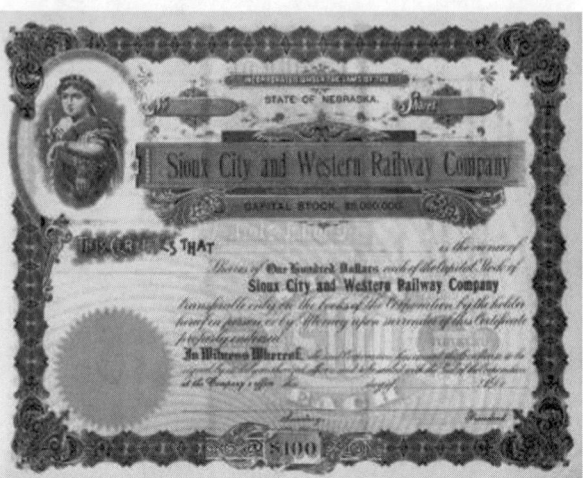

*SI940-20-10, 1xxx, v, u/u certificate, GOES, grey
  . . . . **$15.00**

Sioux Oil Co. (CO par 5¢)

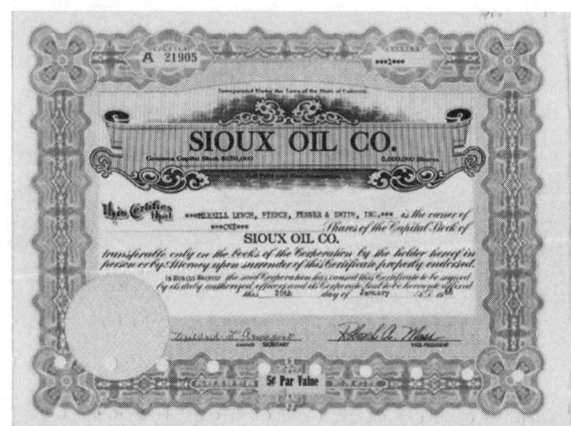

*SI980-20-10, 1968, v, 1 sh., orange **$3.00**

Skil Corporation (DE par $2)

SK100-20-10, 1969, v, 52 sh. on a less than 100 sh.
  certificate, 12" x 8", blue **$4.00**

Skippack & Perkionen Bus Company
   (PA par $100)

SK210-20-10, 19xx, v - Lincoln, unissued certifi-
  cate, grey **$10.00**

Smith Motor Truck Corporation (par $10)

SM190-20-10, 1916, t, 10 sh., green **$20.00**

Smoky Valley Mining & Milling Company (NV 1¢)

SM310-20-10, 19xx, v, unissued certificate, grey
. . . .$6.00

Smuggler Mining Company, Ltd. (NV par 10¢)

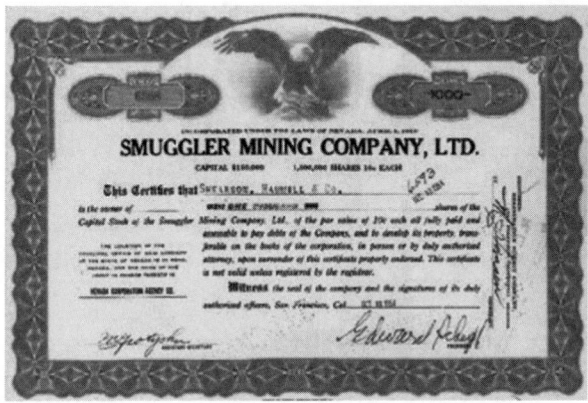

*SM510-30-10, 1954, v, 1,000 sh., orange. . .$4.00

Frequently encountered types of cancellation:

- **punch out cancels of small holes, sometimes forming words**
- **punch out cancels of larger holes**
- **cut out cancels made with a knife or scissors**
- **slit cancels made with a knife**
- **pen cancels**
- **rubber stamp cancels**

UNLISTED TYPES & VARIETIES

Readers are welcome to contact the author directly at:

> **Rainer Stahlberg**
> **P.O. Box 1044**
> **Rooseveltown, New York 13683**

Socony Mobil Oil Company, Inc. (NY)

*SO190-40-10, 1963, v, u/c $1,000 bearer 4-1/4% debenture due 1993, ABN, 10-1/4" x 15-1/4", blue. $5.00

Socorro Uranium Corporation (NM par 1¢)

*SO230-20-10, 1955, v, 80,000 sh., GOES, 10" x
5-3/4", grey **$8.00**

Sohio/BP Trans Alaska Pipeline Finance Inc.

SO400-30-10, 1975, v, $1,000 8-5/8% note due
1983, green **$6.00**

*SO400-35-10, 1975, v, $5,000 8-5/8% note due
1983, ABN, 12" x 8", orange **$6.00**

*SO400-40-10, 1975, v, $25,000 8-5/8% note due
1983, o/p name changed to Sohio/BP Tran-
salaska Pipeline Capital Inc., green **$6.00**

Somerset and Kennebac Railroad Company

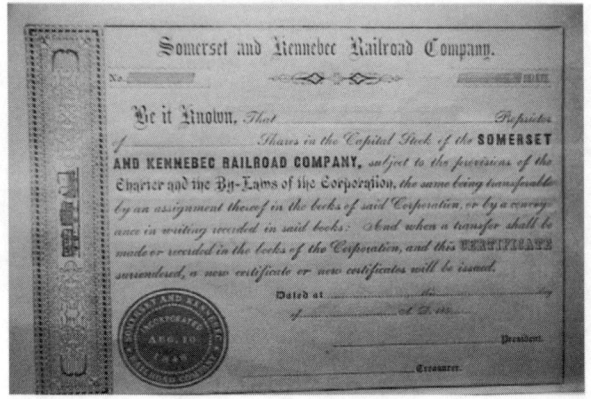

*SO570-20-10, 185x, v, u/u certificate, black on
light blue **$8.00**

Somerville Horse Railroad Company (par $50)

SO610-20-10, 1866, 6 sh., black **$50.00**

Soo Line Co-Operative Association (MN)

SO710-20-10, 1915, 1 sh., grey, about the size of a
check **$9.00**

State of South Carolina

*SO780-20-10, 187x, v, $500 Consolidation 6%
stock, due 1893, ABN, green **$35.00**
SO780-25-10, 1871, v, £100 6% sterling funded
debt., grey **$22.00**
SO780-30-10, 1872, v, $2 scrip bond, grey
. . . .**$35.00**

South Coast Life Insurance Company (TX)

*SO820-30-10, 1961, v, 100 sh., Steck-Austin, 11"
x 8-3/4", green $4.00

The State of South Dakota

SO890-30-10, 1921, v, $1,000 5-1/2% State High-
way Bond due 1931, green $15.00

South Denver Water Company (CO)

SO920-40-10, 1913, v, $100 collateral trust 5-20
year 6% sinking fund gold bond w. coupons,
green $66.00

The South Georgia Railway Company
(par $100)

SO960-20-10, 1917, 20 sh., grey $55.00

South Porto Rico Sugar Company

SO1070-20-10, 1957, v, 12 sh. on a less than 100
sh. certificate, o/p par value $5, blue $10.00

The South Riverside
Land & Water Company (par $100)

*SO1220-20-10, 1896, v, 3-1/2 sh., green
.................................$100.00

South Utah Mines & Smelters (ME)

SO1280-30-10, 1910, v, 100 sh., orange $8.00

Southern Bell Telephone and Telegraph
Company (NY)

SO1340-30-10, 1939, v, $1,000 3% 40-year deben-
ture, orange.......................$20.00
SO1340-40-10, 1977, v, $1,000 3% 40-year deben-
ture, ABN, blue $16.00

The Southern Development Company
(NJ par $100)

SO1380-20-10, 19xx, unissued certificate, brown
.................................$6.00

Southern Pacific Company (DE no par)

SO1480-20-10, 1959, v, 20 sh. on a less than 100
sh. certificate, blue $16.00
SO1480-30-10, 1978, v, 500 sh., green $21.00

The Southern Quarry Company (par $50)

SO1520-20-10, 1903, 10 sh., grey $10.00

This catalog has listings in an alphabetical format. The reason is simple: Companies diversify as they grow. For example, the Canadian Pacific Railway company recently split into five
companies. They represent the railway, hotels, shipping, airline, and petroleum interests of
the company. During World War II, the Singer sewing machine company made guns and
other defense-related equipment, so where should we list it? It's far easier to use a strict
alphabetical order, rather than to confuse the reader with topical classifications.

Southern Railway Company

*SO1560-30-10, 1925, v, 100 sh., red **$6.00**
SO1560-40-10, 1942, v, 10 sh., preferred, brown
...............................**$10.00**

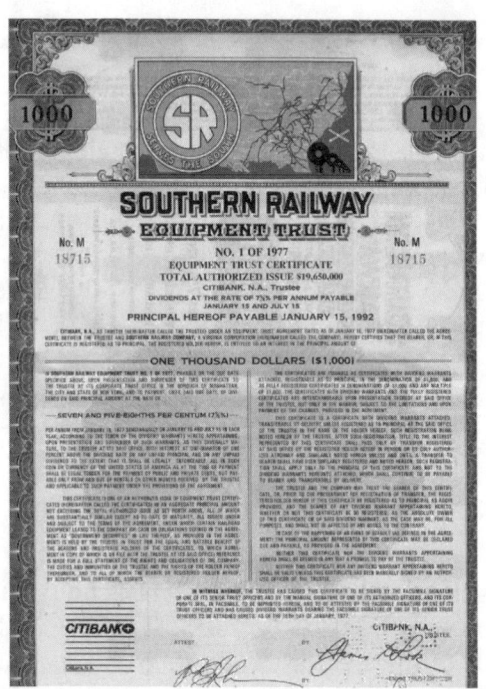

*SO1560-60-10, 1977, v, u/c $1,000 equipment
trust, No. 1 of 1977, 7-5/8% bond, ABN, 9-1/2"
x 13-1/2", blue **$5.00**

UNLISTED TYPES & VARIETIES
Readers are welcome to contact the author
directly at:

Rainer Stahlberg
P.O. Box 1044
Rooseveltown, New York 13683

Southern States Guaranty Company (FL)

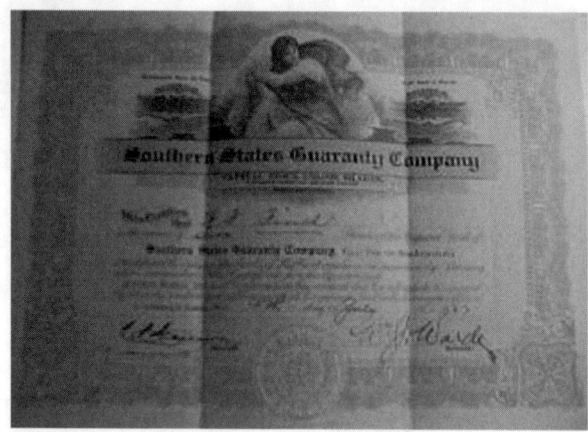

*SO1620-20-10, 1927, v, 5 sh., 12" x 8-1/2",
orange...........................**$3.00**

Southwestern Land and Power Co. (ME par $100)
SO1690-20-10, 1903, v, 100 sh., grey border
...............................**$5.00**

The Southwestern Railroad Company (GA par $100)
SO1740-20-10, 1917, v, 20 sh. on a less than 100
sh. certificate, brown **$10.00**

Spectex Industries, Inc. (NY 1965, par 1¢)
SP120-20-10, 1972, 100 sh., Corpex-Wolberg, 12"
x 8", green **$4.00**

*SP120-20-15, 1972, 50,000 sh., Corpex-Wolberg,
12" x 8", green **$5.00**

Spectro Manufacturing and Sales, Inc. (CO par $1)

*SP150-20-10, 19xx, v, u/c with pin hole "SAM-PLE," GOES, 10-3/4" x 8-1/2", grey on gold
.....................................$3.00

Speed Wrap Incorporated (CO no par)

*SP190-20-10, 19xx, v, u/c certificate, GOES, 11" x 8-1/2", orange $3.00

The value of a stock certificate depends on:
- rarity
- the issuer
- signatures
- quality of engraving
- overall appearance
- condition
- date of issue

*SP190-20-15, 19xx, v, u/c pinhole "SAMPLE," GOES, 11" x 8-1/2", orange............$3.00

Spencer Shoe Corporation (MA par $1)

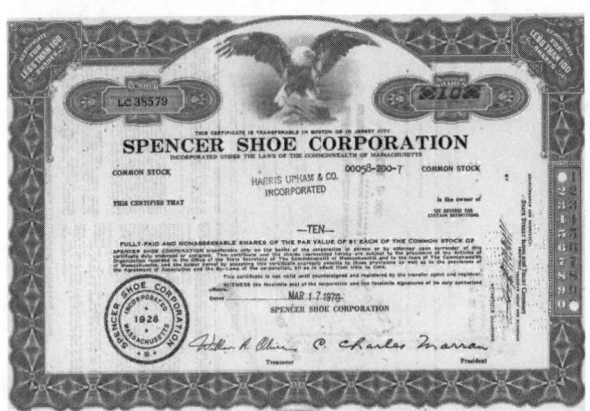

*SP260-20-10, 1970, v, 10 sh. on a less than 100 sh. certificate, ABN, 12" x 8", orange $3.00

*SP260-30-10, 1970, v, 100 sh., green $3.00

The Sperry Corporation (DE par $1)

*SP320-30-10, 1954, v, 100 sh., mauve....**$12.00**

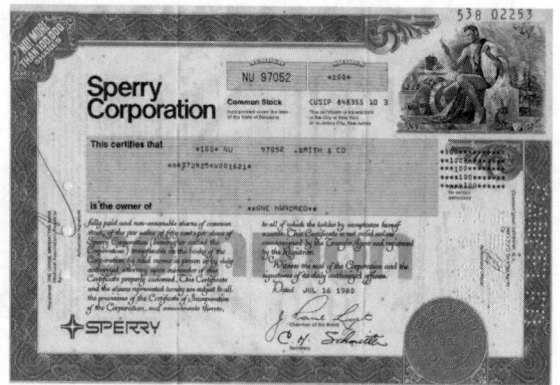

*SP320-40-10, 1980, v, 100 sh. (par 50¢), SCB, 12" x 8", bright blue **$5.00**

Spiral Metal Company, Inc. (DE 1975, par 1¢)

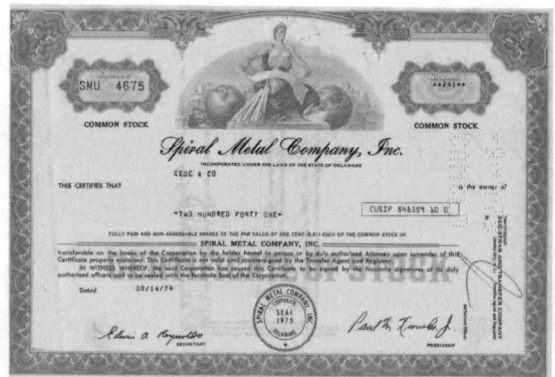

*SP470-30-10, 1979, v, 241 sh., SCB, 12" x 8", orange **$4.00**

Spokane-Wild Rose Oil & Gas Co. (WA par 10¢)

SP660-20-10, 1921, v, 1,000 sh., orange border **$30.00**

Spring City Oil Co. (MN par $1)

*SP770-20-10, 1905, v, 500 sh., 11" x 8", brown border **$55.00**

The Spring Gulch Tunnel Company (par $1)

Yreka, CA mining district.
SP800-20-10, 19xx, v, unissued certificate, green **$20.00**

The Springfield Oil and Gas Company (OK par $5.00)

SP840-20-10, 19xx, unissued certificate, green **$6.00**

Stafford Meadow Coal, Iron and City Improvement Company of Scranton (PA)

*ST270-40-10, 1858, v, $100 6% 1ˢᵗ mortgage bond, signed by Thomas Philo Remington, grey **$40.00**

The H.A. Stahl Properties Company (DE par $100)

*ST370-30-10, 1925, v, 28 7% preferred shares, GOES Litho, 12" x 9-1/4", orange **$6.00**

Standard Federal Bank (USA par $1)

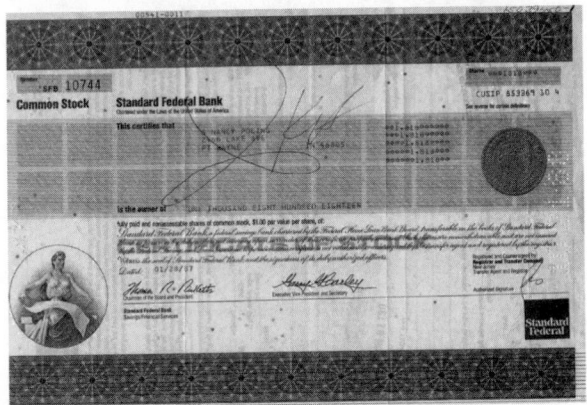

*ST460-30-10, 1987, v, 1,818 sh., SCB, 12" x 8", blue **$4.00**

Standard Oil Company (IN)

ST520-60-10, 1977, v, $5,000 9.20% debenture due 2004, orange **$10.00**

> *It is generally assumed that only 5% of certificates survive to reach collectors.*

*ST520-65-10, 1977, v, $10,000 9.2% debenture due 2004, blue **$8.00**

Standard Oil Company (NJ)

ST530-60-10, 1976, v, $10,000 6-1/2% debenture due 1998, o/p name changed to Exxon Corporation, purple **$9.00**

*ST530-65-10, 1978, v, $100,000 6-1/2% debenture due 1998, o/p name changed to Exxon Corporation, red **$9.00**

The Standard Oil Company (OH)

*ST540-60-10, 1977, v, $10,000 8-1/2% bond due 2007, blue **$24.00**

Standard Silver-Lead Co. (WA par $1)
ST620-30-10, 1960, v, 100 sh., Spokane Litho
Company, green $7.00

Stanley Consolidated Mining and Milling Company (WA par $1)

ST680-20-10, 19xx, v, u/u certificate, GOES, grey
. . . .$3.00

Stanley Mining Company (ID par $0.10)
ST710-20-10, 19xx, v, unissued certificate, black
. . . .$6.00

Stanwood Oil Corporation
ST780-20-10, 1945, v, unissued certificate, green
. . . .$6.00

Star Motors, Incorporated (DE)

ST820-20-10, 1924, v, 1 sh., red. $65.00

State Acceptance Corporation (ND par $1)

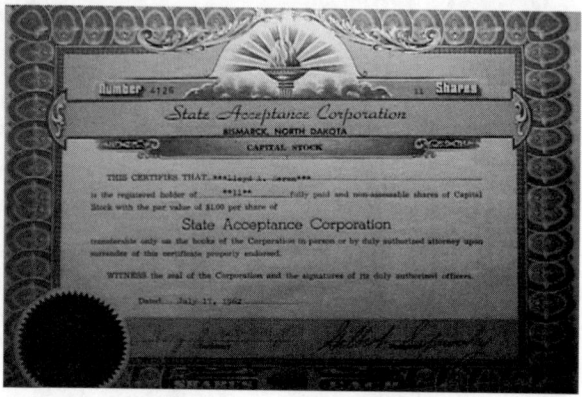

ST930-20-10, 1962, v, 11 sh., blue $5.00

State Line and Union Rail Road Co. (WI par $100)

ST950-20-10, 18xx, v, u/u certificate, Cameron,
Amberg & Co., Printers, Chicago; 10" x 6",
brown border $35.00

Stauffer Chemical Company (DE)

ST1020-40-10, 1975, v, $1,000 4-7/8% subord.
debenture due 1991, blue $5.00

Sterling Debenture Corporation (NY 1906)

ST1120-10-10, 1907, certificate to purchase 2 sh., of the American Telegraphone Company at $10 per share, brown $20.00

Sterling Precision Corporation (DE 1955, par 10¢)

*ST1200-20-10, 1963, v, 50 sh. on a less than 100 sh. certificate, ABN, 12" x 8", purple. $4.00

*ST1200-30-10, 1962, v, 100 sh., ABN, 12" x 8", blue $4.00

The Sterling Silver Mining Company (AZ territory, par $5)

Tombstone district.

*ST1240-30-10, 1890, v, 500 sh., grey. . . .$160.00

John B. Stetson Company (PA no par)

Founded in 1865 with $10 worth of fur and hand tools. Today, the Stetson hat is a mark of quality. They are made in St. Joseph, Missouri.

ST1430-20-10, 1935, v, 25 sh. on a less than 100 sh. certificate, green $40.00

Steubenville and Indiana Rail Road Company (par $50)

ST1580-20-10, 1862, v, 5 sh., grey $15.00

Stevens Mining Company (ME par $100)

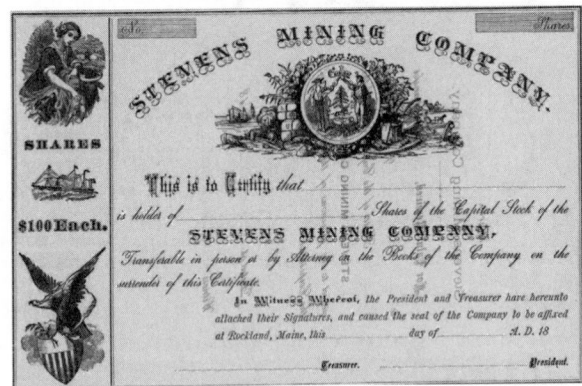

*ST1630-20-10, 18xx, v, u/u certificate, w/o imprint, thin paper, 10-1/4" x 6-1/2", green $5.00

Steve's Homemade Ice Cream, Inc.

*ST1670-30-10, 1986, v, 100 sh., blue $10.00

D.B. Stewart Company (par $100)

ST1720-20-10, 189x, v, u/u certificate, brown $4.00

The Sticktite Fly Paper Company (WI par $100)

ST1750-20-10, 1909, v, 5 sh., GOES, 11" x 8", brown border......................$32.00

The Stissing Bank (par $100)

ST1770-30-10, 1858, v, 120 sh., grey......$14.00

Stormont Mining Company of Utah (UT par $1)

ST1890-30-10, 1883, v, 100 sh., green....$125.00

Stratus Services Group, Inc.

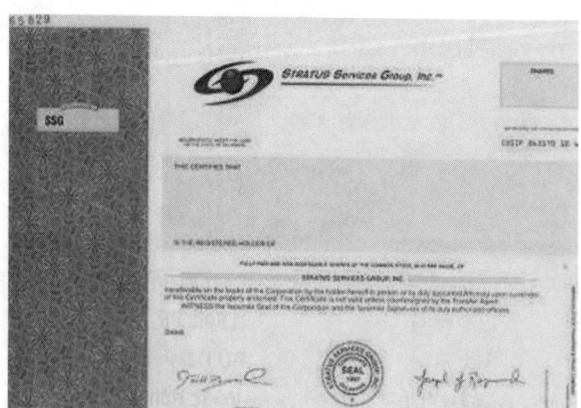

ST1950-20-10, 19xx, v, u/u certificate, red
.................................$10.00

Strauss-Erkhardt Co. Inc. (par $5)

ST1980-20-10, 19xx, v, u/u certificate, blue
.................................$3.00

Strongheart Building & Loan Association (PA)

ST2090-30-10, 1927, $50 deferred certificate of indebtness, green $5.00

This catalog has listings in an alphabetical format. The reason is simple: Companies diversify as they grow. For example, the Canadian Pacific Railway company recently split into five companies. They represent the railway, hotels, shipping, airline, and petroleum interests of the company. During World War II, the Singer sewing machine company made guns and other defense-related equipment, so where should we list it? It's far easier to use a strict alphabetical order, rather than to confuse the reader with topical classifications.

Stud Timber Co., Inc. (MT par $1.00)

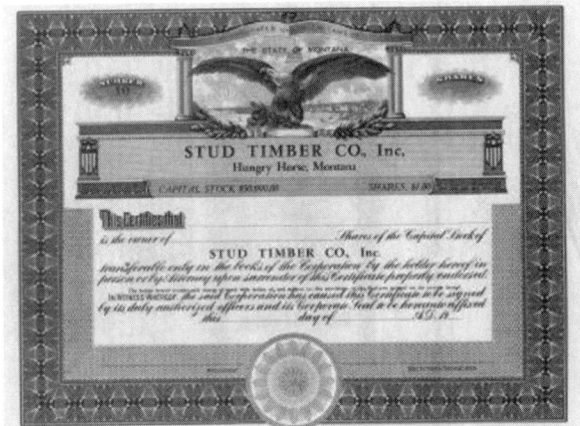

*ST2220-20-10, 19xx, v, u/u certificate, green
.....................................$15.00

Studebaker Corporation (DE)

ST2250-40-10, 1957, v, 5 sh. on a less than 100 sh.
certificate, green $5.00

*S2250-50-10, 1954, v - blacksmith shop, 100 sh.,
purple $10.00

*ST2250-60-10, 1964, v - SC w. modern tools, 100
sh. (par $1), SCB, 12" x 8-1/4", green....$5.00

Studebaker-Packard Corporation

*ST2270-30-10, 1954, v, 8 sh. on a less than 100
sh. certificate, ABN, 12" x 8", green $4.00
ST2270-35-10, 1958, v, 25 sh. on a less than 100
sh. certificate, green $4.00

*ST2270-40-10, 1955, v, 100 sh., o/p par value
change, blue $5.00

*ST2270-45-10, 1964, v, 100 sh., green $5.00
ST2270-55-10, 1962, v, 100 convert. pref. sh.,
yellow..............................$5.00

Studebaker-Worthington, Inc. (DE)

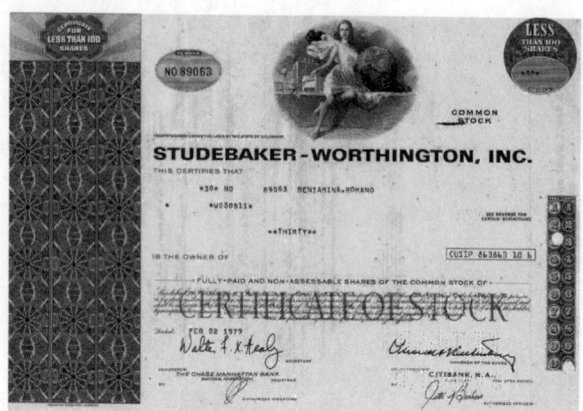

*ST2290-20-10, 1979, v, 30 sh. on a less than 100 sh. certificate, ABN, 12" x 8", blue $3.00

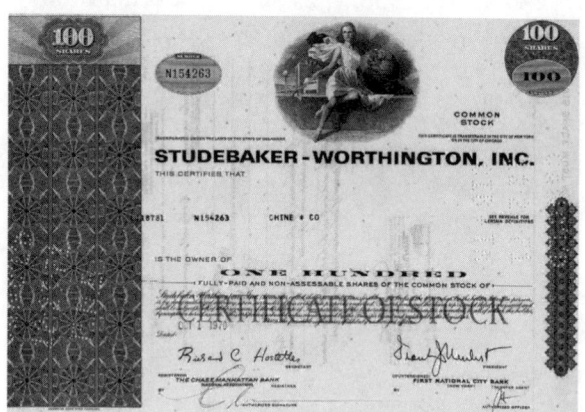

*ST2290-30-10, 1970, v, 100 sh., ABN, 12" x 8", green $3.00

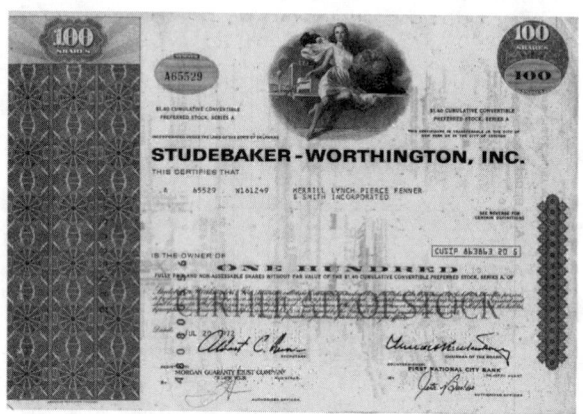

*ST2290-40-10, 1972, v, 100 series A $1.40 cumul. conv. preferred sh., ABN, 12" x 8", brown $4.00

Student Loan Marketing Association (US 1972)

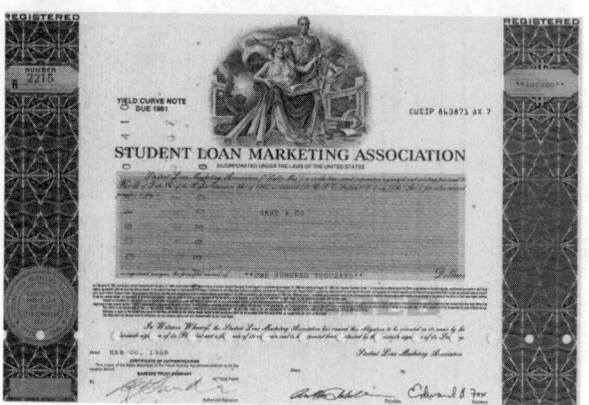

*ST2330-40-10, 1986, v, $100,000 yield curve note, due 1991, ABN, 12" x 8", blue $4.00

Suffield Gold, Silver and Copper Mining Company (par $25)

SU130-20-10, 186x, v, unissued certificate, grey $10.00

Sun Oil Company (PA par $1)

*SU330-20-10, 1972, v, 22 sh. on a less than 100,000 sh. certificate, ABN, 12" x 8", blue $4.00

Sunday Lake Mining Company (WI par $25)

*SU350-20-10, 1887, v, 100 sh., 11" x 8", green
  border $85.00

Sunray Mid-Continent Oil Company (DE par $1)

SU370-20-10, 1955, v, 10 sh. on less than 100 sh.
  certificate, red $5.00

*SU370-25-10, 1955, v, 10 sh. on a less than 100
  sh. certificate, Dutch revenue imprint, orange
  . . . .$4.00
SU370-30-10, 1955, v, 10 sh. on a less than 100 sh.
  certificate, orange $4.00

> ***It is generally assumed that only 5% of certificates survive to reach collectors.***

The Superior Oil Company (CA)

*SU470-40-10, 1956, v, $1,000 3-1/4% bond due
  1981, green $6.00

Superior Portland Cement, Inc. (WA)

*SU500-30-10, 19xx, v, u/u 100 class B shares,
  blue $7.00

Superior Rapid Transit Railway Co. (WI par $100)

*SU520-20-10, 1892, v, 133 sh., 11-1/2" x 8-1/2", grey border $60.00

Supervised Shares, Inc. (DE 1932, par 10¢)

*SU540-30-10, 1933, v, 358 sh., Hamilton Bank Note - New York, 12" x 8", blue $4.00

Surrey Sleep Products, Inc. (NY)

SU600-20-10, 19xx, v, unissued certificate, orange $4.00

SU600-25-10, 19xx, unissued pref. certificate, green $4.00

Susquehanna & Lehigh Turnpike Company

SU740-20-10, 180x, water stains $20.00

Swarthmore National Bank and Trust Company (U.S. par $100)

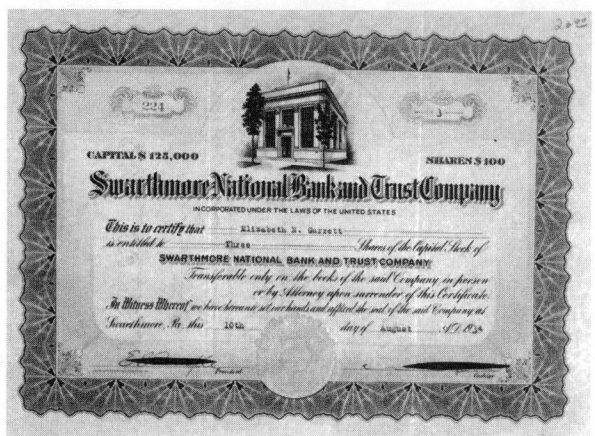

*SW130-20-10, 1934, 3 sh., 11-1/2" x 8", brown border $6.00

Syracuse Rapid Transit Railway Company (NY)

SY250-20-10, 189x, v, unissued certificate, orange $15.00

American International, $5

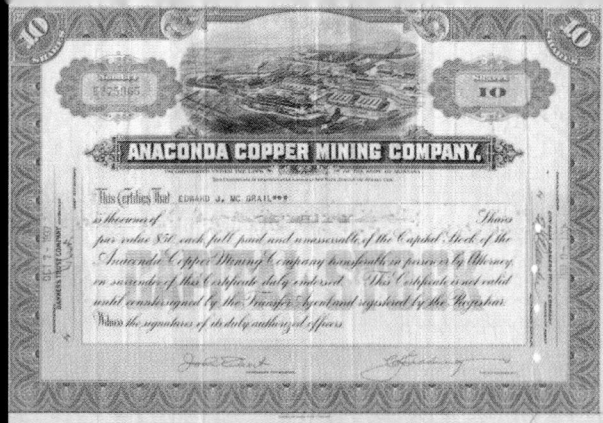

Anaconda Copper Mining Company, $10

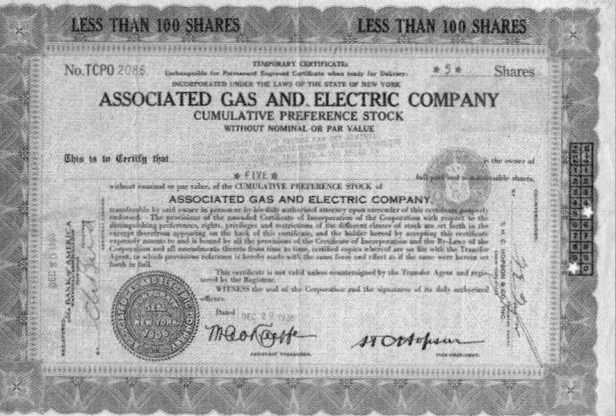

Associated Gas and Electric Company, $4

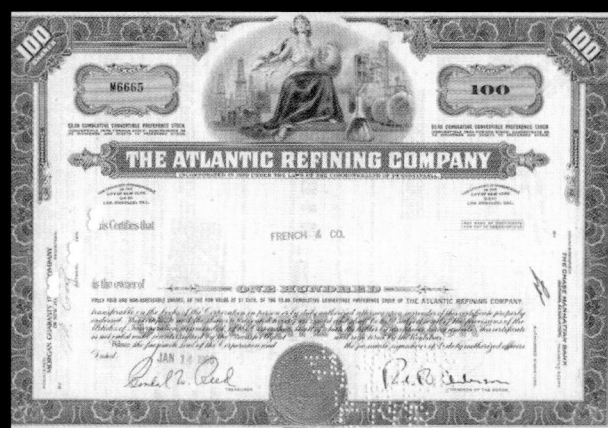

The Atlantic Refining Company, $4

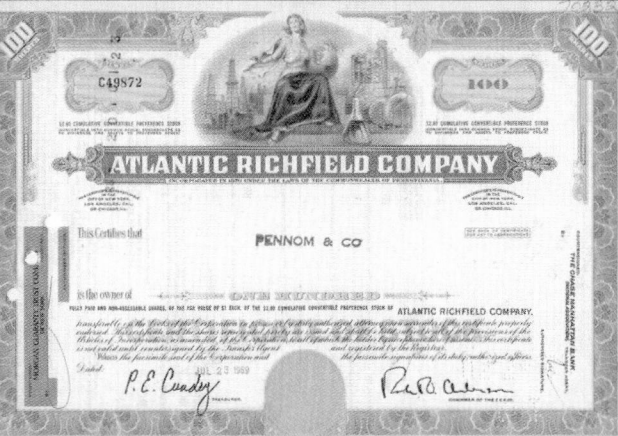

Atlantic Richfield Company, $4

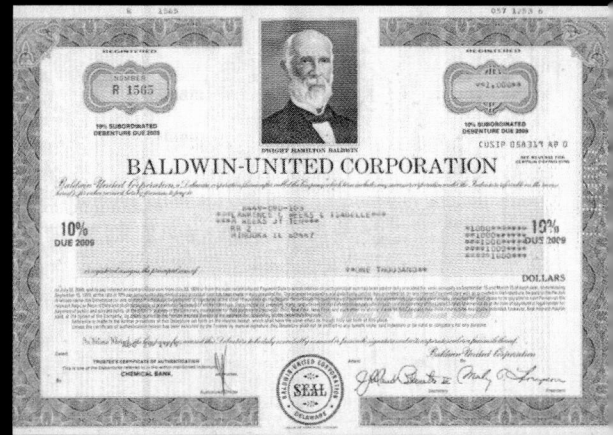

Baldwin-United Corporation, $4

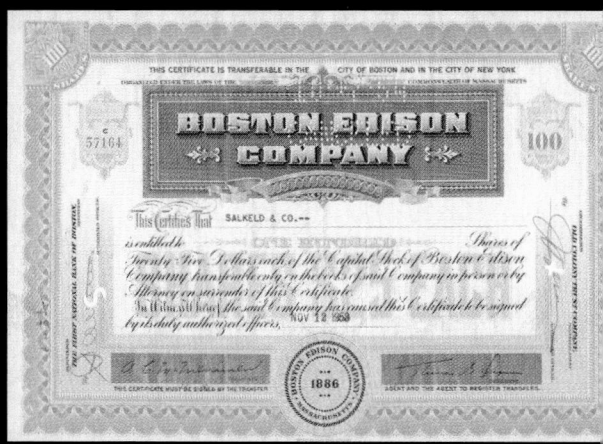

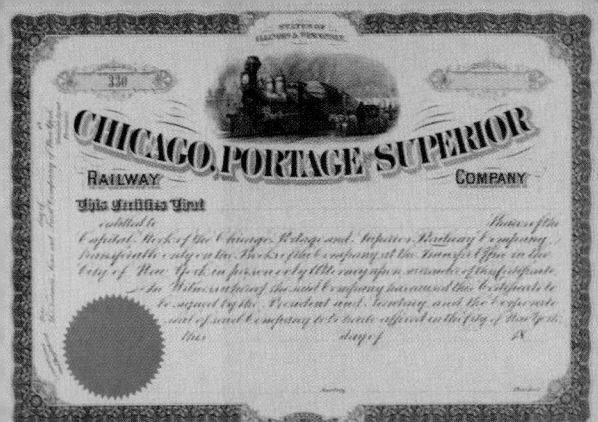

Chicago, Portage and Superior Railway Company, $30

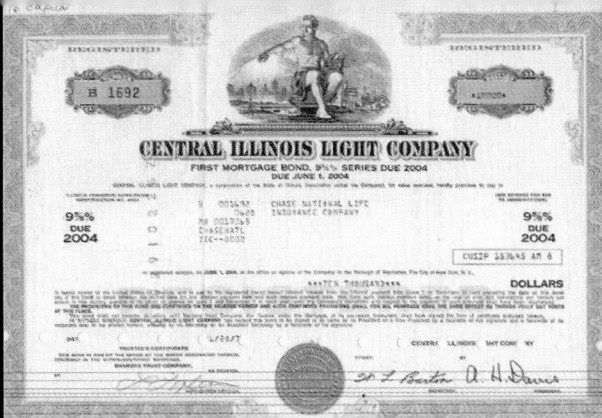

Central Illinois Light Company, $5

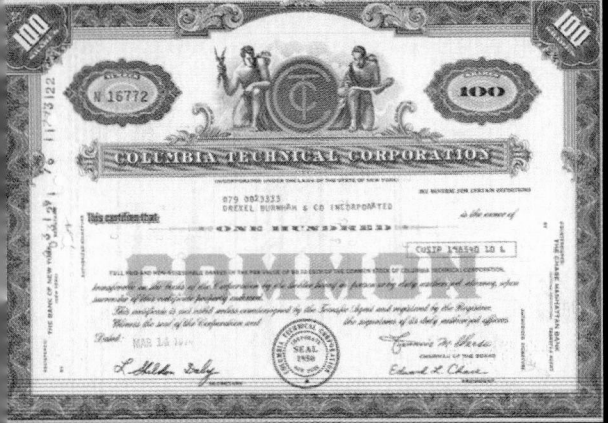

Columbia Technical Corporation, $4

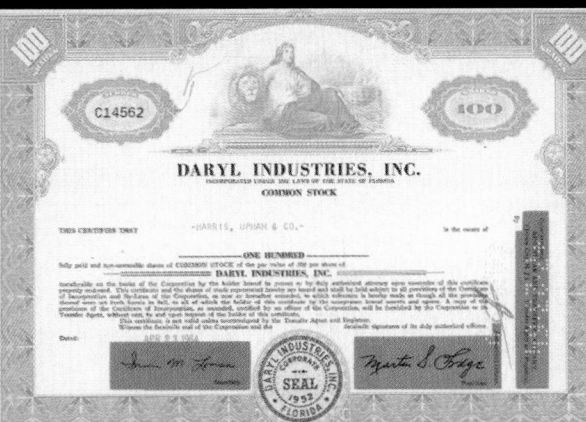

Daryl Industries, Inc., $4

First Financial Bancorp, Inc., $4

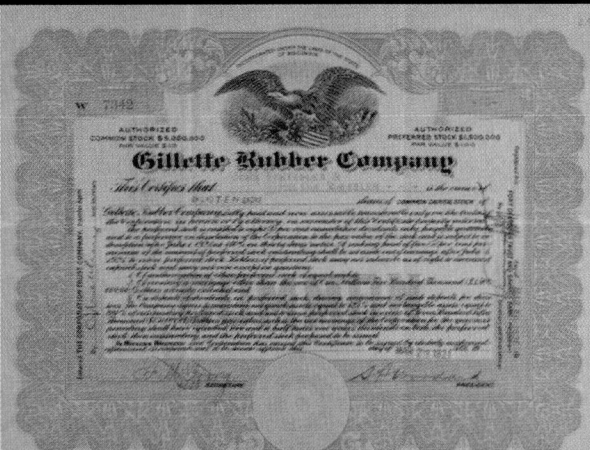

Gillette Rubber Company, $25

Hazel Green Mining Company, $30

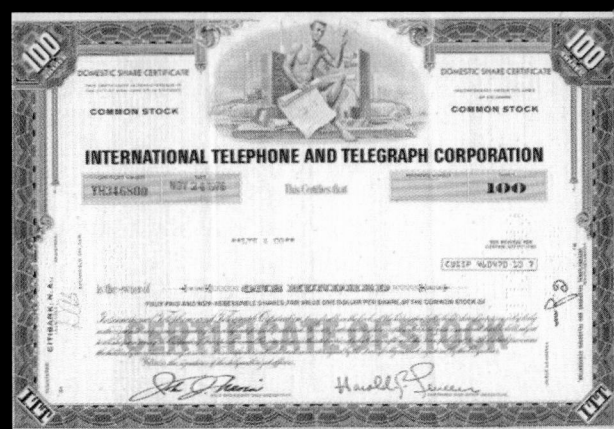

Jolliffe Importers, Inc., $3

Lehigh Valley Transit Company, $5

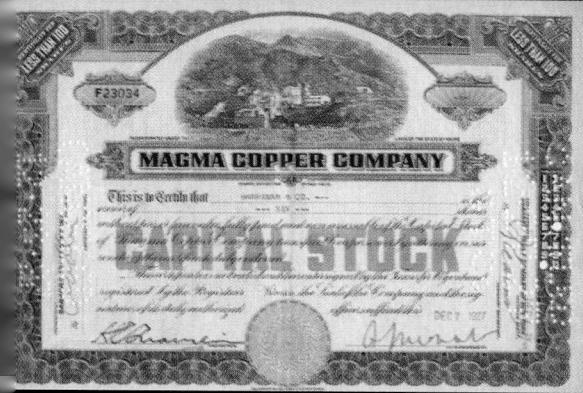

Magma Copper Company, $4

The Natal Day Mining & Milling Co., LTD, $13

Kohinoor Blende Mining Corp., $125

Chester A. Martin, Inc., $4

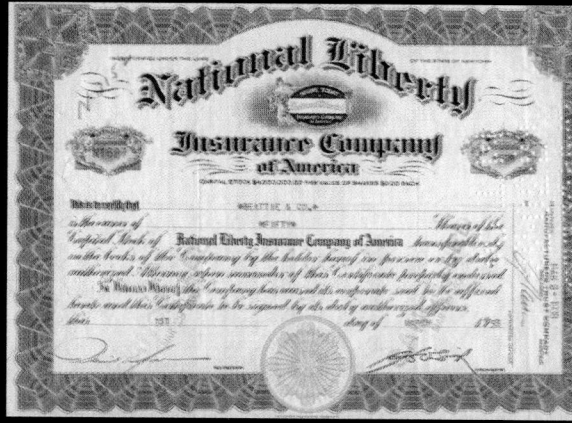

Mount Olive Consolidated Coal-Coke Co., $15

National Liberty Insurance Company of America, $6

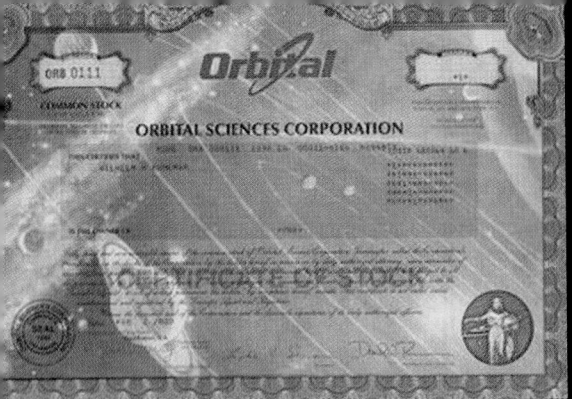

Orbital Sciences Corporation, $40

The Pennsylvania Railroad Company, $4

The Reliable Mining Co., $45

Seatrain Line

Pabst Brewing Company, $200

Quebrada Grande Mining and Development Company

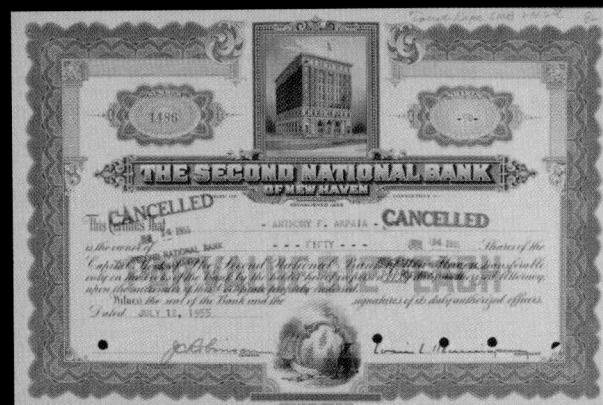

Rochester Gas and Electric Corporation, $4

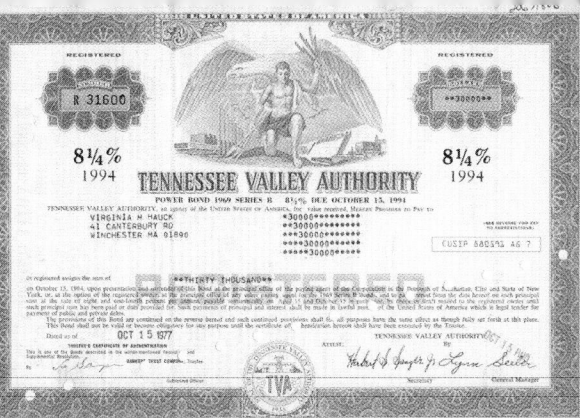

Tennesse Valley Authority, $76

Trout Mining Company, $4

Tuolumne Copper Mining Company, $6

United States Lines Company, $7

Vulcanized Rubber and Plastics Company, $4

S.D. Warren Company, $4

Xoma Corp...

...le Corporation

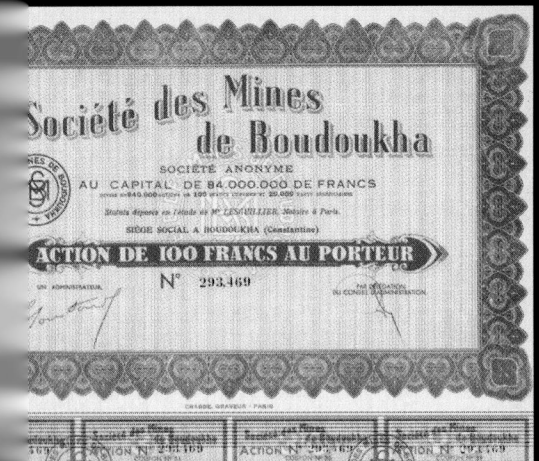

a, Société des Mines de Boudoukha S.A., $4

Argentina, Compañía Azucarera Tucumana S.A., $5

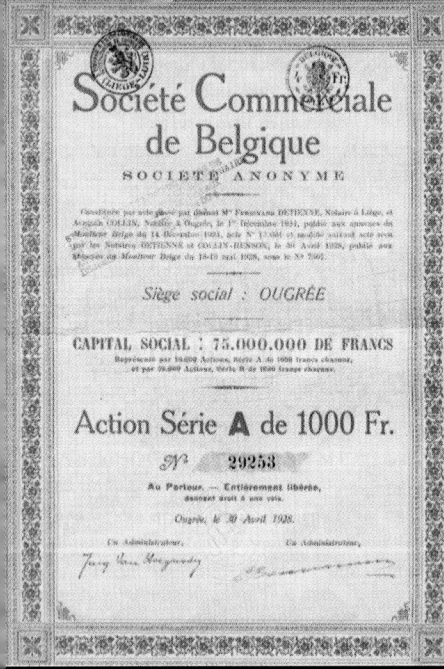

um, Société Commerciale de Belgique S.A., $3

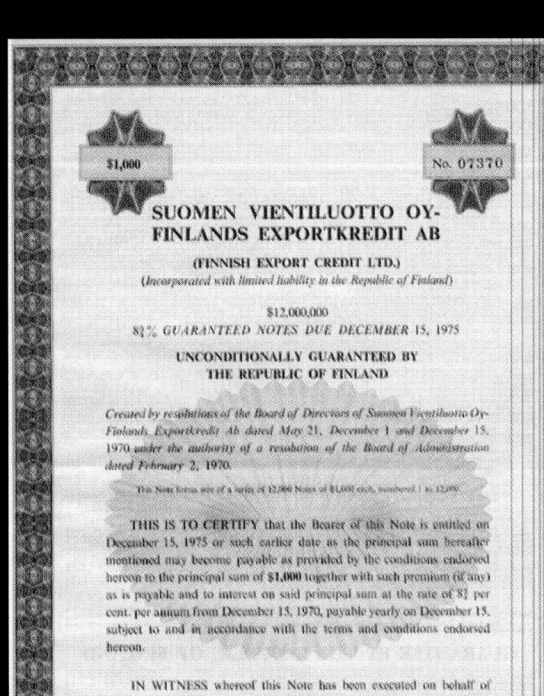

Brazil, Banco do Café, $3

a, British Columbia Power Corporation Limited, $5

France, Anciens Etablissements A. Binet S.A., $3

Great Britain, National Coke & Oil Company Ltd., $3

Germany, Schatzan Des Deutsches Reichs, $3

Hungary, 3rd Peale Loan, $30

Greece, Antrakorucheion Aliberou, $4

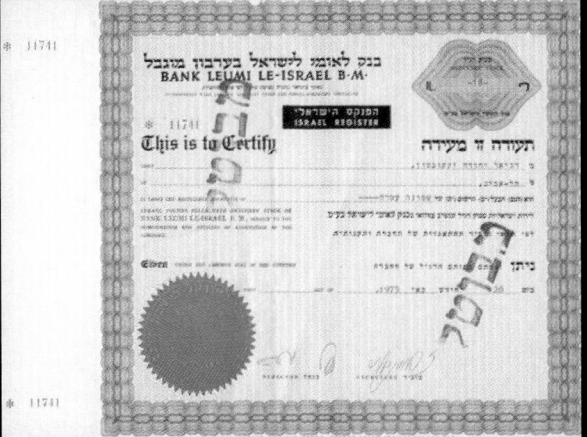

Israel, Bank Leumi Le-Israel B.M., $5

Japan, Asahi Glass Company, Limited, $3

Japan, Kurosaki Refractories Co. Ltd., $3

Nichi Co., Ltd., $3

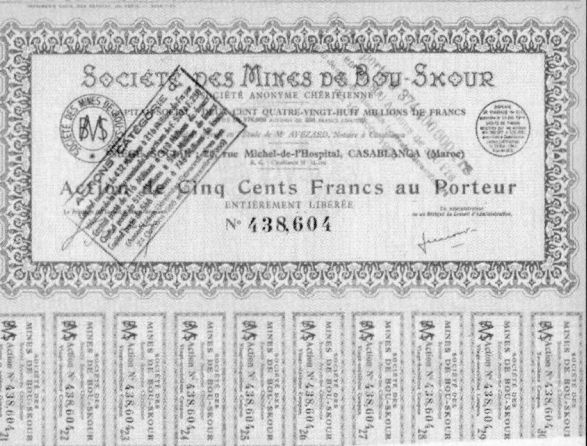

Morocco, Sociéte des Mines de Bou-Skour, $5

Compagnie Minière du Souss, $4

Netherlands, American Natural Gas Corporation, $3

Nederlandsch-Indische Spoorweg-Maatschappij, $4

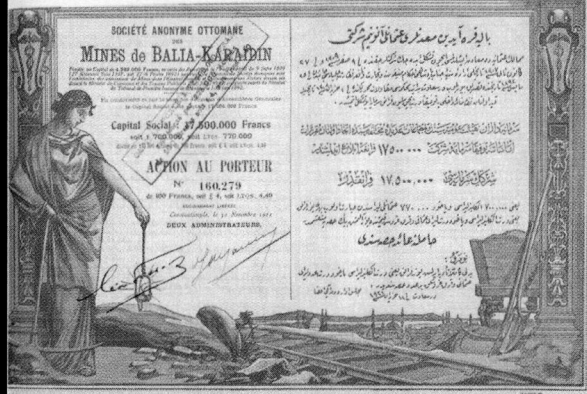

T

Tacoma Boatbuilding Co.

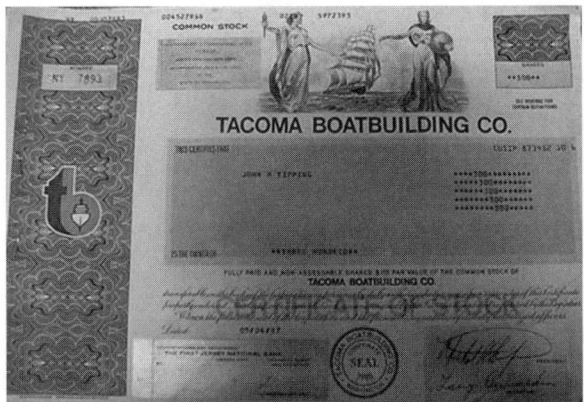

*TA50-20-10, 1987, v, 300 sh., blue. $5.00

Tallulah Falls Railway Company (GA)
TA120-20-10, 1xxx, v, 1 sh., preferred stock, brown
. . . .$40.00

Tamarack and Chesapeak Mining Company (par $1)
*TA200-20-10, 1904, v, 2,000 sh., grey $5.00

Tecopa Consolidated Mining Company (par $1)

*TE110-20-10, 1910, v - Chief Tecopa, 100 sh., 9" x 11", brown $65.00

Tehama Crusade Placers Ltd. (NV)
TE200-20-10, 193x, unissued certificate, grey
. . . .$8.00

Telepost Company

*TE320-30-10, 1913, v, 1sh., series A, class II convertible stock, blue-grey. $5.00
TE320-40-10, 1909, v, 100 sh., series A class II conver., brown $6.00

Tenabo Mining and Smelting Company (NV)
TE470-30-10, 1910, 100 sh., green $10.00

Tenneco Corporation

*TE530-60-10, 1976, v, $25,000 6-1/4% subordinated debenture, blue $6.00

Tennessee Brewing Company (par $100)
TE590-20-10, 1885, v, 8 sh., grey $77.00

Tennessee Northern Railway Company (TN par $100)

TE640-20-10, 1901, 4 sh., brown........$43.00

Tennessee Valley Authority (USA)

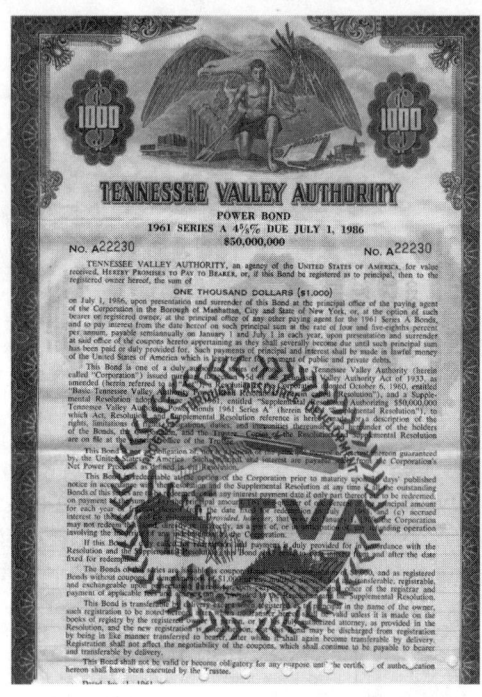

*TE730-50-10, 1961, v, $1,000 4-5/8% series A bond due 1986; De La Rue Banknote Co., 9" x 15-1/4", green.....................$7.00

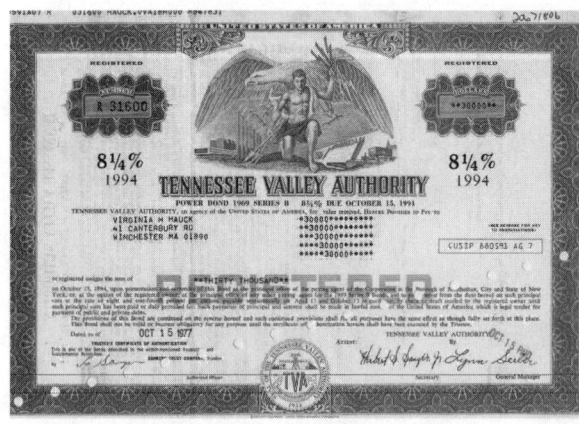

*TE730-60-10, 1974, v, $1,000 8-1/4% power bond 1969 series B, due 1994, Federated Banknote Company, 12" x 8", purple.............$7.00

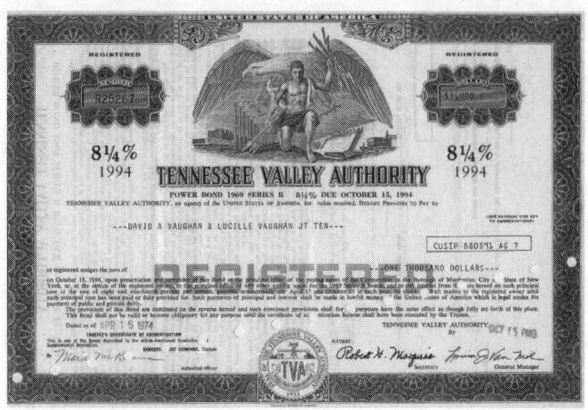

*TE730-60-15, 1977, v, $30,000 8-1/4% power bond 1969 series B, due 1994, signature variety, SCB, 12" x 8", purple.................$5.00

TE730-80-10, 1989, v, $100,000 7% power bond, blue.....................$10.00

TE730-90-10, 1990, v, $12,000 7% power bond due 1997, blue $10.00

Terminal Elevator Company (AL par $100)

TE820-20-10, 18xx, v, u/u certificate, A. Hoen & Co, black.........................$27.00

Terre-Haute and Richmond Rail-Road Company (IN par $50)

TE880-10-10, 1853, 1 sh., grey $30.00

The Terry Steam Turbine Company (CT par $5)

*TE1020-20-10, 1961, 50 sh., EAW, 11-3/4" x 8", green...........................$4.00

Texaco Inc. (DE)

*TE1120-60-15, 1976, v, $1,250,000 8-1/2%
debenture bond, due 2006, ABN, 12" x 8", blue
..................................$10.00

TE1120-60-10, 1979, v, $25,000 8-1/2% debenture
bond, due 2006, blue................$10.00

Republic of Texas

TE1150-20-10, 1840, v, $500 8% bearer bond,
Southern Banknote Co., black $175.00

TE1150-30-10, 1845, v, $100 certificate of stock in
the 10% consolidated fund, w. coupons, brown
..................................$175.00

Texas Eagle Oil and Refining Company (DE)

*TE1200-30-10, 1920, v, 262 sh., blue......$5.00

Texas Hydro-Electric Corporation

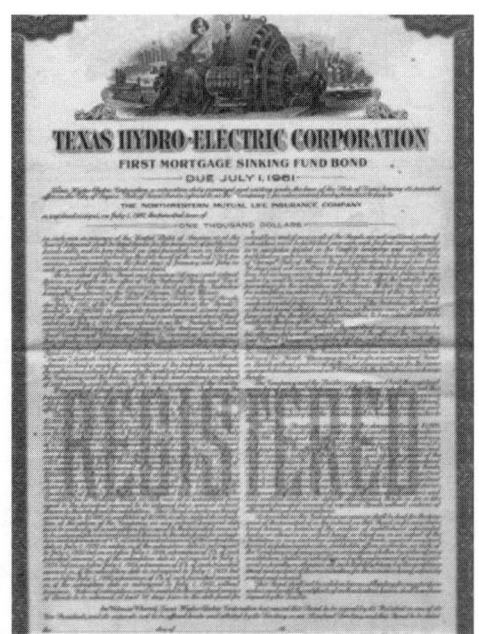

*TE1260-30-10, 19??, $1,000 1st mortgage sinking
fund bond due 1961, purple $15.00

The Texas and Pacific Railway Company (par $100)

TE1340-30-10, 1954, v, 12 sh. on a less than 100
sh. certificate, red..................$22.00

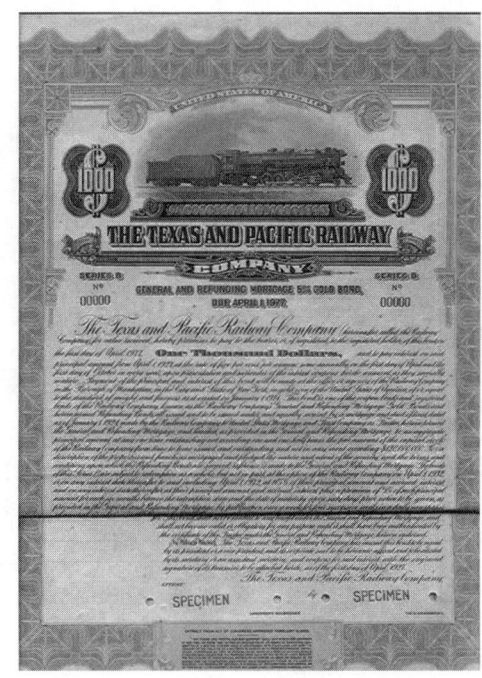

*TE1340-50-10, 1927, v, s $1,000 series B 5% gold
bond, brown $90.00

Texas Southern Oil & Gas Company (TX 1954, par $0.25)
TE1400-30-10, 1954, v, 100 sh., brown **$15.00**

Texas Star Flour Mills (TX par $100)

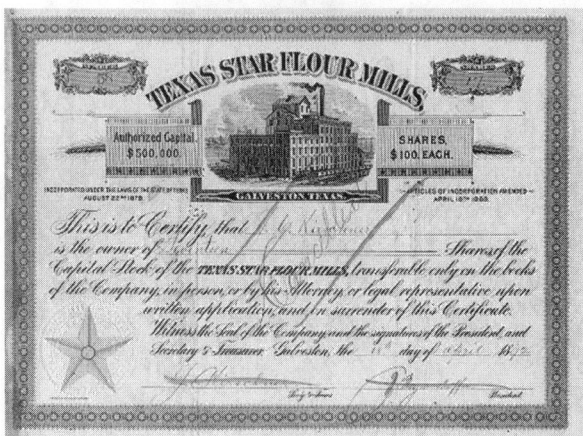

TE1430-20-10, 1892, v, 17 sh., green. **$25.00**

Thayer Oil and Gas Co. of Indiana (DE par $1)
TH160-30-10, 1919, v, 500 sh., grey **$10.00**

Thiokol Chemical Corporation (DE 1930, par $1)

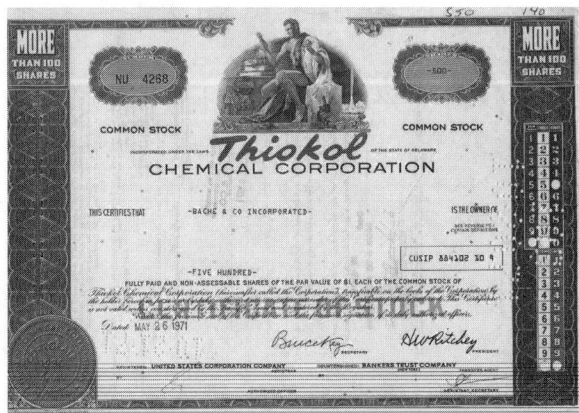

TH300-30-10, 1971, v, 500 sh. on a more than 100 sh. certificate, SCB, 12" x 8", green **$4.00**

Third National Bank (TN)
TH370-40-10, 1972, v, $25,000 7-1/2% debenture due 2002, ABN, green **$6.00**

Thompson Brothers Lumber Company (TX par $100)

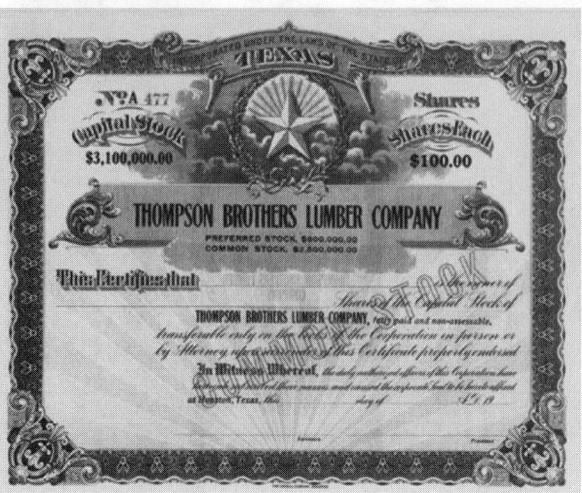

TH470-20-10, 19xx, v, u/u certificate, 10" x 8-1/2", grey **$4.00**

J.M. Thompson Lumber Company (TX par $100)
TH500-20-10, 1904, v, 20 sh., brown **$45.00**

Thompson & Tucker Lumber Company (TX par $500)

TH530-20-10, 1912, v, 4 sh., brown **$7.00**

Thomson Divide Mining Company
TH560-30-10, 1931, v, 1,000 sh., 10" x 5-3/4", brown **$6.00**

Three Rivers Development Co. (MT par $1)

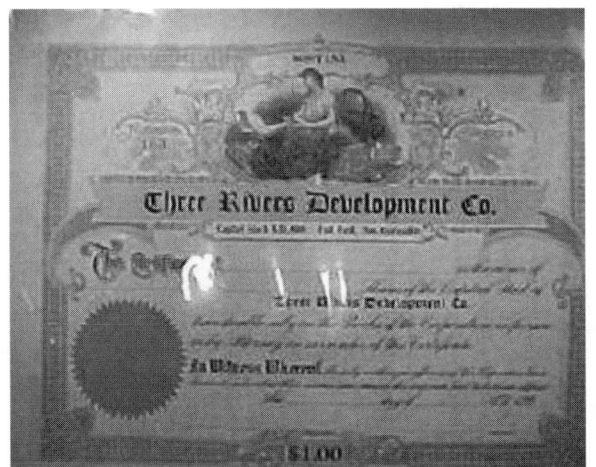

*TH590-20-10, 189x, v, u/u certificate, orange
....................................$5.00

Thunder Cave Corporation (UT)

Formed to raise money for the "Thunder Cave" book about the adventures of Jasper, Zebbie and the Grand Wigwah. Most certificates were signed by John S. (Jack) Sears the illustrator.

*TH630-20-10, 1931, v, 1 sh., green $46.00

Thwaites Furniture Company (MI)

*TH660-30-10, 1924, v, 100 sh., brown $5.00

Tigerton Canning Company (WI par $100)

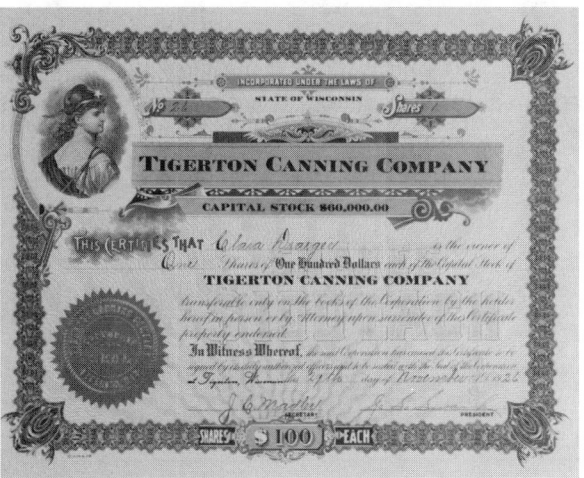

*TI100-20-10, 1926, v, 1 sh., GOES, 11" x 8", brown border $18.00

The value of a stock certificate depends on:

- rarity
- the issuer
- signatures
- quality of engraving
- overall appearance
- condition
- date of issue

The Times Investment Company, Times Printing Company of Seattle (WA)

*TI190-40-10, 1920, v, u/c $1,000 7% gold note, brown on beige $22.00

Timlow Builders, Inc. (PA no par)

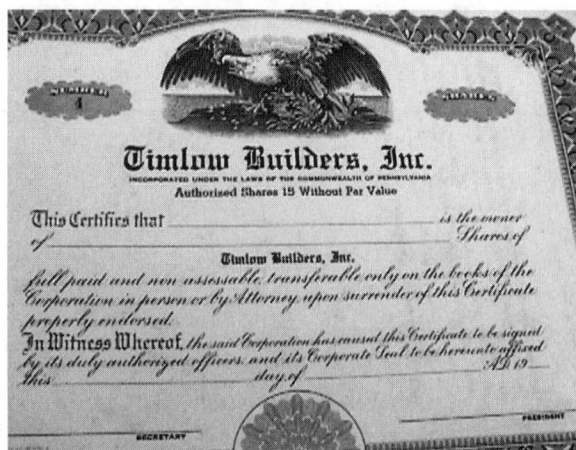

*TI220-20-10, 19xx, v, u/u certificate, green
. . . .$3.00

The Tioga National Bank and Trust Company

*TH250-20-10, 1938, v, 1 sh., green $10.00

Tobacco Products Corporation (VA 1912, no par)

*TO60-20-10, 1925, v, 10 sh. on a less than 100 sh. certificate (par $100), ABN, 11-1/2" x 7-1/2", brown $6.00

*TO60-30-10, 1925, v, 100 sh. (par $100), ABN, 11-1/2" x 7-1/2", olive green $6.00
TO60-35-10, 1930, v, 100 sh., brown $9.00
TO60-40-10, 1932, v, 100 sh., class A, blue
. . . .$9.00

Tobacco Shares Group Securities Inc.
TO90-30-10, 19xx, v, 1,000 sh. certificate . . **$10.00**

Toledo and Ohio Central Railway Company (OH par $100)
TO230-20-10, 19xx, v, unissued certif, FBN, green
. . . .**$15.00**

Toman, Inc. (IN no par)

TO400-20-10, 19xx, v, u/u certificate, w/o imprint, 11" x 7-1/2", green border. **$3.00**

Tombstone Mill and Mining Company (CT)

TO430-30-10, 1882, v, 200 sh., grey on beige, with stockholders report **$425.00**

> ***It is generally assumed that only 5% of certificates survive to reach collectors.***

Tonopah "76" Consolidated Mining Company (NV par $1)

TO510-30-10, 1912, v, 500 sh., brown . . .**$20.00**

Tonopah Divide Mining Company (NV 1912 par $1)

TO540-30-10, 1919, v, 100 sh., orange **$7.00**

Tonopah Gold, Silver, Copper, Water & Milling Co. (SD par $1)
TO570-30-10, 1906, v, 500 sh., brown **$20.00**
TO570-35-10, 1906, v, 1,000 sh., brown . . .**$20.00**

Tonopah and Goldfield Railroad Company (NV par $100)
TO590-30-10, 19xx, v, u/u pref. certificate, grey-blue. **$43.00**

Tonopah Mining Company of Nevada (DE par $1)

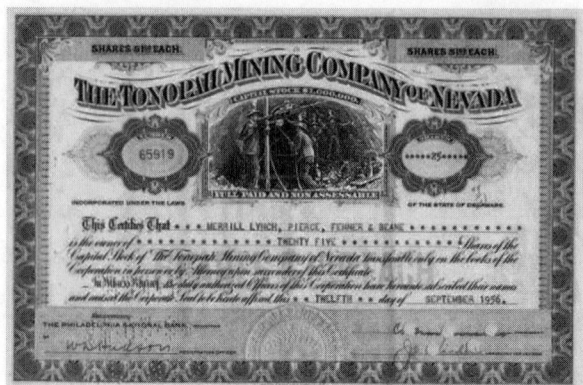

*TO620-20-10, 1956, v, 25 sh., SBN, brown
..................................$10.00

Tonopah Wall Street Mining Company (AZ territory 1905)

TO660-30-10, 1905, v, 500 sh., ...$20.00

Tonopah Western Consolidated Mining Company

*TO690-30-10, 19??, v, 1,000 sh., green $6.00

Topper Corporation (DE)

A very large toy company.
TO750-30-10, 1973, v, 1,000 sh., green....$28.00

Toulumme Copper Mining Company (AZ par $1)

TO830-30-10, 1913, v, 100 sh., brown.....$6.00
TO830-35-10, 1922, v, 100 sh., brown.....$7.00

Tractor Supply Co. (IL)

*TR70-20-10, 1962, v, 85 class A sh. on a less than 100 sh. certificate, brown............$10.00

Trail Mines, Inc. (CO)

*TR180-30-10, 1954, v, 25,000 sh., grey....$4.00

Trans World Airlines, Inc.

TR300-20-10, 1973, 5 sh., blue $5.00

The value of a stock certificate depends on:

- rarity
- the issuer
- signatures
- quality of engraving
- overall appearance
- condition
- date of issue

*TR300-50-10, 1961, v, $500 6-1/2% subordinated income debenture, orange..............$5.00

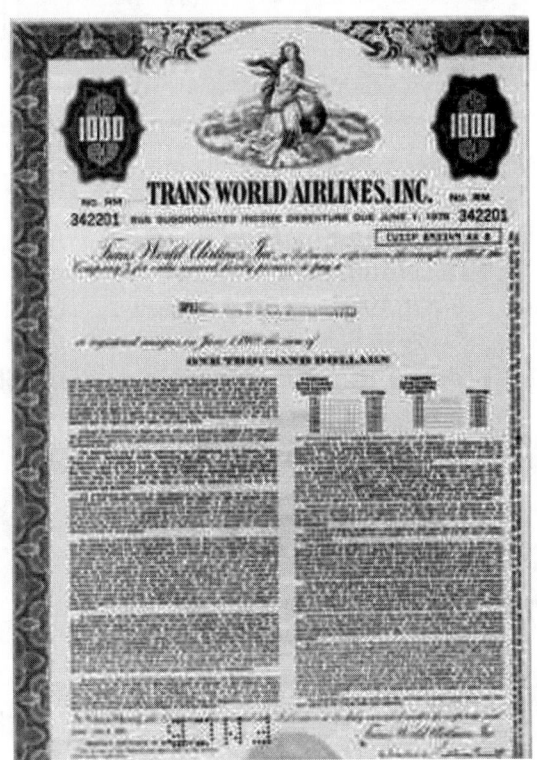

*TR300-55-10, 1961, v, $1,000 6-1/2% subordinated. income debenture bond, green.....$5.00

Transamerica Financial Corporation (DE)

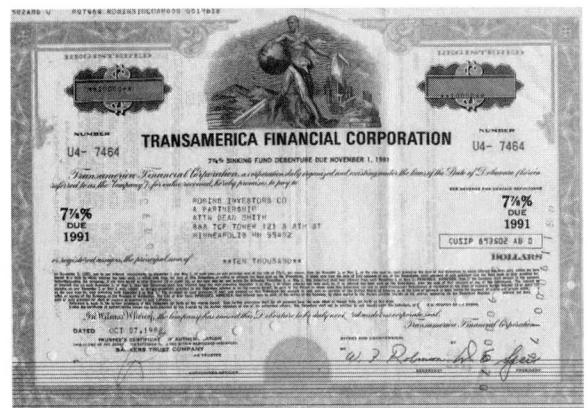

*TR370-40-10, 1982, v, $10,000 7-7/8% sinking Fund debenture due 1991, SCB, 12" x 8", yellow $4.00

Trans-Beacon Corporation (DE 1933 par $1)

Early television company originally founded as Television Industries.

TR400-30-10, 1965, v, 100 sh., orange $4.00

*TR400-35-10, 1969, v, 100 sh., Corpex-Wolberg, 12" x 8", orange....................$4.00

Transcoastal Industries Corp. (NJ 1949, par $1)

TR450-30-10, 1968, v, 100 sh., blue $4.00

Transocean Gulf Oil Company (DE)

TR580-40-10, 1968, v, $1,000 bond, green $10.00

TR580-45-10, 1969, v, $1,000 guaranteed debenture due 1984, bearer bond, blue $6.00

*TR580-50-10, 1972, v, $1,000 7-1/2% guaranteed
bearer debenture due 1987, ABN, 9" x 13-1/2",
red $5.00

Transierra Gold Mining Company (CA)

*TR640-30-10, 1947, 1,000 sh., orange $4.00

Transtates Petroleum Inc. (NY)

*TR670-30-10, 1953, v, 100 sh., orange . . .$10.00

George A. Treadwell Mining Company (WV par $10)

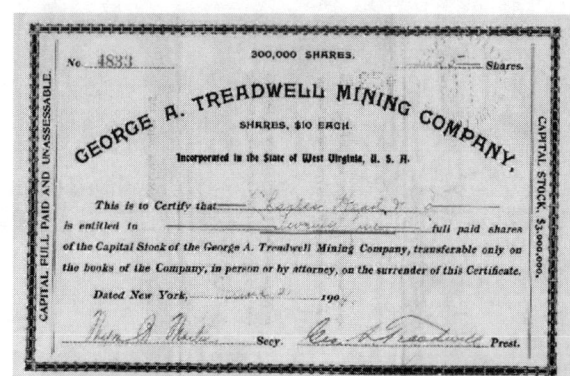

*TR740-20-10, 1902, i/u 25 sh., grey. $30.00

The Tri-Bullion Smelting and Development Company

TR810-30-10, 1908, v, 100 sh., green $7.00

The Tronton Rail Road Company (par $50)

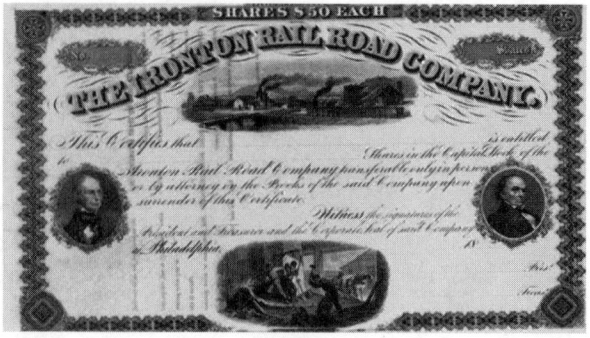

*TR950-20-10, 18xx, v, u/u certificate, grey
. . . .$6.00

Tropical Shells, Inc. (FL no par)

TR980-20-10, 19xx, v, unissued certificate, green
...................................$5.00

Trout Mining Company (DE 1958, par $1)

TR1050-20-10, 1974, v, 16 sh., FLB, 11-3/4" x 8",
orange $4.00

Troy Hill Passenger Railway Company (PA par $50)

TR1180-20-10, 18xx, v, u/u certificate, Mackenzie Davis & Company, Pittsburgh, PA; purple
................................$13.00

The Trustees of Kenwood Lodge No. 303, Free and Accepted Masons (WI)

TR1260-20-10, 19??, v, $100 1st mortgage 5% gold bond, reddish brown..............$6.00

Tucker Corporation (DE 1946, par $1)

TU140-20-10, 1947, t, 10 class A sh., green
................................$100.00

Tung-Sol Electric Inc. (DE 1925, par $1)

TU260-20-10, 1959, v, 19 sh. on a less than 100 sh. certificate, SBN, 12" x 8-1/4", orange .$4.00

This catalog has listings in an alphabetical format. The reason is simple, companies diversify as they grow. For example, the Canadian Pacific Railway company recently split into five companies. They represent the railway, hotels, shipping, airline and petroleum interests of the company. During World War II, the Singer sewing machine company made guns and other defense-related equipment, so where should we list it? It's far easier to use a strict alphabetical order, rather than to confuse the reader with topical classifications.

TU260-30-10, 1955, v, 100 sh., SBN, 12" x
8-1/4", blue **$4.00**

Tuolumne Copper Mining Company (AZ territory, par $1)

TU360-20-10, 1923, v, 66 sh. on a less than 100
sh. certificate, Western Bank Note & Eng. Co.
Chicago, 12-1/4" x 8", green **$6.00**
TU360-30-10, 1916, v, 100 sh., brown. **$8.00**

TWA

TW60-20-10, 2001, v, 1 sh. certificate, red
. . . .**$15.00**

Twenty Mile Oil Company (par $1)

TW120-20-10, 1919, v, 500 sh., grey. **$5.00**

Twenty Third Street Railway Company (NY)

TW170-20-10, 19xx, v, unissued certificate,
ABN, grey **$10.00**
TW170-25-10, 1912, v, 100 sh., grey. **$15.00**

U

Umatilla Tonopah Mining Company (NV par $1)

*UM60-30-10, 1928, 1,000 sh., grey $7.00

The Uncas National Bank of Norwich (par $100)

UN60-20-10, 19xx, v, unissued certificate, grey
.................................$15.00

The Uncle Sam Oil Company (AZ par $1)

Believed to be a fraudulent company.

*UN120-30-10, 1911, v, 2,450 sh., grey on blue
   paper $13.00
UN120-35-10, 1917, v, 5,000 sh., yellow...$20.00
UN120-55-10, 1921, v, $500 2% 20-year gold
   bond, yellow $22.00

The Union Bank

UN240-10-10, 1860, 10 sh., light brown border
..............................$22.00

Union Boot and Shoe Company (MA 1908, par $30)

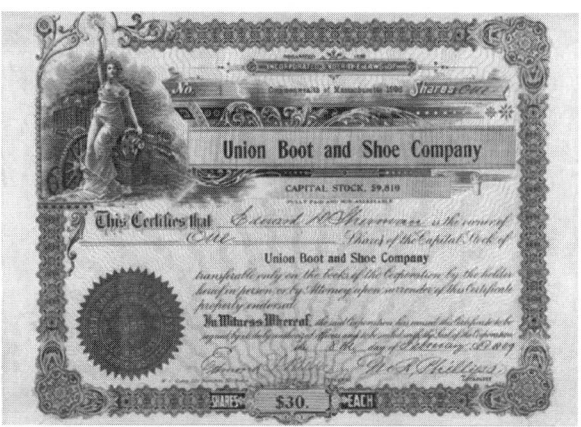

*UN270-20-10, 1909, v, 1 sh., grey $20.00

Union Carbide Corporation (NY)

UN310-40-10, 1977, v, $1,000 7-1/2% debenture
   due 2006, green $10.00

Union Consolidated Mining Co. (CA) Mines in Virginia District, NV.

UN340-30-10, 1927, v, 500 sh., 9" x 4", grey on
   yellow............................$7.00

The Union Corporation (NJ 1938, par 50¢)

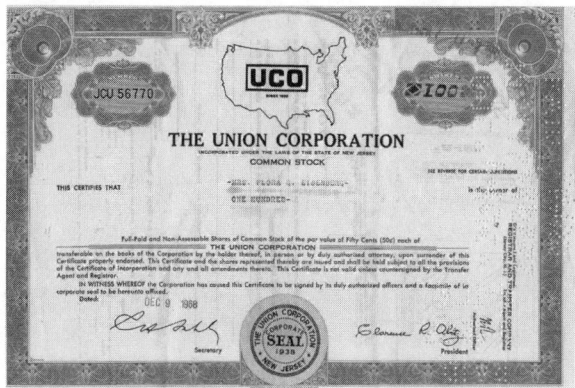

*UN370-30-10, 1968, v - UCO, 100 sh., SCB, 12"
   x 8", orange $4.00

Union Extension Mining Company
UN420-20-10, 1928, v, 2,500 sh., brown **$5.00**

Union Labor Temple Association (CA par $1)
UN520-20-10, 1918, v, 4 sh., brown **$4.00**

Union Mutual Insurance Company
UN620-20-10, 1876, v, 1 sh., grey **$25.00**

The Union National Bank (par $50)

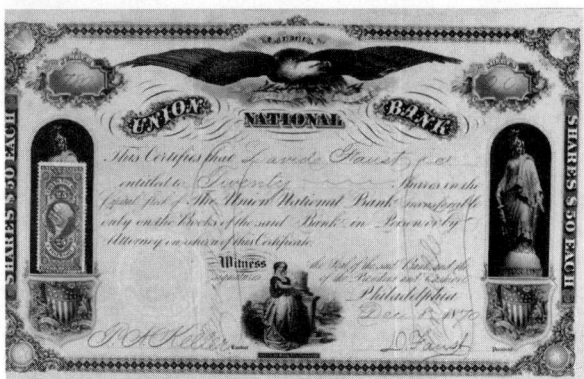

*UN660-20-10, 1870, v, 20 sh., revenue stamp, 11" x 6-1/2", brown border **$50.00**

Union National Bank of Ashland, Wisconsin (incorp. under National Bank Laws)

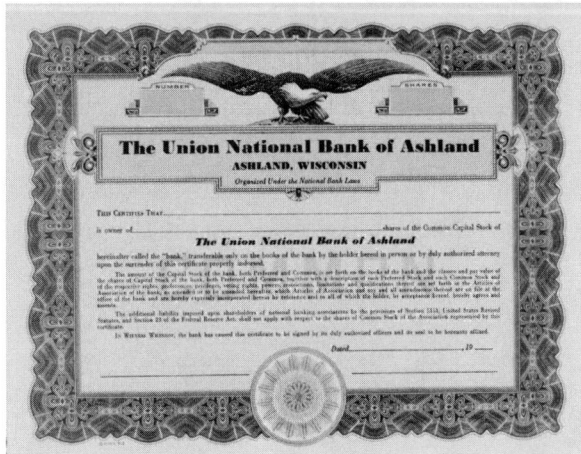

*UN680-20-10, 19xx, u/u certificate, GOES, 11" x 9", green border **$10.00**

Union Pacific Corporation (UT)
UN740-40-10, 1974, v, 100 sh. (par $10), orange
. . . . **$4.00**

*UN740-45-10, 1979, v, 100 sh. (par $5), ABN, 12" x 8", orange **$4.00**

*UN740-50-10, 1980, v, 100 sh., o/p par value of $2.50, ABN, 12" x 8", orange **$4.00**
UN740-52-10, 1980, v, 100 sh. (par $2.50), ABN, 12" x 8", brown **$5.00**
UN740-55-10, 1982, v, 100 sh., par $2.50, orange
. . . . **$4.00**
UN740-60-10, 1980, v, 200 sh. (par $2.50), green
. . . . **$4.00**
UN740-65-10, 1980, v, 1,000 sh. (par $5), brown
. . . . **$5.00**
UN740-80-10, 1969, v, $100 4-3/4% conv. debenture due 1999, green **$7.00**
UN740-85-10, 1969, v, $1,000 4-3/4% conv. debenture due 1999, green **$6.00**

Union Pacific Equipment Trust
UN750-40-10, 1981, v, $20,000 sinking fund trust certificate, due 1990, orange **$4.00**

Union Passenger Railway Company of Philadelphia (PA par $50)

UN780-20-10, 1932, v, 50 sh., grey **$13.00**
UN780-40-10, 18xx, v, u/u $1,000 7% loan, brown
and green **$50.00**

The Union Supply Company (CO no par)

UN830-20-10, 19xx, v, u/c certificate, GOES, 11"
x 8-1/2", grey on gold **$3.00**

Union Thrall Oil Company (par $10)

UN880-20-10, 1915, v, 1 sh., green **$10.00**

Unit Petroleum Corporation (MT par $1)

UN930-20-10, 19xx, v, u/u certificate, dark green
. . . . **$8.00**

United Air Lines Inc. (DE)

UN980-40-10, 1967, v, $1,000 5% sub. debenture
bond, due 1991, ABN, 12" x 8", purple . . . **$5.00**

UN980-45-10, 1967, v, $10,000 5% sub. deben-
ture bond due 1991, blue **$5.00**

*UN980-55-10, 1977, v, $1,000 4-1/4% subordi-
nated debenture bond, brown **$7.00**

United Cigar Stores

UN1040-40-10, 1924, v, 50 pref. sh. on a less than
100 sh. certificate, green. **$10.00**
UN1040-50-10, 1927, v, 100 sh., 6% cum. pref.,
orange **$10.00**

United Cigar-Whelan Stores Corporation

*UN1050-30-10, 1937, t, 100 sh., blue. **$3.00**

The United Corporation (DE 1929)

UN1080-20-10, 1937, v, 10 sh., red **$4.00**

> ### It is generally assumed that only 5% of certificates survive to reach collectors.

*UN1080-25-10, 1940, v, 16 sh. on a less than 100
sh. certificate(no par), ABN, 11-3/4" x 8", green
. . . .**$4.00**

*UN1080-35-10, 1949, v, 100 sh. (par $1), ABN,
11-3/4" x 8", orange **$4.00**

United Drug, Inc. (DE 1933, par $5)

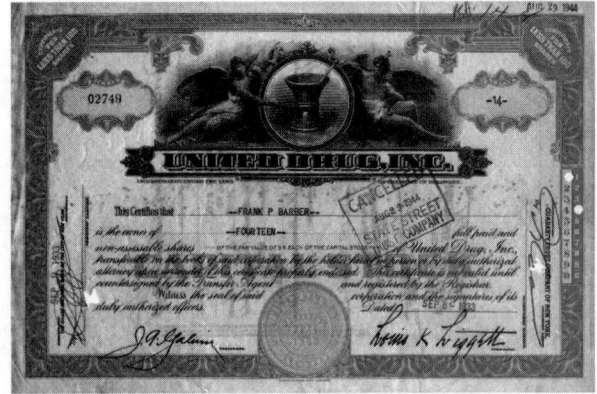

*UN1170-20-10, 1933, v, 14 sh. on a less than 100
sh. certificate, ABN, 11-1/2" x 7-1/2", orange
. . . .**$4.00**

United Electric Railways Company (RI)

*UN1220-20-10, 19xx, v, u/u certificate, ABN, blue $7.00

United Mining and Leasing Company (CO par 10¢)

*UN1470-20-10, 19xx, v, u/c certificate with "SAMPLE," GOES, 11" x 8-1/2", grey . . .$3.00

The United New Jersey Rail Road and Canal Company (NJ par $100)

UN1540-20-10, 1903, v, 16 sh., grey $25.00

*UN1540-30-10, 1915, v, 11 sh. on a less than 100 sh. certificate, green $8.00
UN1540-35-10, 1937, v, 5 sh. on a less than 100 sh. certificate, green $18.00
UN1540-40-10, 1955, v, 10 sh. on a less than 100 sh. certificate, green $8.00
UN1540-50-10, 1931, v, 100 sh., orange . . .$12.00

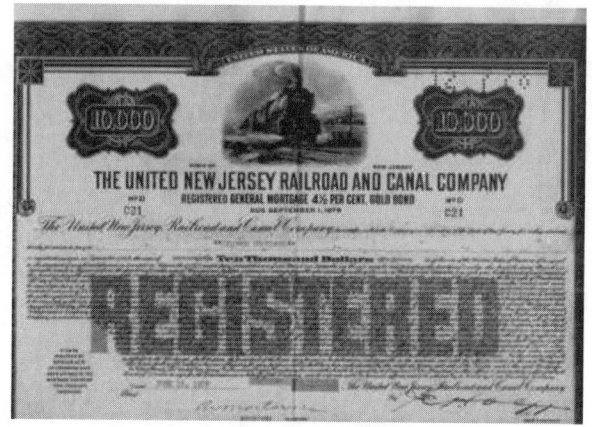

*UN1540-70-10, 1962, v, $10,000 4-1/2% general mortgage gold bond, green $7.00

United Properties of California (DE)

UN1670-30-10, 1911, v, $1,000 conv. debenture bond, brown $5.00

This catalog has listings in an alphabetical format. The reason is simple: Companies diversify as they grow. For example, the Canadian Pacific Railway company recently split into five companies. They represent the railway, hotels, shipping, airline, and petroleum interests of the company. During World War II, the Singer sewing machine company made guns and other defense-related equipment, so where should we list it? It's far easier to use a strict alphabetical order, rather than to confuse the reader with topical classifications.

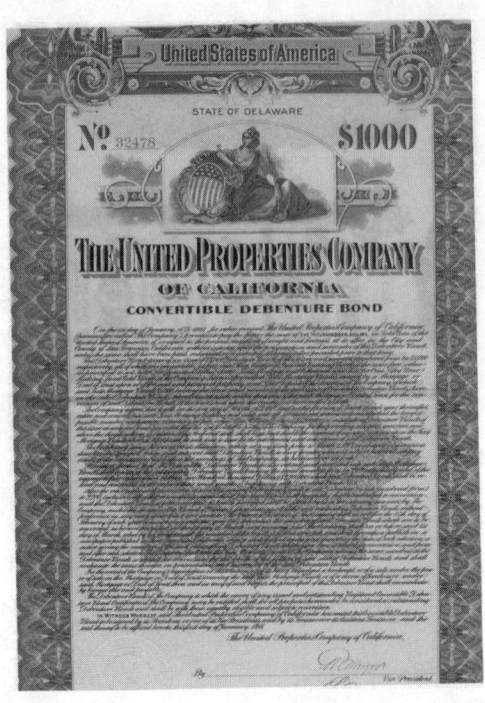

*UN1670-35-10, 19xx, v, u/u $1,000 conv. debenture bond, 50-year gold bond, Britton & Rey, S.F., 9-1/4" x 14-1/2", green............$6.00

United Railways & Electric Company of Baltimore (MD)
UN1720-20-10, 1899, v, green............$9.00

United States of America
UN1910-70-10, 1944, v, savings bond series E, grey..............................$31.00

United States Banknote Corporation (VA par $1)
UN2000-30-10, 1965, v, 100 sh., green.....$4.00

United States Building, Mutual Loan and Accumulating Fund Association (NY)
UN2030-20-10, 189x, v, u/u certificate, green
.....................................$4.00

United States Ceramic Tile Company (DE par $5)
UN2100-20-10, 1972, v, 100 sh., green.....$5.00

The United States Gasoline Corporation (CO)
UN2360-30-10, 1929, v, 500 sh., brown and multi-colored $15.00

The United States Gold Corporation (CO par $1)

*UN2410-30-10, 1909, v, 1,000 sh., brown
.....................................$25.00

United States Gypsum Company (par $4)

*UN2460-30-10, 1968, v, 100 sh., green....$4.00
UN2460-40-10, 19xx, v-s, u/u specimen certificate for not more than 100,000 sh., brown ...$18.00

The United States Leather Company (NJ)
UN2750-30-10, 1943, v - bull, 100 sh., blue
.....................................$15.00

United States Lines Company (NJ 1893)
UN2780-30-10, 1924, 100 sh. certificate of deposit, orange $15.00
UN2780-40-10, 1947, t, 10 sh. (par $1), green
.....................................$4.00

*UN2780-50-10, 1943, t, 100 sh. (par $1), ABN,
   12" x 8", orange $4.00
UN2780-55-10, 1951, v, 100 sh., orange $7.00

*UN2780-70-10, 1950, v, 42, 4-1/2% pref. sh. on a
   less than 100 sh. certificate (par $10), ABN, 12"
   x 8", brown $7.00
UN2780-75-10, 1961, v, 3 sh. on a less than 100 sh.
   certificate, green $7.00

United States Lines Inc.

*UN2785-65-10, 1931, v, 4 pref. sh. on a less than
   100 sh. certificate, orange $25.00

United States Mining & Smelting Company (PA)

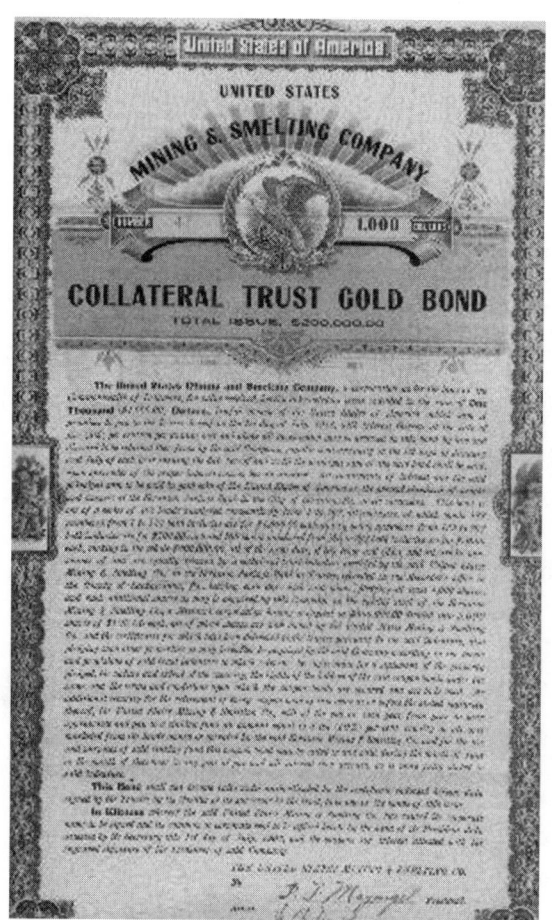

*UN2860-40-10, 1903, v, $1,000 collateral trust
   gold bond w. coupons, green $10.00

United States Motor Company (NJ)

*UN2890-20-10, 1911, v, 100 sh., brown
   . . . .$125.00

United States & Overseas Corporation
(DE no par)

*UN2930-20-10, 1930, v, 50 sh. on a less than 100 sh. certificate with attached warrant, ABN, 11-1/2" x 7-1/2", orange **$5.00**

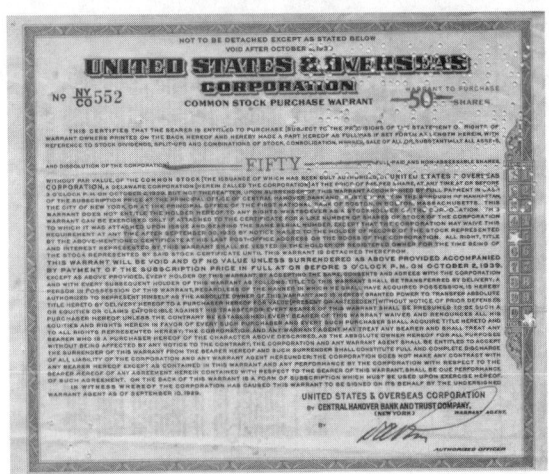

** UN2930-20-11, attached common stock purchase warrant, valid until 1939.

United States Pipe and Foundry Company
(NJ par $20)

*UN2980-20-10, 1937, v, 40 sh. on a less than 100 sh. certificate, ABN, 11-1/2" x 7-1/2", red .**$4.00**

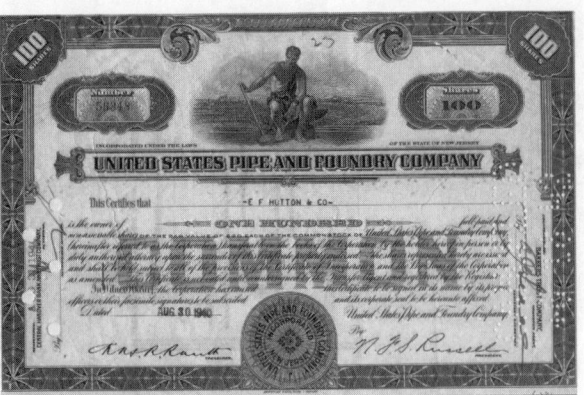

*UN2980-30-10, 1940, v, 100 sh., ABN, 11-1/2" x 7-1/2", brown **$4.00**

United States Plywood Corporation

*UN3010-30-10, 1955, v, 100 sh., green **$6.00**

United States Sealed Postal Card Company

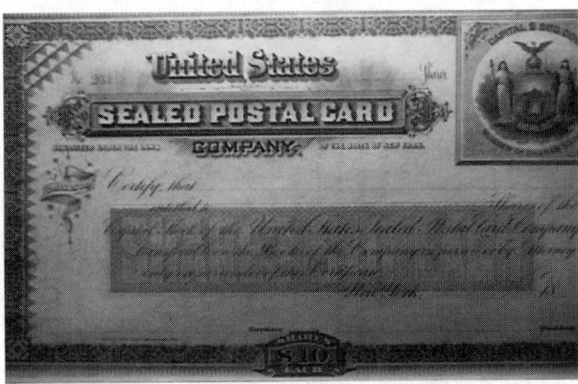

*UN3300-20-10, 18xx, v, u/u certificate, brown
. . . .**$12.00**

United States Steel Corporation
UN3390-20-10, 1932, v, 4 sh. on a less than 100 sh. certificate, brown **$8.00**

*UN3390-30-10, 1948, v, 3 sh. on a less than 100
sh. certificate, ABN, 12" x 8-1/2", green ..$6.00
UN3390-35-10, 19xx, v, 80 sh. on a less than 100
sh. certificate, green $6.00

*UN3390-45-10, 1947, v, 1 sh., 7% pref. (par
$100) on a less than 100 sh. certificate, olive
green...........................$25.00

*UN3390-55-10, 1921, v, 100 pref. sh., red
................................$10.00

United Stores Corporation (DE no par)

*UN3450-20-10, 1931, v, 1 sh. on a less than 100
voting share trust certificate, ABN, 11-1/2" x
7-1/2", yellow.....................$4.00

*UN3450-30-10, 1931, v, 100 voting trust sh.,
ABN, 11-1/2" x 7-1/2", red $4.00

United Traction Company of Pittsburgh (PA par $50)

UN3580-20-10, 189x, 100 sh., unissued certificate,
green............................$8.00

United Western Minerals Company (DE 1955, par 10¢)

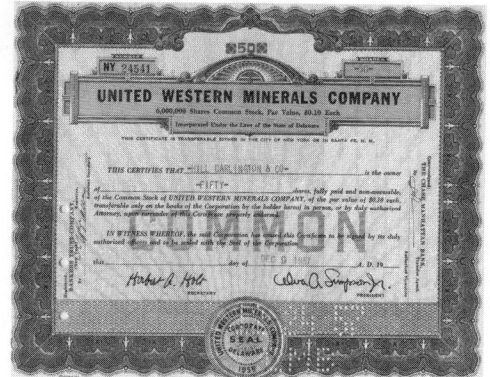

*UN3710-20-10, 1957, 50 sh., GOES, 11" x
8-1/2", green......................$4.00

United Whelan Corporation

*UN3740-20-10, 1967, v, 75 sh. on a less than 100 sh. certificate, brown. $4.00

UN3740-25-10, 1967, v, 1 sh. on a less than 100 sh. certificate, o/p name changed to Perfect Film & Chemical Corporation, olive. $4.00

UN3740-35-10, 1967, v, 100 sh., green $4.00

Unity Consolidated Mining Company (AZ)

UN3770-30-10, 1906, v, 1,000 sh., grey . . .$15.00

Universal Garage Corporation (MA)

*UN3810-20-10, 19xx, unissued pref. sh. (par $25) certificate, George J. Morse Co., 10-3/4" x 8-1/4", brown $3.00

Universal Motors Company (DE par $5)

UN3840-30-10, 1916, t, 100 sh., black. $25.00

Universal Oil Products Company (DE)

*UN3870-30-10, 1975, v, 100 sh., green $4.00

University Computing Company (TX 1965)

UN3910-20-10, 1972, v, 10 sh., o/p DE incorporation $6.00

UN3910-50-10, 1978, v, $5,000 bond $10.00

University National Life Insurance Co.

UN3950-20-10, 1959, v, 500 sh., green $4.00

Upper Coos Railroad (VT par $100)

Certificate issued under the lease to Maine Central Railroad Company.

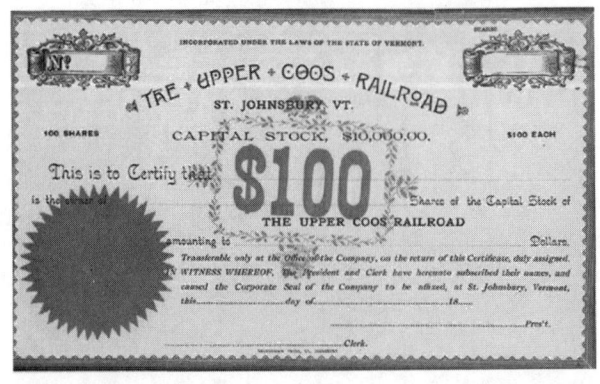

*UP110-30-10, 18xx, u/u 100 sh. certificate, grey $3.00

UP110-35-10, 1890, v, 100 sh., green $20.00

Uris Buildings Corporation (NY 1960, par 10¢)

UR210-30-10, 1967, v, 100 sh., blue $4.00

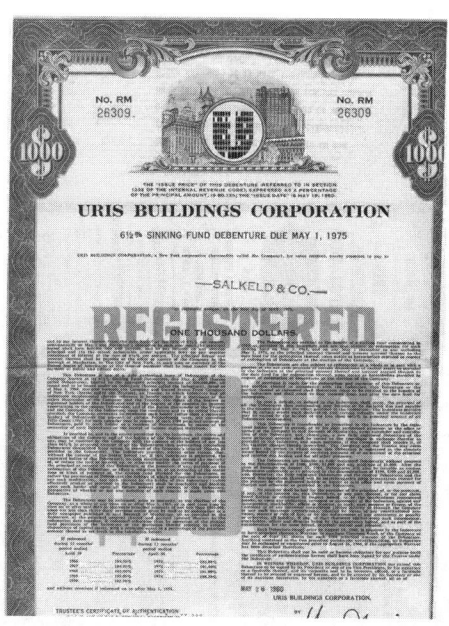

*U210-50-10, 1960, v, $1,000 6-1/2% sinking fund
debenture due 1975, SCB, 9-1/2" x 14", brown
. . . .$5.00

The Uronon Fire Resisting Co.
(ME par $50)

UR310-20-10, 19xx, v, unissued certificate, brown
. . . .$6.00

The U.S. Automatic Ore Reduction Company (CO par $1)

US50-30-10, 1898, v, 200 sh., dark brown
. . . .$25.00

U.S. Beryllium Corporation

*US120-30-10, 1962, v, 100 sh., green $6.00

U.S. Photo Supply Co., Inc. (DE 1955, par 10¢)

*US430-20-10, ND, v, 15 sh., purple. $3.00

U S Staple Corporation (CO no par)

*US510-20-10, 19xx, v, u/c with pinhole "SAM-
PLE," GOES, 10-3/4" x 8-1/2", gold border
. . . .$3.00

USLife Common Stock Fund a class of the capital stock of USLife Funds Inc. (MD)

*US550-30-10, 1976, v, 100 sh. on a not over 1000
sh. certificate, no printers name, 12" x 8", l. blue
. . . .$4.00

Utah-Apex Mining Company (ME)

UT100-20-10, 1935, v, 1 sh. on a less than 100 sh.
  certificate, orange $8.00
UT100-25-10, 1937, v, 10 sh. on a less than 100 sh.
  certificate, orange $10.00

*UT100-30-10, 1925, 100 sh., brown. $8.00
UT100-35-10, 1934, 20 sh., orange $8.00

Utah Galena Corporation (UT par $1)

*UT190-30-10, 1936, v, i/u 200 sh., green. . .$9.00

The value of a stock certificate depends on:

- rarity
- the issuer
- signatures
- quality of engraving
- overall appearance
- condition
- date of issue

Utah International Finance Corp. (DE 1968)

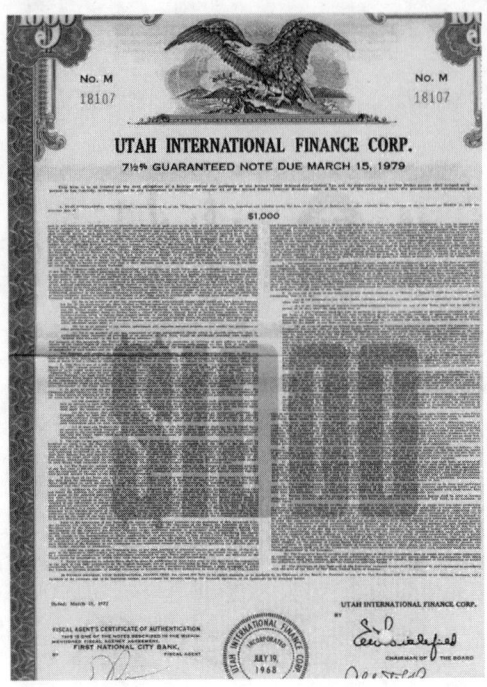

*UT240-30-10, 1972, v, $1,000 7-1/2% guaranteed
  note due 1979, SCB, 9-3/4" x 14", reddish brown
  . . . .$4.00

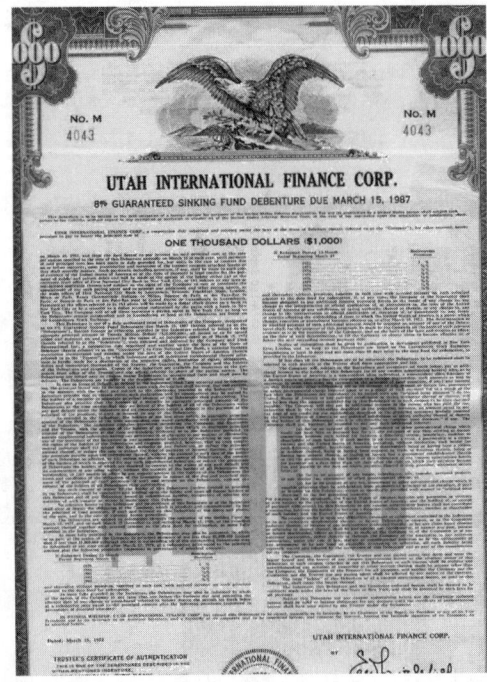

*T240-35-10, 1972, v, $1,000 8% guaranteed sink-
  ing fund debenture due 1987 w. coupons, SCB,
  10" x 14", red purple $4.00

Utah Metal and Tunnel Company

*UT340-30-10, 1935, v, 100 sh., green $4.00
UT340-35-10, 1931, v, 1,000 sh., brown $5.00

Ute Uranium Inc.

UT460-20-10, 1954, v, 50 sh., orange $10.00

Utica and Black River Railroad Company

UT570-40-10, 1890, v, $1,000 1st mortgage 4%
   gold bond, brown $31.00

UNLISTED TYPES & VARIETIES

Readers are welcome to contact the author directly at:

    Rainer Stahlberg
    P.O. Box 1044
    Rooseveltown, New York 13683

Utility Equities Corporation

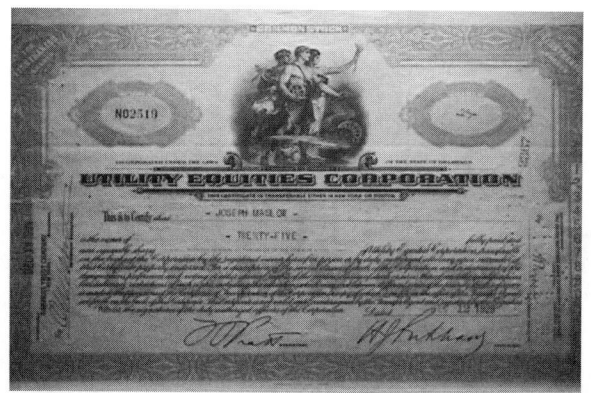

*UT600-20-10, 1929, v, 25 sh. on a less than 100
   sh. certificate, orange $5.00

UV Industries Inc. (ME par $1)

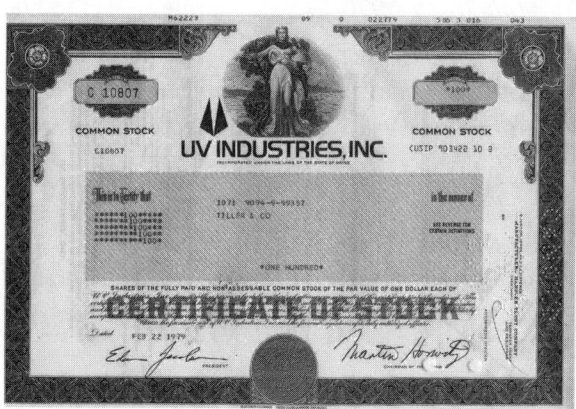

*UV110-30-10, 1979, v, 100 sh., SCB, 12" x 8",
   purple $4.00

V

Vadsco Sales Corporation

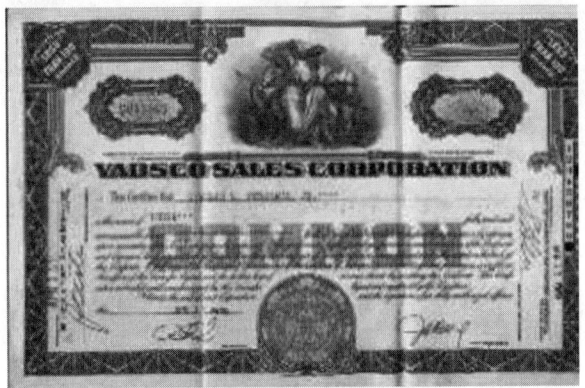

VA140-20-10, 1920, v, 3 sh., purple $4.00

Valentino Antonucci Inc. (no par)

VA210-20-10, 19xx, v, unissued certificate, blue
. . . .$4.00

Valley Gold Mines, Inc. (NV par 5¢)

VA240-20-10, 19xx, v, unissued certificate, orange
. . . .$12.00

Van Dyne Telephone Co. (WI par $50)

VA290-20-10, 1920, v, 1 sh., 11" x 8", grey border
. . . .$35.00

Vandalia Railroad Company (IN-IL par $100)

VA310-20-10, 1907, v, 10 sh., brown $60.00

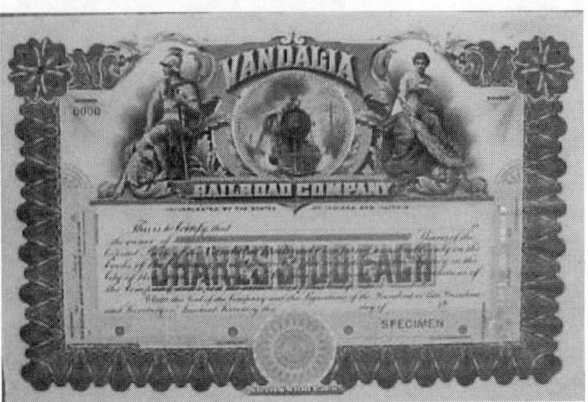

VA310-25-10, 19xx, v, u/s certificate, blue
. . . .$14.00

Venezuelan Petroleum Company (DE par $100)

VE170-30-10, 1953, v, 100 sh., brown $5.00

Ventnor City (NJ)

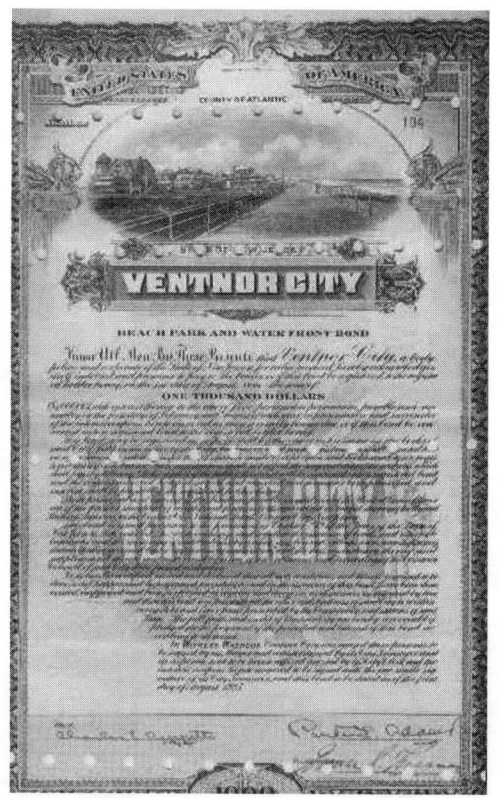

VE220-40-10, 1925, v, $1,000 bond, green
. . . .**$15.00**
VE220-45-10, 1927, v, $1,000 General Improve-
ment bond, brown. **$8.00**
VE220-50-10, 1928, v, $1,000 Water Works Bond
w. coupons, brown **$8.00**

Vernal Mining Company of Goldfield (AZ territory, par $1)

VE320-30-10, 1914, v, 500 sh., grey **$36.00**

Vernon Dental Supply Company (UT)

VE350-20-10, 1925, v, 15 sh., black **$7.00**

Vernon, Greensburgh & Rushville Railroad Company (IN)

VE370-40-10, 1880, $1,000 first mortgage bond
due 1920, green **$60.00**

Viacom, Inc. (DE 1986, par $0.01)

The owner of Paramount, Nicklelodeon, Music
First, MTV, Showtime and Simon & Schuster.

VI40-30-10, 19xx, v, u/u specimen certificate for
class B common shares, blue **$18.00**

The Victor Buildings (IL)

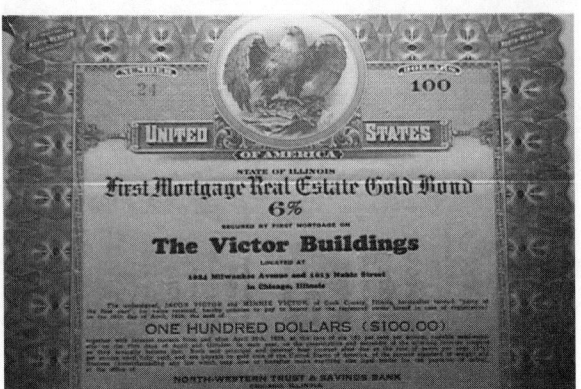

*VI140-40-10, 1926, v, $100 6% 1st mort. real estate gold bond, green **$5.00**

Victoria Consolidated Mining Company (UT par 10¢)

The mine was located in the Tintic District of Utah.

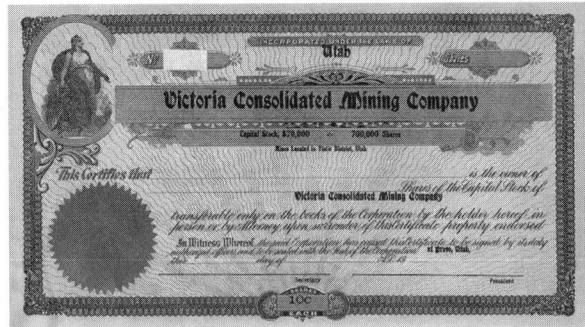

*VI170-20-10, 19xx, v, u/u certificate, grey
. . . .**$6.00**

Victoria Gold Mines, Inc. (AZ par 10¢)

*VI200-30-10, 1968, v, 5,000 sh., GOES, 10-3/4" x 8-1/4", grey **$4.00**

Vim Tractor Company (WI par $10)

*VI300-20-10, 1921, v, 7-1/2 sh., GOES, 11" x 8", green border **$100.00**

Virginia-Carolina Railway Company (par $100)

*VI410-20-10, 1xxx, v, u/u certificate, green
. . . .**$8.00**

The Virginia Coal and Iron Company (VA)

*VI440-20-10, 1935, v, 25 sh. on a less than 100 sh. certificate, SBN, 11" x 8", orange **$4.00**
VI440-25-10, 1952, v, 25 sh. on a less than 100 sh. certificate (par $100), brown **$6.00**

The Virginia Investment Association
VI500-20-10, 1890, 10 sh., red brown $7.00

Virginia Office Supplies, Incorporated (VA par $25.00)

VI570-20-10, 19xx, u/u certificate, brown . .$3.00

Virginia Railway and Power Company (VA par $100)
VI610-40-10, 19xx, v, u/u non-cumulative pref. stock less than 100 sh. certificate, 12" x 8", blue
. . . .$6.00

The Virginian Railway Company

VI640-50-10, 1946, v, $5,000 series B 1st lien and refunding bond 3%, due 1995, brown . . .$17.00

Vitaglass Corporation (NY no par)

VI750-30-10, 1928, 1,000 sh., W.N. Perrin & Company, Inc., New York; 11" x 7-1/2", brown
. . . .$3.00

Vogue Instrument Co. (NY 1948, par $0.01)

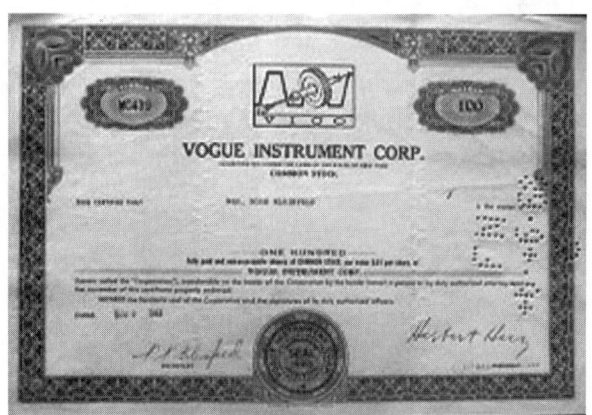

VO150-30-10, 1963, v, 100 sh., blue $4.00

VO150-35-10, 1970, v, 100 sh., Haserouck, Thistle & Co., 11-3/4" x 8", blue. $3.00

The Vondy Corporation (CO par $1)

*VO240-10-10, 19xx, c, u/c certificate with pin-hole "SAMPLE," GOES, 10-3/4" x 8-1/2", gold
. . . .$3.00

Vornado, Inc. (DE)

VO300-30-10, 1970, v, 100 sh., green $4.00

The Vose Mining Company (MT par $1)

VO410-20-10, 189x, v, u/u certificate, brown
. . . .$15.00

Vulcan Coal Company (VA)

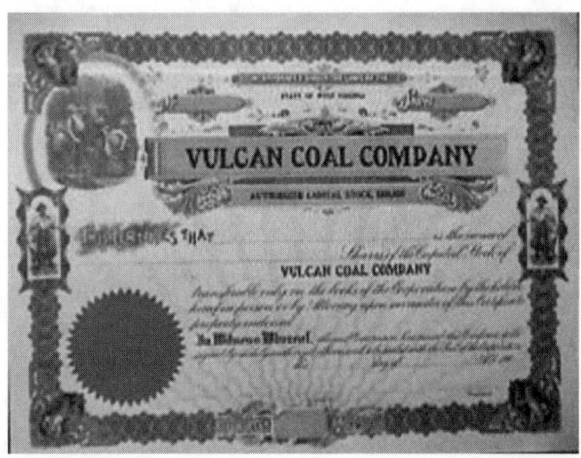

*VU160-20-10, 19xx, v, u/u certificate, grey
. . . .$4.00

Vulcan Oil Company, Inc.

*VU200-30-10, 1921, v, 100 sh., blue $3.00

The Vulcanized Rubber Company (ME 1916, par $100)

*VU260-30-10, 1939, v, 100 sh., ABN, 11-1/4" x 7-3/4", brown $4.00

Vulcanized Rubber and Plastics Company (ME no par)

*VU270-20-10, 1954, v, 13 sh., 12" x 8", green
. . . .$4.00

W

Wabash Magnetics, Inc. (IN no par)

WA60-20-10, 1961, v, 100 sh., ABN, 11-3/4" x
8", green **$4.00**

Wabash Railroad Company (MI-OH-IN-IL-MO-IA)

WA100-20-10, 1890, v, 10 sh. (Missouri)
(par $100), green. **$50.00**
WA100-40-10, 197x, v, $500 bond, series A 4% due
1981, purple **$7.00**
WA100-45-10, 198x, v, $500 bond, series B 4-1/4%
due 1991, orange. **$7.00**
WA100-50-10, 198x, v, $1,000 bond, series B 4-1/4%
due 1991, brown **$7.00**

The Wachovia Corporation

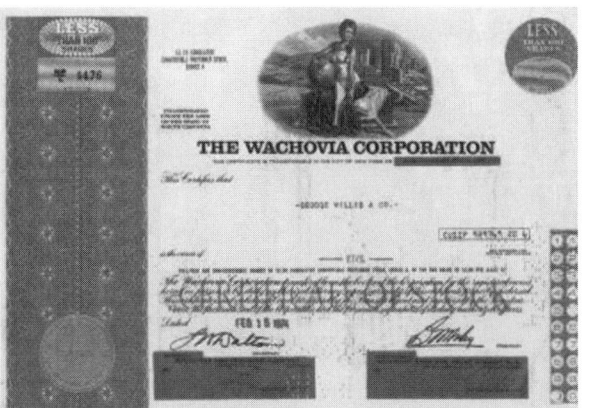

WA160-20-10, 1974, v, 5 sh. on a less than 100 sh.
certificate, green **$5.00**

Wagner Palace Car Company (par $100)

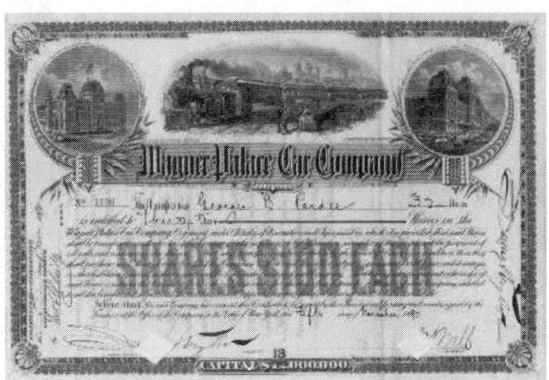

WA290-20-10, 1890, v, 32 sh., signed by William
Webb who was the son-in-law of William
Vanderbilt, brown and grey **$50.00**

The Wakefield Land and Investment Company (RI)

WA420-20-10, 189x, v, u/u certificate, grey
. . . . **$5.00**

Walden Bancorp, Inc. (MA 1995, par $1)

WA510-20-10, 1996, v, 1,179 sh., ABN, 12" x 8",
green **$4.00**

Waldorf System Incorporated (MA no par)

WA540-20-10, 1923, t, 74 sh., brown **$6.00**

Walker Hotel Corporation (DE no par)

WA570-20-10, 19xx, v, u/u certificate, orange
. . . .**$6.00**

Wall Street Mining Company (par $1)

WA600-20-10, 1910, v, 21,500 sh., green
. . . .**$45.00**

The Wallkill Valley Railway Company (NY)

WA630-20-10, 1868, v, $500 7% 1st mort. sinking
fund debenture, brown **$36.00**

Walmil Realty Co., Inc. (NY)

WA650-20-10, 1955, v, 2 sh., green **$5.00**

Waltham Watch Company (MA par $1)

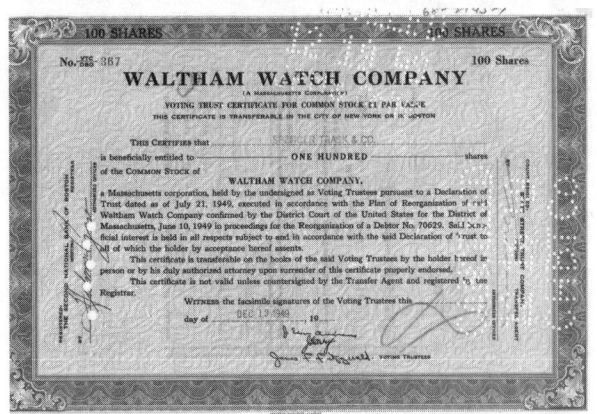

WA700-30-10, 1949, 100 voting trust stock, ABN,
12" x 8", olive green **$3.00**
WA700-35-10, 1949, 100 voting trust stock, orange
. . . .**$3.00**

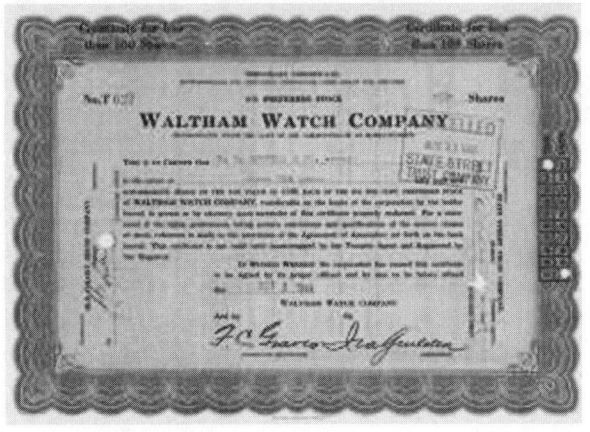

WA700-45-10, 1944, t, 10 pref. sh., green . . **$3.00**

Ward Apartments (IL)

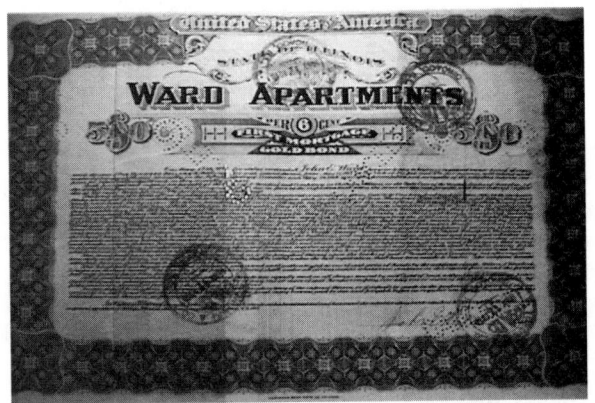

*WA1030-40-10, 1919, v, $500 6% 1st mortgage bold bond $5.00

The Ward Electric Light and Power Company (CO par $1)

WA1060-20-10, 1897, v, 50 sh., grey......$15.00

Ware River Rail Road Company (MA par $100)

*WA1090-20-10, 1944, v, 1 sh., grey......$10.00

Warner-Lambert Company (DE)

WA1130-30-10, 1973, v, 156 sh., orange ...$10.00

UNLISTED TYPES & VARIETIES

Readers are welcome to contact the author directly at:

Rainer Stahlberg
P.O. Box 1044
Rooseveltown, New York 13683

S.D. Warren Company (MA 1918)

*WA1180-20-10, 1953, v, 5 sh. on a less than 100 sh. certificate, ABN, 11-1/2" x 7-1/2" brown $4.00
WA1180-30-10, 1932, v, 100 sh., blue......$5.00

Warren & Ouachita Valley Railway (AR par $100)

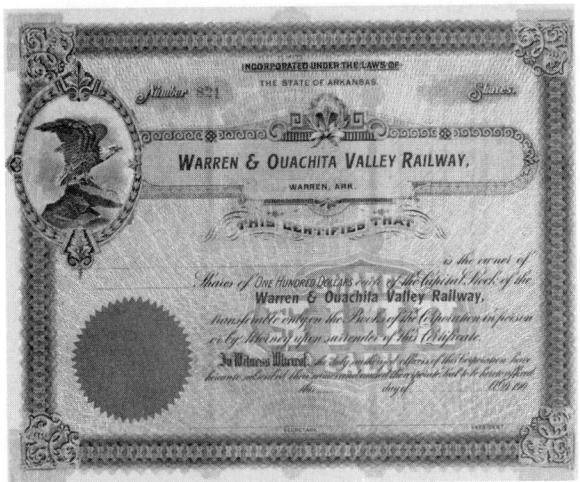

*WA1210-20-10, 190x, v, u/u certificate, w/o imprint, 10" x 8-1/4", grey $6.00

Washington, Baltimore and Annapolis Electric Railroad Company (par $50)

WA1270-20-10, 19xx, 100 sh., u/u certificate, orange............................$15.00

Washington County Railroad Company (ME par $100)

WA1300-20-10, 189x, u/u certificate, grey $15.00

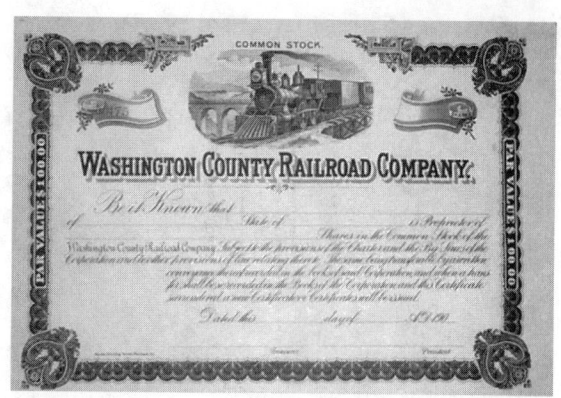

*WA1300-25-10, 190x, u/u certificate, bluish
...................................$17.00

Washington Gas Light Company (DC no par)
WA1340-20-10, 1977, v, 5 sh. on a less than 100 sh.
certificate, brown $5.00

Washington Market Company (DC par $50)
WA1380-20-10, 1915, v, 25 sh., grey......$10.00

*WA1380-25-10, 19xx, v, u/u certificate, grey
...................................$10.00

The Washington Post Company

*WA1420-30-10, 1971, v, 100 class B shares, blue
...................................$5.00

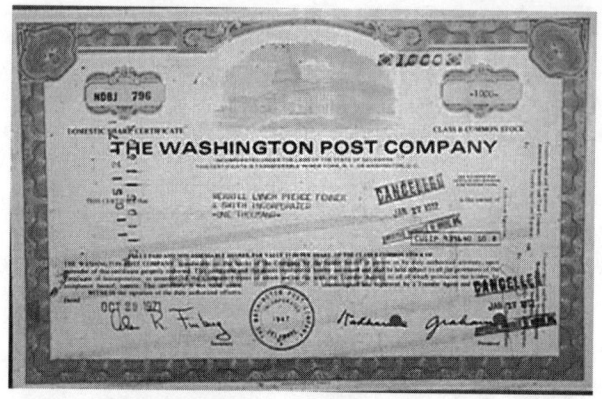

*WA1420-35-10, 1971, v, 1,000 class B sh. certifi-
cate, orange.......................$5.00

Washington Railway and Electric Company (DC par $100)
WA1470-20-10, 19xx, v, u/u certificate, brown
...................................$12.00
WA1470-30-10, 193x, v, unissued 100 pref. sh. cer-
tificate, green $7.00

Washington Realty Company (WI par $10)

*WA1500-2010, 1922, 250 sh., revenue stamp,
11-1/2" x 8", green border $40.00

Washoe Mercantile Company (MT par $5)
WA1570-20-10, 189x, v, u/u certificate, grey border
...................................$6.00

Watertown Brick Company (WI no par)

*WA1700-20-10, 1925, v, 10 sh., GOES, 11" x 8", brown border. $30.00

Waukesha Motors Company (1906)

*WA1840-30-10, 1968, v, 100 sh., brown $24.00

The Waumandee Railway Company (WI par $100)

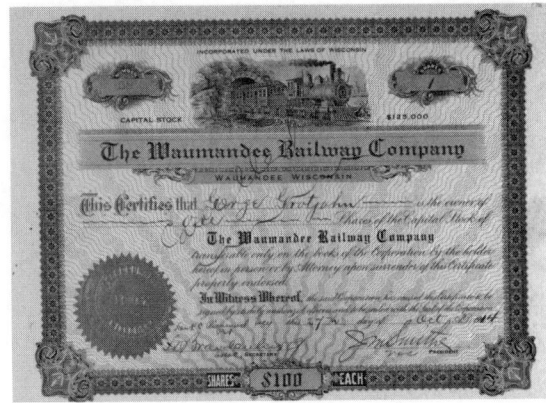

*WA1860-20-10, 190x, v, u/u certificate, 11" x 8", brown border. $30.00

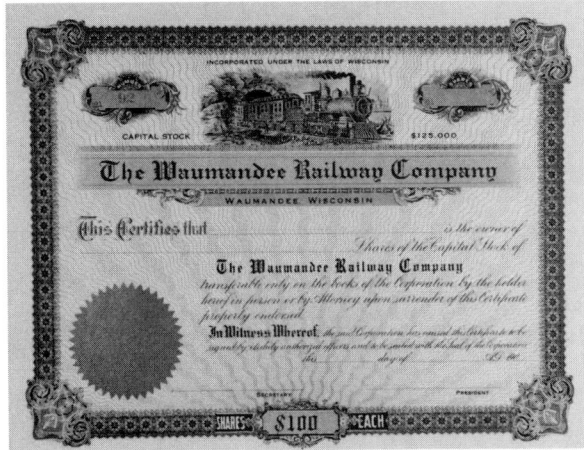

*WA1860-21-10, 1914, v, 1 sh., 11" x 8", brown border $45.00

Waverley Co-Operative Bank of Belmont, Mass. (MA par $200)

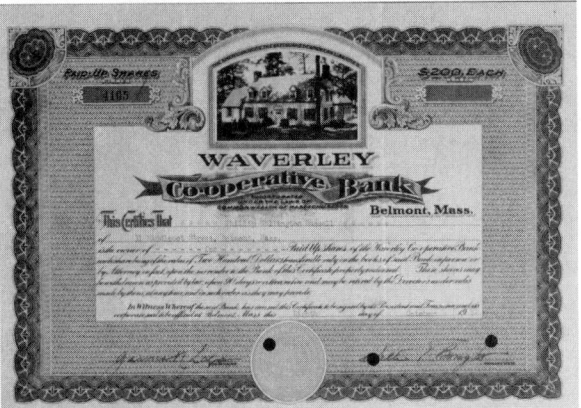

*WA1890-20-10, 1951, v, 1 sh., 11-1/2" x 8", green border $12.00

The Waverly Short Line (IA par $20)

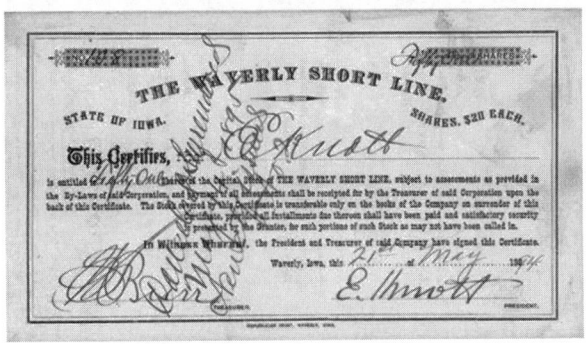

*WA1900-20-10, 1894, 51 sh., blue. $34.00

Weatherford Milling Co. (OK par $100)
WE110-20-10, 1918, v, 50 sh., green $8.00

Weaver & Shasta Wagon Road Company (CA)
WW200-20-10, 18xx, v, u/u certificate, brown, small certificate. $50.00

Webster Manufacturing Company (WI par $100)

WE290-20-10, 1906, v, 10 sh., 10-1/2" x 8", brown border. $50.00

The Weems Steamboat Company of Baltimore City

WE330-20-10, 189x, v, u/u certificate, brown $22.00

Weinschel Engineering Co., Inc. (DE 1952, par $1)

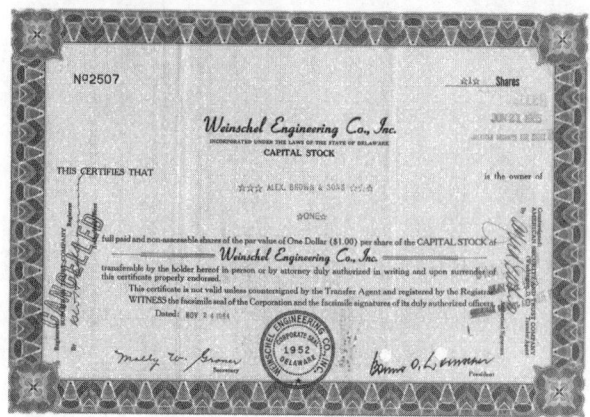

WE380-20-10, 1964, 1 share, SCB, 11-3/4" x 8-1/4", blue. $3.00

WE380-20-15, 1971, 10 sh., signature variety, SCB, 12" x 8-1/4", blue $3.00

Weisman Big Muddy Oil Company (WY par $1)

WE430-20-10, 19xx, v, u/u certificate, 11" x 8-1/2", brown $6.00

The West Chester and Philadelphia Rail Road Company (par $50)

WE900-20-10, 1856, v, 21 sh., brown $50.00

West End Street Railway Company (MA par $50)

WE930-20-10, 19xx, v, u/u certificate, green
. . . .$12.00

*WE930-25-10, 1919, v, 50 sh., green $8.00

West Indies Sugar Company (DE 1932, par $1)

*WE1020-30-10, 1944, v, 100 sh., EAW, 11-3/4" x 8", green $4.00

West Iron Gate Land Company

WE1050-20-10, 189x, v, u/u certificate, greyish
. . . .$14.00

West Jersey Bancshares, Inc. (NJ 1989, par $0.01)

*WE1080-30-10, 1994, v, 400 sh., o/p par value changed to "No Par Value", ABN, 12" x 8", red
. . . .$4.00

West Jersey and Seashore Railroad Company (NJ par $50)

WE1110-20-10, 1934, v, 15 sh. on a less than 100 sh. certificate, green $12.00

West Philadelphia Passenger Railway Company (PA 1857, par $50)

WE1240-20-10, 1859, v, 10 sh., black $49.00
WE1240-30-10, 1886, v, 50 sh., light brown
. . . .$20.00
WE1240-40-10, 1939, v, 1 sh., brown $10.00

This catalog has listings in an alphabetical format. The reason is simple: Companies diversify as they grow. For example, the Canadian Pacific Railway company recently split into five companies. They represent the railway, hotels, shipping, airline and petroleum interests of the company. During World War II, the Singer sewing machine company made guns and other defense-related equipment, so where should we list it? It's far easier to use a strict alphabetical order, rather than to confuse the reader with topical classifications.

West Shore Railroad Company (NY)
Became part of New York Central Railroad Company.

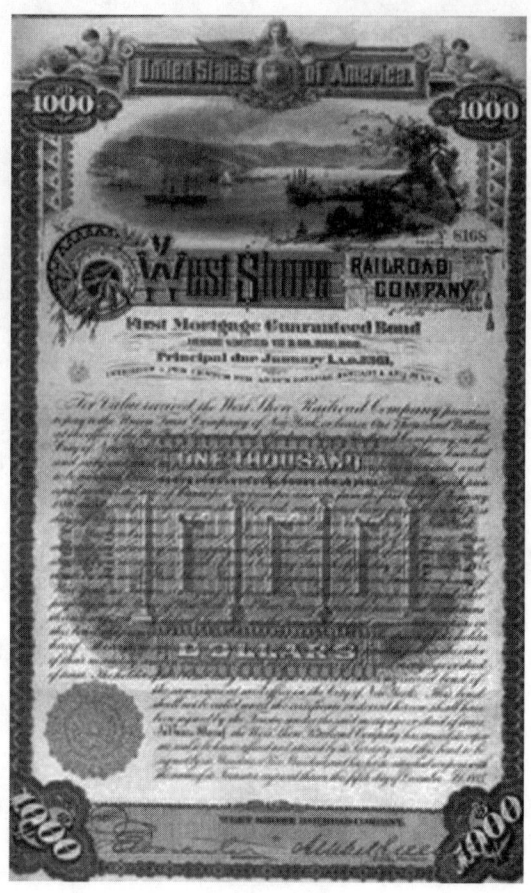

*WE1320-40-10, 1885, v, $1,000 4% 1st mortgage guaranteed bond, due 2361, green $12.00

*WE1320-45-10, 1886, v, $500 1st mortgage guaranteed bond, 4% due 2361, brown $5.00
WE1320-55-10, 1923, v, $1,000 first mortgage guaranteed bond, orange...............$8.00

*WE1320-65-10, 1952, v, $1,000 first mortgage 4% guar. bond due 2361, ABN, 13-3/4" x 9-1/4", orange $4.00

*WE1320-65-15, 1953, v, $1,000 1st mortgage 4% guranteed bond due 2361, ABN, 13-3/4" x 9-1/4", orange.....................$4.00

The West Spanish Peak Mining Co. (WI par $1)

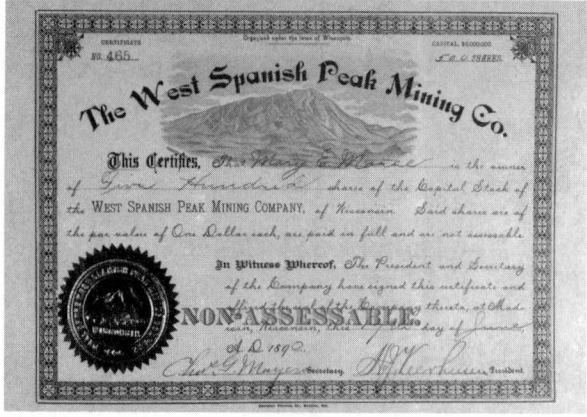

*WE1340-20-10, 1890, v, 500 sh., 11-1/2" x 9", l. brown border $250.00

The Western Corporation (CO par $100)

*WE1380-10-10, 19xx, v, u/c certificate with pin-hole "SAMPLE," GOES, 11-1/4" x 8-1/2", orange $3.00

Western Maryland Railway Company (MA-PA 1917, no par)

*WE1490-20-10, 1917, v, 10 sh. on a less than 100 sh. certificate, d. green $11.00

WE1490-30-10, 1953, v, 100 sh., blue $5.00

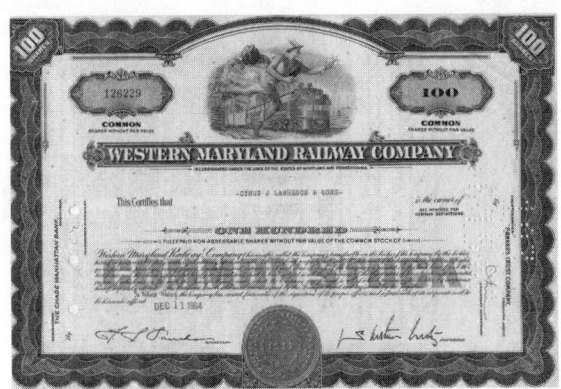

*WE1490-35-10, 1964, v, 100 sh., ABN, 12" x 8", blue $6.00

WE1490-50-10, 1955, v, 50 second pref. sh. on a less than 100 sh. certificate, olive green. .$10.00

Western Moulding Co., Inc. (WI par $50)

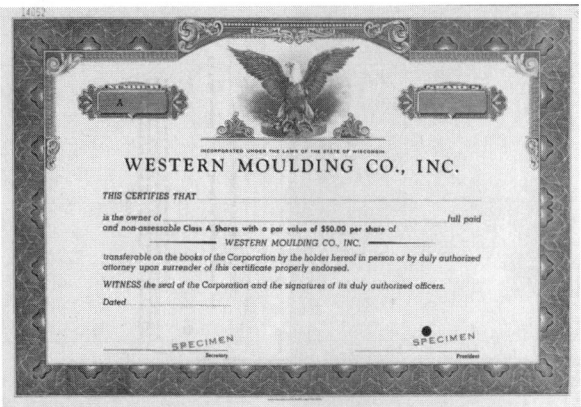

*WE1530-20-10, ND, v, u/c specimen certificate, 12" x 8", green border $7.00

The Western Pacific Railroad Company (CA)

WE1590-30-10, 1950, v, 100 sh., SBN, brown
. . . .$10.00

Western Power Corporation (NY)

WE1650-30-10, 19xx, v, u/u 100 sh. certificate, green. $6.00

Western Reserve Life Insurance Company (TX par $10)

*WE1710-20-10, 1950, v, 2 sh., GOES, 10-3/4" x 8-1/2", grey. $3.00

Western Security Oil Company (AZ par $1)

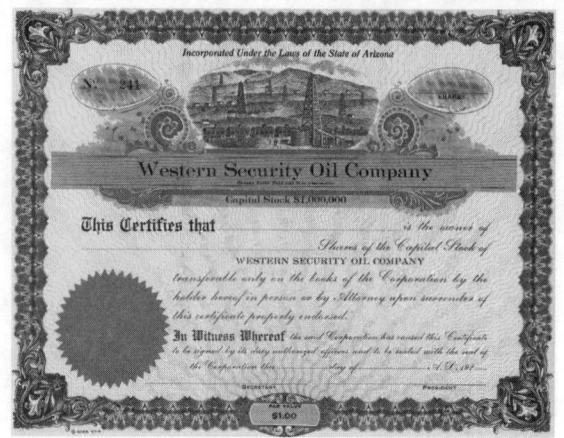

WE1820-20-10, 192x, v, u/u certificate, GOES, 10-3/4" x 8-1/4", grey **$3.00**

Western Union Corporation (DE par $2.50)

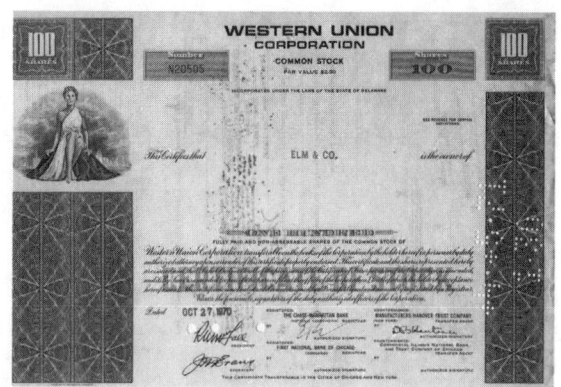

WE2020-30-10, 1970, v, 100 sh., Federated Banknote Co., 12" x 8", red **$4.00**

Western Union Computer Utilities, Inc. (DE par $0.15)

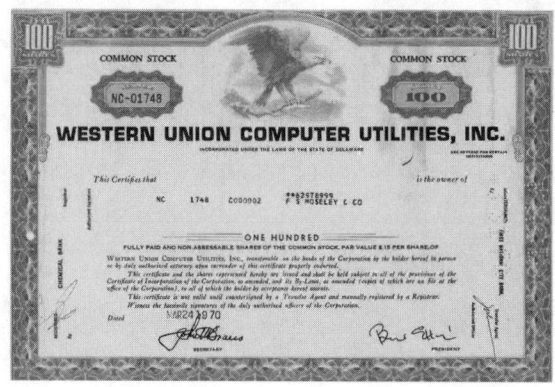

WE2030-30-10, 1970, v, 100 sh., Federated Banknote Co., 12" x 8", orange **$4.00**

Western Union International, Inc.

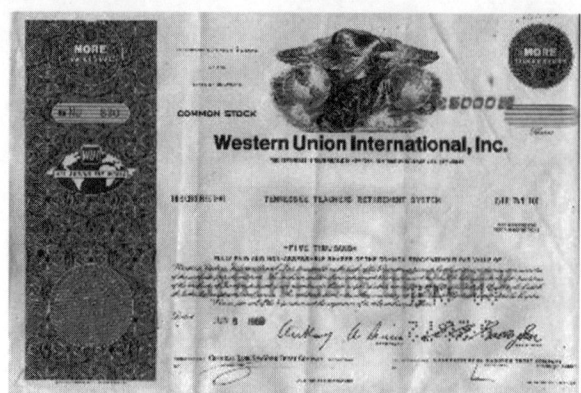

WE2040-30-10, 1969, v, 5,000 sh. on a more than 100 sh. certificate, green **$4.00**

Western Union Telegraph Company (NY)

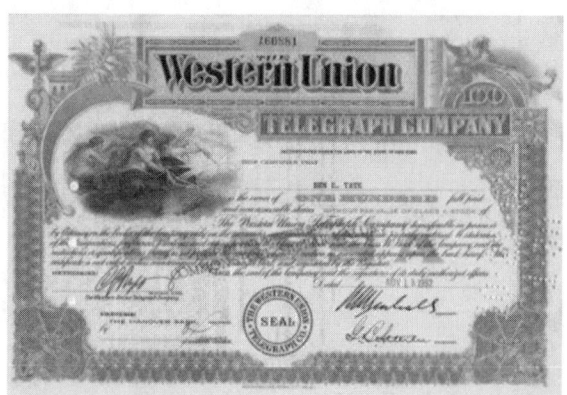

WE2060-30-10, 1952, v, 100 class A sh. (no par), red **$12.00**
WE2060-35-10, 1969, v, 100 sh. (par $2.50), brown **$5.00**

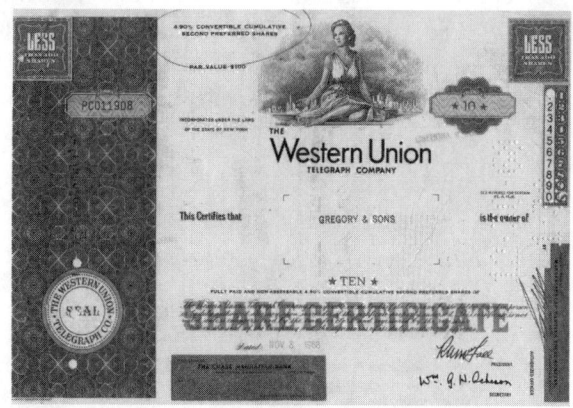

WE2060-50-10, 1968, v, 10 sh., of second 4.90% cumul. conv. pref. stock on a less than 100 sh. certificate (par $100), De la Rue Banknote Co., 12" x 8", reddish brown **$5.00**

Westgate Metal Products Co.
(CA 1922, par $10)

WE2100-20-10, 1922, v, i/u 10 sh., The Mysell
Rollins Co., 11-1/2" x 9", green border ...$4.00

Westinghouse Air Brake Company (PA)

WE2130-40-10, 1951, v, 5 sh. on a less than 100
sh. certificate, SBN, orange $15.00

The Westminster Corporation
(CO 1957, par $1)

The company took over Oiltex Corporation and
subsequently was struck off the companies register in 1959.

WE2200-20-10, 1959, v, 25 sh., green border
.....................................$3.00

> ## It is generally assumed that only 5% of certificates survive to reach collectors.

Westmore Incorporated
(NJ 1958, par $0.40)

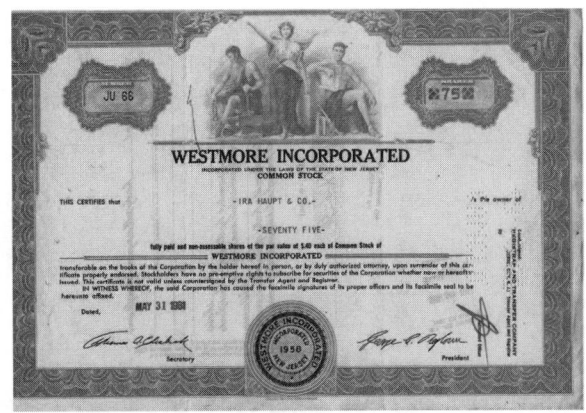

WE2210-20-10, 1961, v, 75 sh., CBN, 12" x 8",
orange...........................$4.00

WE2210-30-10, 1961, v, 100 sh., SCB, 12" x 8",
green............................$4.00

Wexford Construction Corporation
(NY par $100)

WE2380-20-10, 19xx, v, u/u certificate, J. Meyers
Inc., NY, 11" x 8-1/4", green $4.00

Wheeler Fibre Glass Boat Corporation (DE 1960, par 10¢)

*WH110-30-10, 1961, v, 100 sh., SBC, 11-3/4" x 8-1/4", brown $3.00

Whippany River Railroad Company (NJ par $100)

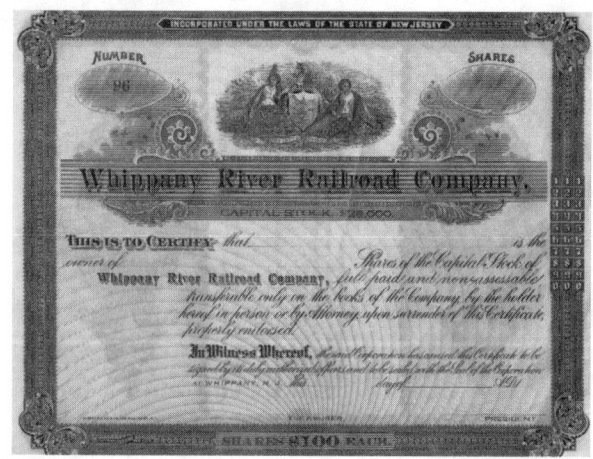

*WH210-20-10, 1xxx, v, u/u certificate, green
. . . .$19.00

White Caps Gold Mining Company (NV par $1)

WH290-20-10, 1925, 50 sh., orange $9.00

The value of a stock certificate depends on:
- rarity
- the issuer
- signatures
- quality of engraving
- overall appearance
- condition
- date of issue

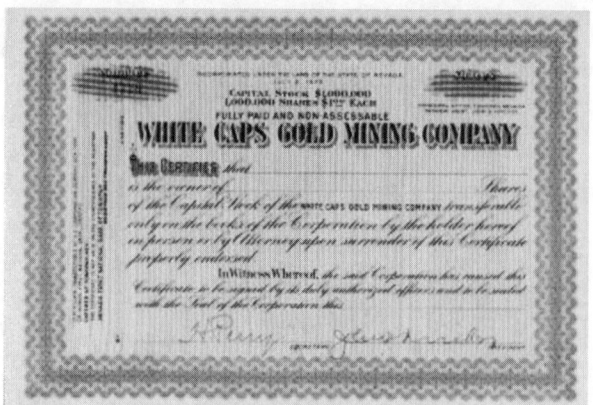

*W290-30-10, 19xx, u/u certificate, orange. . $4.00

White Motor Corporation (OH par $1)

Maker of heavy duty trucks.

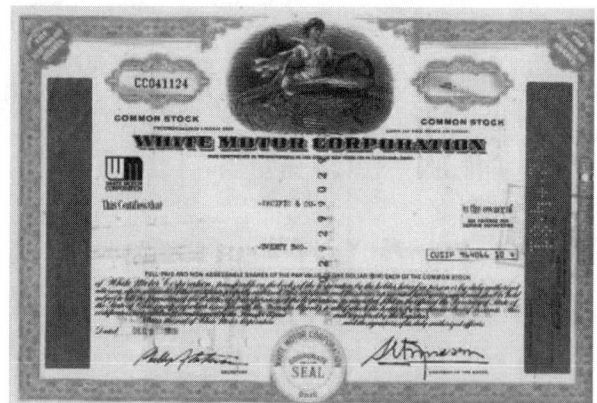

*WH370-20-10, 1978, v, 22 sh. on a less than 100 sh. certificate, orange $5.00
1980, v, 100 sh., red $5.00

The Whitehall Club (OH par $10)

*WH430-20-10, 1940, v, 72 sh., grey $25.00

The Wicklow Mining Company (WI par $1)

*WI130-20-10, 1906, v, 2,500 sh., 11" x 8", orange border $65.00

Willows Warehouse Association (CA par $100)

WI610-20-10, 188x, v, u/u certificate, olive and grey $9.00

Willys Corporation

WI650-30-10, 1921, 20 8% cumul. conver. 1st pref. stock certificate of deposit, orange $20.00

Winona Copper Company (MI)

WI740-20-10, 1918, v, 23 sh., green. $50.00

Winona & St. Peter Rail Road Company in Dakota (Dakota territory, par $100)

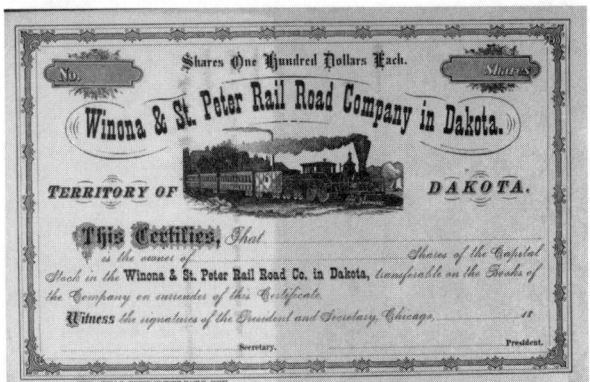

*WI760-20-10, 18xx, v, u/u certificate, 10-1/2" x 6", brown border. $20.00

Winston-Salem Southbound Railway Company

WI780-40-10, 1915, v, $1,000 first mort. 50-year 4% bond, green. $20.00

Winther Motors, Inc. (DE $10)

*WI820-20-10, 1923, v, 50 class A sh., GOES, 10" x 7", orange border. $8.00

Wisconsin Central Railway Company

WI1130-30-10, 1950, v, 100 sh., yellow . . .$76.00

Wisconsin and Colorado Silver Mining Co. (CO par $50)

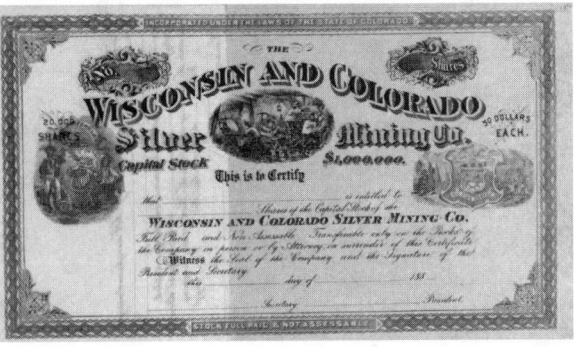

*WI1160-20-10, 188x, v, u/u certificate, 10-1/2" x 5-1/2", blue border on pink $15.00

> *It is generally assumed that only 5% of certificates survive to reach collectors.*

The Wisconsin Edison Company, Incorporated
A utility/operator of Milwaukee's city rail service.

*WI1210-20-10, 1916, v, 10 sh. on less than 100 sh. certificate, green $10.00
WI1210-30-10, 1913, v, 100 sh., purple $6.00

Wisconsin General Finance Corporation (DE no par)

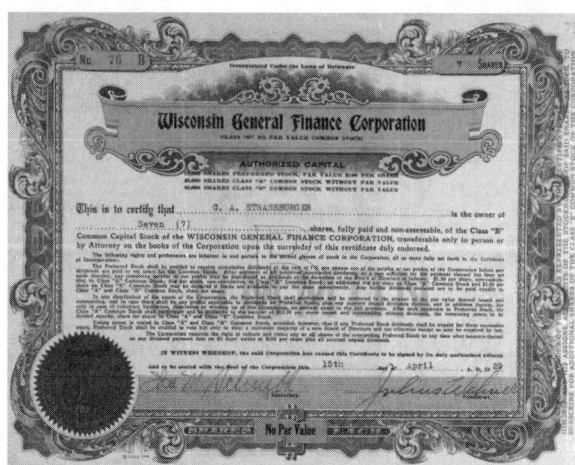

*WI1410-20-10, 1929, 7 class B sh., 11" x 8", brown border. $9.00

UNLISTED TYPES & VARIETIES
Readers are welcome to contact the author directly at:

Rainer Stahlberg
P.O. Box 1044
Rooseveltown, New York 13683

Wisconsin Interurban System (WI)

*WI1425-40-10, 1913, v, $500 5-1/2% 20-year 1st mortgage gold bond, 9-1/2" x 12", brown border $80.00

Wisconsin Investment Company (DE 1929)

*WI1440-15-10, 1930, 98/100th sh., scrip certificate, void after 1932, 11" x 8", blue. $4.00
WI1440-20-10, 1930, t, 20 sh., orange. $4.00

*WI1440-25-10, 1930, v, 93 class A sh. on a less than 100 sh. certificate (no par), 11" x 7-1/2", green border $10.00

*WI1440-26-10, 1931, v, 100 class A sh., ABN, 11" x 7", orange $10.00

*WI1440-27-10, 1932, 2/10th class B sh., scrip certificate, void after 1934, 11" x 8", brown . .$4.00

*WI1440-28-10, 1931, 1 class B sh. on a less than 100 sh.,certificate, 11" x 8", orange $5.00

*WI1440-30-10, 1929, t, 40 pref. sh. on a less than 100 sh. certificate (par $10), 11" x 8", brown border $4.00

*WI1440-33-10, 1930, 24 series A pref. sh., 11" x 8", brown $5.00

*WI1440-35-10, 1933, 2 sh., pref. (par $10), ABN,
10-3/4" x 7-3/4", purple $4.00

*WI1440-40-10, 1934, 100 pref sh. (par $10),
ABN, 11" x 8", blue $4.00

Wisconsin Iron Mining Co. (WI $1)

*WI1500-20-10, 1902, v, 75 sh., revenue stamp,
10" x 8", brown border $65.00

Wisconsin Iron & Steel Company (WI par $25)

*WI1530-20-10, 1890, v, 1 sh., 10-1/2" x 8-1/2",
grey border $105.00

Wisconsin and Michigan Railway Company (WI)

*WI1560-40-10, 1905, v, $1,000 4% general mort-
gage bond, orange border $90.00

Wisconsin Shipbuilding & Navigation Corporation (DE par $10)

*WI1610-20-10, 1920, v, 18 sh., GOES, 11" x 8", brown border.....................$60.00

*WI1610-30-10, 1920, v, 35 pref. sh., GOES, 11" x 8", brown border...................$60.00

This catalog has listings in an alphabetical format. The reason is simple: Companies diversify as they grow. For example, the Canadian Pacific Railway company recently split into five companies. They represent the railway, hotels, shipping, airline, and petroleum interests of the company. During World War II, the Singer sewing machine company made guns and other defense-related equipment, so where should we list it? It's far easier to use a strict alphabetical order, rather than to confuse the reader with topical classifications.

Wisconsin Western Railroad (WI par $100)

*WI1660-20-10, 1xxx, u/u certificate, 8" x 6", brown.............................$15.00

Wolf & Wisconsin Rivers Railroad Company (WI par $100)

*WO170-20-10, 1888, 1 pref. sh., 10" x 5-1/2", brown border $120.00

The Woman's Gold Mining Company (CO)
WO210-30-10, 1893, v, 100 sh., grey $15.00

UNLISTED TYPES & VARIETIES
Readers are welcome to contact the author directly at:

Rainer Stahlberg
P.O. Box 1044
Rooseveltown, New York 13683

Wood-Hagerbarth Cattle Company, Limited (ID)

WO430-30-10, 1909, v, 2,500 sh., grey ...**$25.00**

Woodburn Mining Company (MT par 5¢)

WO460-20-10, 19xx, v, unissued certificate, brown
..................................**$8.00**

Woodruff Sleeping and Parlor Coach Company

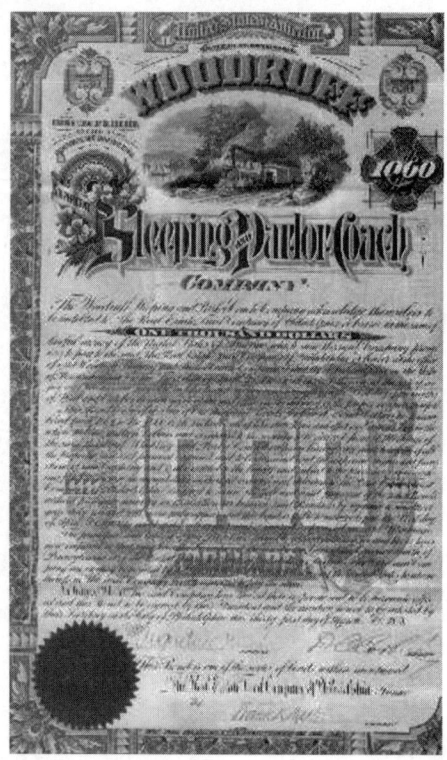

WO490-40-10, 1888, v, $1,000 bond w. coupons,
Homer Lee Bank Note Co., brown......**$45.00**

Woodings Pneumatic Oil Co. (WI par $50)

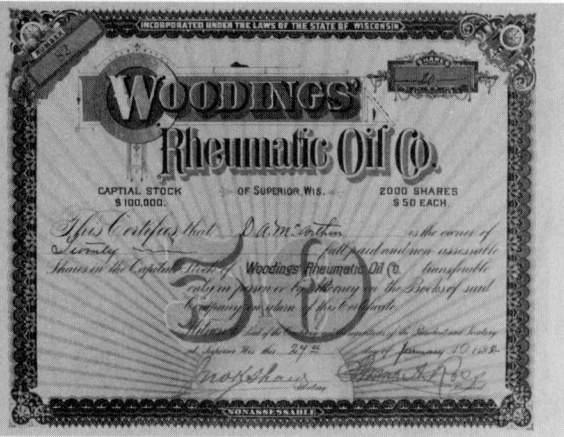

WO510-20-10, 1897, v, 20 sh., 11" x 8-1/2",
brown border **$50.00**

Woods Brothers Corporation (NE)

Real estate and construction company.
WO520-30-10, 19xx, v, u/u 6% conv. pref. share
certificate, green...................**$9.00**

Woods Mobilette Company (1913 par $1)

WO540-30-10, 1915, v, 250 sh., green ...**$130.00**

WO540-35-10, 1915, v, 200 sh., brown
..............................**$125.00**

F.W. Woolworth Co.

WO570-30-10, 1977, v, 500 sh., green border
..............................**$12.00**

Worcester Consolidated Street Railway Company

WO670-40-10, 1930, $10,000 cert. of deposit, first and refunding gold bonds, brown **$6.00**

WO670-45-10, 1930, $9,000 cert. of deposit, first and refunding gold bonds, yellow **$6.00**

WO670-50-10, 1930, $5,000 cert. of deposit, first and refunding gold bonds, red **$6.00**

WO670-55-10, 1930, $3,000 cert. of deposit, first and refunding gold bonds, green **$6.00**

WO670-60-10, 1930, $2,000 cert. of deposit, first and refunding gold bonds, blue **$6.00**

WO670-65-10, 1930, $1,000 cert. of deposit, first and refunding gold bonds, orange **$6.00**

World Oil Company (TX unincorporated Trust Estate, par $1)

*WO950-30-10, 1923, v - oil wells, 400 sh., GOES, 11" x 8-1/2", green **$4.00**

Worldmark Press, Inc. (NY 1957, par 10¢)

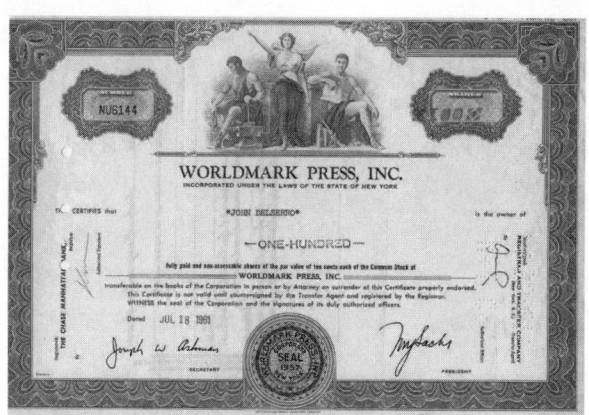

*WO1050-30-10, 1961, v, 100 sh., SCB, 12" x 8", brown **$4.00**

Worthington Co-Operative Exchange, Inc. (IN)

WO1400-20-10, 19xx, v, unissued certificate, grey **$10.00**

Wright Oil Company (DE par $1)

*WR160-30-10, 1919, v, 200 sh., brown . . .**$10.00**

Wrigley Pharmaceutical Co. (DE)

Old time fraud, W.W. Wrigley wanted to cash in on the popularity of Wrigley's chewing gum and started his own company.

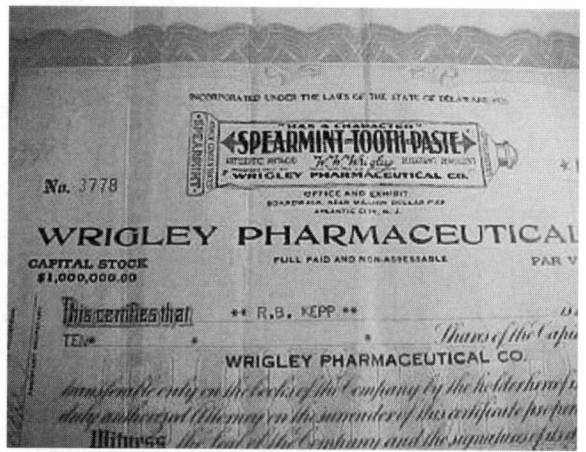

*WR200-20-10, 1925, v, 10 sh., orange **$17.00**

It is generally assumed that only 5% of certificates survive to reach collectors.

WTC Air Freight

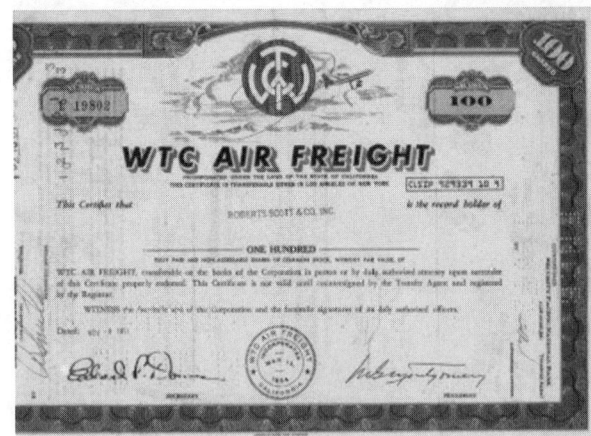

*WT100-30-10, 1971, v, 100 sh., blue **$15.00**

Wyandotte County, Kansas

WY70-20-10, 1888, v, $500 7% road improvement
   bond **$6.00**

The Wyoming Chief Oil & Refining Company (WY par $1)

*WY170-30-10, 1919, v, 500 sh., orange . . .**$12.00**

X

Xerox Corporation
XE60-30-10, 1964, v, 100 sh., ABN, blue . .**$10.00**
XE60-40-10, 1983, v, $10,000 extendable note,
    orange **$10.00**
XE60-45-10, 1986, v, $100,000 extendable note,
    orange **$10.00**

XL Gold Dredging Company (WY)
XL50-20-10, 1911, v, 100 sh., SBN, orange
    . . . .**$35.00**

Xoma Corporation (DE)

*XO80-20-10, 1993, w, 58 sh., warrant void after
    1995, Thomas de la Rue, 12" x 8", brown .**$3.00**

X T Land and Cattle Company
(NM territory, par $100)

*XT80-20-10, 19xx, brown on beige **$8.00**

**The value of a stock certificate
depends on:**

- **rarity**
- **the issuer**
- **signatures**
- **quality of engraving**
- **overall appearance**
- **condition**
- **date of issue**

Y

The Yankee Oil and Drilling Company (CO par 1 mil)
YA60-30-10, 1918, v, 5,000 sh., brown **$15.00**

Yardney Electric Corporation (NY 1944)
YA140-20-10, 1971, v, 5 sh. on a less than 100 sh. certificate, blue **$4.00**

The Yellow Jacket Silver Mining Co. (NV territory)
Gold Hill mining district.
YE90-30-10, 1887, v, 100 sh., grey small certificate **$50.00**

The Yellow Tiger Consolidated Mining Company (NV par 10¢ assessment is limited to 2¢ per share per annum)
YE130-30-10, 1923, 10,000 sh., brown **$10.00**

City of Yonkers (NY)
YO100-30-10, 1862, $25 7% loan, black ...**$55.00**

Yonkers Racing Corporation
YO140-30-10, 1982, v, $100 6% 20-year subord. debenture due 1984, olive............**$18.00**

York Railways Company (PA par $50)

YO190-30-10, 1922, v, 100 sh., green **$8.00**
YO190-40-10, 1916, v - trolley car, 25 pref. sh., blue..............................**$10.00**
YO190-45-10, 1927, v, 29 pref. sh. on a less than 100 sh. certificate, ABN, grey border **$7.00**

The County of Yuba, California
YU50-20-10, 1857, v, $500 10% bond w. coupons, brown **$125.00**

Yukon Basin Gold Dredging Company (AZ par $1)
YU100-30-10, 1908, v, 100 sh., green **$35.00**

Yuscaran Mining Company of New York (NY par $100)
YU80-30-10, 1887, v, 100 sh., black **$55.00**

Z

The Zanesville Terminal Railroad Company (OH par $100)

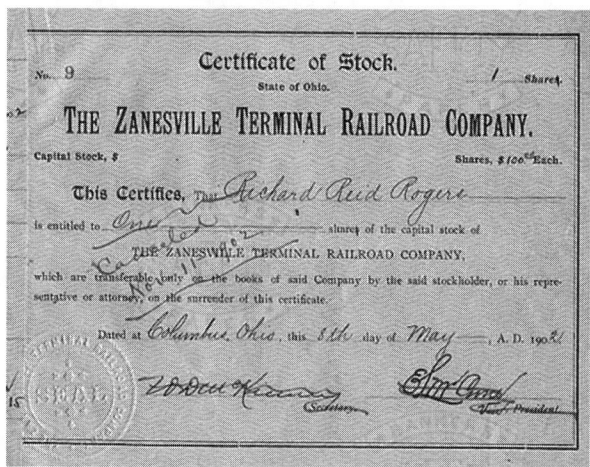

*ZA55-20-10, 1902, 1 sh., black border on green
...................................$21.00

Zanzibar Mining Company of Nevada (NV 10¢)

ZA70-30-10, 1920, 1,000 sh., blue $25.00

Zapata Corporation (DE)

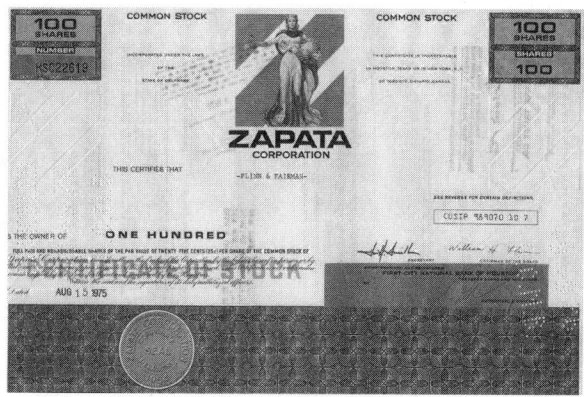

*ZA100-20-10, 1976, v, 4 sh. on a less than 100 sh. certificate (par 25¢), SCB, 12" x 8", blue. ..$4.00

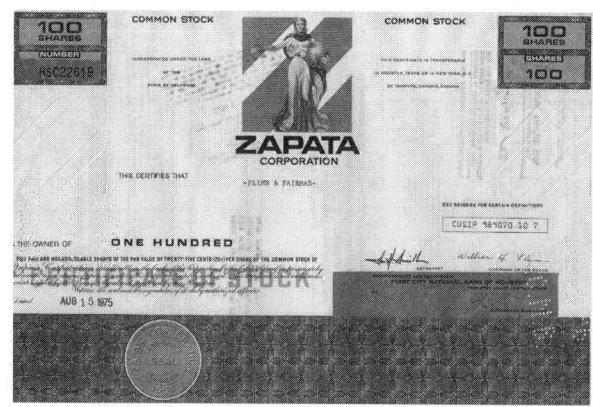

*ZA100-20-15, 1976, v, 1 sh. on a less than 100 sh. certificate (par 25¢), registrar changed, SCB, 12" x 8", blue $4.00

*ZA100-30-10, 1975, v, 100 sh. (par 25¢), SCB, 12" x 8", green $4.00

Zapata Norness Incorporated (DE 1954)

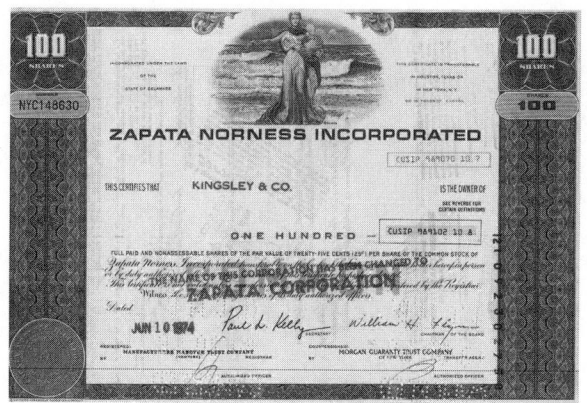

*ZA120-30-10, 1974, v, 100 sh. (par 25¢), o/p name changed to Zapata Corporation, SCB, 12" x 8", green $5.00

Zenith Laboratories, Inc. (NJ par $0.09)

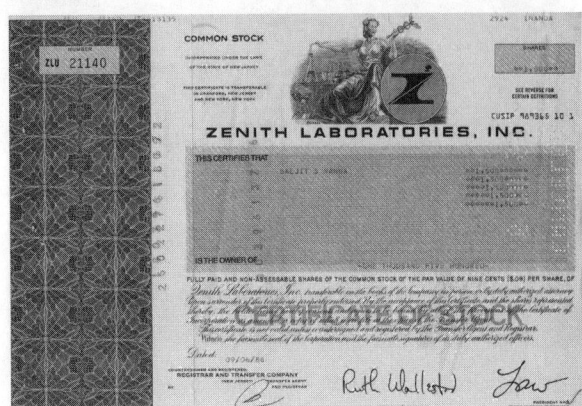

*ZE100-30-10, 1988, v, 1,500 sh., SCB, 12" x 8",
blue $4.00

UNLISTED TYPES & VARIETIES

Readers are welcome to contact the author directly at:

**Rainer Stahlberg
P.O. Box 1044
Rooseveltown, New York 13683**

Zenith Lamp Shade Corporation (NY par $100)

*ZE130-20-10, 19xx, v, u/u certificate, J. Meyers
Ins., NY, 10-3/4" x 8-1/2", blue $4.00

Zion's Co-Operative Mercantile Institution (par $100)

ZI100-20-10, 1880, v, 2 sh., green $700.00

Countries

A

Algeria

Société des Mines de Boudoukha S.A., Boudoukha (Constantine)

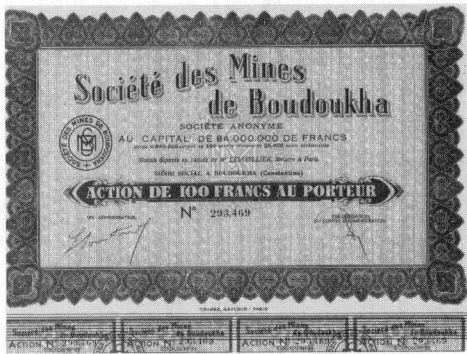

MI160-20-10, ND, 100 F bearer sh., Crabbe, Graveur - Paris, 10-3/4" x 7-1/4", blue....**$4.00**

Protectorate of Annam and Tonkin

50-20-10, 1896, v, Emprunt, 2-1/2% Obligation de 100 F.............................**$40.00**

Argentina

Compañia Azucarera Tucumana S.A., Buenos Aires (1895)

AZ140-50-10, 1959, v, 1 bearer sh. (par 100 Pesos), w/o imprint, 8-1/4" x 10-1/2", red border
......................................**$5.00**

Banco Agricola Commercial del Rio la Plata
BA180-20-10, 1888, 250 sh. blue-grey **$15.00**

Banco de Crédito-Real

BA210-20-10, 1887, v, 10 sh.=1,000 Pesos provisional certificate, 14" x 10-1/4", blue border on green................................**$7.00**

Buderus Roechling S.A.

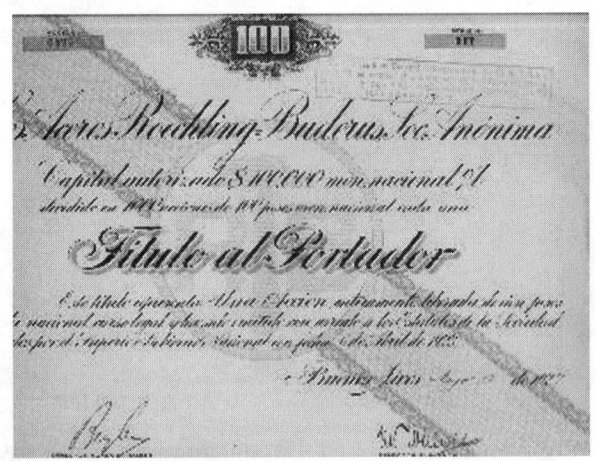

BU10-20-10, 1924, $100.000 bearer sh., black
..................................**$6.00**

S.A. Colonia de Riego Atuel Sud, Buenos Aires

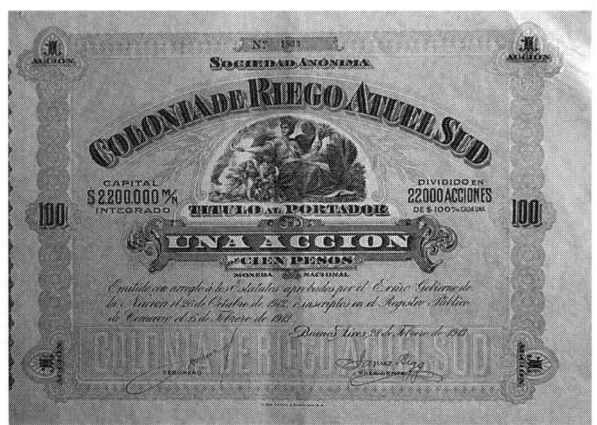

*CO170-20-10, 1913, v, 1 sh. (par 100 P), brown
................................$7.00

Credit Foncier Argentin

CR110-20-10, 1906, v, bearer sh. w. coupons, red on yellow $12.00

La Emilia Industrias Textiles

EM170-20-10, 1946, v, bearer sh. w. coupons, 8" x 11", red...........................$4.00

Molinos Rio de la Plata S.A., Buenos Aires

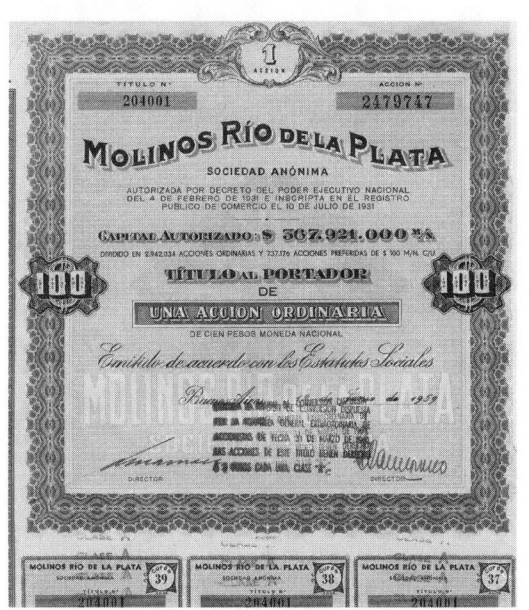

*MO190-20-10, 1959, 1 bearer sh. (par 100 pesos) w. coupons, Atlas Offset, 7-1/2" x 11-1/2", green border on light green......$5.00

Armenia

Armenia
40-30-10, 1993, 500 Dram Government bond, multicolored $5.00

Australia

Dundas Mines No Liability (S. Aus., par 2/6)
DU210-20-10, 1949, 100 sh., brown $7.00

The Midland Railway Company of Western Australia, Limited.
MI110-40-10, 1961, 200 sh. second mortgage deb. stock, green........................$5.00

Mount Zeehan (Tasmania) Silver-Lead Mines Limited

*MO220-20-10, 1896, v, 8 sh. (par £1), grey
................................$12.00

The value of a stock certificate depends on:
• rarity
• the issuer
• signatures
• quality of engraving
• overall appearance
• condition
• date of issue

The Union Consolidated Copper Mines (par £1)

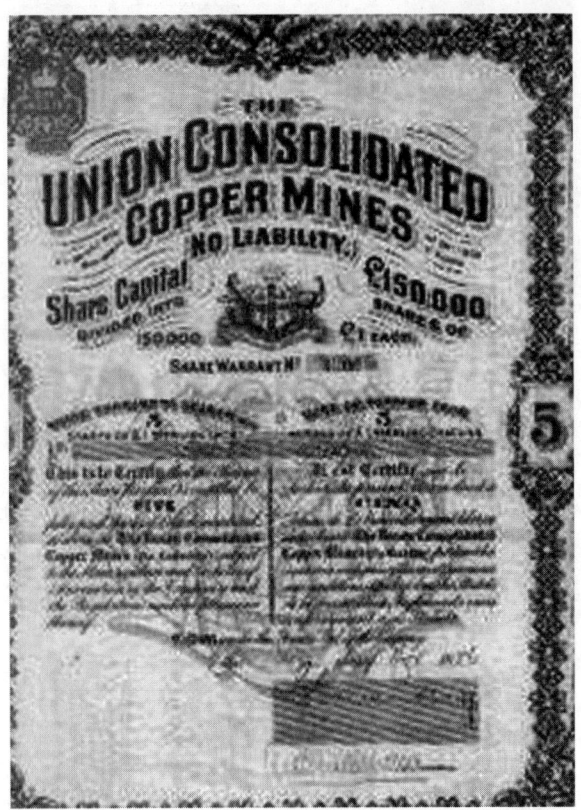

*UN70-20-10, 1906, v, 5 sh., text in English and French, 14" x 20", brown $8.00

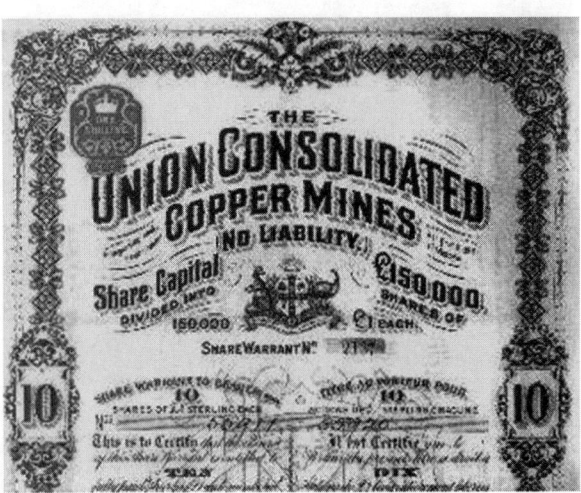

*UN70-25-10, 1906, v, 10 sh., text in English and French, British revenue imprint, green $8.00

Austria

Staatsschuldverschreibung, Public Debt Office

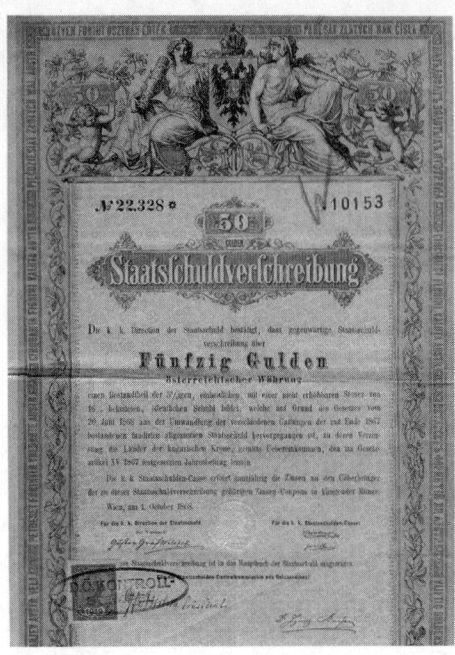

*70-20-10, 1868, v, 50 Florins 5% bond, text in 13 languages, 1919 revenue stamp, 9-1/2" x 14-3/4", light brown $5.00

*70-25-10, 1868, v, 100 Florins 5% bond, with coupons. Text in 13 languages, 9-1/2" x 15", light brown $7.00

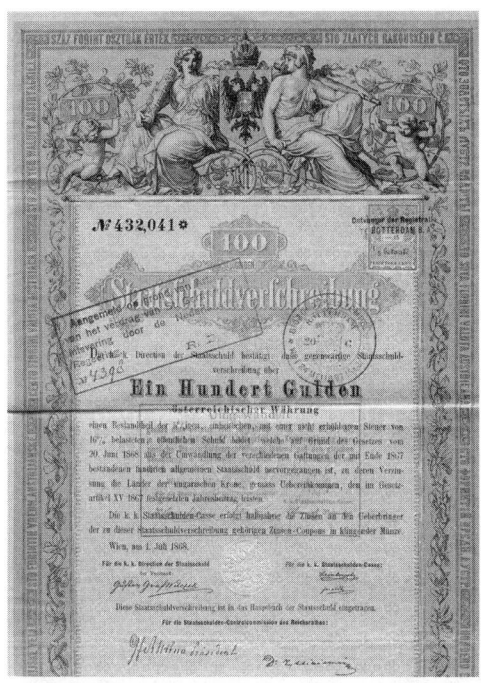

*70-25-11, 1868, v, 100 Florins 5% bond w. coupons, text in 13 languages, Dutch revenue stamp, 9-1/2" x 15", light brown $7.00

*70-65-10, 1920, v, 200 Kr. 4% bond w. coupons
. . . .$5.00

> *It is generally assumed that only 5% of certificates survive to reach collectors.*

Staats-Rente-Obligation

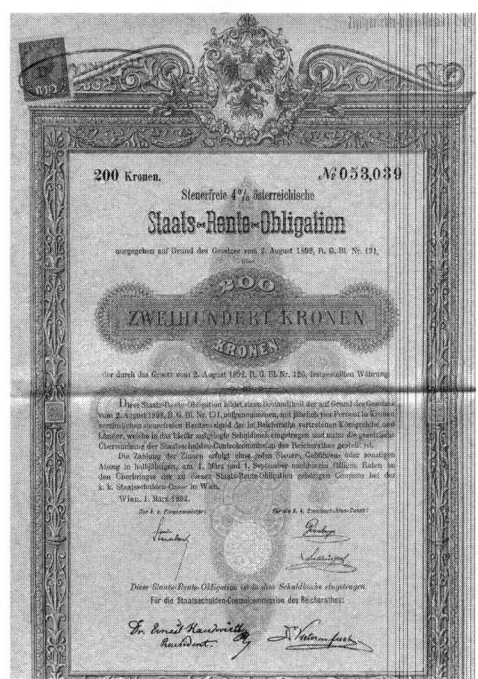

*100-30-10, 1893, v, 200 Kronen 4% bond, 1919 revenue stamp, w/o imprint, 10" x 15", red
. . . .$7.00

Kriegsanleihe

*130-20-10, 1915, v, 100 Kronen war bond, blue
. . . .$10.00

*130-30-10, 1916, v, 200 Kr. 5-1/2% war bond, text in 8 languages, w/o imprint, 9-1/2" x 15-1/4", green border $6.00

*130-35-10, 1916, v, 1,000 Kr. 5-1/2% war bond, text in 8 languages, w/o imprint, 9-1/2" x 14-1/2", brown and green border $7.00

Anlehen der k.k. Reichssupt. Wien

*150-20-10, 1917, v, 1,000 Kronen 4-1/2% bond due 1977 w. coupons, 9-1/2" x 14", blue $10.00

Austrian Government Guaranteed Conversion Loan 1934-1959

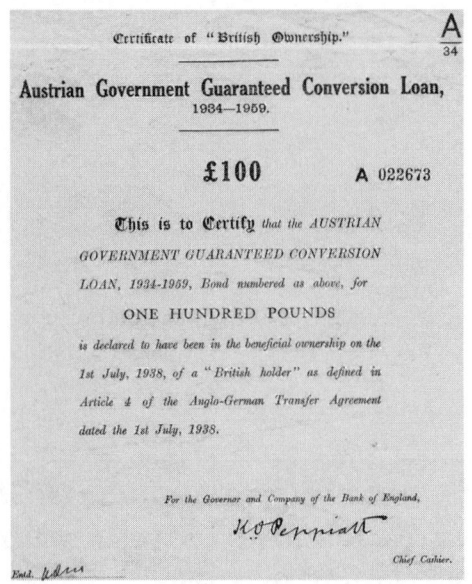

*180-20-10, 1938, £100 certificate of "British Ownership" issued by the Bank of England, 8" x 8-1/2", blue. $4.00

Republic of Austria

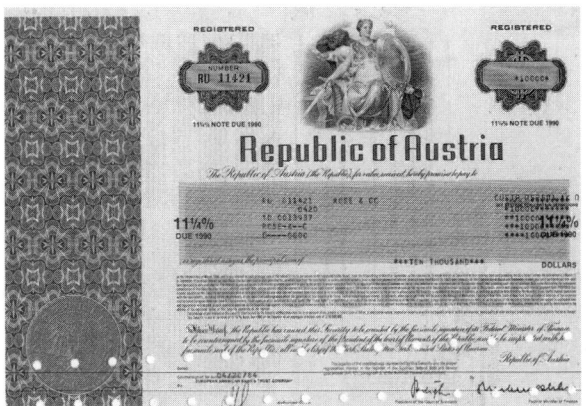

*230-30-10, 1984, v, $10,000 11-1/4% bond due 1990, ABN, 12" x 8", brown $4.00

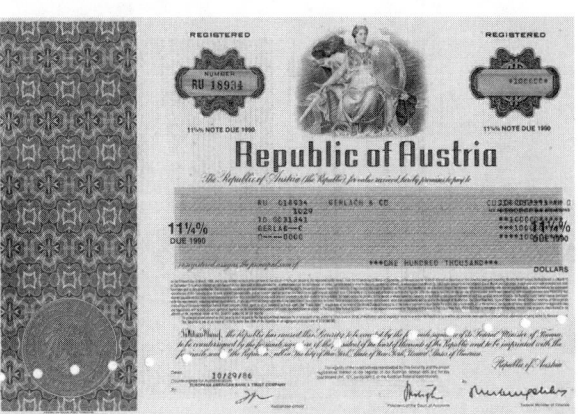

*230-30-15, 1986, v, $100,000 11-1/4% bond due 1990, countersign variety, ABN, 12" x 8", brown $5.00

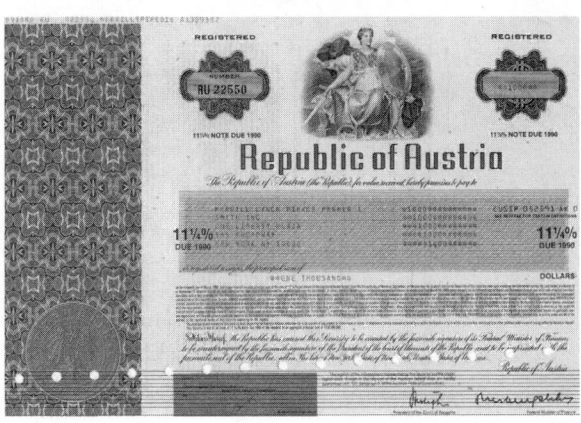

*230-30-20, 1990, v, $1,000 11-1/4% loan, counter sign variety with signature strip, ABN, 12" x 8", brown $4.00

Brünner Local-Eisenbahn-Gesellschaft

*BR410-20-10, 1909, 200 Kronen bearer sh., green-beige......................$12.00

Commission für Verkehrsanlagen in Wien

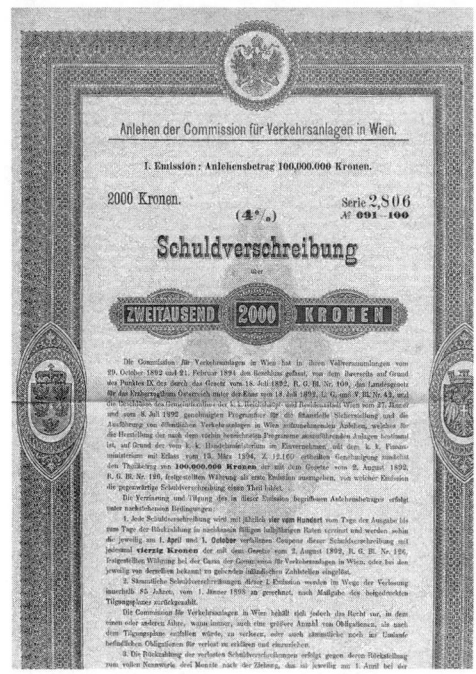

*CO240-20-10, 1894, v, 2,000 Kr. 4% loan w. coupons, w/o imprint, 9-3/4" x 15", blue border $6.00

City of Graz

GR90-40-10, 1921, 10,000 Kronen 5% bond Schuldverfschreibung, blue $10.00

Stadtanleihe Linz

*LI180-20-10, 1923, v, 10,000 Kronen 5% bond,
brown and green $15.00

Carl Ludwig-Bahn,
Eisenbahnstaatsshuldverschreibung

*LU130-40-10, 1902, v, 400 Kronen 4% bond w.
coupons, grey and brown $45.00

Hotel Continental AG.

HO280-30-10, 1916, v, 200 Kronen bearer stock,
brown $19.00

"IRIAG" Intern. Rohölindustriegesellschaft

*IR90-30-10, 1920, 25 bearer shares, 200 Kronen
w. coupons, text in French-German-Czech,
green. $30.00

Oesterreische Gesellschaft vom Roten Kreuze

*OE250-15-10, 1882, v, 10 Gulden bond, grey
. . . .$8.00

*OE250-20-10, 1916, v, 20 Kronen, bond text in nine languages, Gesellschaft für Graphische Industrie, Wien; 12" x 9-1/2", red on beige
..................................$6.00

Österreichisches Bau-Los Em

A lottery loan issued under the Federal Housing and Settlement Fund.

*OS320-25-10, 1921, 300 Kr. building lottery bond, w/o imprint, 11" x 7", brown on beige
..................................$5.00

*OS320-30-10, 1921, v, 1,200 Kr. building lottery bond, text in German-French-English, w/o imprint, 11" x 7", brown on light blue $5.00

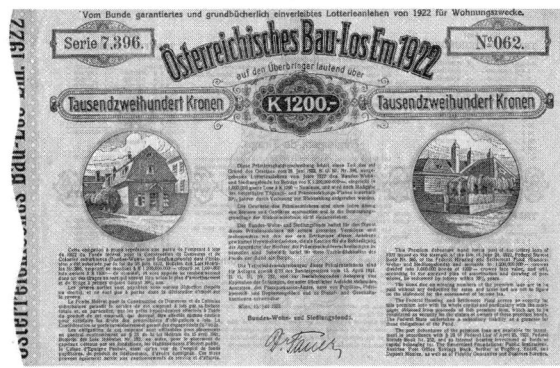

*OS320-35-10, 1922, v, 1,200 Kr. building lottery bond, text French-German-English, w/o imprint, 11" x 7", black on light purple $5.00

Wiener Bankvereins, Wien

*WI170-20-10, 1872, v, 100 Gulden interim certificate for bearer sh., w. coupons, grey $20.00

Wolford, Wien

*WO170-30-10, 1988, 100 S. Ch. bearer sh., multicolored $34.00

B

Bahamas

Basic Resources International (Bahamas) Limited (par $0.03)

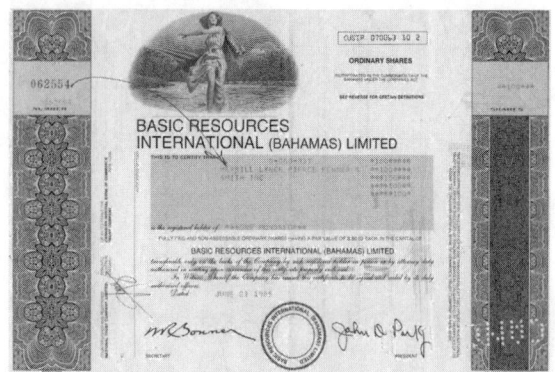

*BA140-20-10, 1985, v, 100 sh., Canadian Banknote Co., 12" x 8", green $3.00

Belgian Congo

Société Belge pour la Commerce au Katanga, Elizabethville

*BE170-20-10, 1928, 500F bearer stock w. coupons, 9" x 14-1/2", green $8.00

Compagnie des Chemins de Fer Katanga-Dilolo-Leopoldville

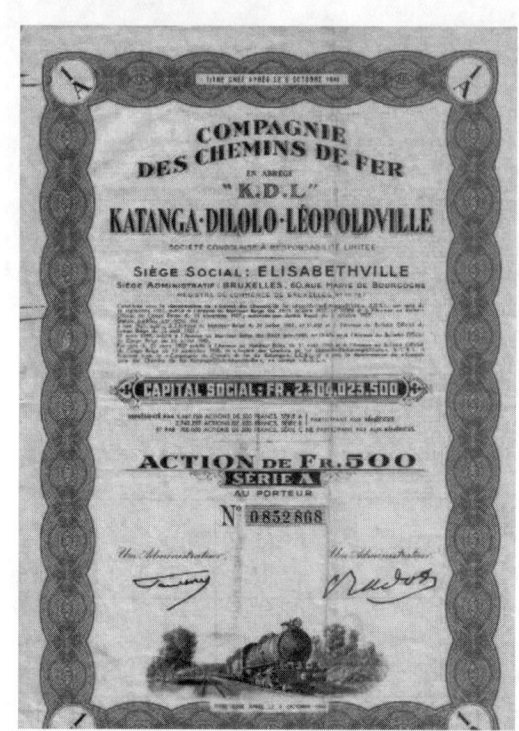

*CH180-30-10, ND, 500 F series A bearer sh., 8-1/2" x 12-1/2", red.................$10.00

*CH180-40-10, ND, 500 Fr. series B bearer stock, blue................................$3.00

Société des Chemins de Fer Vicinaux du Congo, Aketi

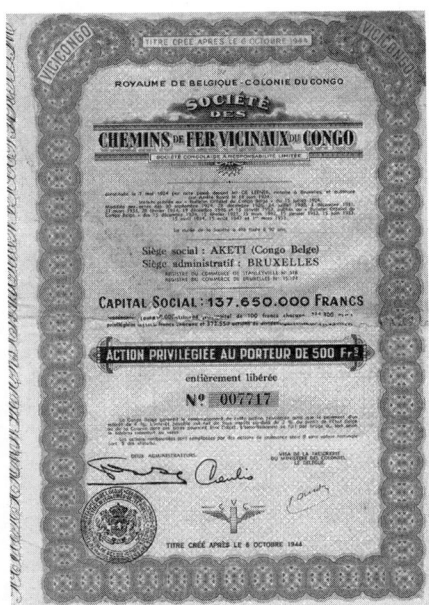

*CH310-30-10, 1953, 500 F bearer pref. stock w. coupons, Belgian Congo revenue rubber stamp, Imprimerie Industrielle et Financiere, Bruxelles, 8-1/2" x 11-3/4", red $5.00

Société Coloniale Minière en abrégé : "COLOMINES", Kule-Matundu

*CO240-20-10, 1952, v, 1 bearer sh., Desoer, 8-1/2" x 12-1/2", brown $4.00

Société Congolaise de Gestion Immobilière, COGIMO, Léopoldville

*CO310-30-10, ND, 5,000 F bearer sh. w. coupons, green $3.00

Compagnie Géologique et Minière des Ingéniurs et Industriels Belges, "GÉOMINES", Manono

*GE90-30-10, 1952, 4 bearer sh. Qualification certif. (250 Congo F), Imprimerie Industrielle et Financiére - Bruxelles, 8" x 10-3/4", red . .$3.00

Société Internationale Forestière & Minière du Congo (FORMIERE)

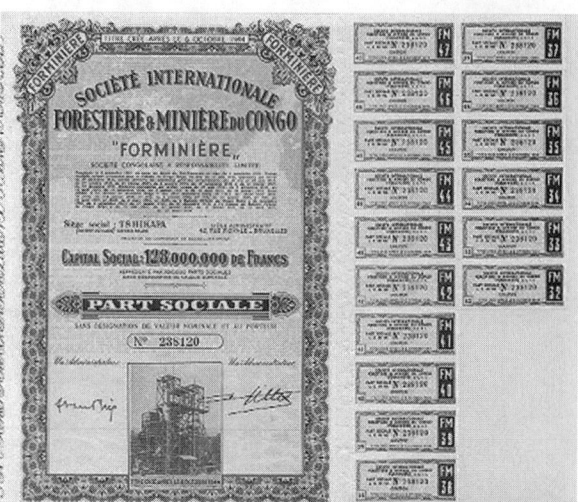

*IN180-30-10, 1944, v, no par bearer sh. w. coupons, blue $9.00

Société des Mines d'Or Kilo-Moto, Kilo

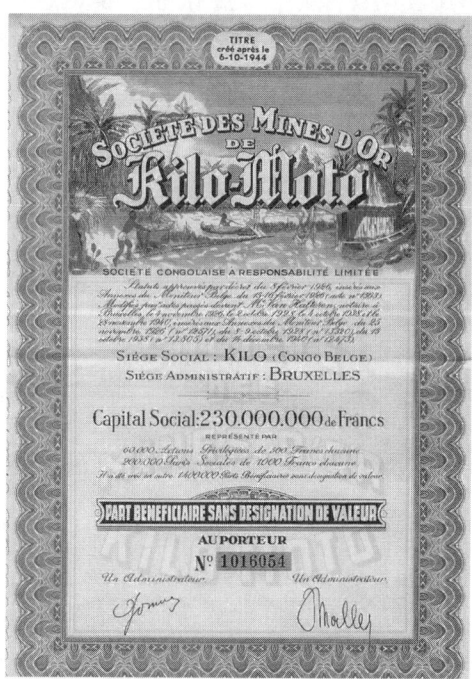

*MI190-20-10, 19xx, v, beneficial part (no par), Etablissements J. Deheneffe, Bruxelles; 8-3/4" x 12-3/4" red border. $5.00

*MI190-30-10, 19xx, v, 5 bearer sh., brown border
. . . .$6.00

Société Miniére de Bafwaboli "SOMIBA", Stanleyville

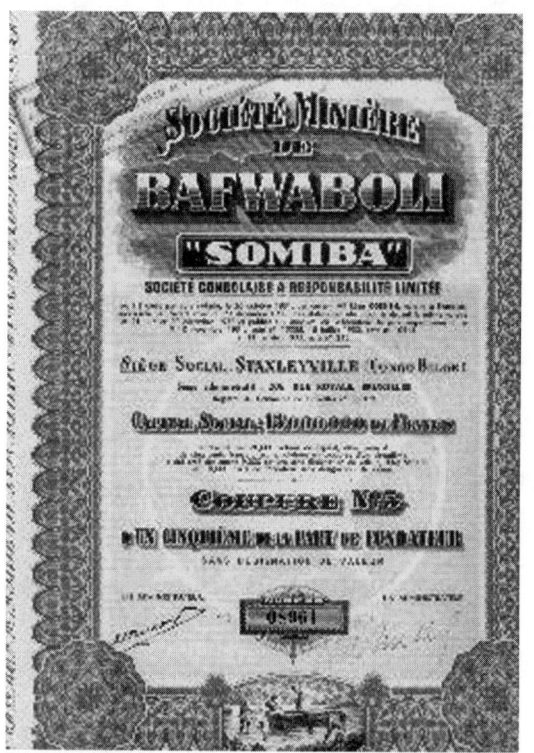

*MI310-20-10, 1933, v, bearer stock, green . $3.00

Sucrerie et Raffinage l'Afrique Centrale SUCRAF, Bukavu

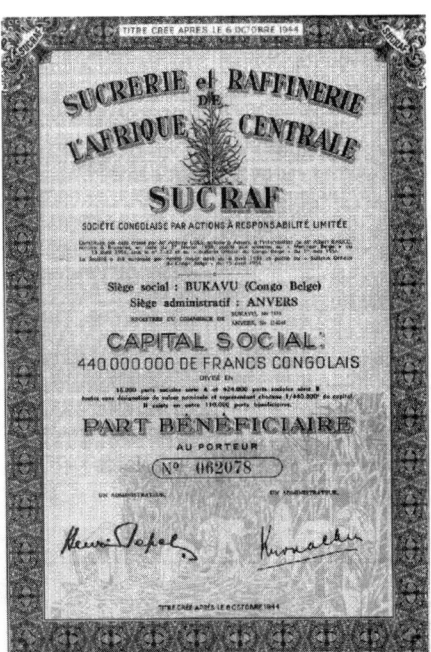

*SU140-20-10, 1956, bearer sh., brown border
. . . .$3.00

Union Pharmaceutique Congolaise UNICONGO, Elisabethville

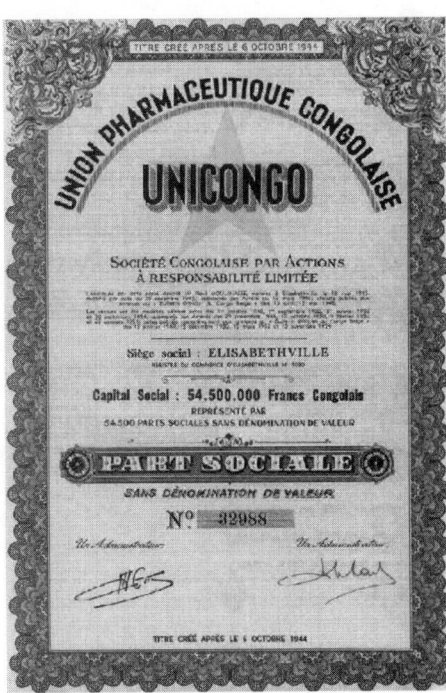

*UN120-20-10, 1954, v, bearer sh., green border
. . . .$3.00

Belgium

Société Industrielle des Applications Chimiques, Bruxelles

*AP260-20-10, 1928, 500 F bearer sh. w. coupons,
blue. $4.00

Ateliers de Construction de Familleureux S.A.

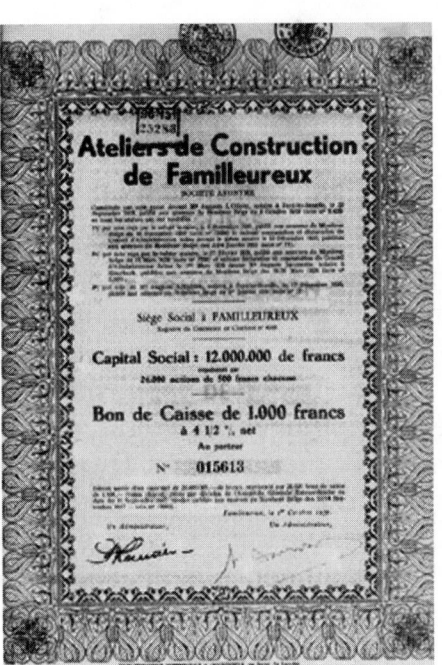

*AT150-30-10, 1937, 1,000 F 4-1/2% bond, green
. . . .$3.00

S.A. Ateliers de Construction de la Meuse

*AT180-20-10, 1946, v, 1 bearer stock, brown
....$6.00

Ateliers Germain-Anglo S.A.

AT210-20-10, 1963, v, bearer sh., brown border on
pink..$3.00

This catalog has listings in an alphabetical format. The reason is simple: Companies diversify as they grow. For example, the Canadian Pacific Railway company recently split into five companies. They represent the railway, hotels, shipping, airline, and petroleum interests of the company. During World War II, the Singer sewing machine company made guns and other defense-related equipment, so where should we list it? It's far easier to use a strict alphabetical order, rather than to confuse the reader with topical classifications.

Automobiles Impéria-Excelsior S.A., Nessonvaux (Liége)

*AU160-20-10, 1928, 1 ordinary bearer sh.,
green..$4.00

Compagnie Auxiliaire Industrielle S.A., Bruxelles

*AU210-30-10, 1897, v, 100 F pref. bearer stock,
brown..$4.00

Société Belge d'Entreprises en Chine, Bruxelles

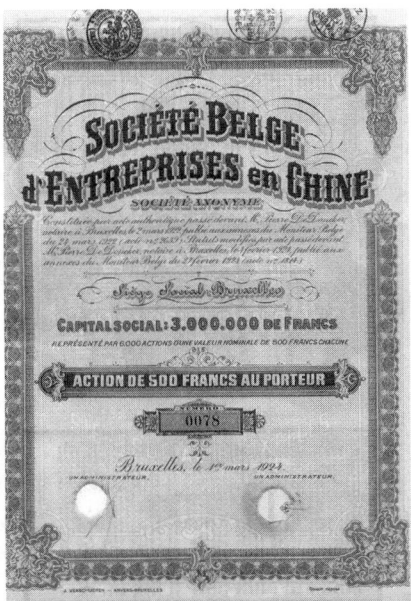

BE110-20-10, 1924, 500 F bearer sh. w. coupons, Belgian and Dutch revenue rubber stamps, J. Verschueren-Anvers-Bruxelles, 8-3/4" x 12-1/2", blue-green..................$5.00

Compagnie Belge de Participations, de Gestion et d'Entreprises S.A., C.B.P.G.E., Bruxelles

BE340-20-10, 1957, 1 bearer sh. (no par), red $3.00

Société Filiale Belge-Néerlandaise d'Aluminium (Procédés Peniakoff), Bruxelles

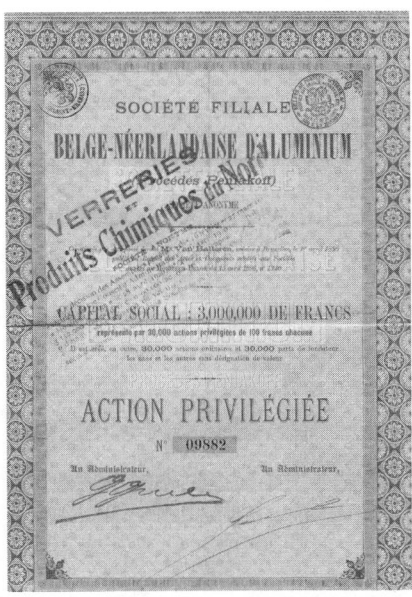

BE410-30-10, 1920, 100 F pref. bearer sh. w. coupons, o/p Verreires et Produits Chimiques du Nord, Imprimerie Industrielle et Financiére (SA), 10-1/4" x 13-1/2", red............$4.00

Compagnie Centrale d'Électricité de Moscou, Liége

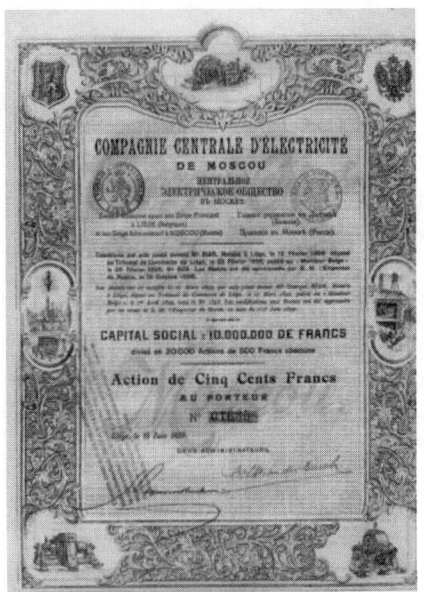

CE150-20-10, 1899, v, 500 F bearer sh. w. coupons, Belgian revenue rubber stamp, blue $5.00

S.A. du Centre des Appalaches - The Central Appalachian Company Limited, Kentucky

CE200-20-10, 1892, v, 500 F bearer stock w. coupons, green **$22.00**

Charbonnages d'Alexinatz, S.A. en liquidation, Bruxelles

The company was founded in 1914. Its principal objective was to mine the coal deposits of Kraljevatz and Novi-Kraljevats near Alexinatz in the Serbian part of Yugoslavia. With the 1946 Yugoslav government decree nationalizing the assests, the company went into liquidation.

*CH110-20-10, 1949, part social sh. (no par), Imprimerie Industrielle et Finacière (IMIFI), Bruxelles; 8-3/4" x 12-1/2", green **$3.00**

Compagnie Charbonnages de Pobedenko

CH210-20-10, 1898, v, 100 F bearer sh., red on light green **$7.00**

Compagnie de Chemin de Fer Beira au Zambèze (Mozambique), Bruxelles

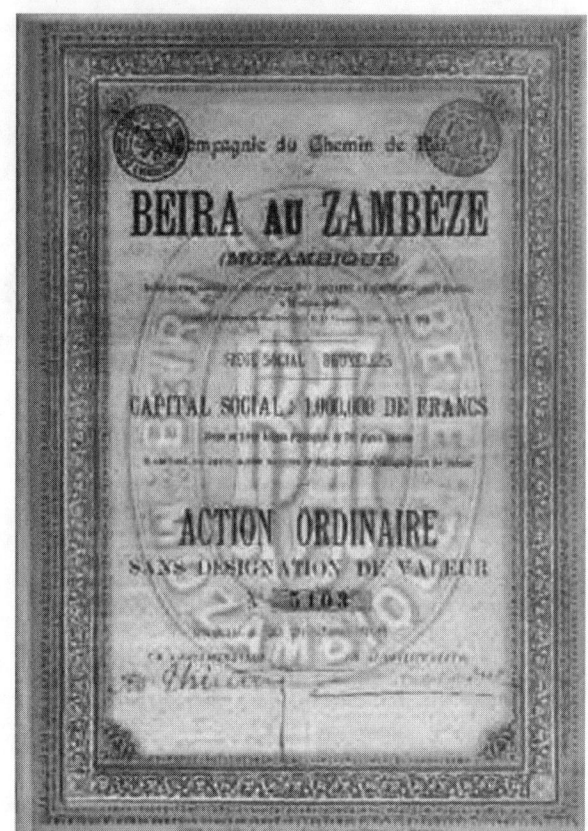

*CH380-20-10, 1898, v, 1 bearer sh. (no par), red **$5.00**

Compagnie Générale de Chemins de Fer et de Tramways en Chine S.A., Bruxelles

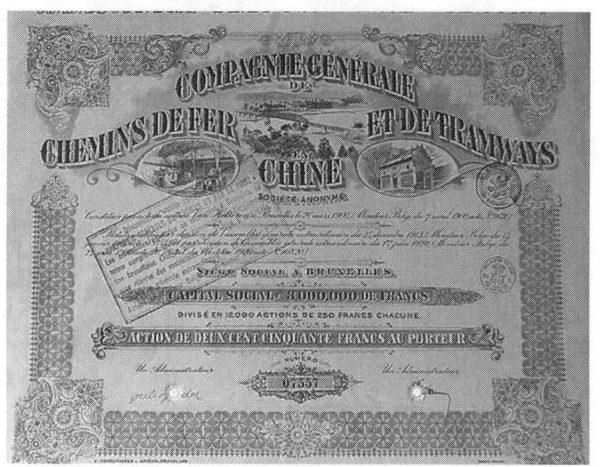

*CH510-20-10, 1920, v, 250 F bearer sh. w. coupons, l. brown border **$5.00**

S.A. la Coloniale Industrielle (pour l'étude et la mise en valour d'Entrepises coloniale

CO130-20-10, 1899, v, bearer sh., red on green
paper $44.00

Société Commerciale de Belgique S.A., Ougrée

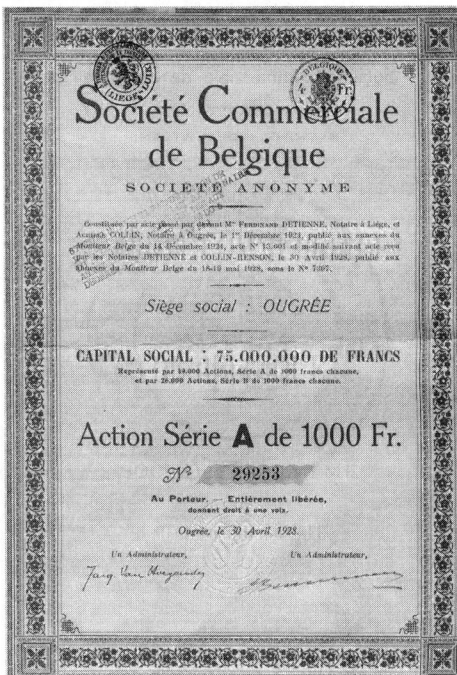

*CO280-20-10, 1928, 1,000 F series A bearer sh.
w. coupons, Maison Desoer, S.A. Liége; 9-1/4" x
13-1/2", brown border $3.00

The value of a stock certificate depends on:

- rarity
- the issuer
- signatures
- quality of engraving
- overall appearance
- condition
- date of issue

Société d'Electricité & de Mécanique S.A., Gand

*EL160-20-10, 1956, 5,000 F 5% bearer bond,
Impr. de la Bourse S.A. Anvers; 8-3/4" x
12-1/2", red border $3.00

Societè Espagnole Nitramites S.A.

ES120-20-10, 1890, 100 F bearer sh., Imp. Travaux
Publics S.A. Bruxelles, red. $3.00

Établissements Industriels de Berdiansk

*ET150-20-10, 1899, v, bearer sh. w. coupons, text
French on the front, French-Russian on the back,
blue $15.00

Société Anonyme des Établissements Sud-Américains Gratry, Bruxelles

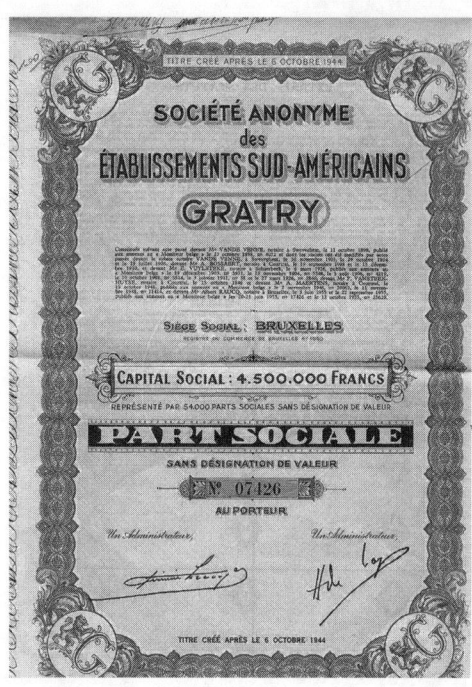

*ET380-20-10, ND, v, social part (no par), Imprimerie Industrielle et Financiére, Bruxelles; 8-3/4" x 11-1/2", green $3.00

Compagnie Fermière de Charbonnages de Prokhorow

FE160-20-10, 1909, 1 bearer sh. w. coupons, brown $10.00

Compagnie Financiére d'Exploitations Forestiere & d'Impregnations des Bois, FORFINA, Brussels

FI170-20-10, 1926, v, 500 F bearer sh. w. coupons, 8-3/4" x 14", green border $5.00

Les Fonderies Broxelloises en abrege Fobrox S.A., Vilvorde

FO180-30-10, 1950, v, Founder's bearer sh., red $5.00

Forges et Fonderies REMY, (no par) Yves-Gomezée

*FO270-20-10, 1954, 1 bearer sh. (no par) w. coupons, Imprimerie de Coker, Anvers, 8-1/2" x 12-1/2", blue $3.00

Compagnie Glaces du Midi de la Russie, Bruxelles

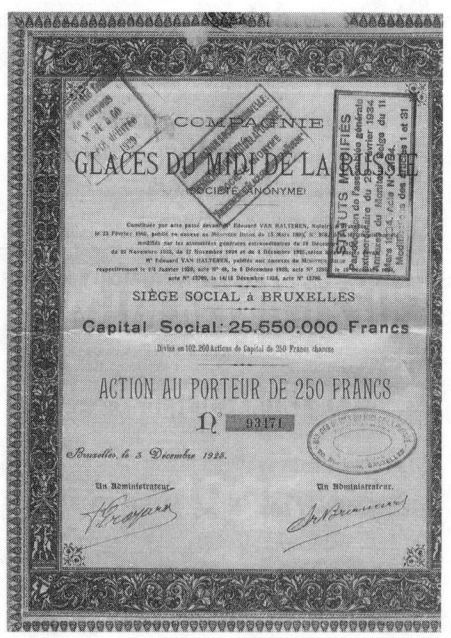

*GL90-20-10, 1925, 250 F bearer stock w. coupons, Dutch revenue imprint, J. Delacre & Fils, Charleroi, 9-3/4" x 13-1/2", reddish......$4.00

Hanin Maréchal

HA190-20-10, ND, 500F bearer capital stock, lilac $3.00

Société Immobilière, Financière & d'Entreprises Industrielles (S.I.F.E.I.), Bruxelles

IM170-20-10, 1927, 100 F bearer sh., Imprimerie Industrielle et Financière S.A., Bruxelles; 10-3/4" x 7", rose-red border $3.00

Compagnie Immobilière du Littoral-Ouest S.A., Bruxelles

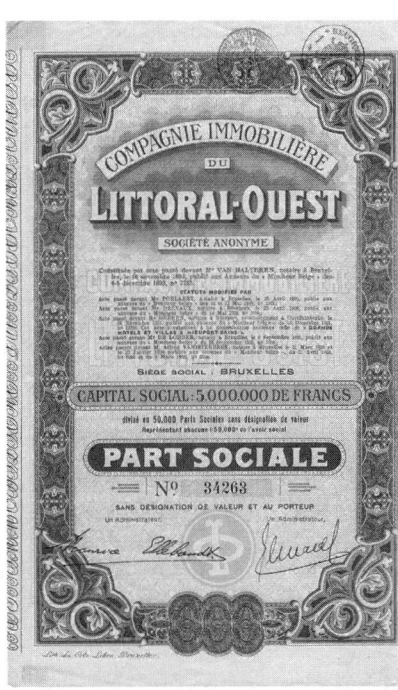

IM250-20-10, ND, v, social part (no par), w. Belgian revenue rubber stamps, Lith. La Cote Libre, Bruxelles; 7" x 11-1/2", green $3.00

Compagnie Industrielle de Belgique S.A.

IN130-20-10, ND, v, founder bearer sh. (no par), red.................................$3.00
IN130-30-10, 1898, v, 100 F bearer sh., light blue $12.00

Societe Internationale de participation aux Industries Chimique

IN270-20-10, ND, v, 1 bearer sh., no par value, brown $4.00

Société Civile Jeux de Spa

JE110-20-10, 1959, bearer sh., yellowish brown
...............................$40.00

City of Liege

LI160-25-10, 1905, v, 100 F bearer bond w. coupons, 9-1/4" x 10-3/4", grey $10.00
LI160-40-10, 1925, 100F bearer bond w. coupons, beige-brown $10.00

La Lowa S.A. d'Importation & d'Exportation au Congo Belge et autres Pays d'Outre-Mers, Anvers

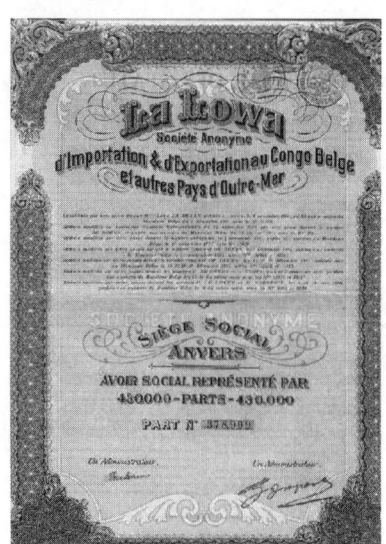

LO210-20-10, 1925, bearer sh., blue border
...............................$3.00

S.A. Belge Lukolela-Plantations, Liège

LU160-20-10, 1961, v, bearer sh., green $3.00

Manufactures Royales de Corsets P.D., (no par) Bruxelles

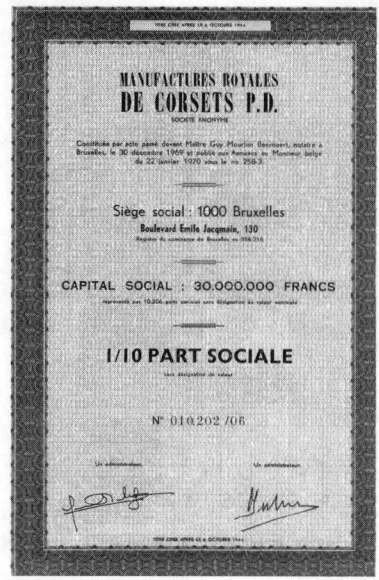

MA110-20-10, 1970, 1/10 social part (no par) w. coupons, Protecto Cy, Bruxelles, 8-1/2" x 12-1/2", blue.....................$3.00

Meubelfabrieken Aubry NV, Antwerp

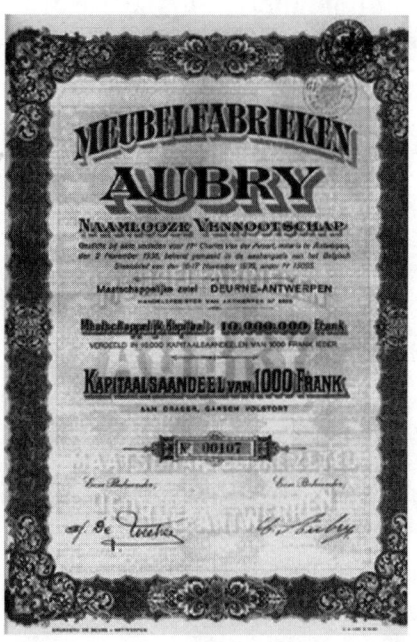

ME290-20-10, 1938, 1,000 F bearer stock, blue
...............................$3.00

Minerva Motors S.A.

MI170-20-10, 1930, 1/10 sh. bearer stock, blue
................................$35.00
MI170-25-10, 1930, bearer stock w. coupons, blue
................................$24.00

Compagnie de Mines et Minerais, Bruxelles

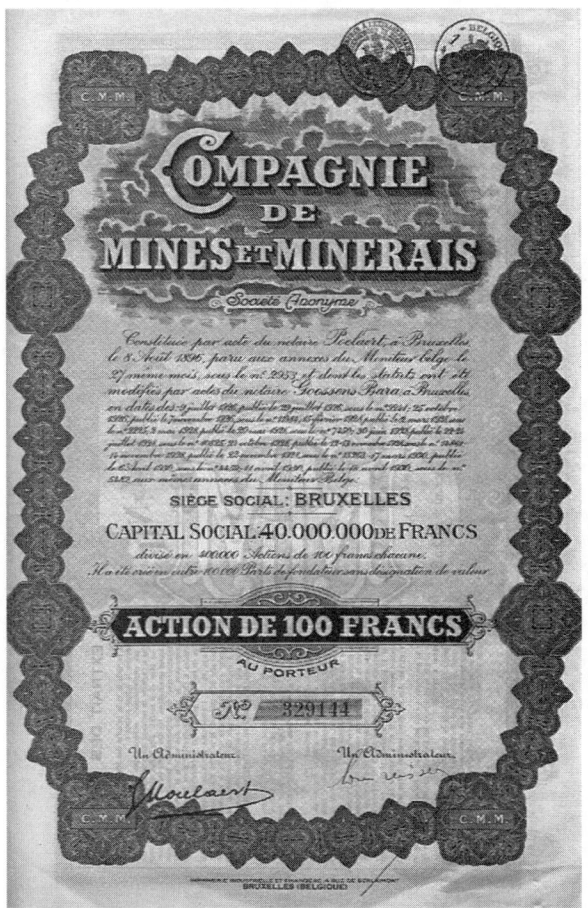

*MI220-20-10, 1930, v, 100 F bearer sh. w. coupons, green $4.00

> *It is generally assumed that only 5% of certificates survive to reach collectors.*

Société Minière du Canada S.A., Bruxelles

*MI310-20-10, 1910, Dividend bearer sh. (no par), Belgian revenue rubber stamp, Imp. Industrielle et Financière (Soc. An.), Bruxelles, 10-1/2" x 13-3/4", turquoise............$4.00

Société Minière Joltaia-Rieka S.A.

*MI510-20-10, 1899, v, 100 F bearer stock, brown
................................$9.00

*MI510-30-10, 1899, v, "action de Jouissance," olive $7.00

Minerva Motors S.A., Anvers

MI720-30-10, 1910, v, 1/10 of a sh., Typ. & Lith. J. Verschueren-Anvers, blue $6.00

S.A. de Mines de Mertola (Portugal), Liége

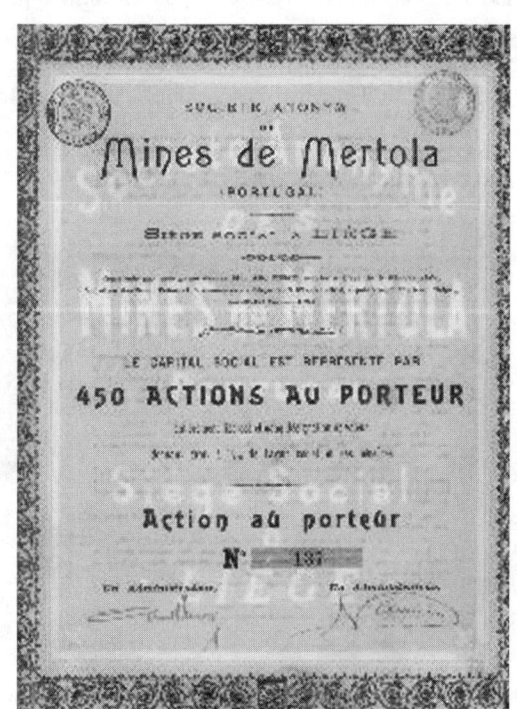

*MI820-20-10, 1904, 450 sh. bearer stock, brown $3.00

S.A, Mines d'Or de Katchkar

MI860-20-10, 1911, v, 100 F pref. bearer stock, brown $13.00

les Mines d'Or de Porcecito, Bruxelles

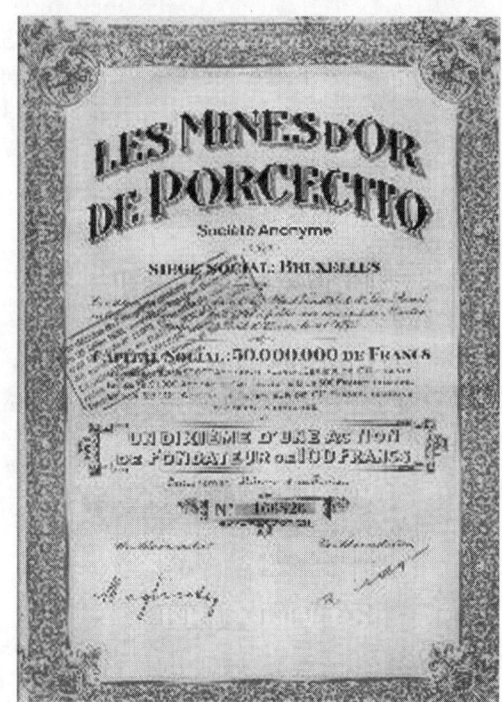

*MI880-20-10, 1928, 1/10 bearer sh. (par 100 F), red.................................$3.00

Mines du Pedroso S.A., Anvers

*MI910-20-10, 1912, 300 F bearer sh., green $3.00

Les Nouvelles Usines Bollinckx S.A., Buysinghen

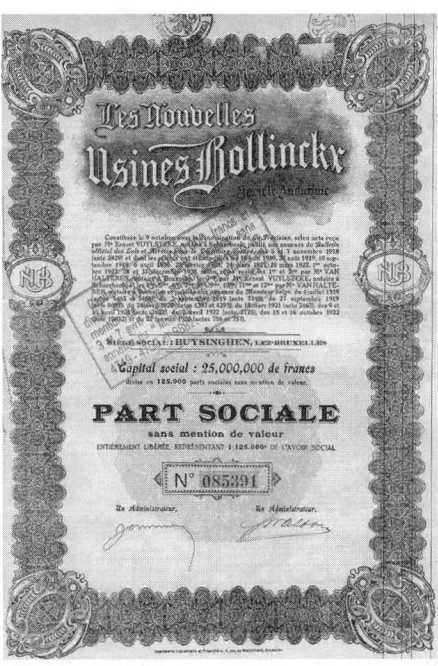

NO120-20-10, 1926, v, bearer sh. w. coupons, Belgian revenue rubber stamps, Imprimerie Industrielle et Financière, Bruxelles; 8-1/4" x 12-1/4", grey border $3.00

Opales de Binche S.A.

OP60-20-10, 1911, 100 F bearer stock, blue on beige $3.00

Le Peigné S.A., Verviers

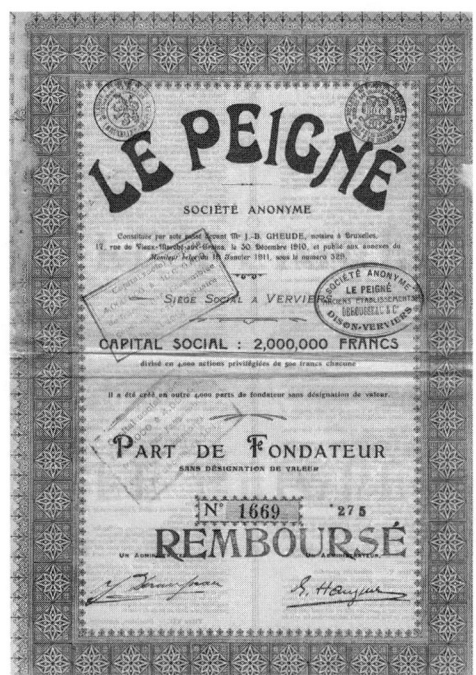

PE130-20-10, 1910, 500 F Founder's bearer sh. w. coupons, w. Belgian revenue rubber stamps, Imprimerie G. Piquart, Bruxelles; 10" x 14", red border $3.00

PE130-40-10, 1910, 500 F pref. bearer sh. w. coupons, w. Belgian revenue rubber stamps, Imp. Ch. Vinche, Verviers; 10" x 14-1/2", green border. $4.00

Pétroles de Boryslaw S.A.

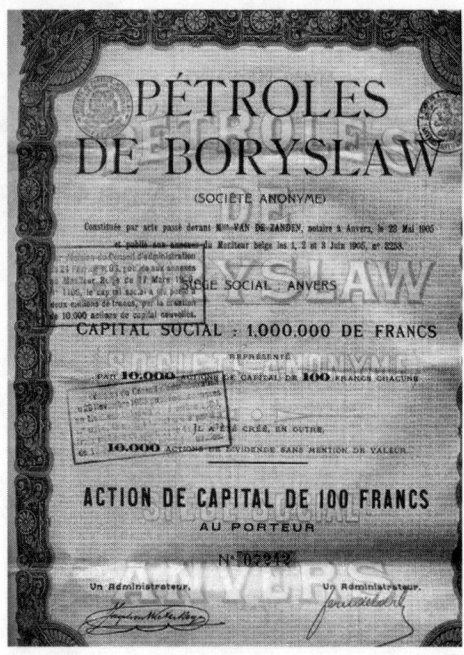

PE440-20-10, 1905, 100F bearer sh., brown
. . . .$4.00

S.A. des Produits Réfractories Céramiques et Terres Plastques de Seilles-lez-Andenne, Seilles

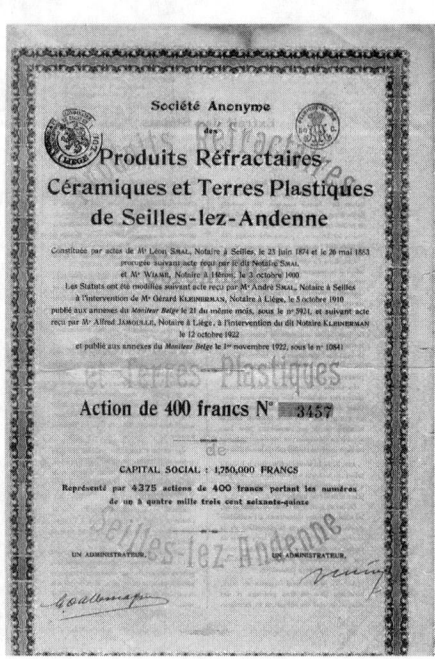

PR180-20-10, 1923, 400 F bearer sh. w. coupons, w. Belgian revenue rubber stamps, w/o imprint, 8-1/2" x 12-3/4", brown border. $3.00

Raffinerie Nationale de Petroles, Bruxelles

RA150-20-10, 1928, v, 1 bearer sh., green
. . . . $3.00

Tramways d'Athénes et du Pirée, Brussels

TR110-30-10, 1900, v, 100 F preferred bearer stock, green. $3.00

Compagnie Générale du Tramways de Buenos-Ayres S.A., Bruxelles

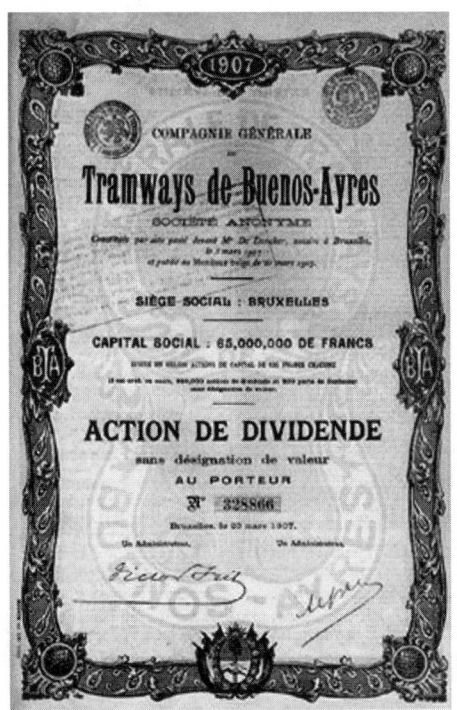

TR140-20-10, 1907, v, bearer sh., blue border on beige **$6.00**

Tramways et l'Eclairage Electriques de Saratov, Brussels

TR220-20-10, 1907, v, 1 bearer sh., l. brown **$7.00**

Les Tramways de Kiew S.A., Bruxelles

TR290-20-10, 1905, 100 F bearer sh., 12" x 10", red border **$5.00**

S.A. des Tramways Napolitains, Bruxelles

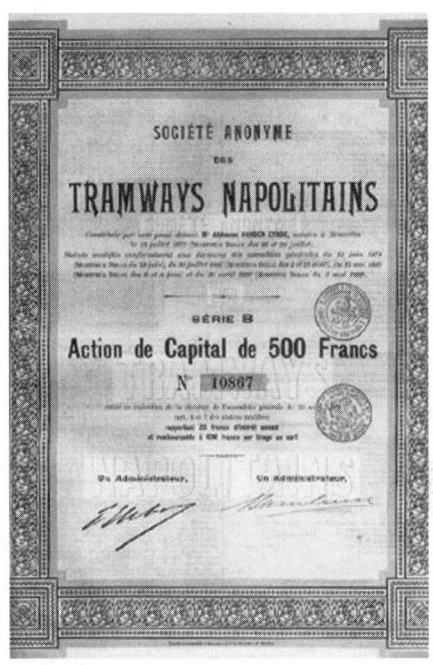

TR360-20-10, 1899, 500 F bearer sh., green **$3.00**

Trust Colonial S.A., Bruxelles

TR520-20-10, 1899, v, bearer sh. of dividends, w. coupons, 10" x 14-1/4", light blue **$15.00**

Union Tuileries de Briquetteries

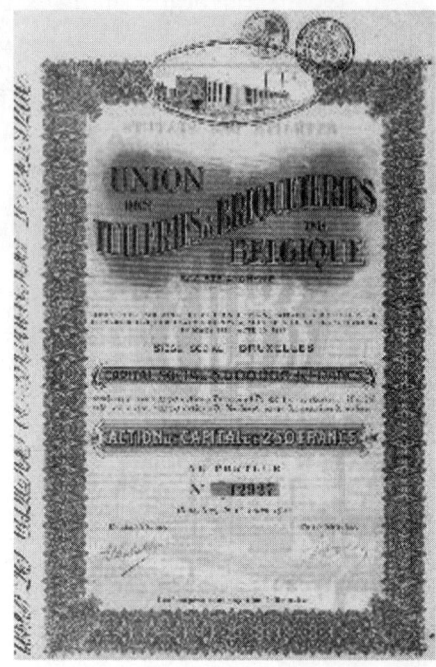

*UN180-20-10, 1921, v, 250 F bearer sh., green
......................................$3.00

Usines Cotonnieres de Belgique S.A., Gand

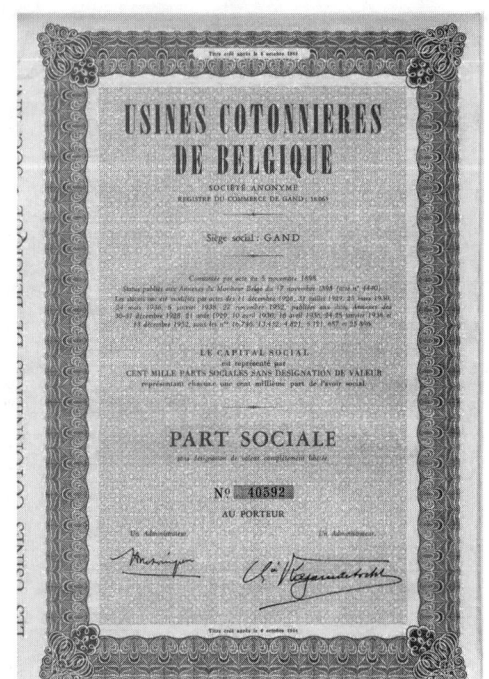

*US180-20-10, ND, bearer social part (no par) w.
coupons, L. Vanmelle S.A., Gand; 8-1/2" x
12-1/2", green border $3.00

Bolivia

Republica de Bolivia
60-20-10, 1870, v, 1,000 Bolivar Emprestito, blue
..................................$22.00

Banco Potosi, Sucre
BA60-10-10, 1889, v, 1 sh. (par 100 Bolivianos),
blue-green border..................$22.00

Brazil

Apolice Consolidacao da divida fluctuante do estado Amazonas
AP60-20-10, 1900, v, Rs500$000, juro annual
Rs35$000 bond, grey $20.00

Apolice da Divida Publica, Republica dos Estados unidos do Brazil

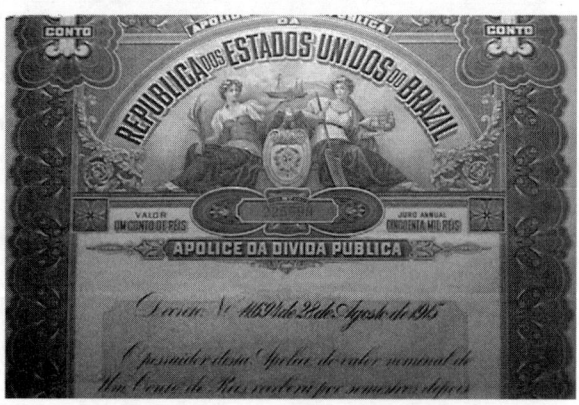

*AP90-20-10, 1915, v, 1 conto, annual dividend of
Rs50$000, green....................$45.00

This catalog has listings in an alphabetical format. The reason is simple: Companies diversify as they grow. For example, the Canadian Pacific Railway company recently split into five companies. They represent the railway, hotels, shipping, airline, and petroleum interests of the company. During World War II, the Singer sewing machine company made guns and other defense-related equipment, so where should we list it? It's far easier to use a strict alphabetical order, rather than to confuse the reader with topical classifications.

Banco do Café
Issued mortgage letters to increase coffee sales.

*BA140-20-10, 19xx, u/u 100 milreis 7% bond, 7"
x 3-1/2", pink $3.00

Sociedade Uniád Eborense
EB160-20-10, 1895, v, 400$000 reis, multicolored
. . . .$180.00

Bulgaria

Banque de Sofia, S.A.

BA170-20-10, 1917, 100 gold Leva bearer stock
w. coupons, in Bulgarian and French, Giesecke
& Devrient, 14½" x 10¼", green $4.00

Bulgarskaya Fondava Banka
BU140-20-10, 1917, 100 Leva bearer stock, multicolored $6.00

Mezdun Turgovia Industria
Sofia industrial company.

ME150-20-10, 1920, v, 1,000 Leva bearer stock
w. coupons, green. $8.00

Petroles Bulgaria S.A., Sofia

*PE170-20-10, 1927, v, 200 Leva, green...$15.00

Serial Eksporti a d-Sofia

Grain export company of Sofia.

*SE80-20-10, 1941, 10 bearer sh.s 10,000 Leva, blue border $6.00

Zora AG

*ZO80-20-10, 1921, v, 100 Leva bearer sh., multi-colored $5.00

Peoples Republic

60-30-10, 1952, 30 Leva savings bond, reddish-brown $10.00

Burma

G. McKenzie and Co., Rangoon

MC180-20-10, 1921, 100 sh. (par 10 Rupees)
................................$15.00

Moola Oil Co., Ltd., Rangoon

MO220-20-10, 1920, 100 sh. (par 10 Rupees), A.B.M. Press, light blue..............$27.00

MO220-40-10, 1936, par 10 Rupees, S.V.P. Works, light blue $22.00

Rangoon Para Rubber Estates Ltd., Rangoon

RA260-20-10, 1935 ....$6.00

Suburban Land Development Co., Ltd., Rangoon

SU210-20-10, 1930, par 10 Rupees $15.00

Upper Burmah Ruby Exploration and Trading Co., Ltd.

UP120-20-10, 1889, 5 shillings $20.00

C

Cameroon

Les Cafés du Cameroun, Douala

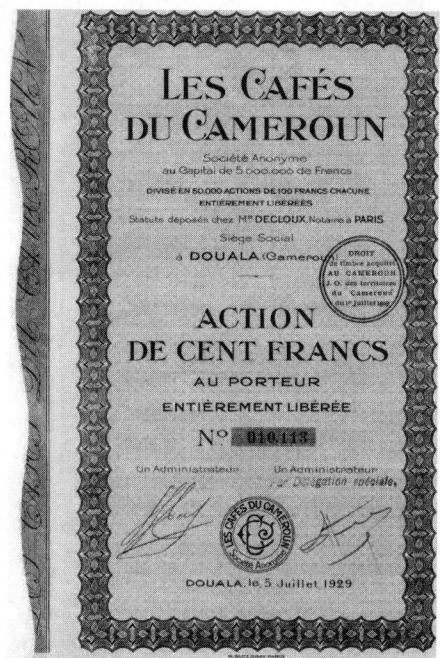

*CA30-20-10, 1929, 100 F bearer sh. w. coupons, Cameroon revenue rubber stamp, R. Blitz, Grav. Paris, 6-1/4" x 9-1/2", blue border $5.00

Canada

2736411 Canada Inc. (Can no par)

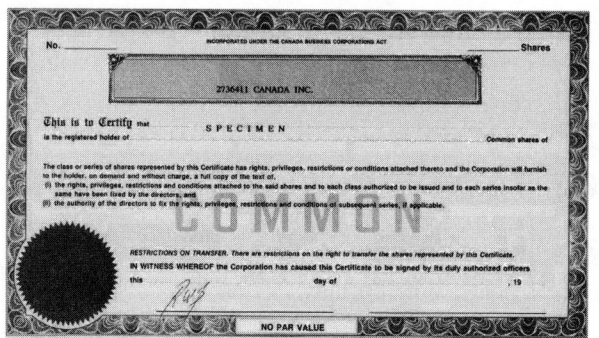

*160-10-10, 19xx, specimen certificate, D&D, 11" x 6-1/4", brown $4.00

927636 Ontario Inc. (ON no par)

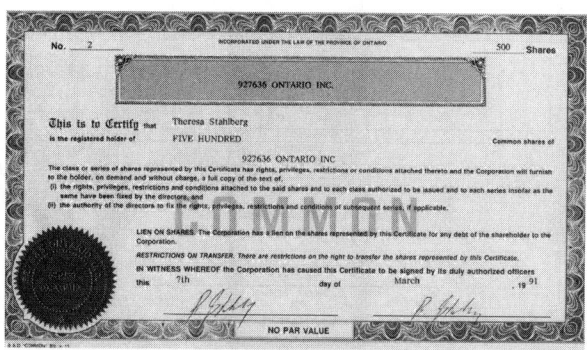

*190-10-10, 1991, i/u 500 sh., D & D Common, 11" x 6-1/2", brown $3.00

Air Canada

*AI130-40-10, 19xx, v, specimen non voting certificate, text in English and French, green $12.00

This catalog has listings in an alphabetical format. The reason is simple: Companies diversify as they grow. For example, the Canadian Pacific Railway company recently split into five companies. They represent the railway, hotels, shipping, airline, and petroleum interests of the company. During World War II, the Singer sewing machine company made guns and other defense-related equipment, so where should we list it? It's far easier to use a strict alphabetical order, rather than to confuse the reader with topical classifications.

Aluminum Company of Canada, Limited

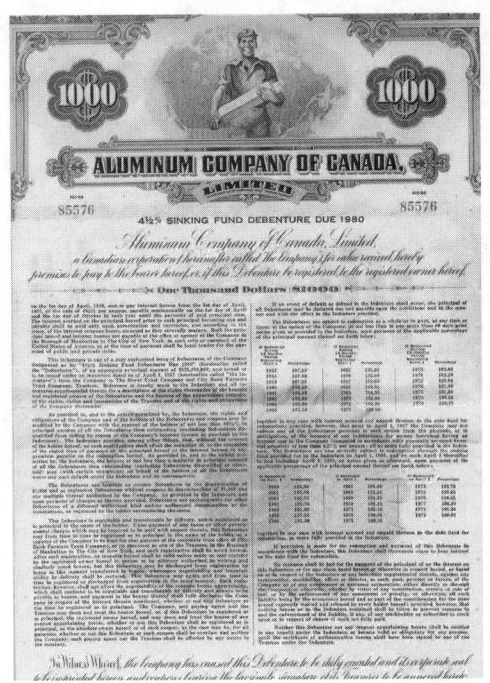

AL210-50-10, 1957, v, u/c $1,000 4-1/2% sinking fund debenture due 1980, ABN, 10-1/4" x 15-1/4", brown $6.00

Ardeen Gold Mines, Limited (ON par $1)

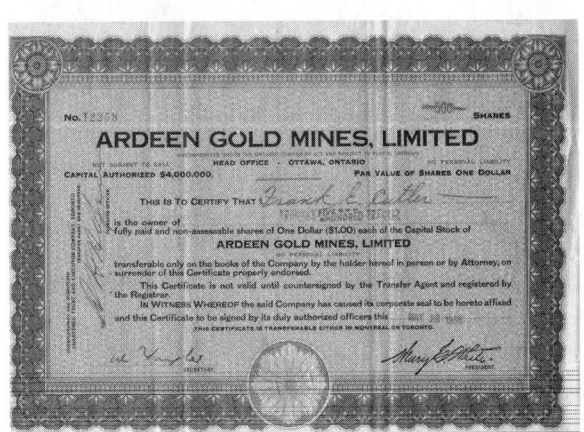

AR150-20-10, 1936, i/u 500 sh., British American Bank Note Co. Ltd., 12" x 8-3/4", green border $5.00

The Atlantic, Quebec and Western Railway Company

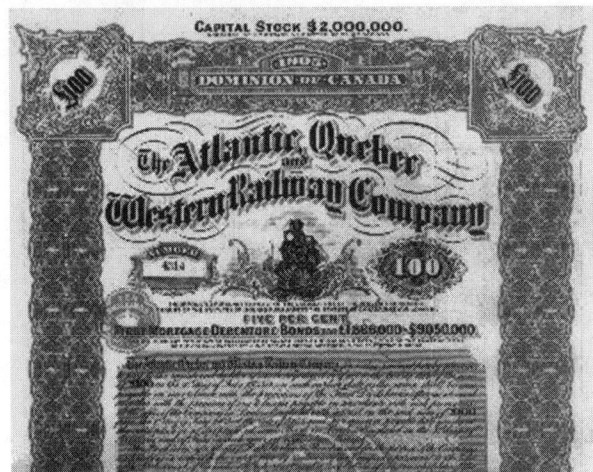

AT270-20-10, 1910, v, $100 5% 1st mortgage bond w. coupons, with English revenue imprint, 11" x 16", green $15.00

Atlantic & St. Lawrence Railroad Company

AT310-20-10, 1958, v, 1 sh. £100, grey $23.00

Bailey Cobalt Mines, Limited (ON par $1)
BA130-20-10, 1921, 1,000 sh., on a not over 1,000 sh. certificate, grey on white $6.00

Barry-Hollinger Gold Mines, Limited (ON par $1)
BA350-20-10, 1925, 200 sh., on a not over 200 sh. certificate, blue border $8.00

Brett Tretheway Mines, Limited (par $1)
BR130-20-10, 1936, v, 200 sh., green $5.00

Bre-X Minerals Ltd.

One of the great mining hoaxes of recent years, a good example of "salting" gold samples.

BR190-30-10, 1997, v, 100 sh., red **$40.00**

British Columbia Hydro and Power Authority

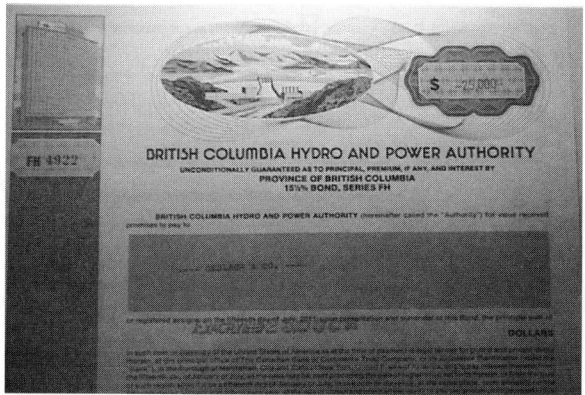

*BR310-40-10, 1981, v, $25,000 Provincially guaranteed 15% bond, series FH, brown and blue **$6.00**

British Columbia Power Corporation Limited (Can 1928, no par)

*BR410-20-10, 1954, v, 10 sh., Canadian Bank Note Company, Limited; 12" x 8", blue . . .**$5.00**

British Columbia Resources Investment Corporation (BC 1979)

These were issued in 1979 and every household received one.

BR480-20-10, 1979, v, 5 bearer sh., orange **$5.00**

British Controlled Oilfields Limited

*BR540-20-10, 1931, v, 50 shares voting trust certificate, green **$4.00**

Canada General Fund (1954) Limited

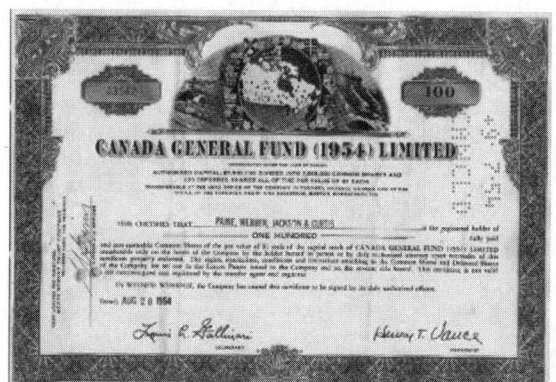

*CA160-20-10, 1954, v, 100 sh., green **$4.00**

Canadian Collieries (Dunsmuir) Limited

*CA230-20-10, 1913, v, 10 pref. sh. (par $100), British revenue imprint, green **$10.00**

Canadian Export Gas & Oil Ltd.
(AB par 16-2/3¢)

*CA370-30-10, 19xx, v, 100 sh., voided certificate, SBN, 11-1/2" x 8-1/4", green **$4.00**

Canadian Homestead Oils Limited (AB)
CA510-30-10, 1974, 100 sh., orange **$6.00**

Canadian Javelin Limited
One of the largest stock market frauds in North America.

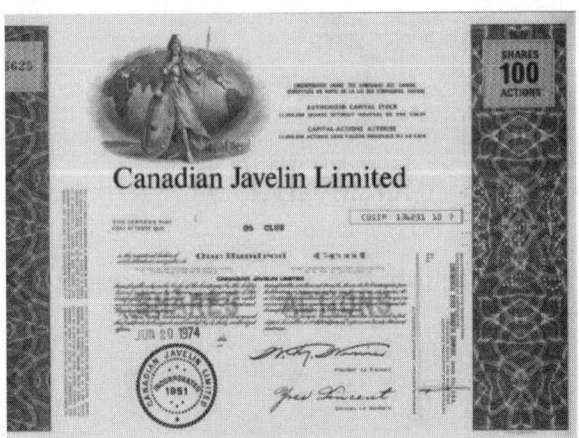

*CA610-30-10, 1974, v, 100 sh., text in English and French, green **$4.00**

The Canadian Metal Company, Limited
CA710-20-10, 1906, 5 sh., brown. **$10.00**

Canadian National Railway Company

*CA800-50-10, 1976, $1,000 8-3/8% bond due 1986, Can. Banknote Co., 9-1/4" x 13", blue **$5.00**

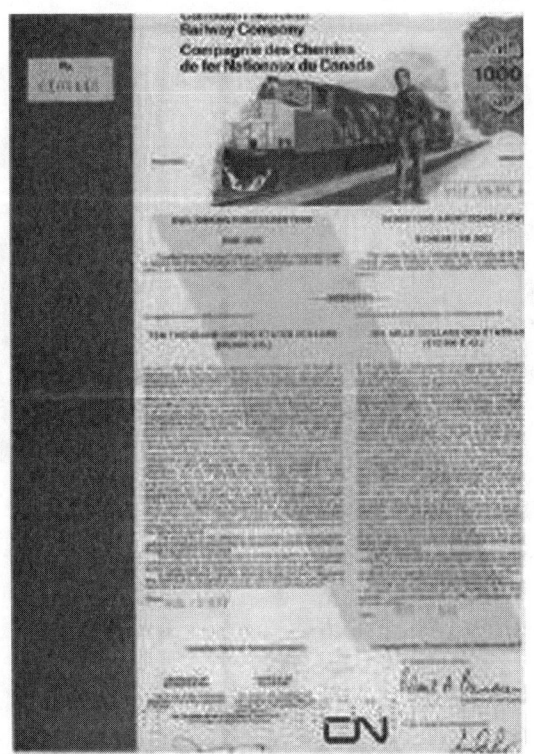

*CA800-55-10, 1977, v, $10,000 8-3/8% bond, 9-1/4" x 13", brown **$5.00**

Chieftain Development Co. Ltd. (AB)
CH240-30-10, 1981, v, 100 sh., deep orange
............................$4.00

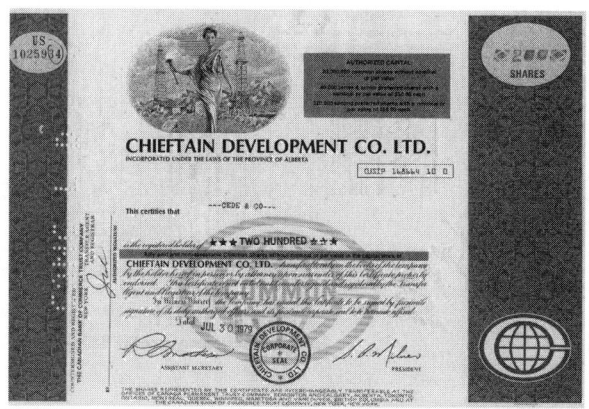

*CH240-40-10, 1979, v, 200 sh. (no par), Canadian
Bank Note, 12" x 8", red..............$4.00

Cobalt Century Mines, Limited (ON par $1)
CO160-20-10, 1932, v, 400 sh., brown border
................................$5.00

La Compagnie de Construction Lafontaine (QC 1907, par $25)

*CO280-20-10, 190?, v, 1 sh., grey $5.00

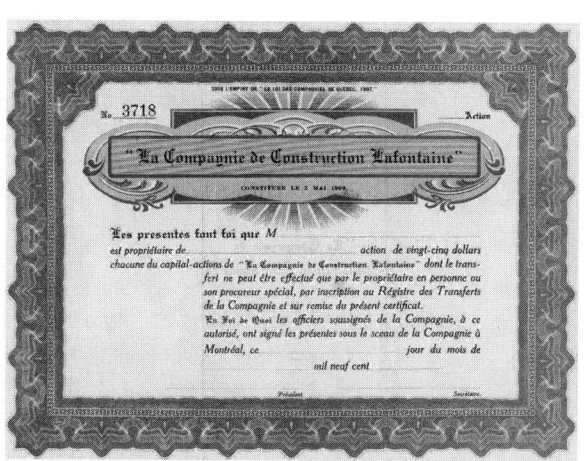

*CO280-30-10, 19xx, u/u certificate, text in
French, 10-3/4" x 8-1/4", brown $3.00

The Consolidated Tin Corporation Limited (Can no par)
CO600-20-10, 1932, 1,666 sh., brown......$5.00

Czobor Micro Information Co. International Corp. (Can no par)

*CZ30-20-10, 1987, 550,000 sh., 10-1/4" x 8-1/4",
green............................$7.00

Dominion Steel and Coal Corporation Limited
DO190-20-10, 1958, f, 45 class B sh., brown
................................$6.00

Dominion Stores Limited (Can 1919, no par)
DO220-20-10, 1929, v, 100 sh., orange....$14.00

Eco Energy International Corp. (NB no par)

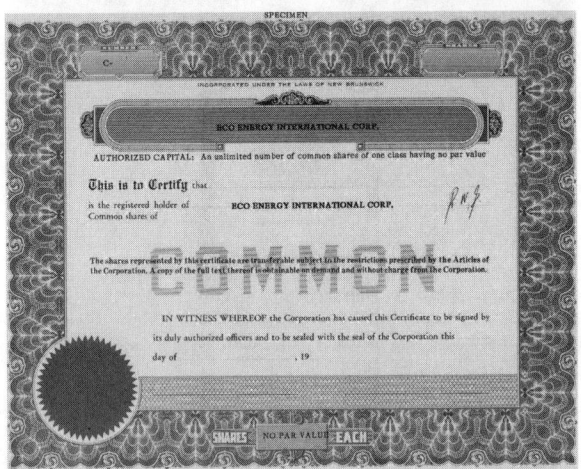

*EC160-10-10, 19xx, specimen certificate, N&G Ltd., 11" x 8-1/2", brown **$4.00**

Fiske Gold Mines, Limited (QC par $1)

*FI160-20-10, 1926, 100 sh., GOES, 11" x 8-1/2", green border **$5.00**

Flanagan-Skead Mines Limited (par $1) Toronto

FL70-20-10, 1928, v, 1,000 sh., brown border
. . . .**$6.00**

The Ford Motor Company of Canada, Limited

*FO190-20-10, 1905, 8 sh., signed by John S. Grey, grey border, rare **$250.00**

Francana Oil & Gas Ltd. (Can)

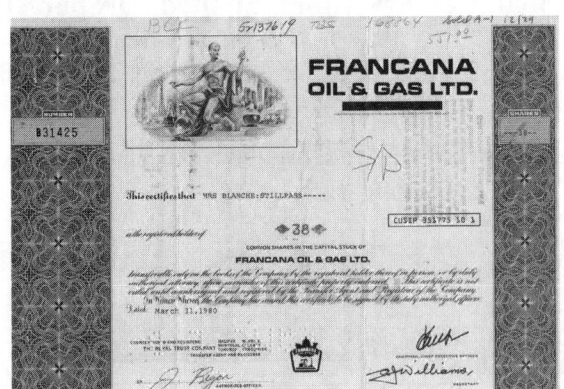

*FR70-20-10, 1980, v, 38 sh., B.A. Bank Note Ottawa, 12" x 8", green **$4.00**

Genesee Mining Company, Limited (ON)

*GE170-20-10, 1918, v, 125 sh., aqua **$5.00**

Genstar Limited (Can)

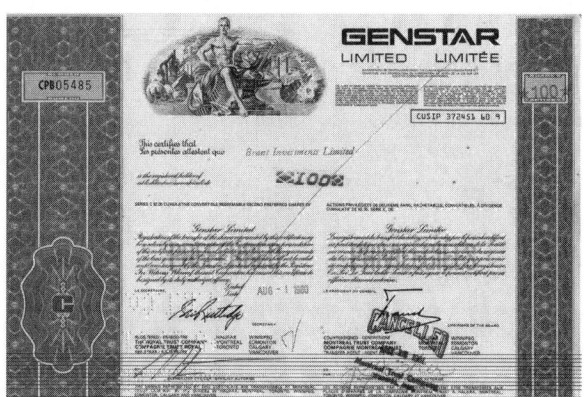

*GE210-40-10, 1980, v, 100 series C $2.35 convert. redeemable 2nd pref. shares, British American Bank Note Ottawa, 12" x 8", red $6.00

Grace Lake Gold Mines, Limited (ON no par)
GR100-20-10, 1928, 1,000 sh., brown border
. . . .$5.00

Grover Daley Mines, Ltd. (QC par $1)

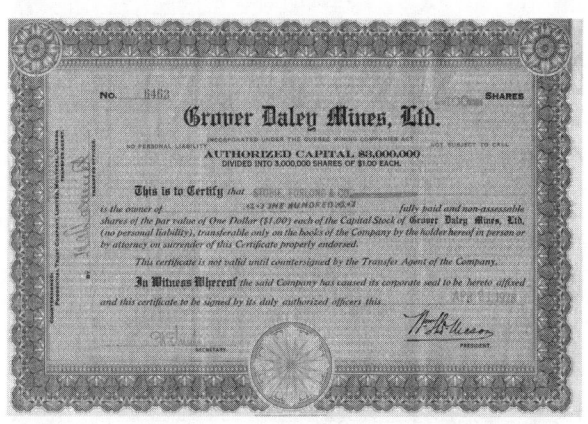

*GR290-20-10, 1928, 100 sh., British American Banknote Co. Ltd., Ottawa, 12" x 8-1/4", green
. . . .$5.00

Hudson Bay Mining and Smelting Co., Limited (Can no par)
HU150-30-10, 1946, v, 25 sh., on a less than 100 sh., certificate, brown $6.00

Imperial Oil Limited (Can. no par)
The company incorporated 16 refiners in southwestern Ontario in 1860. In 1896, the majority interest was sold to the Standard Oil group and in 1899, Imperial took over all of Standard's Canadian assets. 1907 marked the opening of the first gasoline station in Vancouver. With the discovery of the Leduc oil field in Alberta, Imperial became the largest producer of oil.

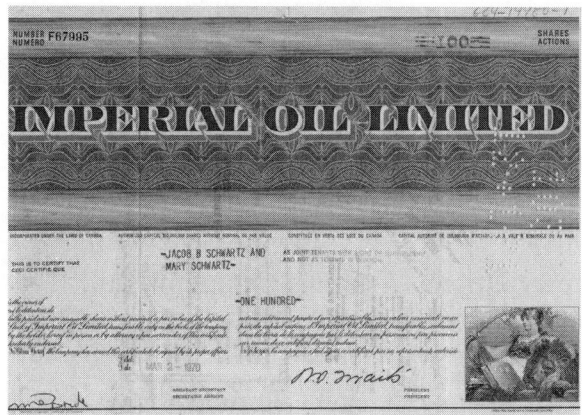

*IM210-50-10, 1970, v, 100 sh., Canadian Bank Note Company, Limited; 12" x 8", red . . .$4.00

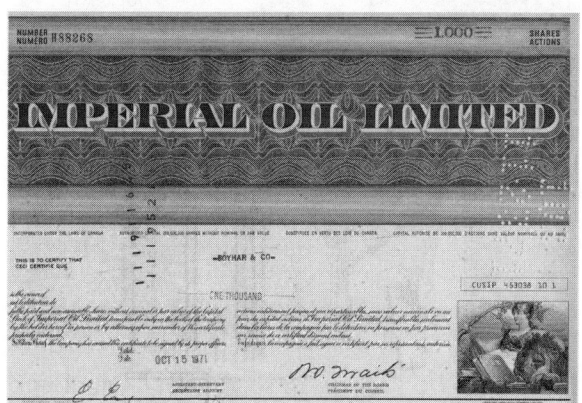

*IM210-50-15, 1971, v, 1,000 sh., signature variety, Canadian Bank Note Company, Limited; 12" x 8", red $5.00

It is generally assumed that only 5% of certificates survive to reach collectors.

IntelCom Group Inc. (Can no par)

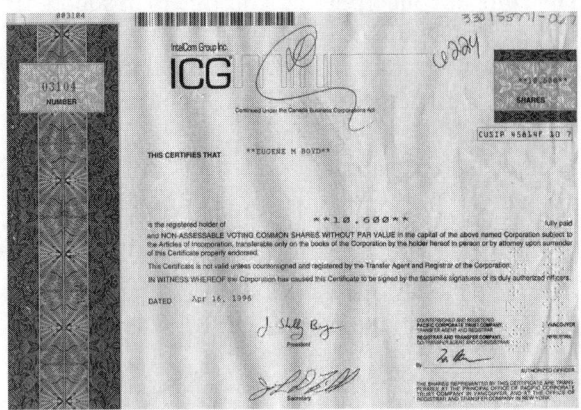

*IN240-20-10, 1996, 10,600 sh., certificate, Canadian Bank Note Co., 12" x 8", green .**$4.00**

International Asbestos Company, Ltd.

IN260-20-10, 1943, 100 sh., blue border ...**$12.00**

International Nickel Company of Canada Limited (Can)

*IN290-40-10, 1938, v, 10 sh. (no par), Can. Bank Note Co., 11-1/2" x 7-1/2", green........**$4.00**

The value of a stock certificate depends on:

- • rarity
- • the issuer
- • signatures
- • quality of engraving
- • overall appearance
- • condition
- • date of issue

*IN290-60-10, 1951, v, 10 $5 pref. sh., on a less than 100 sh., certificate, Canadian Bank Note Company, Limited; 11-1/2" x 7-1/2", brown **$4.00**

*IN290-70-10, 1939, v, 100 sh., $5 pref., Canadian Bank Note Company, 11-1/2" x 7-1/2", orange **$4.00**

*IN290-70-15, 1954, v, 100 sh., pref. stock (par $5), signature variety, Canadian Bank Note Co. Ltd., 11-1/2" x 7-1/2", orange **$4.00**

ISE Canadian Finance Limited (ON)

A subsidiary of International Standard Electric
Company (DE 1918)

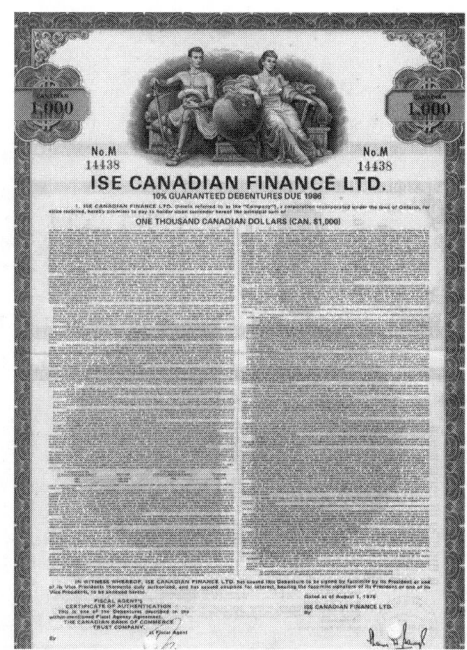

IS110-40-10, 1976, CAD $1,000 10% guaranteed
debenture due 1986, ABN, 9-1/4" x13-1/2",
green $4.00

The Keirstead & Mersereau
Fox and Fur Company (Can par $10)

KE170-20-10, 1914, v, 10 sh., orange $24.00

Kirkland Central Mining Company,
Limited (ON par $1)

KI190-20-10, 1926, v, i/u 2,500 sh., Canada
Litho, 11-1/4" x 9", grey border $7.00

KI190-30-10, 1937, i/u 500 sh., GOES, 11" x
8-1/2", green border $6.00

Kirkland Consolidated Mines, Limited
(ON 1934, par $1)

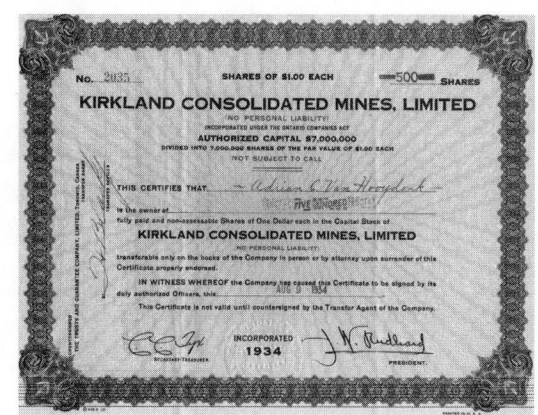

KI210-10-10, 1934, i/u 500 sh., GOES, 11" x
8-1/4", grey border $5.00

Kirkland-Eastern Gold Mines, Limited
(ON par $1)

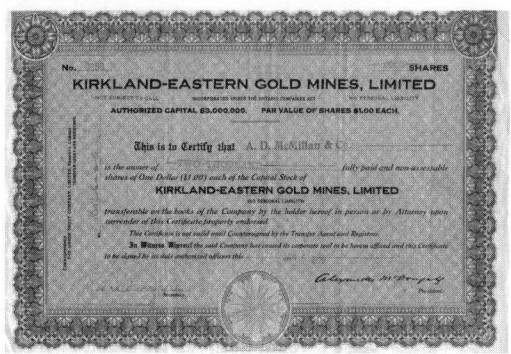

KI250-20-10, 1929, 2,000 sh., British American
Banknote Co. Limited, Ottawa, 12" x 8", green
border $8.00

Kitsault Eagle Silver Mines, Limited (BC)

KI310-20-10, 1928, v, 25 sh., green......**$20.00**

Kodiak Petroleums Ltd. (AB no par)

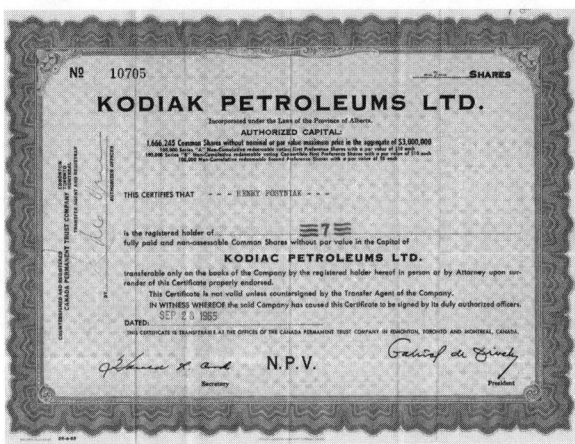

KO210-20-10, 1965, 7 sh., British American
Bank Note Company, Limited, 10-3/4" x 8", red
..................................**$3.00**

Letson Gold Mines Limited (ON)

LE160-20-10, 1915, v, 10 sh., green.......**$10.00**

UNLISTED TYPES & VARIETIES

Readers are welcome to contact the author
directly at:

Rainer Stahlberg
P.O. Box 1044
Rooseveltown, New York 13683

Lucky Cross Mines of Swastika, Limited (ON par $1)

LU190-30-10, 1911, v, 350 sh., green **$11.00**

Manitoba Basin Mining Co. Limited (Can no par)

MA160-20-10, 1935, 40 sh., orange........**$4.00**

Massey-Ferguson Limited (Can no par)

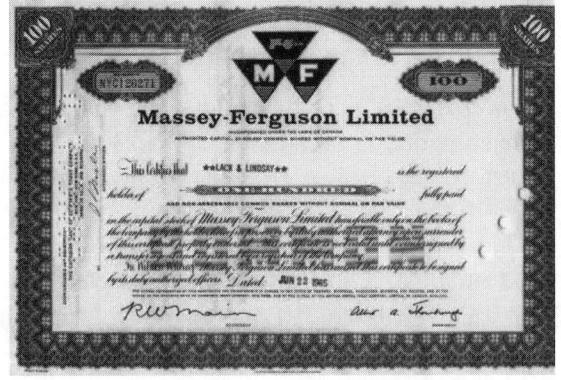

MA410-40-10, 1965, v - tractor, 100 sh., green
..................................**$5.00**
MA410-45-10, 1976, v, 100 sh., brown **$4.00**

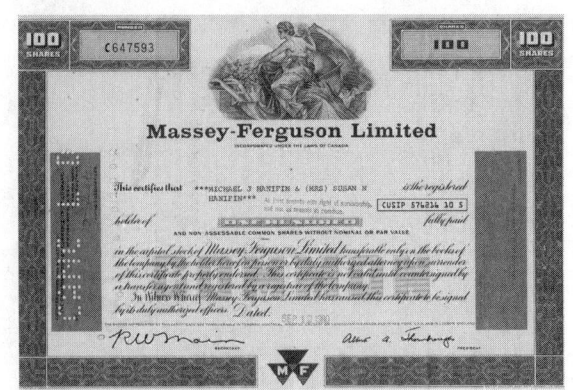

MA410-50-10, 1980, v, 100 sh., British American
Bank Note Company Limited, 12" x 8", green
..................................**$4.00**

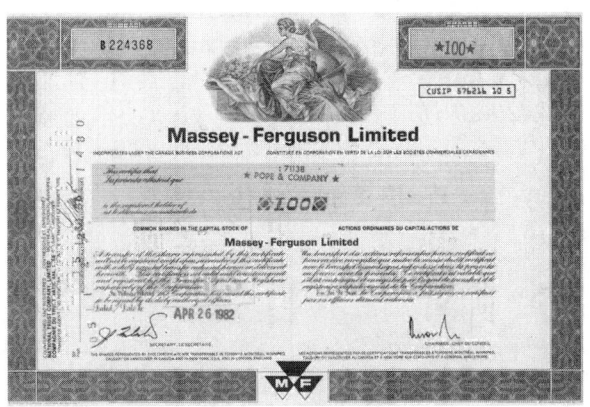

*MA410-55-10, 1982, v, 100 sh., British American Bank Note Company Limited, 12" x 8", blue
. . . .$4.00

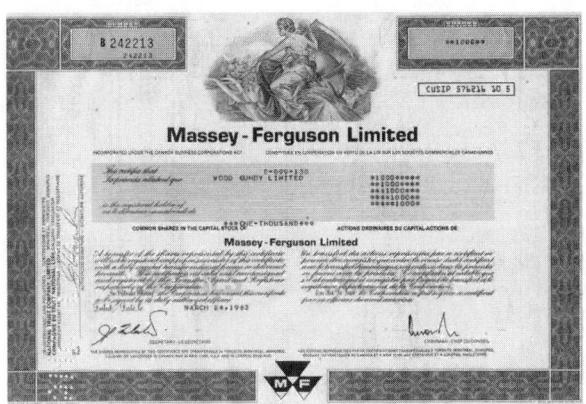

*MA410-60-10, 1983, v, 1,000 sh., British American Bank Note Inc., 12" x 8", blue $5.00

Melzer Mines Limited (ON no par)

*ME140-30-10, 1930, 5,000 sh., British American Banknote Co. Ltd., Ottawa, 11-3/4" x 8-1/2", orange $4.00

The Mexican Electric Light Company, Limited

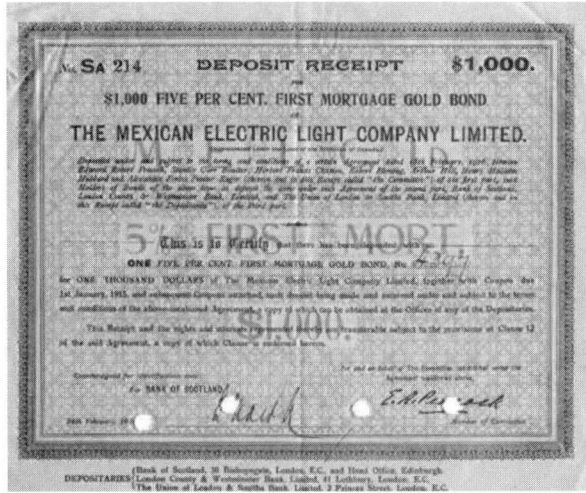

*ME470-20-10, 1916, $1,000 deposit receipt for 5% 1st mortgage gold bond, the bond issue was arranged in London, England; pink on green
. . . .$5.00

Millcrest Mining Company, Limited (ON par $1)

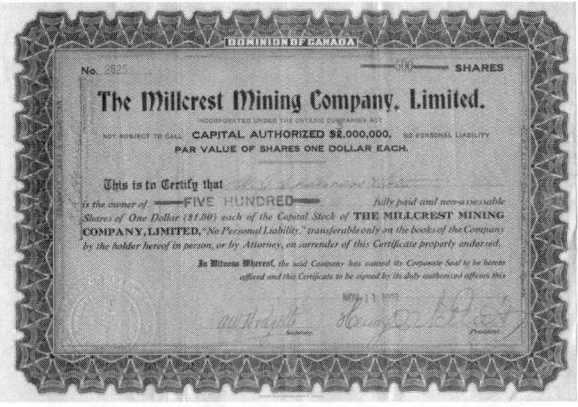

*MI190-20-10, 1927, 500 sh., British American Bank Note Co. Ottawa, 11" x 7-1/2", blue
. . . .$6.00

It is generally assumed that only 5% of certificates survive to reach collectors.

Minnetonka Gold Mines, Limited (BC)

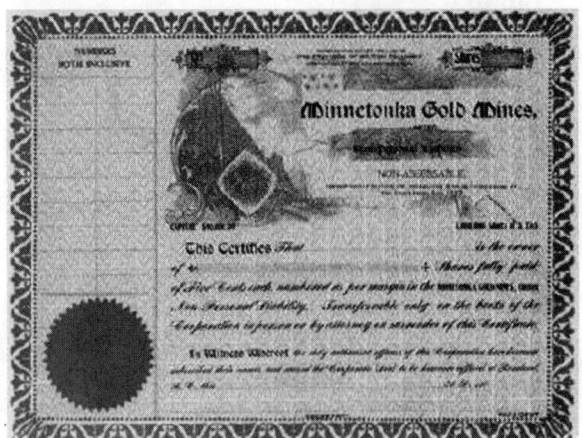

*MI270-20-10, 19xx, v, u/u certificate, brown border on blue $10.00

Monarch Gold Miners Syndicate Ltd. (MN par $1)

MO250-20-10, 1937, 500 sh., green. $4.00

City of Montreal

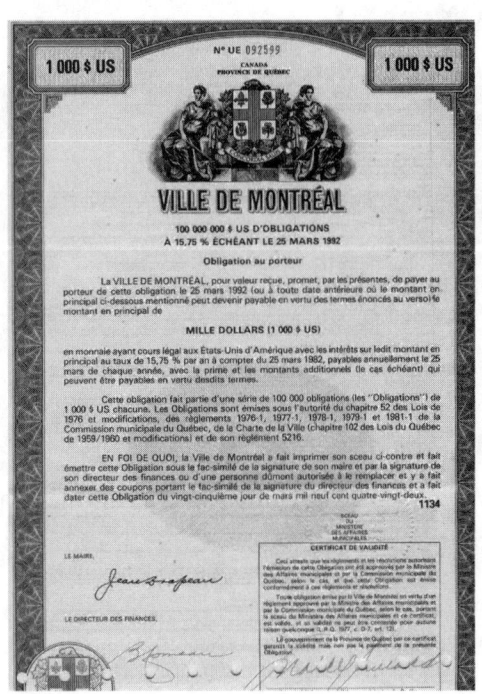

*MO390-50-10, 1982, v, $1,000 15.75% US debt, Yvon Boulanger Ltee., 9" x 12-3/4", green
. . . .$7.00

The Montreal and Boston Consolidated Mining and Smelting Company, Limited (ON par $5)

MO420-20-10, 1905, v, 100 sh., green $80.00

New-Era Walls Limited (Can.)

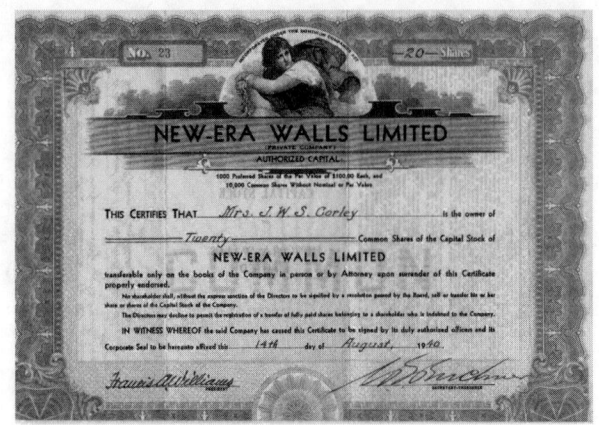

*NE170-20-10, 1940, v, i/u 20 sh. (no par), GOES, 12-1/4" x 9-1/2", orange. $3.00

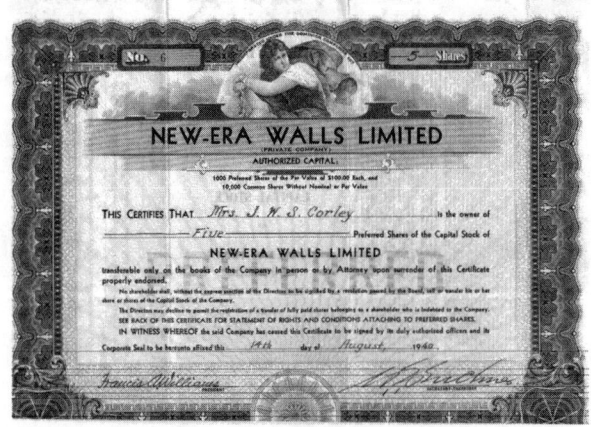

*NE170-30-10, 1940, v, i/u 5 pref. sh. (par $100), GOES, 12-1/4" x 9-1/2", green $3.00

Norcon Oil Company Limited (Can par $1)

NO320-20-10, 1930, v, 829 sh., green. $4.00

The value of a stock certificate depends on:
- rarity
- the issuer
- signatures
- quality of engraving
- overall appearance
- condition
- date of issue

The North Saskatchewan Land Company, Limited, Can.

*NO410-20-10, 1911, v, 10 sh. (par $100), British revenue imprint, blue $10.00

Okalta Oils Limited (Can par 90¢)

*OK80-30-10, 1960, v, 100 sh., rose $4.00

County of Oxford Province of Ontario

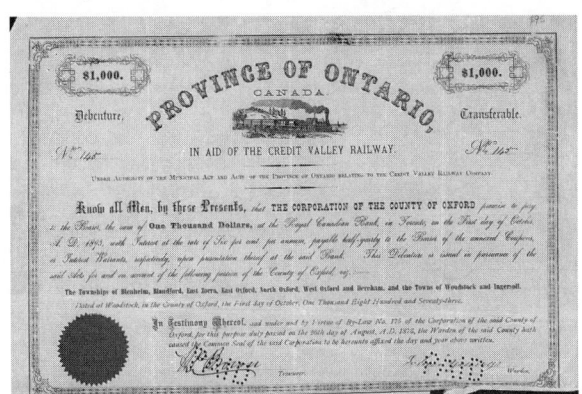

*OX80-20-10, 1873, v, $1,000 6% debenture in aid of the Credit Valley Railway, grey on white
...................................$25.00

Peel-Elder Limited (ON no par)

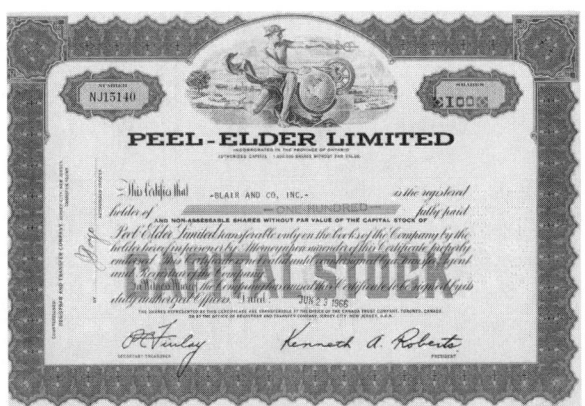

*PE130-30-10, 1966, v, 100 sh., British American Banknote Co., 12" x 8", brown $3.00

Peruvian Investment and Finance Limited (Can)

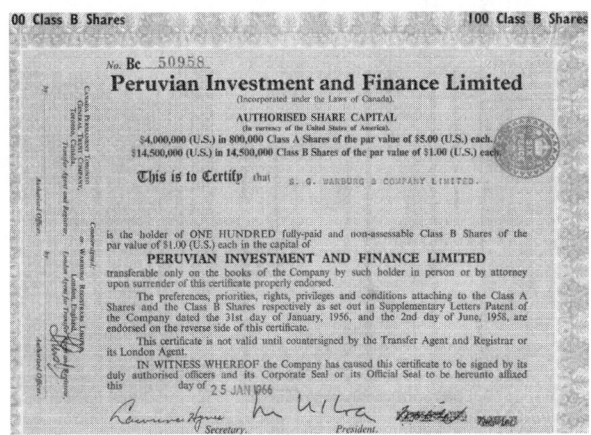

*PE430-30-10, 1966, 100 class B sh. (par US $1); Burrup, Mathieson & Co. Ltd., London, England; 11-1/2" x 6-3/4", orange $3.00

Pontiac Mines and Power Company, Limited (QC no par)

PO280-20-10, 1925, 100 sh., brown border
...................................$6.00

Robb-Montbray Mines Limited (ON par $1)

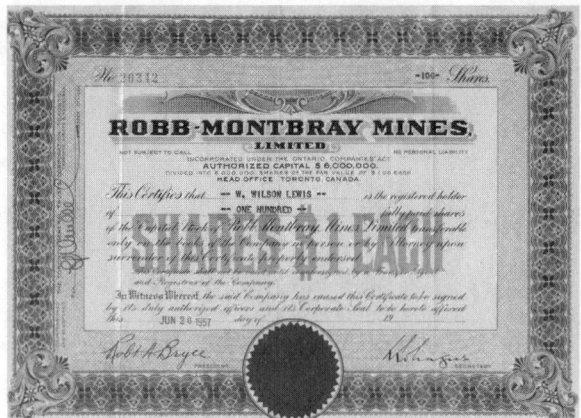

*RO80-20-10, 1957, 100 sh., Alexander & Cable Co., Ltd., Toronto; 12" x 8-1/4", blue border $3.00

St. Onge Land Development Company, Limited (Can)

*SA80-20-10, 19xx, v, u/u certificate (par $10), w/o imprint, 10-3/4" x 8-1/2", green......$3.00

The value of a stock certificate depends on:

- **rarity**
- **the issuer**
- **signatures**
- **quality of engraving**
- **overall appearance**
- **condition**
- **date of issue**

Ste. Anne Investment Corporation (QC 1926, no par)

*SA190-20-10, 19xx, u/u certificate, Charles F. Dawson Ltd. Montreal, 10-3/4" x 7-3/4", green $3.00

Ste. Anne Paper Company, Ltd. (QC 1925)

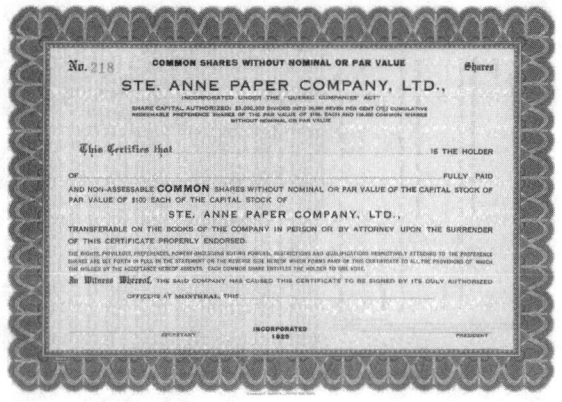

*SA210-20-10, 19xx, u/u certificate (no par), Charles F. Dawson Ltd, Montreal, 10-3/4" x 8", brown $3.00

*SA210-30-10, 19xx, u/u 7% pref. sh., certificate (par $100), Charles F. Dawson Ltd, Montreal, 10-3/4" x 8", green $3.00

San Antonio Land and Irrigation Company, Limited (Can par $100)

SA310-20-10, 1912, v, 10 sh., green.......**$20.00**

Sarnoil Limited (ON par $1)

*SA470-30-10, 1962, 1,000 sh., Northern Miner Press Limited, Toronto; 11-1/4" x 8-1/4", green
.................................**$3.00**

Province of Saskatchewan

SA570-50-10, 1976, v, $10,000 30 yr, 8.70% debenture green....................**$6.00**

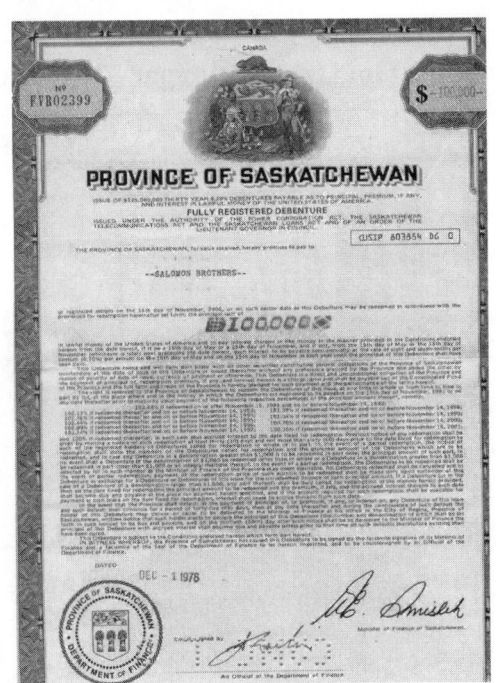

*SA570-55-10, 1976, v, $100,000 30 yr 8.70% debenture, Can. Banknote Co., 9-1/4" x 13", green..............................**$7.00**

The Saskatchewan Mining and Development Company, Limited (par $1)

SA620-30-10, 1911, v, 5,000 sh., green....**$10.00**

The Shawinigan Water and Power Company (par $100)

SH120-30-10, 1915, warrant to subs. for 1 sh., at a rate of $105.00 per sh., orange.........**$7.00**

Strange Lake Mining Co. Ltd. (NB no par)

*ST310-10-10, 19xx, specimen certificate, 10-1/2" x 8-1/4", green **$3.00**

Texas Prairie Lands Limited (Can par $100)

TE190-20-10, 1913, v, 10 sh., green **$7.00**

Trans Empire Oils Ltd. (Can 1950, par $1.25)

*TR240-20-10, 1955, v, 25 sh., British American Banknote Co., 12" x 8", green **$4.00**
TR240-30-10, 1956, v, 100 sh., green **$4.00**

Vancouver Kraft Company Limited (BC)

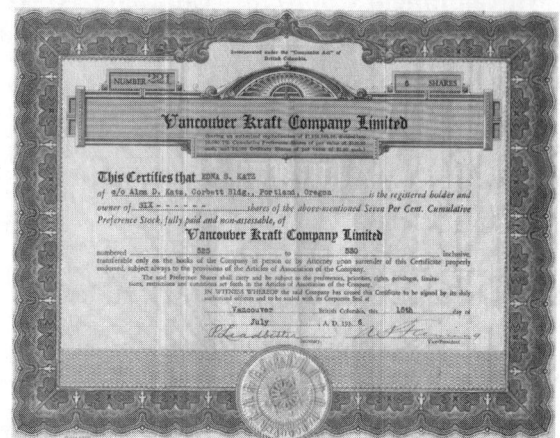

*VA110-20-10, 1936, 42 sh. (par $1), GOES, 11" x 8-1/2", brown border................$3.00

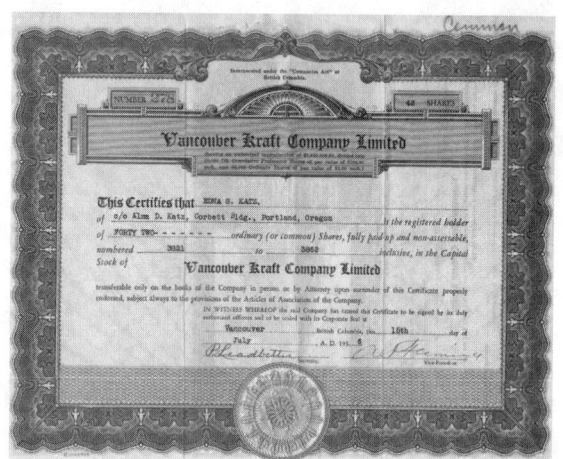

*VA110-30-10, 1936, 6 sh. (par $100), GOES, 11" x 8-1/2", green border................$4.00

Varity Corporation

Successor to Massey-Ferguson.

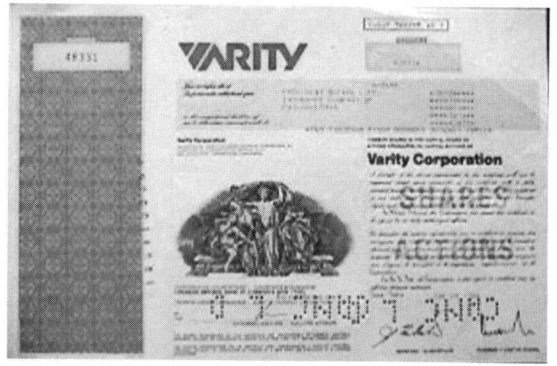

*VA150-20-10, 1988, v, 2,873 sh., text in English and French, red....................$4.00

Victoria Baseball and Athletic Company Limited

VI80-20-10, 1952, 1 sh. (par $25), green border
....$21.00

West Canadian Oil & Gas Ltd. (CAN par $1.25)

*WE190-30-10, 1958, v, 100 sh., British American Bank Note Co. Ltd. Ottawa, 12-1/4" x 8-1/4", blue................................$4.00

Western Tin Mines Limited

WE220-30-10, 1965, v.................$5.00

Westricia Gold Syndicate (par $10) Toronto

WE250-20-10, 1937, 10 units, brown border
....$6.00

Wettlaufer Lorrain Silver Mines, Limited (ON par $1)

*WE280-20-10, 1912, 500 sh., The Broun-Green Co., N.Y., 11-1/2" x 8-1/2", brown border
....$8.00

Cayman Island

Mariculture, Limited

*MA80-20-10, 1970, v, 200 sh., revenue stamp affixed, green $36.00

Ceylon

Co-Operative Federal Bank of Ceylon, Ltd. (par 100 Rupiahs)

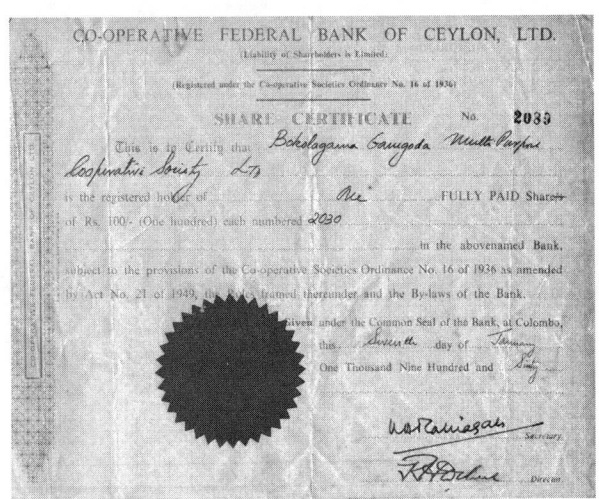

*CO180-20-10, 1960, 1 sh., w/o imprint, 9-1/4" x 7-1/4", l. green $3.00

Chile

Compania Salitrera de Tarapaga y Antofagasta, Santiago

*S160-30-10, 1934, v, 1 sh., w. coupons, Universo, 11-1/4" x 7-1/4", blue................$7.00

China

Government of the Chinese Republic

90-40-10, 1913, v, £20 reorganization loan, orange $60.00

110-40-10, 1914, Republique de China, Emprunt Industriel du Gouvernement, 5% Obligation de 500 F, brown $45.00

*150-40-10, 1919, v, £100 Chinese Government Treasury note (Vickers loan), British revenue imprint, green....................$37.00

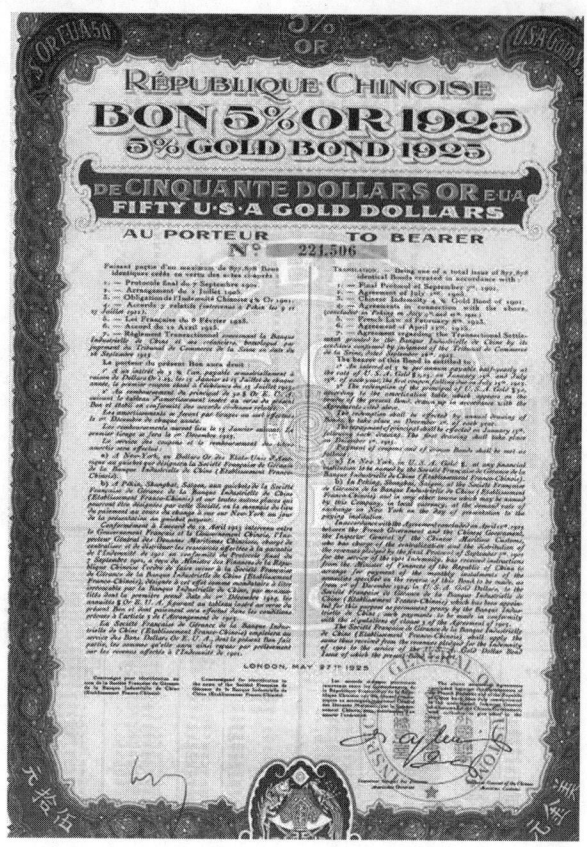

*200-30-10, 1925, Republic of China, US $50 5% gold bearer bond w. coupons, used to reorganize the debt from the Boxer rebellion and secured by Maritime Customs Revenues and internal Chinese salt taxes, brown on yellow.....**$50.00**

320-35-10, 1926, v, $5 (Canton Currency) Second Nationalist Government Lottery Loan of the 15th year of the Republic, 7-1/4" x 5", deep lilac
..................................**$10.00**

320-40-10, 1938, The 27th Year Gold Loan of the Republic of China, US $5, blue w. coupons
..................................**$10.00**

320-50-10, 1938, The 27th Year Gold Loan of the Republic of China, US $10, brown w. coupons
..................................**$15.00**

340-20-10, 1940, The 29th Year Gold Loan of the Republic of China, US $10, first issue, reddish
..................................**$50.00**

360-30-10, 1940, v, US $5 Reconstruction gold loan w. coupons, in Chinese, blue **$5.00**

360-40-10, 1940, v, US $10 Reconstruction gold loan w. coupons, in Chinese, purple......**$5.00**

Banque Industrielle de Chine

*BA50-30-10, 1913, v, 500 F bearer sh. w. coupons, text in French and Chinese, French revenue rubber stamp, 12-3/4" x 16-3/4", beige and grey border **$44.00**

Central Bank of Manchukuo

CI60-30-10, 1932, 100 sh., 10,000 Yuan, black and tan................................**$45.00**

Lung Tsing-U-Hai Railway

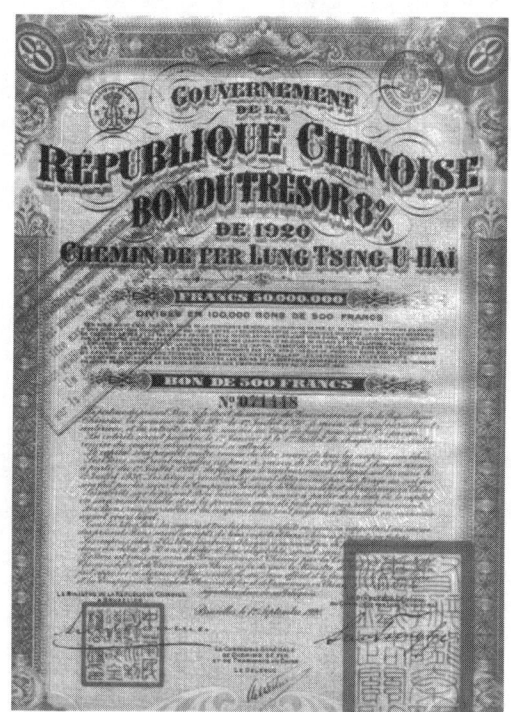

*L120-30-10, 1920, v, 500 Franc 8% bond w. coupons, Brussels, 10-1/2" x 15", brown.**$20.00**

LU120-40-10, 1921, 50 Francs 8% bond, French, 9-1/2" x 14", green $15.00

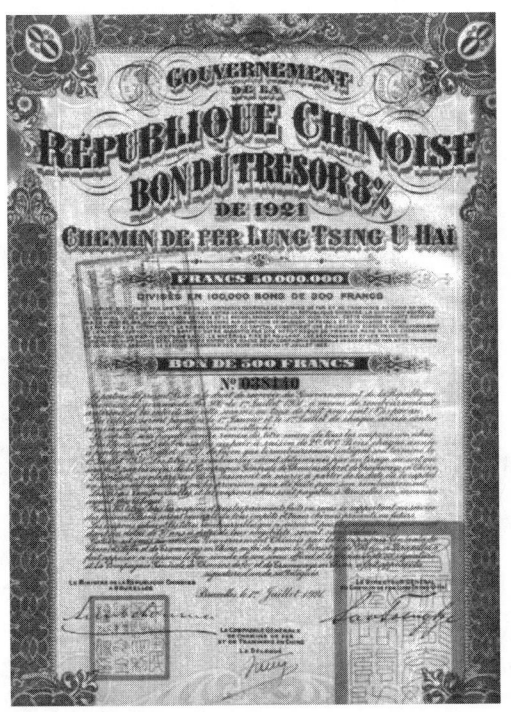

*L120-50-10, 1921, 500 Francs, 8% bond w. coupons, Brussels, 10-1/2" x 15, green $20.00

Shanghai-Nanking Railway

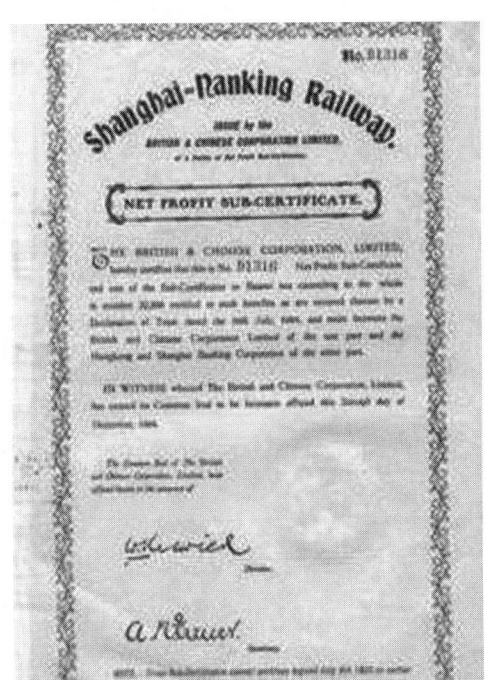

*SM110-30-10, 1904, net profit sub-certificate, grey $5.00

Sinkiang Province
SI140-30-10, 1941, v, 25 Yuan Military Construction Loan Bond, Chinese and Uighur, lilac
. . . .$45.00

**Tientsin-Pukow Railway,
Chinese Government**

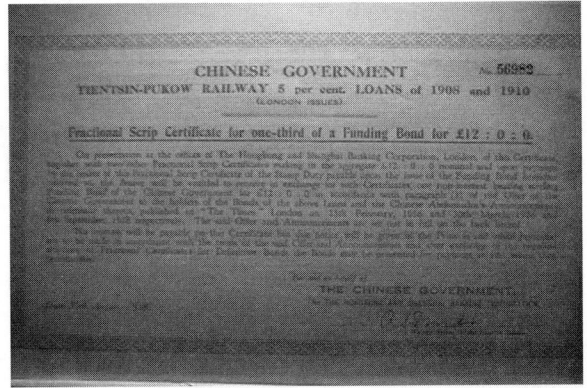

*TI90-30-10, 1938, Fractional Scrip Certificate for a funding bond for £12-1/3 on the 5% loans of 1908 and 1910 (London Issues), light red
. . . .$25.00

Colombia

Republic of Colombia
60-30-10, 1940, v, $1,000 3-1/2% external sinking fund bond due 1970, in English, green. . .$15.00

This catalog has listings in an alphabetical format. The reason is simple: Companies diversify as they grow. For example, the Canadian Pacific Railway company recently split into five companies. They represent the railway, hotels, shipping, airline, and petroleum interests of the company. During World War II, the Singer sewing machine company made guns and other defense-related equipment, so where should we list it? It's far easier to use a strict alphabetical order, rather than to confuse the reader with topical classifications.

Costa Rica

The Costa Rica Railway Company, Limited

Keith Minor used the proceeds of a £650,000 loan to lay a 102 mile railroad. The land grant for the adjoining lands formed the basis for the United Fruit Company.

CO160-20-10, 1890, v - Bernardo Soto, £100 second debenture 6%, 13" x 16", brown **$35.00**

Cuba

Compania Azucarera Vertientes-Camagüey de Cuba

AZ70-20-10, 1951, v, 76 sh., on a less than 100 sh., certificate, orange **$20.00**
AZ70-30-10, 1961, v, 100 sh., Spanish-English certificate, ABN, blue **$10.00**
AZ70-35-10, 1970, v, 100 sh., green. **$15.00**

Banco Español de la Isla de Cuba

BA160-20-10, 1925, v, 49 centavo Certicado de Agreedor, brown. **$50.00**

Banco Territorial de Cuba

BA260-40-10, 1911, v, bond, green **$25.00**

Cuba International Oil Company (par US $1 gold)

CU160-30-10, 1917, v, 500 sh., green **$42.00**

Ferrocarriles Consolidados de Cuba - Consolidated Railways of Cuba

FE90-40-10, 1936, v, 100 pref. sh., English and Spanish, green **$23.00**

Compañia Minera "El Tesoro de Fiñales"

MI80-20-10, 1915, v, 1 sh., orange **$32.00**

Trinidad Industrial S.A., Propietaria de la Fabrica de Cigarros "EVA" (par 100 pesos)

TR90-20-10, 1943, v, 1 sh., blue **$20.00**

Czechoslovakia

State Loan

50-40-10, 1922, v, £100 series E, text in English and Czech, British revenue imprint, olive border
. . . .**$10.00**

D

Denmark

**Chr. Jensens Møbelsnedkeri, Haslev a/s,
Haslev**

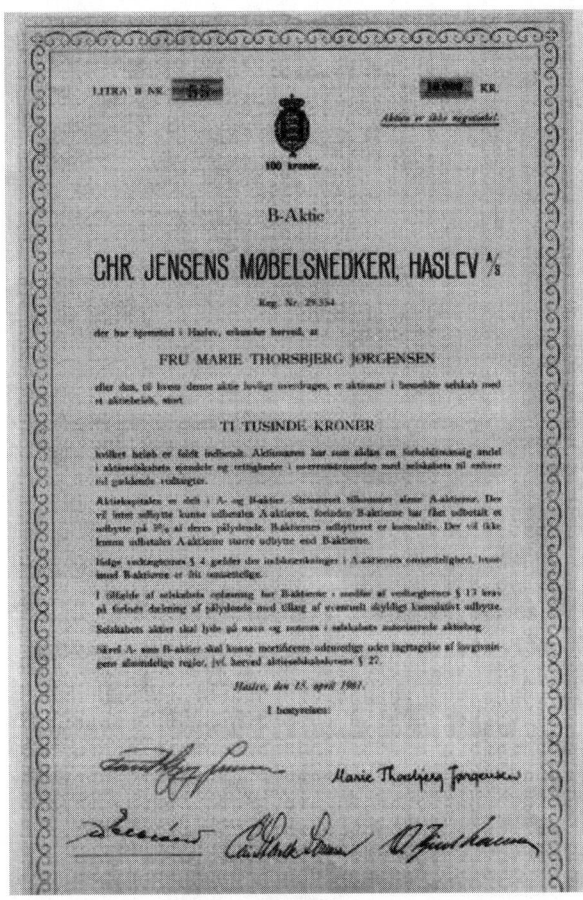

*JE90-30-10,*1961, 10,000 Kroner series B sh.,
  8-1/2" x 13-1/2", brown on beige **$7.00**

E

Ecuador

Compañia Azucarera Valdez S.A., Guayaquil

*AZ90-20-10, 1942, v, 1 sh. (par 1,000 Sucres), Capital 10,000,000 S, Ecuadorian revenue stamps, Imprenta Papeleria "Mercurio" Guayaquil, 14-1/2" x 11", light blue **$4.00**

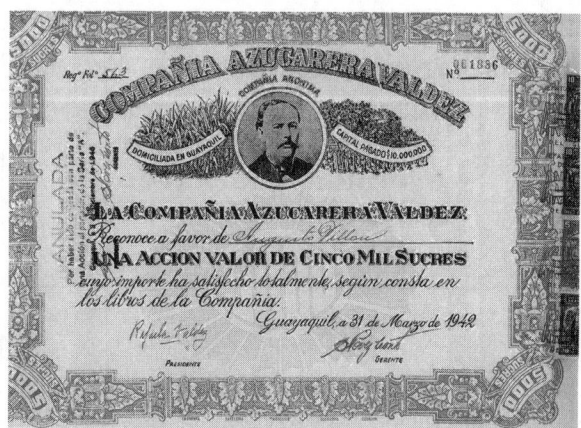

*AZ90-25-10, 1942, v, 1 sh. (par 5,000 Sucres), Capital 10,000,000 S, Ecaudorian revenue stamps, Imprenta Papeleria "Mercurio" Guayaquil, 13-3/4" x 11", green **$4.00**

*AZ90-35-10, 1946, v, 1 series A sh. (par 10,000 Sucres), capital 20,000,000 S, Ecaudorian revenue stamps, w/o imprint, 13-1/4" x 9-1/4", green **$3.00**

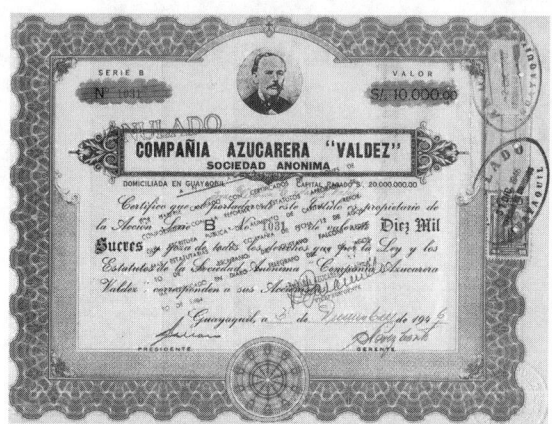

*AZ90-40-10, 1946, v, 1 series B sh. (par 10,000 Sucres), capital 20,000,000 S, Ecuadorian revenue stamps, w/o imprint, 13-1/4" x 9-1/4", brown **$3.00**

*AZ90-50-10, 1949, v, 1 series C bearer sh. (par 10,000 S), capital 40,000,000 S, Ecuadorian revenue stamps, w/o imprint, 12-1/4" x 9-1/2", blue **$3.00**

Compañia Continental de Inversiones S.A., Guayaquil

*CO80-20-10, 1955, v, 1 series A bearer sh. (par 1,000 S), Ecuadorian revenue stamps, w/o imprint, 11" x 10-1/4", green **$3.00**

Compania Minera Pillzhum
MI190-20-10, 1896, v, 5 Sucre certificate, brown **$8.00**

Egypt

Crédit Foncier Égyptien S.A.

*CR90-40-10, 1951, £E10 bearer bond, text in French and Arabic, green-blue **$5.00**

The Egyptian Delta Light Railways, Limited
EG110-30-10, 1901, v, bearer warrant for 1 preference sh. w. coupons, British revenue imprint, blue **$7.00**

Land Bank of Egypt (par £5)

*LA70-20-10, 1905, v, 1 sh., warrant, text in English, French and Arabic, multicolored **$9.00**

Société de Nouveautés BENZOIN

*NO110-20-10, 1951, v, 5 bearer shares, text in French and Arabic, red **$6.00**

Shepheard's & Egyptian Hotels Company
SH90-20-10, 1959, 25 sh. **$14.00**

Travaux d'Irrigation du Gouvernement Égyptien Assouan et Assiout

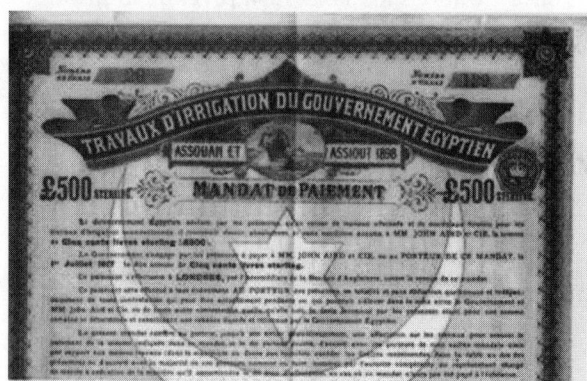

*TR110-40-10, 1898, v, £500 Mandat de Paiment, red **$10.00**

It is generally assumed that only 5% of certificates survive to reach collectors.

S.A. de Wadi Kom-Ombo, Cairo

*WA70-20-10, 1905, v, 1 bearer sh. (par £4) w. coupons, green **$14.00**

*WA70-40-10, 1944, v, 10 bearer sh. (par £4) w. coupons, blue **$14.00**

F

Finland

Nokia Corporation

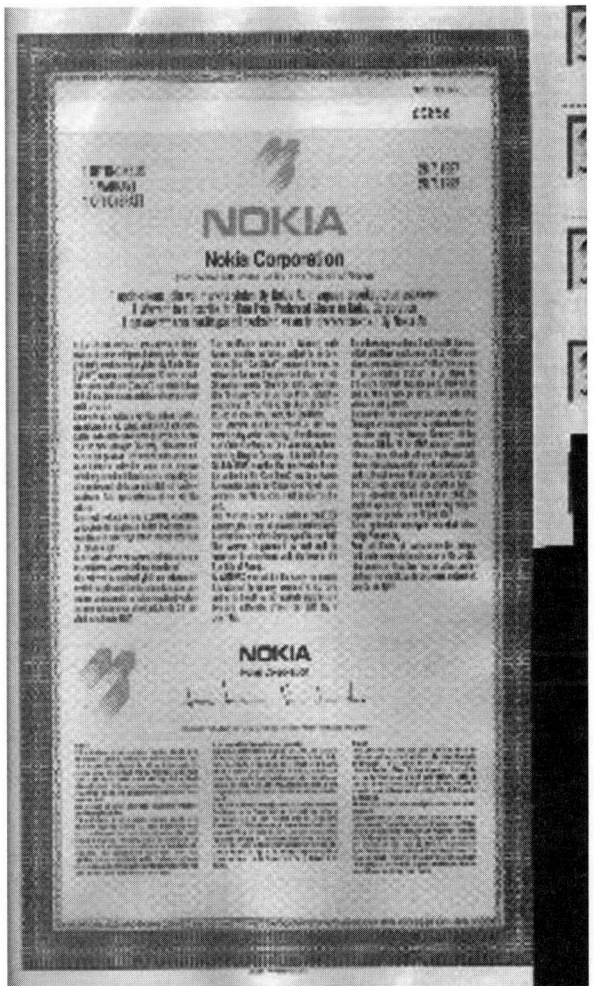

*NO190-30-10, 19??, 1 bearer sh. w. coupons, text
Finnish-Swedish-English, blue..........$5.00

UNLISTED TYPES & VARIETIES

Readers are welcome to contact the author directly at:

Rainer Stahlberg
P.O. Box 1044
Rooseveltown, New York 13683

Suomen Vientiluotto Oy

Finlands Exportkredit AB, Finnish Export Credit
Ltd. was created to foster export of Finnish
goods and services.

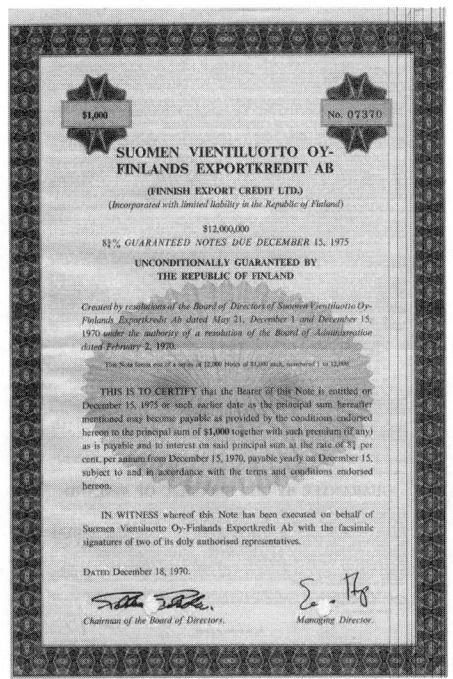

*SU230-30-10, 1970, $1,000 8-3/4% guar. notes
due 1975, Thomas de la Rue & Company, Limited; 8-1/2" x 12", blue.................$3.00

France

Société Française des Aciers Basset S.A., Paris

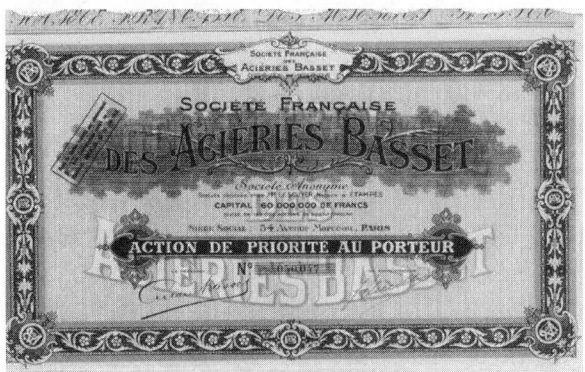

*AC60-20-10, 1921, 1 pref. bearer sh., blue
...................................$3.00

Société Algérienne de Développement et d'Expansion, SOCALDEX, Paris

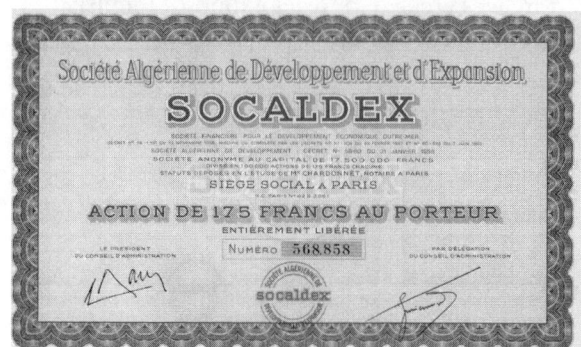

AL100-20-10, ND, 175 F bearer sh. w. coupons, Imprimerie Spéciale de Banque, 10-1/2" x 6-1/2", green $3.00

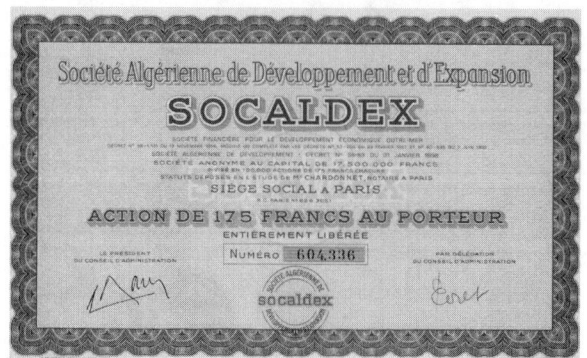

AL100-20-15, ND, 175 F bearer sh., w. coupons, signature variety, Imprimeria Spéciale de Banque, 10-1/2" x 6-1/2", green $3.00

Compagnie d'Alimentation d'Installations Frigorifiques S.A., Paris

AL130-20-10, 1920, v, 250 F bearer sh., w. coupons, w. French revenue rubber stamps, Imprimerie Richard, Paris, 12-3/4" x 8-3/4", grey border on green $3.00

S.A. Ancien Établissements Caffort Frères

AN70-20-10, 1923, 100 F bearer stock, green $5.00

Anciens Etablissements A. Binet S.A., Paris

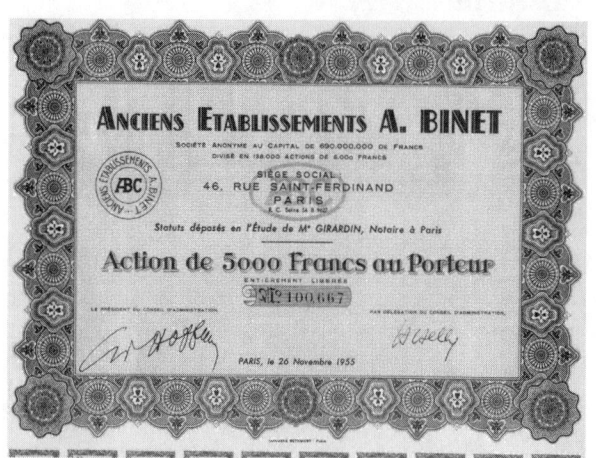

AN120-20-10, 1955, 5,000 F bearer sh. w. coupons, Imprimerie Bethmont - Paris; 10-3/4" x 8", maroon border $3.00

Anciens Établissements G.-G. Bomier, Boulogne-Billancourt (Seine)

AN150-20-10, 1959, v, 5,000 F bearer sh. w. coupons, Fortin Paris-Nevers, 10-1/2" x 7-3/4", blue on pink $3.00

> ***It is generally assumed that only 5% of certificates survive to reach collectors.***

Anciens Etablissements H. Desmidt & Cie. S.A., Paris

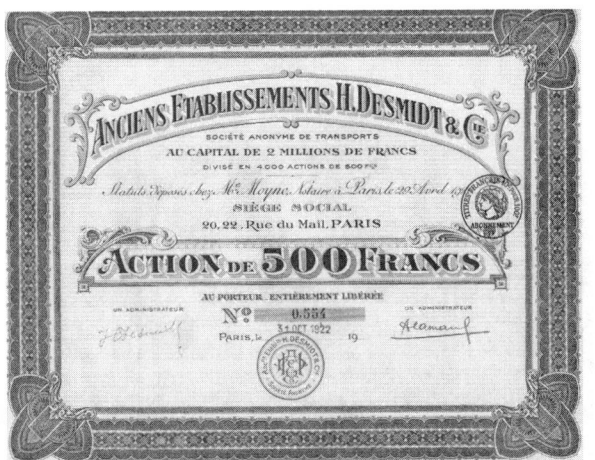

AN180-20-10, 1922, 500 F bearer sh. with coupons, French revenue rubber stamp, Imp. G. Michel, Paris; 12" x 9-1/2", blue **$3.00**

S.A. des Anciens Établissements Ducos & Sarrat, Bordeaux

AN210-20-10, 1926, 100 F bearer stock w. coupons, blue on green. **$3.00**

S.A. des Anciens Établissements LaCloche Frères, Paris

AN300-20-10, 1928, 100 F bearer sh., brown **$3.00**

S.A. des Anciens Etablissements Marcel Olivier Elbeuf

Drapery manufacturer.

AN380-20-10, 1929, v, 100 F bearer sh., brown frame. **$4.00**

S.A. Anciens Etablissements Ruelle et Cie. et Leduc Réunis, Blanc Misseron, Quiévrechain (Nord)

AN410-20-10, 1923, 100 F bearer sh. w. coupons, Imp. Louis Jeanrot - Paris; 12-1/4" x 8-1/4", black and pale orange border **$3.00**

Anglo-French Company for the Manufacture of Sperm Oil

AN460-20-10, 1857, v, 1 bearer sh. (par 100 F), text in English and French, brown **$100.00**

Societe des Appareils Boirault S.A., Paris

*AP100-20-10,*ND, 100 F bearer sh., w. coupons, w. French revenue rubber stamp, Ch. Crabbe, Paris; 10-3/4" x 8-3/4", green. **$3.00**

Société d'Applications et de Fabrications Industrielles S.A., S.A.F.I., Puteaux (Seine)

AP150-20-10, ND (1956), 3,500 F bearer sh. w. coupons, Imprimerie des Papiers de Valeurs - (Bernard Frères Paris); 10-3/4" x 8", blue border
. . . .$3.00

Societe d'Applications Techniques S.A., Paris

AP180-20-10, ND, 300 F bearer stock w. coupons, Imp. Fano-Emonet - Paris; 10-1/2" x 7", blue on pink border $3.00

UNLISTED TYPES & VARIETIES

Readers are welcome to contact the author directly at:

Rainer Stahlberg
P.O. Box 1044
Rooseveltown, New York 13683

Société Ardennaise de Forge (La Manestamp) S.A., Paris

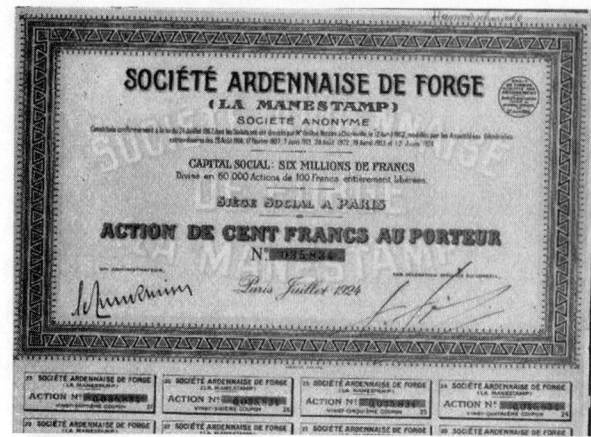

AR70-20-10, 1924, 100 F bearer sh., green
. . . .$3.00

Atlas Aviation Lyon

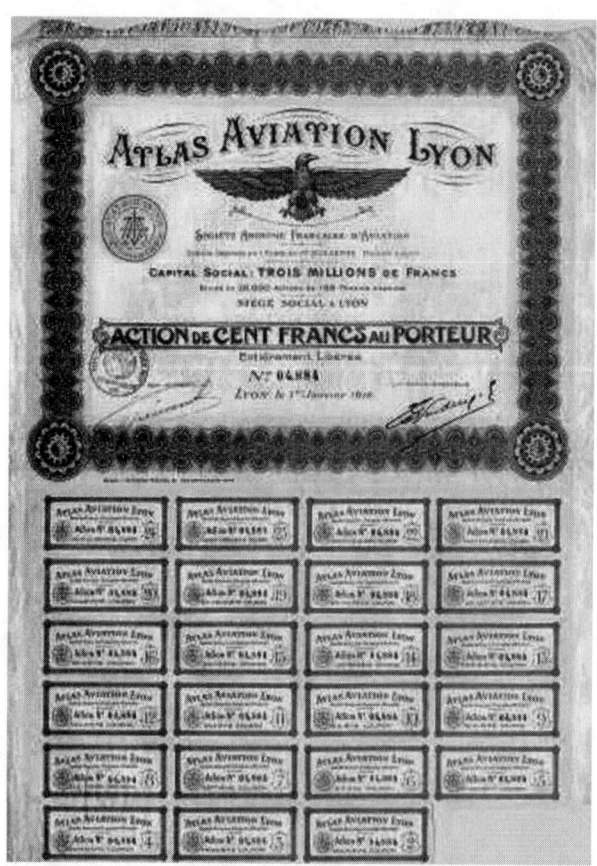

AT100-20-10, 1918, v, 100F bearer stock, green
. . . .$60.00

L'Azote Français S.A., Paris

AZ80-20-10, ND, 100F bearer sh. certificate w. coupons, Marcel Charles Verneau & cie., Paris; 12-1/4" x 8-1/4", blue on beige.........**$3.00**

Compagnie Générale de Boulets et Agglomérants S.A., Paris

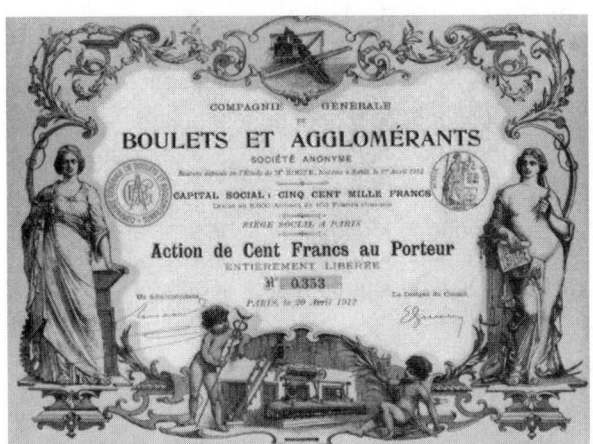

BO90-20-10, 1912, v, 100 F bearer sh., light brown **$12.00**

This catalog has listings in an alphabetical format. The reason is simple, companies diversify as they grow. For example, the Canadian Pacific Railway company recently split into five companies. They represent the railway, hotels, shipping, airline and petroleum interests of the company. During World War II, the Singer sewing machine company made guns and other defense-related equipment, so where should we list it? It's far easier to use a strict alphabetical order, rather than to confuse the reader with topical classifications.

Société Bretonne d'Études Miniéres et d'Exploitation des Mines de Pontpéan S.A., Saint Brieuc

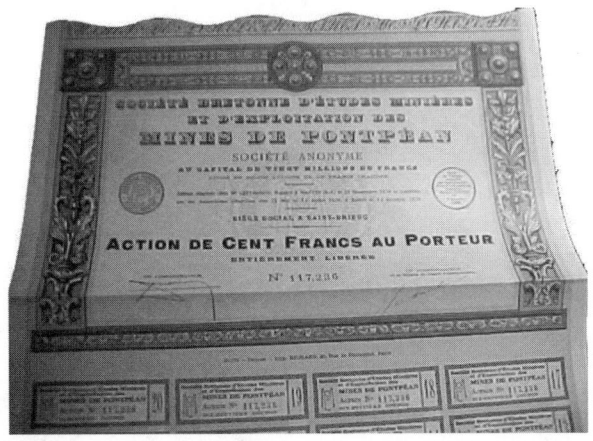

BR100-20-10, ND, 100 F bearer sh., brown
.................................**$3.00**

Société Calaisienne des Pates a Papier S.A.

CA60-20-10, 1961, 100 new F bearer sh., red on yellow.........................**$3.00**

Carrieres et Scieries de Bourgogne Févre & Cie. S.A.

CA100-20-10, 1955, v, 5,000 F bearer stock, brown
.................................**$3.00**

S.A. des Casinos de Royan

CA130-20-10, 19??, 125F bearer stock, blue
.................................**$3.00**

Société Centrale des Banques de Province, Paris

*CE100-20-10, 1926, 125 F class B bearer sh. w. coupons, brown $3.00

S.A. des Chantiers Navals de l'Ouest, Paris

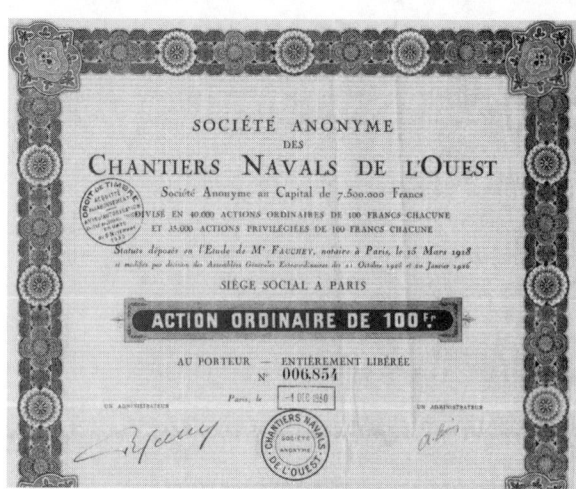

*CH100-20-10, 1930, 100 F bearer sh. w. coupons, w. French revenue rubber stamp, Breger Ainé et Cie. Paris; 10-1/2" x 9-1/2", brown border on light beige $3.00

UNLISTED TYPES & VARIETIES

Readers are welcome to contact the author directly at:

Rainer Stahlberg
P.O. Box 1044
Rooseveltown, New York 13683

Compagnie des Charbonnages d'Ekatherine S.A.

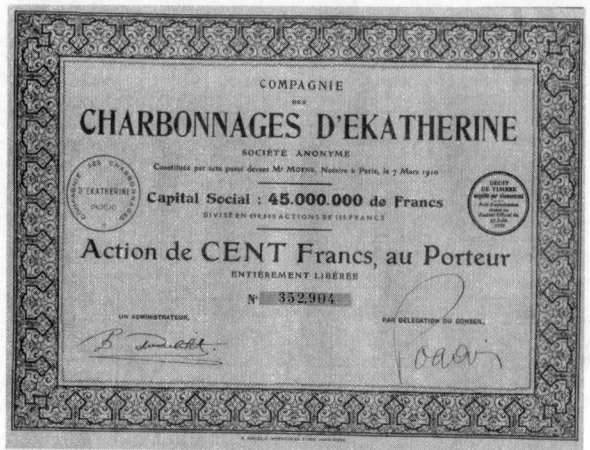

*CH140-20-10, 1929, 100 F bearer sh. w. coupons, P. Forveille Imprimeur de Titres, Paris; 12" x 8-1/2", blue on grey $3.00

Charbonnages de Millau, Millau

CH180-20-10, 1927, v, 100 F bearer sh., w. coupons, 12" x 8-1/2", grey border $10.00

Société des Charbonnages de Ninh-Bihn S.A.

French Indochina coal company.

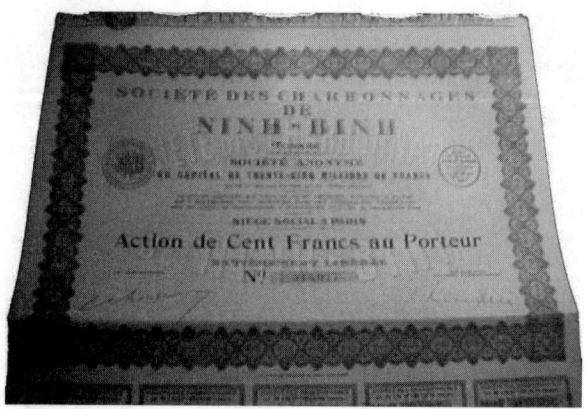

*CH210-20-10, 1929, 100 F bearer stock w. coupons, brown $4.00

Charbonnages de la Seo de Urgel
Concessions "Minerva" and "Eliga."

*CH260-20-10, 1893, v, bearer sh., brown
..................................$12.00

Charbons Actifs & Procédés Èdouard Urbain S.A., Paris

*CH300-30-10, 1927, v, 250 F series A bearer stock, red..........................$3.00

Chargeurs Réunis S.A., Compagnie Française de Navigation a Vapeur, Le Havre

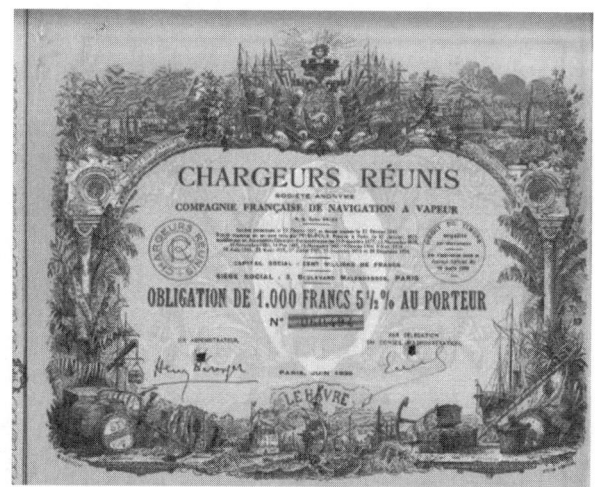

*CH340-40-10, 1939, v, 1,000 F 5-1/2% bearer bond w. coupons, brown $10.00

S.A. Chemin de Fer de la Basse-Egypte
CH400-30-10, 1896, v, 500 F bearer pref. stock, blue on brown.......................$7.00

Chemin de Fer et Bassin Houiller du Var S.A., Paris

*CH430-40-10, 1873, v, 100 F 6% bearer bond, green..............................$7.00

It is generally assumed that only 5% of certificates survive to reach collectors.

S.A. Chemin de Fer d'Intérét Local de L'Hérault, Paris

*CH550-30-10, 1890, v, preferred bearer sh., grey on green $4.00

Compagnie de Chemin de Fer d'Intéret Local Poitiers a Saumur S.A.

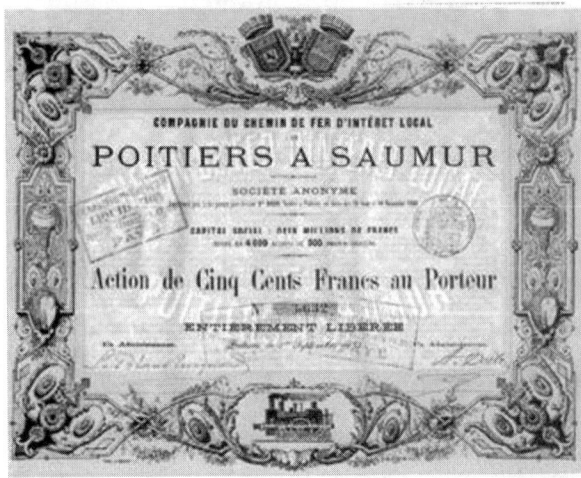

*CH580-20-10, 1873, v, 500 F bearer sh., grey on blue $23.00

Compagnie du Chemin de Fer du Nord

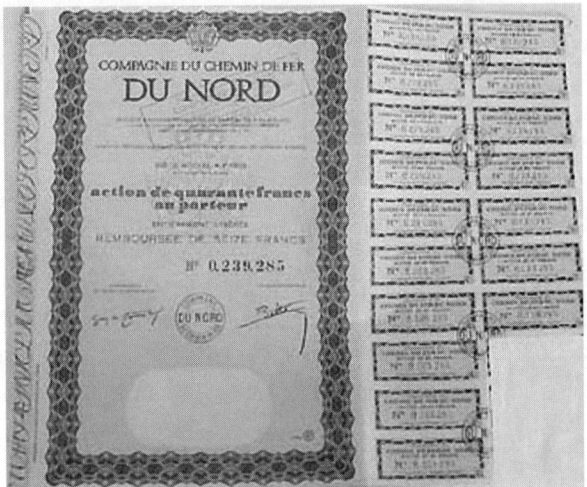

*CH630-30-10, 1965, v, bearer sh., w. coupons, purple $4.00

S.A. Chemin de Fer Transcaucasien

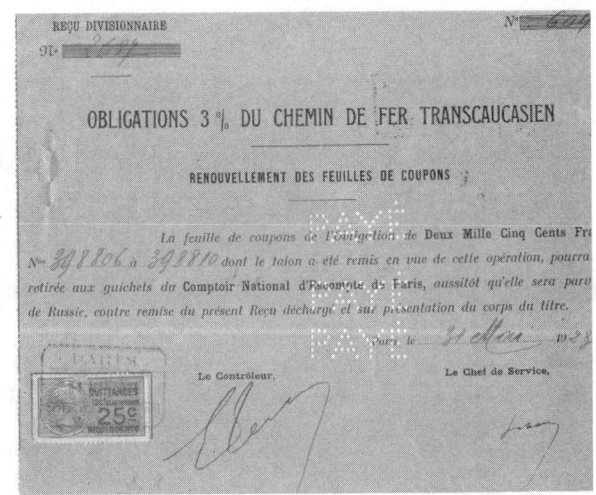

*CH700-40-10, 1923, 2,500 F 3% receipt for coupons, 8-1/4" x 6-1/4", grey paper $2.00

This catalog has listings in an alphabetical format. The reason is simple: Companies diversify as they grow. For example, the Canadian Pacific Railway company recently split into five companies. They represent the railway, hotels, shipping, airline, and petroleum interests of the company. During World War II, the Singer sewing machine company made guns and other defense-related equipment, so where should we list it? It's far easier to use a strict alphabetical order, rather than to confuse the reader with topical classifications.

Compagnie des Chemins de Fer Garantis des Colonies Françaises, Cái dúong lúa ó Saigon di Mýtho, Paris

CH770-30-10, 1901, v, 500 F bearer sh., green
.... $15.00

CH770-50-10, 1901, v, 500 F bearer bond, brown on yellow $25.00

The value of a stock certificate depends on:

- rarity
- the issuer
- signatures
- quality of engraving
- overall appearance
- condition
- date of issue

Compagnie de la Chine et des Indes, Paris

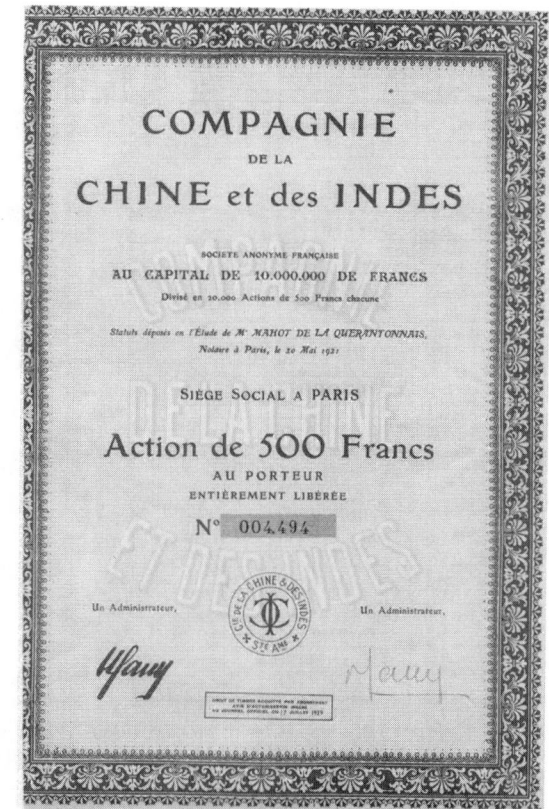

CH790-20-10, 1929, 500 F bearer sh. w. coupons, w/o imprint, 9" x 12-1/4", blue border
.... $4.00

Cinéchromographique Exploitation S.A.

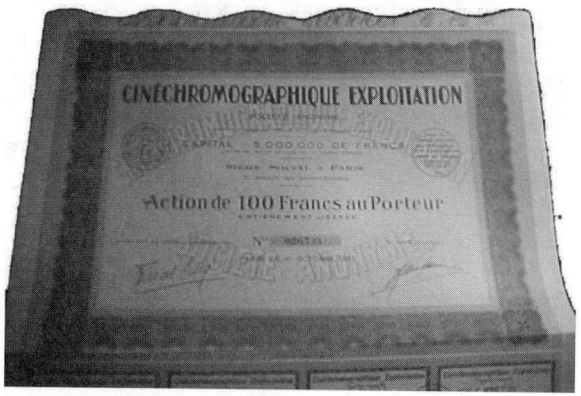

CI140-20-10, 1921, 100 F bearer sh., pink
.... $4.00

S.A. Coloniale de Mines, Paris

*CO100-20-10, 1930, v, 100 F bearer sh. w. coupons, P. Forveille Imprimeur de Titres, Paris-Rodez; 11" x 9", brown $3.00

Société Générale des Comptois Franco-Africains, Paris

CO140-20-10, 1925, v, 100 F bearer sh. w. coupons, blue border. $12.00

Comptoir Lyon-Alemand Affinage - Metaux Précieux S.A., Paris

CO180-20-10, 1933, 125 F bearer sh. w. coupons, Bernard Frères, Paris; 8" x 12", brown on light brown $3.00

Comptoir Tuilier du Nord, Marcq-en-Barœul (Nord)

CO280-20-10, 1963, v, 100 F bearer sh. w. coupons, Imprimerie Spéciale de Valeurs Mobiliéres, 7-3/4" x 10-1/2", green $3.00

UNLISTED TYPES & VARIETIES

Readers are welcome to contact the author directly at:

Rainer Stahlberg
P.O. Box 1044
Rooseveltown, New York 13683

Conserveries L.R. Orange, Chemin de la Deymarde, á Orange (Vaucluse)

*CO330-20-10, ND, v, 100 F bearer sh. w. coupons, Imprimerie des Papiers de Valeurs, Bernard Frères, Paris; 10-3/4" x 5-1/4" (certificate part only), blue $3.00

S.A. de Constructions Métalliques de Bèthune, Béthune (P.-de-C.)

CO370-20-10, 1929, 100 F bearer stock w. coupons, 12" x 7-3/4", brown. $3.00

Corporation Minière du Mexique S.A., Paris

*CO440-20-10, 1923, 100 F bearer sh. w. coupons, black on blue background $5.00

Société Corse et Continentale d'Exploitations Forestieres, S.A.C.C.E.F., Paris

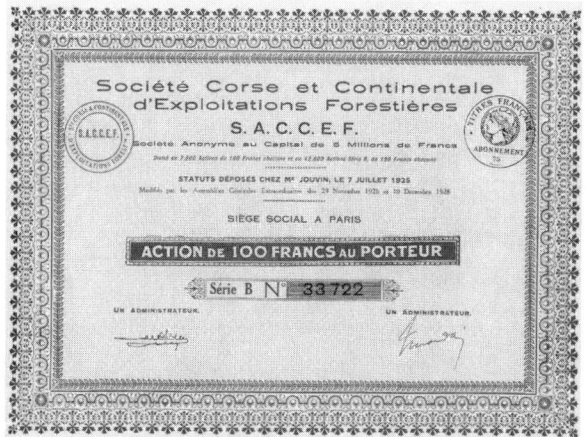

*CO500-20-10, ND, 100 F bearer sh., w. coupons, w. French revenue rubber stamps, Imp. D. et B., Paris; 10-3/4" x 8", blue $3.00

Crédit Foncier Argentin

*CR100-20-10, 1906, v, 500 F bearer sh., w. coupons, brown. $4.00

The value of a stock certificate depends on:
- rarity
- the issuer
- signatures
- quality of engraving
- overall appearance
- condition
- date of issue

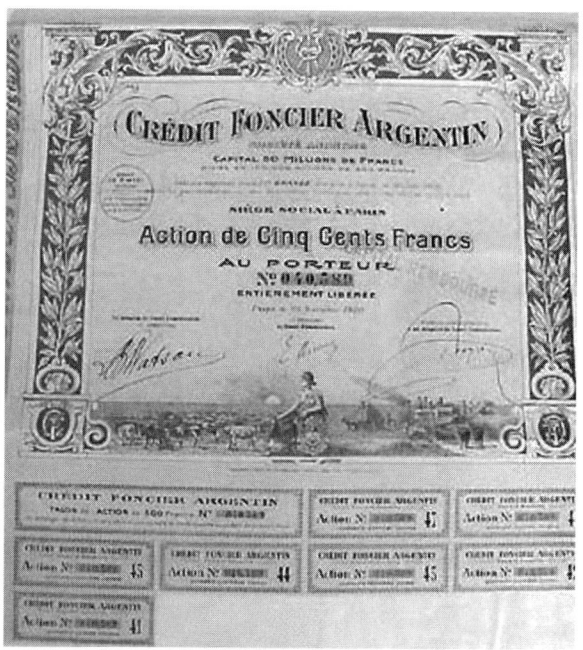

*CR100-30-10, 1920, v, 500 F bearer sh. w. coupons, brown $5.00

Crédit Foncier du Brésil et de l'Amérique du Sud, Paris

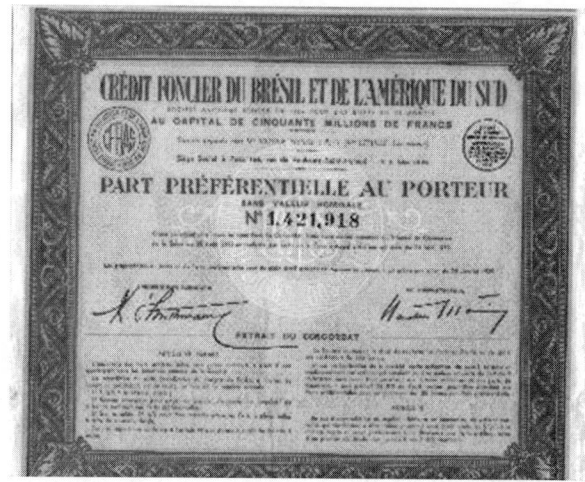

*CR130-40-10, 1929, pref. bearer sh., brown
. . . . $5.00

Crédit Foncier Continental S.A., Paris

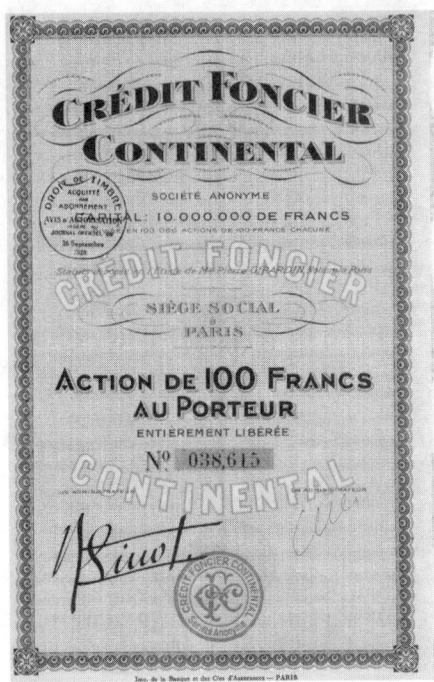

*CR160-30-10, 1928, 100 F bearer sh. w. coupons,
Imp de la Banque et des Cies d'Assurances -
Paris; 6" x 9-1/2", grey border on blue $3.00

Société des Cultures Diakandapé S.A.

*CU100-20-10, 1928, v, 100 F bearer sh., w.
coupons, 10" x 8", blue border on pink . . .$4.00

Société Dauphinoise de Constructions Mécaniques S.A.

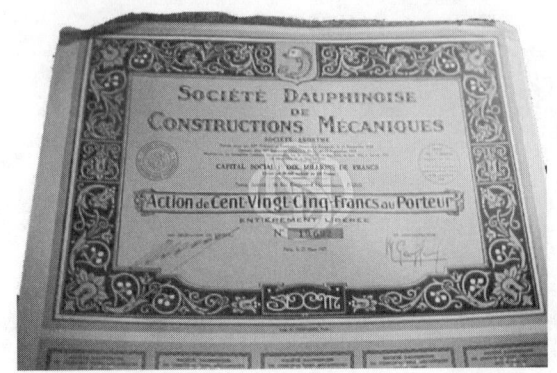

*DA80-20-10, 1925, v, 125 F bearer stock w.
coupons, brown $5.00

S.A. du Domaine de Cavalés

*DO110-20-10, 1934, 250 F bearer stock w.
coupons, brown $3.00

Compagnie d'Electricité du Sénégal, Paris

*EL80-50-10, 1925, v, 500 F 6% bond w. coupons,
w/o imprint, 12" x 9", blue $3.00

Elesca S.A., Paris

*EL120-20-10, ND, 3,000 F bearer sh. w. coupons, Imprimeria Fano-Émonet, Paris; 7-1/4" x 10-1/2", blue border $3.00

Entreprise Coopérative Française, Paris

*EN160-20-10, 1922, v, 100 F bearer sh. w. coupons, brown. $3.00

S.A. Entreprises et de Travaux, Bordeaux 1905

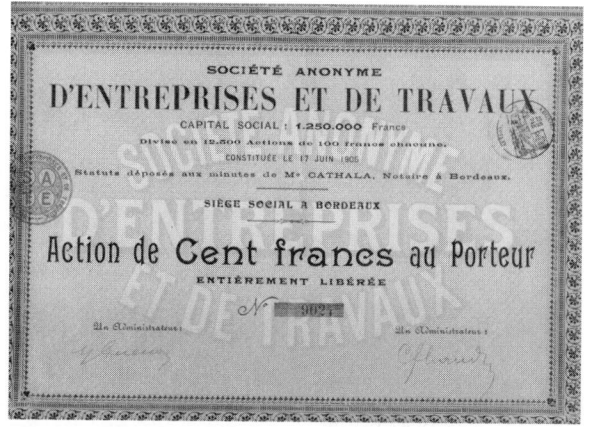

*EN240-30-10, ND, 100 F bearer sh. w. coupons, French revenue rubber stamp (1933), Bordeaux - Imprimerie G. Gounouilhau; 13-3/4" x 9-3/4", blue border $3.00

Société d'Équipement des Voies Ferrées et des Grands Réseaux Électriques S.A., Paris

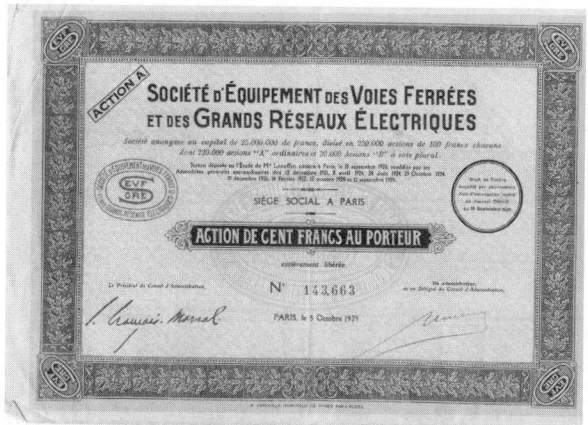

*EQ100-30-10, 1929, series A 100 F bearer sh., w. coupons, P. Forveille Imprimeur de Titres Paris-Rodez; 11-1/2" x 8-1/4", blue border on beige $3.00

It is generally assumed that only 5% of certificates survive to reach collectors.

*EQ100-40-10, 1935, series B bearer sh. w. coupons, Imprimeria Spéciale de Banque - Paris, 9-1/2" x 6-3/4", brown $3.00

Établissements J. Bte. Bigotte, Entreprise Générale de Batiments et Fabrication Industrielle S.A. Tourcoing (Nord)

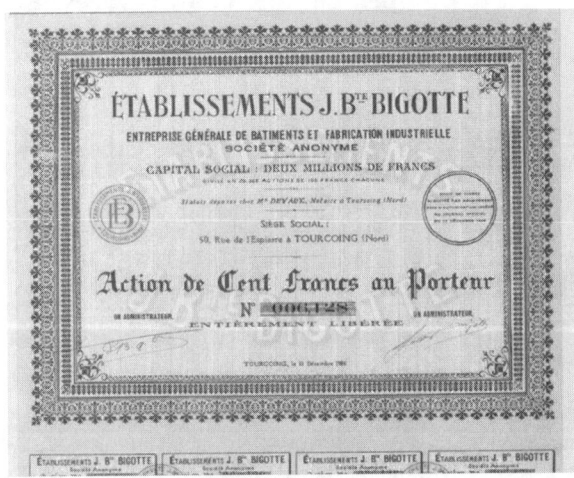

*ET80-20-10, 1926, 100 F bearer sh. w. coupons, brown $3.00

S.A. des Etablissements Courmont, Cambrai

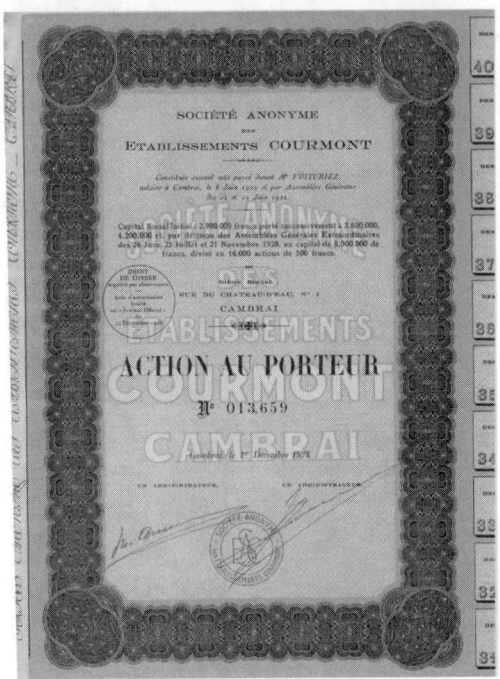

*ET140-20-10, 1928, 500 F bearer sh. w. coupons, no printers name, 7-1/2" x 11-3/4", blue $3.00

Etablissements Duchesne & Cie. S.A., Villeurbanne-les-Lyon (Rhône)

*ET170-20-10, 1924, 1 (500 F) bearer sh. w. coupons, 12-1/4" x 8", green $3.00

S.A. Etablissements Industriels de E.-C. Grammont et de Alexandre Grammont, Paris

*ET300-20-10, 1926, v, 100 F bearer stock, light brown $8.00

S.A. Etablissements Mehuys, Croix

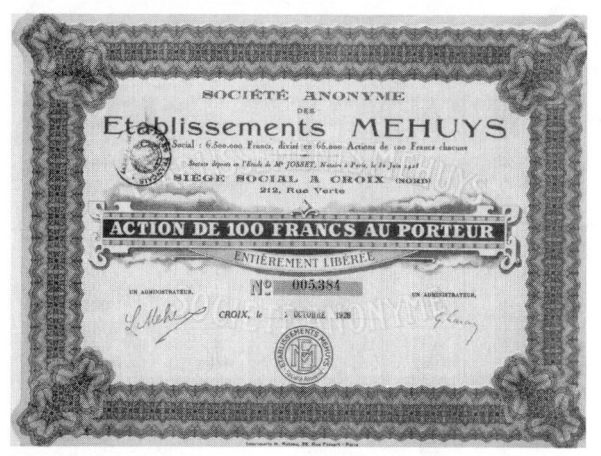

*ET370-20-10, 1928, v, 100 F bearer sh., w. coupons, Imprimerie H. Rateau - Paris; 12" x 9", brown border on green $3.00

Etablissements Mourier L. Barraya & Cie., Paris

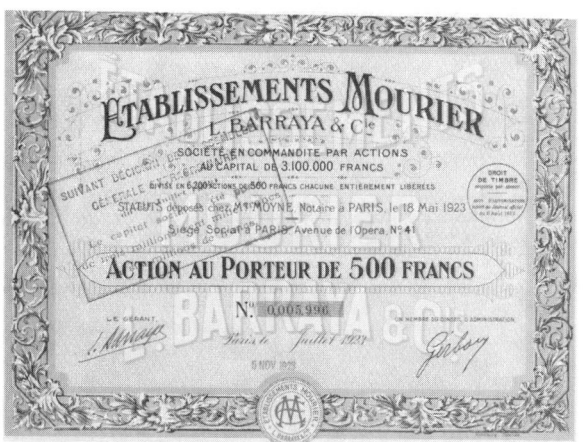

*ET410-20-10, 1923, v, 500 F bearer sh., w. coupons, capital 3,100,000 F, Robaudy, Cannes; 11-3/4" x 9", blue $3.00

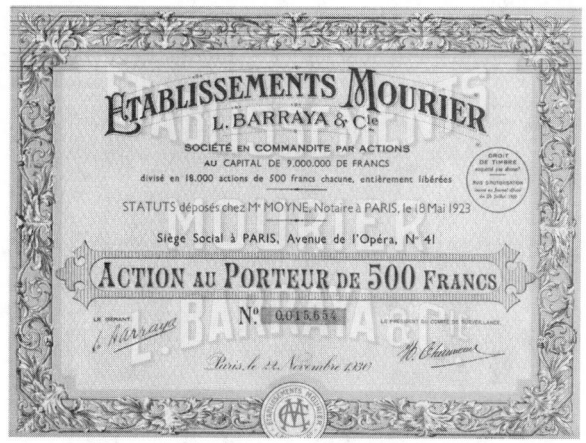

*ET410-25-10, 1936, v, 500 F bearer sh. w. coupons, capital 9,000,000 F, Imp. Robaudy - Cannes; 11-3/4" x 9-1/4", blue $3.00

This catalog has listings in an alphabetical format. The reason is simple: Companies diversify as they grow. For example, the Canadian Pacific Railway company recently split into five companies. They represent the railway, hotels, shipping, airline, and petroleum interests of the company. During World War II, the Singer sewing machine company made guns and other defense-related equipment, so where should we list it? It's far easier to use a strict alphabetical order, rather than to confuse the reader with topical classifications.

Établissements H. Vernet S.A., Paris

*ET510-30-10, 1929, 100 F series A bearer sh., w. coupons, Imp. de la Banque et Cie. d'Assurances- Paris; 12" x 8-3/4", red border on green $3.00

Société Française d'Etudes & d'Exploitation de Phosphates en Tunisie

*ET570-20-10, 1908, v, 250 F bearer stock, brown $8.00

Euro Disneyland S.C.A.

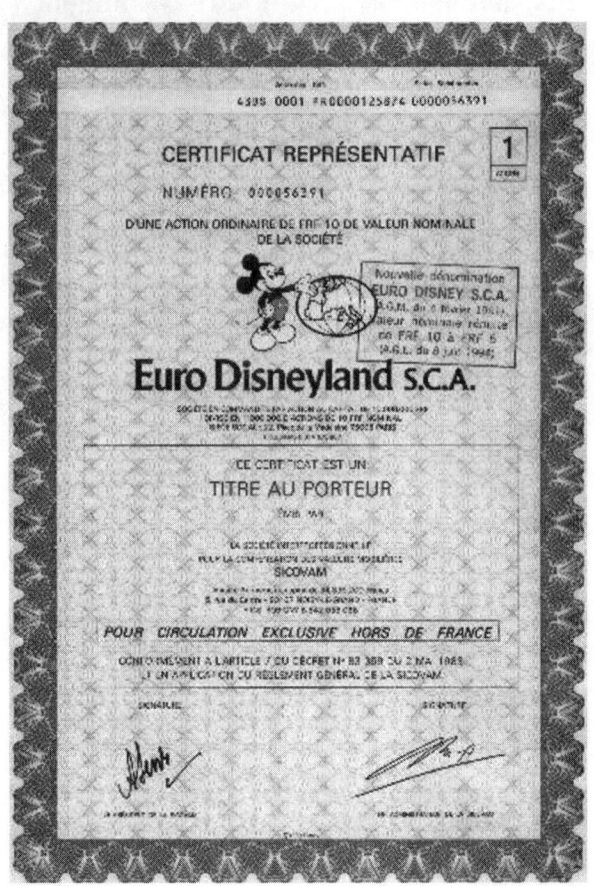

*EU100-40-10, 1963, one bearer sh. for outside of France, blue and pink.................$7.00

UNLISTED TYPES & VARIETIES

Readers are welcome to contact the author directly at:

Rainer Stahlberg
P.O. Box 1044
Rooseveltown, New York 13683

Compagnie Européenne de Matériels C.E.M.A., Paris

*EU150-20-10, 1963, 50 F bearer sh., w. coupons, Baguenier-Desormeaux, 7-3/4" x 10-3/4", blue
...................................$3.00

Société Française d'Exploitations Auriferes, Paris

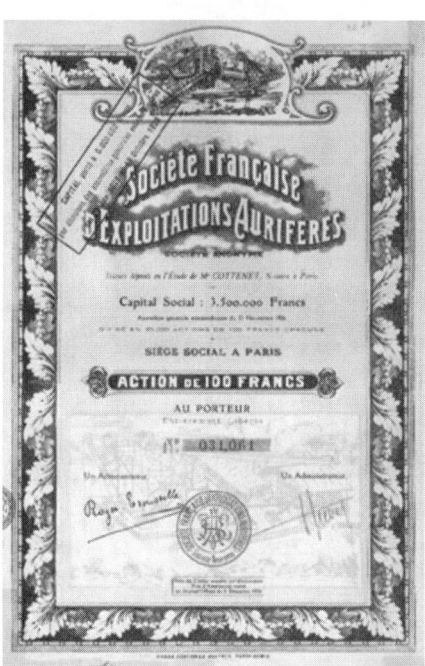

*EX100-20-10, 1926, v, 100 F bearer sh., grey-blue
...................................$9.00

Société d'Exploitation des Brevets Jacques Arthuys S.A., ARTHEL, Paris

EX140-20-10, 19xx, u/u 500 F certificate, blue border $4.00

Explosifs Minélite S.A., Paris

*EX200-30-10, 1928, v, 100 F bearer "jouissance" sh., red $3.00

Société Anonyme pour la Fabrication des Produits "Asphaltoid", Huningue (H-Rhin)

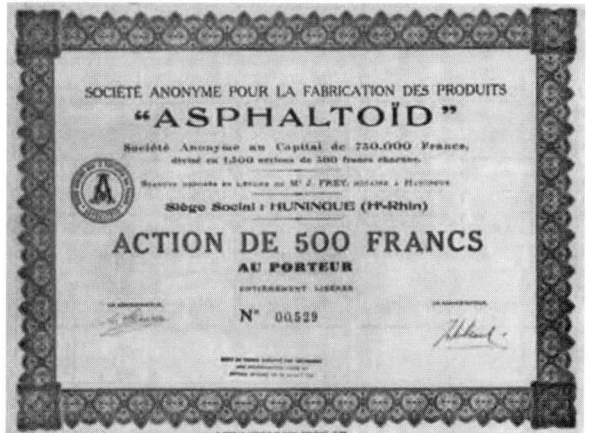

*FA50-20-10, 1934, v, 500 F bearer sh., blue on yellow...........................$3.00

Flandria S.A., Malo-les Bains
Cement manufacturer.

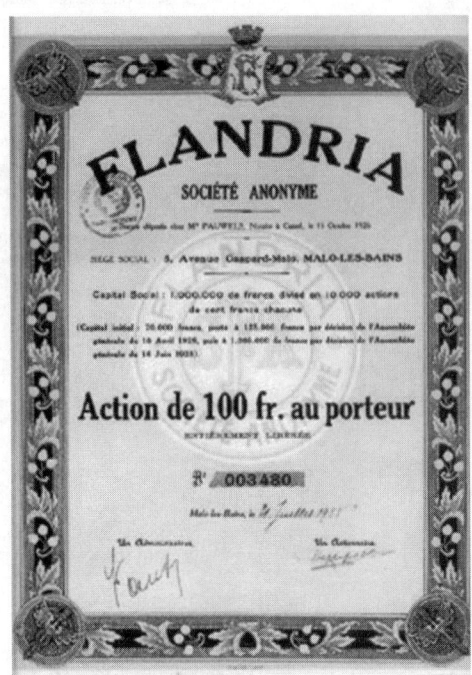

FL50-20-10, 1928, v, 100 F bearer sh., brown
. . . .$3.00

La Foncière Tassy Mont-Blanc

FO180-40-10, 1928, v, 100 F preferred bearer
stock, blue. $4.00

S.A. Fonderies & Ateliers de Plaisance & du Rhone

FO210-20-10, 1918, 100 F bearer stock, blue
. . . .$4.00

S.A. Fonderies de Vaugirard
FO270-20-10, 1923, 100 F bearer stock w.
coupons, blue $7.00

Force & Distribution S.A., Paris

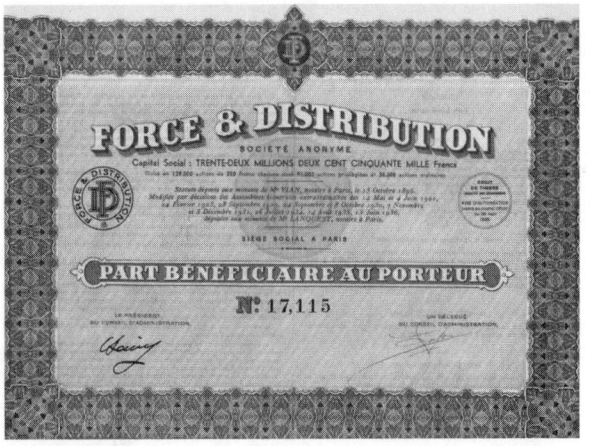

FO310-40-10, 1936, 250 F bearer sh. w. coupons,
Imprimeria Chaix, Paris; 12-1/2" x 8-3/4", red
border $3.00

S.A. des Forges & Ateliers de la Fournaise, St. Denis (Seine),

*FO350-20-10, 1936, 100 F bearer sh. w. coupons, André Wellhoff, Imp. Paris; 12-1/2" x 8-3/4", blue border $3.00

Cie. Franco-Americaine des Métaux et de Minerais S.A., COFRAMET, Paris

*FR100-20-10, 1924, 100 F bearer sh., blue
. . . .$3.00

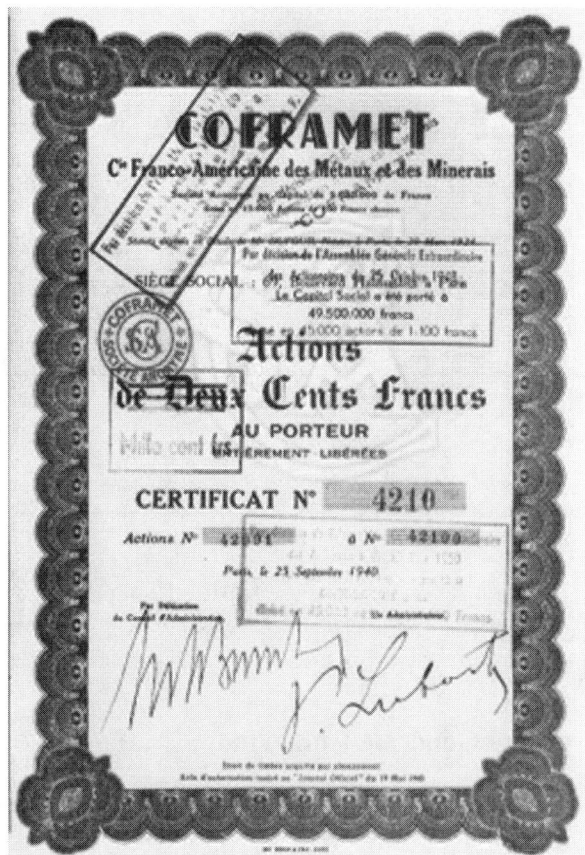

*FR100-40-10, 1940, 200 F bearer sh., brown
. . . .$3.00

Franco Canadienne de Participations S.A., Paris

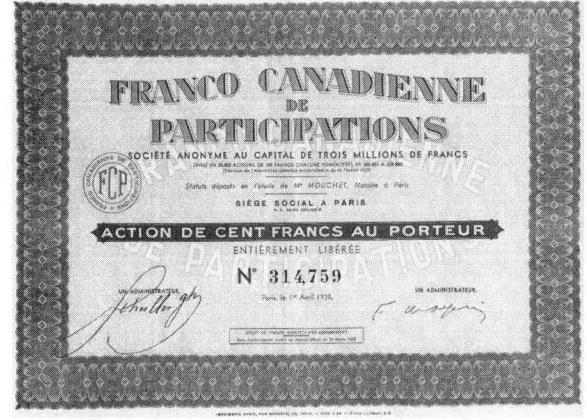

*FR140-20-10, 1939, 100 Franc bearer stock w. coupons, Imprimerie Chaix, 12-1/2" x 8-1/2", blue. $4.00

Société Générale de Contre-Assurances S.A., Paris

GE80-20-10, 1924, 100 F bearer sh. w. coupons, French revenue rubber stamp, H. Baguenier-Desormeaux Paris, 10-3/4" x 7-3/4", light brown **$3.00**

Société Générale Isothermos S.A., Paris

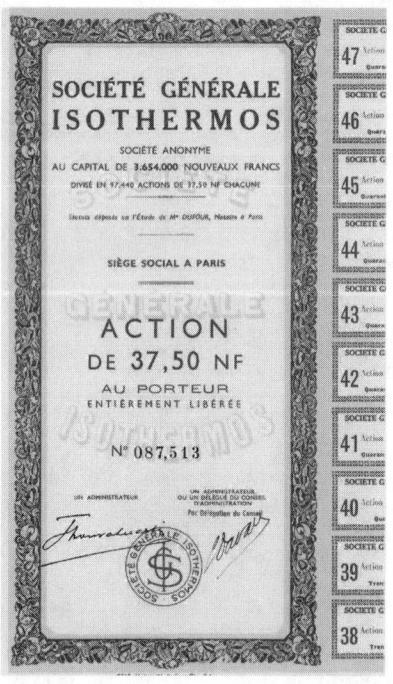

GE140-20-10, ND, 37.50 NF bearer sh. w. coupons, capital 3,654,000 NF, Hammerlé, Petit et Cie., 5-1/2" x 10-1/2", light brown **$3.00**

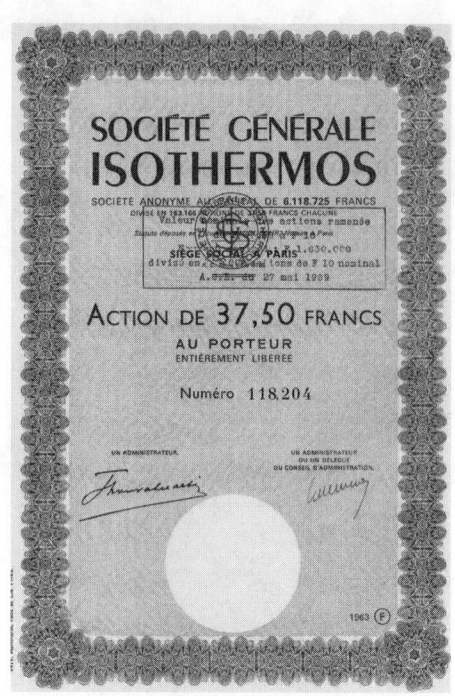

GE140-30-10, 1963, 37.50 F bearer sh. w. coupons, capital 6,118,725 F, Hammerlé, Petit et Cie., 7-1/2" x 10-1/2", light brown.......**$3.00**

Compagnie Générale Transatlantique S.A., Paris

GE200-40-10, 1928, v, 150 F class B bearer sh., w. coupons, 10-3/4" x 7-3/4", blue border **$12.00**

La Holding Française S.A., H.O.L.F.R.A., Paris

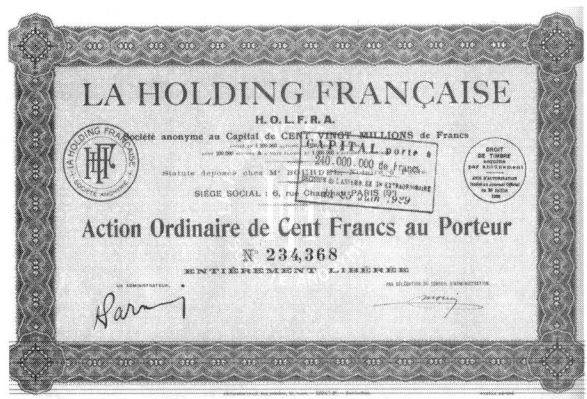

*HO80-20-10, 1928, 100 F bearer sh., w. coupons, Impremerie Chaix, Paris; 12-3/4" x 8-1/4", red border on green.....................$3.00

Hotel de Paris S.A.

*HO120-30-10, 1946, 1,000 F bearer sh., green
...................................$5.00

Société Hotelière de Beausoleil

HO150-20-10, 1926, 500F bearer stock w. coupons, blue $7.00

Société Hôteliere des Centres, de Pèlegrines Catholiques S.A., Paris

*HO190-50-10, 1946, 500 F 6-1/2% bearer bond w. coupons, P. Forveille Imprimeur de Titres, 12-1/2" x 8-3/4", lilac, w. annex $4.00

*HO190-50-11, - Annex to the above bond w. coupons, Imp. G. Soulas, 9-1/2" x 7", blue, see above

---

The value of a stock certificate depends on:
- rarity
- the issuer
- signatures
- quality of engraving
- overall appearance
- condition
- date of issue

Cie. Hoteliére de Marseille et de la Riviera, Paris

HO250-40-10, 1920, v, 93 F 5% bond, blue on
orange $3.00

Societè des Hotels et Bains de Mer d'Hossegor S.A., Paris

HO310-40-10, 1934, 1,000 F 3% bearer bond w.
coupons, P. Forveille Imprimeur de Titres,
14-1/4" x 7-1/2", green $3.00

Société Hydro-Electrique du Verdon, Paris

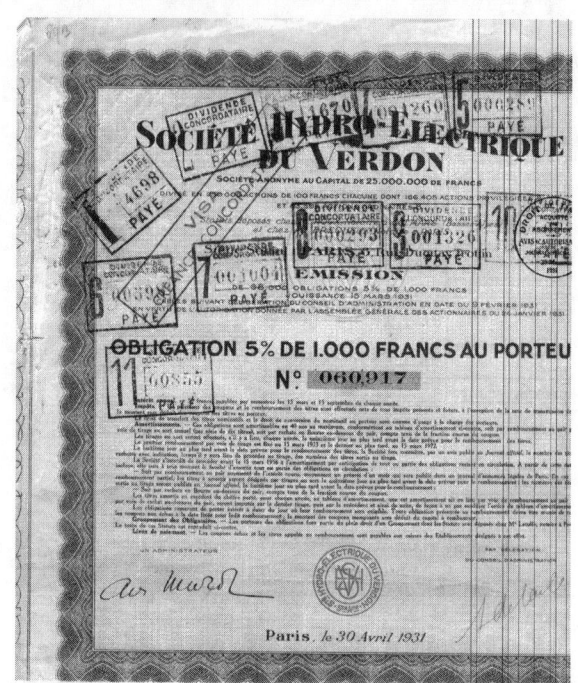

HY50-40-10, 1931, 1,000 F 5% bearer bond w.
coupons, Imp. de la Banque et des Cies d'Assurances - Paris, 9-1/2" x 10-1/4", blue border
. . . . $3.00

S.A. Immobilière du Loquidy, Nantes

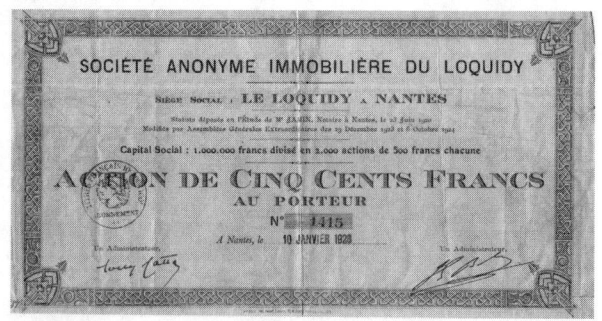

IM90-20-10, 1928, 500 F bearer sh., w. coupons,
Imp. André Clouet, Nantes; 10-3/4" x 5-1/2", red
lilac. $3.00

> **It is generally assumed that only 5% of certificates survive to reach collectors.**

Société Immobilière de Paris et du Littoral S.A., Paris

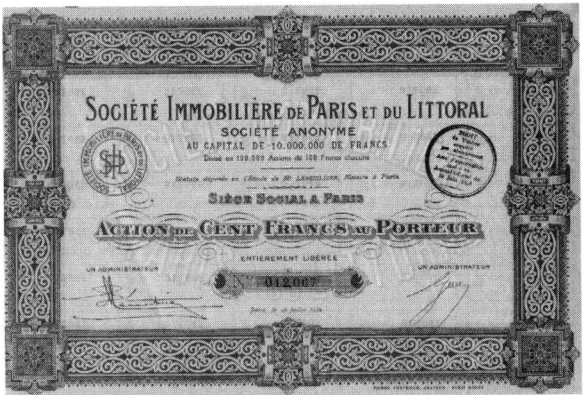

IM170-20-10, 1924, 100 F bearer sh., w. coupons, Pierre Forveille, Graveur, Paris-Rodez; 12-1/4" x 8", reddish-brown border **$3.00**

Societe Anonyme Immobilière Saint-Jean, Clermond-Ferrand

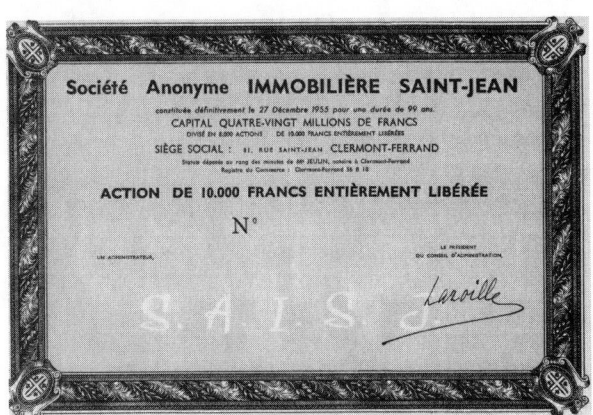

IM210-30-10, 1955, u/u 10,000 F bearer stock certificate w. coupons, Imp. G. De Bussac, Clermont-FD, 10-1/2" x 7" (certificate only), blue **$3.00**

Société Immobilière Ilot Wagram S.A., Paris

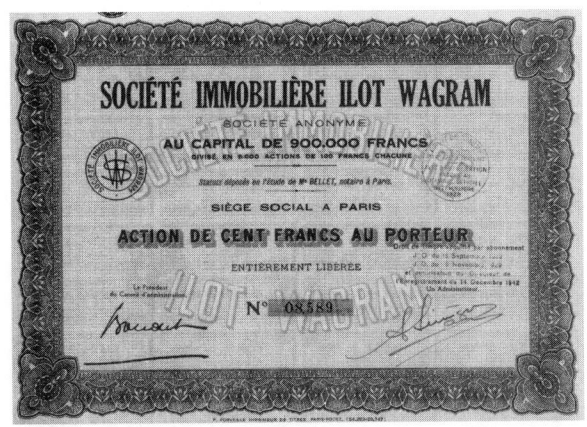

IM300-20-10, 1942, 100 F bearer sh. w. coupons, P. Forveille Imprimeur de Titres, Paris-Rodez; 10-1/2" x 7-1/2", purplish border **$3.00**

Société Anonyme Industrielle et Commerciale (S.I.C.), Paris

IN100-15-10, 1919, v, 100 F bearer sh. w. coupons, capital 225,000 F, 7-3/4" x 10-3/4", blue **$3.00**

IN100-20-10, ND, 100F bearer stock w. coupons, capital raised to 500,000 F, w/o imprint, 7-3/4" x 10-3/4", blue **$3.00**

L'Industrielle de Matériaux Ancien Etablissements Bonnel & Co., Saint-Quentin

*IN150-20-10, 1928, v, 250 F bearer sh., red
..................................$4.00

Société Industrielle de Verreire

*IN210-20-10, 1928, 100 F bearer sh. w. coupons, 14" x 12", green $3.00

le Kétol S.A.

KE70-20-10, 1926, v, 100 F bearer stock, green
..................................$3.00

J. Laveissiere Fils & Cie., Paris

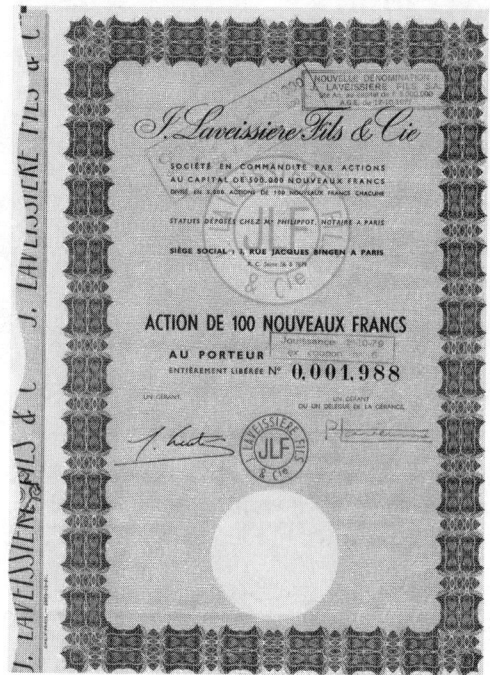

*LA80-30-10, 1979, 100 New Franc bearer sh., Chaix-Paris, 7-3/4" x 10-3/4", blue $3.00

Ligne Internationale D'Italie

*LI70-20-10, 1868, v, 525 F bearer bond, blue
..................................$10.00

Société Maritime Française S.A., Paris

*MA100-30-10, 1917, v, 250 F bearer sh., w.
coupons, 12-3/4" x 8-1/2", brown border .**$3.00**

Compagnie Maritime de la Seine, Paris

*MA190-20-10, 1899, v, 100 F founder's bearer sh.,
12-3/4" x 9-1/4", brown **$15.00**

Mediterranean Electric Telegraph

*ME100-20-10, 1854, v, 1 bearer sh., of £10, grey
. . . .**$45.00**

UNLISTED TYPES & VARIETIES

Readers are welcome to contact the author
directly at:

**Rainer Stahlberg
P.O. Box 1044
Rooseveltown, New York 13683**

Les Métalliques Françaises S.A., Paris

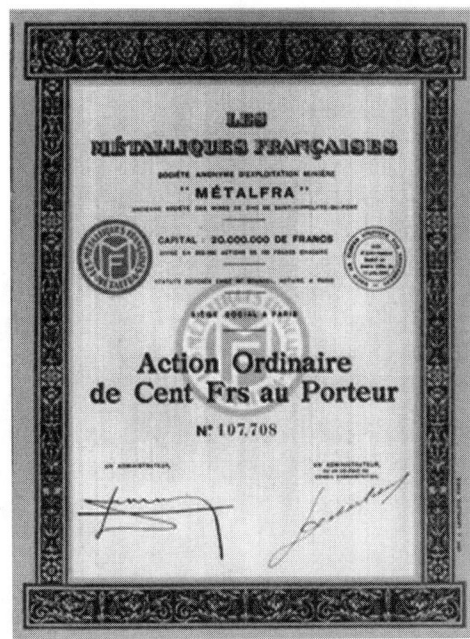

*ME210-20-10, ND, 100 F bearer sh., brown
. . . .**$3.00**

Société Metallurgique de l'Oural-Volga S.A., Paris

*ME270-20-10, 1899, v, 500 F bearer sh. w.
coupons, blue **$11.00**

Minas Pedrazzini S.A. Minas Pedrazzini Gold and Silver Mining Co., Sonora, Mexico

Mines in Arizpe.

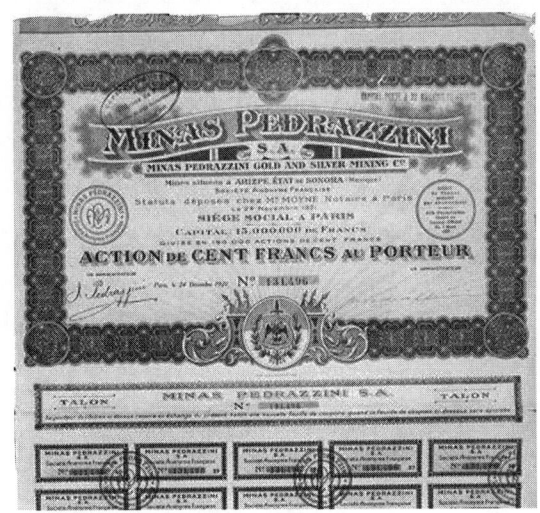

*MI120-20-10, 1921, v, 100 F Founder's bearer
stock w. coupons, brown **$6.00**

*MI120-25-10, 1921, v, 100 F bearer sh. w. coupons, capital 15,000,000 F; brown $4.00

*MI120-30-10, 1924, v, 100 F bearer sh. w. coupons, capital 22,000,000 F; brown $4.00

*MI120-35-10, 1926, v, 100 F bearer sh. w. coupons, capital 35,000,000 F; brown $4.00

Compagnie Française des Mines d'Akhtala (Caucase)

*MI150-20-10, 1887, v, 500 F bearer sh., brown $11.00

Compagnie des Mines d'Arras S.A.

MI180-20-10, 1926, v, 100 F bearer sh., green $3.00

Mines de la Betica Province Almeria (Espagne)

MI210-20-10, 1909, 250 F bearer stock w. coupons, brown $15.00

Mines du Djebel-Sekarna S.A., Paris

*MI250-20-10, 1925, v, 1/10 bearer sh. (no par), brown $5.00

Mines d'Entifa (Maroc) S.A., Paris

MI300-20-10, 1923, 100 F bearer sh., brown
. . . .**$3.00**

Mines et Industries S.A., Paris

MI340-20-10, 1940, v, 100 F bearer sh. w. coupons, Imp. Spéciale pour Titres, Paris; 10-1/2" x 8-3/4", blue border **$3.00**

Compagnie Miniere Franco-Tunisienne, Paris

MI410-20-10, 1929, v, 100 F bearer sh. w. coupons, brown. **$4.00**

Société Minière du Gard S.A., Paris

MI450-20-10, 1900, v, 100 F bearer sh., blue
. . . .**$4.00**

Compagnie Miniere du Laos, Paris

MI510-20-10, 1928, 100 F bearer stock w. coupons, Imp. Martin-Mamy, Crouan & Roques, Lille-Paris; 11-1/2" x 8-1/2", red **$5.00**

The value of a stock certificate depends on:

- rarity
- the issuer
- signatures
- quality of engraving
- overall appearance
- condition
- date of issue

Compagnie Française des Mines d'Or du Canada, Paris

*MI600-20-10, 1929, 100 F bearer sh. w. coupons, blue $4.00

Les Mosaïques Noël S.A., Paris

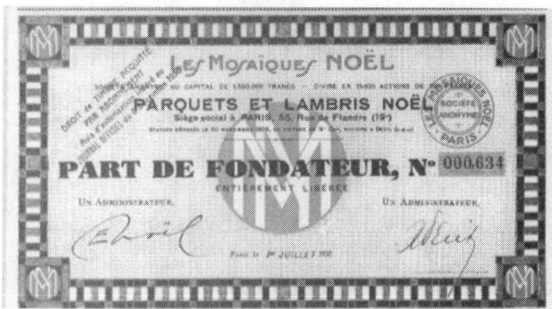

*MO110-20-10, 1930, v, founder's bearer sh., green-red $3.00

Le Nickel Calédonien

The company operating the nickel and cobalt mines in New Caledonia.

*NI70-20-10, 1907, v, 250 F bearer stock, blue-grey $11.00

S.A. Normande Produits Alimentaires

*NO120-20-10, 1929, 100 F founder bearer certificate w. coupons, blue $4.00

Nouvelle Compagnie Générale Électrique "Nancy" S.A., Nancy

*NO210-40-10, 1957, Beneficial Interest w. coupons, Imprimerie Spéciale de Banque, 10-1/2" x 7", blue border $3.00

Compagnie Nouvelle des Mines de Villemagne S.A., Paris

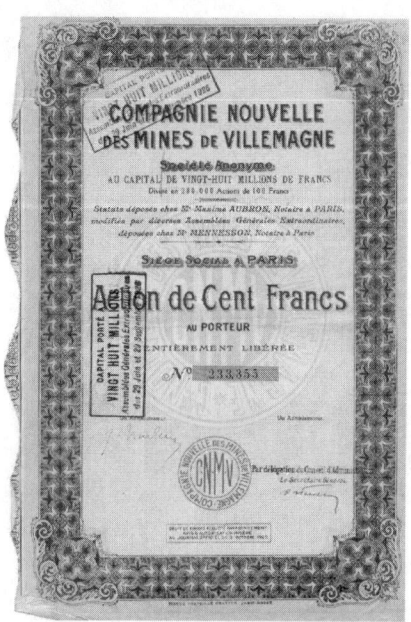

*NO240-20-10, 1926, 100 F bearer sh., w. coupons, Pierre Forveille Graveur, Paris-Rodez; 8" x 12-1/4", grey border $3.00

Paul Olmer & Cie. S.A., Paris

*OL50-30-10, 1928, v, 500 F bearer sh., series B; blue $5.00

Omnium Colonial Français S.A., Paris

*OM80-20-10, 1900, 100 F bearer sh., w. coupons, French revenue rubber stamp, 13" x 11", red border on green $5.00

Palladium S.A., Argenteuil (Seine-et-Oise)

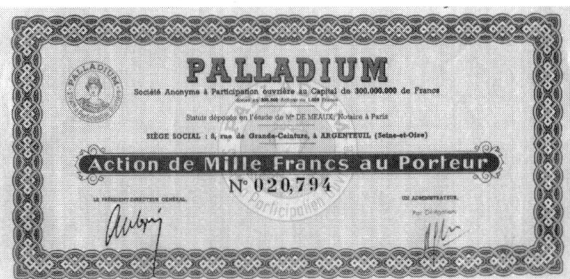

*PA60-20-10, ND, 1,000 F bearer sh., Imprimerie Chaix, Paris; 10-1/2" x 5-1/4", brown $3.00

Société Anonyme des Parfums D'Arys

PA110-20-10, 1918, v, 500 F bearer stock, brown $4.00

Compagnie de Participations et de Gestion, Lyon

*PA160-20-10, 1936, 100 F bearer sh., w. coupons, P. Forveille, Imprimeur de Titres, Paris-Rodez; 12-1/2" x 8-1/4", blue border $3.00

> *It is generally assumed that only 5% of certificates survive to reach collectors.*

La Perrodière Société Agricole d'Èlevage S.A., Rillé (Indre-et-Loire)

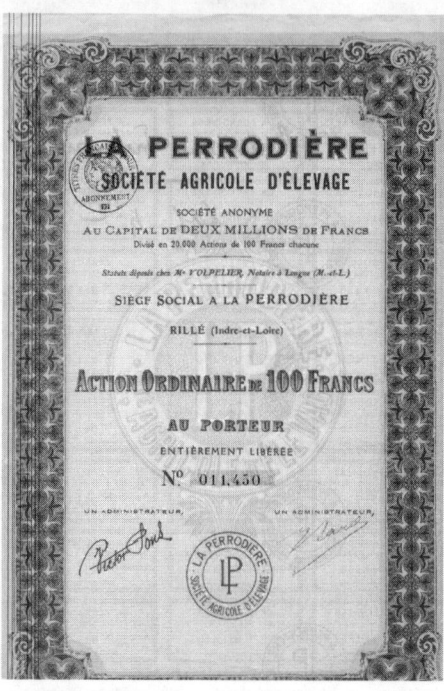

*PE110-20-10, ND, v, 100 F bearer sh. w. coupons, French revenue rubber stamp, 8" x 12", brown $3.00

Société Pétroles Bellik á Grosnyi, Paris

*PE200-20-10, 19??, 500 F bearer sh. w. coupons, blue on beige. $4.00

Société des Pétroles Monte-Carlo, Tourcoing

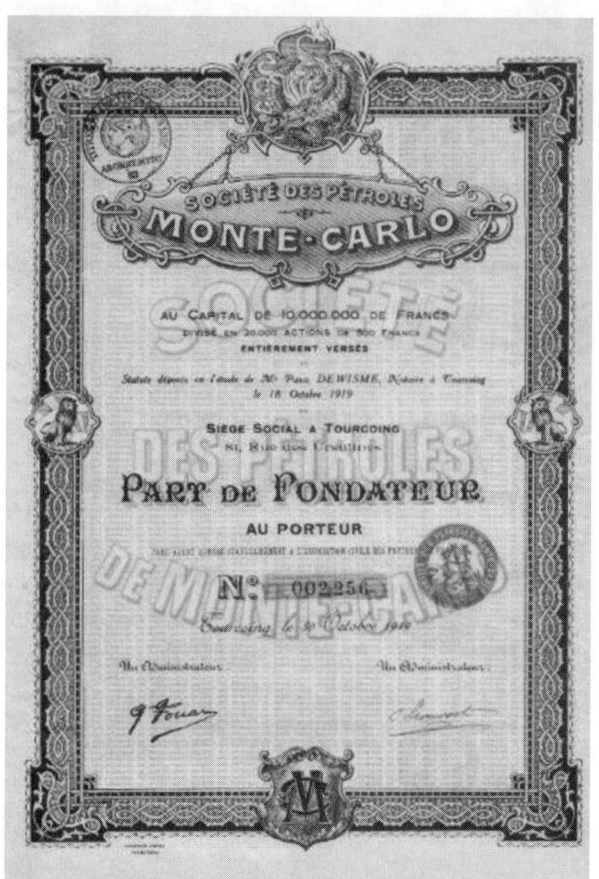

*PE250-20-10, 1919, v, 500 F founder's bearer sh. w. coupons, 8" x 12", brown $12.00

Société des Phosphates de Fauzan

PH100-20-10, 1925, 100 F founder bearer stock, purple $3.00

This catalog has listings in an alphabetical format. The reason is simple: Companies diversify as they grow. For example, the Canadian Pacific Railway company recently split into five companies. They represent the railway, hotels, shipping, airline, and petroleum interests of the company. During World War II, the Singer sewing machine company made guns and other defense-related equipment, so where should we list it? It's far easier to use a strict alphabetical order, rather than to confuse the reader with topical classifications.

Les Produits C.B.C.; C., C. Buelens & Cie., Amiens

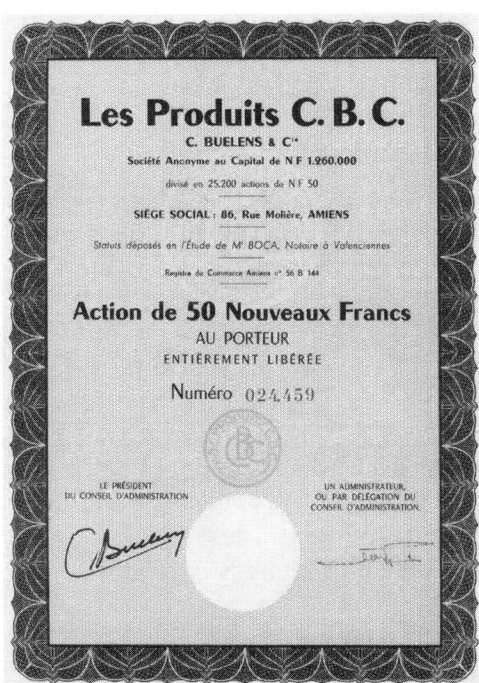

PR120-30-10, ND, 50 new F bearer stock w. coupons, Imprimeria Spéciale de Valeurs Mobilieres - Paris, 7-1/2" x 10-1/2", blue on yellow $3.00

Produits Chimiques de France et Blancs de Comines

PR150-20-10, 1931, v, 100 F bearer sh., brown $3.00

Société Civile de Reconstruction de la Région de Noyon

RE70-40-10, 1922, v, 500 F 6% bearer bond, blue $3.00

UNLISTED TYPES & VARIETIES

Readers are welcome to contact the author directly at:

**Rainer Stahlberg
P.O. Box 1044
Rooseveltown, New York 13683**

Le Sac S.A., Strasbourg

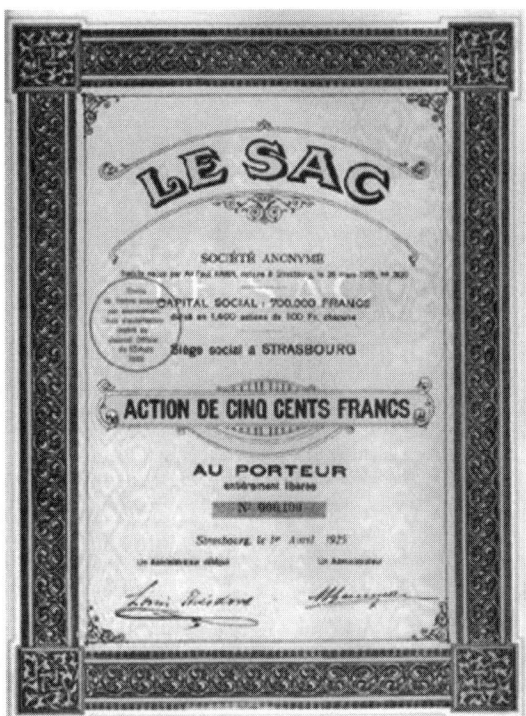

SA40-20-10, 1925, 500 F bearer sh., brown border $3.00

Société des Salines de Tunisie, Paris

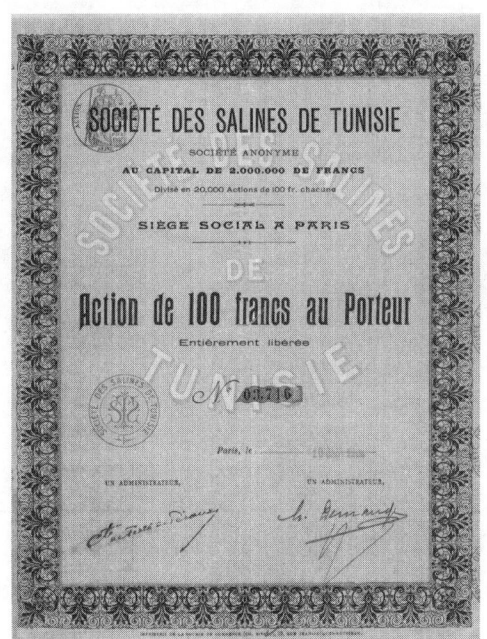

SA80-20-10, 1908, 100 F bearer stock w. coupons, Impremerie de la bourse de commerce, 8-1/2" x 11", blue $4.00

S.A. la Salubrité Urbaine, Paris

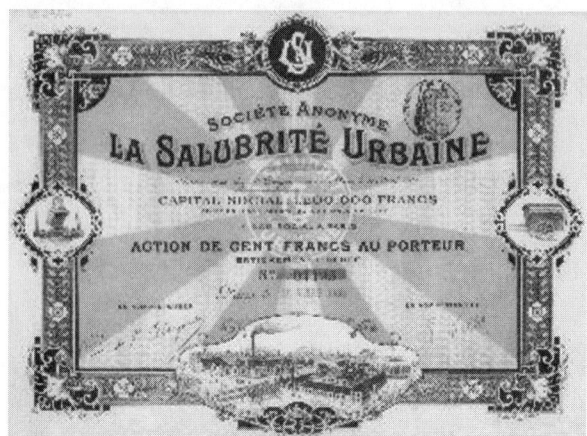

*SA110-20-10, 1905, v, 100 F bearer sh. $5.00

Societe des Sels Gemmes & Houilles de la Russie Meridionale S.A.

SE100-20-10, 1911, 250 F bearer stock,
   brown and green $8.00

Société de Signalisation de Chemin de Fer (Brevet Cousin et César), Paris

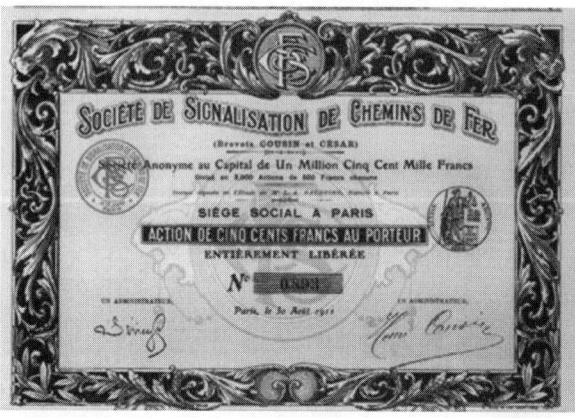

*SI100-20-10, 1911, v, 500 F bearer sh., grey
. . . .$5.00

> *It is generally assumed that only 5% of certificates survive to reach collectors.*

La Soie Artificielle d'Amiens S.A., Paris
Artificial silk manufacturing company.

*SO110-20-10, 1926, 100 F bear sh. w. coupons,
   Imp. Rapide Moderné - Paris, 12-3/4" x 9", grey
   border on pink $3.00

La Soie de Compiègne S.A., Paris

*SO140-20-10, ND, v, 100 F bearer sh., green
. . . .$3.00

Stadium de Paris

*ST60-20-10, 1934, 100 F bearer stock w. coupons,
   l. green $5.00

Société Stéphanoise de Constructions Mécaniques, St. Etienne

*ST100-20-10, 1968, 50 NF bearer sh. w. coupons, A. Mulcey, St. Etienne, 6-3/4" x 11-3/4", blue border $3.00

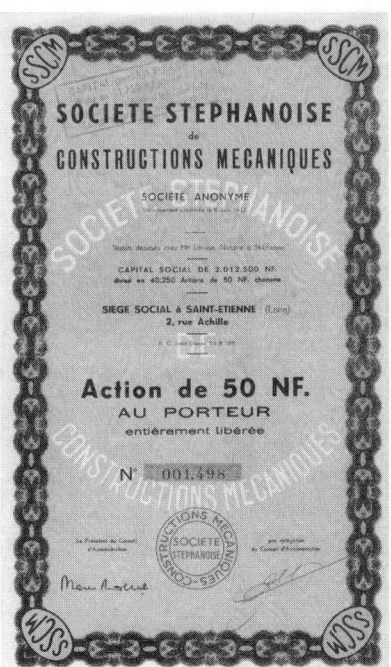

*ST100-30-10, 19??, 50 F bearer sh., brown
. . . .$3.00

Syndicat Lyonnais de Madagascar S.A.

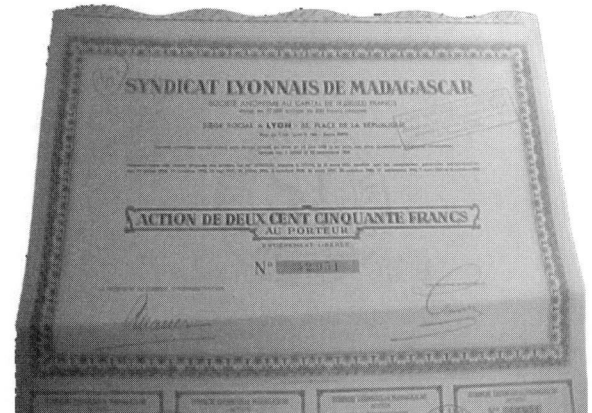

*SY100-20-10, 1956, 250 F bearer stock w. coupons, grey $5.00

Syndicat Mana S.A., Paris

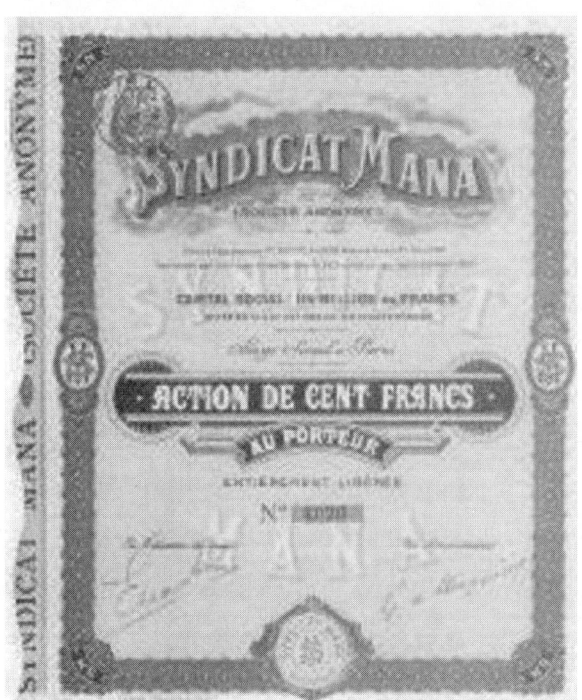

*SY140-20-10, ND, v, 100 F bearer sh., grey
. . . .$3.00

Tanneries Augere & Gentilly Réunies S.A.

TA100-20-10, ND, v, 100 F bearer sh. w.
coupons, 10" x 15", reddish brown border
....$3.00

Taxis-Citroen S.A.

Andre Citroen founded the company in 1919. The
company is known for its innovative designs.

TA180-20-10, 1924, v, 100 F bearer stock, brown
on yellow $45.00

Telegraphes & Telephones sans fil

TE150-20-10, 1901, v, bearer stock, rose red
....$24.00

Compagnie des Tramways Électriques de l'Ariège S.A., Saint Girons

TR100-20-10, 1908, v, bearer sh., blue
....$16.00

Les Travaux Textiles S.A., Paris

TR200-20-10, 1925, 500 F bearer sh. w. coupons,
French revenue rubber stamp, Imp. F. Van
Buggenhoudt S.A., Bruxelles; 8-1/2" x 12-1/4",
grey border $3.00

Tuileries Mécaniques d'Halluin, Halluin (Nord)

TU100-20-10, 1927, 1,000 F bearer sh. w. coupons, Pierre Forveille, Graveur Paris, 11-3/4" x 8", green $3.00

Tuileries du Nord & du Pas-de-Calais S.A., Marcq-en-Barœul (Nord)

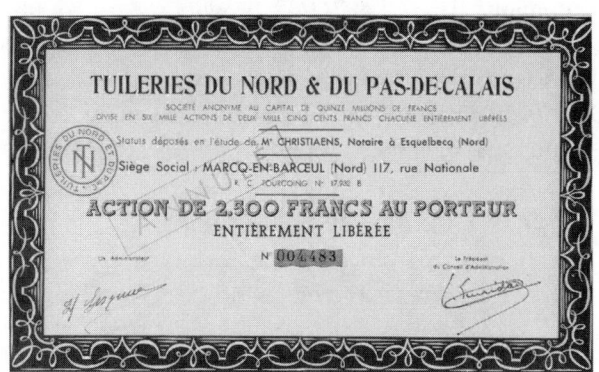

TU130-20-10, ND, 2,500 F bearer sh. w. coupons, w/o imprint, 10-1/4" x 6-1/2", blue $3.00

The value of a stock certificate depends on:

- **rarity**
- **the issuer**
- **signatures**
- **quality of engraving**
- **overall appearance**
- **condition**
- **date of issue**

Tuileries des Tarterets Gilardoni Frères, Essonnes (S. et O.)

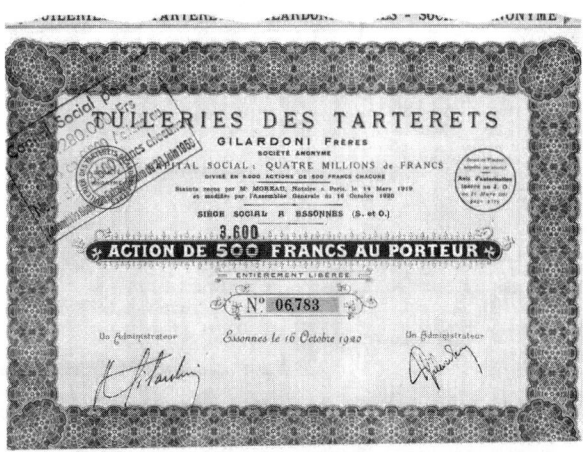

TU200-30-10, 1920, 3,600 F (o/p on 500) bearer sh. w. coupons, Union des Arts Graphiques, 12-3/4" x 8-1/2", lilac. $3.00

TU200-40-10, 1956, 3,600 F bearer sh. w. coupons, Imp. Watelet-Arbelot - Paris, 10-1/2" x 10", purple border on yellow . . .$3.00

Union des Beurreries de France S.A., Paris

UN50-20-10, 1910, v, bearer sh., French revenue rubber stamp, brown border $3.00

Union Rurale d'Électricité S.A., Paris

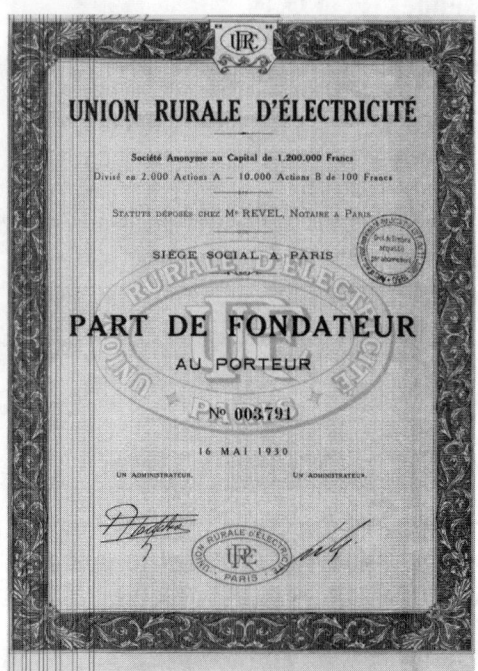

*UN120-20-10, 1930, v, Founder's bearer sh. w. coupons, Barthe & Cie., 9" x12", grey-blue border $3.00

Compagnie Universellè Cinematographique

*UN160-20-10, 1919, v, 100 F bearer stock, 10" x 8-1/2", brown $15.00

S.A. de Usines Franco-Russes

*US80-20-10, 1881, v, 500 F bearer stock, black $9.00

S.A. de la Vieille Cure de Cenon, Cenon-Bordeaux (Gironde)

VI90-20-10, 1952, v, 2,500 F bearer sh., w. coupons, 10-1/2" x 7-3/4", brown border . . $8.00

La Viscamine, Pontcharra-sur-Breda (Isére)

VI160-20-10, 1928, v, founder's bearer sh. w. coupons, blue background $9.00

Voyer & Compagnie S.A., Paris

*VO190-20-10, 1973, v, 50 F bearer sh. w. coupons, Imprimerie Spéciale de Valeurs Mobiliéres, 7-3/4" x 10-3/4", blue border on blue $3.00

Washington Palace S.A., Paris

WA100-20-10, 1920, 500 F bearer sh., blue on
green $4.00

French Congo

**Compagnie Générale Sangha-Likouala,
Brazzaville**

SA80-20-10, 1931, v, 1 bearer sh., brown
. . . .$7.00

French Equatorial Africa

**Compagnie de l'Afrique Française S.A.,
CAFRA, Pointe-Noire**

AF40-20-10, 1924, 2,500 C.F.A. bearer sh., Hélio
& Typo Aulard - Paris, 10" x 7-1/2", green
. . . .$5.00

French Guyana

**Société d'Exploitations Minières de l'Inini
(SEMI)**
EX60-20-10, ND, 5 bearer sh. (par 250 F) w.
coupons, grey-blue $4.00

UNLISTED TYPES & VARIETIES

Readers are welcome to contact the author directly at:

**Rainer Stahlberg
P.O. Box 1044
Rooseveltown, New York 13683**

Union Minière de la Haute Mana S.A., Cayenne

*UN60-20-10, ND, 1 bearer sh. (par 250 F) w. coupons, Imp. J.O.L. I - Paris, 8-1/2" x 12-3/4", green $4.00

French India

Savana S.A.
S30-20-10, 1952, v - elephants and oxen, 250 F stock $20.00

French Indochina

Société Agricole du Song-Ray, Saigon

*AG50-20-10, 1927, v, 10 Piaster bearer sh. w. coupons, 10-1/2" x 7-1/2", brown $12.00

Société des Cafés de l'Indochine, S.C.A.F.I., Saigon

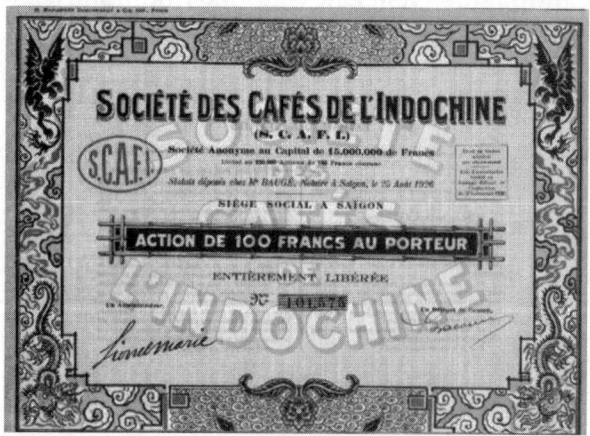

*CA40-20-10, 1926, v, 100 F bearer sh. w. coupons, multi-colored border on brown. . . .$12.00

Compagnie de Chemins de Fer Garantis des Colonies Françaises, Cai duong lua ò Saigon di Mytho
CH90-20-10, 1921, 500 F bearer stock, brown
. . . .$30.00

G

Germany

Schuldverschreibung

*40-20-10, 1911, 1,000 M Colonial 4% bond,
  brown on yellow................**$60.00**
40-40-10, 1925, v, 1,000 RM, 8" x 11" **$6.00**

Anleihe des Deutschen Reichs
60-20-10, 1922, 5,000 M, Schuldverschreibung,
  green............................**$5.00**
60-30-10, 1922, 10,000 M Schuldverschreibung,
  green............................**$3.00**

Schatzanweisung des Deutsches Reichs

*80-40-10, 1923, v, 100,000 Mark Reichswährung,
  7-15% bond w. coupons, Reichsdruckerei,
  8" x 11-1/2", black on green...........**$3.00**

Steuergutschein, Tax Payment Note

*100-30-10, 1937, v, 20 RM note, blue-green
  border.........................**$15.00**

Konversionskasse für Deutsche Auslandsschulden (Conversion Office for German Foreign Debts)

120-40-10, 1936 $1,000 3% bond due 1946, orange
. . . .**$40.00**

120-50-10, 1938, Fractional certificate, brown
. . . .**$36.00**

Federal Republic of Germany, German Government International Loan 1930-Extension issue of 1953

140-30-10, $1,000 5% bond due 1980, green
. . . .**$15.00**

Schuldverscreibung

*160-30-10, 1938, v, 100 RM 4-1/2%, red and grey border **$7.00**

> ***It is generally assumed that only 5% of certificates survive to reach collectors.***

*160-50-10, 1938, v, 1,000 RM 4-1/2% bond, red and grey border **$10.00**

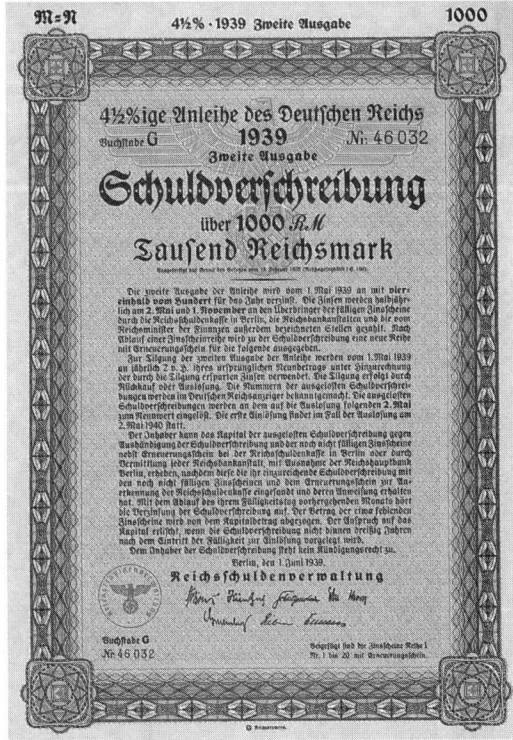

*160-60-10, 1939, v, 1,000 RM 4-1/2% bond, red and grey border **$11.00**

160-70-10, 1940, v, 1,000 RM 4-1/2% bond,
red and grey border.................$10.00

Schatzanweisung der Deutsches Reich

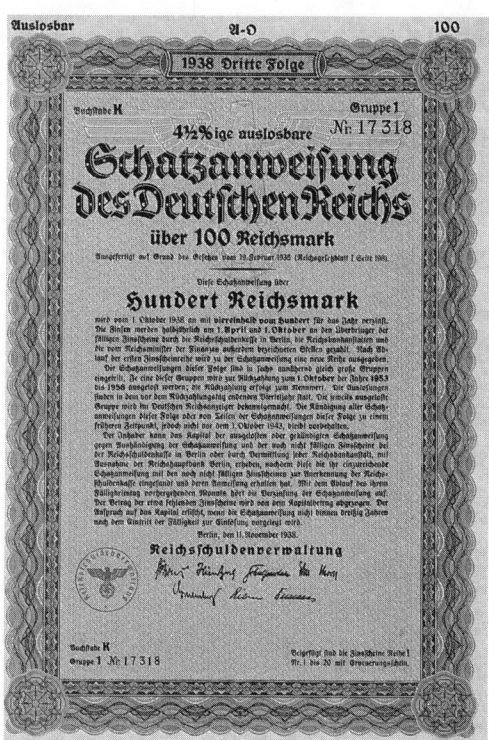

180-30-10, 1938, v, 100 RM 4-1/2% bond,
green and brown border $12.00

180-35-10, 1938, v, 500 RM 4-1/2% bond,
green and brown border $12.00

180-50-10, 1941, v, 1,000 RM 3-1/2% bond due
in 1956, red.......................$12.00

Aachener Lederfabrik AG, Aachen

AA60-20-10, 1929, 200 RM bearer sh., green
...................................$29.00

Aachener und Münchener Feuer-Versicherungs-Gesellschaft

AA90-20-10, 1970, 1 sh. (par 50 DM), green
...................................$3.00

AA90-25-10, 1962, 100 DM sh., green.....$3.00

AA90-30-10, 1970, 100 DM sh., blue $3.00

Aachener Rückversicherungs-Gesellschaft

AA120-20-10, 1988, 1 sh.(par 50 DM), purple
...................................$5.00

Achterbahn AG, Kiel

AC60-20-10, 1988, v, 1 bearer sh. (5 DM), multi-colored $10.00

AGAB

*AG60-20-10, 19??, 2 bearer sh., w. coupons,
green $3.00

AGIB AG for Grundbesitz und
Industriebeteligungen

AG100-30-10, 1980, 50 DM bearer sh., blue
. . . .$3.00

*AH60-20-10, 1989, 1 bearer sh. (50 DM), blue
. . . .$7.00

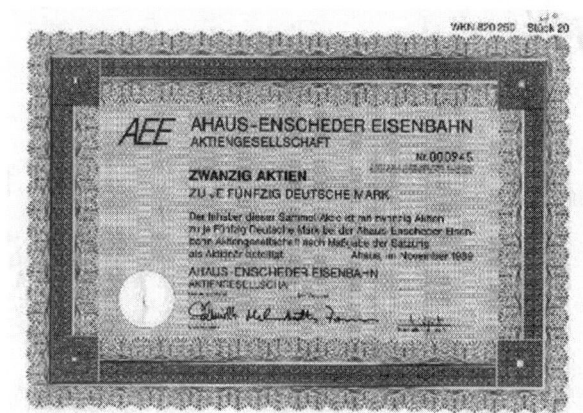

*AH60-25-10, 1988, v, 20 sh. (50 DM), brown
. . . .$5.00

AKJ Allgemeine Leasing AG

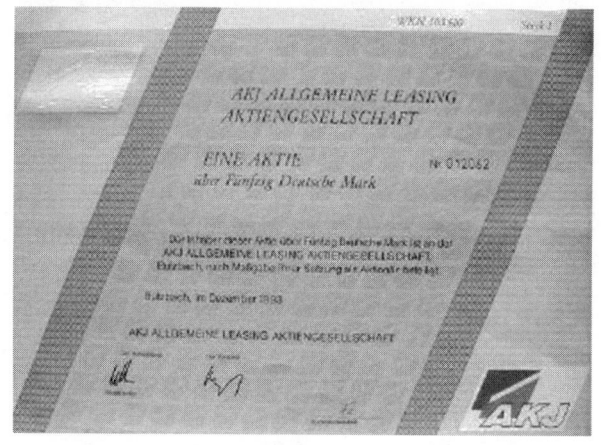

*AK90-20-10, 1993, 50 DM bearer sh. w. coupons,
blue $9.00

Ahaus-Enscheder Eisenbahn AG, Ahaus

*AG100-35-10, 1996, 50 DM bearer sh., blue
. . . .$3.00

Allgemeine Tanklager

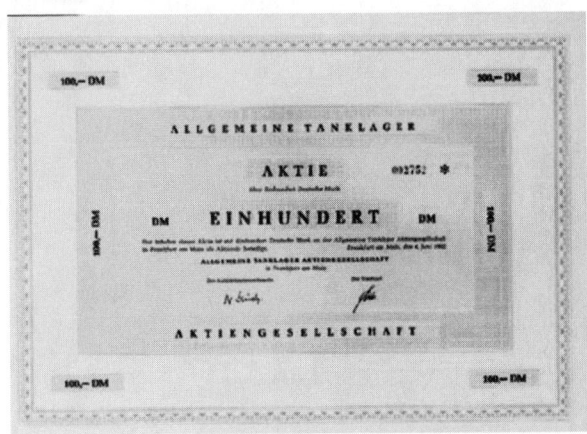

*AL110-30-10, 1962, 100 DM bearer certificate, yellow $3.00

Atlantis AG
AT100-20-10, 1969, v, 50 DM sh., deep blue
. . . .$8.00

Badische Anilin & Soda Fabrik (BASF)
BA60-40-10, 1971, v, 50 DM bearer sh., grey
. . . .$4.00
BA60-45-10, 1961, v, 100 DM, bearer sh., red
. . . .$5.00

*BA60-50-10, 1971, v, 200 DM bearer sh., green
. . . .$9.00
B30-55-10, 1961, v, 500 DM bearer sh., brown
. . . .$10.00

Beate Uhse AG
BE60-20-10, 1999, 1 Euro bearer sh., blue
. . . .$15.00

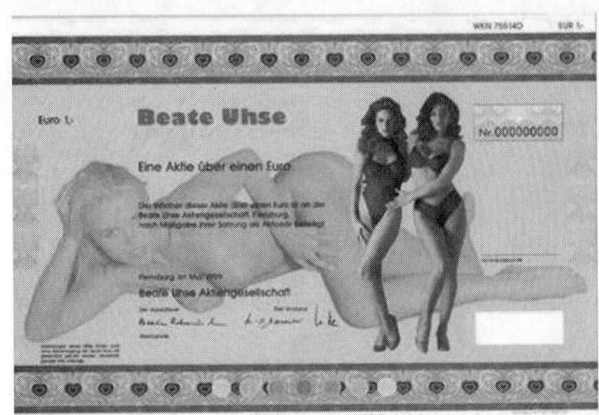

*BE60-25-10, 1999, 1 Euro specimen certificate, blue $15.00

C. Beckstein Pianoforte AG, Berlin
BE90-30-10, 1996, v, 500 DM sh., blue and brown
. . . .$22.00

AG Bergbau, Blei und Zinkfabrikation zu Stolberg und in Westfalen, Aachen

*BE250-20-10, 1901, v, 300 M bearer sh. w. coupons, dark green on light green $70.00

Bergedorfer Eisenwerk AG

*BE280-30-10, 1907, v, 1,000 M bearer sh., grey on blue $70.00

Berzelius Umwelt-Service AG, Frankfurt

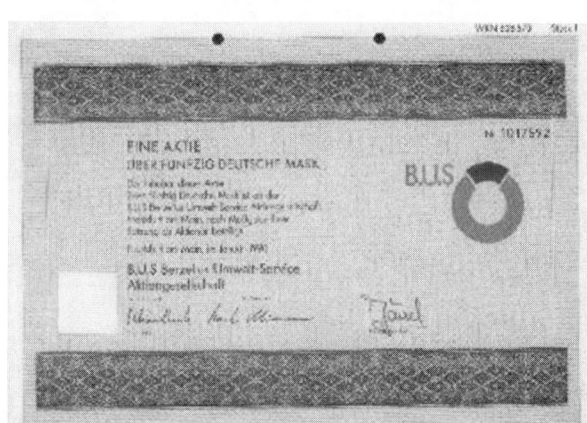

*BE340-30-10, 1990, v, 50 DM bearer sh., blue on green $4.00

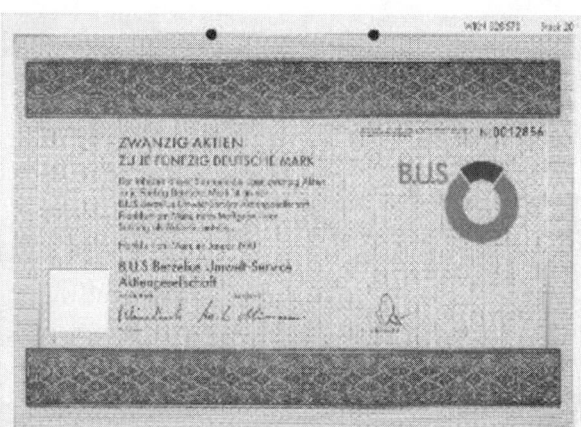

*BE340-40-10, 1990, v, 20 bearer sh., 1,000 DM, red on pink $4.00

Buderus AG

BU50-20-10, 1992, 1 sh., 50 DM, blue $15.00

CeWe Color Holding AG, Oldenburg

*CE80-20-10, 1992, v, 1 bearer sh. (50 DM), grey
. . . .$3.00

Chemische Fabrik Joh. Fritz Neuhaus A.G., Saargebiet

*CH160-30-10, 1923, v, 1,000 M sh., series B, green $10.00

der Chicken Club

*CH210-20-10, 19xx, v - naked woman, 1 sh.,
    dark green $10.00

Condomi AG
CO120-20-10, 1999, v, 1 bearer sh., red ...$25.00

Daimler-Benz AG, Stuttgart
DA140-50-10, 1942, v, 500 RM 4% Bond, green
    ....$12.00

DEGUSSA (Deutsche Guld und Silberscheideanstalt)
DE120-40-10, 19??, 50 DM bearer bond, brown
    ....$5.00

Deutsche Post AG

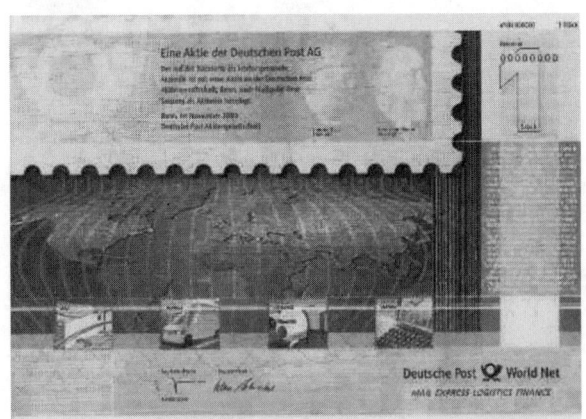

*DE320-40-10,19xx, v, u/s 1 bearer sh., yellow
    and blue........................$8.00

Deutsche Spiegelglas AG, Freden/Leine

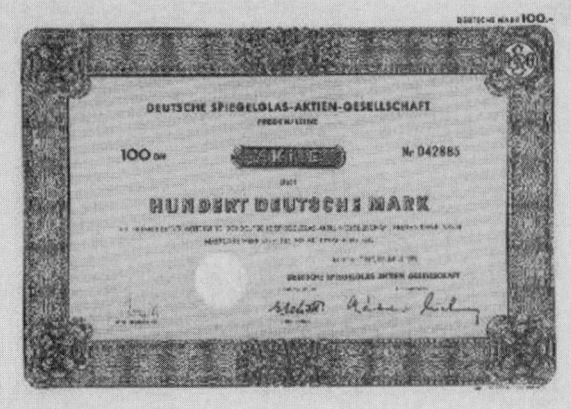

*DE380-30-10, 1971, 100 DM bearer sh., brown
    ....$7.00

Gebr. Dickertmann Hebezeugfabrik AG

*DI60-30-10, 1987, v, bearer sh. (100 DM),
    green..............................$3.00

This catalog has listings in an alphabetical format. The reason is simple: Companies diversify as they grow. For example, the Canadian Pacific Railway company recently split into five companies. They represent the railway, hotels, shipping, airline, and petroleum interests of the company. During World War II, the Singer sewing machine company made guns and other defense-related equipment, so where should we list it? It's far easier to use a strict alphabetical order, rather than to confuse the reader with topical classifications.

Ehlebracht AG

*EH60-40-10, 1994, preferred bearer sh. (50 DM),
blue $3.00

Anleihe der Stadt Elberfeld
EL60-40-10, 1922, v, 1,000 M 5% bond, 9" x 15",
grey-green.......................$15.00

The value of a stock certificate depends on:

- rarity
- the issuer
- signatures
- quality of engraving
- overall appearance
- condition
- date of issue

Erdöl-Bohrgesellschaft Plockhorts

*ER80-40-10, 1934, bearer sh., green $8.00

Erdölgesellschaft Oelerse, Hannover
Mining company.

*ER110-40-10, 1926, v, 1 bearer sh., green
................................$11.00

FAG Kugelfischer Georg Schäfer K Ga A

*FA60-30-10, 1985, 1 bearer sh. (DM 50), blue and grey $3.00

*FA60-35-10, 1985, 2 bearer sh. (100 DM), pink and brown........................$3.00

*FA60-50-10, 1986, 1 pref. bearer sh. (DM 50), blue and grey $4.00

*FA60-55-10, 1986, 2 pref. bearer sh. (100 DM), pink and brown....................$4.00

UNLISTED TYPES & VARIETIES

Readers are welcome to contact the author directly at:

**Rainer Stahlberg
P.O. Box 1044
Rooseveltown, New York 13683**

I.G. Farben

*FA260-40-10, 1953, v, 100 RM bearer sh. certificate w. coupons, brown $4.00

*FA260-45-10, 1953, v, 200 RM bearer sh. w. coupons, green $6.00

Flachglass AG Delog-Detag, Fürth (Bayern)

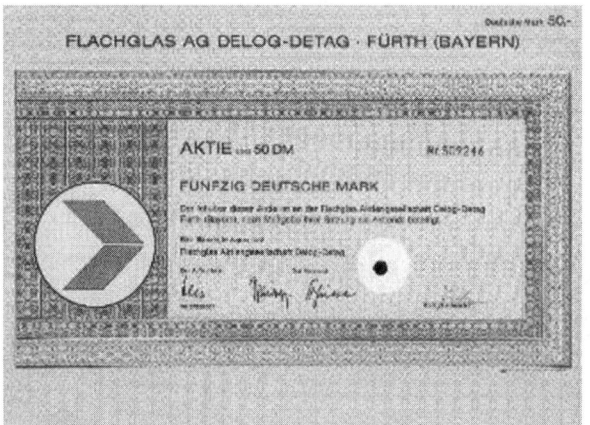

*FL70-30-10, 1972, v, 50 DM bearer sh., pink and brown $6.00

Fuchs Petrolub AG

*FU70-40-10, 1988, 3,000 DM 5% bond, brown $3.00

AG für Glasindustrie

GL80-30-10, 1888, 1,000 M bearer stock w. coupons, brown on yellow **$70.00**

Glasfabrik Eckamp-Altwasse AG

GL110-30-10, 1952, v, 200 DM bearer sh., green
. . . .**$9.00**

Vereinigte Grauwarse und Basalte AG

*GR80-30-10, 1921, 1,000 Mark bearer stock, Buchdruckerei Johann Balfer, Köln; 9" x 11", grey-green. **$4.00**

Heidelberger Zement AG

HE120-40-10, 1991, v, 20 sh. (50 DM), dark grey
. . . .**$15.00**

Henkel KgaA, Düsseldorf

*HE400-60-10, 1985, v, 10 pref. bearer sh. (50 DM), blue. **$6.00**

Fr. Hesser AG, Stuttgart-Bad Cannstatt

*HE620-30-10, 1981, 100 DM sh., blue
. . . .**$12.00**

Hoesch AG, Dortmund

HO150-40-10, 1943, 1,000 RM bearer sh., blue
...............................$20.00

Kamerun-Eisenbahn-Gesselschaft auslandsgeschäfle Wagner Computer

KA90-20-10, 1973, 50 DM, brown........$7.00

Korf-Stahl AG, Baden-Baden

KO180-30-10, 1972, v, 1 bearer sh. (50DM), reddish brown $3.00

Fried. Krupp AG Hoesch-Krupp

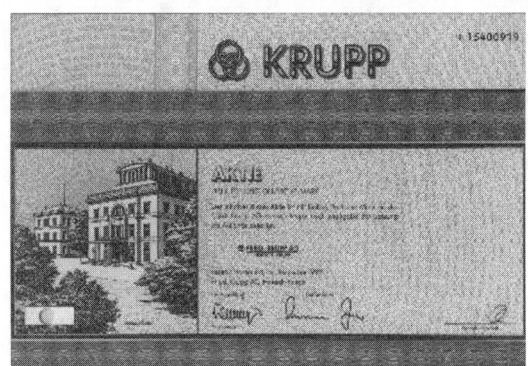

KR410-50-10, 1992, v, 50 DM bearer sh., lilac
...............................$12.00

Leifheit AG

LE160-30-10, 1984, 50 DM bearer sh., green
...............................$3.00

Lindner Holding KgaA

LI150-30-10, 1991, 50 DM sh............$5.00

Lowaland-Werke Bitzer & Co., AG, Düsseldorf

LO430-40-10, 1948, 1,000 RM bearer sh., grey
...............................$27.00

Lufthansa AG

LU170-40-10, 1968, 50 DM sh..........$12.00
LU170-45-10, 1966, v, 1,000 DM sh., brown
...............................$20.00

MAHO AG

MA150-30-10, 1992, 50 DM, blue........$4.00

MAN AG, München

*MA280-50-10,*1986, v, 2 pref. bearer shares (100 DM), green **$4.00**

Mannesmann AG, Dusseldorf

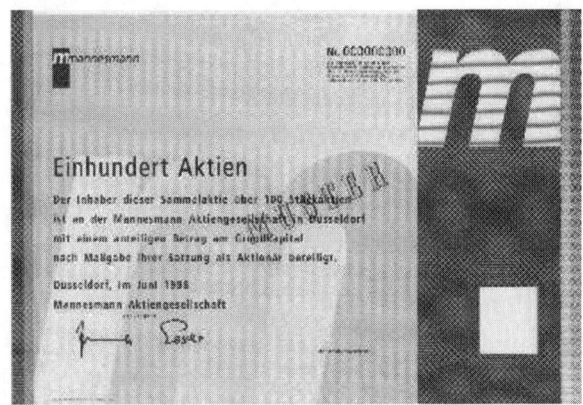

MA310-50-10, 1998, v, 100 sh., bearer sh., green **$3.00**

Mitsubishi Oil Co. Ltd.

MI430-30-10, 1985, 1 option, grey **$9.00**

Muldentalwerke AG in Freiberg, Freiberg

MU270-30-10, 1922, 1,000 M bearer sh. w. coupons, brown **$15.00**

MU270-35-10, 1923, 1,000 M bearer sh. w. coupons, purple border **$15.00**

Niedersächsische Bergbaugesellschaft "Rote Erde", Hannover

NI110-30-10, 1926, v, 50 RM, green **$5.00**

Oehringen Bergbau AG zu Berlin

OE140-30-10, 1925, v, 100 RM bearer sh., blue on green $15.00

K.K. Priv. Prag-Duxer Eisenbahn

PR150-30-10, 1896, 300 M 3% bond, light brown $9.00

Moritz Prescher Nachfolger AG, Leipzig

PR220-30-10, 1926, v, 100 RM, blue $25.00

Preussag AG, Berlin/Hannover

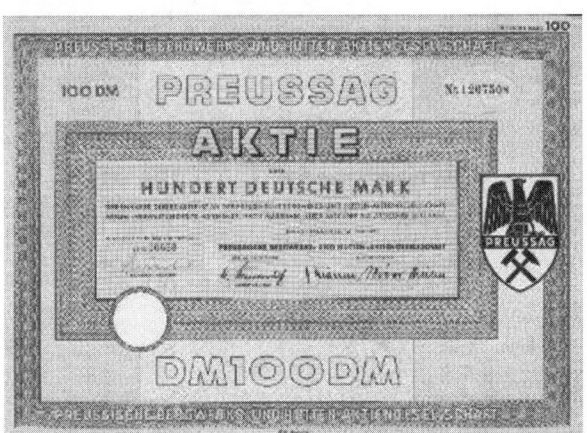

PR290-50-10, 1961, v, 100 DM bearer sh., grey $8.00

Friedr. Wilh. Remy & Cie. AG

RE140-30-10, 1923, 1,000 M bearer stock, brown on yellow $5.00

Rheinelektra AG

*RH170-30-10, 1983, 1 bearer sh., 50 DM, blue $4.00

Rheinisch-Westfälische Kalkweke AG

RH200-40-10, 1963, 100 DM 6% bond due 2000, blue $3.00

Rosenthal-Porzallan AG

RO330-40-10, 1942, 100 RM bearer sh., brown $30.00

Ruhrstahl AG

RU160-60-10, 1954, v, 100 DM 7% bearer bond, grey $8.00
RU160-65-10, 1954, v, 1,000 DM 7% bearer bond, brown $8.00

Hermann Schött AG

SS150-30-10, 1951, 100 DM bearer stock, grey $4.00

Schramm AG, Offenbach/Main

*SC210-30-10, 1977, v, 1,000 DM bearer sh., grey on green $4.00

Schramm Lack- und Farbenfabriken AG

SC240-30-10, 1951, v, 100 DM bearer stock, brown $3.00
SC240-40-10, 1965, v, 100 DM bearer stock, brown $3.00
SC240-50-10, 1977, v, 1,000 DM bearer stock, green $3.00

SKW Trostberg AG

*SK230-40-10, 1995, 10 bearer sh. (par 50 DM), grey $3.00

Jooss Söhne AG für Hoch-, Tief- und Eisenbetonbau in München

*SU160-30-10, 1921, v, 1,000 M sh.......$12.00

Stader Lederfabrik AG

ST90-30-10, 1950, 100 DM bearer stock, green
. . . .$11.00

R. Stahl AG

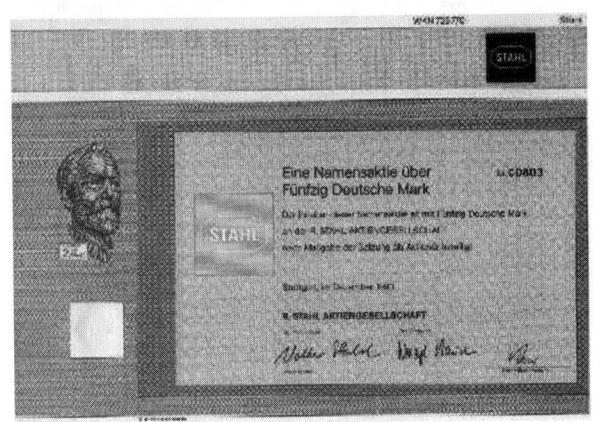

ST120-30-10, 1993, u/u 1 sh. (50 DM), grey, blue
and pink $3.00

ST120-40-10, 1993, u/u 1 pref. sh. (50 DM) certificate, grey, blue and pink $3.00

Stahlberg A.G. für Metallwarenerzeugung zu Köln a. Rh.

ST220-30-10, 1922, v, 1,000 Mark bearer sh.,
brown $11.00

The value of a stock certificate depends on:

- rarity
- the issuer
- signatures
- quality of engraving
- overall appearance
- condition
- date of issue

Süddeutsche Boden-Creditbank

SU140-50-10, 1942, v, 1,000 RM 4% debenture, multicolored border $8.00

Südzucker AG Mannheim/Ochsenfürt

*SU260-40-10, 1990, 1 pref sh. (50 DM), green
.................................$5.00

Thyssen AG

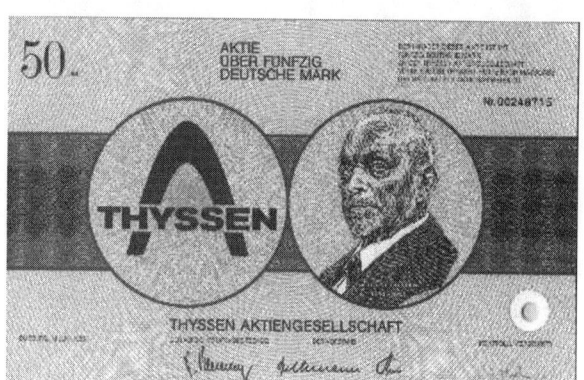

*TH180-50-10, 1986, v, 50 DM sh., blue
.................................$13.00

Tonwarenindustrie Wiesloch AG, Wiesloch/ Baden

*TO220-40-10, 1974, v, 100 DM bearer stock, clue
.................................$6.00

*TO220-50-10, 1984, v, 50 DM bearer stock, green
.................................$5.00

Triumph Werke Nürnberg AG

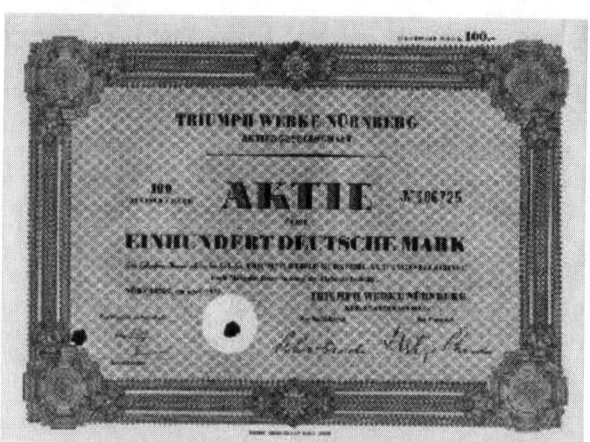

*TR140-30-10, 1951, v, 100 DM bearer sh., blue
.................................$18.00

Uhlig & Weiske Mühlenwerke Aktiengesellschaft in Bad Lausick

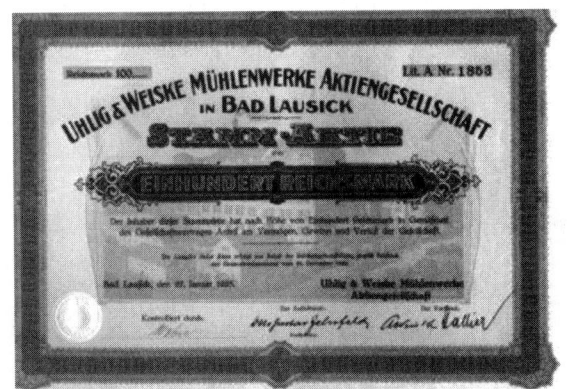

*UH150-30-10, 1925, v, 100RM bearer stock, brown on green $27.00

*UH150-35-10, 1928, v, 100RM bearer stock, brown on green $24.00

Union Baugesellschaft auf Actien, Berlin
UN180-30-10, 1933, 100 M bearer sh., brown
. . . .$9.00

Varta AG

*VA140-30-10, 1977, v, 10 sh. (500 DM), brown and pink $13.00

Wagner Computer, Kamerun-Eisenbahn-Gesellschaft

*WA140-30-10, 1973, v, bearer sh. (50 DM), brown $4.00

Wallbergbahn AG, Rottach-Egern, Bayern

*WA260-30-10, 1950, v, 100 DM bearer sh., grey-blue. $40.00

WCM Beteiligungs-und Grundbesitz-AG, Heidenheim/Brenz

*WC80-30-10, 1994, v, 1 bearer sh. (50 DM), blue $3.00

Westend Terrain und Beteiligungges AG

WE200-30-10, 1982, v, 50 DM sh. certificate,
   grey $3.00

Wibau AG

WI120-30-10, 1983, 1 sh. (50 DM), green . . .$7.00

Wilke-Werke AG, Braunschweig

*WI240-40-10, 1950, v, 1,000 DM bearer sh.,
   blue $6.00

Windhoff Aktiengesellschaft

WI310-30-10, 1993, 50 DM bearer sh.,
   green and blue $5.00

Wintershall AG, Celle

*WI380-30-10, 1951, v, 100 DM bearer sh.,
   green $15.00

F. Wöhlert'schen Maschinenban-Anstalt und Eisengiesseerei AG

WO110-20-10, 1881, v, 600 RM bearer stock,
   brown $10.00

Great Britain

The 600 Group Limited

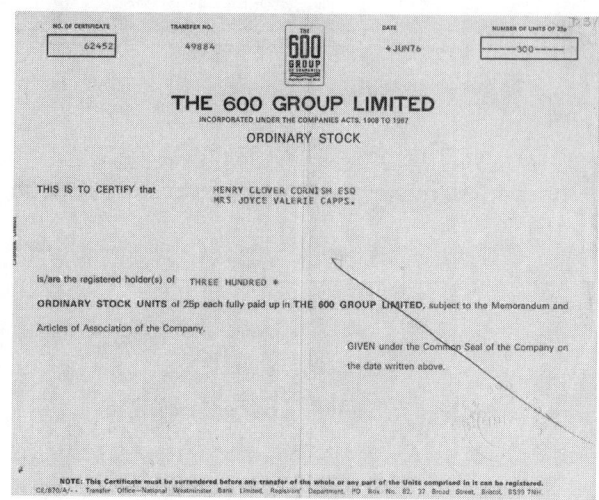

*160-30-10, 1976, v, 300 sh. (par 25p), Caustons,
   London; 9-3/4" x 8", black on white $3.00

The African Transcontinental Telegraph Company Limited

AF80-20-10, 1894, 100 sh., grey $120.00

This catalog has listings in an alphabetical format. The reason is simple: Companies diversify as they grow. For example, the Canadian Pacific Railway company recently split into five companies. They represent the railway, hotels, shipping, airline, and petroleum interests of the company. During World War II, the Singer sewing machine company made guns and other defense-related equipment, so where should we list it? It's far easier to use a strict alphabetical order, rather than to confuse the reader with topical classifications.

Akroyd & Smithers P.L.C.

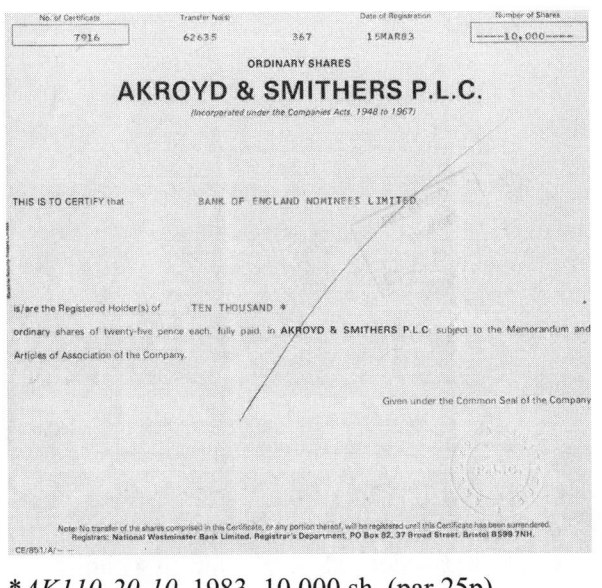

*AK110-20-10, 1983, 10,000 sh. (par 25p),
Waterlow Security Printers Limited, 8-3/4" x 8",
blue on white. $3.00

Alders Paper Mills Limited

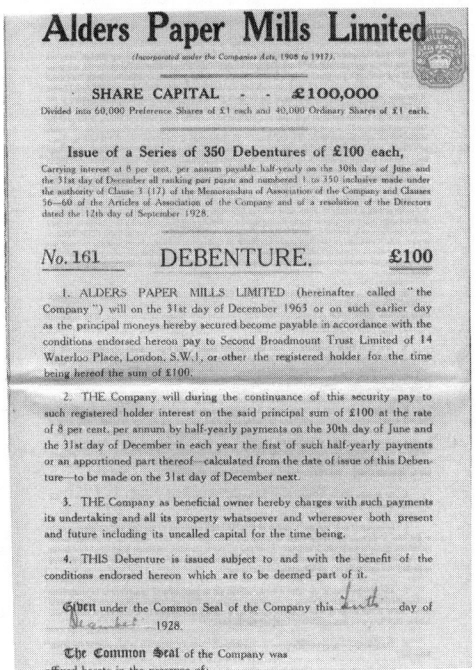

*AL80-40-10, 1928, £100 8% debenture, w/o
imprint name, 11-1/4" x 17-1/2", grey $5.00

The Anchor Chemical Company Limited
(par 5 shillings)

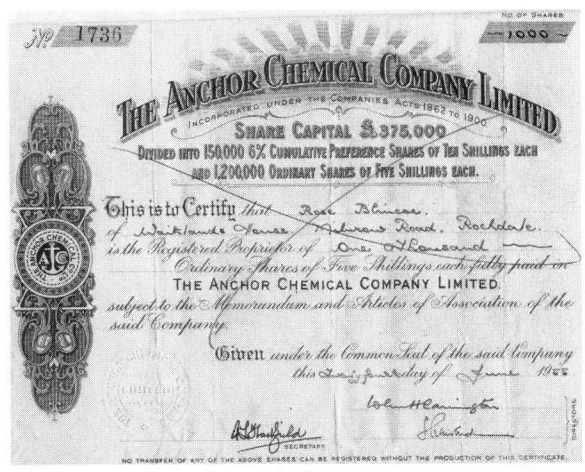

*AN170-40-10, 1955, 1,000 sh., 10-1/2" x 9-1/2",
grey. $3.00

Anglian Unit Trust

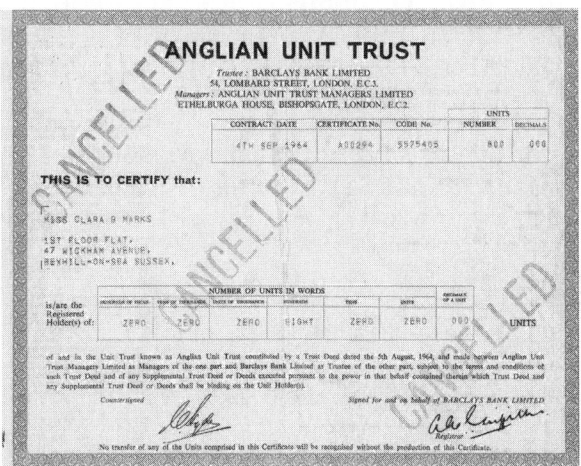

*AN390-20-10, 1964, 800 units, Thomas de la Rue
& Co., 10-1/4" x 7-3/4", orange. $3.00

Anglo-Argentine Tramways Company Limited

*AN430-40-10, 1910, v, £20 6% bond, red . .**$5.00**

Anglo-Belgian Company of Egypt Limited.

AN460-20-10, 1919, v, 1 bearer sh. (par £5), text in English and French, green **$7.00**

Compagnie Anglo-Française Marocaine Limited (par £1), London

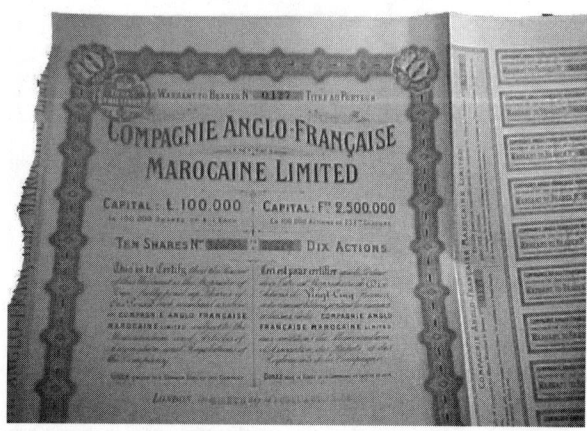

*AN490-20-10, 1908, 10 shares w. coupons, text in English and French, brown. **$12.00**

Associated Leisure Limited

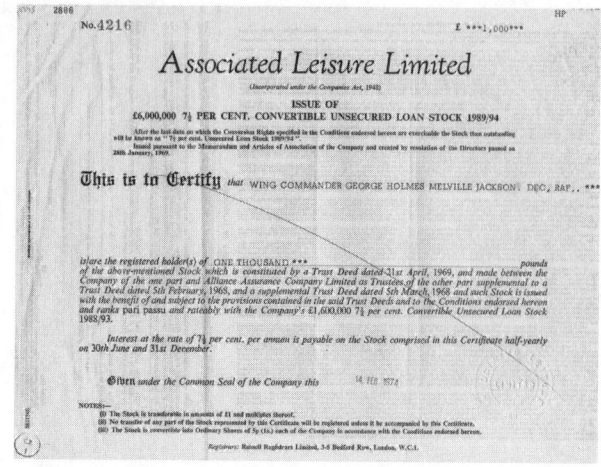

*AS300-40-10, 1974, £1,000 7-1/2% conver. unsecured loan stock 1989/94, Burrup, Mathieson & Co. Ltd., London; 11" x 8", blue on white
. . . .**$3.00**

Associated Leisure Public Limited Company (par 5p)

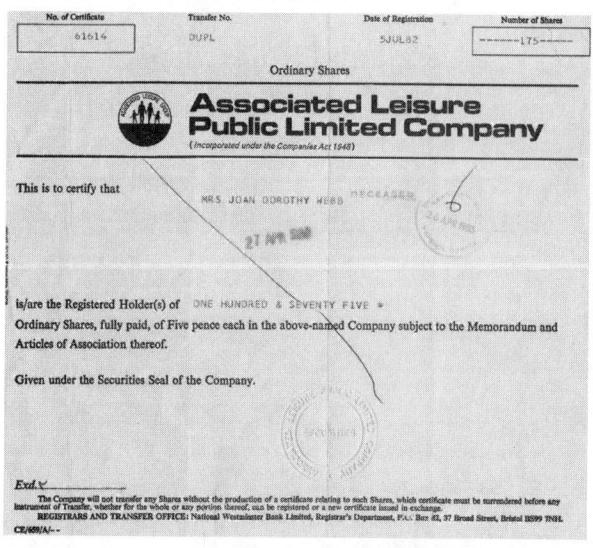

*AS310-20-10, 1982, 175 sh., Burrup, Mathieson & Co. Ltd., London; 9" x 8", black on white
. . . .**$3.00**

It is generally assumed that only 5% of certificates survive to reach collectors.

Bambergers Limited

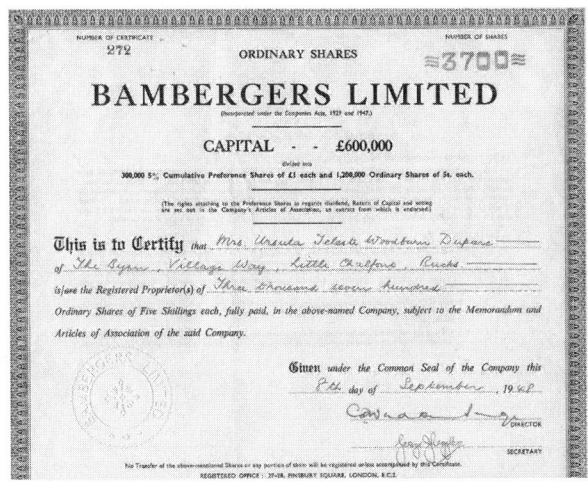

*BA170-30-10, 1948, 3,700 sh. (par 5/-), St. Clements Press, Ltd., Kingsway; 11-3/4" x 10", grey border $3.00

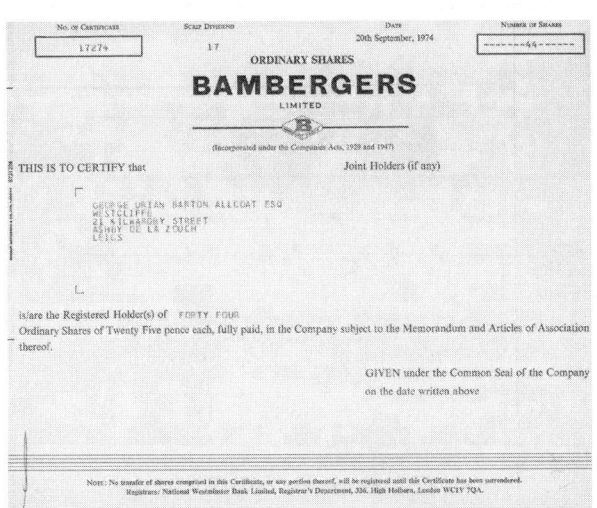

*BA170-40-10, 1974, v, 44 sh. (par 25p), Burrup, Mathieson & Co., Ltd., London; 10" x 8" $3.00

Banner Gold Mine, Limited

Mine located close to Oroville, Butte County, CA.
*BA230-20-10, 1896, i/u 3,500 sh. (par £1), brown $15.00

Barcelona Traction, Light and Power Company Limited (par $100 gold)

*BA320-30-10, 1923, v, 1 sh. warrant, text in English and French, Waterlow & Sons, brown $5.00

Barker & Dobson Group p.l.c.

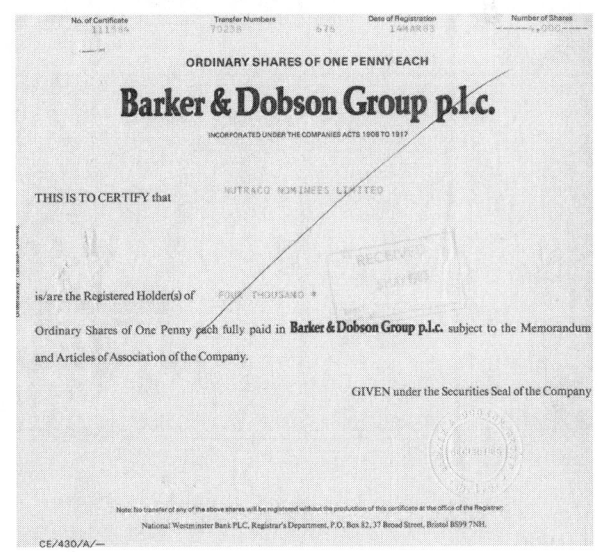

*BA380-20-10, 1983, 4,000 sh. (par 1p), Greenaway - Harrison Limited; 9" x 8", black on white $3.00

Bent's Brewery Company, Limited, Liverpool

BE190-40-10, 1923, £1,150 6% irredeemable
    debenture, black $10.00

Birmid Qualcast Limited

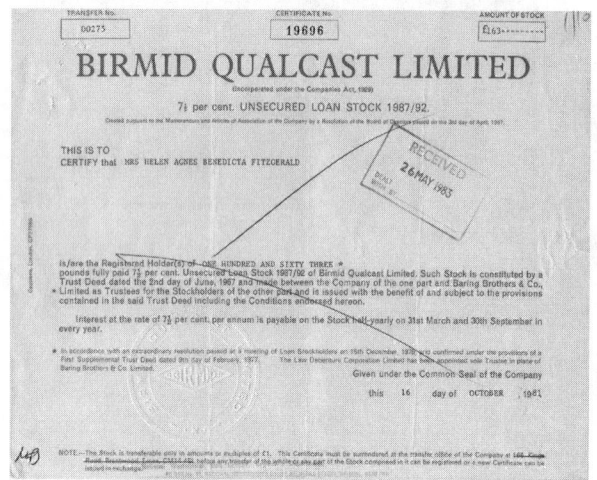

BI240-40-10, 1981, £163 7-1/2% unsecured loan
    stock of 1987/92, Caustons, London; 10" x 8"
    . . . .$3.00

Blue Circle Industries Limited

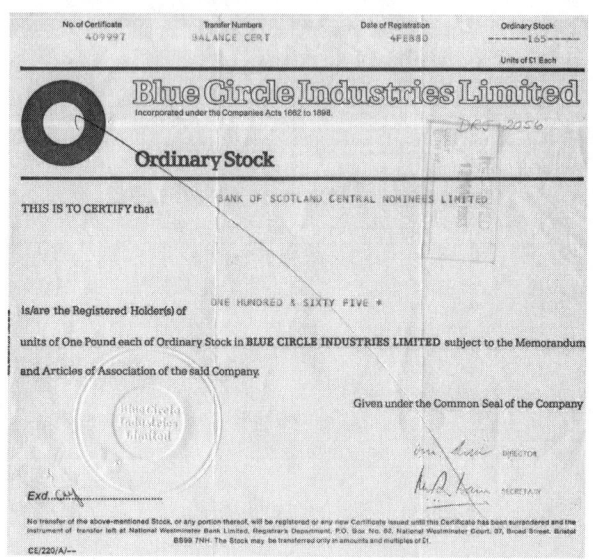

BL370-20-10, 1980, v, 165 sh. (par £1), Burrup,
    Mathieson & Co. Ltd., London; 9" x 8", blue on
    white $3.00

Brazendale and Company, Limited

BR310-20-10, 1951, 50 sh. (par £), The Solici-
    tors' Law Stationery society, Limited, London;
    11-1/2" x 9", blue border $3.00

British Gas plc

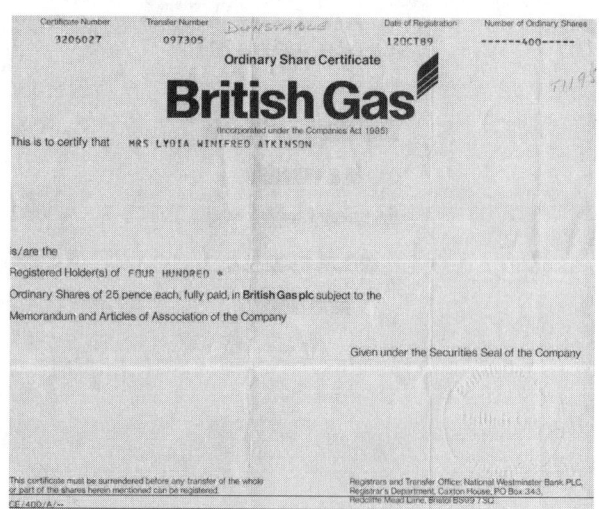

BR440-40-10, 1989, 400 sh. (par 25p), w/o
    imprint, 9" x 7-1/2", blue on white. $3.00

The value of a stock certificate depends on:
- rarity
- the issuer
- signatures
- quality of engraving
- overall appearance
- condition
- date of issue

The British Honduras Company, Limited

*BR470-20-10, 1863, 1 sh. (par £5), black
................................**$15.00**

The British Molybdenite Company, Limited (par £1)

BR610-20-10, 1906, 5 sh., brown........**$10.00**

British Vita Company Limited

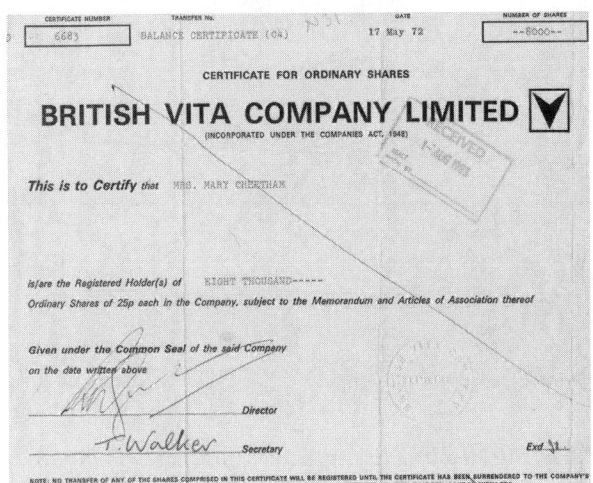

*BR840-20-10, 1972, 8,000 sh. (par 25p), 10" x 8", black on white.....................**$3.00**

Brixton Estate Limited

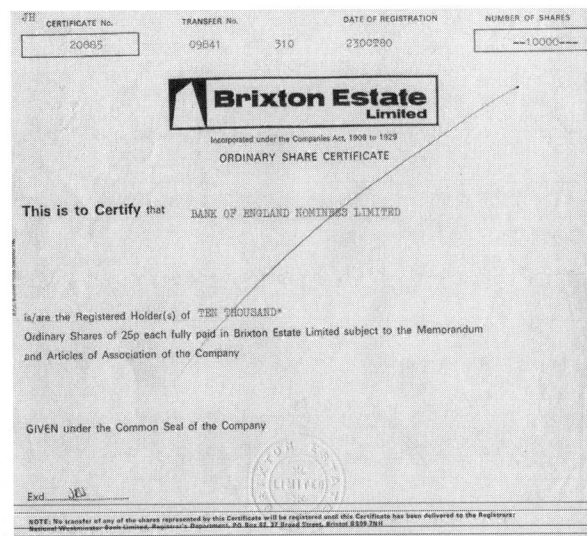

*BR900-20-10, 1980, v, 10,000 sh. (par 25p), B.P.C. Business Forms (Security) Ltd., 9" x 8", blue on white **$3.00**

Brooke Bond Liebig Limited

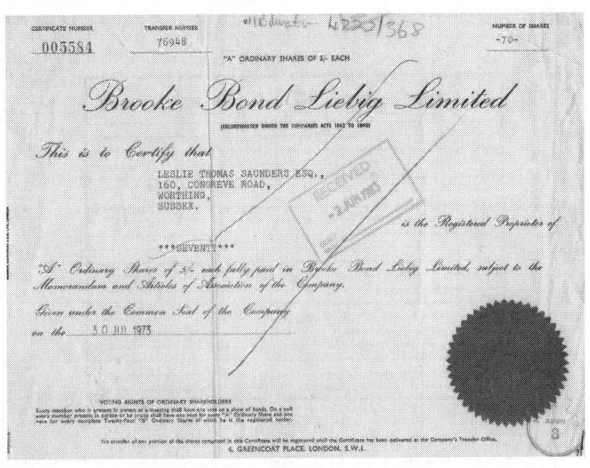

*BR1020-20-10, 1973, 70 "A" sh. (par 5/-), Burrup, Mathieson & Co. Ltd.; 9-3/4" x 7-1/2"
................................**$3.00**

Bryant Holdings Limited

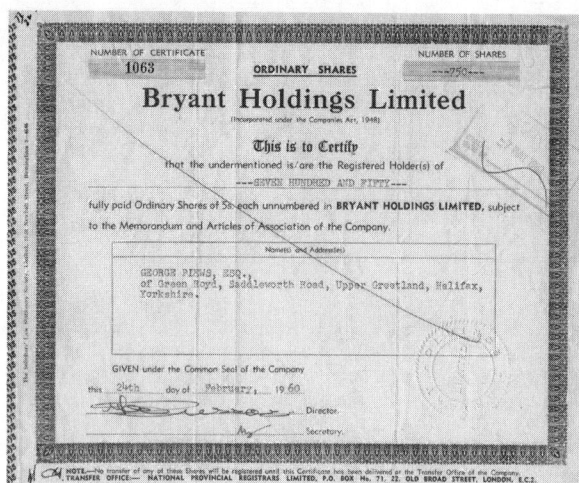

*BR1200-20-10, 1960, 750 sh. (par 5/-), The Solicitor's Law Stationery Society, Limited, Birmingham; 10" x 8", blue on white $3.00

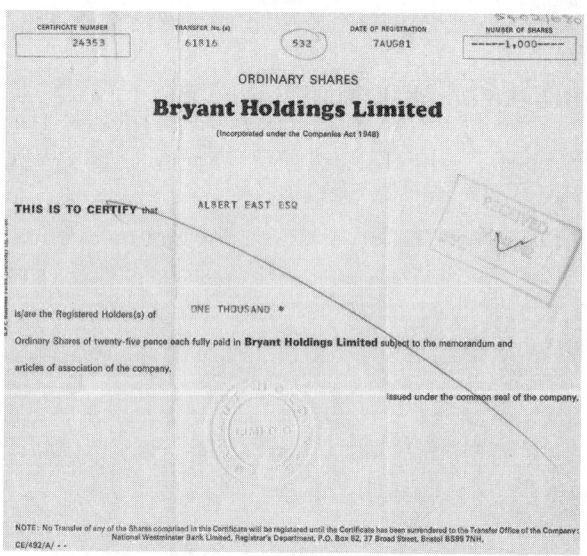

*BR1200-30-10, 1981, 1,000 sh., B.P.C. Business Forms (Security) Ltd.; 9" x 8", blue on white $3.00

H.P. Bulmer Holdings Limited

BU280-20-10, 1977, v, 500 sh. (par 25p), Burrup, Mathieson & Co. Ltd.; 9" x 7-1/4", green on white $3.00

Cable and Wireless Public Limited Company

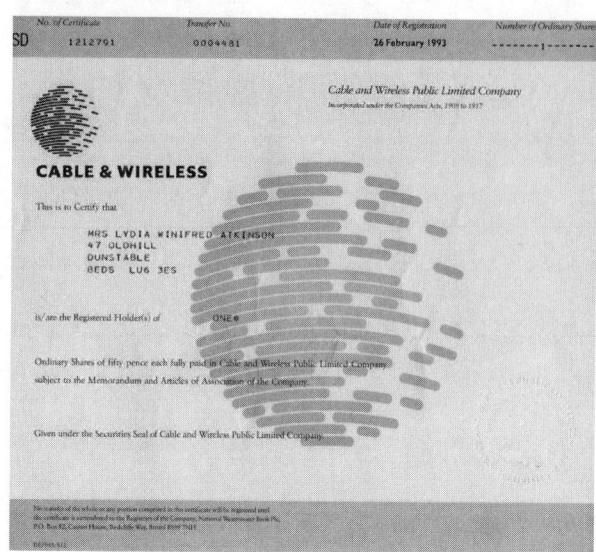

*CA60-20-10, 1993, v, 1 sh. (par 50p), BPCC Waterlow Fetty, 9" x 8", blue...........$3.00

Camp Bird Limited

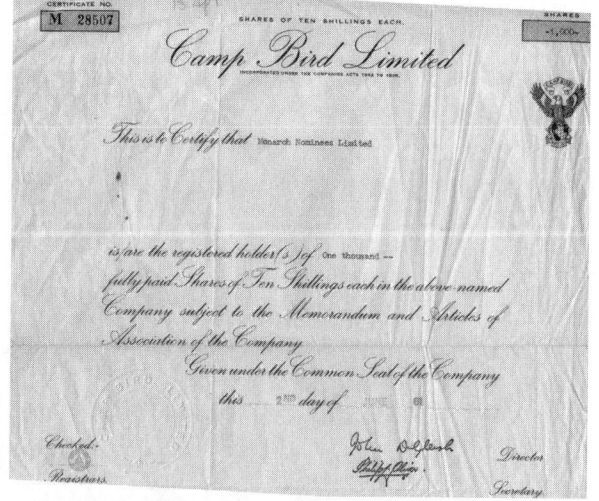

*CA180-40-10, 1961, v, 1,000 sh. (par 10/-), w/o imprint, 10-1/2" x 9-1/2", black on white $3.00

Change Wares Limited

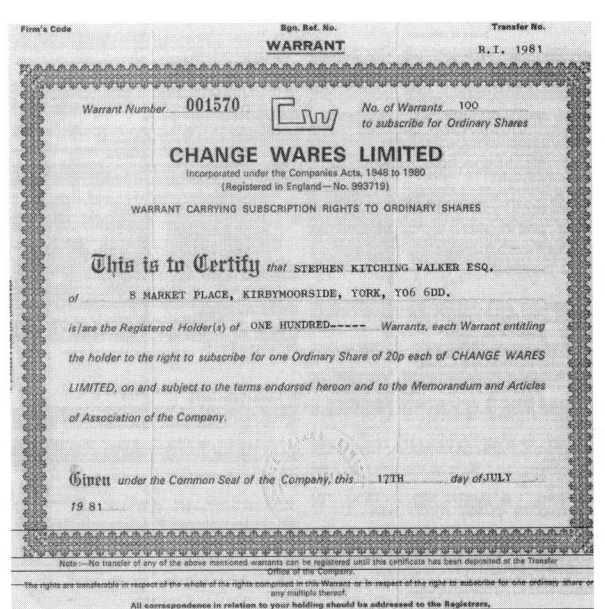

*CH120-20-10, 1981, w, 100 warrants shares 20 p each, S. Straker & Sons Ltd., London; 8-3/4" x 8-1/2", red border, red on white **$3.00**

The Chilian Northern Railway Company Limited

CH250-40-10, 1912, v, £20 6% first mort. debenture, orange **$15.00**

*CH250-50-10, 1912, v, £100 debenture, green **$15.00**

CH250-60-10, 1913, v, £20 debenture, red **$15.00**
CH250-70-10, 1913, v, £100 6% debenture, green **$15.00**

Christie-Tyler Limited

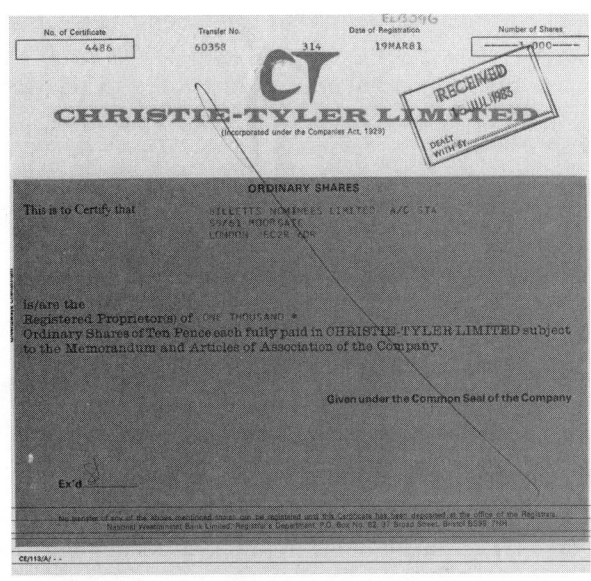

*CH590-40-10, 1981, 1,000 sh. (par 10p), Greenaways Cheltenham, 9" x 8", reddish-orange **$3.00**

Clarkson Old Brewery Barnsley Limited (par £10)

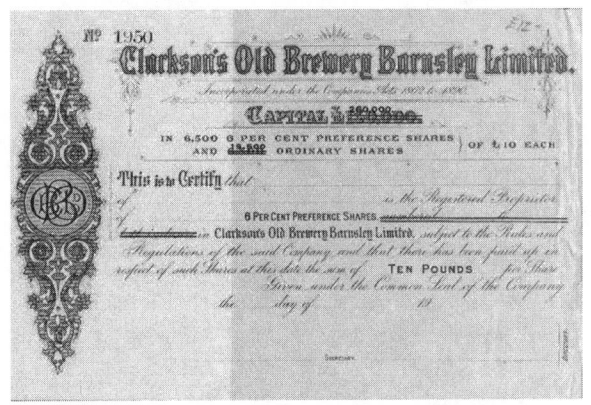

*CL230-40-10, 19xx, v, u/u 6% pref. sh., certificate, capital £260,000 over £130,000, grey **$5.00**

Coates Brothers & Company, Limited

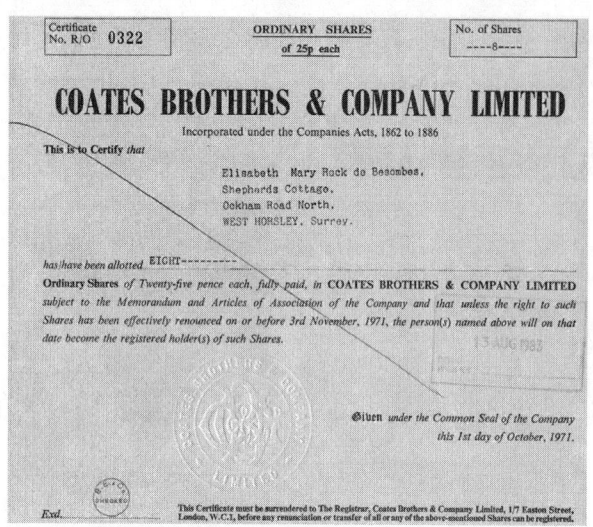

*CO70-40-10, 1971, 8 sh. (par 25p), w/o imprint, 8-1/4" x 7", blue on grey $3.00

Colombian National Railway Company

The interest upon this debenture is guaranteed by the Government of the Republic of Colombia.

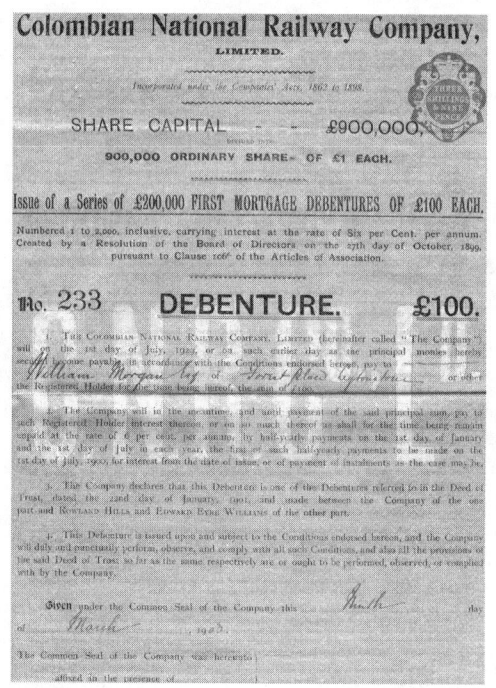

*CO230-40-10, 1903, £100 6% 1st mortgage debenture, w/o imprint, 11" x 17-1/2", blue border $8.00

The Commonwealth Oil Corporation Limited

*CO330-20-10, 1927, v, 36,100 deferred ordinary shares, (par 1/-) 12" x 11", grey $5.00

Computer and Systems Engineering p.l.c.

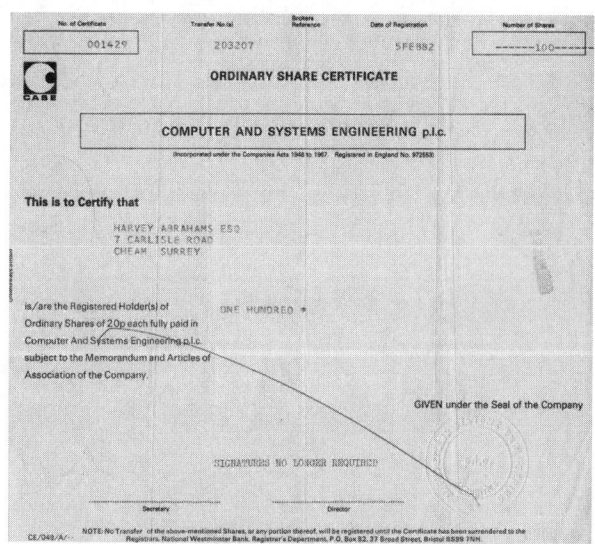

*CO370-20-10, 1982, 100 sh. (par 20p), Greenaways Stroud, 8-3/4" x 8", black on white $3.00

Wm. Cory & Son, Limited

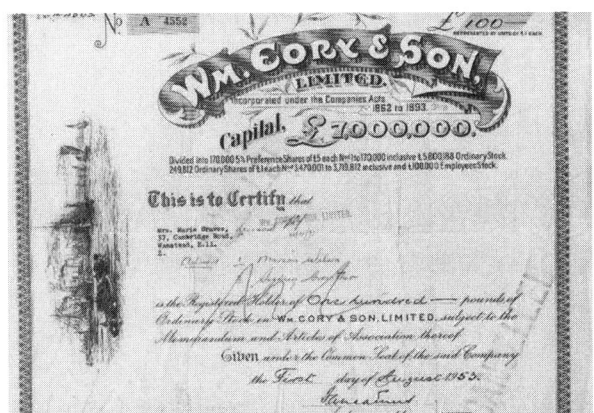

*CO430-30-10, 1953, v, 100 sh. (par £1), grey
..................................$5.00

Crittall-Hope Limited

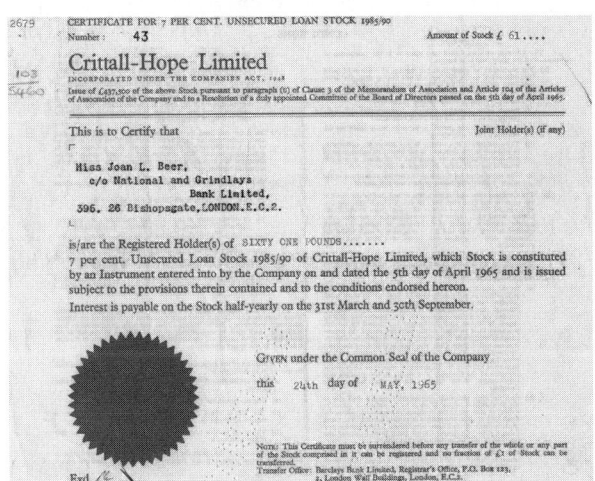

*CR180-40-10, 1965, £61 7% unsecured loan
1985/90, Waterlow London, 10" x 8", red
..................................$3.00

The value of a stock certificate depends on:

- rarity
- the issuer
- signatures
- quality of engraving
- overall appearance
- condition
- date of issue

The De La Rue Company Limited

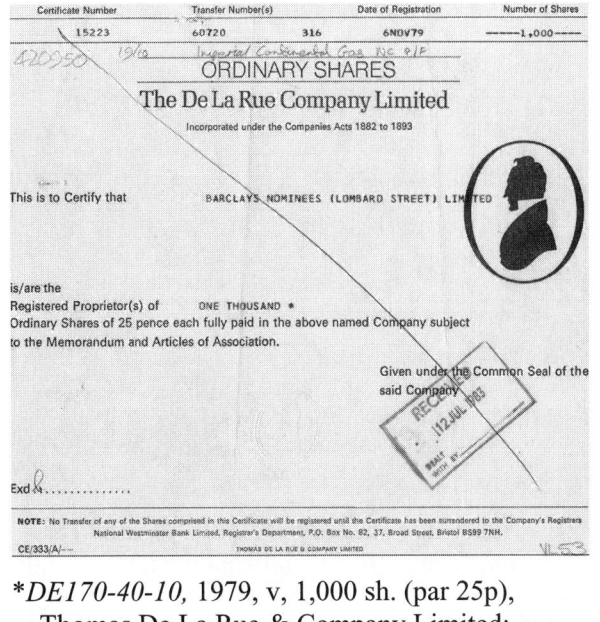

*DE170-40-10, 1979, v, 1,000 sh. (par 25p),
Thomas De La Rue & Company Limited;
8-3/4" x 8", green...................$4.00

Delta Group p.l.c.

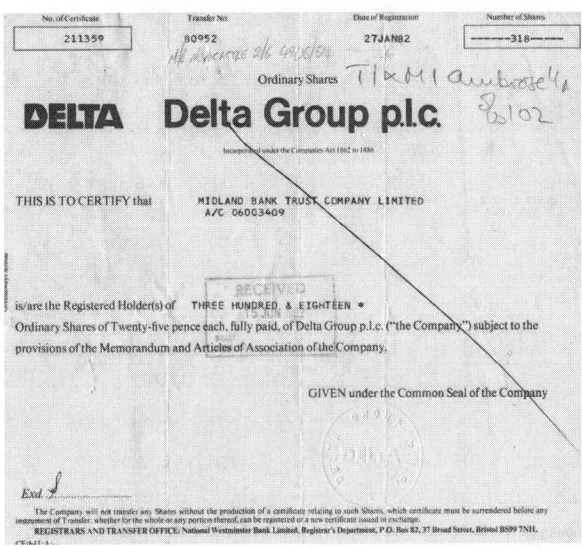

*DE230-30-10, 1982, 318 sh. (par 25p), Green-
aways Stroud, 9" x 8", blue on white.....$3.00

Delta Metal Company, Limited

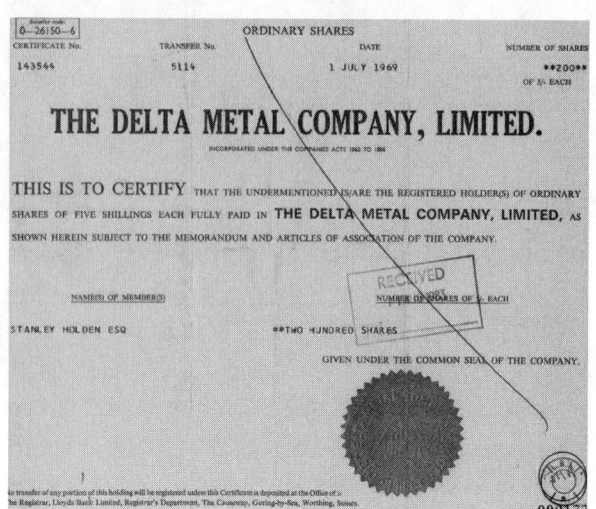

*DE250-40-10, 1969, 200 sh. (par 5/-), Smith & Guzman Ltd.; 10" x 8", brown on white...**$3.00**

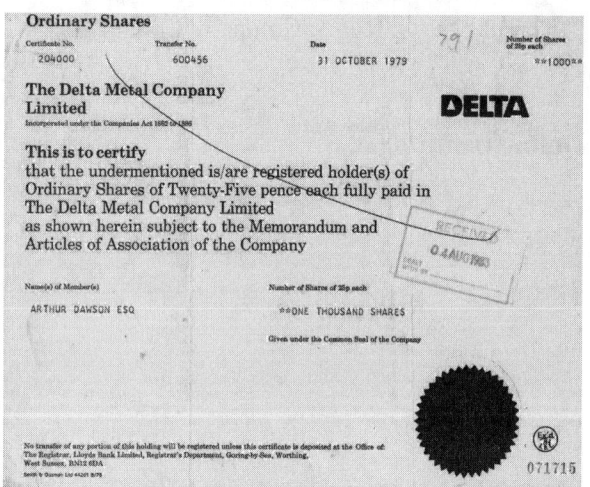

*DE250-50-10, 1979, 1,000 sh. (par 25p), Smith & Guzman Ltd.; 10" x 8", blue on white **$3.00**

Doornkop Gold Mining Company

The company was struck off the register in 1899.
DO230-20-10, 1896, 20 sh. (par £1).......**$5.00**

> *It is generally assumed that only 5% of certificates survive to reach collectors.*

Duport Limited

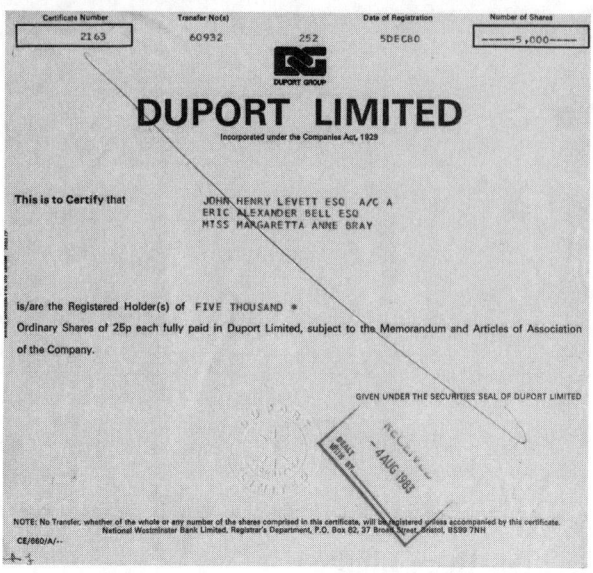

*DU260-40-10, 1980, 5,000 sh. (par 25p), Burrup, Mathieson & Co. Ltd., London; 9" x 8", blue on white **$3.00**

The Easton & Church Hope Railway Co. (Par £20)

EA130-30-10, 188x, unissued certificate, red **$8.00**

Elys (Wimbledon) Limited

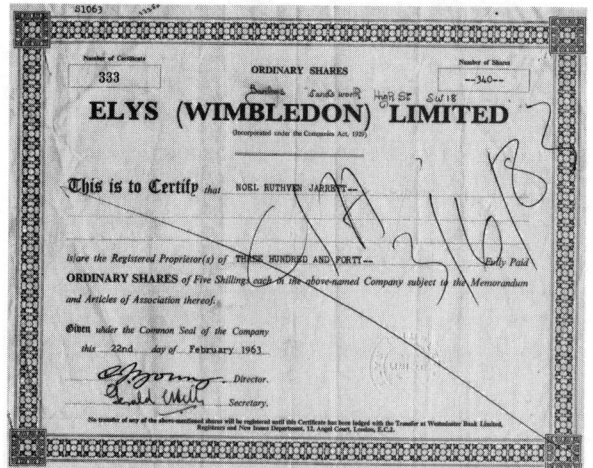

*EL280-30-10, 1963, 340 sh. (par 5/-), HJR&L, 11-1/4" x 8-1/2", green on white **$3.00**

Evered and Company Holdings Limited

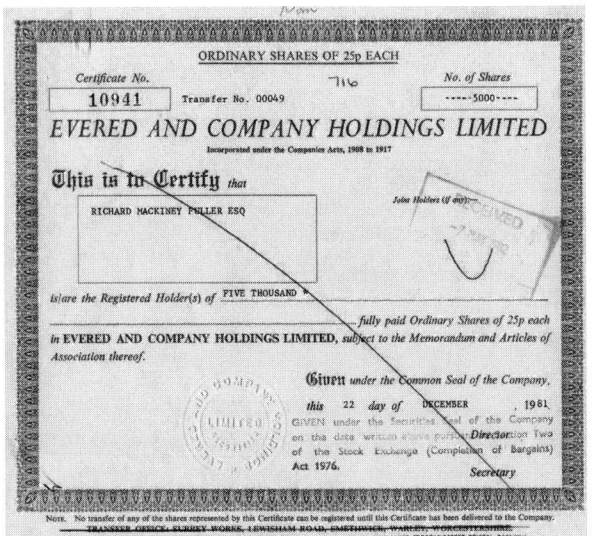

*EV130-30-10, 1981, 5,000 sh. (par 25p), Burrup, Mathieson & Co. Ltd., London; 9" x 8", green on white $3.00

Ferranti plc

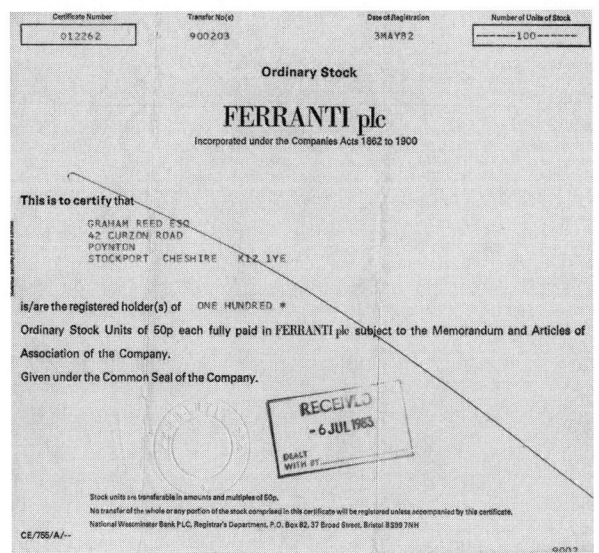

*FE350-40-10, 1982, 100 sh. (par 50p), Waterlow Security Printers Limited, 9" x 8", dark blue on white $3.00

The Fleming Mercantile Invesment Trust Public Limited Company

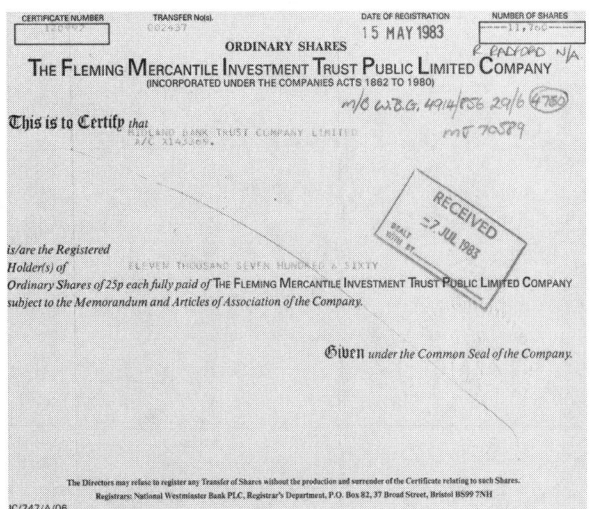

*FL120-40-10, 1983, 11,760 sh. (par 25p), w/o imprint, 9" x 7-1/2", black on white $3.00

Ford International Capital Corporation
Incorporated in the State of Delaware U.S.A.

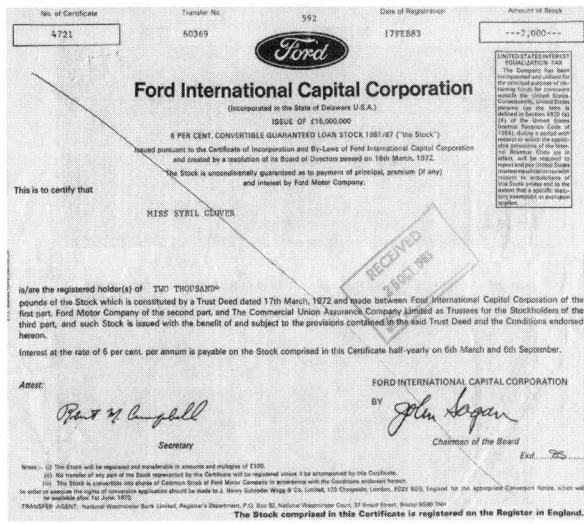

*FO250-40-10, 1983, v, £2,000 6% convertible guaranteed stock 1981/87, B.P.C. Business Forms (Security) Ltd.; 10" x 8", blue $3.00

Theo. Garvin Limited

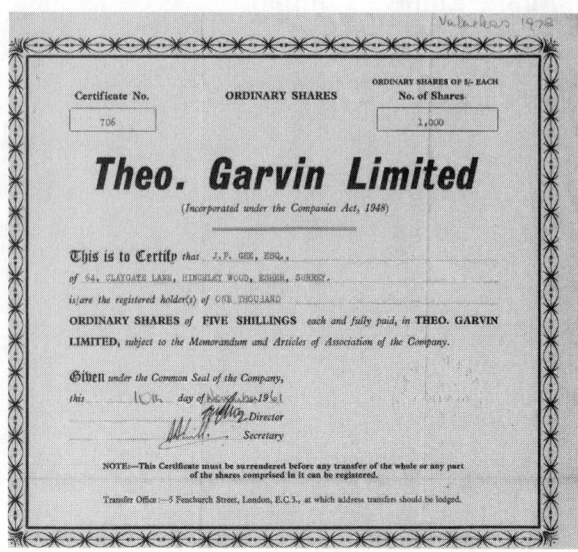

*GA180-30-10, 1961, 1,000 sh. (par 5/-), w/o imprint, 10" x 8-3/4", blue on white **$3.00**

Gold-Run Klondike Mining Company, Limited

*GO150-20-10, 1902, 10 bearer sh., in English and French, English tax stamp, l. blue. **$80.00**

Grainger & Smith Limited (par 10/-)

*GR110-30-10, 1958, v, 1,000 sh., brown on yellow **$3.00**

R. Green Properties Limited

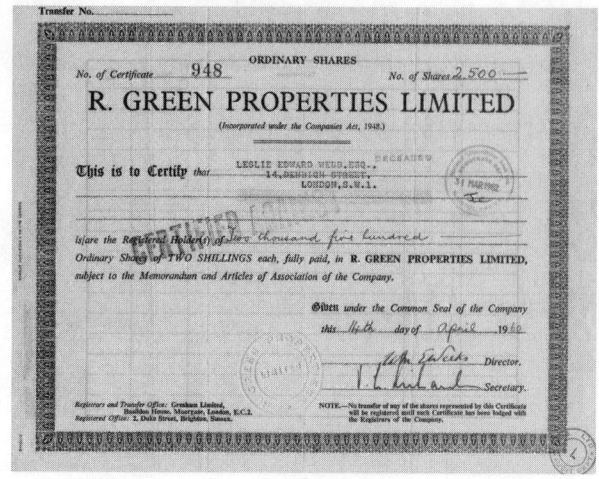

*GR290-30-10, 1960, 2,500 sh. (par 2/-), Burrup, Mathieson & Co. Ltd., London; 10" x 8", black border **$4.00**

Guinness Peat Group Public Limited Company

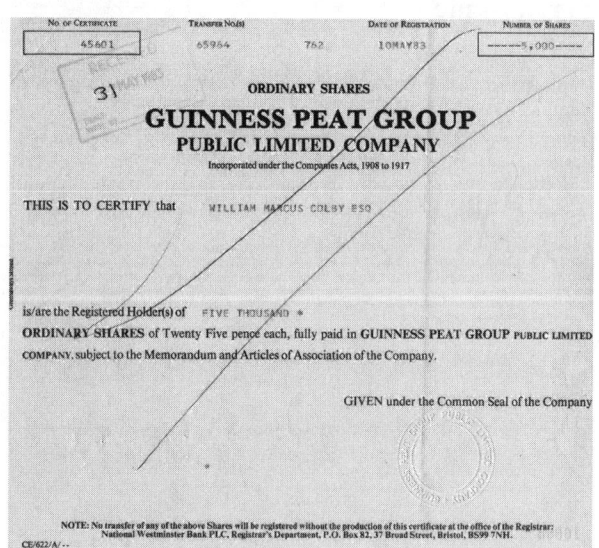

*GU220-40-10, 1983, 5,000 sh. (par 25p), Greenaways Stroud, 9" x 8", black on white **$3.00**

Hambros Limited

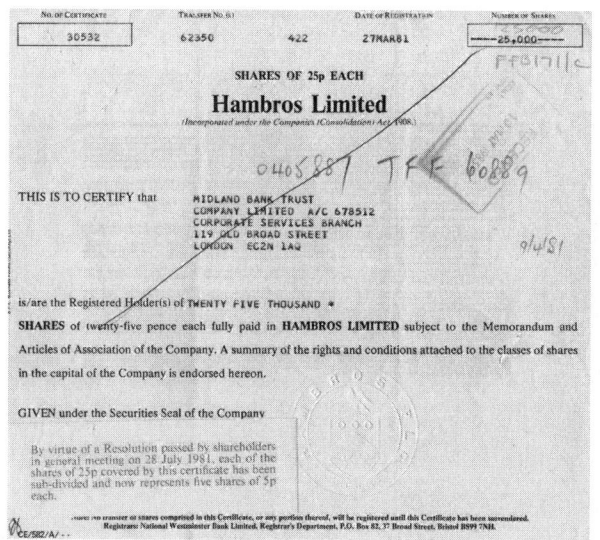

*HA190-40-10, 1981, 25,000 sh. (par 25p), B.P.C. Business Forms (Security) Ltd., 9" x 8", blue on white $3.00

Harris Queensway PLC

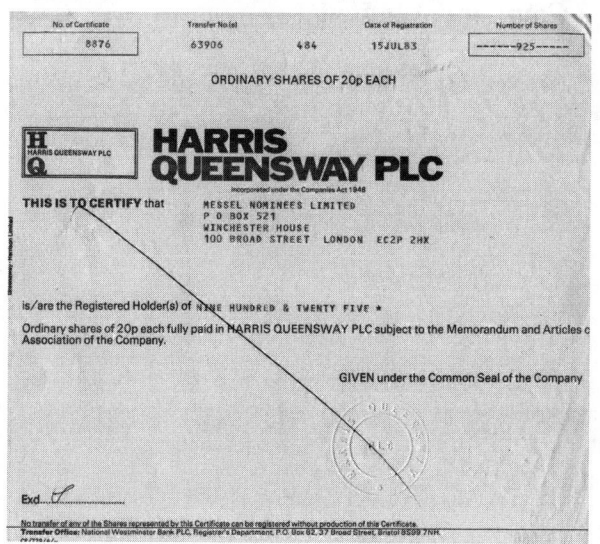

*HA280-30-10, 1983, v, 925 sh. (par 20p), Greenaway-Harrison Limited, 8-3/4" x 8", green on white $3.00

Haslemere Estates Limited

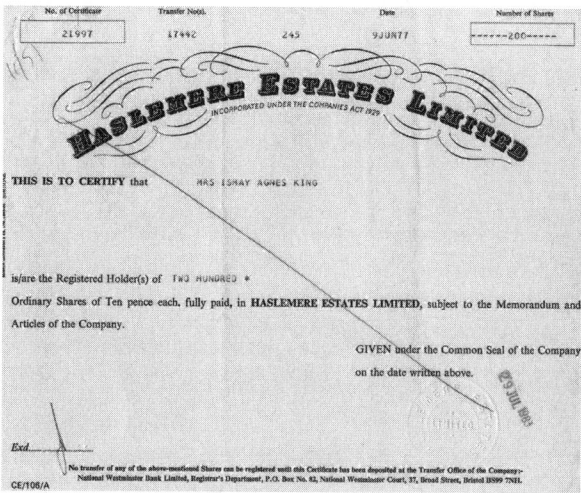

*HA380-40-10, 1977, v, 200 sh. (par 10p), Burrup, Mathieson & Co., Ltd., 10" x 8", black on white $3.00

Huelva Central Copper Mining Company

Registered in 1896 as Central Copper Mines of Spain. Changed name to Huelva in 1899 and went into voluntary liquidation in 1902.

HU120-20-10, 1900, v, 5 bearer sh., warrants (par £1) w. coupons, text in English and French, British revenue imprints, blue border $5.00

India General Navigation Railway Company Limited

IN160-40-10, 1915, v, 500 Rupiahs 5% bearer debenture, green $20.00

This catalog has listings in an alphabetical format. The reason is simple, companies diversify as they grow. For example, the Canadian Pacific Railway company recently split into five companies. They represent the railway, hotels, shipping, airline, and petroleum interests of the company. During World War II, the Singer sewing machine company made guns and other defense-related equipment, so where should we list it? It's far easier to use a strict alphabetical order, rather than to confuse the reader with topical classifications.

Industrial Finance and Investment Corporation PLC

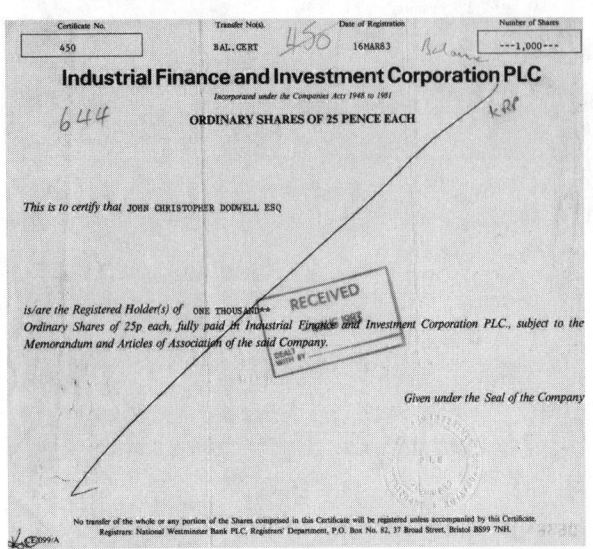

*IN230-30-10, 1983, 1,000 sh. (par 25p), w/o imprint, 9" x 8", black on white $3.00

The Industrial & General Trust Limited

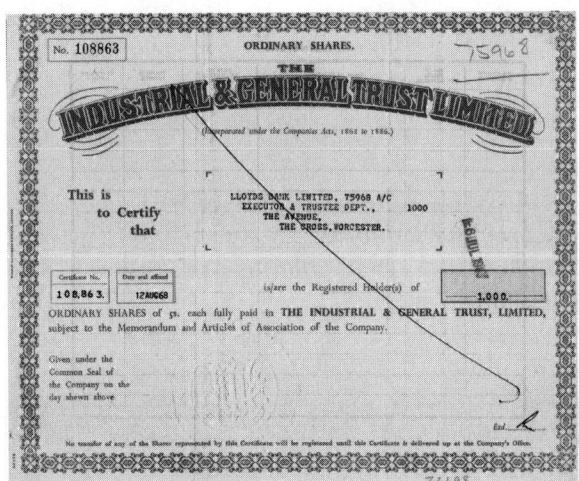

*IN260-50-10, 1968, 1,000 sh. (par 5/-), Burrup, Mathieson & Co., Ltd., 10" x 8", gold on white $3.00

> ### It is generally assumed that only 5% of certificates survive to reach collectors.

Inter-City Investment Group p.l.c.

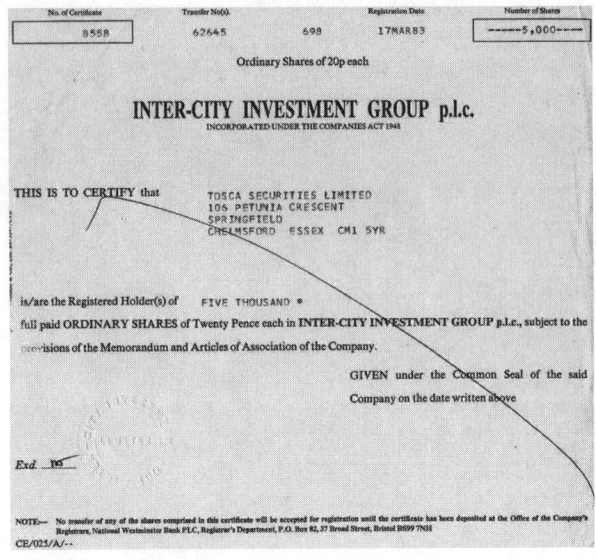

*IN450-30-10, 5,000 sh. (par 20p), Burrup, Mathieson & Co., Ltd., 8-3/4" x 8", blue on white $3.00

Jerusalem Electric & Public Service Company, Limited

*JE240-20-10, 1945, 100 pref. sh., Arabic-English-Hebrew text $15.00
JE240-30-10, 1948, 200 pref. sh., Hebrew, Arabic and English, blue and brown $15.00

The Jewish Colonial Trust (Judische colonialbank)

The money raised by the company was authorized by the Second Zionist Conference in 1899 in Switzerland. Theodor Herzl as head of the conference offered to resettle Jews of the Diaspora in Europe back to what later became the State of Israel. Written in five languages (English, Hebrew, Russian, German and French).

JE350-20-10, 1914, v, 1 sh., of £1, with coupons, blue **$90.00**

Jones, Stroud (Holdings) Limited

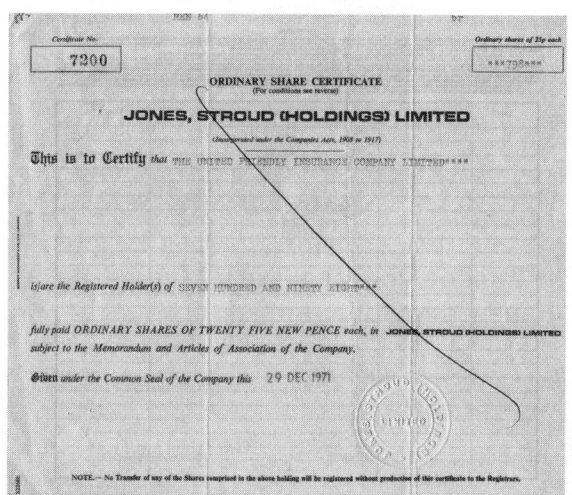

*JO170-30-10, 1971, 798 sh. (par 5np), Burrup, Mathieson & Co., Ltd., 9-1/2" x 8", blue on white **$3.00**

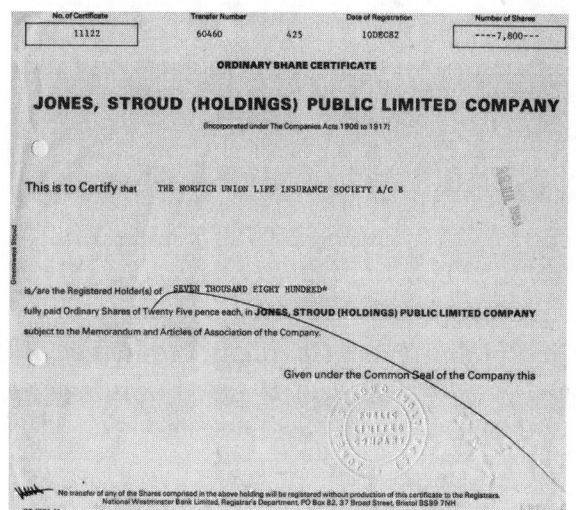

*JO170-40-10, 1982, 7.80 sh. (par 25p) Greenaways Stroud, 8-3/4" x 8", blue on white . .**$3.00**

Kemsley Newspaper Limited

This company's assets included the *Sunday Times* and was acquired by Roy Thompson in 1959.

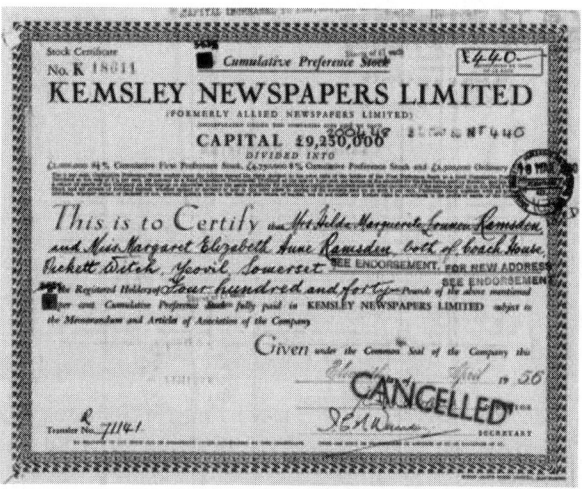

*KE250-30-10, 1956, 440 sh (par £1) blue . .**$7.00**

Kirby's Limited

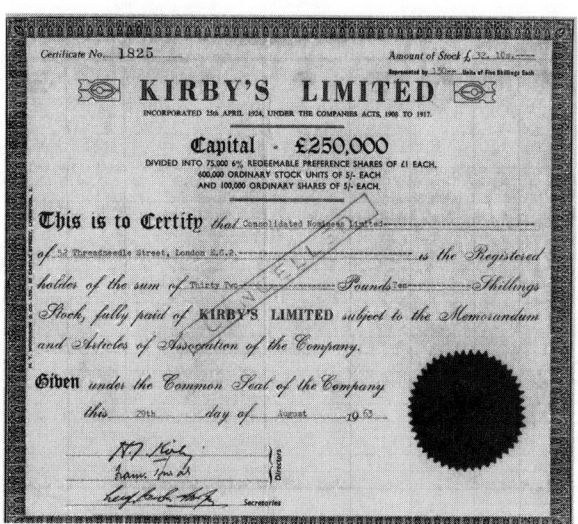

*KI280-30-10, 1963, v, 130 sh. (par 5/-), H.T. Woodrow & Co., Ltd., Liverpool; 11" x 10", black border **$4.00**

The value of a stock certificate depends on:
- rarity
- the issuer
- signatures
- quality of engraving
- overall appearance
- condition
- date of issue

La Reforma Mines of Mexico Limited (par £1)

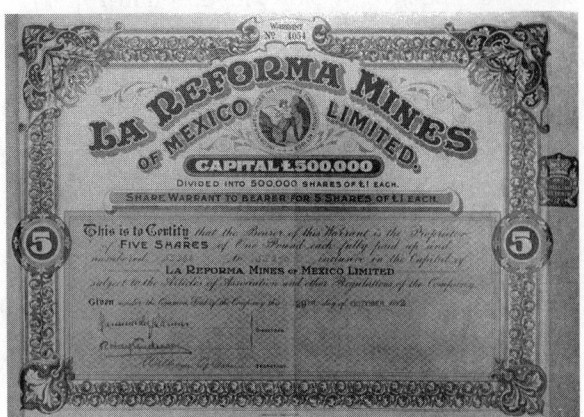

LA130-20-10, 1912, v, sh. warrant for 5 shares, British revenue imprint $4.00

Charles Laffitte Company Limited
LA250-20-10, 1866, £20 sh. certificate, grey
. . . .$15.00

The Leopoldina Terminal Company, Limited

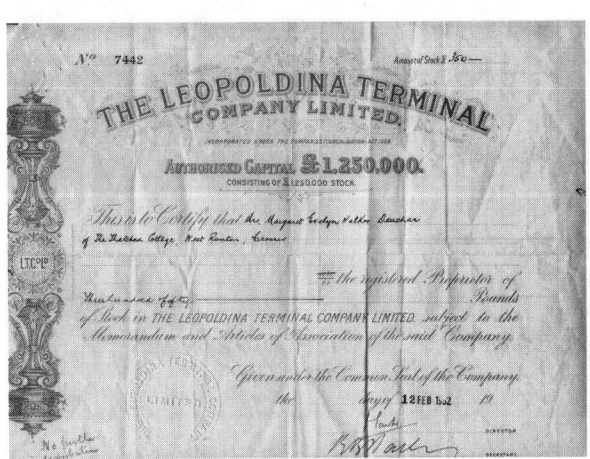

LE190-30-10, 1952, v, £350 stock, w/o imprint, 12" x 10", green on white $4.00

The Liberator Permanent Benefit Building & Investment Society
The failure of Liberator caused ruin for 25,000 families and damaged the Building Society movement.
LI110-20-10, 1985, 1 sh. (par £30), 9" x 8", black on white $20.00

London Merchant Securities Limited

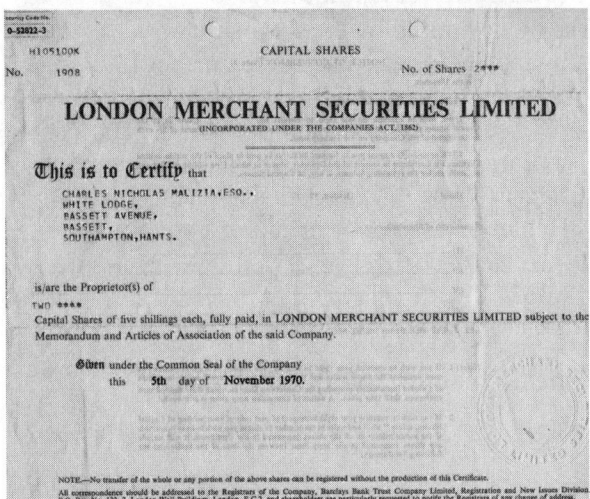

LO240-50-10, 1970, 2 sh. (par 5/-), Metcalfe Cooper & Hepburn Ltd., London; 10" x 8", green on white $3.00

The London and Rhodesian Mining and Land Company, Limited

LO310-30-10, 1909, v, £100 sh. transfer certificate, red $18.00

The London Trust Company Limited
LO410-20-10, 1908, v, 6,350 sh., 11" x 10", grey on white $8.00

Lonrho Limited

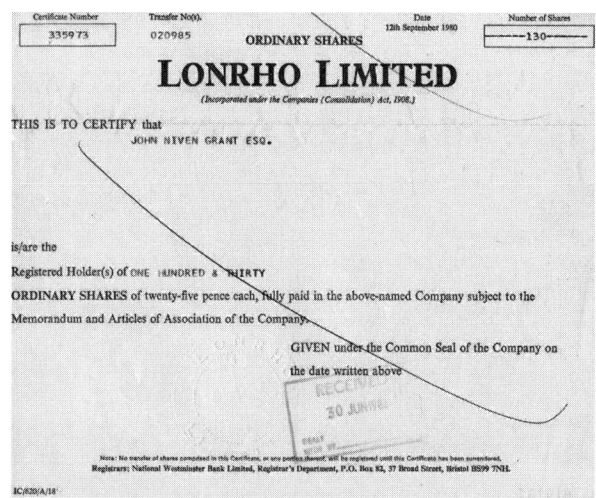

*LO510-40-10, 1980, 130 sh. (par 25p), w/o
imprint, 9" x 7-1/4", brown on white $3.00

The Loveden Mine Syndicate Limited
Mine in Mysore, India.

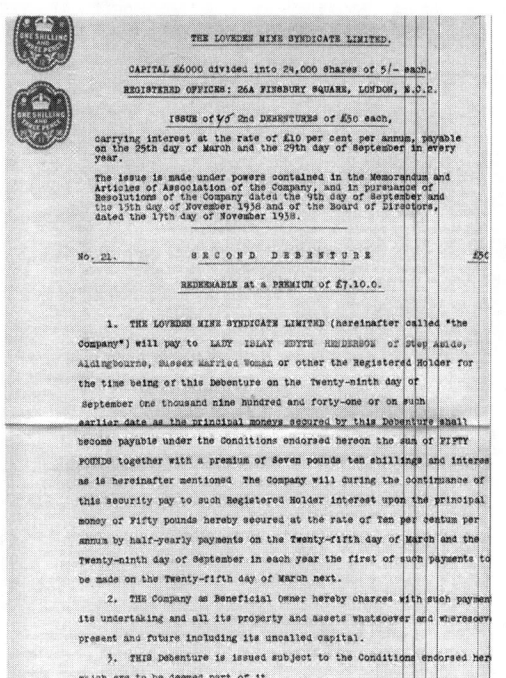

*LO820-40-10, 1938, £50 2nd debenture 10%, due
1941, British revenue imprints, typewritten doc-
ument, 10" x 16" $7.00

Manáos Improvements Limited (Brazil)

*MA250-40-10, 1909, v, £20 6% debentures w.
coupons, blue $10.00

David Martineau & Sons, Limited

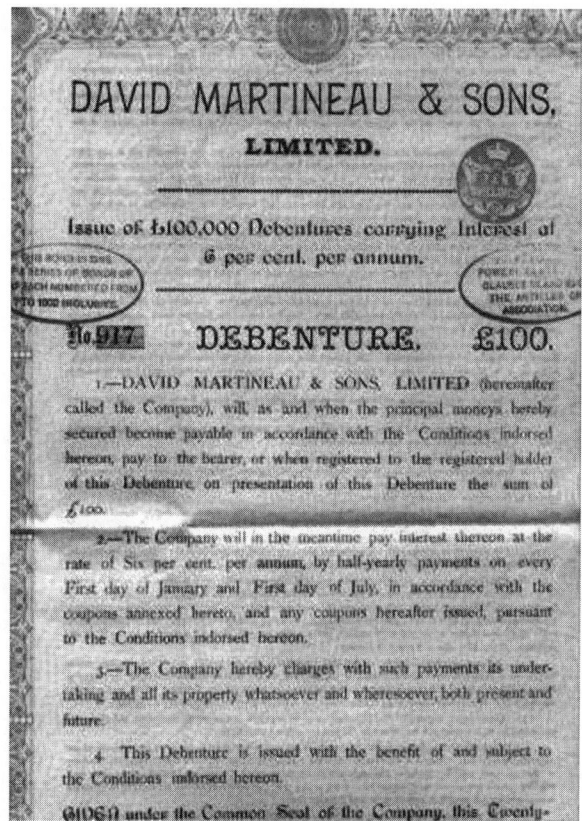

*MA370-40-10, 1890, £100 6% debenture w.
coupons, red border $4.00

May & Hassel Limited

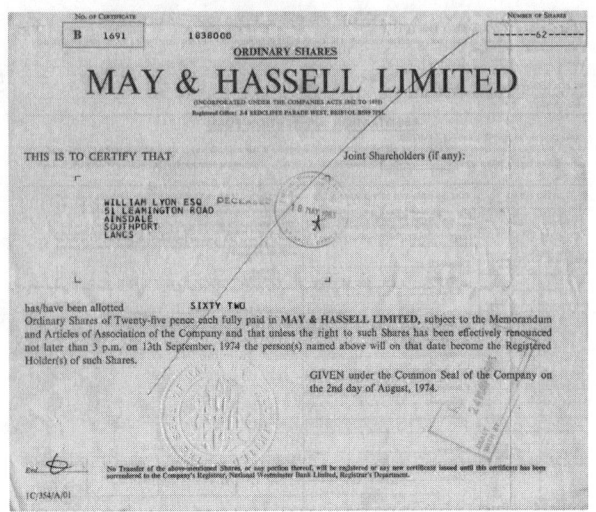

*MA490-40-10, 1974, 62 sh. (par 25p), w/o
   imprint, 9-3/4" x 8", red on white........$3.00

The Metal Box Company Limited

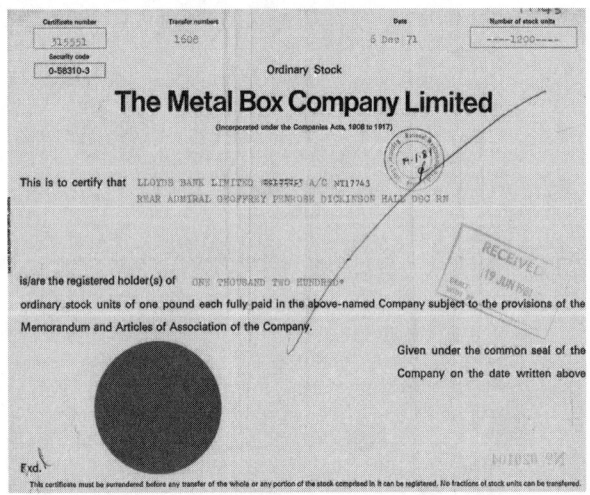

*ME420-40-10, 1971, 1,200 sh. (par £1), The
   Metal Box Company Limited, 9-3/4" x 8",
   black on white......................$3.00

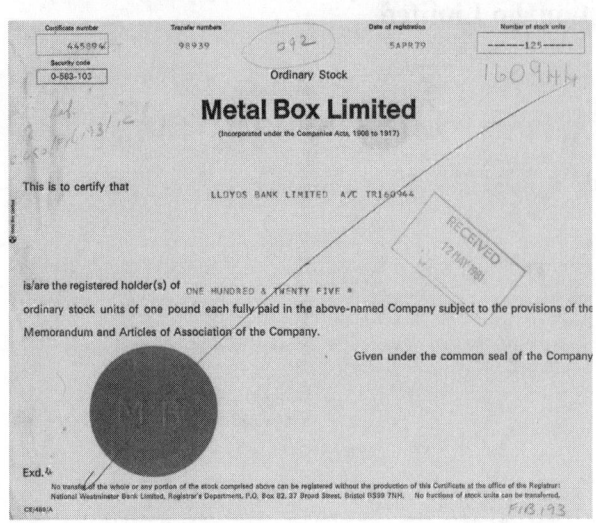

*M420-50-10, 1979, 125 sh. (par £1), Metal Box
   Limited, 9-3/4" x 8", black on white.....$3.00

The Mexican Central Railway Securities Company, Limited

*ME840-30-10, 1899, v, £100 4% "B" debenture,
   Sir Joseph Causton & Sons Limited, Bank Note
   Engravers, London; green and black $10.00

Mexico Tramways Company

ME870-40-10, 1916, $500 deposit receipt, gen.
   consol. first mortgage 50-year 5% gold bond,
   Bank of Scotland, black on blue and green
   ....$6.00

Mining, Ranching, Cotton and Tobacco Lands of Rhodesia, Limited, London (par 5/-)

MI280-30-10, 1931, 15 sh., green border....**$8.00**

Mohar Investment Co. Limited (par £1)

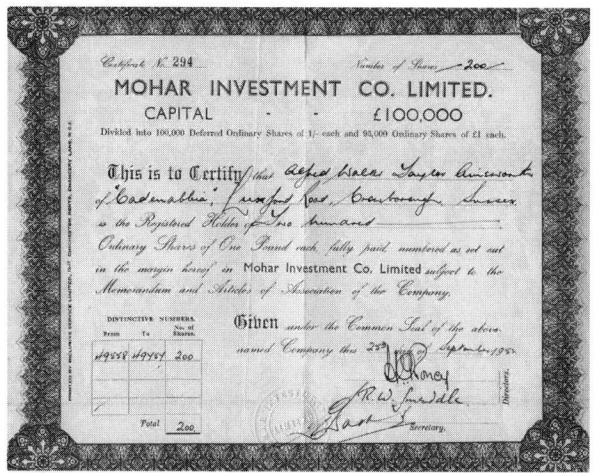

MO190-30-10, 1952, 200 sh., blue.......**$3.00**

Multitone Electronics plc

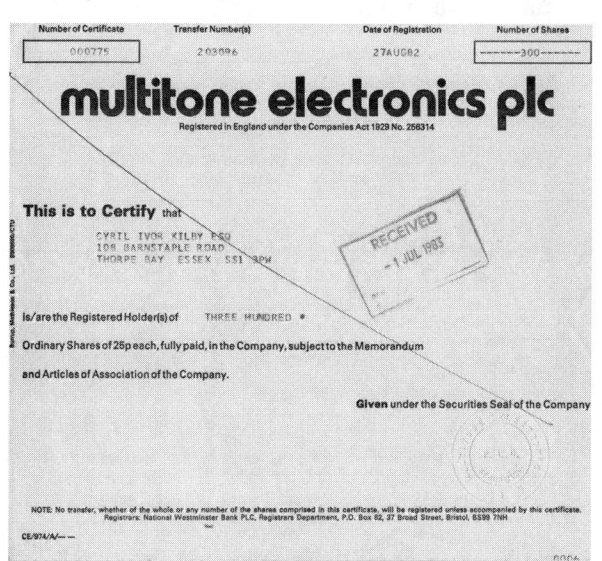

MU220-30-10, 1982, 300 sh. (par 25p), Burrup, Mathieson & Co., Ltd., 9" x 8", black on white
..................................**$3.00**

The National Coke & Oil Company, Limited

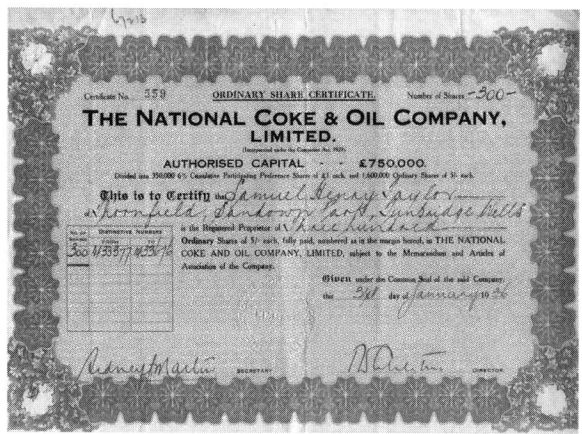

NA120-30-10, 1936, 300 sh. (par 5/-), Rapkin & Co. Limited, 12-3/4" x 9-1/4", light red
..................................**$3.00**

National Provincial Bank Limited (par £1)

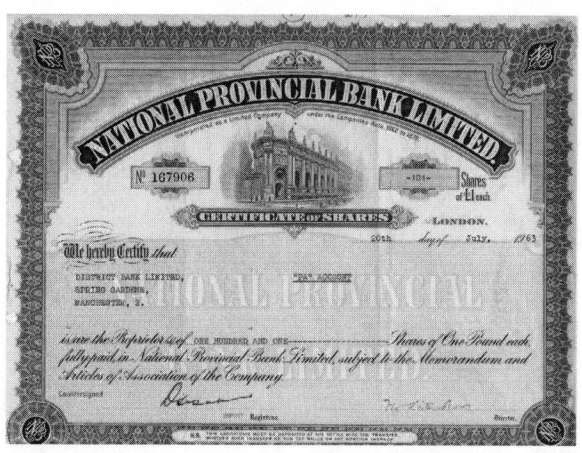

NA270-30-10, 1963, v, 101 sh., Waterlow & Sons Limited, London; 12-1/4" x 9-1/2", green
..................................**$4.00**

The value of a stock certificate depends on:

- **rarity**
- **the issuer**
- **signatures**
- **quality of engraving**
- **overall appearance**
- **condition**
- **date of issue**

Wm. Neill & Son (St. Helens) Limited

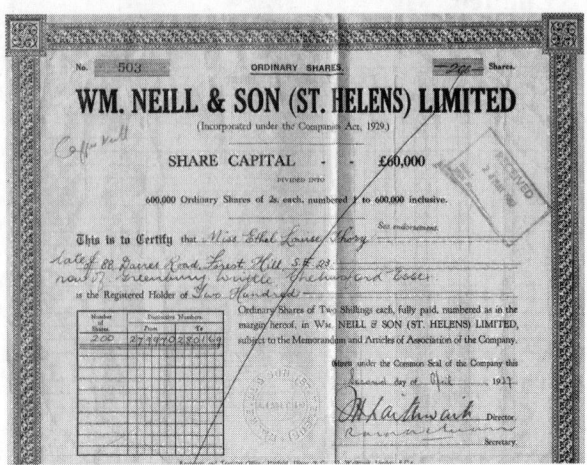

*NE210-30-10, 1937, 200 sh. (par 2/-), St. Clements Press Ltd., 12-3/4" x 11-3/4", black on white $3.00

New Goldfields of Venezuela Limited (par 5/-)

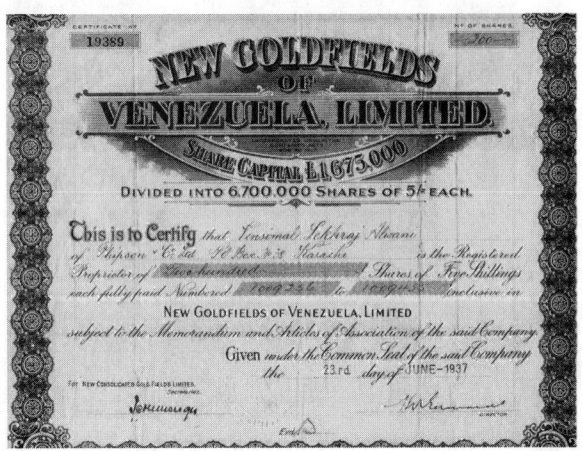

*NE630-30-10, 1937, 200 sh., w/o imprint, 12-1/2" x 11", blue $5.00

Oak Investment Corporation, Limited, Wound up 1929.

OA80-20-10, 1927, v, 1 sh. (par £1), 11" x 10", grey $4.00

> **It is generally assumed that only 5% of certificates survive to reach collectors.**

The Oceana Consolidated Company, Limited (par 5/-)

*OC110-30-10, 1933, v, 25 sh., bearer stock, British revenue imprints, brown $6.00

The Ontario Porcupine Goldfields Development Company, Limited

ON330-20-10, 1913, 25 sh. (par £1), blue on white $7.00

The Pacific Timber Company Limited (par 25 shillings)

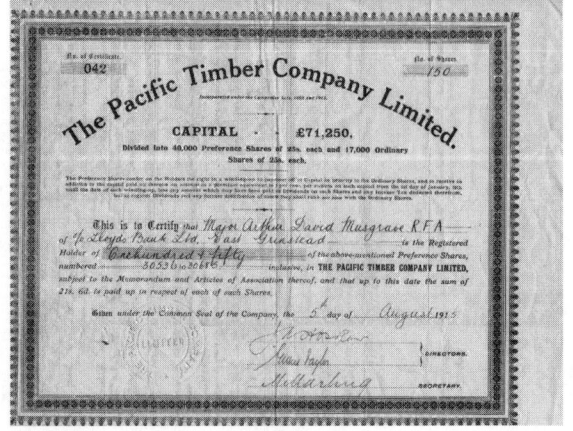

*PA90-40-10, 1915, 150 pref. sh., no printers name, 12" x 10", green $3.00

Petroleum Revenues Company Limited

PE670-30-10, 1911, 5 deferred sh. (par 1/-) w. coupons, English tax stamp, in English and French, rose $6.00

PE670-50-10, 1914, 5 preferred sh. (£1) w. coupons, English & French tax stamp, in English and French, red $6.00

Pierpoint & Bryant Limited

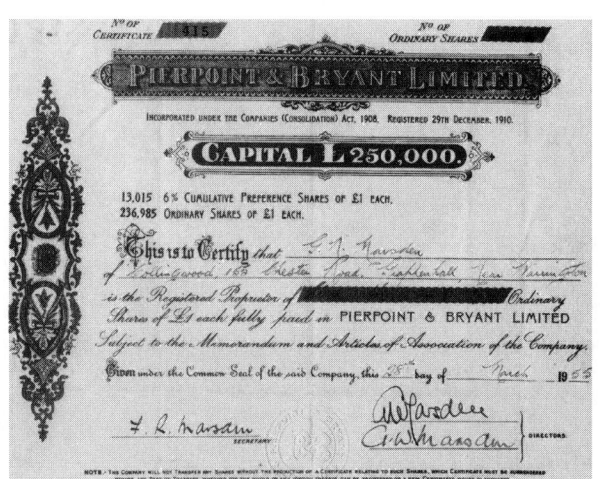

*PI190-30-10, 1955, v, 1,100 sh. (par £1), w/o imprint, 10-1/2" x 9", green $4.00

Port of London Authority

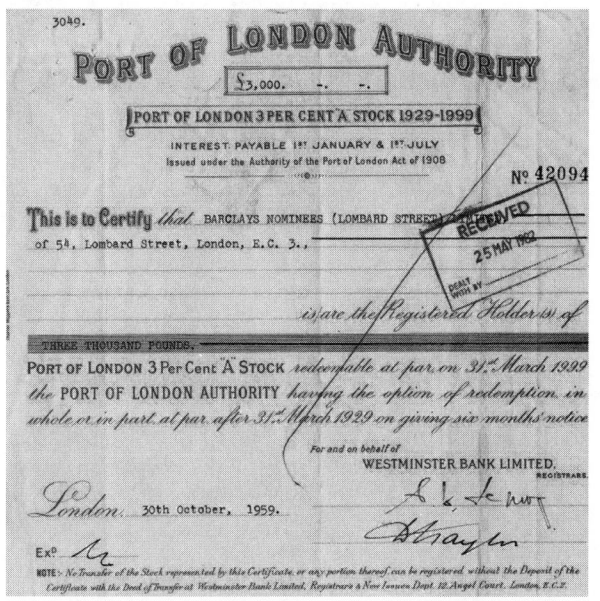

*PO330-50-10, 1959, £3,000 3% "A" stock, 9" x 8-1/2", red $4.00

PowerGen plc

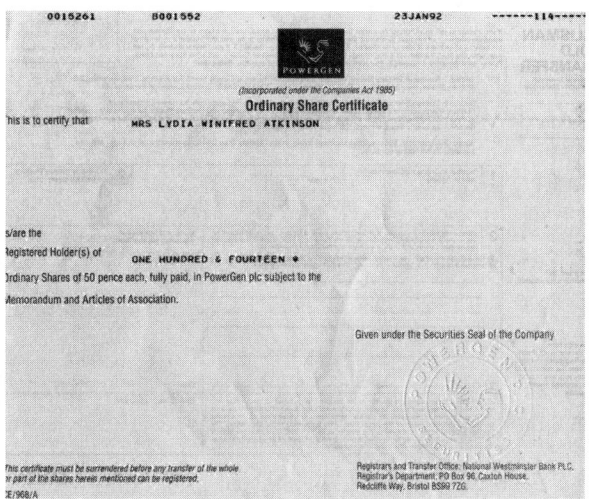

*PO510-20-10, 1992, v, 114 sh. (par 50p), w/o imprint, 8-3/4" x 7-1/4", green on white . .$3.00

William Press & Son, Limited

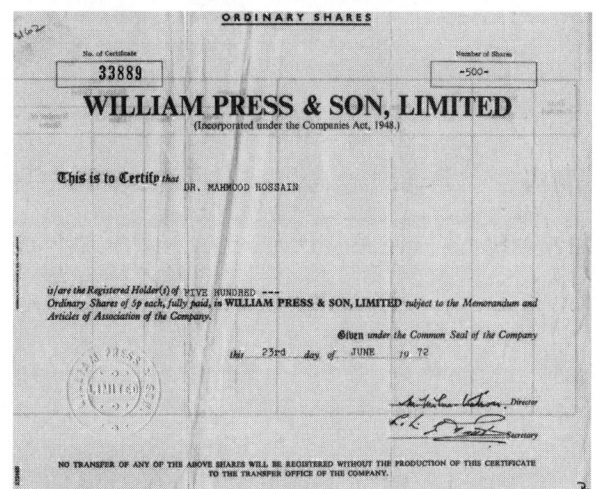

*PR190-30-10, 1972, 500 sh. (par 5p), Burrup, Mathieson & Co., Ltd., 9-3/4" x 8", brown on white $3.00

This catalog has listings in an alphabetical format. The reason is simple: Companies diversify as they grow. For example, the Canadian Pacific Railway company recently split into five companies. They represent the railway, hotels, shipping, airline, and petroleum interests of the company. During World War II, the Singer sewing machine company made guns and other defense-related equipment, so where should we list it? It's far easier to use a strict alphabetical order, rather than to confuse the reader with topical classifications.

The Prince of Wales Hotel Company, Southport, Limited

*PR290-30-10, 1962, 40 sh. (par 5/-), blue . .$5.00

Ransome Hoffman Pollard Limited

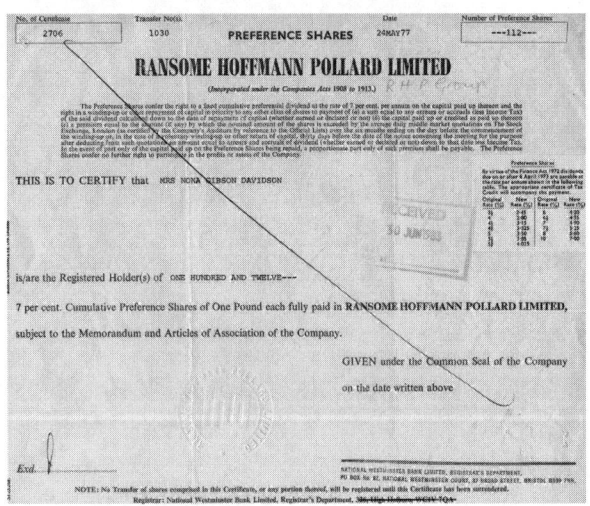

*RA240-40-10, 1977, 112 7% cumul. preference sh. (par £1), Burrup, Mathieson & Co., Ltd.; 9-3/4" x 8", green on white............$3.00

The value of a stock certificate depends on:

- rarity
- the issuer
- signatures
- quality of engraving
- overall appearance
- condition
- date of issue

J.P. & G. Reed, Limited (par £1)

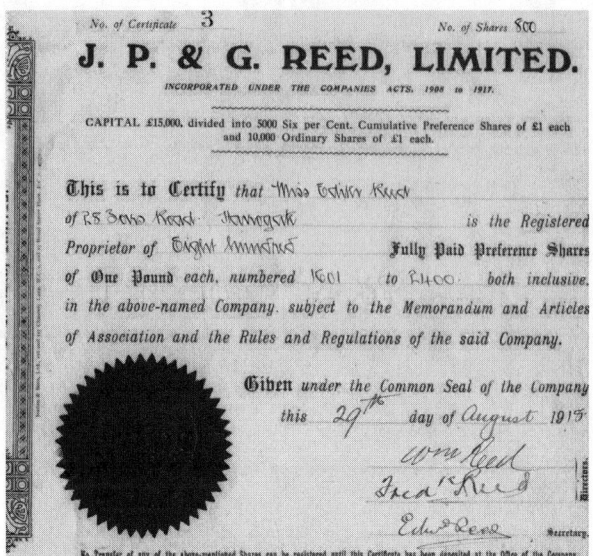

*RE170-20-10, 1918, 800 6% cumulative pref. sh. (par £1), Jordan & Sons, Ltd., 9" x 9", red $4.00

RIT and Northern p.l.c.

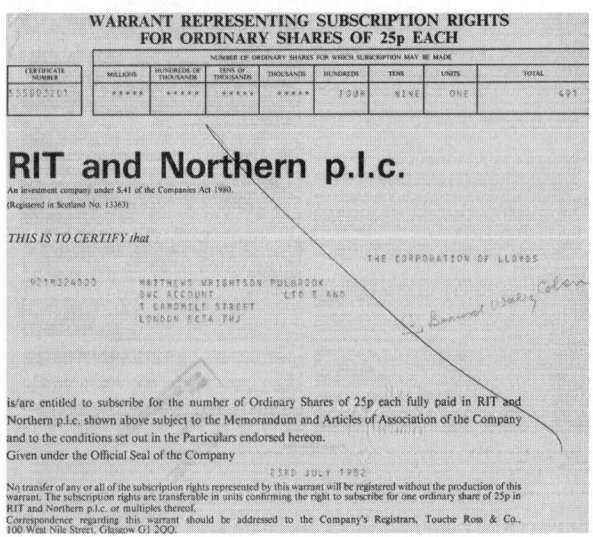

*RI300-30-10, 1982, w, 491 sh., warrant (par 25p), w/o imprint, 9" x 8", black on white $3.00

E S & A Robinson (Holdings) Limited

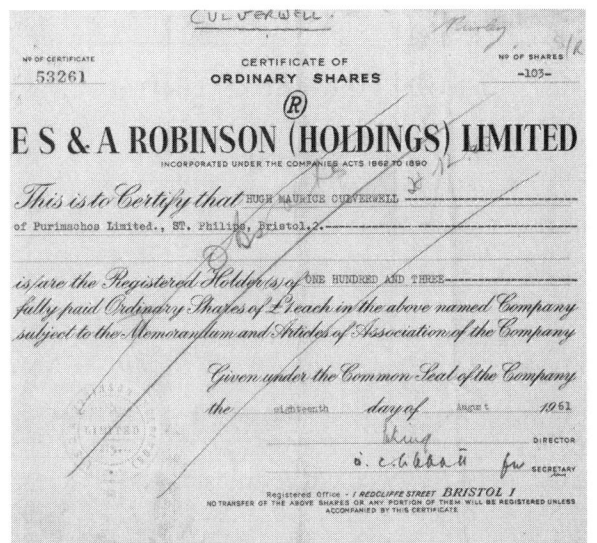

*RO130-40-10, 1961, 103 sh. (par £1), w/o imprint, 9-3/4" x 8", black on white **$3.00**

Rochdale Property & General Finance Company Limited (par £5)

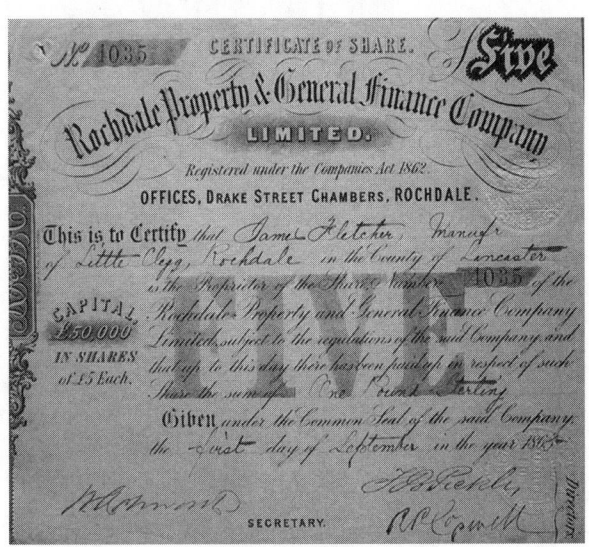

*RO180-20-10, 1863, 1 sh., black on grey
. . . . **$10.00**

> **It is generally assumed that only 5% of certificates survive to reach collectors.**

Roche Plant Group Limited

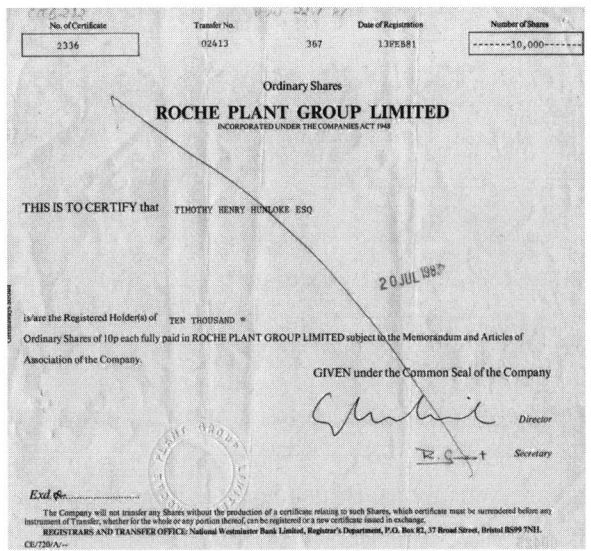

*RO210-30-10, 1981, 10,000 sh. (par 10p), Greenaways Stroud, 9" x 8", black on white **$3.00**

Rodez Coal Company Limited

RO290-40-10, 1912, £20 6% second charge debenture, red **$4.00**

Rolls-Royce plc

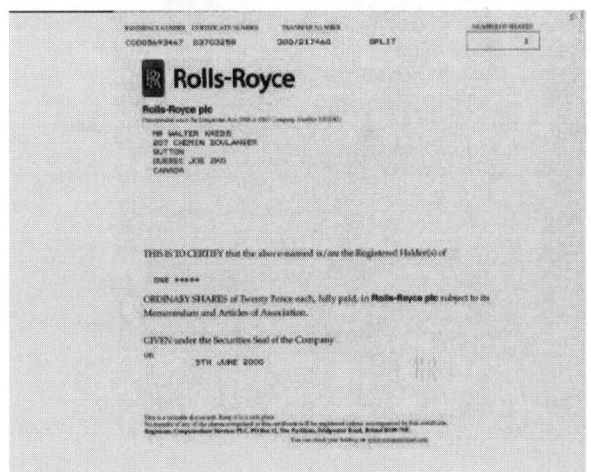

*RO420-40-10, 2000, v, 1 sh., blue **$40.00**

Saga Holidays Limited

SA160-30-10, 1982, 1,120 sh. (par 20p), Greenaways Cheltenham, 10" x 8", black on white
. . . . **$3.00**

The Salvador Railway Company Limited

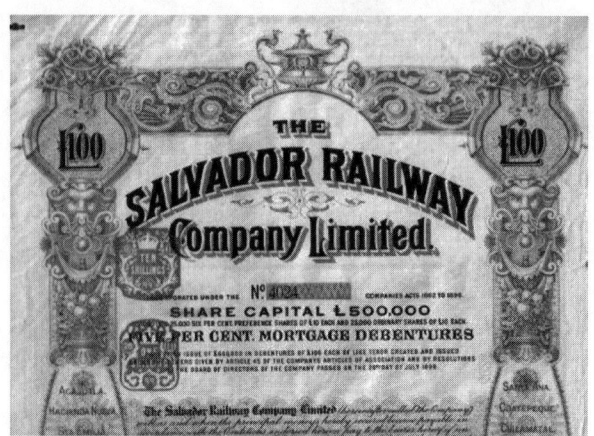

*SA250-40-10, 1899, v, £100 5% mortgage deben-
ture w. coupons, British revenue imprints, 12" x
18-1/2", red $25.00

The San Cebrian Railway and Collieries Company, Limited, S.A. del Ferro-Carril y de las Minas de Carbon de San Cebrian

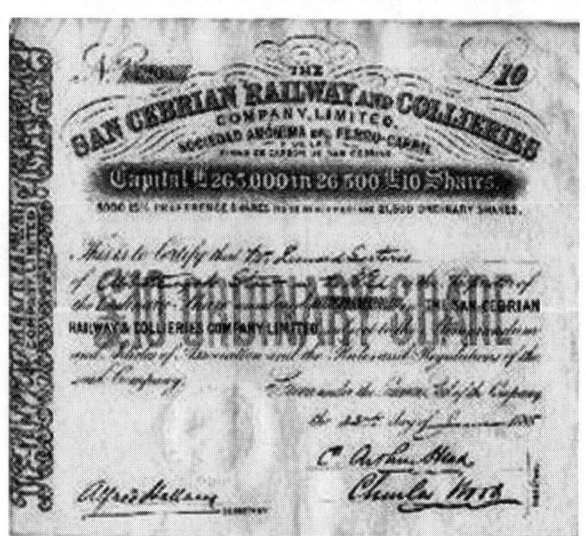

*SA400-20-10, 1885, 1 sh. (par £10), 9" x 8",
brown $9.00

UNLISTED TYPES & VARIETIES

Readers are welcome to contact the author
directly at:

Rainer Stahlberg
P.O. Box 1044
Rooseveltown, New York 13683

Sefton Corn Mills Limited (par £1)

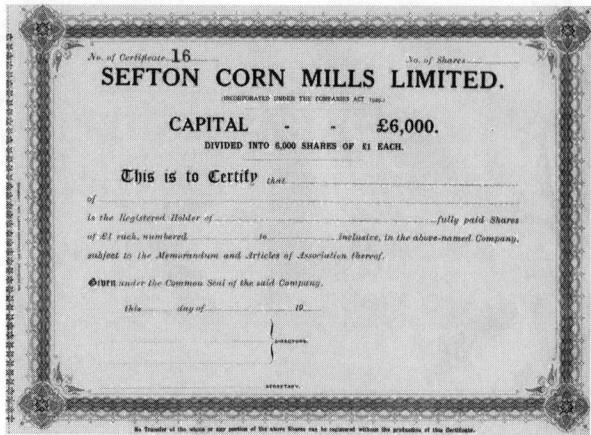

*SE220-30-10, 19xx, u/u certificate, 11-1/4" x
8-3/4", blue $3.00

Slough Estates plc

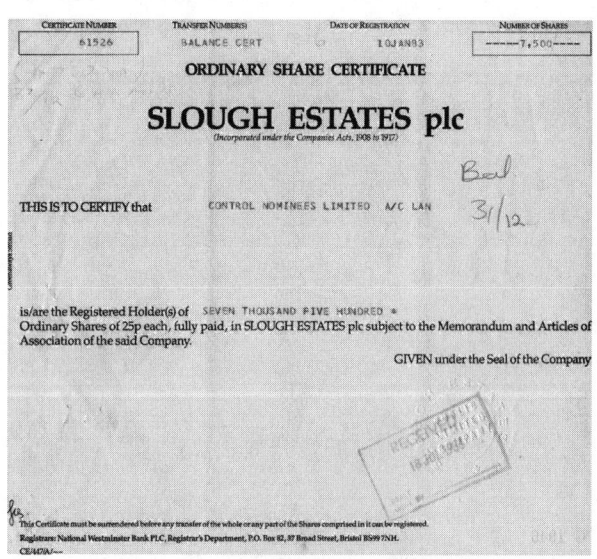

*SL210-40-10, 7,500 sh. (par 25p), Greenaways
Stroud, 9" x 8", black on white $3.00

Sonora Silver Mining Company, Limited

SO270-40-10, 1887, £10 first mort. debenture w.
coupons, black $10.00

The South American Copper Company, Limited (par 2/-)

*SO410-20-10, 19xx, 100 sh., w/o imprint, 12-3/4" x 11-1/4", blue $4.00

Spassky Copper Mine Limited (par £1) London

*SP80-30-10, 1913, v, 1 sh., text in English and French, lilac $4.00

The Stock Conversion and Investment Trust Limited

ST340-40-10, 1981, 300 sh. (par 25p), B.P.C. Business Forms (Security) Ltd.; 10" x 8", blue on white $3.00

Strong & Fisher (Holdings) Limited

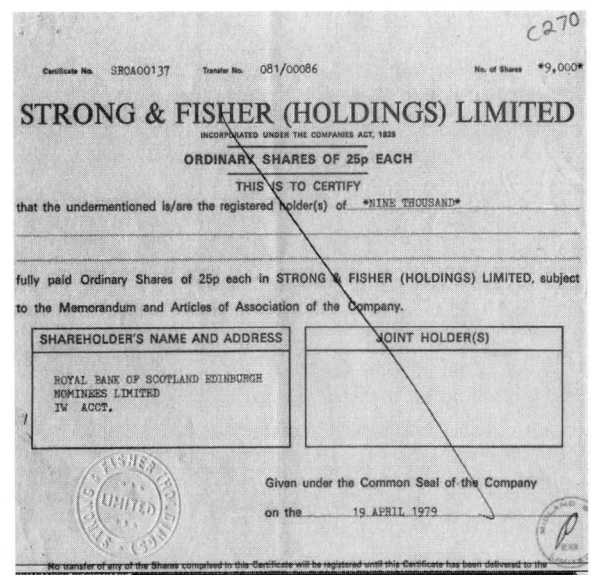

*ST460-30-10, 1979, 9,000 sh. (par 25p), HJPS, 9" x 8", blue on white $3.00

Tate & Lyle Investments Limited

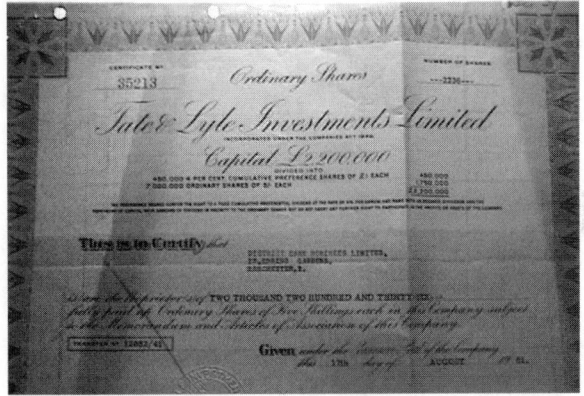

*TA140-50-10, 1961, 2,236 sh., (par 5/-), brown $5.00

The value of a stock certificate depends on:
- rarity
- the issuer
- signatures
- quality of engraving
- overall appearance
- condition
- date of issue

Tecalemit Limited

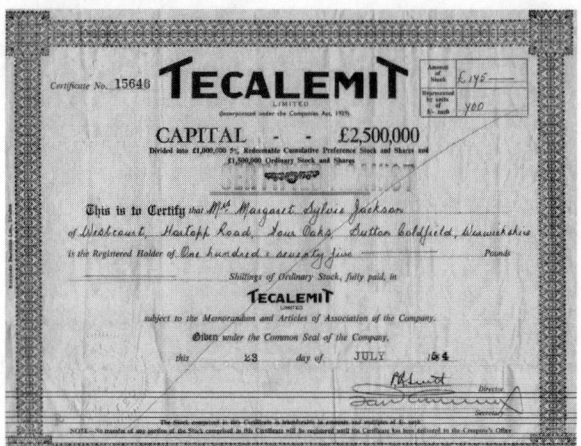

*TE110-30-10, 1954, 400 sh. (par 5/-), Rayward
Brothers Ltd., London; 11-1/2" x 9-1/2",
red on white $3.00

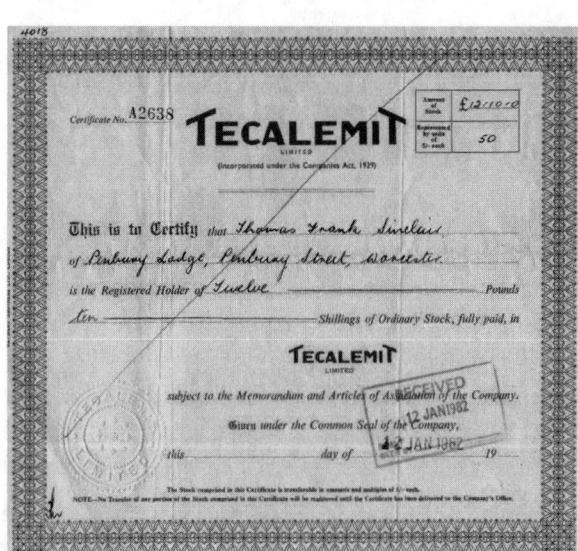

*TE110-35-10, 1962, 50 sh. (par 5/-), Rayward
Brothers Ltd., London; 9-1/4" x 8-1/4",
red on white $3.00

Thorn Electrical Industries Limited

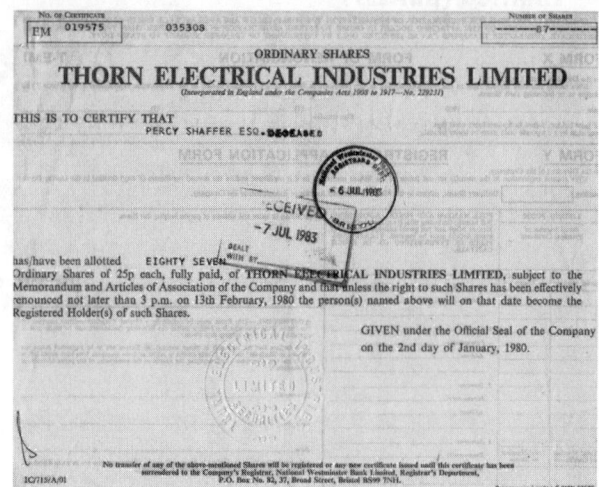

*TH190-30-10, 1980, 87 sh. (par 25p), Green-
aways London, 9" x 7", green on white . . .$3.00

Thorn EMI plc

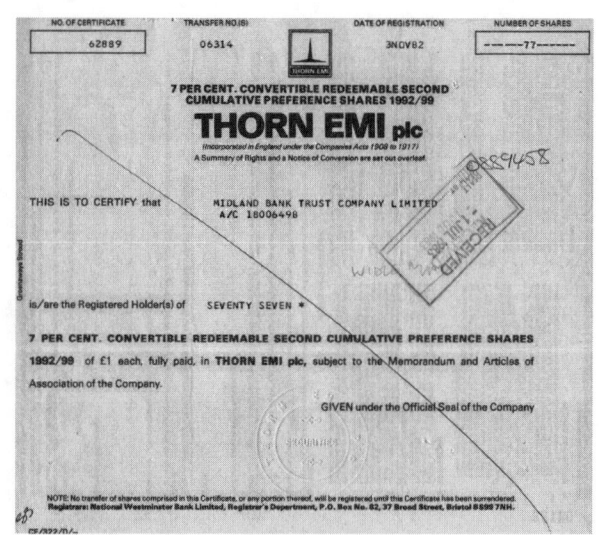

*TH200-20-10, 1982, v, 77 7% conver. pref.
sh.(par £1), Greenaways Stroud, 9" x 8", red on
white
. . . .$3.00

This catalog has listings in an alphabetical format. The reason is simple: Companies
diversify as they grow. For example, the Canadian Pacific Railway company recently
split into five companies. They represent the railway, hotels, shipping, airline, and
petroleum interests of the company. During World War II, the Singer sewing machine
company made guns and other defense-related equipment, so where should we list it?
It's far easier to use a strict alphabetical order, rather than to confuse the reader with
topical classifications.

The Trustees Corporation, Limited

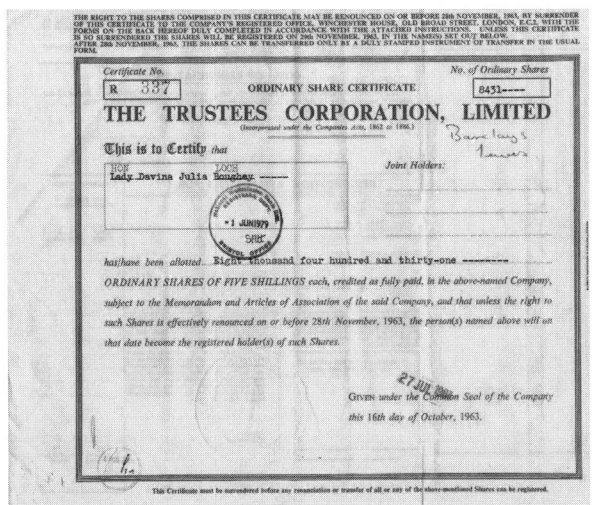

*TR360-40-10, 1963, 8,431 sh. (par 5/-), Burrup, Mathieson & Co., Ltd., London; 10-1/2" x 8-1/2", red on white $3.00

Turner & Newall plc

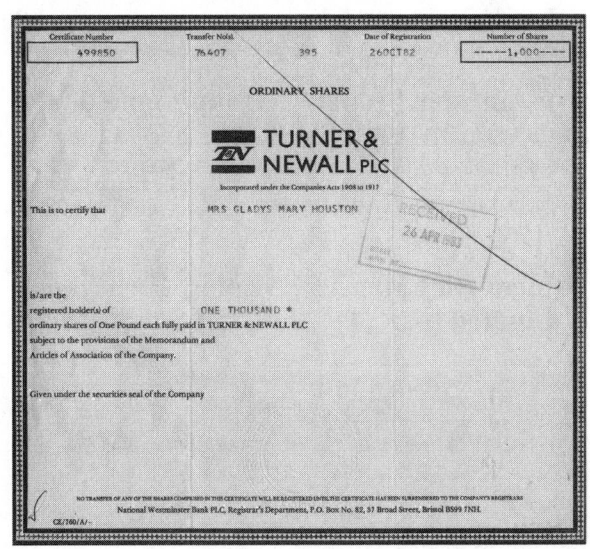

*TU280-30-10, 1982, 1,000 sh. (par £1), 8-3/4" x 8", green border $3.00

UBM Group Limited

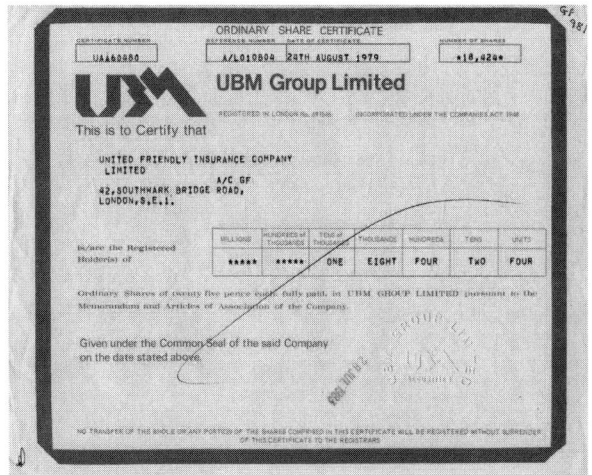

*UB90-30-10, 1979, v, 18,424 sh. (par 25p), w/o imprint, 9-3/4" x 8", deep orange border $3.00

Unilever Limited (par £1)

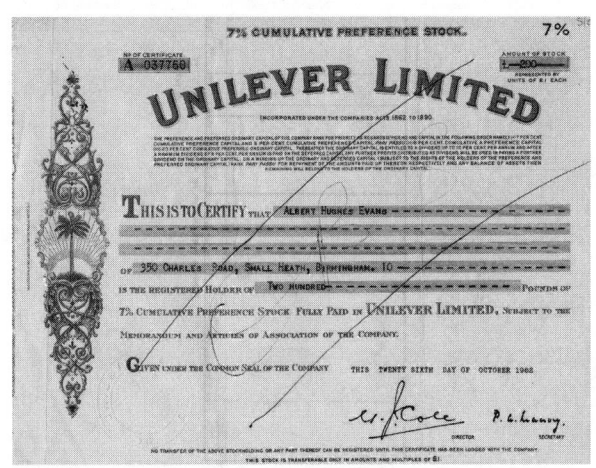

*UN160-70-10, 1962, £200 7% cum. pref. stock, 10-1/2" x 8-1/4", black.................$3.00

UNLISTED TYPES & VARIETIES

Readers are welcome to contact the author directly at:

Rainer Stahlberg
P.O. Box 1044
Rooseveltown, New York 13683

The Venezuela Central Railway Company, Limited

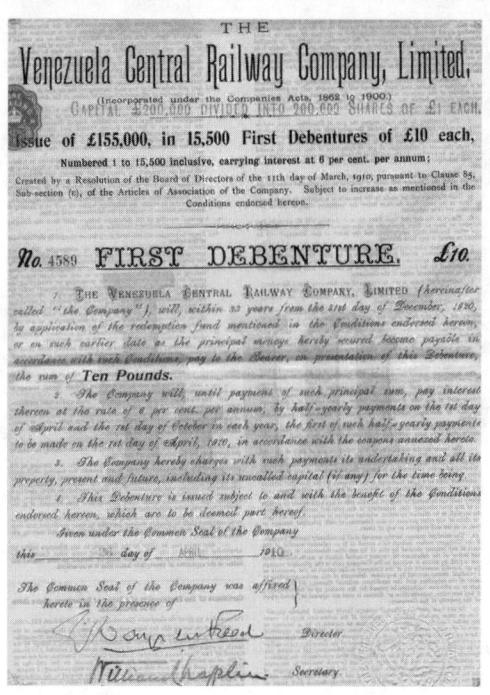

*VE240-40-10, 1910, £10 6% 1st debenture w. coupons, Doherty & Co., Printers; 13-1/2" x 16-1/4", green $5.00

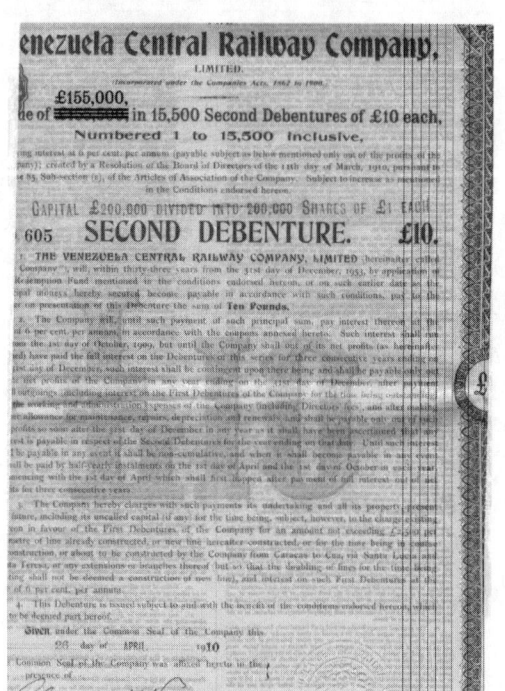

*VE240-45-10, 1910, £10 6% 2nd debenture w. coupons, Doherty & Co., Printers; 13-1/2" x 16-1/4", brown $5.00

The Viking Whaling Company Limited

VI210-20-10, 1931, v, 100 sh., w. coupons, brown $160.00
VI210-25-10, 1939, v, 1 sh., w. coupons, brown $350.00

Vosper Limited

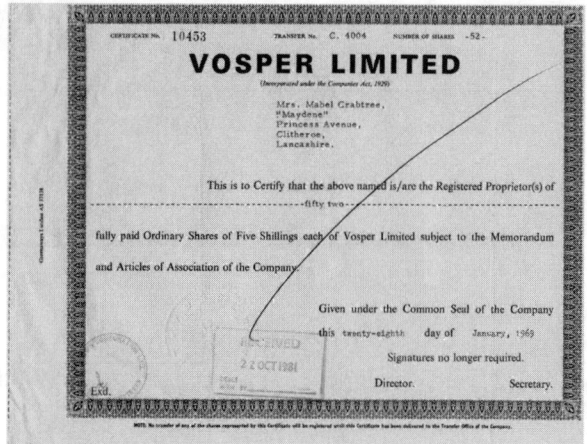

*VO380-30-10, 1969, 52 sh. (par 5/-), Greenaways London; 11" x 8", blue on white $3.00

Westminster Property Group Limited

WE350-40-10, 1973, 100 sh. (par 20p), Burrup, Mathieson & Co., Ltd., London; 10" x 8", black on white $3.00

Whitworth Finance & Mining Corporation Limited (par £1)

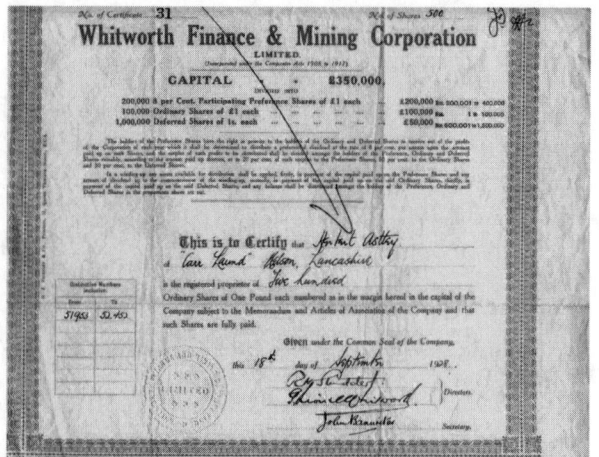

*WH280-30-10, 1928, 500 sh. (par £1), no printers name, 11-1/2" x 11-1/4", red $3.00

Wimbledon Stadium Limited
WI300-30-10, 1964, £40 deferred stock, pink and
yellow **$60.00**

Greece

Kingdom of Greece

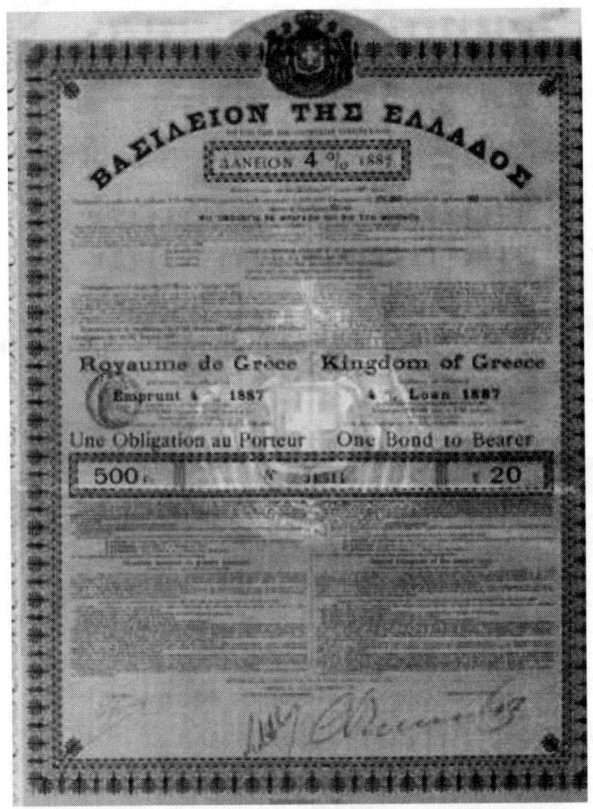

*30-30-10, 1887, v, £20 or 500 Francs 4% bond,
text in Greek-French-English, secured by
monopolies of salt, petroleum, playing cards,
matches, cigarette paper and emery of Naxos.
brown **$8.00**

*30-60-10, 1898, £100 2-1/2% bond, in Greek-
French-English, 11-1/2" x 15-3/4", blue . .**$4.00**

Antrakorucheion Aliberou

*AN240-20-10, 1926, v, 1 bearer sh., Greek revenue stamp, 15-3/4" x 10-3/4", grey border on
orange. **$4.00**

*It is generally assumed that only 5% of certificates
survive to reach collectors.*

Banque de Thessalie S.A. Volo

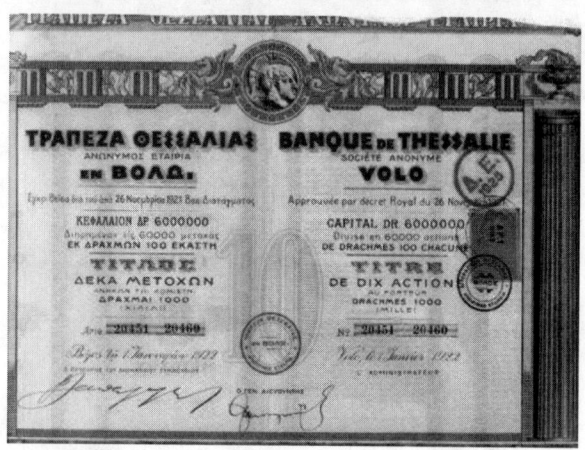

BA330-30-10, 1922, v, 10 sh. (par Dr. 1000) bearer stock w. coupons, brown **$9.00**

Privileged Company to Foster the Production and Trade of Currants

FO230-20-10, 1905, v, 250 F bearer stock, green **$10.00**

S.A. des Glacieres de Patissia

GL130-20-10, 1922, v - penguins, 25 sh. w. coupons, brownish **$20.00**

Hellenic Electric Railways Co. Ltd., Athens

HE230-40-10, 1963, 10 debenture bonds 1,500 Drachmas, 7% loan, blue **$3.00**

HE230-45-10, 1964, 10 debenture bonds 1,500 Drachmas 7% loan, lilac. **$3.00**

Piraus-Athens-Peloponnesus Railroad Company

PI330-20-10, 1887, v, bearer stock certificate, grey **$10.00**

Société Hellénique Anonyme de Produits et Engrais Chimiques, Athens

PR260-30-10, 1971, v, 10 sh. (par 180 Dr), grey **$3.00**

> ## The value of a stock certificate depends on:
>
> - • **rarity**
> - • **the issuer**
> - • **signatures**
> - • **quality of engraving**
> - • **overall appearance**
> - • **condition**
> - • **date of issue**

Thessalonian Railways

TH130-20-10, 1886, v, 1 bearer sh. par £10, British revenue imprint, brown and blue
............................$10.00

Guernsey

The Metals Extraction Corporation Limited (par £1)
ME20-20-10, 1907, 500 sh., black........$8.00

UNLISTED TYPES & VARIETIES

Readers are welcome to contact the author directly at:

Rainer Stahlberg
P.O. Box 1044
Rooseveltown, New York 13683

H

Hungary

Royal Hungarian Bonds

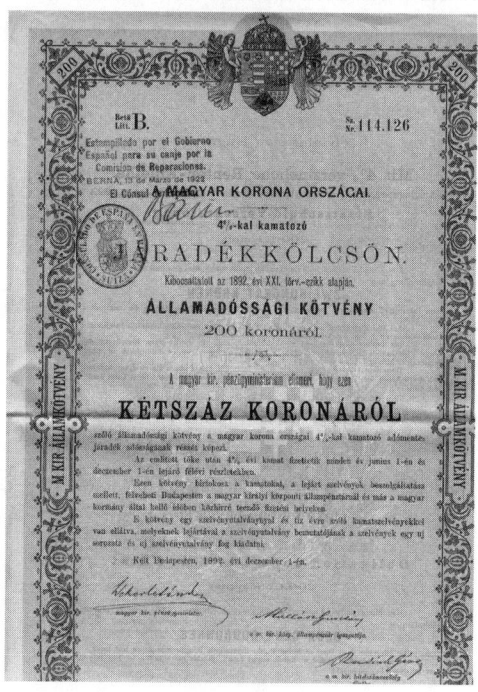

*60-40-10, 1892, v, 200 Korona 4% bond w. coupons, Hungarian-German-French-English-Spanish revenue rubber stamp, 9-3/4" x 15-1/2", grey $7.00

This catalog has listings in an alphabetical format. The reason is simple: Companies diversify as they grow. For example, the Canadian Pacific Railway company recently split into five companies. They represent the railway, hotels, shipping, airline, and petroleum interests of the company. During World War II, the Singer sewing machine company made guns and other defense-related equipment, so where should we list it? It's far easier to use a strict alphabetical order, rather than to confuse the reader with topical classifications.

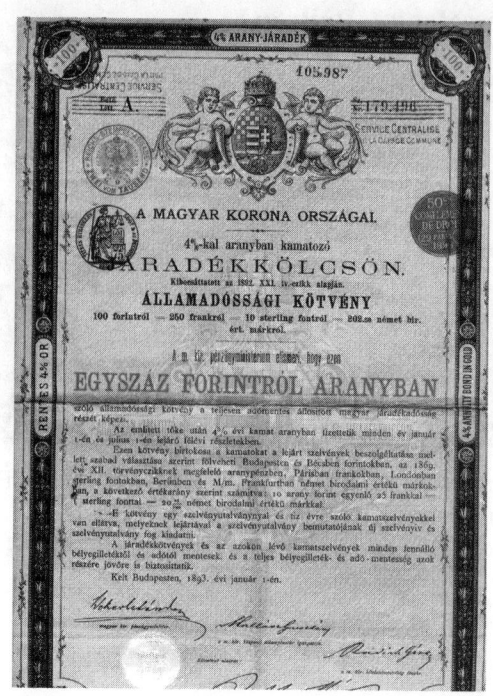

*60-50-10, 1893, v, 100 Korona, 4% gold bond, German and French revenue imprints, 10-1/2" x 15-3/4", black on beige $7.00

*60-70-10, 1897, v, 200 Korona 3-1/2% bond w. coupons, text in Hungarian-German-English, 9-3/4" x 15-1/2", grey.................$7.00

*60-90-10, 1903, v, 200 Korona 4% bond w. coupons, grey $5.00

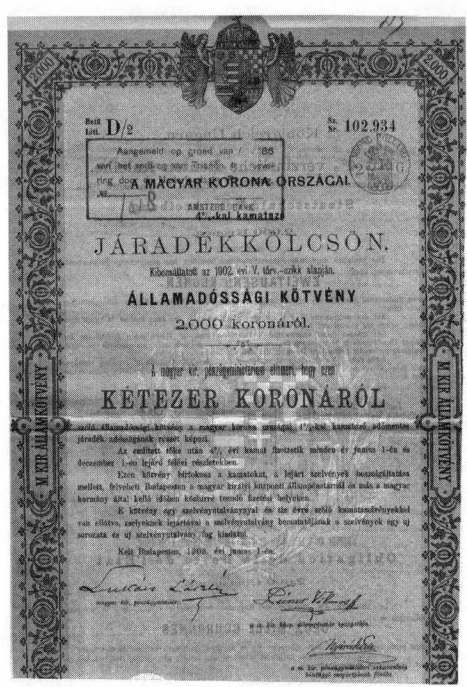

*60-95-10, 1903, v, 2,000 Korona, 4% bond w. coupons, Dutch revenue rubber stamp, 9-3/4" x 15-1/2", grey on pink $7.00

Government Bearer Bond
110-50-10, 1912, v - King and Queen, 100 Korona, brown $10.00

*110-70-10, 1919, 480 Korona=£20 4-1/2% consolidated redeemable state debt w. coupons, 10" x 15", British revenue imprint, brown $6.00

Magyar Korona Orszagai War Bond
170-30-10, 1917, v, 10,000 Korona 5-1/8% bearer bond, blue border $12.00

Belvàrosi Takarèkpènztàr Rèszvèny Tàrsasàg, Inner City Credit Union

*BE110-40-10, 1897, v, 2,000 Korona 4-1/2% bond w. coupons, Dutch revenue rubber stamp, text in Hungarian-German-French, Czettel és Deutsch, Bpest; 10" x 15-1/2", blue and grey $7.00

*BE110-60-10, 1911, v, 200 Korona 4-1/2% bond, Dutch revenue rubber stamp, text in Hungarian-German-French, Gráfikai Intèzet, Bpest, 10" x 15-3/4", green and grey...............$7.00

Beregszászi Tetöcserép és Téglagyár-Részvénytársaság

*BE210-20-10, 1918, 1,000 Korona bearer sh. w. coupons, Republic of Czechoslovakia revenue rubber stamp of 1922, w/o imprint, 10-3/4" x 7-3/4", grey......................$9.00

Györ-Sopron-Ebenfurti Vasut, Raab-Oedenburg-Ebenfürtner Eisenbahn, Budapest

GY260-30-10, 1884, 200 Gulden bearer sh., text in Hungarian and German, beige.........$17.00

*GY260-70-10, 1940, 40 RM loan certificate, text in Hungarian and German, Giesecke & Devrient $15.00

Magyar Ákìlános Hòssènbànya Rèszvèny Tàrsalat - Ungarische Allgemeine Kahlenbergbau AG

*MA180-20-10, 1869, v, 200 Gulden, text in Hungarian and German, grey..........$40.00

Magyar Földhitel Intèzet
Hungarian Mortgage Credit Union.

MA280-30-10, 1895, v, 2,000 Korona 4% bond
due 1922, w. coupons, Dutch revenue rubber
stamps, text in Hungarian-German-French, Franklin-Társulat nyomdája, 10" x 16-1/2", green
and grey $7.00

Magyar Jelzálog-Hitelbank Budapest, Budapest Credit Union

MA340-20-10, 1884, v, 100 Forint 4% bond w.
coupons, Dutch revenue stamp, Hungarian-
German-French, Lègràdy Testvèrek, Budapest;
14" x 9", blue $7.00

MA340-30-10, 1894, v, 200 Korona 3% bond,
Dutch revenue rubber stamp, Hungarian-
German-French, Lègràdy Testvèrek, Budapest,
15" x 10", grey on beige. $7.00

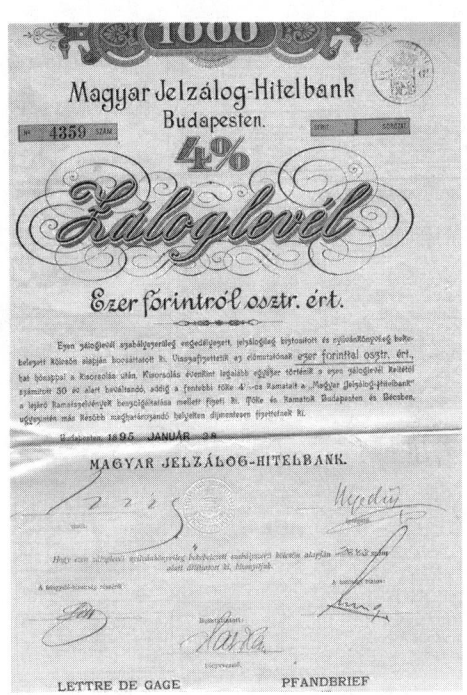

MA340-40-10, 1895, v, 1,000 Forint 4% bond w.
coupons, Dutch revenue rubber stamp, Lègràdy
Testvèrek, Budapest; 9-3/4" x 17-1/4", purple
. . . .$7.00

*It is generally assumed that
only 5% of certificates survive
to reach collectors.*

*MA340-60-10, 1900, v, 100 Forint 4%, annual draw for prizes, text in French-Hungarian-German, Légràdy Testvérek, Budapest, 11-1/2" x 8", grey on beige. $5.00

*MA340-70-10, 1906, v, 100 Korona 3% series 1880 loan, text in French-Hungarian-German, Légrady Testvérek, Budapest; 11-1/2" x 9", dark grey on light grey $5.00

The value of a stock certificate depends on:

- rarity
- the issuer
- signatures
- quality of engraving
- overall appearance
- condition
- date of issue

*MA340-80-10, 1909, v, 200 Korona 4-1/2% bond w. coupons, Dutch revenue rubber stamp, Lègràdy Testvèrek, Budapest; 11" x 16", purple on green $7.00

*MA340-90-10, 1910, v, 1,000 Korona 4-1/2% bond w. coupons, Dutch revenue rubber stamp, Hungarian-German-French, Lègràdy Testvèrek, Budapest, 11" x 16", blue on green $7.00

*MA340-100-10, 1915, v, 2,000 Korona 4-1/2%
bond w. coupons, Dutch revenue imprint, Hungarian-German-French, Légràdy Testvérek,
Budapest, 11" x 16", brown on green $7.00

*MA340-100-15, 1918, v, 2,000 Korona 4-1/2%
bond with coupons, signature variety, Dutch
revenue imprint, Hungarian-German-French,
Lègrády Testvèrek, Budapest, 11" x 16",
brown on green $7.00

Magyar Országos Központi Takarékpénztár, Central Credit Union of Hungary

*MA420-30-10, 1910, v, 2,000 Korona 4-1/2%
bond w. coupons, Dutch revenue rubber stamp,
Hungarian-German-French, Franklin-Társulat
nyomdája, 10" x 16-1/2", purple $7.00

Pesti Hazai Elsö Takarékpénztár-Egyesület, First United Credit Union of Pest

*PE330-30-10, 1906, v, bearer sh., text in Hungar-
ian and German, brown $3.00

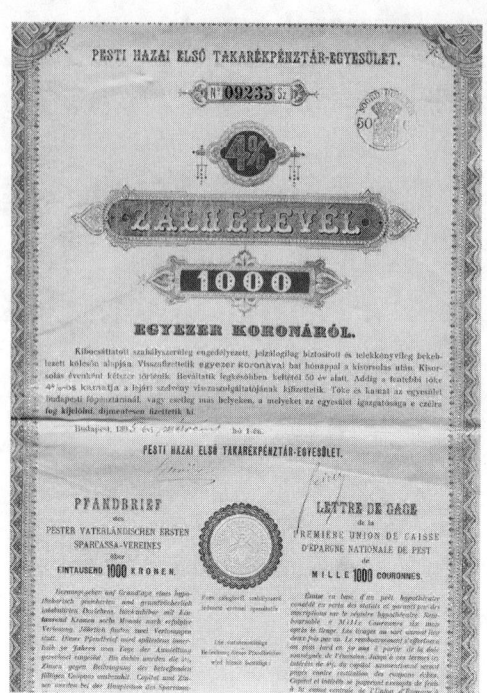

*PE330-50-10, 1895, v, 1,000 Korona 4% bond w. coupons, Dutch revenue rubber stamp, Hungarian-German-French, 10" x 16-1/2", green .$7.00

Pesti Magyar Kereskedelmi Bank
Hungarian Commercial Bank of Pest.

*PE420-40-10, 1895, v, 2,000 Korona 4% bond w. coupons, text in Hungarian-German, Dutch revenue rubber stamp, Nyomatott Kertész Józsefnél, Budapest, 15-3/4" x 9-3/4", grey on pink
..................................$7.00

Salgó-Tarjáni Vilamossági Részvény-Társaság, Salgó-Tarján
A manufacturer of light bulbs.

*SA170-20-10, 1896, v, 100 K bearer sh., green
..................................$10.00

Temesvár-Módosi Helyi Érdekü Vasut Részvénytársaság

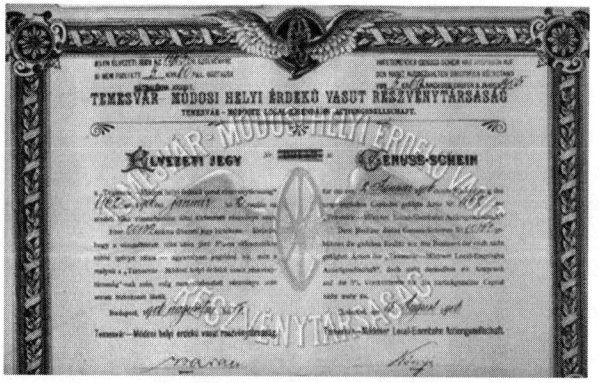

*TE100-30-10, 1906, v, bearer sh., blue
..................................$14.00

Urikány-Zsilvölgyi Magyar Köszénybánya-Részvénytársaság; Urikány-Zsilthaler Ungarische Kohlenbergwerks AG, Budapest

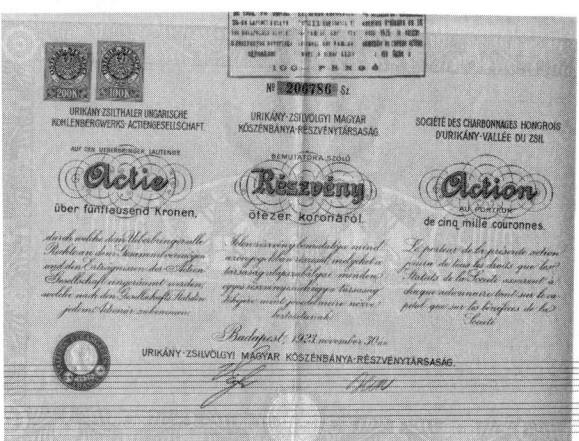

*UR180-30-10, 1923, 5,000 Korona bearer sh., French revenue imprint, light blue $7.00

```
┌─────────────────────────────────┐
│ The value of a stock certificate │
│ depends on:                      │
│                                  │
│    • rarity                      │
│    • the issuer                  │
│    • signatures                  │
│    • quality of engraving        │
│    • overall appearance          │
│    • condition                   │
│    • date of issue               │
└─────────────────────────────────┘
```

People's Republic

Second Peace Loan

These loans were considered a tax, and were very unpopular. The 10-year loans were cashed in as fast as possible, and uncancelled certificates are very scarce.

*2PR90-20-10, 1951, v, i/u 200 Forint Loan certificate, red $30.00

Third Peace Loan

*2PR120-20-10, 1952, v, i/u 200 Forint Loan certificate, brown. $30.00

I

India

Most of these certificates are listed courtesy of Krause Publications. They come from an article based upon a large private collection purchased some time ago and subsequently broken up. Indian terms for large numbers are: Lac (Lakh)=100,000 and Cror=10,000,000

Acme Oil Mills, Ltd., Calcutta
AC130-20-10, 1919, par 10 Rupees **$3.00**

Adarsh Chitra Ltd., Bombay
AD60-30-10, 1937, par 10 Rupees, red-brown and blue. **$3.00**

Agra Electric Supply Company Limited, Calcutta

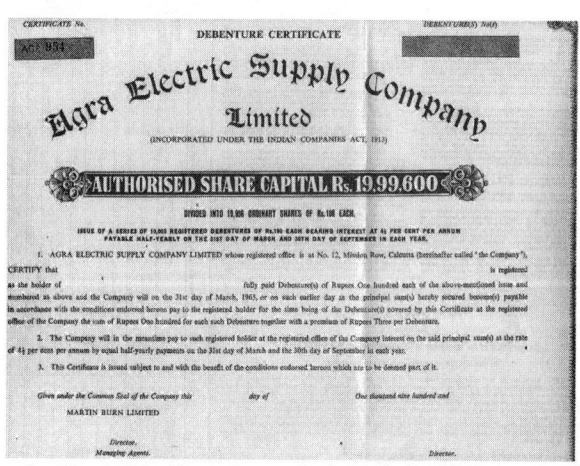

*AG200-40-10, 19xx, u/u Rs. 100 4-1/2% debenture, Martin Burn Limited Managing Agents, w/o imprint, 14" x 11-3/4", red. **$3.00**

Agra United Mills, Ltd., Calcutta
AG290-30-10, 1921, par 10 Rupees **$3.00**
AG290-40-10, 1921, par 100 Rupees pref. . . . **$4.00**

Agricultural Products Ltd., Poona
AG370-30-10, 1941/42, par 10 Rupees, blue on green **$3.00**
AG370-40-10, 1941, par 50 Rupees pref., blue on pink. **$4.00**

Ahmedabad Advance Spinning and Weaving Co., Ltd., Ahmedabad
AH230-30-10, 1897, 1,000 Rupees **$11.00**

Ahmedabad Astodia Manufacturing Co., Ltd., Bombay
AH260-20-10, 1922, v - goddess and mills, 1 sh. (par Rs 100), violet. **$7.00**

Ahmedabad Jupiter Spinning, Weaving and Manufacturing Co. Ltd., Ahmedabad
AH290-20-10, 1920, par 125 Rupees, black on light green. **$5.00**
AH290-25-10, 1935, par 125 Rupees. **$4.00**
AH290-50-10, 1935, par 125 Rupees pref., red, black on yellow **$6.00**

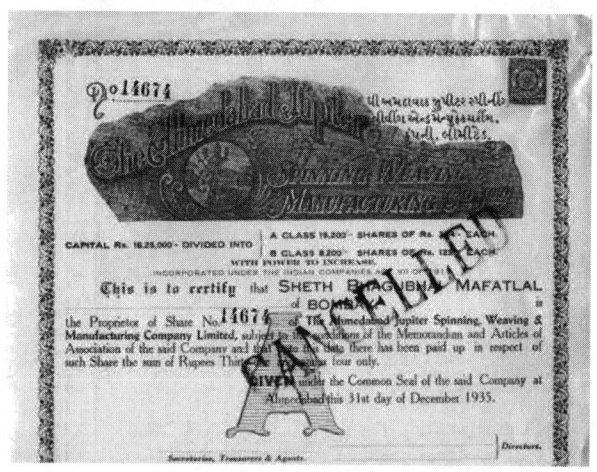

*AH290-60-10, 1935, 1 sh. series A (par 31Rs, 4 Annas), green on light green **$5.00**
AH290-65-10, 1935, series B, par 31 Rupees 4 Annas on 125 Rupees, brown-violet and green, red. **$6.00**
AH290-70-10, 1936, par 125 Rupees, dark blue on light blue paper **$4.00**
AH290-75-10, 1942, par 125 Rupees. **$3.00**
AH290-80-10, 1942, par 100 Rupees pref., brown and blue on light blue **$4.00**
AH290-85-10, 1943, par 100 Rupees pref., brown and blue on pink **$4.00**
AH290-90-10, 1947/48, par 12 Rupees 8 Annas series A pref., orange-brown and blue on tan **$3.00**
AH290-95-10, 1952, par 125 Rupees, brown-violet and blue on pink. **$3.00**
AH290-100-10, 1952, par 100 Rupees pref. **$4.00**

AH290-105-10, 1952, par 12 Rupees 8 Annas
 series A pref. $3.00
AH290-110-10, 196x, par 125 Rupees, blue,
 black on pink. $3.00

Ahmedabad Merchants's Spinning Mills Co., Ltd., Ahmedabad

AH320-20-10, 1897/1906, 1,000 Rupees, light blue
 . . . .$7.00

Ahmedabad New Edward Manufacturing Co., Ltd., Ahmedabad

AH350-20-10, 1917, par 250 Rupees $5.00

Ahmedabad New Spinning and Manufacturing Co., Ltd., Ahmedabad

AH370-30-10, 1895, 1,000 Rupees. $10.00

Ahmedabad New Textile Mills Co., Ltd., Ahmedabad

AH390-30-10, 1941, par 250 Rupees $6.00
AH390-40-10, 1941, par 125 Rupees pref.,
 orange-brown $8.00
AH390-50-10, 1946/48, par 500 Rupees on 250
 Rupees. $4.00
AH390-60-10, 1946/48, par 125 Rupees pref. $3.00

Ahmedabad Sarangpur Mills Co., Ltd., Ahmedabad

AH500-40-10, 1947, v - factory, black on light
 green $4.00

Ahmedabad Spinning and Weaving Co., Ltd., Ahmedabad

AH560-30-10, 1921, v - portraits and mills, 1 sh.
 (par Rs 100), brown and blue $5.00
AH560-40-10, 1921, par 100 Rupees, green and
 brown $4.00

Ahmedabad Vishnu Cotton Mills Co., Ltd., Ahmedabad

AH620-20-10, 1920, par 125 Rupees, blue. . .$6.00

Akbar Manufacturing and Press Co., Ltd., Bombay

AK130-20-10, 1917, par 50 Rupees $4.00

Akhil Bharat Printers, Ltd., Bombay

AK210-30-10, 1947, par 100 Rupees, dark blue on
 light blue. $3.00

Alcock, Ashdown & Co. Ltd., Bombay

AL160-30-10, 1944, par 100 Rupees, red . . .$3.00
AL160-40-10, 1954, par 100 Rupees, blue. . .$3.00

All India General Insurance Co., Ltd., Bombay

AL280-30-10, 1944, par 100 Rupees $3.00

All India Loc Co. Ltd., Calcutta

AL310-20-10, 1927, par 10 Rupees, dark blue
 . . . .$3.00

All India Publicity Corporation, Ltd., Bombay

AL340-20-10, 1924, par 40 Rupees $3.00

Alliance Cotton Manufacturing Co., Ltd., Bombay

AL420-20-10, 1915, par 100 Rupees $5.00

Al'Worth Products Ltd., Bombay

AL540-30-10, 1947, par 1 Rupee founder's stock
 . . . .$4.00
AL540-35-10, 1947, par 100 Rupees, tan. . . .$3.00
AL540-45-10, 1947, par 100 Rupees pref. . . .$5.00

Ambaji Taranga Light Railway Co., Ltd., Bombay

AM90-20-10, 1916, par 100 Rupees $7.00

Ambica Air Lines Ltd., Bombay

AM180-20-10, 1947, v - airplane, 26 sh.
 (par Rs 25), brown on tan. $3.00
AM180-30-10, 1947, par 100 Rupees pref. . .$5.00

Amrut Oil Mills Ltd., Bombay

AM400-30-10, 1946, 100 Rupees,
 dark blue on grey $3.00
AM400-40-10, 1946, 100 Rupees pref.,
 dark blue on light blue $3.00

Ananta Mills Limited., Ahmedabad
AN40-30-10, 1930, par 100 Rupees, light green
. . . .**$4.00**
AN40-35-10, 1930, v, 2 sh over 1 sh. (par Rs 20
over Rs 100), Indian revenue imprint **$3.00**
AN40-40-10, 1940. (par Rs 20 over on Rs 50 over
Rs 100), light green on blue paper **$3.00**
AN40-45-10, 1940, par 20 Rupees, green on light
green **$3.00**

Anantapur Gold Field Ltd.
AN70-20-10, 1906/19, green. **$10.00**
AN70-30-10, 1914, preferred, blue **$10.00**
AN70-35-10, 1914/19, preferred **$10.00**

Apollo Mills, Ltd., Bombay
AP250-20-10, 1920, par 100 Rupees, brown
. . . .**$6.00**
AP250-25-10, 1921, par 50 Rupees over Rs 100,
brown **$5.00**
AP250-30-10, 1921, par 2 Rupees over Rs 100,
brown **$4.00**
AP250-40-10, 1942, par 2 Rupees **$3.00**

**Aryan Champion Insurance Co., Ltd.,
Bombay**
AR470-30-10, 1941, par 25 Rupees **$3.00**

Aryan Life Assurance Society Ltd., Bombay
AR500-30-10, 1940, par 10 Rupees, blue on yellow
. . . .**$4.00**

Ashok Insurance Co., Ltd., Ahmedabad
AS300-30-10, 1944, par 100 Rupees **$4.00**
AS300-40-10, 1944, par 25 Rupees pref. **$4.00**

Ashwin Industries Ltd., Baroda
AS370-30-10, 1945, par 1 Rupee **$6.00**
AS370-35-10, 1945, 100 Rupees, grey blue . .**$4.00**
AS370-40-10, 1945, 100 Rupees pref., tan . . .**$3.00**

Asiatic Chemical Works, Ltd., Calcutta
AS410-20-10, 1920, par 10 Rupees, red and dark
blue **$4.00**

Assam Co. Ltd.
AS550-20-10, 1865, £20 . . . .**$32.00**
AS550-30-10, 1923, £1 . . . .**$5.00**

Assam Bengal Cement Co., Ltd., Calcutta
AS580-30-10, 1938/47, par 1 Rupee **$3.00**
AS580-35-10, 1938/47, par 10 Rupees, dark green
on tan **$3.00**
AS580-45-10, 1938/47, par 100 Rupees pref.
. . . .**$4.00**

Assam Frontier Tea Co., Ltd.
Became the Suddia Road Tea Co.
AS640-20-10, 1911, £10 stock **$8.00**

**Associated Advertisers and Printers Ltd.,
Bombay**
AS930-30-10, 1937, par 10 Rupees, brown . .**$3.00**
AS930-40-10, 1944, par 4/10 Rupees, brown
. . . .**$3.00**

Assur Veerje Mills, Ltd., Bombay
AS1020-20-10, 1920, par 100 Rupees **$4.00**

Automatic Tools, Ltd., Calcutta
AU250-20-10, 1920, par 10 Rupees **$3.00**

Badham Pile and Company Ltd., Bombay
BA140-20-10, 1910, par 70 Rupees, brown-violet
. . . .**$5.00**

Balaghat Gold Mines Ltd.,
Formerly Balaghat Gold Mining Co., Ltd.
BA370-20-10, 1919/32, par 10/- **$4.00**
BA370-30-10, 1919/32, par 10/- preferred . . .**$5.00**

Balaghat Gold Mining Co. Ltd.
Formerly the Balaghat-Mysore Ltd.
BA400-20-10, 1896/1919, £1 . . . .**$11.00**

Balaghat-Mysore Gold Mine Ltd.
BA430-20-10, 1890/94, £1 . . . .**$12.00**

Balaghat-Mysore Gold Mining Co., Ltd.
BA460-20-10, 1886/90, £1 . . . .**$15.00**

Balaghat-Mysore Mines Ltd.
BA470-20-10, 1894/96, £1 . . . .$12.00

Bank of Bengal (1876)

*BA530-20-10, 1898, v, 9 sh. (par Rs 500), black
. . . .$7.00

Bank of Bombay
BA570-20-10, 500 Rupees $4.00

Bank of Bougal
BA600-20-10, 500 Rupees $4.00

Bank of Calcutta Ltd.
BA630-20-10, £25 . . . .$11.00

Bank of Hindustan, China and Japan, Ltd.
BA720-20-10, 1863, v - arms, 1 sh. (par £100),
    mauve paper $35.00
BA720-25-10, 1864, v - arms, 1 sh. (par £100),
    brown-orange paper $25.00

Bank of Madras
BA760-20-10, 500 Rupees $6.00

Baroda Calico Industrial Mills Co., Ltd., Baroda
BA870-30-10, 1931, par 100 Rupees $8.00

Baroda Crystal Glass Works Ltd., Baroda
BA900-30-10, 1944, par 10 Rupees, black on tan
. . . .$6.00
BA900-40-10, 1944, par 10 Rupees pref.,
    green on tan. $8.00

Baroda Steels Ltd., Baroda
BA1000-30-10, 1944, par 10 Rupees deferred
. . . .$6.00
BA1000-40-10, 1944, 2 sh. (par Rs 10), Indian tax
    stamps, blue on yellow $5.00
BA1000-50-10, 1944, par 100 Rupees pref.
. . . .$8.00

Bellary Press Co., Ltd., Bombay
BE220-20-10, 1900, 275 Rupees, light blue
. . . .$9.00

Bengal Bridge and Bolt Co., Ltd.
BE340-20-10, 1920, par 10 Rupees $3.00

Bengal Canning and Condiment Works Ltd., Calcutta
BE370-20-10, 1920, par 10 Rupees, brown-orange
. . . .$3.00

Bengal Central Flotilla Co. Ltd.
BE400-20-10, 18xx, £10 . . . .$14.00

Bengal Gold and Silver Mining Co., Ltd.
BE430-20-10, 1894, 100 Rupee bond, red and
    black on green $15.00

Bengal Iron Co. Ltd.
BE460-30-10, 1936/37 . . . .$4.00

Bengal Iron and Steel Co. Ltd.
BE470-20-10, £1 stock $6.00
BE470-30-10, £10 pref. stock $12.00

Bengal Mills Co., Ltd.
BE510-20-10, £10 pref. Stock $7.00

Bengal National Bank, Ltd., Calcutta
BE570-20-10, 1908, par 100 Rupees $8.00

Bengal Shellac Factory, Ltd., Calcutta
BE680-20-10, 1920, v, 1 sh. (par Rs 10),
    multicolored $4.00

Berar Manufacturing Co. Ltd., Bombay
BE810-20-10, 1922, par 200 Rupees, brown
. . . .$4.00

Berar Oil Works, Ltd., Akola
BE850-20-10, 1913, 250 Rupees **$6.00**

Bhagirathi Jute Mills Ltd., Calcutta
BH60-20-10, 1920, par 10 Rupees, green on pink
. . . .**$3.00**
BH60-30-10, 1920, par 100 Rupees pref. **$5.00**

Bhairab Electric Supply Ltd., Bhairab, Bengal
BH100-30-10, 1946, par 10 Rupees, green. . .**$3.00**
BH100-40-10, 1946, par 100 Rupees pref. . . .**$5.00**

Bharat Laxmi Cotton Mills Co., Ltd., Ahmedabad
BH390-20-10, 1921, par 100 Rupees,
red on yellow **$3.00**

Bharatkand Textile Manufacturing Co., Ltd., Ahmedabad
BH480-30-10, 1943, par 200 Rupees, green
. . . .**$5.00**
BH480-40-10, 1943, par 200 Rupees pref. B
. . . .**$5.00**
BH480-50-10, 19xx, par 50 Rupees pref. C
. . . .**$3.00**
BH480-60-10, 1948/49, par 100 Rupees pref. D,
orange **$3.00**
BH480-70-10, 1952, par 500 Rupees over 250 Rs.
. . . .**$3.00**
BH480-80-10, 1952, par 100 Rupees pref. D
. . . .**$3.00**

Bhilupur Ginning and Manufacturing Co., Ltd., Baroda
BH630-20-10, 1914, par 100 Rupees, red
. . . .**$11.00**

The Bikaner Government
BI150-50-10, 1929, 500 Rupees 5-1/2% bond
. . . .**$60.00**
BI150-60-10, 1929, 25,000 Rupees 5-1/2% three
year bond (free of all state taxes) **$60.00**

Bombay Banking Co., Ltd., Bombay
BO280-20-10, 1907, v - arms, par 50 Rupees,
dark blue on red **$10.00**

Bombay Baroda Assurance Co., Ltd., Baroda
BO310-20-10, 1929, v - arms, par 25 Rupees
. . . .**$10.00**

Bombay Brick and Tile Manufacturing Co., Ltd., Bombay
BO340-20-10, 1914, par 100 Rupees. **$5.00**
BO340-30-10, 1916, par 100 Rupees. **$6.00**

Bombay Canning and Fruit Products co., Ltd., Bombay
BO370-30-10, 1939, par 20 Rupees, dark blue on
light blue. **$3.00**

Bombay Cotton Manufacturing Co., Ltd., Bombay
BO400-20-10, 1891, par 500 Rupees, blue . .**$6.00**
BO400-30-10, 1906, par 500 Rupees, green .**$4.00**
BO400-40-10, 1912, par 500 Rupees, dark blue
. . . .**$4.00**
BO400-50-10, 1924, par 500 Rupees, dark blue
. . . .**$4.00**
BO400-60-10, 1924, par 10 Rupees pref. . . .**$3.00**

Bombay Cotton Press Co., Ltd., Bombay
BO410-20-10, 1884, par 125 Rupees. **$8.00**

Bombay Electric Supply and Tramways Co., Ltd., Bombay
BO450-20-10, 1905, par £10 . . . .**$8.00**
BO450-30-10, 1905, par £10 pref. **$10.00**
BO450-50-10, 1933/46, par 50 Rupees, blue
. . . .**$3.00**
BO450-60-10, 1933/46, par 50 Rupees pref.
. . . .**$3.00**

Bombay Fire Insurance Co., Ltd., Bombay
BO480-20-10, 1896, 1,000 Rupees **$6.00**

Bombay Industrial Mills Co., Ltd., Bombay
BO520-30-10, 1920, v - factory, par 100 Rupees,
dark brown on brown-violet. **$3.00**

Bombay Merchants Bank Ltd., Bombay
BO560-20-10, 1910, 1 sh. (par Rs 100), light green
. . . .**$8.00**
BO560-30-10, 1918/19, par 100 Rupees,
light green. **$8.00**

Bombay Neon Sign Co., Ltd., Bombay

BO600-30-10, 1938, par 100 Rupees, light blue
  paper **$5.00**

Bombay Potteries and Tiles Limited, Bombay

BO640-30-10, 1946, v - pottery items, 1 sh. (par Rs
  100), yellow under-print **$4.00**

BO640-40-10, 1946, par 100 Rupees pref. . . .**$7.00**

BO640-50-10, 1946, par 100 Rupees 2nd pref.
  . . . .**$5.00**

Bombay Talkies, Ltd., Bombay

BO750-30-10, 1942, v, 1 sh. (par 100 Rupees),
  grey-green **$4.00**

BO750-40-10, 1934/42, par 100 Rupees pref., grey
  green **$4.00**

Bombay Tyre and Rubber Co., Ltd., Bombay

BO780-30-10, 1940/43, par 100 Rupees **$5.00**

Bombay Woolen Manufacturing Co., Ltd., Bombay

BO890-30-10, 1920/22, par 100 Rupees, pink
  under-print **$4.00**

British India Corporation, Ltd., Cawnpore

BR210-30-10, 1920, par 10 Rupees **$3.00**

BR210-40-10, 1920, 100 Rupees pref. **$4.00**

BR210-50-10, 1921, par 7 Rupees 8 Annas
  . . . .**$3.00**

BR210-60-10, 1921, 100 Rupees pref. **$4.00**

BR210-70-10, 1928, par 2 Rupees 8 Annas
  . . . .**$3.00**

BR210-80-10, 1928, par 5 Rupees **$3.00**

BR210-90-10, 1928, 100 Rupees pref. **$4.00**

BR210-100-10, 1932, par 1 Annas **$3.00**

BR210-110-10, 1932/35, par 1 Rupee **$3.00**

BR210-120-10, 1932, 100 Rupees pref. **$3.00**

British India General Insurance Cp., Ltd., Bombay

BR260-20-10, 1919, v - flags, 1 sh. (par Rs 100)
  . . . .**$4.00**

Broach Electric Supply and Development Corporation Ltd., Bombay

BR560-30-10, 1929, v, 10 sh. (par Rs 10), brown
  . . . .**$3.00**

Broach Fine Counts Spinning and Weaving Co., Ltd., Bombay

BR590-20-10, 1918, v - factory, 1 sh. (par Rs 250),
  purple **$5.00**

Budderpore Tea Co., Ltd.

BU190-20-10, 19xx, par £1 . . . .**$4.00**

Martin Burn Limited, Calcutta

*BU410-30-10, 1946, v - elephant head, Rs. 500
  5% convertible note, w. Indian revenue stamp,
  Waterlow & Sons Limited, London. 14" x
  11-1/4", brown **$3.00**

Buxa Timber and Trading Co., Ltd.

BU610-20-10, 1921, blue on grey **$4.00**

Calcutta Soap Works, Ltd., Calcutta

CA180-20-10, 1919, par 10 Rupees, brown,
  orange and green **$4.00**

Cement and Stone Products, Ltd., Madras

CE190-40-10, 1937, par 10 Rupees, blue and
  brown **$3.00**

CE190-50-10, 1937, par 100 Rupees pref. . . .**$7.00**

Central Bank of India Ltd., Bombay

CE240-30-10, 1923, v - Britannia, par 50 Rupees
  . . . .**$7.00**

Central India Mining Co., Ltd., Bombay
CE450-30-10, 1910/22, par 10 Rupees,
   brown-violet on yellow-orange.........**$3.00**

**Central Provinces Portland Cement Co.,
   Ltd., Calcutta**
CE680-20-10, 1919, par 10 Rupees, red.....**$3.00**

Central Tipperah Tea Co., Ltd., Calcutta
CE810-30-10, 1918/19, par 25 Rupees, dark blue
   and purple........................**$10.00**
CE810-40-10, 1920, par 25 Rupees, dark blue and
   brown-violet......................**$5.00**

Central Travancore Rubber Co., Ltd.
CE870-20-10, 19xx, par £1 ....**$5.00**
CE870-30-10, 19xx, par £1 pref. **$6.00**

Cherra Tea Co., Ltd.
CH160-20-10, 1881, £10 ....**$12.00**

**Chinubhai Labhai and Brothers Ltd.,
   Ahmedabad**
CH280-30-10, 1929, par 1 Rupee, lilac **$8.00**

Chitale Agricultural Products Ltd., Bombay
CH370-20-10, 19xx, par 10 Rupees.......**$3.00**
CH370-30-10, 19xx, 100 Rupees..........**$6.00**
CH370-40-10, 19xx, par 50 Rupees pref.....**$6.00**
CH370-50-10, 1946, 100 Rupees, dark blue
   on purple.........................**$4.00**

Chowringhee Properties Limited
CH520-40-10, 1915, 500 Rupees 5-1/2% 1st mortgage debenture, unusually wide (17"+) ..**$12.00**

**Cine Industries and Recording Co., Ltd.,
   Bombay**
CI330-30-10, 1940, par 100 Rupees, brown and
   pink.............................**$5.00**

**Coal Mining and State Minerals Ltd.,
   Bombay**
CO60-40-10, 1945, v - miner, 10 Sh. (par Rs 10),
   green............................**$3.00**

Coke Consumers' Combine (Calcutta) Ltd.
CO180-20-10, 1919, par 10 Rupees, dark blue on
   light blue.........................**$4.00**

**Colaba Spinning and Weaving Co., Ltd.,
   Bombay**
CO240-20-10, 1876, par 1,000 Rupees, pink
   under-print.......................**$8.00**

Crescent Insurance Co., Ltd., Bombay
CR120-20-10, 1921, v - arms, par 100 Rupees
   ....**$3.00**
CR120-40-10, 1944, v - arms, par 15 Rupees, 10
   Anna, 8 Pies; brown and orange-brown...**$3.00**

Crescent Mills Co., Ltd., Bombay
CR160-20-10, 1907, par 100 Rupees, blue on light
   green............................**$6.00**

Currimbhoy Mills Co., Ltd., Bombay
CU370-20-10, 1913, par 250 Rupees, brown
   ....**$7.00**

**Dacca Button Manufacturing Co., Ltd.,
   Calcutta**
DA130-20-10, 1920, par 10 Rupees, green
   underprint........................**$4.00**

**Dalbhoom Gold and Minerals Prospecting
   Co., Ltd., Calcutta**
DA260-20-10, 1917, par 10 Rupees, green ..**$5.00**
DA260-30-10, 1917, par 10 Rupees pref. ...**$7.00**

Darjeeling Himalayan Railway Co. Ltd.
DA390-30-10, Par 100 Rupees...........**$8.00**

Datta Chemical Works, Ltd., Calcutta
DA510-30-10, 1920, par 10 Rupees, pink ...**$4.00**

Dawn Match Co., Ltd., Rampur
DA640-40-10, 1944, par 10 Rupees, dark blue
   ....**$4.00**

Delhi Electric Supply and Traction Co. Ltd.
DE210-30-10, 19xx, par £1 ....**$10.00**

Departmental Service Stores Ltd., Bombay

DE490-40-10, 1946, par 10 Rupees, lilac and blue
on grey paper $3.00
DE490-50-10, 1946, 100 Rupees pref......$4.00

Diamond Spinning and Weaving Co., Ltd., Bombay

DI110-20-10, 1920, par 100 Rupees, blue-green
underprint $4.00
DI110-30-10, 1920, par 100 Rupees pref. ...$4.00

Digvijay Tiles and Potteries Ltd., Jamnagar, Nawanagar

DI230-30-10, 1945, v, 3 sh. (par Rs100), green and
brown $9.00
DI230-40-10, 1945, par 100 Rupees pref., brown,
orange and blue....................$12.00

Dumra Gold Prospecting Syndicate, Ltd., Calcutta

DU260-20-10, 1890, par 1 Rupee founders sh.
...................................$7.00
DU260-30-10, 1890, par 1 Rupees........$9.00

Duncan Stratton & Company, Ltd., Bombay

DU320-30-10, 1947, par 10 Rupees, blue ...$3.00
DU320-40-10, 1947, par 10 Rupees pref....$4.00
DU320-50-10, ND, par 5 Rupees.........$3.00
DU320-60-10, ND, par 5 Rupees pref......$4.00

Dwarka Cement Company, Limited, Bombay

DW60-30-10, 1921, 1 sh. (par 100 Rs), multicolored..............................$3.00
DW60-40-10, 1921, par 100 Rupees pref. ...$4.00

East India Coal Company, Limited, Dammodan Valley, Province of Bengal

EA120-20-10, 1860, v, £10 stock, brown
...................................$10.00

East India Irrigation and Canal Co.

EA150-20-10, 1860, £20, blue on red......$17.00

East Indian Iron Co.

EA210-20-10, 1854, £10 stock..........$40.00

East Indian Junction Railway Co.

EA240-20-10, 1847, £50, black on blue paper
...................................$90.00

East Indian Railway Co.

EA400-20-10, 1856, £1,000............$35.00

East and West Insurance Co., Ltd., Bombay

EA630-30-10, 1914/44, par 50 Rupees, brown on
tan...............................$3.00

Eastern Bank, Limited., Bombay

EA670-20-10, 1910, 15 sh. (par £10), Bombay
Register, light green...............$15.00

Eastern Life Assurance Co., Ltd., Karachi

EA700-30-10, 1944, par 50 Rupees, red and black
...................................$4.00

Eastern Petroleum and Finance Company, Limited, Bombay

EA790-20-10, 1921, 12 sh. (par £1).......$3.00

Ebrahimbhoy Pabaney Mills Co., Ltd., Bombay

EB210-20-10, 1918, par 250 Rupees, green
underprint.........................$5.00

Eclat Coal Co., Ltd., Calcutta

EC130-20-10, 1919, par 10 Rupees, green ..$4.00

Elak (Southern India) Rubber Co., Ltd.

EL60-20-10, 1910/15, green $8.00

Electro Industries Ltd., Patan, Baroda

EL180-30-10, 1949, v - Indian god, 1 sh. (par Rs
25), red..........................$9.00

Elliot & Company, Limited, Calcutta

EL260-20-10, 1920, 20 sh. (par Rs 100), Indian
revenue imprint $5.00

Elphinstone Spinning and Weaving Mills Co., Ltd., Bombay

EL350-20-10, 1919, par 100 Rupees, yellow, green underprint $4.00

*EL350-30-10,*1919, par 100 Rupees pref.. . . .$4.00

English Press and Manufacturing Co. Ltd., Bombay

EN330-20-10, 1898, 1 sh. (par 100 Rupees)
. . . .$9.00

Estate and Finance Ltd., Bombay

ES360-30-10, 1947, 5 sh. (par Rs 1,000) $3.00

Exchange Bank of India and Africa, Ltd., Bombay

EX180-30-10, 1943, v - elephant and giraffe, par 100 Rupees, blue and tan $6.00

EX180-40-10, 1943, par 100 Rupees pref.. . . .$7.00

Exchange Talkies of India, China and Africa Ltd., Bombay

EX340-30-10, 1950, par 10 Rupees, light green
. . . .$3.00

EX340-40-10, 1950, par 25 Rupees pref.. . . .$6.00

Express Oil Mills Co., Ltd., Calcutta

EX420-20-10, 1919, par 10 Rupees, green and red
. . . .$4.00

Fazulbhoy Mills, Ltd., Bombay

FA150-20-10, 1906, par 250 Rupees, brown on light green. $7.00

Framjee Petit Spinning and Manufacturing Co., Ltd., Bombay

FR180-20-10, 1910, par 1,000 Rupees, green
. . . .$6.00

Freezite Limited, Bombay

FR240-30-10, 1942, 100 Rupees $4.00

Fulchand Govindlal & Company Limited, Messr., Ahmedabad

FU250-20-10, 1921, par 5 Rupees, red and dark blue on light green $12.00

Gaekwar Industrials, Ltd., Baroda

GA90-20-10, 1920, v - founder, 1 sh. (par Rs 100), brown on yellow brown $8.00

Gaekwar Oil and Chemical Co., Ltd., Baroda

GA120-20-10, 1920, par 100 Rupees, brown
. . . .$7.00

Gaekwar Umbrella Manufacturing Co., Ltd., Baroda

GA150-20-10, 1908, par 100 Rupees, text in Hindi, violet. $12.00

Gaya Sugar Mills Ltd., Bihar

GA290-20-10, 1946, 100 Rupees, ...$4.00

GA290-30-10, 1946, series A par 10 Rupees
. . . .$3.00

GA290-40-10, 1946, 100 Rupees pref.. . . . . .$5.00

GA290-50-10, 1946, series A pref. (par 10 Rupees)
. . . .$4.00

Glory Insurance Co. Ltd., Holkar State (Indore)

Later known as the Central India Insurance Co., Ltd.

GL180-30-10, 1946, v - sunface, 1 sh. (par Rs 100), Indian revenue stamps, blue on tan
. . . .$8.00

Gold Fields of Dharwar (India) Ltd.

GO160-20-10, 1904/10, £1 . . . .$12.00

Gold Fields of Mysore Ltd., Mysore

GO210-20-10, 1886, £1 . . . .$24.00

GO210-25-10, 1898, £1 . . . .$24.00

Gold Fields of Mysore and General Exploration Co., Ltd., Mysore

Formerly Gold Fields of Mysore Ltd.

GO220-20-10, 1902, £1 . . . .$18.00

Gopal Mills Co., Ltd.

GO390-40-10, 1942, v - factory, par 100 Rupees
. . . .$6.00

GO390-50-10, 1942, v - factory, 1 pref. sh. (par Rs 100), green and purple on yellow. $6.00

Great India Fire Insurance Co., Ltd., Bombay

GR180-20-10, 1918/19, v - map of India, par 20 Rupees, blue on green................$5.00

Guide Rail Road Feeder Lines Co., Ltd., Almatti District, Bijapur

GU190-30-10, 1936, par 10 Rupees, dark blue and pink $9.00

Gujarat Candle Factory and Asbestos Works Co., Ltd., Tardeo, Bombay

GU230-20-10, 1907, v, 1 sh. (par Rs 100), dark blue..........................$9.00

Gujarat Cotton Mills Co. Ltd., Ahmedabad

GU250-20-10, 1921, par 125 Rupees, dark blue on tan.....................................$4.00

GU250-30-10, 1939, par 15 Rupees, brown on yellow $3.00

GU250-40-10, 1944/46, par 15 Rupees, brown on yellow.................................$3.00

Gujarat Swadeshi Stores Co. Ltd., Ahmedabad

GU330-20-10, 1910/18, par 20 Rupees, Praja Bandhu $5.00

GU330-30-10, 1919, par 20 Rupees, Shri Ganesh $5.00

GU330-35-10, 1925, par 10 Rupees.......$4.00

Gwalior Paint and Chemical Industries Ltd., Gwalior

GW70-30-10, 1943, par 1 Rupee $4.00

GW70-40-10, 1943, par 10 Rupees, brown ..$3.00

GW70-50-10, 1943, v, 10 pref. sh. (par 100 Rupees), blue $7.00

Messrs Hargovandas Jivandas & Sons Ltd., Bavnagar

HA260-30-10, 1933, 1 sh. (par Rs 1), green on orange...........................$13.00

HA260-40-10, 1933, par 1 Rupee pref......$11.00

Hatim Mills, Ltd., Surat

HA390-20-10, 1910, par 100 Rupees, red-violet $4.00

HA390-30-10, 1910, par 100 Rupees pref....$6.00

Hemp Jute Mills Ltd.

HE220-20-10, 1875 ....$30.00

Himabhai Manufacturing Co., Ltd., Ahmedabad

HI250-20-10, 190x, par 1,000 Rupees, green on light green..........................$5.00

HI250-30-10, 19xx, par 125 Rupees, lilac underprint..........................$4.00

HI250-40-10, 1946, par 125 Rupees, dark blue on pink....................................$4.00

HI250-50-10, 1946, 1/60 sh (par Rs 2, 1 Anna 4 Pies) $3.00

HI250-60-10, 19xx, v - male portrait, par 250 Rupees, brown and yellow-orange.......$3.00

HI250-70-10, 19xx, par 250 Rupees pref. ...$5.00

Himansurai Indo-International Talkies, Ltd., Bombay

HI280-30-10, 193x/46, 2,500 Rupees $8.00

Hindu Co-operative Bank, Ltd., Karachi

HI330-30-10, 1935, par 10 Rupees, green and blue $10.00

Hindu Insurance Co., Ltd., Lahore

HI360-30-10, 1941, par 1 Rupee, blue paper $6.00

Hindustan Co-operative Insurance Society Ltd., Lahore

HI420-20-10, 1909, par 100 Rupees, green, red, and blue $6.00

Hindustan Electric and Accumulators Manufacturing Co., Ltd., Bombay

HI450-30-10, 1937, par 10 Rupees, brown ..$3.00

HI450-40-10, 1937, par 100 Rupees pref. ...$5.00

Hindustan Soap and Candle Works Ltd., Ahmedabad

HI520-20-10, 1918, 1 sh. (par 125 Rupees) $7.00

Hindusthan Ltd., Bombay

HI560-20-10, 1918, par 100 Rupees, brown $10.00

Hosur Gold Mines Ltd., Bangalore, Mysore.
Formerly the Hosur Gold Mines of Dharwar Ltd.
HO240-20-10, 1907/09, £1.............$9.00

Hosur Gold Mines of Dharwar Ltd., Bangalore, Mysore
HO250-20-10, 1909/10, £1.............$9.00

Hutti (Nizam's) Gold Mines Ltd., Hyderabad
HU370-20-10, 1901/20, £1............$10.00

Hyderabad (Sind) Mercantile Co-Operative Bank, Ltd., Hyderabad (Sind)
HY200-30-10, 1937/39, par 20 Rupees, red
.................................$7.00

Hyderabad Starch Products Ltd., Hyderabad
HY230-30-10, 1944, par 50 Rupees.......$4.00

Imanshah Transport Co., Ltd., Ahmedabad
IM70-20-10, 1920, par 25 Rupees, blue-green
.................................$5.00

Imperial Bank of India
IM170-30-10, 500 Rupees $5.00

Government of India
IN90-20-10, 1867, £100 bond...........$40.00
IN90-25-10, 1870, bond $40.00

India Collective Farms Ltd., Calcutta
IN130-30-10, 1944, par 10 Rupees.........$3.00
IN130-40-10, 1944, 100 Rupees pref. $4.00

India General Construction Corporation, Calcutta
IN180-30-10, 1946, par 10 Rupees, grey-green on yellow...........................$3.00

The India General Navigation & Railway Company Limited
IN210-40-10, 1915, v, 500 Rupiah 5% bearer bonds, green $8.00

India Oil Plastics Ltd., Calcutta
IN270-30-10, 1944, par 10 Rupees, ochre ...$3.00
IN270-40-10, 1944, par 100 Rupees pref. ...$4.00

India Spinning and Weaving Co., Ltd., Ahmedabad
IN340-20-10, 1920, par 100 Rupees $8.00

India Timber, Mines and Products, Ltd., Calcutta
IN370-20-10, 1920, par 10 Rupees, red.....$4.00

India United Mills, Ltd., Bombay
IN420-30-10, 1946, par 1 Rupee deferred ...$3.00
IN420-40-10, 1946, par 10 Rupees, pink underprint
.................................$3.00

Indian Cement Co., Ltd. Bombay
IN450-30-10, 1937, par 10 Rupees $3.00

Indian Clock Manufacturing Co., Ltd., Bihar
IN470-30-10, 1944, par 10 Rupees, lilac on yellow
.................................$3.00
IN470-40-10, 1944, par 50 Rupees pref. $6.00
IN470-50-10, 1944, par 100 Rupees pref. ...$6.00

Indian and Colonial Goldfields Ltd.
IN510-20-10, 1896/1912, £1 ....$8.00

Indian Consolidated Gold Mining Co., Ltd.
Became Kempinkote Gold Fields Ltd.
IN540-20-10, 1881/90, £1 ....$17.00

Indian Cotton Co., Ltd., Bombay
IN570-20-10, 1886/1915, 125 Rupees, pink .$7.00

Indian Cotton Oil Co., Ltd., Bombay
IN580-20-10, 1914, 100 Rupees, dark blue and yellow $3.00
IN580-30-10, 1918, 100 Rupees, dark blue and green...........................$3.00
IN580-40-10, 1914, 250 Rupees pref. $5.00

Indian Financial Journals, Ltd., Calcutta

IN610-30-10, 1935, par 10 Rupees, light blue **$6.00**
IN610-40-10, 1935, par 100 Rupees pref., light
   blue **$6.00**

Indian Glace Kids Ltd., Calcutta

IN640-20-10, 1919, par 10 Rupees, brown
   and yellow-orange **$4.00**

Indian Globe Insurance Co., Ltd., Bombay

IN660-30-10, 1937, v - Laxmi seated on globe with
   two lions, par 50 Rupees, brown and tan . . **$5.00**

Indian Industrial Bank, Ltd., Calcutta

IN690-20-10, 1920, v - the border is of line draw-
   ings of various coins struck in India over the last
   22 centuries, 10 sh. (par Rs 10), brown and green
   . . . . **$30.00**

Indian Iron and Steel Co., Ltd.

IN710-30-10, 193x, par 10 Rupees. **$3.00**
IN710-40-10, 193x, par 100 Rupees. **$3.00**

Indian National Airways, Ltd.

IN760-30-10, 1944, par 1 Rupee, deferred. . . **$3.00**
IN760-40-10, 1944, par 10 Rupees. **$4.00**
IN760-50-10, 1944, par 10 Rupees pref. **$5.00**
IN760-60-10, 1946, par 10 Rupees, red **$3.00**

Indian National Bank Ltd., Calcutta

IN780-30-10, 1946, par 10 Rupees, dark blue on
   light green. **$5.00**
IN780-40-10, 1946, par 25 Rupees **$8.00**
IN780-50-10, 1946, par 50 Rupees pref. . . . **$6.00**

Indian Newspaper Co., Ltd., Bombay

IN800-20-10, 1913, par 50 Rupees **$4.00**

Indian Specie Bank, Ltd., Bombay

IN850-20-10, 1909/13, par 100 Rupees. **$7.00**

Indian Tea Co. of Cachar Ltd.

IN900-20-10, £10 stock **$12.00**

Indian Textile Journal Co., Ltd., Bombay

IN930-20-10, 1898, 250 Rupees, lilac on pink
   . . . . **$7.00**

Indo-Burma Steam Navigation Co., Ltd., Calcutta

IN960-20-10, 1920, par 10 Rupees, blue **$3.00**

Indora Malwa United Mills Ltd., Bombay

IN1000-30-10, 1949, par 100 Rupees, green and
   orange. **$5.00**

Indore State Bullion Exchange

IN1030-30-10, 1887, bond **$13.00**
IN1030-50-10, 1940, par 50 Rupees **$8.00**
IN1030-60-10, 1950, green **$6.00**

Industrial Bank of Western India, Ltd., Ahmedabad

IN1110-20-10, 1920, par 100 Rupees **$10.00**
IN1110-30-10, 19xx, par 25 over 100 Rupees. . **$8.00**
IN1110-40-10, 19xx, par 10 over 25/100 Rupees
   . . . . **$18.00**

Industrial and Exchange Bank of India, Ltd., Bombay

IN1130-20-10, 1921, par 10 Rupees **$6.00**

Investment Corporation Ltd., Kottayam, Travancore

IN1470-30-10, 1946, par 10 Rupees, green . . **$3.00**

Irrawaddy Petroleum Oil Syndicate Ltd., Bombay

IR330-20-10, 1920, par 10 Rupees, red **$6.00**

IR330-30-10, 1921, par Rs 2 8 Annas, red and green **$3.00**

Jain Vidyottejak Sahakari Mandal Ltd., Bombay

JA120-30-10, 1933, par 25 Rupees. **$8.00**

Jaipur Tea Co., Ltd.

Became the Jhanzie Tea Association Ltd.

JA150-20-10, 19xx, £5 stock **$7.00**

Jamnadas Nursery Ginning and Pressing Co., Ltd., Bombay

JA230-20-10, 1919, v, par 250 Rupees. **$4.00**

JA230-30-10, 1919, v, 1 pref. sh. (par 250 Rupees) **$8.00**

Jamnagar Sarangdhar Laboratory Ltd., Jamnagar, Kathiawar Nawaganar

JA290-30-10, 1947, par 100 Rupees. **$10.00**

JA290-40-10, 1947, 10 5% pref. shares (par 100 Rupees), lilac **$10.00**

Jamshed Manufacturing Co., Ltd.

JA330-20-10, 1887, par 250 Rupees, pink underprint **$7.00**

JA330-30-10, 18xx, par 250 Rupees. **$5.00**

Jaunpur Sugar Factory, Ltd., Allahabad

JA530-20-10, 1920, par 10 Rupees, brown . .**$3.00**

Messr. Jayantilal Amratlal Co., Ltd., Vankaner

JA650-30-10, 1933, par 1 Rupee **$12.00**

JA650-40-10, 1933, par 1 Rupee pref., green, red and olive-green **$7.00**

JA650-50-10, 19xx, par 249 Rupees. **$6.00**

JA650-60-10, 19xx, par 250 Rupees. **$3.00**

JA650-70-10, 19xx, par 100 Rupees pref. . . .**$3.00**

Jayantilal Amratlal Ltd., Ahmedabad

Agents of the Ananta Mills, Ltd.

JA680-20-10, 1930, par 1 Rupee **$4.00**

JA680-30-10, 1930, par 1 Rupee pref. **$3.00**

JA680-40-10, 19xx, par Rs 250 over 1 Rupee . . .**$3.00**

JA680-50-10, 19xx, par 250 Rupees pref. **$3.00**

JA680-60-10, 19xx, par 100 Rupees pref. **$3.00**

JA680-70-10, 19xx, par 100 Rupees 2nd Pref.**$3.00**

Jhanzie Tea Association Ltd.

Formerly Jaipur Tea Co., Ltd.

JH80-20-10, 19xx, £1 stock **$5.00**

Jibutil (Anantapur) Gold Mines Ltd.

Formerly Jibutil Gold Mines of Anantapur Ltd.

JI80-20-10, 1914, par 10/- **$11.00**

JI80-30-10, 1914, par 10/- pref. **$11.00**

Jivraj Balloo Spinning and Weaving Co., Ltd., Bombay

JI420-20-10, 187x/89, par 1,000 Rupees. . . .**$9.00**

JI420-30-10, 1919, par 1,000 Rupees **$8.00**

JI420-40-10, 1919, ¼ sh (par Rs 1,000), red .**$7.00**

Jubbulpore Portland Cement Co., Ltd., Bombay

JU80-20-10, 1920, par 100 Rupees **$5.00**

Jupiter Airways Ltd., Bombay

JU290-20-10, 1946, par 10 Rupees, dark blue and pink **$3.00**

JU290-30-10, 1946, par 10 Rupees pref. **$3.00**

Jupiter General Insurance Co., Ltd., Bombay

J320-20-10, 1920, v - peacock and elephants, 1 sh. (par Rs 100), brown and tan **$7.00**

J320-30-10, 1920, par 50 Rupees pref. **$6.00**

Kadi Ginning, Pressing and Oil Mill Co. Ltd., Bombay

KA90-20-10, 1910, par 250 Rupees, pink underprint **$5.00**

Kadur Estates Ltd.

Formerly known as Kadur Tea and Produce Co., Ltd.

KA150-30-10, 193x, par 2/- **$3.00**

Kadur Tea and Produce Co., Ltd.

KA180-20-10, Par 2/- **$4.00**

Kaiser-I-Hind Gold Mining Co., Ltd.
KA210-20-10, 1881, par 25 Rupees, pink....$7.00
KA210-30-10, 1887, par 25 Rupees $7.00

Kaiser-I-Hind Insurance Co., Ltd., Bombay
KA240-30-10, 1944, par 20 Rupees, blue on pink
......................................$3.00

The Kalol Cotton Mills Co. Ltd., Kalol, N. Gujarat, Baroda
KA320-20-10, 1920, v - founder's portrait, 1 sh. (par Rs 100), brown $9.00

Kalol Kapadia Spinning and Weaving Co., Ltd., Kalol, N. Gujarat
KA350-20-10, 1920, par 100 Rupees, brown, blue and green.........................$13.00

Kalol Swadesh Mills Co., Ltd., Baroda, Kalol, N. Gujarat
KA380-20-10, 1921, par 100 Rupees, red shadowing.........................$8.00

Kalyan Mills Ltd., Ahmedabad
KA440-30-10, 1932, par 100 Rupees $4.00

Kapadwanj Electricity Co., Ltd., Bombay
KA510-30-10, 1936, par 25 Rupees, dark blue on light blue..........................$4.00
KA510-40-10, 1936, par 25 Rupees pref.....$5.00

The Kapila Textile Mills, Limited., Bangalore City, Mysore
KA540-30-10, 1946, v - factory scenes, 25 def. sh. (par Rs 2), orange-brown, light-blue and orange
......................................$8.00
KA540-40-10, 1946, par 10 Rupees, green, light green and orange....................$6.00
KA540-50-10, 1946, par 100 Rupees, blue, light blue and orange....................$11.00

Karachi Bank, Limited., Karachi
KA620-20-10, 1915, v - camel, 100 sh. (par Rs 100), Indian revenue stamp, light blue ...$18.00

Karnan Steamship Co., Ltd., Calcutta
KA670-20-10, 1920, par 100 Rupees, green. .$4.00

Karnatak Industrial and Plywood Cp., Ltd., Bombay
KA700-30-10, 1945, par 10 Rupees........$3.00
KA700-30-10, 1945, par 100 Rupees pref....$4.00

Karnatak Sugar and Cellulose Works, Ltd., Bombay
KA740-30-10, 1947, par 10 Rupees, green on grey
......................................$3.00
KA740-40-10, 1947, par 100 Rupees pref., green and brown on light orange brown $4.00

Karnatak Vegetable Oils and Refineries Ltd., Hospet
KA770-30-10, 1946, par 10 Rupees, brown..$4.00

Kastoorchund Mills Co., Ltd., Bombay
KA830-20-10, 1914, par 500 Rupees.......$5.00
KA830-30-10, 1917, par 500 Rupees.......$4.00
KA830-40-10, 1921, par 500 Rupees.......$3.00
KA830-50-10, 1926, par 50 Rupees.......$3.00
KA830-60-10, 1926/27, par 50 Rupees $3.00

Kathiawad and Ahmedabad Banking Corporation, Ltd., Ahmedabad
KA970-20-10, 1911, par 100 Rupees.......$7.00
KA970-30-10, 1911, par 100 Rupees pref., green
......................................$9.00

The Kenico Products Ltd., Karachi
KE190-20-10, 1946, par 10 Rupees deferred.$8.00
KE190-30-10, 1946, v - child with fish, u/u certificate (par Rs 100), brown on light green...$6.00

Kerala Calicut Estates Ltd.
Became the Kerala Rubber Co. Ltd.
KE410-20-10, 1920, £1 stock............$7.00
KE410-30-10, 1932, £2 stock............$4.00

Kerala Tea Co., Ltd.
KE450-20-10, 19xx, par 2/- stock $4.00

Keshaw Mills Co., Ltd., Petlad
KE570-30-10, 1942, par 1,000 Rupees $10.00
KE570-40-10, 1942, par 1,000 Rupees pref., black and red $5.00

Khudabadi Amil Co-operative Agricultural Association Ltd., Hyderabad, Sind

KH170-30-10, 1934/41, v - farming scene pictorial, 1 sh. (par Rs 50), blue **$10.00**

Khudabadi Amil Cooperative Credit Bank, Ltd., Hyderabad, Sind

KH180-20-10, 1917, par 10 Rupees **$15.00**
KH180-30-10, 1938, v - founder's photo, 1 sh. (par Rs 10), red **$13.00**

Khudabadi Bhaidbund Co-operative Credit Bank, Ltd., Hyderabad, Sind

KH210-30-10, 1936, par 10 Rupees **$12.00**

Khulna Bagirhaut Railway Co., Ltd., Ahmedabad

KH410-20-10, 1916, par 100 Rupees **$8.00**

Kilachand Mills Limited, Bombay

KI130-20-10, 1920, v - male portrait, 1 sh. (par Rs 25), brown on tan **$6.00**

The Kolar District Board Railway, Mysore

KO150-30-10, 1912, 4% debenture loan . . .**$30.00**

Kolhapur and Southern Maratha Bank Ltd., Kolhapur

KO190-20-10, 1910, par 50 Rupees **$12.00**

Kousanie Tea Co., Ltd.

KO490-20-10, 1874, 100 Rupees **$12.00**

Krishna Textile Trading Co., Ltd., Vankaner (Wankaner)

KR210-30-10, 1942, 1 sh. (par Rs 100), black on light blue **$13.00**

UNLISTED TYPES & VARIETIES

Readers are welcome to contact the author directly at:

Rainer Stahlberg
P.O. Box 1044
Rooseveltown, New York 13683

Kursiong & Darjeeling Tea Company

*KU450-20-10, 1897, 5 sh. (par Rs 50), Indian revenue imprint, brown on beige **$9.00**

Kurwai Motor Transport Co., Ltd., Kurwai

KU570-20-10, 19xx, v - male portrait, u/u certificate (par Rs 10), brown on yellow **$3.00**

Lalubhai Samaldas Peoples' Co-operative Bank, Ltd., Bombay

LA140-20-10, 1928, par 10 Rupees **$10.00**

Land Mortgage Bank of India Ltd. (Credit Foncier Indien)

LA210-20-10, 1866, bond **$15.00**

Laxmi Bank, Ltd., Akola, Berar

LA490-30-10, 1941, v - goddess, par 100 Rupees, brown **$6.00**

Legal Investment and Insurance Co., Ltd.

LE210-30-10, 1935, v - elephant head, par 20 Rupees, red **$5.00**

Link Industries, Ltd., Madras

LI230-30-10, 1946, par 10 Rupees, blue and grey
. . . .**$3.00**

Lister Antiseptics and Dressings Co., Ltd., Calcutta

LI350-30-10, 1937, par 100 Rupees **$4.00**
LI350-40-10, 1937, par 100 Rupees pref., pink
. . . .**$4.00**

LI350-50-10, 1947, par 100 Rupees, pink . . .**$3.00**

LI350-55-10, 1947, par 100 Rupees, blue . . .**$3.00**

Lunawada Shri Sir Wakhatsinghiji Factory Co., Ltd., Lunawada

LU380-20-10, 1921, v - male portrait, woman with peacock; par 100 Rupees, text in Hindi, red, brown and green **$10.00**

Madan Theatres Ltd., Calcutta

MA140-20-10, 1919/21, par 10 Rupees, brown and green **$3.00**

MA140-30-10, 19xx, par 5 Rupees **$3.00**

Madhowji Dharamsi Manufacturing Co., Ltd.

MA180-20-10, 1916, par 100 Rupees, dark brown and brown-orange **$3.00**

MA180-30-10, 1916, par 250 Rupees pref.. . .**$4.00**

Madhorao Scindia Mills, Ltd., Bombay

MA200-20-10, 1917, par 100 Rupees **$3.00**

Madras Cold Storage Ltd., Madras

MA400-30-10, 1937, par 10 Rupees, green . .**$3.00**

Madras Electric Supply Corporation Ltd.

MA420-20-10, 19xx, £1 . . . .**$6.00**

Madras Electric Tramways Co., Ltd.

MA430-20-10, 1893, par £1 (15 Rupees), blue-grey **$10.00**

Madras Gold Mining Company, Limited. (Par 10 rupees)

MA450-20-10, 1880, 50 sh., black **$9.00**

Madras and Southern Mahratta Railway Co. Ltd.

MA490-20-10, £100 . . . .**$24.00**

Madras United Spinning and Weaving Mills Co., Ltd., Madras and Bombay

MA520-20-10, 189x, par 1,000 Rupees **$8.00**

MA520-30-10, 1898, par 250 Rupees, blue-green **$7.00**

MA520-40-10, 1922, par 250 Rupees, dark green and green **$4.00**

Mahalaxmi Mills Ltd., Bhavnagar

MA710-30-10, 1942, par 1 Rupee **$9.00**

MA710-40-10, 1942, par 50 Rupees pref., blue **$8.00**

MA710-50-10, 1946, par 100 Rupees 2nd pref. **$8.00**

MA710-60-10, 1948, par 200 Rupees, green and brown **$6.00**

Maharaja Kishangarh Mills Ltd., Kishangarh

MA740-30-10, 1944, par 10 Rupees, brown .**$6.00**

MA740-40-10, 1944, par 10 Rupees pref. . . .**$8.00**

The Maharani Woolen Mills, Limited., Baroda

MA770-20-10, 19xx, par 100 Rupees **$6.00**

MA770-30-10, 1921, v - female portrait, 1 sh. (par Rs 100) **$7.00**

Maheshwari Devi Jute Mills Ltd., Cawnpore

MA800-30-10, 1943, par 100 Rupees, black on light green **$3.00**

Majuli Tea Co., Ltd., Majuli

Later became the Luckimpore Tea Co. of Assam Ltd.

MA860-20-10, £10 stock, ...**$8.00**

Malabar Forests and Rubber Co., Ltd., Bombay

MA910-30-10, 1921, v - elephant, par 50 Rupees, grey-green **$4.00**

Malabar Timber Co., Ltd.

MA940-20-10, 1920, v - elephant, logging scenes, 5 sh. (par Rs 100), yellow-green **$4.00**

Mangalore Automobiles, Ltd., Mangalore, South Kanara

MA1030-30-10, 1938, v - automobile, par 10 Rupees, dark blue and yellow on light blue **$5.00**

Manockjee Petit Manufacturing Co., Ltd., Bombay

MA1070-20-10, 1894, v - two male portraits, par 1,000 rupees $9.00

Maple Tobacco Co. (India) Ltd., Bombay

MA1110-30-10, 1944, par 100 Rupees, blue on light green $3.00

MA1110-40-10, 1944, par 100 Rupees pref., blue on red $4.00

Mathradas Mills, Ltd., Bombay

MA1210-20-10, 1917, par 500 Rupees $4.00

MA1210-30-10, 1918, par 500 Rupees $3.00

McKenzies Ltd., Bombay

MC230-20-10, 1918, v - two males, par 100 Rupees. $3.00

MC230-30-10, 1941/43, v - two males, par 100 Rupees, blue on light green $3.00

MC230-40-10, 1941/43, v - two males, par 100 Rupees pref., blue $4.00

MC230-50-10, 1943, v - two males, par 100 Rupees 2nd pref. $4.00

Mehar Electric Supply Co., Ltd., Hyderabad, Sind

ME150-30-10, 1939, par 10 Rupees, green and purple $3.00

Mercantile Bank Ltd.

ME240-20-10, 1907, £25 . . . .$25.00

Mercantile Press Co., Ltd., Bombay

ME270-20-10, 1917, par 25 Rupees, black and brown on yellow $5.00

Mica Mining and Trading Company of India Ltd., Calcutta

MI210-30-10, 1942, par 2 Rs 8 Annas deferred $4.00

MI210-40-10, 1942, par 25 Rupees, orange and blue $3.00

MI210-50-10, 1942, par 100 Rupees pref. . . .$5.00

Minerva Mills, Limited., Bombay

MI530-30-10, 1948, v - Minerva, 1 sh. (par Rs 100), brown and tan $3.00

Model Mills, Nagpur, Bombay

MO250-20-10, 1922, par 250 Rupees, black and yellow-green. $3.00

Modern Housing Construction and Properties Ltd., Madras

MO280-30-10, 1946, v - construction scenes, par 10 Rupees, black and grey $3.00

MO280-40-10, 1946, v - construction scenes, par 100 Rupees, black and orange $4.00

Mohanlal Kahandass Ginning and Manufacturing Co., Ltd., Amracti, Bombay

MO320-20-10, 1897, par 100 Rupees, black on red $8.00

Morris Transport Service Ltd., Ahmadabad

MO610-20-10, 1944, v - ship, plane and bus, par 100 Rupees, brown and orange $3.00

MO610-30-10, 1944, v - ship, plane and bus, par 85 Rupees over Rs 100, brown and orange $3.00

MO610-40-10, 1944, v - ship, plane and bus, par 77 Rupees over Rs 85 which is over Rs 100, brown and orange. $3.00

The Motilal Hirabhai Spinning Weaving and Manufacturing Co., Ltd., Anmedabad

MO830-20-10, 1922, v - goddess playing flute, u/u certif., par 100 Rupees, text in Hindi, red on green. $3.00

Mount Rima Mining Co., Ltd.

MO930-20-10, 1908, par 10 Rupees $9.00

Mysore Chemicals and Fertilizers Ltd., Mysore

MY250-30-10, 1943, par 10 Rupees, black, red and green. $6.00

Mysore Spinning and Manufacturing Co., Ltd., Mysore

MY320-20-10, 1922, v - male portrait, par 50 Rupees, brown $7.00

MY320-30-10, 1922, v - male portrait, par 50 Rupees pref. $5.00

MY320-40-10, 1945, v - male portrait, par 50 Rupees............................$3.00

MY320-50-10, 1945, v - male portrait, par 50 Rupees pref. $4.00

Mysore Spun Silk Mills Ltd., Bangalore

MY350-30-10, 1936, v - machinery, par 10 Rupees $8.00

Mysore Spun Silk Mills Ltd., Channapatna

MY355-30-10, 1943, v - machinery, par 10 Rupees $8.00

Nagpur Glass Works, Ltd., Nagpur

NA260-20-10, 1926, par 100 Rupees, brown on blue $5.00

Naneghat Funicular Tramway and Transport Co., Ltd., Poona

NA380-30-10, 1946, v - vehicles, par 25 Rupees deferred, pink on blue................$6.00

NA380-40-10, 1946, v - vehicles, par 100 Rupees, blue on pink $6.00

Narayan Cotton Mills, Ltd., Bombay

NA510-20-10, 1884, par 1,000 Rupees......$8.00

Nath Bank, Ltd., Calcutta

NA720-30-10, 1942, par 25 Rupees, blue on light blue $6.00

National Chemicals, Ltd.

NA750-30-10, 1944, par 1 Rupee..........$3.00

NA750-40-10, 1944, par 10 Rupees, blue and brown $3.00

NA750-50-10, 1944, par 100 Rupees pref. ...$4.00

National Gramophone Record Mfg. Co., Ltd., Bombay

NA780-10-10, 1936/41, par 1 Rupee founder's sh., blue on yellow......................$6.00

NA780-20-10, 1936/41, par 100 Rupees, brown on yellow $4.00

National Industrial Alcohol Ltd., Nagpur

NA810-30-10, 1947, par 10 Rupees, black and red $3.00

NA810-40-10, 1947, par 100 Rupees pref., black and green $4.00

National Information and Publications Ltd., Bombay

NA830-30-10, 1946/47, par 10 Rupees, green................................$3.00

National Iron and Steel Co., Ltd., Calcutta

NA880-30-10, 1937, par 10 Rupees, black and yellow-green $4.00

National Literature Publishing Co., Ltd., Madras

NA920-30-10, 1934, par 10 Rupees, dark blue on light blue..............................$3.00

National Newspapers (India) Company, Limited, Bombay

NA990-40-10, 1928, 100 Rupee 1st Mortgage Debenture 6%......................$5.00

National Safe Deposit and Cold Storage Ltd., Calcutta

NA1040-30-10, 1944, par 10 Rupees, blue-green and tan $3.00

Nevatia Flour Mills, Ltd., Bombay

NE310-20-10, 1915/16, par 100 Rupees, black, yellow and green $5.00

New Berar Co., Ltd., Bombay

NE430-30-10, 1925, par 500 Rupees, 2nd issue $6.00

New Bombay Steamships, Ltd., Bombay

NE480-20-10, 1929, par 100 Rupees.......$6.00

New Citizens Bank of India Ltd., Bombay

NE510-30-10, 1938/39, 500 Rupees deferred sh., pink-orange paper...................$10.00

NE510-40-10, 1938/39, par 25 Rupees, pink-orange paper........................$5.00

NE510-50-10, 1938/39, par 50 Rupees pref., pink-orange paper...................$7.00

New Ginning Pressing and Manufacturing Co., Ltd., Chalisgaon, E.K.

Later became the Chalisgaon Shri Laxmi Narayan Mills Co., Ltd. (1931).

NE590-20-10, 1923, v - Indian gods, 1 sh. (par Rs 100), brown and tan **$8.00**

New India Transport Limited, Madras

NE670-30-10, 1944, par 100 Rupees, dark blue
. . . .**$8.00**

New Kaiser-I-Hind Spinning and Weaving Co., Ltd., Bombay

NE730-30-10, 1946, par 100 Rupees **$4.00**
NE730-40-10, 1946, par 100 Rupees pref. . . .**$3.00**

New Kempinkote Gold Field, Ltd., Kolar, Mysore District

Formerly Kempinkote Gold Fields Ltd.
NE770-20-10, 1901/02, par 5/-, mauve **$12.00**

New Maneckchock Spinning and Weaving Co., Ltd., Ahmedabad

NE840-30-10, 1945, par 100 Rupees, green and brown **$5.00**
NE840-40-10, 1945, par 100 Rupees pref. . . .**$3.00**

New Mofussil Company, Limited, Bombay

NE870-20-10, 1892, v - portrait of Queen Victoria, 1 sh. (par Rs 400), black on pink **$8.00**
NE870-30-10, 1892, 1/4 sh. (par Rs 400) . . .**$13.00**

New Oil Mills Co., Ltd., Bombay

NE910-20-10, 1920, par 25 Rupees **$4.00**

New Pratap Spinning, Weaving and Manufacturing Co., Ltd., Dhulia, West Kandesh

NE950-20-10, 1925, par 100 Rupees, brown on green **$5.00**

New Victoria Mills Co., Ltd., U.P.

NE1010-20-10, 1920. . . . .**$7.00**
NE1010-30-10, 1943, par 1 Rupees deferred .**$3.00**
NE1010-40-10, 1943, par 2 Rupees 8 Annas, black on light green **$3.00**
NE1010-50-10, 1943, par 5 Rupees **$3.00**

Nine Reefs Co., Ltd.

NI250-20-10, 1901, par 5/-. **$11.00**

Nizams Government, Hyderabad

NI590-30-10, 1930, bond **$9.00**

N.K. Chemical Industries Ltd., New Delhi

NK210-30-10, 1944, par 50 Rupees, dark blue on light blue. **$4.00**

Nuddea Mills Co., Ltd.

NU140-20-10, 1920/36 . . . .**$3.00**

Nundydroog Co., Ltd.

Formerly Nundygroog Gold Mining Co., Ltd.
NU260-20-10, 1893/1920, par 10/- **$11.00**

Ogale Glass Works, Ltd., Bombay

OG50-30-10, 1948, par 5 Rupees, dark blue on green. **$3.00**

Orient Pictures Corporation, Ltd.

OR180-20-10, 1929, par 5 Rupees, black . . .**$4.00**
OR180-30-10, 1929, par 5 Rupees pref., red .**$4.00**

Oriental Bank Corporation (1851)

OR210-20-10, 1856, v, 1 sh. (par £25), grey
. . . .**$20.00**

Oriental Gold Mining Co. of India Ltd.

OR250-20-10, £1 . . . .**$6.00**

Oriental Inland Steam Co. Ltd.

OR310-20-10, 1859/65, £10. . . . .**$30.00**

Osmanshahi Mills, Ltd., Hyderabad Deccan
OS160-30-10, 1942, 1 sh. (par Rs 100), with
   revenue stamps, purple $6.00

Oude Railway Company Ltd.
OU110-20-10, 1857 . . . .$20.00

Palai Central Bank, Ltd., Palai, Travancore
PA170-30-10, 1936, par 25 Rupees, green, red and
   dark blue $10.00
PA170-40-10, 1946, par 25 Rupees, dull green
   . . . .$10.00

Patel Garage Ltd., Calcutta
PA400-30-10, 1947, v - garage scene, 30 sh.
   (par 10 Rupees), brown on yellow $3.00
PA400-40-10, 1947, 100 Rupees pref. $5.00

Pearl Mills Ltd., Bombay
PE80-20-10, 1914, par 250 Rupees $4.00

**Petlad Bulakhidas Mills Co., Ltd., Petlad,
Baroda**
PE510-20-10, 1922, par 100 Rupees, violet. .$6.00
PE510-40-10, 1950, par 100 rupees $5.00
PE510-50-10, 1950, par 90 Rupees pref., lilac
   . . . .$5.00

**Pharmaceutical Laboratories of India Ltd.,
Calcutta**
PH90-30-10, 1946, par 100 Rupees, blue, yellow
   and brown $5.00
PH90-40-10, 1947, par 1 Rupee, red, pink and
   brown $3.00
PH90-50-10, 1947, par 10 Rupees, green,
   yellow-green and brown $3.00

Phillips and Co., Ltd., Bombay
PH190-20-10, 1888, par 100 Rupess, pink. . .$9.00
PH190-30-10, 18xx, par 40 Rupees over Rs 100,
   pink $8.00

**Pioneer Indian Paint and Oil Works, Ltd.,
Bombay**
PI210-20-10, 1920, par 25 Rupees, black and
   brown $4.00

**Pioneer Rubber and Industrial Co., Ltd.,
Bombay**
PI240-20-10, 1920/21, par 50 Rupees,
   brown-violet $4.00

Planet Mills Ltd., Bombay
PL80-20-10, 1917, par 100 Rupees, green. . .$5.00

Pondicheri Railway Co. Ltd.
PO270-20-10, 1857 . . . .$37.00

The Poona Bank, Limited, Poona
PO320-20-10, 19xx, par 100 Rupees $25.00
PO320-30-10, 1914, par 100 Rupees $17.00
PO320-40-10, 1915, v - goddess, 1 sh. (par Rs 100)
   . . . .$13.00
PO320-50-10, 1919, par 10 over 100 Rupees
   . . . .$10.00
PO320-55-10, 1919, par 15 Rupees $11.00
PO320-65-10, 1919, par 100 Rupees pref. .$13.00

**Poona Metal Manufacturing Co., Ltd.,
Poona**
PO350-20-10, 1891, par 100 Rupees, green and
   red. $12.00

**Poona Swadeshi Sugar Manufacturing Co.,
Ltd., Bombay**
PO380-30-10, 1934, par 10 Rupees $4.00

**Port Canning and Land Improvement Co.,
Ltd., Bombay**
PO450-30-10, 1938, v - farming, plowing, par 100
   Rupees, orange-brown on green $4.00

Prabhat Mills, Ltd., Bombay
PR70-20-10, 1929, par 10 Rupees, black on light
   blue-green $3.00

Premier Mills, Ltd., Bombay
PR190-20-10, 1917, v - women, par 100 Rupees,
   blue-green. $4.00

Presidency Mills Co., Ltd., Bombay
PR310-20-10, 1917, par 125 Rupees, brown-violet
   on tan $5.00

Progressive Land Building and Trading Co., Ltd., Bombay

PR430-20-10, 1919, par 100 Rupees, dark blue on red **$4.00**

PR430-30-10, 1919, par 100 Rupees pref. . . .**$6.00**

Provincial Union Assurance Ltd., New Delhi

PR500-20-10, 1934, par 25 Rupees, green on light green **$4.00**

Punjab Breeders, Ltd., Bombay

PU170-30-10, 194x, par 100 Rupees, yellow-orange **$5.00**

PU170-40-10, 1945, par 100 Rupees, yellow-orange **$4.00**

Punjab and Cashmere Carpet Co. Ltd.

PU190-20-10, 1884/87 . . . .**$14.00**

Purushotum Spinning and Manufacturing Co., Ltd., Ahmedabad

PU310-20-10, 1895-1931, par 250 Rupees, black on red **$8.00**

PU310-30-10, 1895-1931, par 125 Rupees .**$13.00**

Raghuvanshi Mills, Ltd., Bombay

RA160-20-10, 1929, par 100 Rupees, black and green **$5.00**

Raja Gokaldass Mills, Ltd., Bombay

RA210-20-10, 1918, par 100 Rupees **$5.00**

Rajnagar Spinning, Weaving and Manufacturing Co., Ltd.

RA240-20-10, 1918/19, par 125 Rupees. **$6.00**

RA240-40-10, 1949, 250 Rupees over Rs 125. .**$3.00**

RA240-50-10, 1949, par 50 Rupees pref. **$4.00**

Rajratna Naranbhai Mills Co., Ltd., Petlad, Baroda

RA270-20-10, 1922/24, par 100 Rupees, black and green **$8.00**

RA270-40-10, 1947, par 50 Rupees **$6.00**

RA270-50-10, 1947, par 100 Rupees pref. . . .**$7.00**

RA270-60-10, 1950, par 100 Rupees **$5.00**

RA270-70-10, 1950, par 100 Rupees pref. . . .**$6.00**

RA270-80-10, 1950, par 50 Rupees 2nd pref., light green **$5.00**

Rampur Maize Products Ltd., Rampur

RA410-30-10, 194x, u/u certificate (par 10 Rupees), 1,000,000 sh. issue **$8.00**

RA410-35-10, 1943, 100 sh. (par 10 Rupees), 2,000,000 sh. issue **$6.00**

Rani Travancore Rubber Co., Ltd.

RA510-20-10, 19xx, £1 stock **$5.00**

Ratlam Bombay United Spinning & Weaving Co., Ltd., Bombay

RA820-20-10, 1920, v - factory, oxcart, par 100 Rupees, brown and tan **$4.00**

Ratlam Sugar Mills Coy. Ltd., Ratlam

RA850-30-10, 1942, par 5 Rupees **$6.00**

RA850-40-10, 1942, 3 sh. (par 100 Rupees), with Indian revenue stamps, dark blue on light blue **$8.00**

RA850-50-10, 1942, par 100 Rupees pref. . .**$11.00**

Reserve Bank of India

RE220-30-10, 1931, par 100 Rupees **$8.00**

Ripon Manufacturing Co., Ltd., Bombay

RI250-20-10, 1884, v - male portrait, par 1,000 Rupees **$11.00**

Saikowah (Assam) tea Co., Ltd.

SA160-20-10, £1 stock **$5.00**

SA160-30-10, £1 pref. stock. **$6.00**

Saint Joseph Tile Works Ltd., Palai, Travancore

SA180-30-10, 1946, par 10 Rupees, dark blue on yellow-green **$7.00**

Sangor Elecricity Supply Co. Ltd.

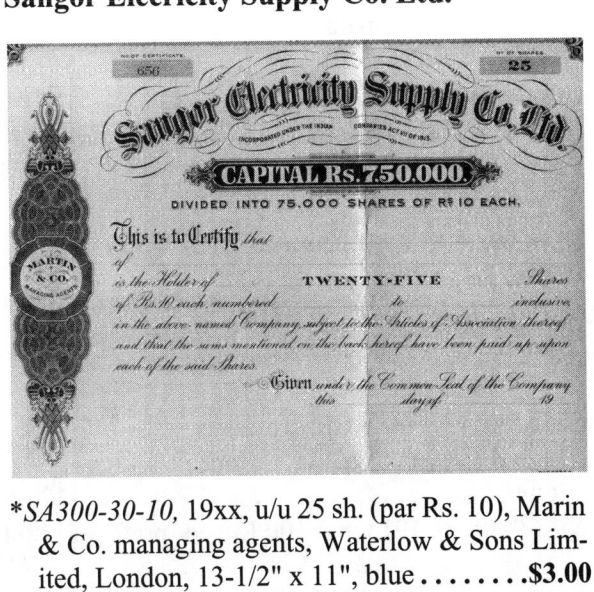

*SA300-30-10, 19xx, u/u 25 sh. (par Rs. 10), Marin & Co. managing agents, Waterlow & Sons Limited, London, 13-1/2" x 11", blue **$3.00**

Saraswili Ginning and Manufacturing Co., Ltd., Ahmedabad

SA410-20-10, 1921, par 100 Rupees, brown and green on light green **$6.00**

Satya Mill Ltd., Bombay

SA540-20-10, 1929, par 100 Rupees **$5.00**

The Satyanarayan Marine & Fire Insurance Company, Limited

SA570-20-10, 1909, v - ship, 1 sh. (par Rs 100), violet **$10.00**

Servants of India Insurance Co., Ltd., Delhi

SE390-30-10, 1932, par 20 Rupees **$3.00**
SE390-40-10, 1932, par 100 Rupees pref., brown on light green **$5.00**

Shamro Vithal Co-operative Bank, Ltd., Bombay

SH110-30-10, 1931, v - male portrait, par 25 Rupees. **$10.00**

Shapurji Broach Mills, Ltd., Sir, Bombay

SH140-20-10, 1917, v - male portrait, par 100 Rupees. **$5.00**
SH140-40-10, 1935, par 100 Rupees conversion **$4.00**
SH140-50-10, 1935/37, v - male portrait, par Rs 2 8 Annas deferred, black and yellow-green .**$3.00**

Sharnrao Vithal Co-operative Credit Society, Ltd., Bombay

SH210-20-10, 1928, v - male portrait, par 25 Rupees **$10.00**

Shatrushailya Iron and Steels Ltd., Jamnagar, Nawanagar

SH270-30-10, 1947, par 100 Rupees, blue-green on red **$6.00**
SH270-40-10, 1947, par 100 Rupees pref.. . . .**$8.00**

Shilotri Bank, Ltd.

SH320-20-10, 1926, par 25 Rupees **$8.00**

Shivrajpur Syndicate Ltd., Bombay

SH410-20-10, 1907, par 10 Rupees **$6.00**
SH410-30-10, 19xx, par 10 Rupees **$4.00**
SH410-40-10, 1923/42, par 10 Rupees **$4.00**

Sholapur Bank, Ltd., Sholapur

SH630-20-10, 1910, par 50 Rupees, blue underprint. **$6.00**

Sholapoor Spinning and Weaving Co., Ltd., Bombay

SH660-20-10, 1898, v - male portrait, factory, par 1,000 Rupees, blue-green. **$10.00**
SH660-30-10, 19xx, v - male portrait, factory, par 1,000 Rupees **$8.00**
SH660-40-10, 1943, v - male portrait, factory, par 1,000 Rupees **$8.00**
SH660-50-10, 1943, v - male portrait, factory, par 100 Rupees pref., blue **$5.00**

Shree Jam Wire Products Co., Ltd., Jamnagar

SH720-30-10, 1943, par 100 Rupees, black on light green. **$5.00**

Shree Life Assurance Co., Ltd., Bombay

SH750-30-10, 1933, par 100 Rupees, brown-violet **$7.00**

Shri Gopal Chamber of Commerce Ltd., Delhi

SH780-20-10, 1920, 1,000 Rupees **$3.00**

Shri Krishna Stores Company, Ltd., Bombay

*SH810-20-10,*1921, v - goddess, 20 sh. (par Rs 25), black on light blue-green **$4.00**

SH810-30-10, 1921, par 25 Rupees pref. **$6.00**

Shri Narayan Sugar Factory Limited (Ganeshwadi, Kurundwad Sr. State)

SH840-30-10, 1943, par 10 Rupees **$15.00**

SH840-40-10, 1943, v - oxcart, god, 1 sh. (par 50 Rupees), dark blue on orange-brown **$22.00**

SH840-50-10, 1943, par 100 Rupees pref. . .**$35.00**

Shri Rajnagar Swadeshi Stores Co., Ltd., Ahmedabad

SH900-20-10, 1919, par 10 Rupees, dark blue
. . . .**$4.00**

Shroff's Bank of India Ltd., Bombay

SH980-30-10, 1944, par 5 Rupees deferred .**$10.00**

SH980-40-10, 1944, par 50 Rupees, lilac and blue on tan **$5.00**

SH980-50-10, 1944, par 50 Rupees pref. **$7.00**

Siddeley Ice Manufacturing Co., Ltd., Bombay

SI150-20-10, 1911, par 100 Rupees **$8.00**

Sika Dominion Ltd.

SI330-20-10, par 1/- **$3.00**

SI330-30-10, par 10/- pref. **$4.00**

Sika (India) Ltd.

SI350-20-10, par 1/- **$4.00**

SI350-30-10, par 10/- pref. **$5.00**

Sonapet Proprietary Gold Mining Co., Ltd., Calcutta

SO260-10-10, 1890, par 1 Rupee founders stock
. . . .**$12.00**

SO260-20-10, 1890, par 1 Rupee **$7.00**

Soonderdass Spinning and Weaving Mills Co., Ltd., Bombay

SO350-20-10, 1896, par 250 Rupees, black on blue-green **$13.00**

South Kolar Gold Mines Ltd.

SO600-30-10, 1945, par 10 Rupees **$4.00**

Southern Mahratta Spinning and Weaving Co., Ltd., Bombay

SO630-20-10, 1882/85, par 250 Rupees . . .**$11.00**

SO630-30-10, 1909, par 250 Rupees **$7.00**

SO630-40-10, 1909, par 250 Rupees pref., black on pink. **$9.00**

Standard Aluminum and Brass Works, Ltd., Bombay

ST150-20-10, 1921, par 100 Rupees, yellow-orange. **$5.00**

Standard Bank Ltd., Bombay

ST170-30-10, 1913, par 100 Rupees, brown on tan **$12.00**

ST170-40-10, 1913, par 100 Rupees pref. . .**$12.00**

Standard Sugar Mills Ltd., Calcutta

ST290-20-10, 1920, par 10 Rupees, black on light green. **$4.00**

Steel Corporation of Bengal Ltd.

ST410-20-10, par 10 Rupees **$4.00**

ST410-30-10, par 100 Rupees pref. **$4.00**

L.A. Stronach and Co. (India) Limited., Bombay

*ST630-20-10, 1927, 1 sh. (par Rs 100), w. revenue stamps, red ruled border, this certificate is drawn by freehand using India ink. **$200.00**

Surat Industrial Mills Co. Ltd., Viramgaum
SU460-20-10, 1920, v - factory, par 500 Rupees, dark green on light green $8.00

Surrat Rice Mill Co., Ltd., Bombay
SU500-20-10, 1906, 200 Rupees, black on yellow $10.00

Swadesh Laxmi Mills, Ltd., Ahmedabad
SW80-20-10, 1921/23, v - goddess Laxmi, par 100 Rupees, dark blue on yellow. $4.00

Swadeshi Oil Mills Co., Ltd., Bombay
SW120-20-10, 1920, v - goddess, par 50 Rupees, brown-violet $5.00

Tata Industrial Bank Ltd.
TA170-20-10, 19xx, par 75 Rupees $4.00

Tata Iron and Steel Co., Ltd., Bombay
TA190-20-10, 1917, par 30 Rupees deferred .$5.00
TA190-30-10, 1917, par 75 Rupees, black and light green. $3.00
TA190-40-10, 1917, par 150 Rupees pref. . . .$5.00

Tata Power Co., Ltd., Bombay
TA210-20-10, 1920, par 1,000 Rupees, brown $3.00
TA210-30-10, 1920, par 1,000 Rupees pref.. .$5.00

Tata Publicity Corporation Ltd., Bombay
TA230-20-10, 1921, par 100 Rupees, brown and green $4.00

Thomson and Taylor Ltd., Bombay
TH250-20-10, 1927, par 10 Rupees, light green $6.00
TH250-30-10, 19xx, par 7 Rupees over Rs 10, light green. $5.00
TH250-40-10, 19xx, par 5 Rupees over Rs 7 over Rs 10, light green $4.00
TH250-50-10, 19xx, par 3/5/7/10 Rupees, light green. $3.00

Toolsidas Tejpal Mills, Ltd., Bombay
TO380-20-10, 1921, par 50 Rupees, dark blue $4.00

Topuldodi (Nizam's) Gold Mines Ltd.
TO420-20-10, 1905/09, £1 . . . .$11.00

Travancore Cables and Rubbers Ltd., Travancore
TR120-30-10, 1938, par 10 Rupees $6.00

Travancore Forward Bank Ltd., Kottayam, Travancore
TR140-20-10, 19xx, par 10 Rupees, brown and purple $17.00
TR140-30-10, 1944, par 10 Rupees, brown and purple $13.00
TR140-35-10, 1944, par 10 Rupees, brown and dark blue. $13.00
TR140-40-10, 1946, par 10 Rupees, brown on light blue. $11.00

Travancore Rubber Co. Ltd.
Became the Paloor (Travancore) Rubber Co., Ltd.
TR180-20-10, 19xx, £1 stock. $5.00

Travancore Wood and Metal Works Ltd., Mundakayan, Travancore
TR220-30-10, 1944, par 10 Rupees, light and dark blue. $5.00
TR220-40-10, 1944, par 10 Rupees pref., brown and dark blue $6.00

Travels Limited, Madras
TR300-20-10, 1946, par 10 Rupees, black on yellow. $3.00

Tricumlal Bhogilal and Co., Ltd., Ahmedabad
TR390-20-10, 1929, par 1 Rupee $8.00

Union Bank of Calcutta
UN70-20-10, 1839, 1,000 Rupees $50.00

Union Life Assurance Co., Ltd.
UN140-30-10, 1940/41, par 1 Rupee 8 Annas deferred, green $3.00
UN140-40-10, 1940/41, v - St. George slaying the dragon, par 100 Rupees $3.00

Union Tea and Trading Co., Ltd., Calcutta

UN310-20-10, 1925, par 20 Rupees, dark blue on
light green........................$4.00

United Iron and Engineering Works, Ltd., Bengal

UN410-30-10, 1941, par 10 Rupees, U.I.E.W. in
underprint, green....................$5.00

UN430-40-10, 1944, par 10 Rupees, full name in
underprint, green....................$4.00

The United Provinces Electric Supply Company Limited, Calcutta

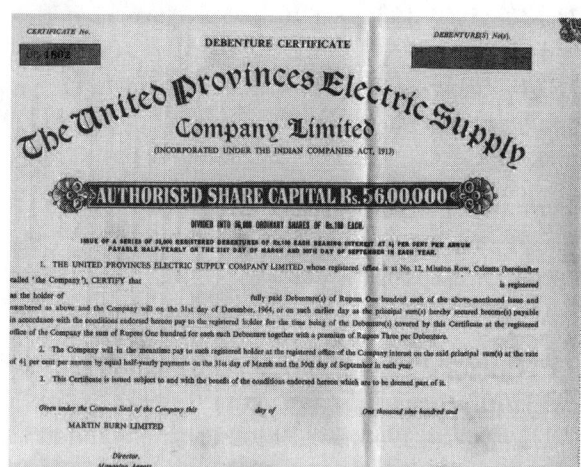

*UN470-40-10, 19xx, Rs. 100 4-1/2% debenture,
due 1964, Martin Burn Ltd. managing agents,
w/o imprint, 14" x 11-3/4", red.........$3.00

United Provinces Oil Mills Co., Ltd., Belanganj, Agra

UN490-20-10, 1921, v - Indian goddess, par 100
Rupees, purple $8.00

United Provinces Sugar co., Ltd.

UN510-30-10, 1942, 10 Rupees..........$3.00

UN510-40-10, 19xx, 10 Rupees, increased capital
....................................$3.00

> *It is generally assumed that only 5% of certificates survive to reach collectors.*

Upper Ganges Valley Electricity Supply Co. Ltd.

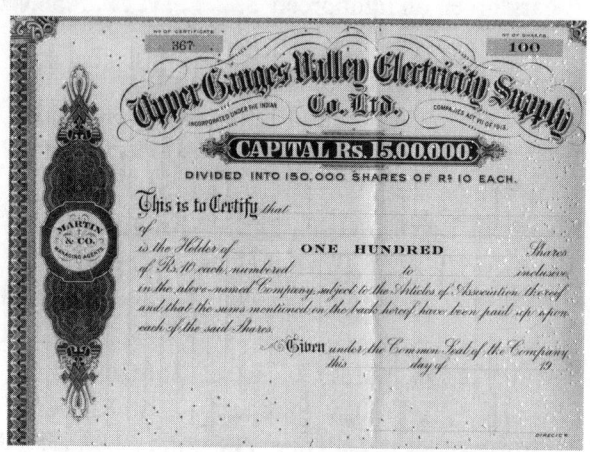

*UP210-20-10, 19xx, u/u 100 sh. (par Rs. 10)
certificate, Martin & Co. managing agents,
Waterlow & Sons Limited, London; 13-3/4" x
11", brown $3.00

Upper Jumna Valley Electricity Supply Co. Ltd.

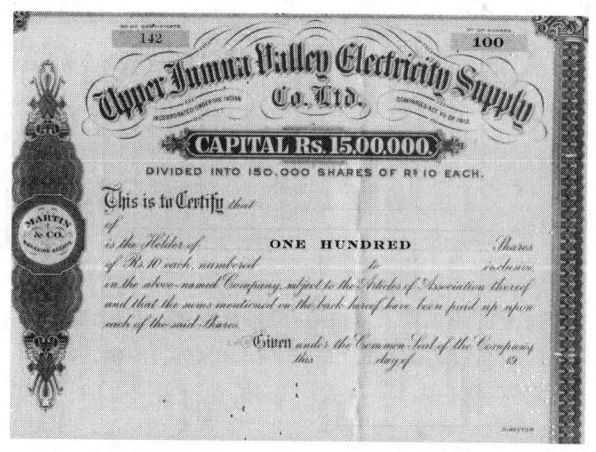

*UP240-20-10, 19xx, u/u 100 sh. (par Rs. 10)
certificate, Martin & Co., managing agents,
Waterlow & Sons Limited, London; 13-3/4" x
11", red............................$3.00

Veerumgaun Spinning and Manufacturing Co., Ltd., Broach

VE150-20-10, 1919, v - portrait of founders, 1 sh.
(Rs 250), 2nd issue, dark blue on yellow .$10.00

Viramgaum Alfred Mills Co., Ltd., Broach

VI170-20-10, 1912, par 500 Rupees, black on red
....................................$8.00

Vishwabharati Insurance Co., Ltd., Bombay
VI220-30-10, 1943, par 100 Rupees, blue on brown
. . . .**$4.00**

Wadia Woolen Mills, Ltd., Bombay
WA130-20-10, 1921, v - sheep, factory; 1 sh. (par
Rs 100) **$4.00**

**Wankaner Electric Supply Co., Ltd.,
Wankaner, Kathiawar Saurashtra**
WA250-30-10, 1949, par 10 Rupees. **$3.00**
WA250-40-10, 1949, par 10 Rupees pref.. . . .**$4.00**

**West Bengal Safe Deposit Vault Ltd.,
Calcutta**

*WE170-20-10, 19xx, u/u certif. (par 10 Rupees),
11-1/2" x 9-1/4", blue **$3.00**

**West Coast Fisheries (Travancore) Ltd.,
Trivandrum**
WE190-30-10, 1946, v - lighthouse, ship, par 10
Rupees, blue, pink and light green **$3.00**
WE190-40-10, 1946, v - lighthouse, ship, par 10
Rupees pref., brown, pink, orange and tan .**$3.00**

Western India Brick Co., Ltd., Bombay
WE270-20-10, 1916, par 100 Rupees, blue . .**$4.00**

Western India Rope Co., Ltd., Bombay
WE290-20-10, 1921, par 100 Rupees. **$5.00**

**The Western Patkoom Gold Prospecting
Syndicate, Ltd., Calcutta**
WE360-20-10, 1890, 1 Founder's sh. warrant (par 1
Rupee), lilac **$13.00**
WE360-30-10, 1890, par 1 Rupees. **$9.00**

**Whittle Spinning and Manufacturing Co.,
Ltd., Broach**
WH170-20-10, 1918, v - two male portraits, par
100 Rupees, dark blue on yellow **$7.00**

James Wright, Ltd., Calcutta
WR190-30-10, 1937, par 1 Rupee deferred . .**$3.00**
WR190-40-10, 1937, par 5 Rupees **$3.00**
WR190-50-10, 1937, par 50 Rupees pref. . . .**$4.00**

Yeshanand Publications Ltd., Bombay
YE140-30-10, 1939, par 100 Rupees **$5.00**

Ireland

Republic of Ireland
30-20-10, 1920 $10 5% gold bond. **$300.00**

**Waterford, Dungarvan and Lismore
Railway Company (par £10)**
WA30-40-10, 1878, 10 sh. 5% pref. stock (par £10),
purple **$15.00**
WA30-50-10, 1898, 7 sh. 5% pref. stock, purple
. . . .**$15.00**

Israel

Bank Leumi Le-Israel B.M.

*BA150-20-10, 1975, v, 18 sh., w/o imprint,
11-3/4" x 8-3/4", blue border **$5.00**

Italy

City of Bari
BA240-20-10, 1868, v, 100 L as issued, repayable
150 L, green $25.00

Società per le Ferrovie Napoletane S.A.

*FE250-20-10, 1910, v, 250 Lire bearer sh. w. coupons, Bruxelles - Imp. F. van Buggenhoudt,
8-1/4" x 14-1/4", blue $6.00

*FE250-30-10, 1926, v, 100 L bearer pref. stock
w. coupons, 13-3/4" x 8-1/2", green border
. . . .$9.00

City of Milano
MI240-20-10, 1886, v, Prestito Unificato, 500 L
4% bond, brown $20.00

Provisional Government of Venice

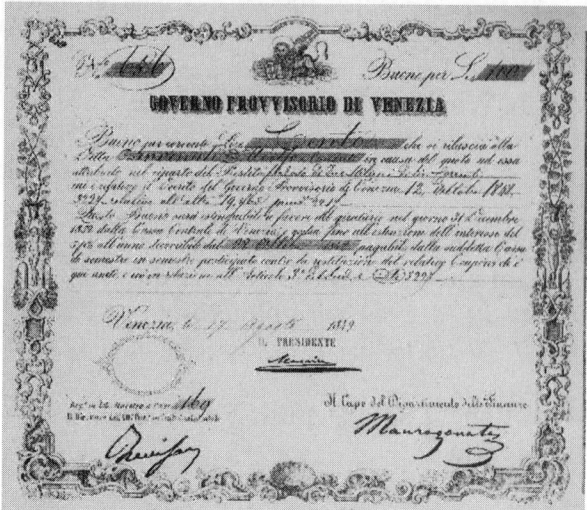

*VE130-10-10, 1849, 100 Lire bond, grey . $25.00

Ivory Coast

Compagnie Agricole Commerciale & Industrielle de Badikaha S.A., Grand-Bassam

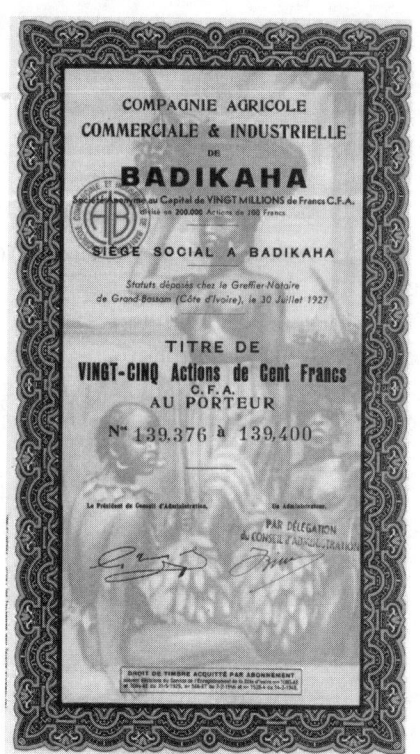

*AG140-20-10, 1927, v, 25 bearer sh. (par 100
C.F.A. Francs), red $12.00

SAFABECAO, Société Anonyme pour la Fabrication du Beurre de Cacao, Abidjan

Société de Plantations de l'Afrique Occidentale S.A., Eloka

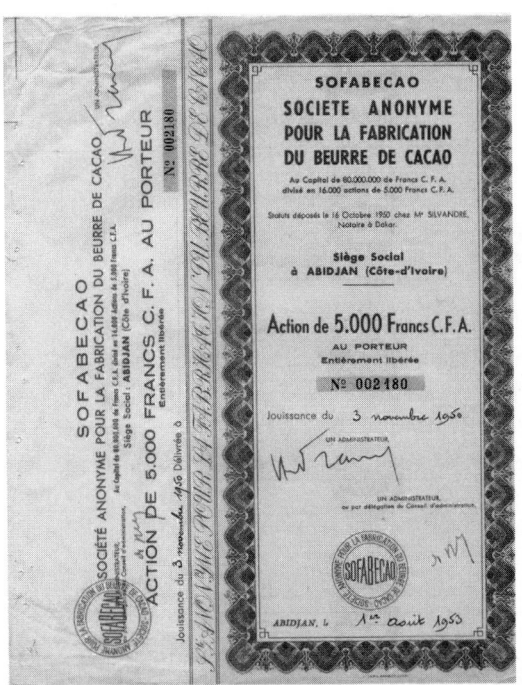

*PL270-20-10, 1933, 500 F bearer sh. w. coupons, D. et B. -Paris, 11-1/4" x 8", red border
. . . .$7.00

*FA110-20-10, 1953, 1 bearer sh., 5,000 C.F.A. Francs, Imp. A. Ramboz, Lyon; 8-1/4" x 10-1/2", brown $5.00

J

Japan

Asahi Glass Company, Limited, Tokyo

*A40-40-10, 1991, v, 1 option, 5,000 DM 4% bond text in German, Giesecke & Devrient Gmbh 1991, 8-1/4" x 11-3/4", brown border.....$3.00

Chubu Steel Plate Co. Ltd., Nagoya

*CH280-40-10, 1991, v, 1 option, 5,000 DM 5% bond text in German, Giesecke & Devrient Gmbh 1991, 8-1/4" x 11-3/4", green border
................................$3.00

Daiwa House Industry Co., Ltd., Osaka

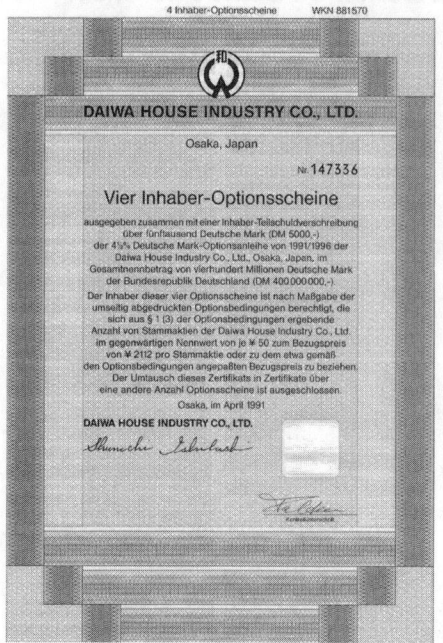

*DA140-40-10, 1991, v, 1 option, 5,000 DM 4-1/2% bond text in German, Giesecke & Devrient Gmbh 1991, 8-1/4" x 11-3/4", brown. . $3.00

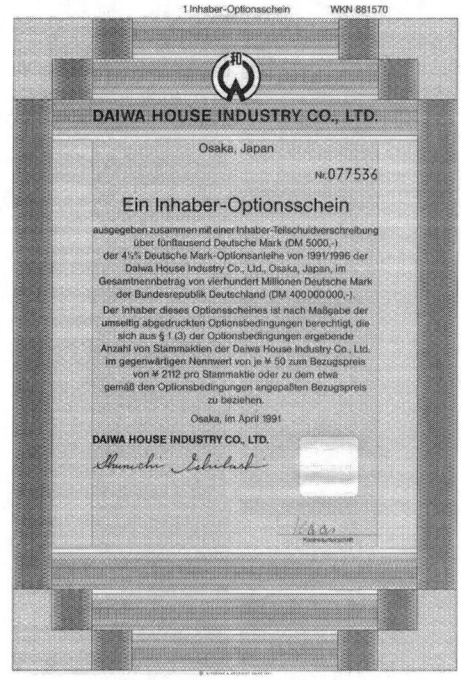

*DA140-45-10, 1991, v, 4 options, 5,000 DM 4-1/2% bond text in German, Giesecke & Devrient Gmbh 1991, 8-1/4" x 11-3/4", pink ...$3.00

Japan Synthetic Rubber Co. Ltd., Tokyo

JA240-40-10, 1989, v, ¥1,325 sh. option, pink
. . . .**$3.00**
JA240-45-10, 1989, v, ¥1,325 sh. option, green
. . . .**$3.00**

Kanaden Corporation, Tokyo

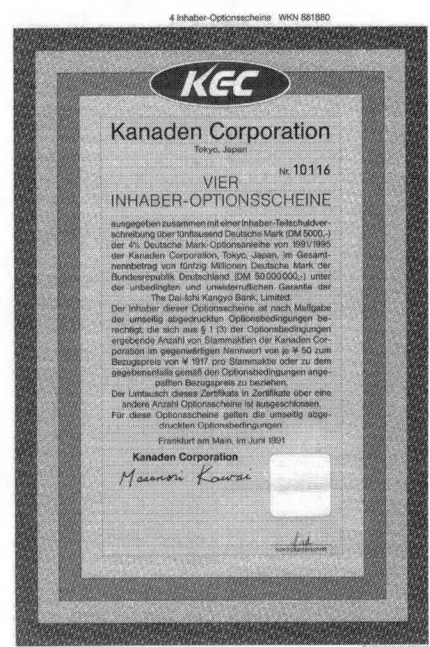

KA140-40-10, 1991, v, 4 options, 5,000 DM 4%
bond text in German, Giesecke & Devrient Gmbh
1991, 8-1/4" x 11-3/4", brown border. **$3.00**

KITZ Corporation (Kabushiki Kaisha Kitazawa Valve), Tokyo

KI120-40-10, 1991, v, 4 options, 5,000 DM
5-1/8% bond text in German, Giesecke & Devrient Gmbh 1991, 8-1/4" x 11-3/4", pink . . . **$3.00**

Kubota Corporation, Osaka

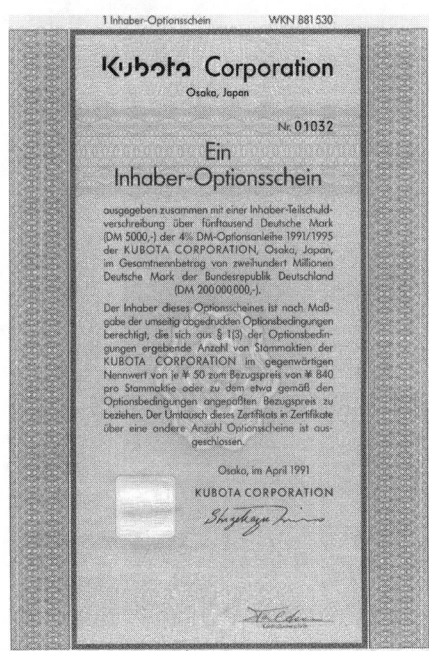

KU140-40-10, 1991, v, 1 option, 5,000 DM 4%
bond text in German, Giesecke & Devrient Gmbh
8-1/4" x 11-3/4", beige brown border **$3.00**

Kurosaki Refractories Co., Ltd., Kitakyushu-shi

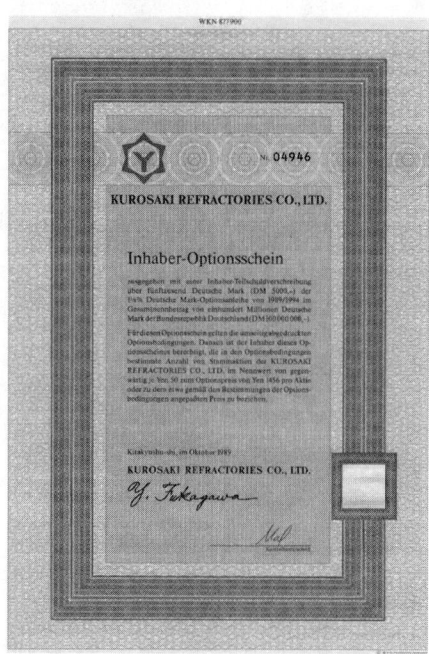

*KU260-40-10, 1989, v, 1 option, 5,000 DM 1-3/8% bond text in German, R-Oldenbourg-Munchen, 8-1/4" x 11-3/4", green border. .**$3.00**

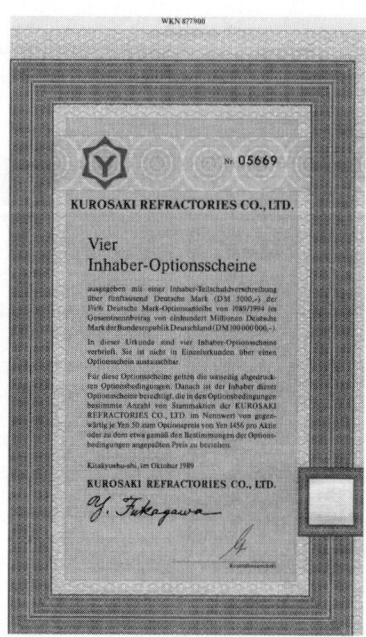

*KU260-45-10, 1989, v, 4 options, 5,000M 1-3/8% bond text in German, R-Oldenbourg-Munchen, 8-1/4" x 11-3/4", beige border **$3.00**

Mitsubishi Oil Co., Ltd.

MI290-40-10, 1991, v, issued in German....**$8.00**

Nichi Co., Ltd., Osaka

*NI190-40-10, 1991, v, 1 option, 5,000 DM 4% bond text in German, Giesecke & Devrient Gmbh 1991, 8-1/4" x 11-3/4", bluish border
..................................**$3.00**

Nippon Electric Company, Limited

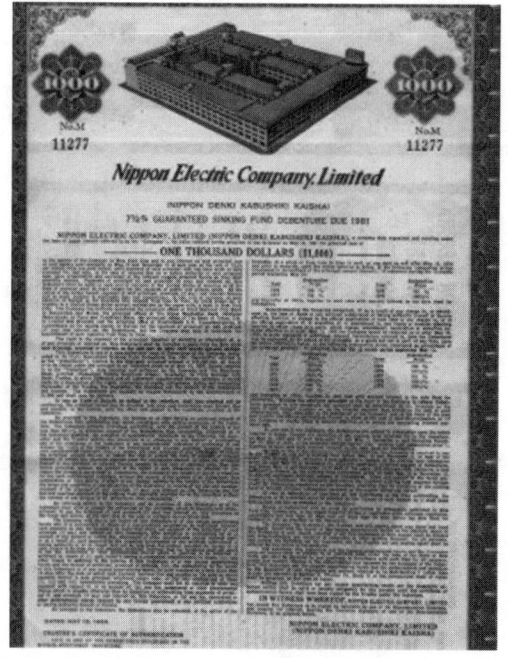

*NI340-70-10, 1969, v, $1,000 7-1/2% guaranteed sinking fund deb. due 1981, blue **$15.00**

The Ohtsu Tire & Rubber Co., Ltd., Osaka

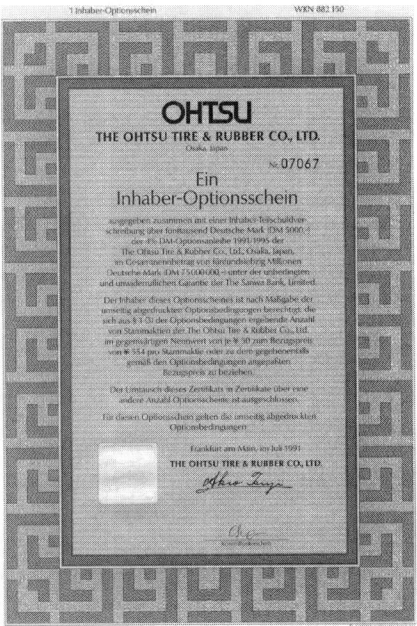

*OH180-40-10, 1991, 1 option, 5,000 DM 4%
bond text in German, Giesecke & Devrient
Gmbh 1991, 8-1/2" x 11-3/4", brown border
................................$3.00

Prima Meat Packers, Ltd., Tokio

*PR190-40-10, 1989, v, 1 option, 5,000 DM 1-5/8%
bond text in German, Giesecke & Devrient
München, 8-1/4" x 11-3/4", green border ..$3.00

Riken Corporation, Tokyo

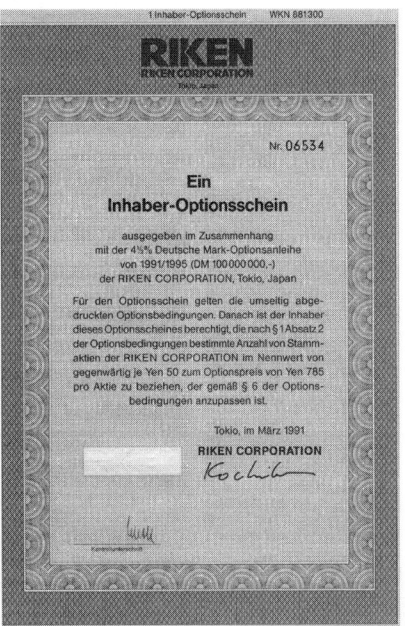

*RI180-40-10, 1991, v, 1 option, 5,000 DM 4%
bond text in German, Giesecke & Devrient
Gmbh, 8-1/4" x 11-3/4", green..........$3.00

Sankyo Aluminium Industry Co., Ltd., Takaoka

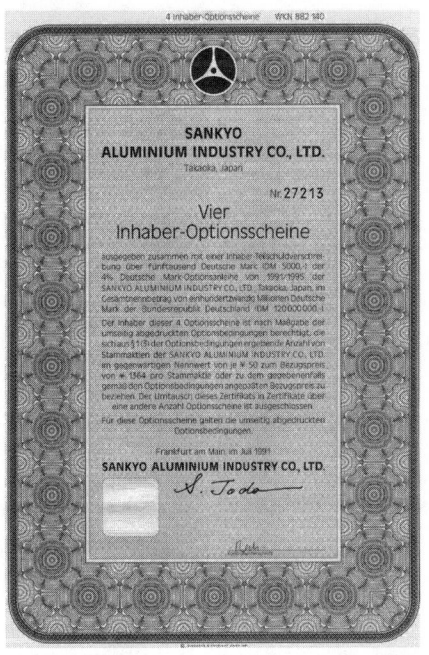

*SA160-40-10, 1991, v, 4 options, 5,000 DM 4%
bond text in German, Giesecke & Devrient
Gmbh, 8-1/4" x 11-3/4", brown and pink..$3.00

Shinko Shoji Co., Ltd., Tokyo

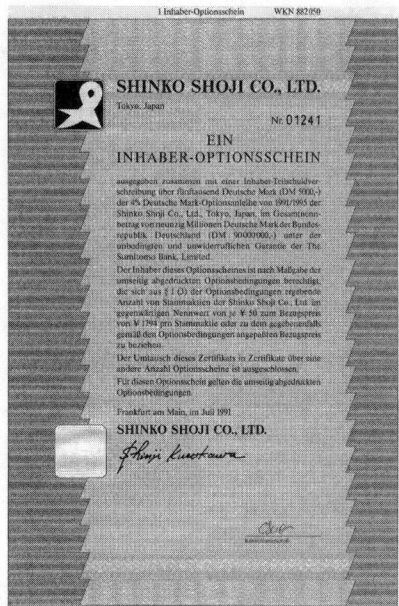

*SH140-40-10, 1991, v, 1 option, 5,000 DM 4% bond text in German, Giesecke & Devrient Gmbh 1991, 8-1/4" x 11-3/4", brown border $3.00

Takashimaya Company, Limited, Osaka

*TA160-40-10, 1989, v, 1 option, 5,000 DM 1-5/8% bond text in German, Giesecke & Devrient München, 8-1/4" x 11-3/4", brown border .. $3.00

Tobu Store Co., Ltd., Tokio

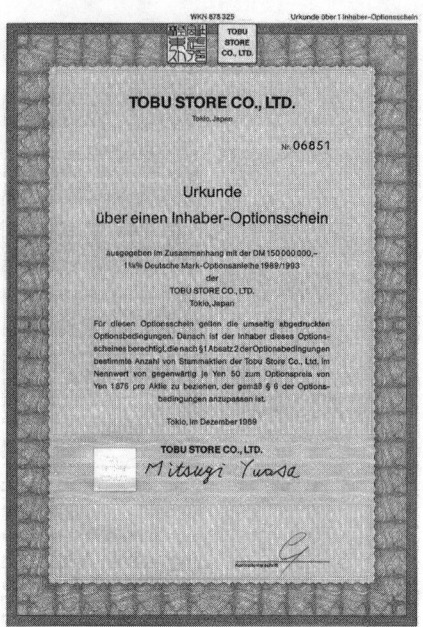

*TO160-40-10, 1989, v, 1 option, 1-5/8% DM bond text in German, R - Oldenbourg - München, blue $3.00

Yamatane Corporation, Tokyo

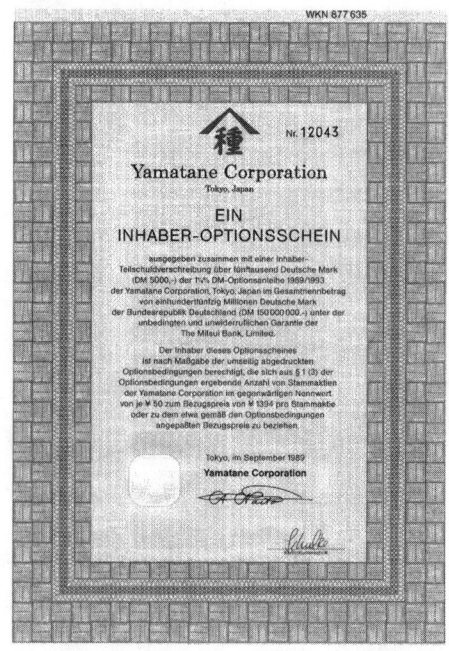

*YA260-40-10, 1989, v, 1 option, 5,000 DM 1-1/4% bond text in German, Giesecke & Devrient München, 8-1/4" x 11-3/4", grey-brown border...................................$3.00

L

Latvia

Latvia National Bank

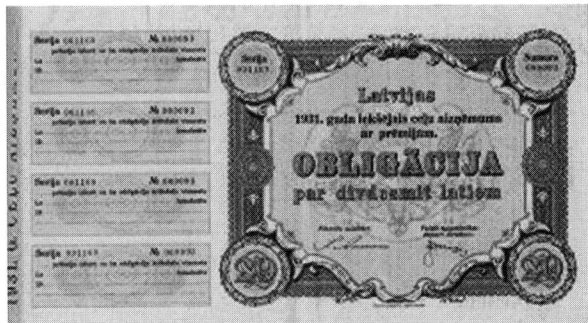

*40-20-10, 1931, 20 Latu 6% bond, w. coupons, 11" x 6", brown on beige **$6.00**

Lebanon

50-20-10, 1949, v, 5,000 pound unissued bond, found after Israel captured Lebanese territory, ornate multicolored. **$20.00**

Luxembourg

ABE, AG für Beteiligungen in Europa

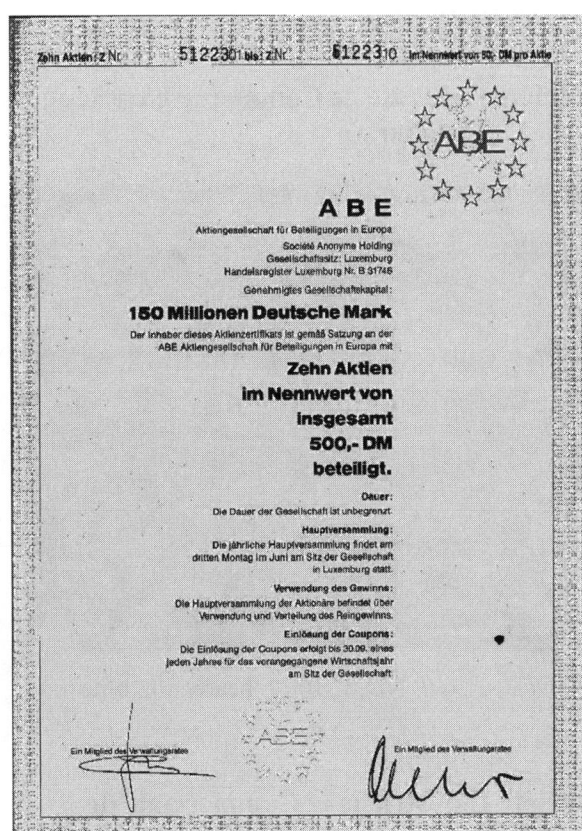

*AB60-20-10, ND, v, 10 sh. (par 50 DM) w. coupons (dated 1992-2021), blue **$10.00**

This catalog has listings in an alphabetical format. The reason is simple: Companies diversify as they grow. For example, the Canadian Pacific Railway company recently split into five companies. They represent the railway, hotels, shipping, airline, and petroleum interests of the company. During World War II, the Singer sewing machine company made guns and other defense-related equipment, so where should we list it? It's far easier to use a strict alphabetical order, rather than to confuse the reader with topical classifications.

M

Madagascar

Société Générale de Commerce Extérieur S.A., Tananarivo

GE130-20-10, ND, v, 100 F bearer sh., blue
. . . . **$4.00**

Société Industrielle et Commerciale de l'Emyrne S.A., Tananarivo

IN140-20-10, 1954, v, 3,000 CFA Franc bearer sh. w. coupons, reddish brown **$4.00**

Mexico

Conversion of Mexican Bonds, deferred 5% stock, London

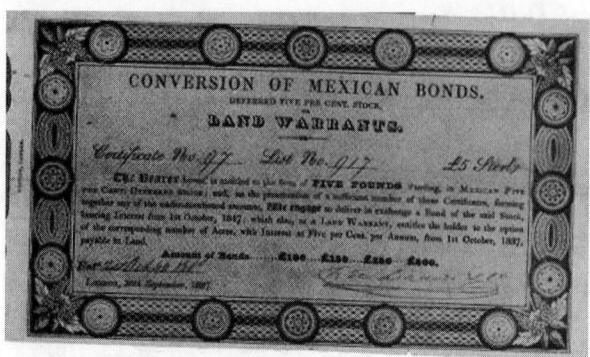

40-20-10, 1837, £5 Land Warrant, Whiting, London, ornate border **$250.00**

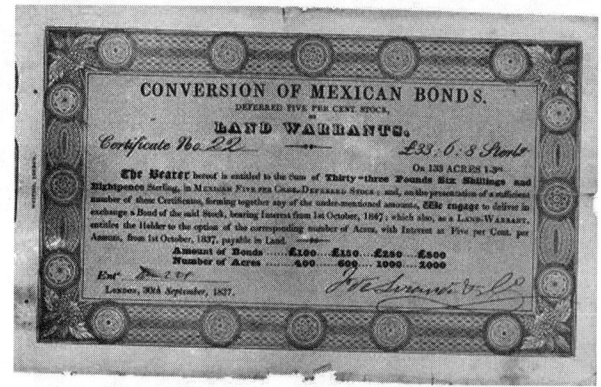

40-25-10, 1837, £33/6/8 or 133-1/3 acres Land Warrant, Whiting, London, ornate border
. . . . **$300.00**

The value of a stock certificate depends on:

- • rarity
- • the issuer
- • signatures
- • quality of engraving
- • overall appearance
- • condition
- • date of issue

Mexican 5% Deferred Stock, London

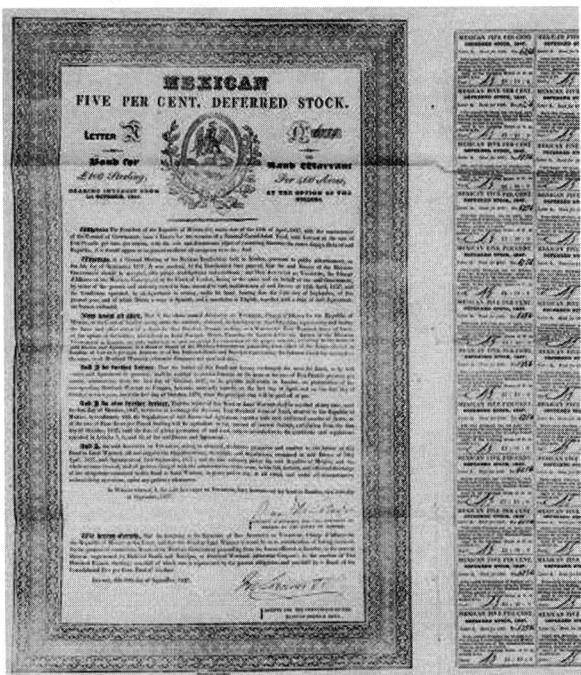

*50-30-10, 1837, v, £100 or 400 acres w. coupons, Whiting, London, black on white......$300.00

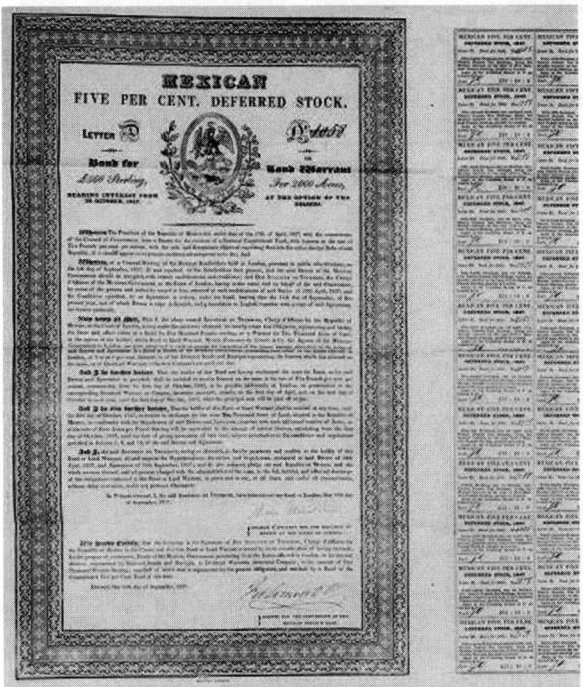

*50-35-10, 1837, v, £500 or 2000 acres w. coupons, Whiting, London, black on white......$350.00

Mexican 3% New Consolidated Stock, Mexico

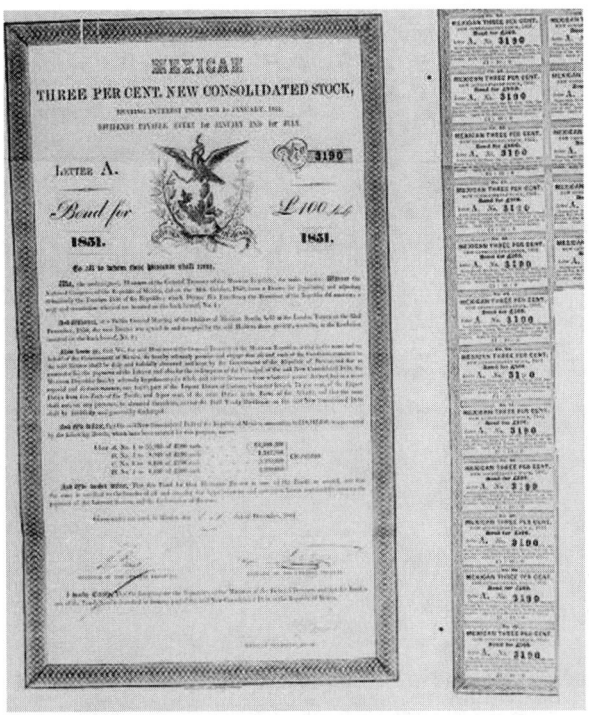

*70-30-10, 1851, v, £100 Letter A bond w. coupons, Letts, Son, and Steer, London, black on white...........................$150.00

Republica Mexicana

90-20-10, 1851, v, 50 Peso, brown on yellow $15.00

90-30-10, 1859, v, 64 Peso 6% bond w. coupons, grey.....................................$15.00

90-40-10, 1862, v, $5 Juarez bond, black on green $15.00

90-45-10, 1863, v, $5 Juarez bond, brown on yellow..................................$15.00

Republica Mexicana, Deuda Interior 6%, México

Interior loan.

*110-20-10, 1859, v, 50 Pesos w. coupons
.................................$200.00

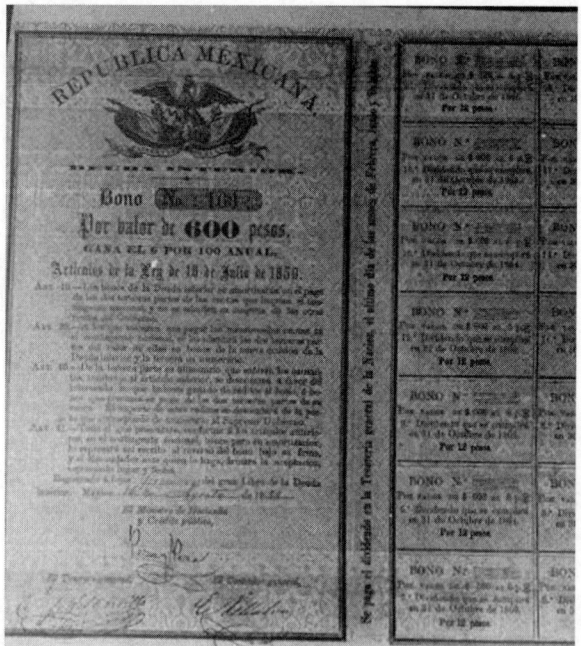

*110-30-10, 1859, v, 600 Pesos w. coupons
.................................$250.00

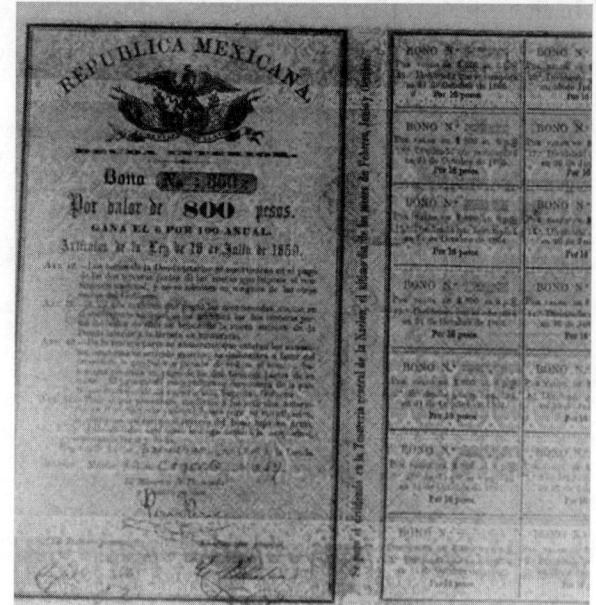

*110-35-10, 1859, v, 800 Pesos w. coupons
.................................$250.00

Mexican Empire, Paris

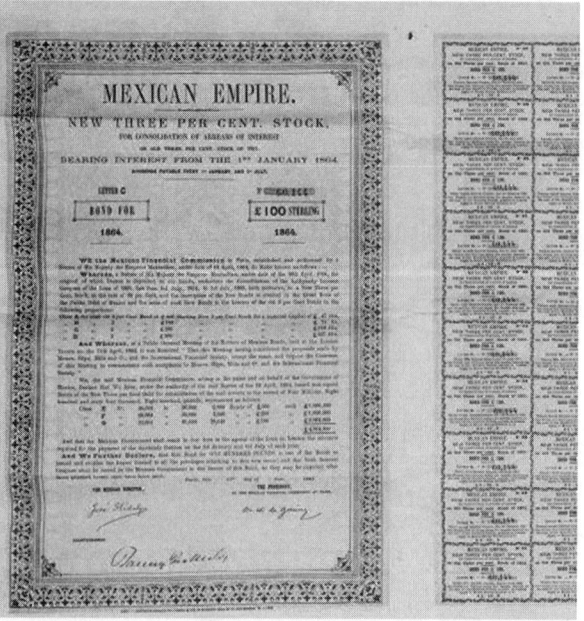

*130-30-10, 1864, £100 letter G Bond w. coupons, crest on back, Paris - Imprimerie Centrale des Chemins de Fer de Napoléon Chaix et Co.; black on light green $140.00

*130-40-10, 1865, 50 Franc deuda publica exterior
w. coupons, black on light blue **$100.00**

Republica Mexicana deuda consolidada, México

*150-30-10, 1885, v, £500 = $2,500 series 8A,
letter H bond, English transfer duty stamp and
German revenue rubber stamp **$100.00**

*150-35-10, 1885, v, £1,000 = $5,000 series 9A,
letter I bond, English transfer duty stamp and
German revenue rubber stamp **$125.00**

Estados Unidos Mexicanos, deuda interior amortizable del 5%, México

*170-30-10, 1896, v, $500 = £100 2nd series letter
F bond, Waterlow & Sons Limited, London
. . . .**$20.00**

*170-40-10, 1899, v, $1,000 = £200 4th series letter
LL bond, Waterlow & Sons Limited, London
................................$35.00

United States of Mexico
4% gold bond of 1904, México.

*190-30-10, 1904, v, $500 U.S. gold = £102/17/7
series B 4% bond w. coupons, text in Spanish-
English-German-French..............$35.00

*190-35-10, 1904, v, $1,000 U.S. gold = £205/15/2
series A 4% bond w. coupons, text in Spanish-
English-German-French.............$50.00

Republica Mexicana Bono de la Deuda Exterior Mexicana
4% 1910, México, external gold loan of 1910.

*210-30-10, 1910, v, Mex $195 = £20 4% bond w.
coupons, text in Spanish-English-German-
French............................$35.00

*210-35-10, 1910, v, Mex $1,950 = £200 =
US$970 4% bond w. coupons, text in Spanish-
English-German-French $50.00

Guaranty Trust Company
Receipt for Coupons or Interest in Arrears, 1922

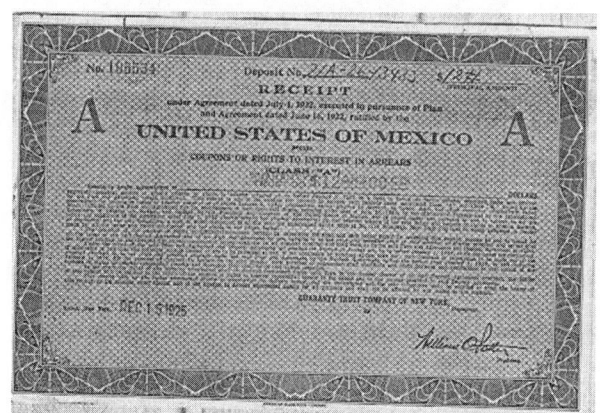

*230-20-10, 1925, $12 class "A" $5.00

This catalog has listings in an alphabetical
format. The reason is simple: Companies
diversify as they grow. For example, the
Canadian Pacific Railway company
recently split into five companies. They
represent the railway, hotels, shipping, airline, and petroleum interests of the company. During World War II, the Singer
sewing machine company made guns and
other defense-related equipment, so where
should we list it? It's far easier to use a
strict alphabetical order, rather than to
confuse the reader with topical classifications.

Estados Unidos Mexicanos, Bono de la Deuda Bancaria, México
Bonds of the banking department.

*250-20-10, 1930, v, 10 Pesos series X class A
bond, w. coupons, OIHM $7.00

*250-25-10, 1930, v, 100 Pesos series X class C
bond, w. coupons, OIHM $10.00

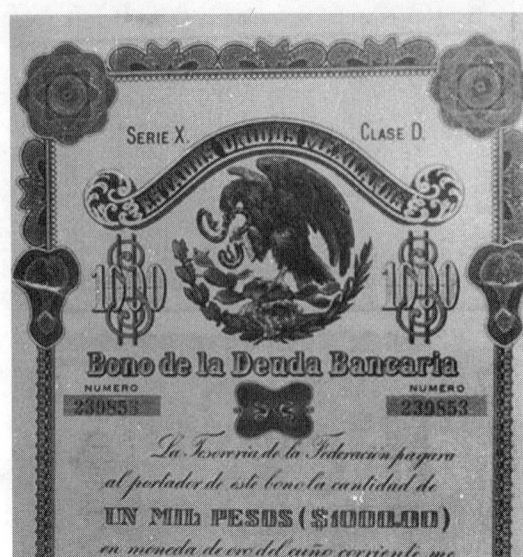

*250-30-10, 1930, v, 1,000 Pesos series X class D bond w. coupons, OIHM $20.00

Republicana Mexicana, Estado Libre y Soberano de Aquascalientes

Free and sovereign state of Aquiscalientes.

*270-30-10, 1910, v, $200 5% Bond, ABN
................................$25.00

Conservative Government of Zuloaga

Fighting against Juarez in the War of Reform (The Three Year War). Issued were 10 to 5,000 Pesos. All are extremely rare.

*310-20-10, 1858, v, 10 Peso 10% bond, thin blue paper.........................$100.00

Compañia Bancaria de Fomento y Bienes Raiges de México S.A. Société Fonciére du Mexique

*BA50-20-10, 1910, v, 100 Peso bearer stock, text in Spanish and French, with French revenue imprint, gold and black..............$15.00

Banco Central Mexicano (1899)

*BA110-30-10, 1908, v, 100 P bearer stock
w. coupons, series A, green $24.00

Banco Yucateco S.A., Mèrida, Yucatan

*BA290-20-10, 1906, v, 1 bearer sh. (par $100)
w. coupons, ABN $12.00

Caja de Prestamos para Obras de Irrigacion y Fomento de la Agriculture S.A.

Institution for Encouragement of Irrigation Works and Development of Agriculture S.A.

*CA150-30-10, 1908, v, $100 US gold or Mex.
Peso 200 or £20/11/6 sterling 35-yr 4-1/2%
Sinking Fund Gold Bond, text English-Spanish-
German-French, German revenue imprint, green
. . . .$10.00

Ferrocarriles Nacionales de Mexico - National Railways of Mexico

*FE160-20-10, 1910, v, 1 2nd pref. sh., 200 Pesos,
blue. $4.00

It is generally assumed that only 5% of certificates survive to reach collectors.

Compañia Industrial de el Oro S.A., México

*IN110-20-10, 1907, v, 1 bearer sh. (par 50P) w. coupons, French revenue imprint, green border on blue background.....................$8.00

Compañía Internacional Minera, S.A., Monterrey, N.L.

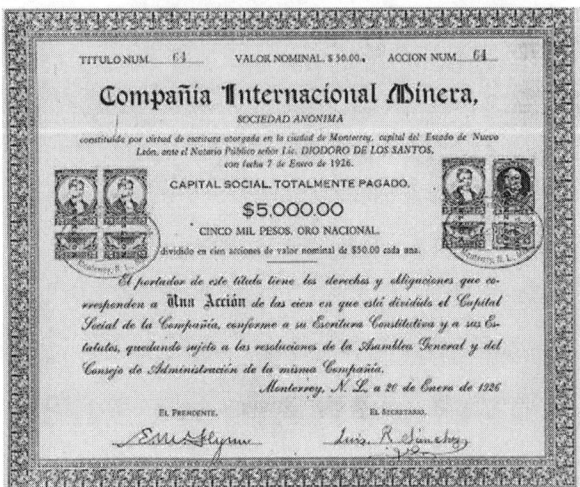

*IN190-30-10, 1926, 1 bearer sh. (par 50 P), green border $5.00

Mexican National Packing Company, Limited

*ME90-40-10, 1922, $1,000 6% first and special mortgage gold bonds, 11-1/4" x 9", grey..$3.00

Compania de Minas la Blanca y Anexas S.A.

*MI170-20-10, 1922, v, 100 Pesos bearer stock, brown $5.00

Compañia Minera la Descubridora, S.A. de El Oro Estado de México, Mexico

MI210-20-10, 1911, 5 sh.. (par 10 Pesos), text in Spanish and French, dark green border on tan background $5.00

MI210-25-10, 1919, v, 1 bearer sh.. (par 100 Pesos), text in Spanish and French, dark blue w. light blue underprint $8.00

Compañia Minera Durango, Monterrey

MI240-20-10, 1924, v, 5 sh.. (par 10 P), green with light green background $5.00

Companie Minera Ignacio Rodriguez Ramos

MI270-20-10, 1910, v, $200 bearer sh., green
. . . .$18.00

Compañia Minera de Los Azules, Mexico

MI310-30-10, 1936, v, 20 P bearer sh., w. coupons, blue. $8.00

Compañia Minera La Paz de México S.A., Mexico

MI370-20-10, 1910, v, 1 bearer sh., green border
..................................**$8.00**

Compañia Minera la Peña y Cazadores, S.A., México

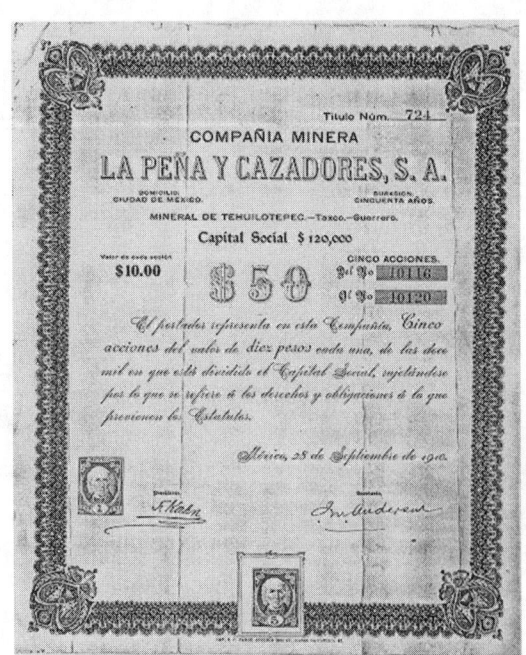

MI410-20-10, 1910, 5 bearer sh. (par 10 Pesos),
w. Mexican revenue stamps, Imp. J.C. Parde,
Sucesor; brown **$8.00**

Compañia Minera La Perla S.A., San Luis Potosi

MI440-20-10, 1901, v, 1 sh. (par 60 P), blue
border, green type....................**$7.00**

Compañia Minera "La Protectora" y Anexas S.A., Mexico

Mine in San Salvador, Estado de Zacatecas.

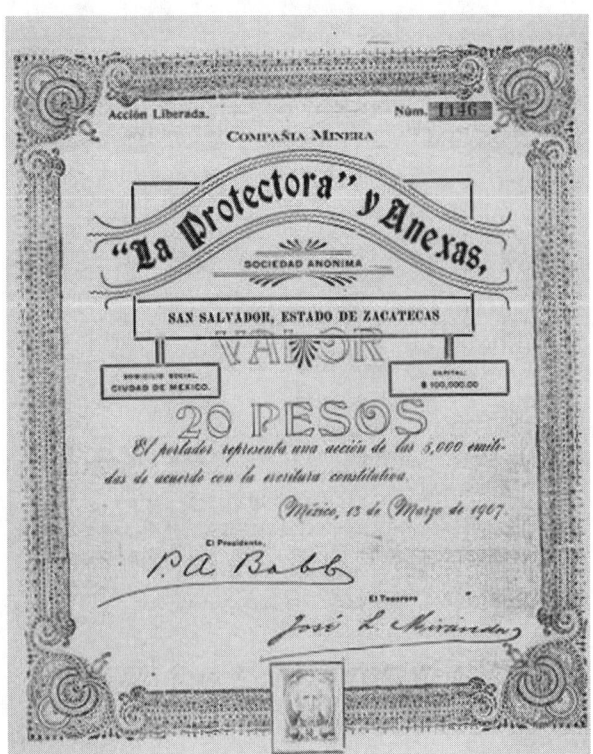

MI470-20-10, 1907, 20 P bearer sh., light purple
border **$8.00**

Companie Minera Nazareno y Anexas S.A.

*MI520-10-10, 1910, v, 1 founder's bearer sh. (par $1 Mex), w. revenue stamp, blue $3.00

Compañia Minera Santa Bernardina y Anexas S.A. Tasco, Guerrero, Mexico

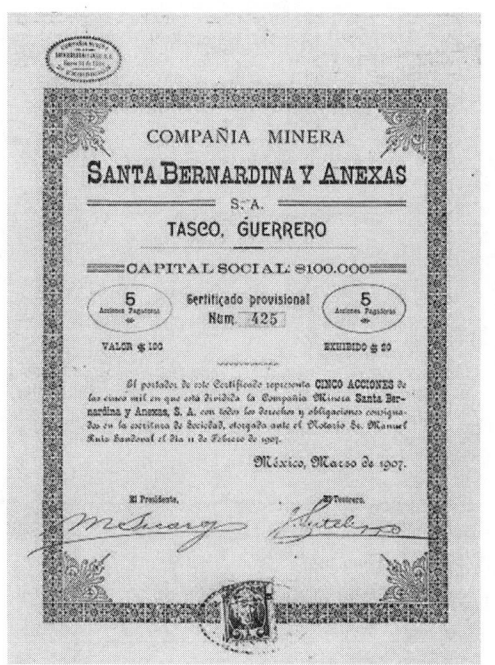

*MI570-20-10, 1907, 5 bearer sh. (par $20), blue border $7.00

Cia. Minera "Los Tres Señores y Anexas," S.A., Mexico

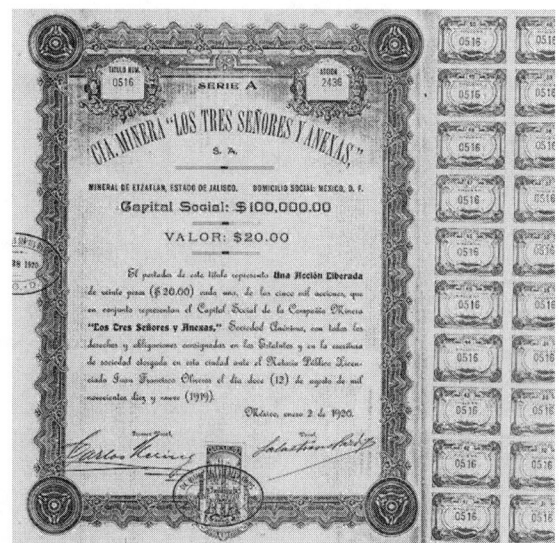

*MI600-20-10, 1920, v, 20 P bearer sh., green $8.00

Negociacion Minera de San Juan, San Antonio y Anexas, S.A., México

NE110-20-10, 1914, v, 1 bearer sh. (par 10 Pesos) w. coupons, w. Mexican revenue stamps, brown $8.00

Negociacion Minera de San Rafael y Anexas, Minerai de Pachuca, Estado de Hidalgo, Mina de "Polo Norte"

*NE140-20-10, 1910, v, 1 sh. ($10) w. coupons, violet. $8.00

*NE140-30-10, 1923, v, 10 bearer sh. (par 0.50 P) w. coupons, text in Spanish-French-English, brown **$8.00**

Negociacion Minera Socavon de San Fernando y Anexas S.A., Mexico

*NE170-20-10, 1919, 1 bearer sh. (par 25 Pesos), brown border on beige background **$8.00**

Negociacion Minera de "Veta Grande." S.A., San Luis Potosi

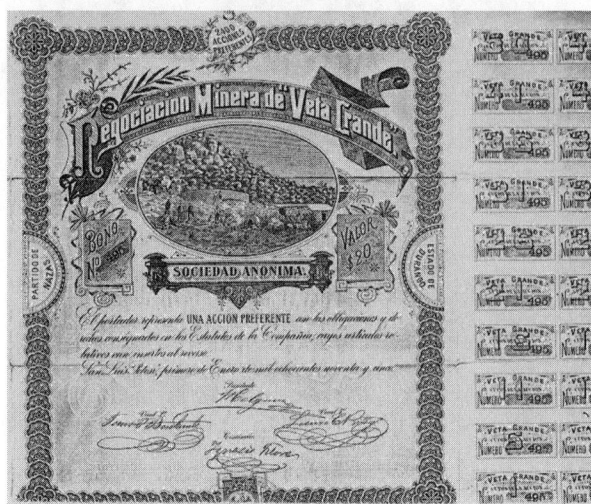

*NE210-20-10, 1895, v, 1 bearer sh., w. coupons, w. Mexican revenue stamp, blue border on beige background........................**$8.00**

Negociacion Minera La Victoria y Anexas en San Pedro S.A., San Luis Potosi

*NE240-30-10, 1935, v, 1 bearer. sh. (par 6 P), brown with grey-blue print............**$7.00**

Securanza Mining Company, S.A., San Luis Potosi

*SE90-20-10, 1910, v, 1 bearer pref. sh. (par 10 P) w. coupons, light green.................$8.00

"La Valenciana" Compañia Cobrera de Teziutlan, S.A., Teziutlan, Estado de Puebla

*VA150-20-10, 1904, v, 100 Pesos bearer sh., green border $8.00

Monte Carlo

Societe des Petroles Monte-Carlo
PE150-20-10, 1928, v, 100 F bearer stock w. coupons $10.00

Morocco

Societe Anglo-Francaise Marocaine Limited
AN120-20-10, 1908, 10 sh of £1=25F w. coupons, brown $10.00

Sociètè des Lièges de la Mamora S.A.
LI110-20-10, 1931, 1 founder bearer sh. (100 F), brown $3.00

S.A. Marocaine du Djebel Chiker (SAMOC), Taza
MA130-20-10, 1927, 100 F bearer sh., brown $3.00

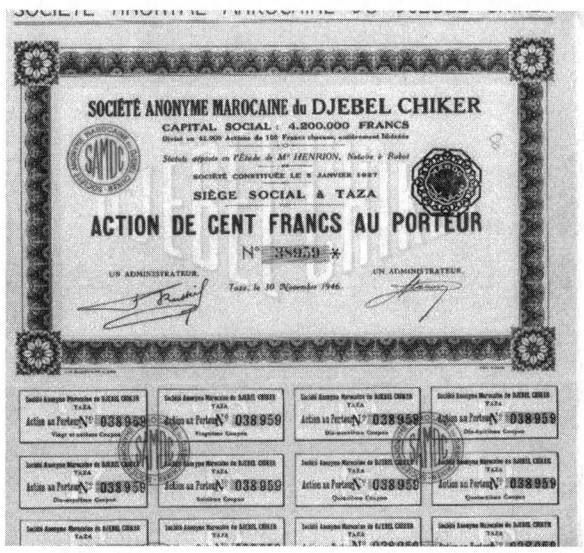

*MA130-30-10, 1946, 100 F bearer sh. w. coupons, brown $3.00

> *It is generally assumed that only 5% of certificates survive to reach collectors.*

Sociéte des Mines de Bou-Skour, Casablanca

MI180-30-10, 1955, 500 F bearer stock w. coupons, Imprimerie Chaix, Paris, 10-1/2" x 5-1/4" (certificate only), reddish.........$5.00

Compagnie Minière du Souss, Meknès

MI360-30-10, 1950, 5 bearer sh. (par 100F) w. coupons, L. Danel, 12-1/2" x 8", green ...$4.00

MI360-35-10, 1950, 10 bearer sh. (par 100 F), blue $4.00

MI360-40-10, 1949, v, 25 bearer sh. (par 100 F), grey on blue $6.00

Companie des Phosphates et du Chemin de Fer de Gafsa

PH160-20-10, 1897, v, 5 Dinar bearer sh. w. coupons, brown $4.00

N

Netherlands Antilles

Beatrice Foods Overseas Finance N.V.

BE40-30-10, $1,000 7-3/4% guaranteed note due 1983, SCB, 9-3/4" x 14", red **$3.00**

This catalog has listings in an alphabetical format. The reason is simple: Companies diversify as they grow. For example, the Canadian Pacific Railway company recently split into five companies. They represent the railway, hotels, shipping, airline, and petroleum interests of the company. During World War II, the Singer sewing machine company made guns and other defense-related equipment, so where should we list it? It's far easier to use a strict alphabetical order, rather than to confuse the reader with topical classifications.

CNA Overseas Capital, N.V.

CN80-30-10, 1970, v - eagle, $1,000 9% guar. note due 1975, ABN, 9-1/2" x 13-1/4", purple **$3.00**

The Long Term Credit Bank of Japan Finance N.V.

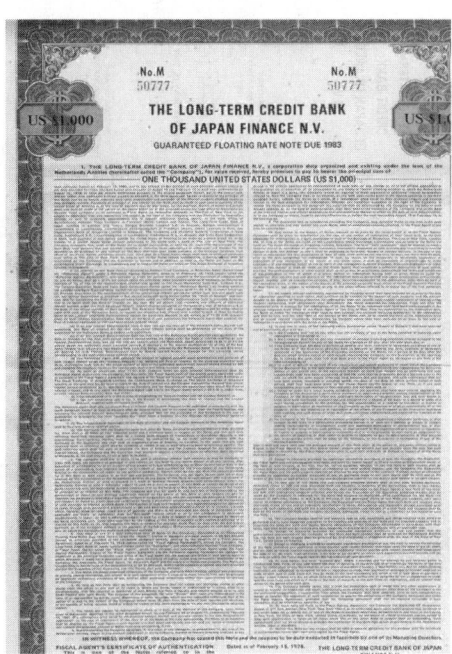

LO180-30-10, 1978, $1,000 guaranteed floating rate note due 1983, ABN, 9-1/4" x 13-1/4", olive **$3.00**

Netherlands

A system similar to American Depositary Receipts (ADR) is found in the Netherlands. One encounters certificates issued mostly in Amsterdam bearing the name of American, British, and corporations from other countries.

American Natural Gas Corporation (Delaware), Amsterdam

AM180-20-10, 1928, 10 bearer sh. w. coupons, Dutch revenue imprint, Druk de Bussy, Amsterdam; 10" x 6-3/4", lilac border on beige $3.00

Central Public Service Company, Amsterdam

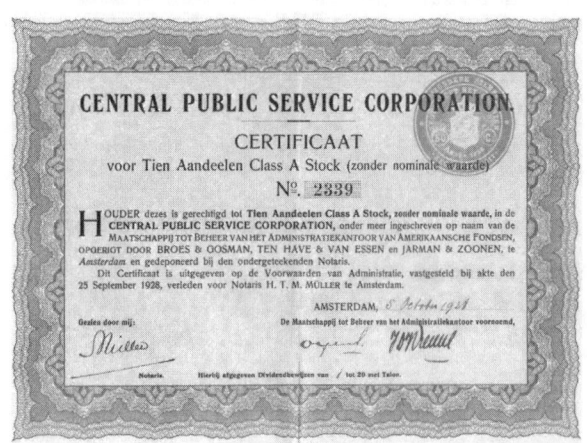

CE120-20-10, 1928, 10 class A bearer sh. w. coupons, Dutch revenue imprint, Joh. Enschedé en Zonen, Haarlem, 9-3/4" x 7", multicolored border $3.00

Central Public Utility Corporation, Amsterdam

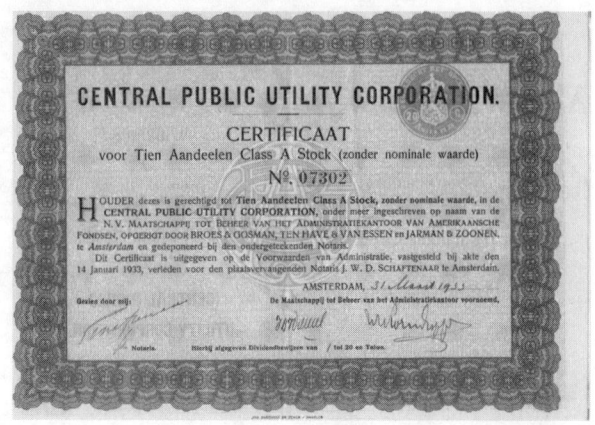

CE150-20-10, 1933, 10 class A bearer sh. w. coupons, Dutch revenue imprint, Joh. Enschedé en Zonen, Haarlem; 9-3/4" x 7", green border on green..............................$3.00

Chicago, Milwaukee, St. Paul and Pacific Railroad Company, Amsterdam

CH250-20-10, 1924, 10 sh. (no par), Dutch revenue imprint, 10" x 7", fancy brown border $6.00

Consolidated Automatic Mechandising Corporation (Delaware), Amsterdam

*CO270-20-10, 1929, 10 bearer sh., Dutch revenue imprint, Druk de Bussy, Amsterdam; 9-3/4" x 7", green border $3.00

N.V. Heiwerken Nederland v/h P. van 't Wout, Rijswijk

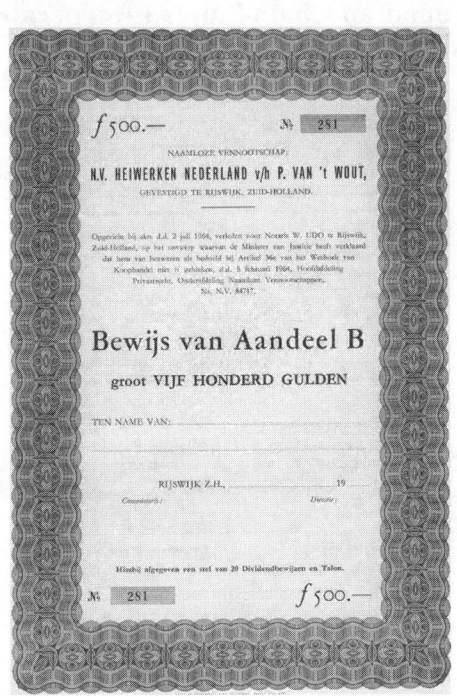

*HE150-30-10, 19xx, v, u/u 500 Gulden class B certificate w. coupons, N.V. Roepers' Drukkerij, Den Haag, 8-1/4" x 11-3/4", blue border . .$3.00

Interborough-Metropolitan Company te New York, Amsterdam

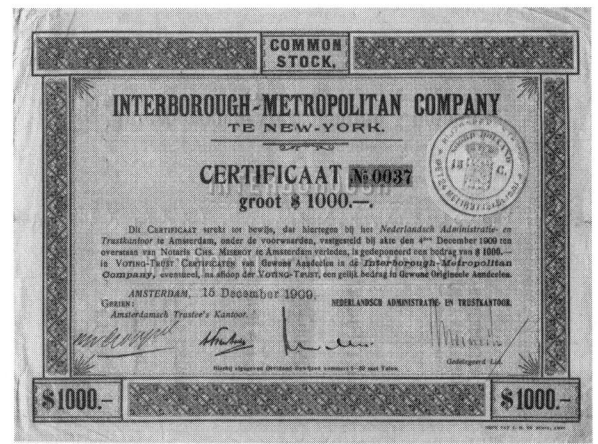

*IN270-30-10, 1909, $1,000 common stock, Dutch revenue rubber stamp, Druk van J.H. Bussy, Amst., 9-3/4" x 7", red border $3.00

N.V. Koninklijke Nederlandsche Petroleum Maatschappij, Royal Dutch Petroleum Company

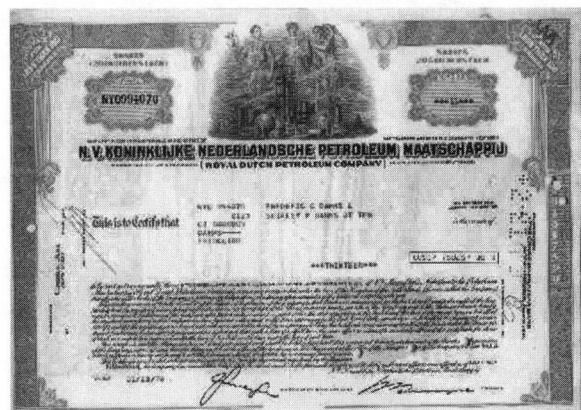

*KO380-50-10, 197?, v, 13 sh. on a less than 100 sh. certif., orange $4.00

The value of a stock certificate depends on:
- rarity
- the issuer
- signatures
- quality of engraving
- overall appearance
- condition
- date of issue

Koninklijke Scholten-Honig N.V., Amersfoort

*KO510-30-10, 1966, v, 100 Gulden (4 x 25) bearer sh. w. coupons, Joh. Enschedé en Zonen, Haarlem; 9" x 13-1/4", blue border **$3.00**

*KO510-40-10, 1966, 1,000 (40 x 25) Gulden bearer stock, w. coupons, Joh. Enschedé en Zonen Haarlem, 9" x 13-1/4", brown **$3.00**

The London & Dominion Trust, Limited te Londen, Amsterdam

*LO390-30-10, 1912, £50 bearer sh. w. coupons, Stoomdr. B. van Mantgem, Hofl., Amst.; 10" x 7-3/4", black border **$3.00**

Metropolitan Chain Stores Incorporated, Amsterdam

*ME350-20-10, 1931, 5 bearer sh. with coupons, Dutch revenue imprint, 9-3/4" x 6-3/4", purple **$3.00**

> *It is generally assumed that only 5% of certificates survive to reach collectors.*

Nationale Trust Company, Amsterdam

*NA330-20-10, 1923, 25 sh. (par £1) invested in the Phoenix Oil and Transport Company, Limited of London, Dutch revenue imprint, Druk de Bussy, 9-3/4" x 6-3/4", blue $3.00

New York & Foreign Investing Corporation, Amsterdam

*NE290-20-10, 1931, 10 bearer sh., Dutch revenue imprint, 9-3/4" x 6-3/4", red $3.00

UNLISTED TYPES & VARIETIES

Readers are welcome to contact the author directly at:

Rainer Stahlberg
P.O. Box 1044
Rooseveltown, New York 13683

Union Pacific Corporation, Amsterdam

*UN230-30-10, 1970, v, 10 sh. (par $10), Joh. Enscgedé en Zonen Haarlem, 11-3/4" x 7-3/4", green $3.00

Netherlands Indies

Cultuur Maatschappij "Boekit Lawang", Batavia

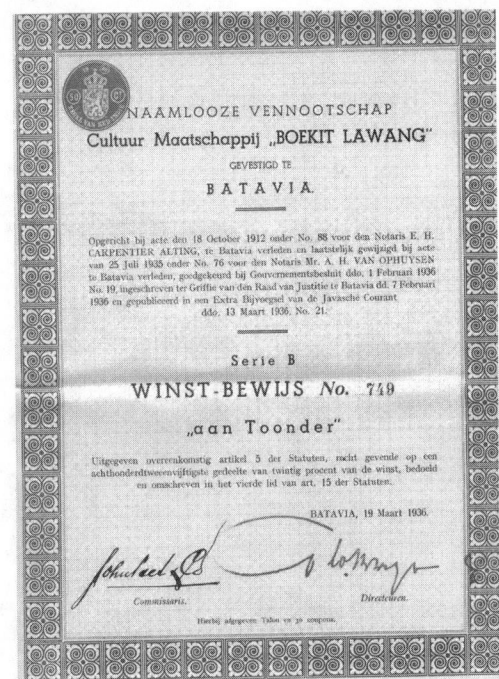

*CU150-30-10, 1936, 1 series B bearer share, w. Dutch revenue imprint, 9-1/2" x 13-1/4", green border $3.00

Cultuur Maatschappij Paseoemah, Batavia

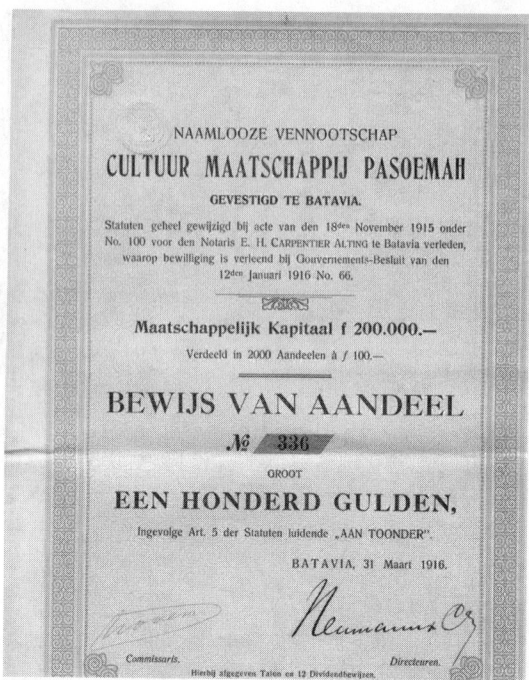

*CU210-20-10, 1916, 1 bearer share 100 Gulden, w. coupons, Typ. Jav. Boekh. & Drukkerrij, - Bat.; 9-1/2" x 13", yellow-orange border . . $3.00

Cultuur Maatschappij "SAMBAWA", Hoofdzetel te Bandoeng (Java)

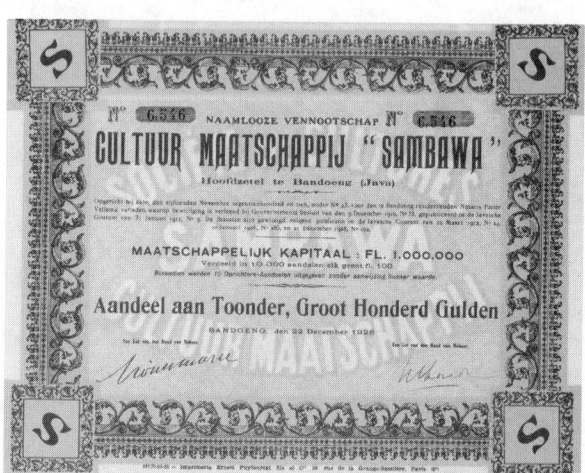

*CU390-30-10, 1928, bearer share of 100 Gulden w. coupons, Imprimerie Ernest Puyfourcat, Paris; 11" x 11", yellowish orange $4.00

Landbouw Maatschappij "Satak", Soerabaia

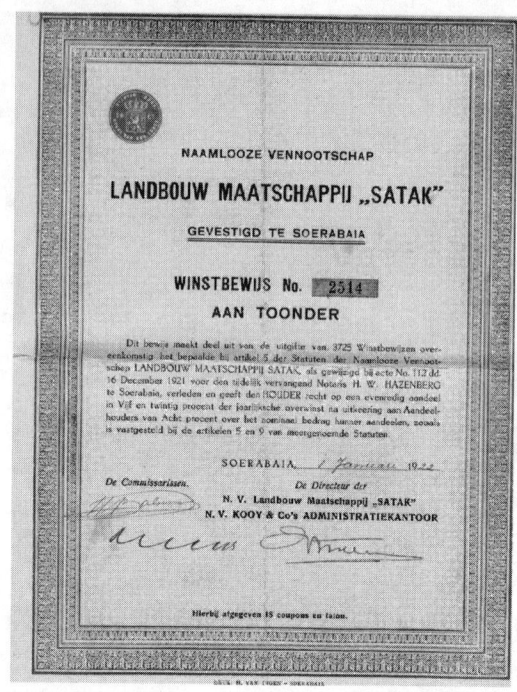

*LA230-20-10, 1922, 1 bearer share, w. Dutch revenue imprint, Druk: H. van Ingen - Soerabaia, 9" x 12-1/2", brown border $3.00

Mijnbouw-Maatschappij Totok, Batavia

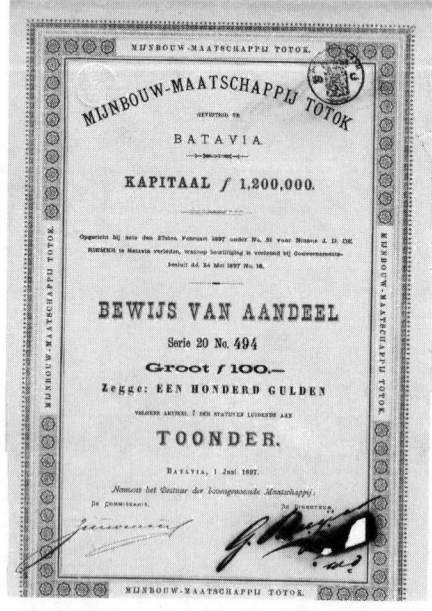

*MI140-20-10, 1897, 100 Gulden bearer stock w. coupons, Typ. G. Kolff & Co. - Batavia, 8-1/2" x 13-1/2", light brown $5.00

Nederlandsch-Indische Spoorweg-Maatschappij

NE130-20-10, 1920, v, 500 Gulden bearer stock w. coupons, Dutch revenue imprint, blue border on green $4.00

The value of a stock certificate depends on:

- **rarity**
- **the issuer**
- **signatures**
- **quality of engraving**
- **overall appearance**
- **condition**
- **date of issue**

Norway

City of Oslo

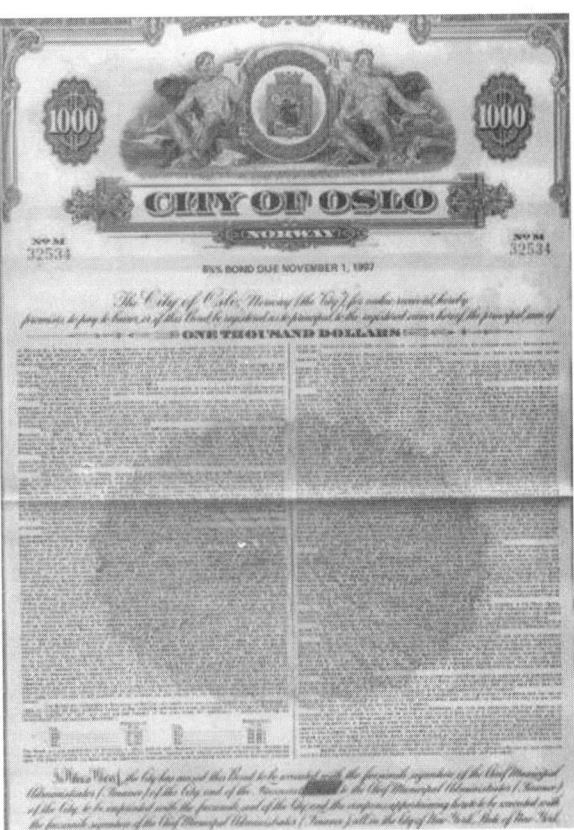

OS180-50-10, 1977, v, $1,000 8-1/2% bond due 1997 w. coupons, brown **$10.00**

P

Panama

Compagnie Universale Canal Interoceanique de Panama

CA70-30-10, 1880, v, 500 F bearer stock w. coupons, blue **$35.00**

CA70-40-10, 1889, v, 50 F bearer stock, reddish orange............................**$35.00**

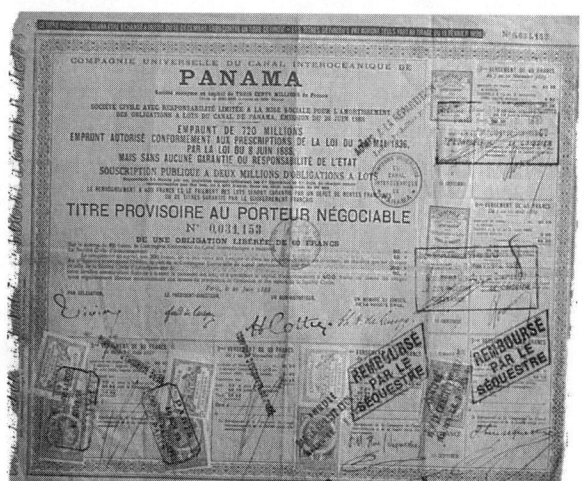

CA70-50-10, 1888, 60 F bearer negotiable provisional title, revenue stamps, red **$30.00**

Peru

Republica del Peru, Obligacion del Tesoro

50-20-10, 1928, 100 gold pounds, brown ..**$10.00**
50-30-10, 1929, 1,000 gold pounds, red ...**$10.00**
50-35-10, 1928, v, 5,000 gold pounds, lilac.**$20.00**

Bono de Desarrollo, Lima

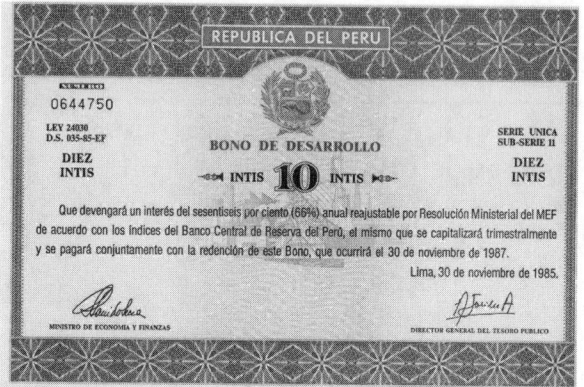

180-30-10, 1985, v, 10 Intis, 66% re-adjustable bond, USB, 8-1/4" x 5-1/2", green.......**$2.00**

180-40-10, 1985, v, 200 Intis, 66% re-adjustable bond, USB, 8-1/4" x 5-1/2", maroon **$2.00**

UNLISTED TYPES & VARIETIES

Readers are welcome to contact the author directly at:

Rainer Stahlberg
P.O. Box 1044
Rooseveltown, New York 13683

Sociedad Agricola Nepeña Limitada, Lima

*AG190-20-10, 1920, v, 1 bearer share (par 100 gold libras), brown $15.00

Philippines

Philippine Long DistanceTelephone Company
PH240-30-10, 19xx, v, 1 sh. on a less than 100 sh. certif., blue $4.00
PH240-40-10, 19xx, v, 100 sh., brown $4.00

Seafront Petroleum and Mineral Resources, Inc. (par 1 centavo)

*SE60-30-10, 1976, v, 500,000 sh., TROJAN 130, 11" x 8-1/2", brown $4.00

Poland

Government of Poland, Rzeczpospolita Polska

*40-30-10, 1931 $5= 44.57 Zloty, serji III, 40 year bond, dark blue.....................$6.00
40-40-10, 1934, 50 Zl. bond w. 9 coupons ..$4.00
40-45-10, 1934, v, 100 Zl 6% bond, red ...$15.00
40-50-10, 1935, v, 100 Zl, 3% bond, 1st issue, blue
...............................$10.00
40-55,10, 1935, v, 100 Zl. 3% bond, 2nd issue, brown $10.00

Katowice

*KA130-20-10, 1929, 680 Zloty bond, brown on blue............................$4.00

Kraj

Tractor and farm equipment manufacturer.

*KR70-20-10, 1920, v, 1 bearer sh. (par 100 Zl.),
brown $9.00

Slaskie Kopalnie i Cynkownie, S.A. des Mines et Usines à Zinc de Silésie, Schlesische AG für Bergbau und Zinchüttenbetrieb, Lipiny

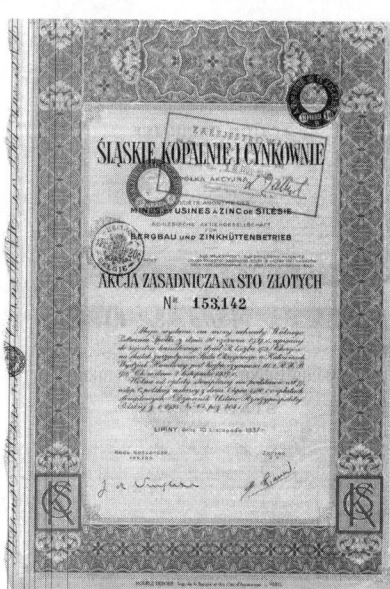

*SL80-30-10, 1937, v, 100 Zloty bearer sh. w. cou-
pons, text in Polish-French-German; Dutch-
French-Belgian revenue imprints, Imp. de la
Banque et des Cies d'Assurances - Paris; 8-1/4"
x 11-1/2", brown-beige. $5.00

Towarzystwo Zakladow Przedzalni Bawelny Tkalni i Blacharni "Zawiercie"

Warsaw cotton and textile mill.

*TO360-30-10, 1929, v, 100 Zloty, brown . . $10.00

Zachodnio Malopolska Akcyjna Spólka Naftowa I Gazowa w Krakowie

(The Petroleum and Natural Gas Limited of Western Little Poland)

*ZA130-30-10, 1923, v, 1,000 Marek bearer bond,
brown $15.00

Portugal

Companhia Colonial de Navegaçáo (1922)

* CO140-40-10, 1954, v, 50 bearer shares, pea
green. $8.00

The Match and Tobacco Timber Supply Company, Lisbon

MA170-20-10, 1924, v, bearer sh. (par £1) w. coupons, text in Portugese-English-French, brown border **$6.00**

S.A. Mines de Mertola

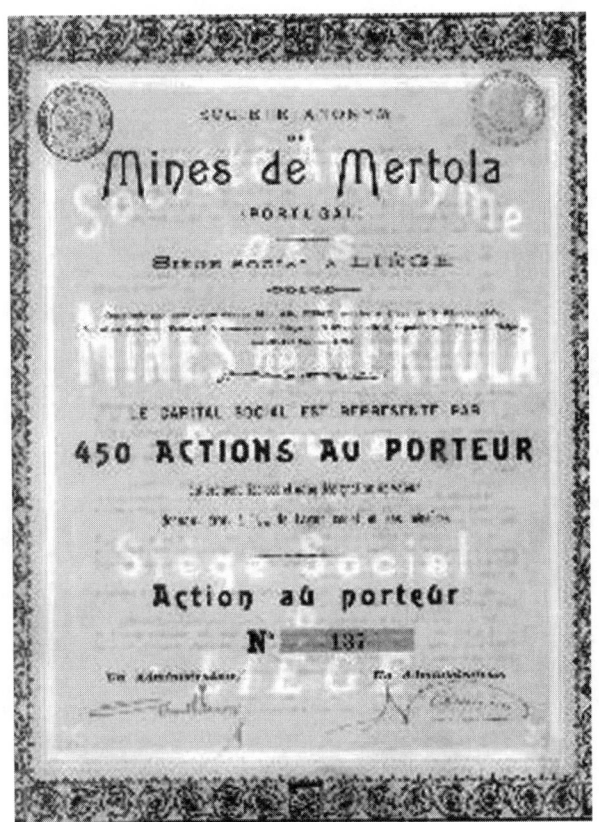

MI220-20-10, 1904, bearer sh., brown **$4.00**

Moagem D'Elvas

MO60-20-10, 1933, 1 sh., black **$4.00**

The value of a stock certificate depends on:

- rarity
- the issuer
- signatures
- quality of engraving
- overall appearance
- condition
- date of issue

Companhia de Mossamedes

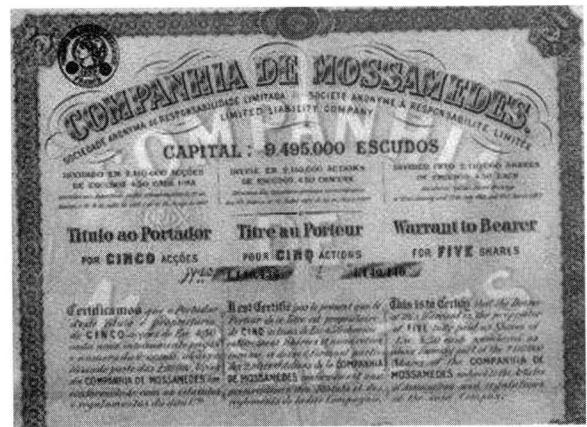

*MO220-20-10, 1937, w, 5 bearer shares w. coupons, text in Portuguese-French-English, French revenue rubber stamp, 13" x 12", red. . . .**$10.00**

Puerto Rico

Banco Espanol de Puerto Rico

B30-20-10, 1895, v, 15 sh. (par $100), brown **$150.00**

Banco Territorial y Agricola

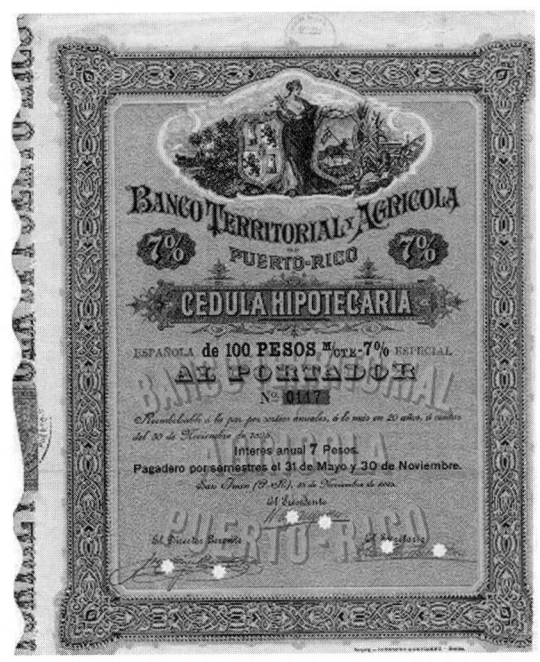

*B60-30-10, 1895, v, 100 Peso 7% mortgage bond, reddish brown. **$26.00**

Puerto Rico Dairy, Inc. (1940)
(PR par $100)

PU40-20-10, 1940, v, 110 sh., orange $20.00

Puerto Rico International Airlines Inc.
(PR 1964)

*PU60-20-10, 1972, v, 100 sh., blue $15.00

Donato Vigil & Cia., Inc. (par $1,000)

*VI40-30-10, 1941, 2 sh., brown $20.00

R

Rio Muni

Colonizadora de la Guinea Continental
S.A., "COGUISA", Bata

*CO140-20-10, 1955, v, 1 bearer sh. (par 50 Pesetas) w. coupons, 14" x 11", multicolored border on pink $10.00

This catalog has listings in an alphabetical format. The reason is simple: Companies diversify as they grow. For example, the Canadian Pacific Railway company recently split into five companies. They represent the railway, hotels, shipping, airline, and petroleum interests of the company. During World War II, the Singer sewing machine company made guns and other defense-related equipment, so where should we list it? It's far easier to use a strict alphabetical order, rather than to confuse the reader with topical classifications.

Romania

Astra Romana

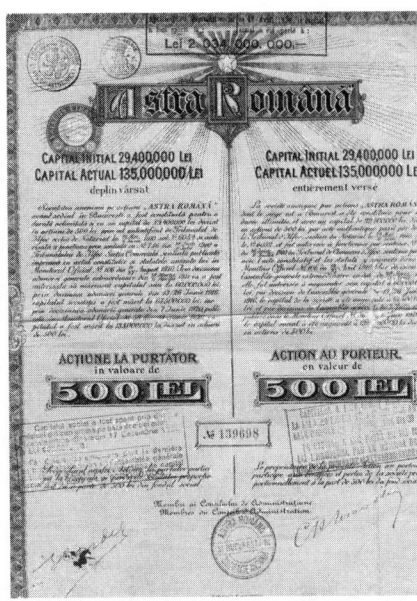

*AS260-30-10, 1924, 500 Lei bearer stock w. coupons, actual capital 135,000,000 Lei, Belgian and French revenue imprints; text in Romanian and French, Taranu & Co., Bucharest, 10-1/2" x 13-1/2", green $3.00

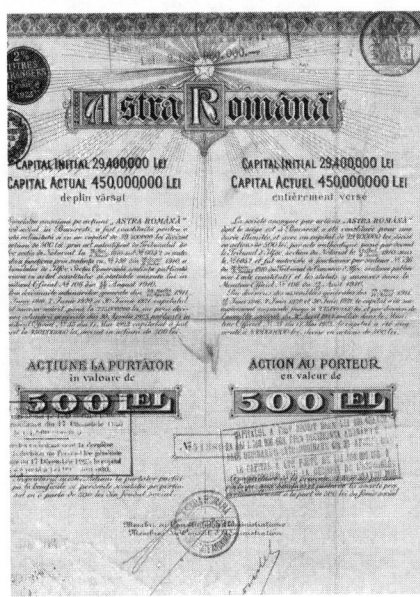

*AS260-35-10, 1924, 500 Lei bearer stock with coupons, actual capital 450,000,000 Lei, text in Romanian and French, French revenue imprint, Stabiliment Grafic Taranu & C. Bucuresti, 11-1/2" x 14", green $3.00

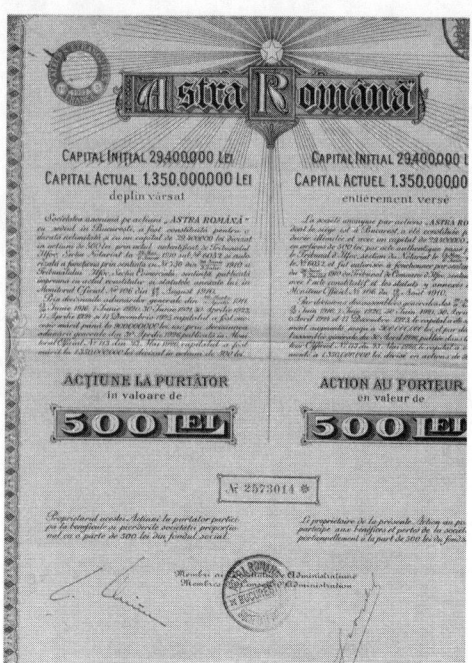

*AS260-37-10, 1925, 500 Lei bearer stock w. coupons, actual capital 675,000,000 Lei, , text in Romanian and French, French revenue imprint, Stab. Taranu & Co. - Bucuresti, 11-1/2" x 14", green $3.00

*AS260-45-10, 1927, 500 Lei bearer share w. coupons, actual capital 1,350,000,000 Lei; text in Romanian and French, French revenue imprint, Stab. Taranu & Co. - Bucuresti, 11-1/2" x 14-1/2", green $3.00

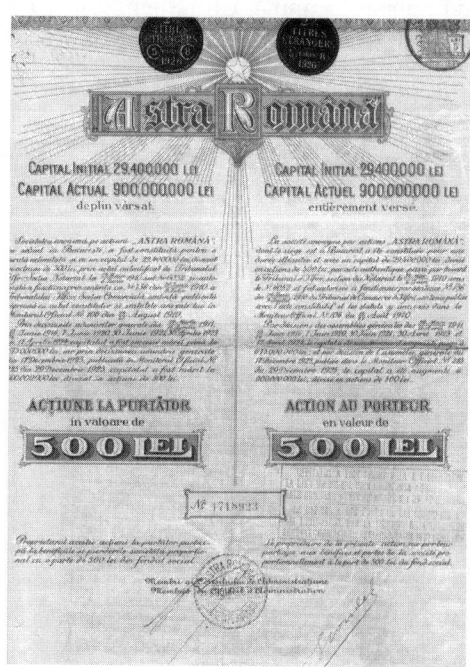

*AA260-40-10, 1926, 500 Lei bearer stock w. coupons, actual capital 900,000,000 Lei, text in Romanian and French, French revenue imprint, Atelierele Socec. & Co. S.A. Bucuresti; 11-3/4" x 14-1/2", green $3.00

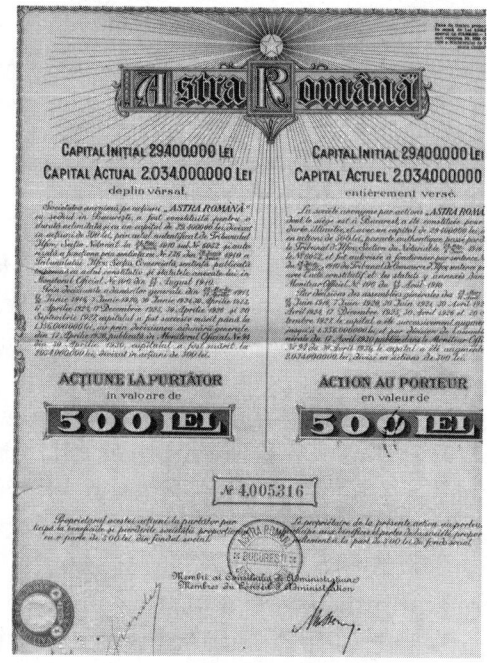

*AS260-50-10, 1931, 500 Lei bearer share w. coupons, actual capital 2,034,000,000 Lei; text in Romanian and French, French revenue imprint, Waldheim-Eberle S.A. Vienne VII, 10-1/2" x 14-1/2", green $3.00

Concordia S.A. Roumanie pour l'Industrie Petrole

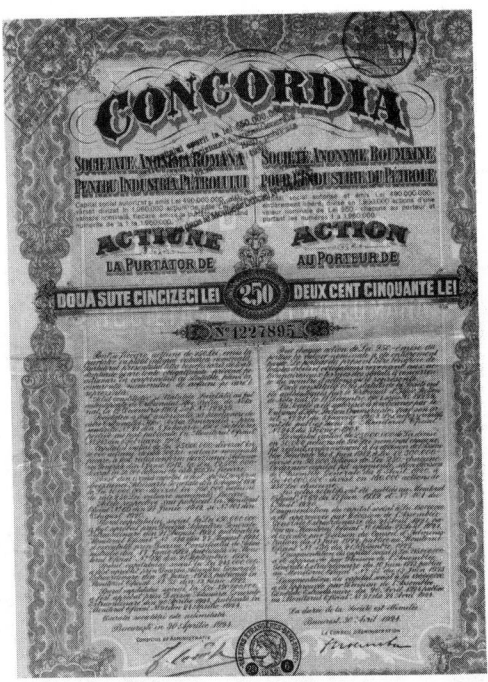

*CO210-20-10, 1924, v, 250 Lei bearer stock w. coupons, text in Romanian and French, French revenue imprint, J. Verschueren - Anvers-Bruxelles, 10" x 14-1/2", reddish $4.00

CO210-25-10, 1922, v, 10 bearer shares (par 250 Lei) w. coupons, text in Romanian and French, blue $4.00

Creditul Carbonifer S.A. Miniera, Bucharest

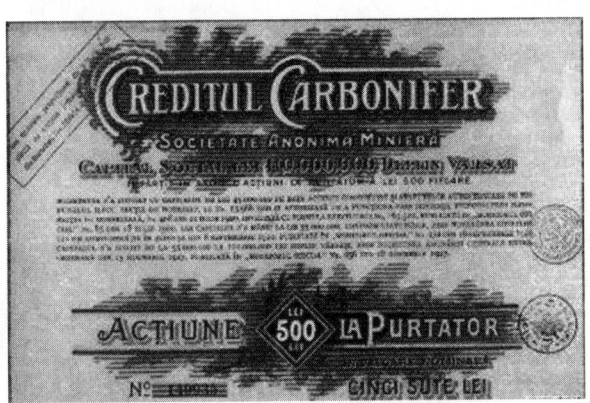

*CR90-30-10, 1927, v, 500 Lei bearer share w. coupons, blue $3.00

Petrol-Block

*PE240-20-10, 1922, v, 500 Lei bearer sh. w. coupons, Capital 30,000,000 Lei, text in Romanian-German-French, green border $3.00

PE240-30-10, 1924, v, 500 Lei bearer stock w. coupons, 4th issue, Capital 200,000,000 Lei, text in Romanian and French, w/o imprint, 10-1/4" x 14", grey on beige $3.00

S.A. Romana de Navigatiur pe Dunare S.R.D.

RO150-30-10, 193x, v, 5 bearer sh. (2,500 Lei) w. coupons, multicolored $12.00

Kingdom of Roumania

*RO200-30-10, 1922, v, £10 bearer bond 4% w. coupons, text in English-Romanian-French, green $15.00

*RO200-40-10, 1922, v, £500 4% consolidation loan, bearer bond w. coupons, text in English-Romanian-French, blue-lilac border....$10.00

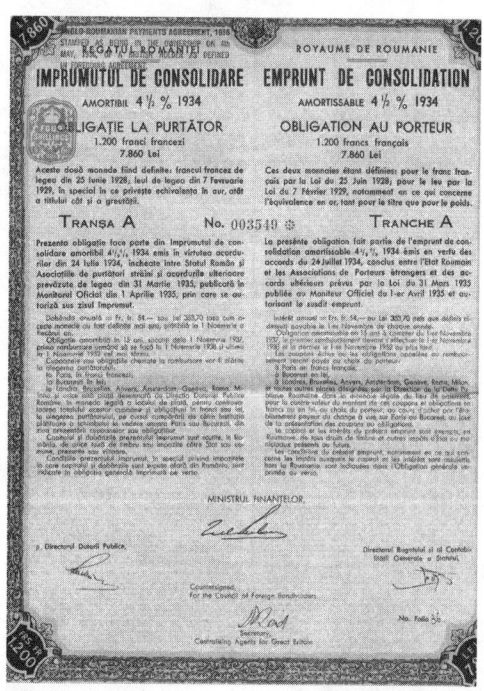

*R200-70-10, 1934, 7,860 Lei = 1,200 FF 4-1/2% Consolidation loan, tranche A, bearer certif. w. coupons, English revenue imprint, E. Marvan, Bucaresti, 10-1/4" x 14-3/4", grey border on green $3.00

*RO200-80-10, 1934, v, Fractional certificate for 20 FF, tranche A, bearer certif., 12" x 9", green border $3.00

Kingdom of Roumania Monopolies Institute

*RO220-30-10, 1929, v, £100 bond, Waterlow & Sons, Limited, London; blue $8.00

Imprumutul de Inzestrare a Tárii

*RO240-30-10, 1934, v, 1,000 Lei 4-1/2% bond,
blue $4.00

Regatul României, Ministerul Finantelor, Datoria Publica a României

*RO260-30-10, 1935, v, 1,000 Lei 3% Consolida-
tion Loan, brown. $5.00

Casa Autonomâ a Fondului Apârârii Nationale

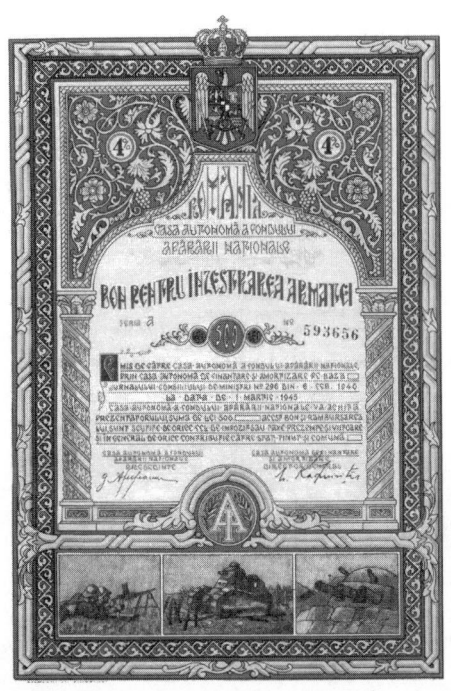

*RO290-60-10, 1940, v, 500 Lei 4% war bond, due
1945, M.O. Impriméria Natiónala, 9" x 12-1/2",
multicolored $7.00

*RO290-70-10, 1941, v, 2,500 Lei 4-1/2% war
bond, blue. $4.00

RO290-75-10, 1941, v, 10,000 4-1/2% Lei War Bond, brown $5.00

RO290-120-10, 1944, v, 1,000 Lei 4% war bond, grey $3.00

RO290-80-10, 1941, v, 100,000 Lei 4-1/2% War Bond, brown $6.00

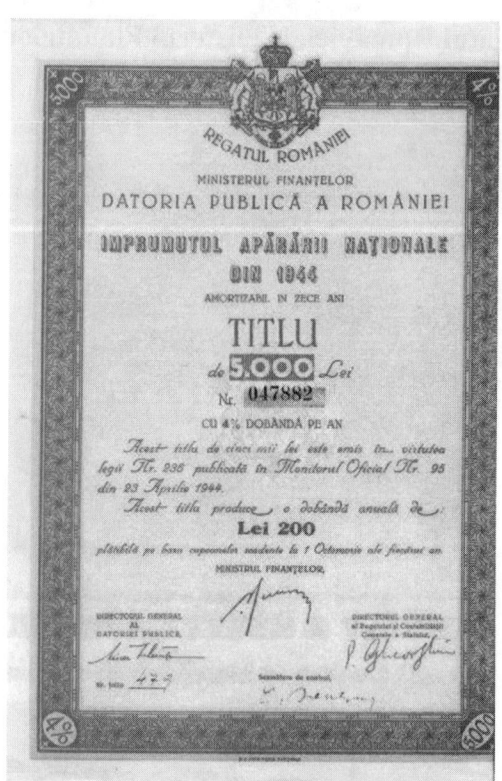

RO290-125-10, 1944, v, 5,000 Lei 4% war bond, brown $3.00

*RO290-130-10, 1944, v, 20,000 Lei 4% war bond, green $3.00

S.A. Románo-Belgiana de Petrol, Bucharest

*RO360-20-10, 1908, v, 250 Lei bearer sh., green $5.00

Steua Romana - Etoile Roumanie S.A.
Petroleum industry company.

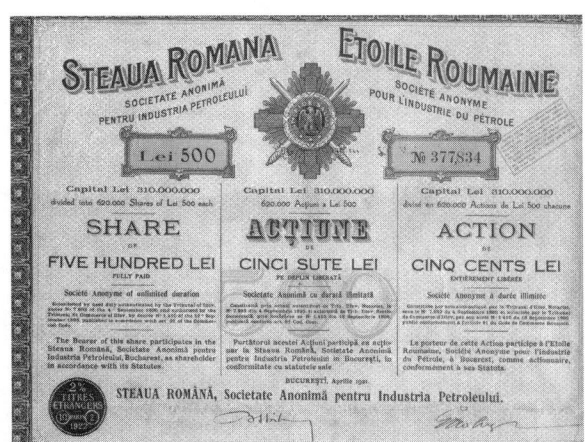

*ST80-20-10, 1921, v, 500 Lei bearer stock w. coupons, text in English-Romanian-French, French revenue imprint, Viellemard Imp. Paris; 13-1/4" x 10", brown $3.00

Uzinele de Fier si Domeniile din Resita S.A., Bucharest

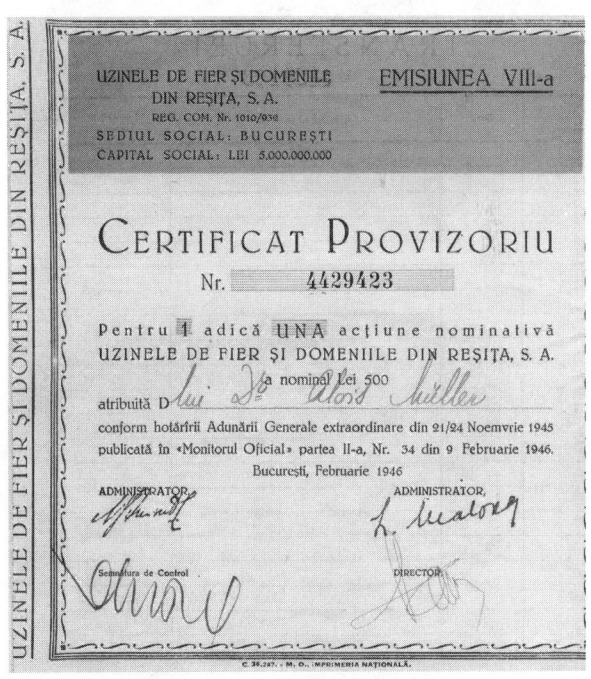

*UZ110-20-10, 1946, t, 1 bearer sh., w. coupons, series VIII-a, M.O., Imprimeria Nationala, 6-1/4" x 7-3/4", rose brown $3.00

*UZ110-25-10, 1946, t, 5 bearer sh., w. coupons, series VIII-a, M.O., Imprimeria Nationala, 6-1/4" x 7-3/4", light brown $3.00

Ruanda

Société Commerciale, Financière et Agricole du Ruanda, SOCOFINA, Kigali

*CO230-20-10, ND, v, 100 F bearer stock, Etabl. d'Imp. Collet-Watrin; 7-3/4" x 11-1/2", brown
...................................$3.00

Russia

4% Bilety (tickets) of the State Bank
In 1857 the interest rates at state banks were reduced from 4% to 3%. In order to avoid the massive withdrawal of funds in 1861 the 300 ruble 4% tickets were introduced forcing the investors to invest in the 41-year notes (info from M. Istomin).
30-10-10, 1860, v, 300 R specimen certificate, brown $80.00

Imperial
50-25-10, 1888, v, 625 R bond, blue $8.00
50-30-10, 1891, v, 125R-500F, 3% bond...$10.00
50-40-10, 1893, v, 500F, 4-1/2% bond, brown
...................................$10.00

*50-45-10, 1894, v, 125 Ruble=404 Reichs Mark=500 French Francs=£19/15/6 3-1/2% bond, text in Russian-English-French-German, brown $5.00

Imperial Land Mortgage Bank for Nobility
80-30-10, 1897, v, 100 R 3-1/2% bond, brown
...................................$6.00

> *It is generally assumed that only 5% of certificates survive to reach collectors.*

*80-35-10, 1898, v, 150 R 3-1/2% bond,
 green-grey border $8.00

Imperial

100-30-10, 1901, 1,000 R, 4% state loan, in Dutch
 "Binnenlandsche Leening van Rusland, red
 ....$4.00

*100-35-10, 1902, v, 100 Rubles 4% state loan w.
 coupons, Russian-French-German, French
 revenue imprint, grey on beige........$10.00
100-37-10, 1902, v, 1,000 Reichsmark 4% bond,
 blue.............................$10.00
100-40-10, 1905, 500 Ruble 5% bond, grey border
 on blue $8.00
100-45-10, 1909, v, 500 F 4-1/2% bond, brown
 ....$4.00
100-60-10, 1915, v - mother Russia, 5% tax free
 bond w. coupons, brown.............$14.00

*100-65-10, 1916, v, 100 R 5-1/2% bond w.
 coupons, w/o imprint, 7-3/4" x 12", brown. . $3.00
100-75-10, 1918, v, 5,000 R 5% interim treasury
 bill, red gold.......................$5.00

U.S.S.R. State Loan (savings bonds)

*610-80-10, 1953, 10 R, 5" x 3-3/4", brown and
 blue............................$2.00

*610-81-10, 1953, 25 R, 5-1/4" x 3-3/4", brown
    and blue..........................$2.00

*610-82-10, 1953, 50 R, 5-3/4" x 4", brown and
    blue..............................$2.00
*610-83-10, 1953, 100 R, 6" x 4-1/4", brown and
    blue..............................$3.00

*611-10-10, 1954, 10 R, 4" x 5-1/2", red....$2.00

*611-11-10, 1954, 25 R, 4-1/4" x 5-3/4", red
    ....$2.00

*611-12-10, 1954, 50 R, 4-1/2" x 6", red....$2.00

UNLISTED TYPES & VARIETIES

Readers are welcome to contact the author directly at:

Rainer Stahlberg
P.O. Box 1044
Rooseveltown, New York 13683

*6*11-13-10,* 1954, 100 R, 4-3/4" x 6-1/4", red
. . . .$3.00

*6*12-10-10,* 1955, 10 R, 5-1/2" x 4", green . .$2.00
*6*12-11-10,* 1955, 25 R, 5-3/4" x 4-1/4", green
. . . .$2.00

*6*12-12-10,* 1955, 50 R, 6" x 4-1/2", green
. . . .$2.00

*6*12-13-10,* 1955, 100 R, 6-1/4" x 5-1/2", green
. . . .$3.00

Société des Aciéres, Forges et Ateliers de Machines de Briansk, St. Petersburg

AC110-20-10, 1912, v, 100 Ruble bearer share, text in Russian and French, brown. $3.00

Akkerman Railway
AK160-40-10, 1913, v, 187.50 R 4-1/2% bond, green. $8.00

Altai Railway
AL280-40-10, 1912, 500 F 4-1/2% debenture, light
green **$8.00**

Armavir-Touapse Railway Company, St. Petersburg

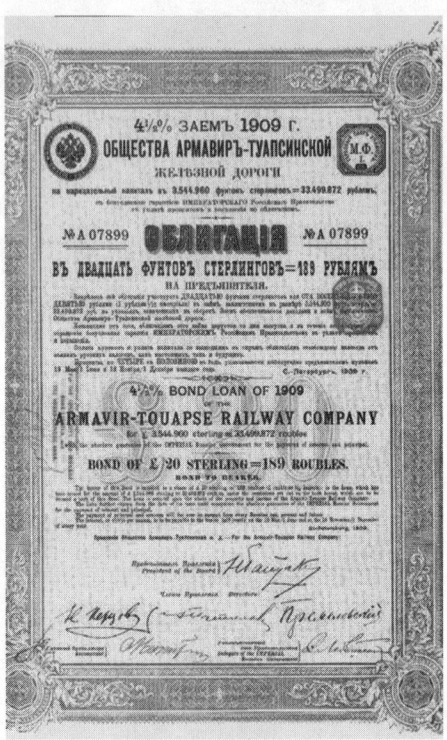

**AR180-40-10,*1909, v, £20=189 Roubles 4-1/2%
bearer bond, British revenue imprint, brown
. . . .**$5.00**

Société Belgo-Russe pour la Fabrication des Glaces

*BE140-40-10, 1912, v, 93.75 Ruble bearer sh.,
text in Russian and French, brown **$6.00**

Compagnie Centrale d'Electricite de Moscou
CE180-30-10, 1899, v, 500 F bearer stock, blue
. . . .**$21.00**

Donetz Railway
DO270-40-10, 1893, v, 125 R 4% bond, green
. . . .**$8.00**

Ferghana Railways,
FE240-40-10, 1914, 187 Ruble 4-1/2% bond,
issued in Petrograd, w. coupons, light purple
. . . .**$8.00**

Grand Russian Railway

*GR70-30-10, 1859, 500 R., black on green . **$8.00**

The value of a stock certificate depends on:
- rarity
- the issuer
- signatures
- quality of engraving
- overall appearance
- condition
- date of issue

Kharkow City Loan

*KH90-50-10, 1911, v, 187.50 R , Dutch revenue imprint, brown $4.00

Koursk-Kharkov-Azof Railway

*KO320-40-10, 1889, v, 500 Mark 4% bond with coupon, text in Russian, French and German, grey.............................$5.00

Societe Miniere et Chimiques Alaguir

MI250-30-10, 1897, v, 250 R bearer stock, blue
....$6.00

City of Moscow

*MO320-55-10, 1908, v, 189 R=£20 5% bearer bond w. coupons, text in Russian and English, 11" x 16", light brown $6.00
MO320-60-10, 1909, v, 500F 5% bond, brown and grey................................$8.00

This catalog has listings in an alphabetical format. The reason is simple: Companies diversify as they grow. For example, the Canadian Pacific Railway company recently split into five companies. They represent the railway, hotels, shipping, airline, and petroleum interests of the company. During World War II, the Singer sewing machine company made guns and other defense-related equipment, so where should we list it? It's far easier to use a strict alphabetical order, rather than to confuse the reader with topical classifications.

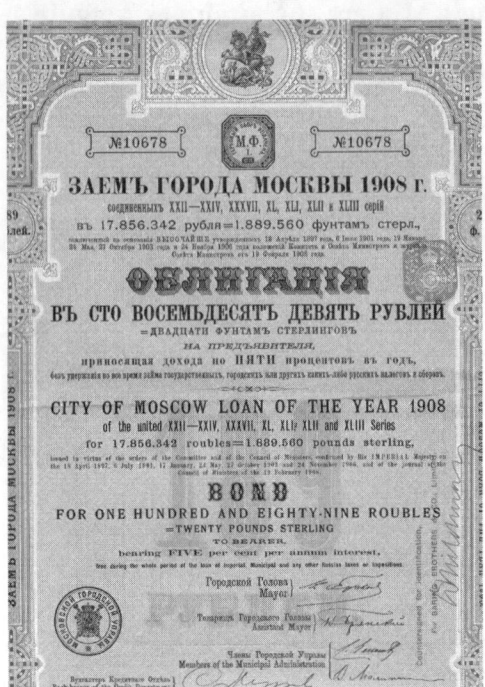

*MO320-70-10, 1912, v, 189 R=£20=504 F Francs=408 Marks=241 Dutch Florins 4-1/2% bearer bond w. coupons, text in Russian-English-French-German, 13" x 18", light brown...**$7.00**

Moscow-Smolensk Railway

*MO360-40-10, 1869, v, 200 Thaler bond w. coupons, text in Russian-German-Dutch, brown **$39.00**

MO360-60-10, 1889, v, 2,000 Mark 4% bond, text in Russian, French and German, grey....**$11.00**

"Naphte" Oil Company, St. Petersburg

*NA240-20-10, 1911, v, 100 Ruble bearer sh. w. coupons, text in Russian and French, 9-3/4" x 13-1/4", blue.......................**$3.00**

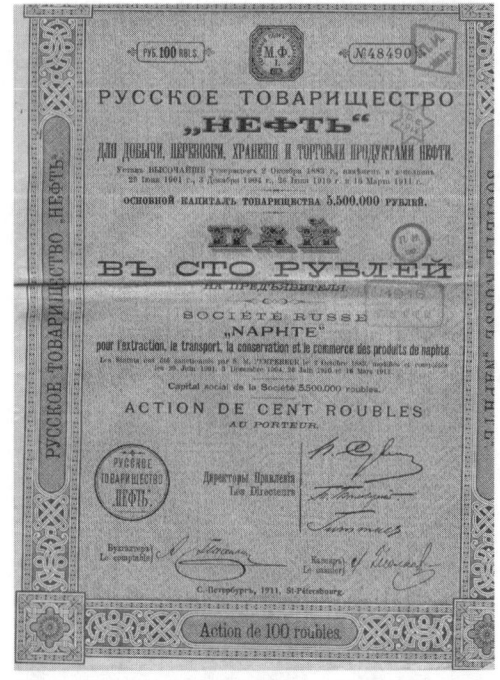

*NA240-20-15, 1913, v, 100 ruble bearer stock w. coupons, text in Russian and French, signature variety, 9-3/4" x 13-1/4", blue **$3.00**

Neftia, pour l'Extraction le transport et le commerce de produits naphta

NE120-30-10, 1914, 100 R bearer sh. with
  coupons. Lilac......................**$7.00**

Peasants Land Bank

PE60-30-10, 1912, 150 Ruble 4-1/2%, green
................................**$12.50**

"Prowodnik" Rubber, Gutta-Percha and Telegraph Company, Riga

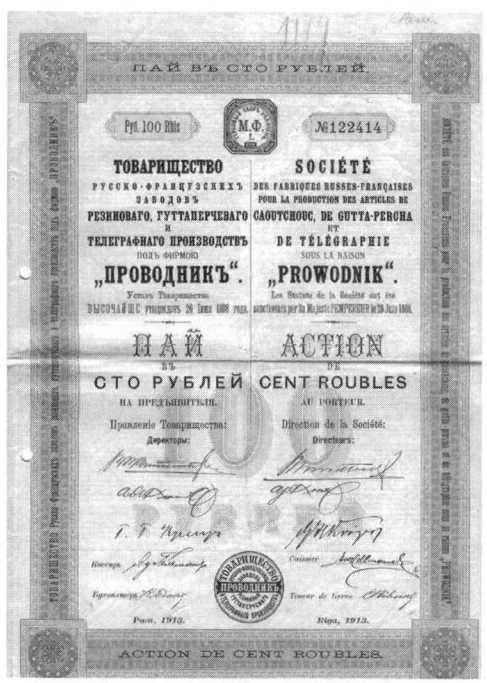

*PR220-30-10, 1913, v, 100 Ruble bearer stock,
  text in French and Russian, w. coupons, 9" x
  12-1/4", brown **$5.00**

Riazan-Uralsk Railway

RI70-40-10, 1897, 187.50 R 4% bond due 1903,
  orange...........................**$15.00**

S.A. Russe de l'Industrie Houillère et Metallurgique dans le Donetz

*RU250-30-10, 1907, v, 112.50 Ruble bearer sh.,
  text in Russian and French, brown.......**$4.00**

The Russian General Oil Corporation, (par £1)

RU310-20-10, 1912, v, 25 bearer sh. w. coupons,
  English-French, orange **$19.50**

Russian Imperial Consolidated Railways

*RU340-40-10, 1889, v, 125 gold Roubles series 2,
  4% bond, blue......................**$6.00**

*RU340-50-10, 1891, v, 125 gold Rubles (625 R) 4% series 3 bond, Dutch revenue rubber stamp, 12" x 16", grey-blue $6.00

Rybinsk Railroad

RY70-30-10, 1895, v, 1/2 Obligation (500 Marks) 4%, green $6.00

RY70-35-10, 1895, 1,000 Mark 4% bond, brown $6.00

St. Petersburg

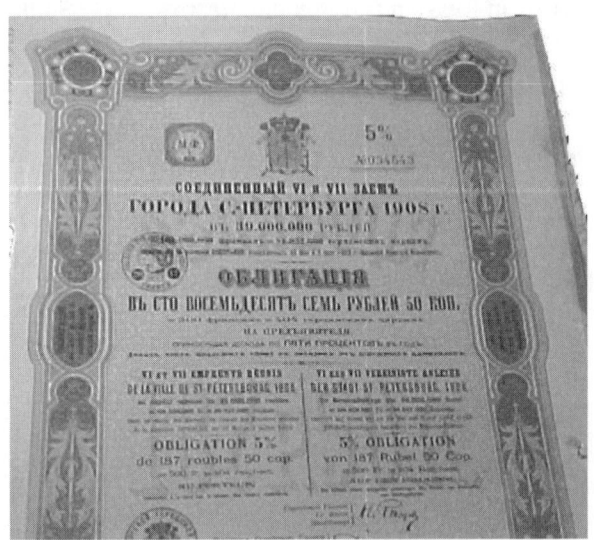

*SA230-40-10, 1908, v, 187.5 R 5% bond, multicolored $6.00

S.A. de St. Petersbourg-Sabountchinskoe pour l'Industrie du Naphthe et le Commerce, Baku

*SA290-30-10, 1912, 100 Ruble bearer sh., brown $5.00

South-East Railway Company

SO290-30-10, 1897, 2,000 Mark 4% bond, text in Russian-Dutch-German, orange $5.00

Troitzk Railway Company

*TR210-40-10, 1913, v, 945 R=£100 4-1/2% bond w. coupons, text in Russian and English, British revenue imprint, 11" x 14", blue border ...$10.00

Ural Railways

UR80-40-10, 1894, 625 R 4% bond, blue ...**$8.00**

Société de l'Usine Mécanique V.G. Stoll et Cie.

*US170-20-10, 1910, v, 100 Rubles, text in Russian and French, brown.............**$8.00**

Warsaw-Vienna Railways

WA230-40-10, 1890, 500 R bond, blue **$8.00**

Wladicaucase Railroad Company

WL80-40-10, 1885, v, 625 R 5 bonds, Dutch revenue rubber stamp, green...........**$5.00**

Post U.S.S.R. Russia

Mavrodi, a pyramid scheme outfit.

*2MA240-10-10, ND, 10 units, 5-3/4" x 2-3/4", red **$1.00**

Trudovogo Collective, Post U.S.S.R. issue

*2TR360-20-10, 19xx, u/u 50 Ruble certificate, MT Goznaka 1989, 7-3/4" x 6", green border on blue...........................**$2.00**

*2TR360-25-10, 19xx, u/u 100 Ruble certificate, MT Goznaka 1989, 7-3/4" x 6", brown border on pink..............................**$2.00**

S

San Marino

Prestito a Premi a vantaggio degli Instituti di Beneficenza e di Previdenza
P30-20-10, 1907, 25 Lira, green and pink . .**$35.00**

Senegal

Crédit Foncier d'Afrique, Dakar

CR240-20-10, 1931, v, 500 F 6% bond w. coupons, 13" x 12", brown **$5.00**

Etablissements A. Lecomte, Dakar

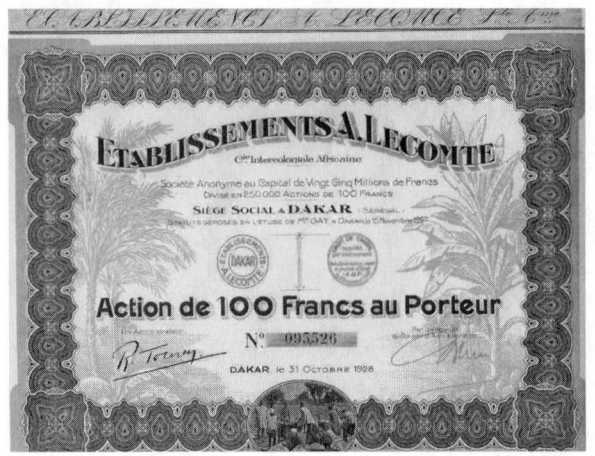

ET50-20-10, 1928, v, 100 F bearer sh., 12-1/2" x 9", grey border **$6.00**

South Africa

East Rand Proprietary Mines, Limited, Transvaal

EA320-20-10, 1927, v, 1 sh., text in English and Afrikaans, 10" x 16", red border **$8.00**

This catalog has listings in an alphabetical format. The reason is simple: Companies diversify as they grow. For example, the Canadian Pacific Railway company recently split into five companies. They represent the railway, hotels, shipping, airline, and petroleum interests of the company. During World War II, the Singer sewing machine company made guns and other defense-related equipment, so where should we list it? It's far easier to use a strict alphabetical order, rather than to confuse the reader with topical classifications.

Golden Valley Citrus Estates Limited (Natal)

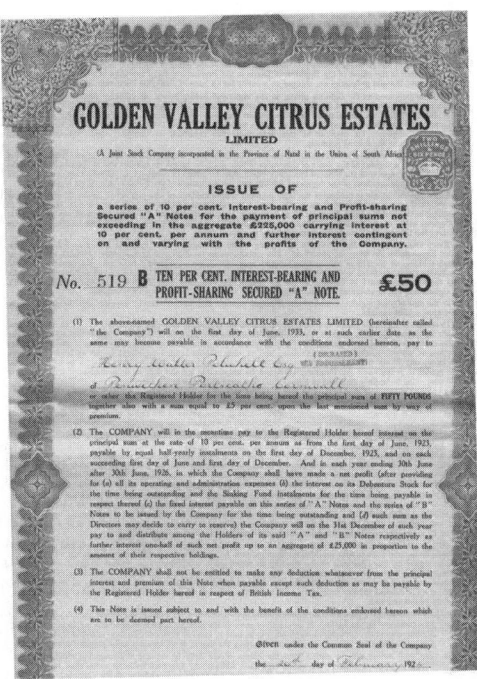

*GO240-30-10, 1924, £50 10% interest bearing and profit sharing secured "A" note, Straker Brothers Limited, 8" x 18", lilac.........$5.00

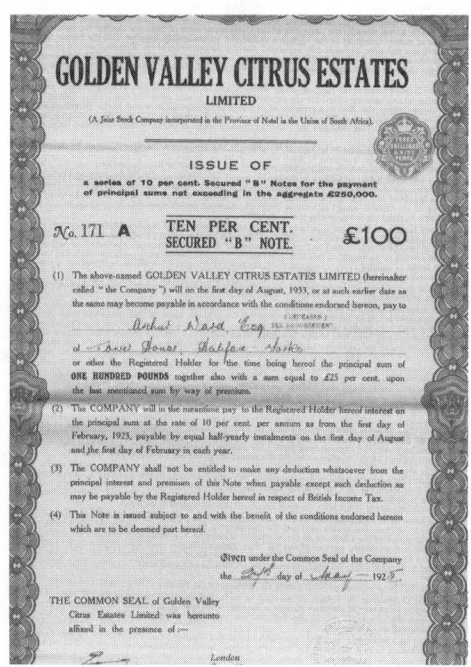

*GO240-35-10, 1925, £100 10% interest bearing and profit sharing secured series "B" note, Bradbury, Wilkinson & Co. Engravers, New Malden, Surrey; 11" x 17-3/4", purple $5.00

New State Areas Limited, (par £1) Johannesburg, Transvaal

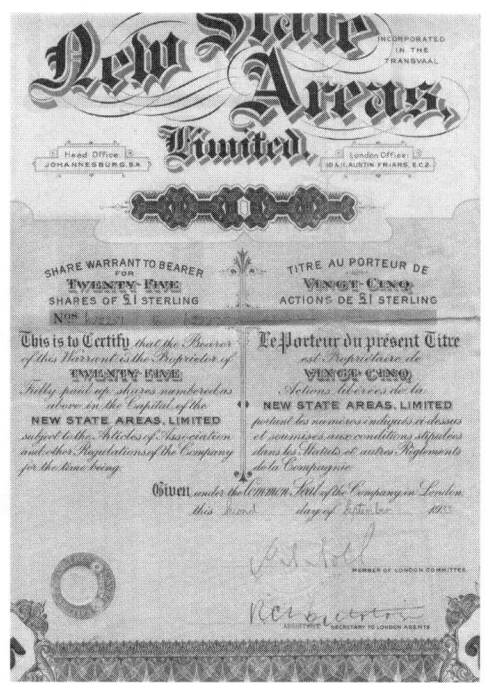

*NE80-20-10, 1933, 25 sh. bearer stock warrant w. coupons, text in English and French, English and French revenue imprints, w/o imprint name, 12-1/2" x 15-1/4", blue................$4.00

The Simmer Deep, Limited

*SI240-30-10, 1907, £100 1st debenture, deep blue $7.00

Union Free State Coal & Gold Mines Limited, (par 5/-) Johannesburg

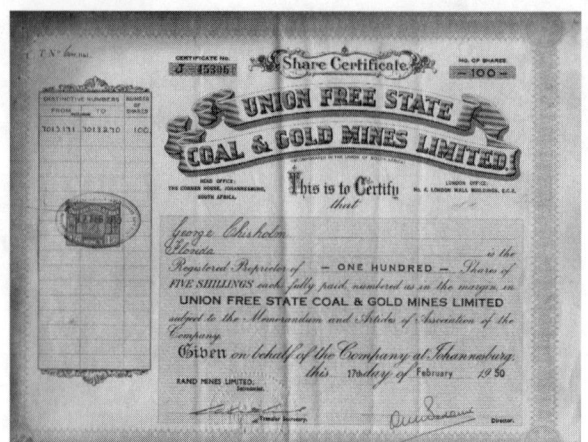

*UN80-30-10, 1950, i/u 100 sh., green $5.00

Spain

Kingdom of Spain

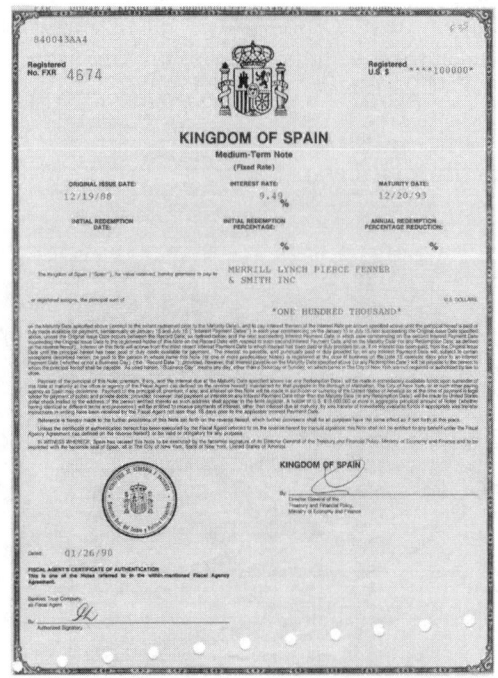

*140-70-10, 1988, v, $100,000 medium term note 9.49%, due 1993, no printers name, 8-1/2" x 11", black on greenish paper $5.00

S.A. Argentifero de Cordoba

*AR160-20-10, 1916, v, 50 Peseta bearer share w. coupons, green $5.00

F. Ballbé S.A., Tarassa (1945)

*BA140-20-10, 1945, 1 sh. (1,000 Peseta) w. coupons, Imp. Juan Morral.-Calvo Sotelo, 13" x 8-1/4", brown border..............$3.00

Bilbaina de Edificacion S.A.

BI70-30-10, 1948, v, 500 Peseta bearer sh., grey border, red-orange. $4.00

Sociedad Española de Carburos Metálicos S.A., Barcelona

An engineering company.

CA240-20-10, 1967, 500 P bearer sh., 12" x 7", brown border. $3.00

Catalana de Gas y Electricidad, S.A., Barcelona (1946)

CA260-40-10, 1973, v, 1 bearer sh. (par 500 P) w. coupons, Rieusset S.A.-Barcelona, 12" x 7-1/4", grey. $3.00

Compañia General de Coches y Automoviles S.A., Barcelona

CO110-20-10, 1910, v, 500 P series A bearer sh. w. coupons, 11" x 9-3/4", green $35.00

S.A. de Distribución, Edición y Librerias, Madrid (1951)

DI260-40-10, 1 class D bearer sh. (par 1,000 P) w. coupons, w/o imprint, 12" x 8-1/2", blue border $3.00

Eléctricas Reunidas de Zaragoza S.A., Zaragoza

EL130-30-10, 1966, v, 500 P bearer sh. w. coupons, 8-1/2" x 12", grey border $5.00

La España Industrial

ES310-20-10, 1850, 2,000 Reales share certificate, black. $13.00

Sociedad General Aguas de Barcelona

GE150-30-10, 1974, 500 Peseta bearer stock, green
.....................................$8.00

Compañia General de Ferrocarriles Catalans

*GE220-40-10, 1924, v, 500 Peseta 6% bond,
brown $5.00

Hidro-Electrica del Duero, Bilbao

*HI90-30-10, 1904, v, bearer sh. w. coupons,
14" x 10", brown on rose $6.00

UNLISTED TYPES & VARIETIES

Readers are welcome to contact the author
directly at:

**Rainer Stahlberg
P.O. Box 1044
Rooseveltown, New York 13683**

Hidroeléctrica Española S.A., Madrid

*HI120-40-10, 1965, v, 500 P bearer sh. w.
coupons, greenish border on blue.......$10.00

S.A. Hidroelectrica Iberica, "Iberduero", Bilbao

HI170-30-10, 1969, v, bearer share w. coupons,
grey border on red $5.00

Hijo de E.F. Escofet S.A., Barcelona (1960)

*HI220-30-10, 1967, 5 bearer sh. (par 500 P) w.
coupons, Inst. Gráf. Oliva de Vilanova S.A.;
13-1/4" x 9-1/4", green border on dark beige
.....................................$3.00

Hilaturas Caralt-Perez S.A., Barcelona

HI240-20-10, 1920, v, 1,000 P series P bearer sh.
w. coupons, brown border $5.00

Compañia Hispano-Americana de Electricidad

HI380-30-10, 1920, v, 500 Peseta series B bearer share w. coupons, brown on pink **$4.00**

Hotel Principe de Asturias

*HO220-30-10, 1921, v, 500 Pesetas bearer sh., green **$10.00**

Industrial Boyer, S.A., Barcelona

IN190-20-10, 1962, 1,000 P bearer sh., 12" x 9", grey border **$3.00**

The value of a stock certificate depends on:

- **rarity**
- **the issuer**
- **signatures**
- **quality of engraving**
- **overall appearance**
- **condition**
- **date of issue**

Industrias Textiles Extremeñas S.A., Badajoz (1954)

*IN240-30-10, 1960, 1 bearer sh. (par 5,000 P) w. coupons, w/o imprint, 11-3/4" x 10", blue border **$3.00**

Indycom S.A., Madrid

IN280-20-10, 1969, 1 bearer sh. w. coupons, red border **$3.00**

Inmobiliaria Fama, S.A., Barcelona (1964)

*IN340-20-10, 1965, 1 bearer sh. (par 1,000 P), w/o imprint, 12-1/2" x 10-1/2", blue border on orange **$3.00**

Islas del Guadalquivir S.A.

IS160-20-10, 1926, v, bearer stock w. 42 coupons, green **$9.00**

Lindner Española, S.A.

*LI160-40-10, ND, 10,000 Peseta sh., light green
..................................$3.00

Locomoción y Garages S.A., Barcelona

*LO300-40-10, 1949, bearer sh. w. revenue stamps
on the back, blue....................$3.00

UNLISTED TYPES & VARIETIES

Readers are welcome to contact the author
directly at:

    Rainer Stahlberg
    P.O. Box 1044
    Rooseveltown, New York 13683

La Maquinista Terrestre y Maritima, Barcelona (1855)

*MA240-50-10, 1952, 1 bearer sh. (par 500 P),
Seix y Barral -Barcelona, 13-1/2" x 9", green
..................................$5.00

Minas de Carmenes S.A.
MI200-30-10, 1903, v, 500 Peseta series A bearer
stock, blue and brown................$17.00

Minas de Hierro de Arditurri
MI280-20-10, 1905, v, 250 Peseta bearer stock,
brown $15.00

Compañia Minera Ignacio Rodriguez Ramos S.A.

*MI340-30-10, 1910, v, 500 Peseta bearer sh., text
in Spanish-English-French, green $3.00

Compañia Minero-Metalurgica los Guindos S.A., Madrid

MI390-30-10, 1920, v, 500 Peseta bearer sh., 15" x 8", brown $5.00

Palacio de Hielo y del Automovil de Madrid S.A.

PA180-30-10, 1921, v, 500 pesetas bearer sh. w. coupons, green $25.00

Compañia Petrolifera Iberica, S.A.

PE260-30-10, 1957, 1,000 Peseta bearer sh. w. coupons, o/p Intransferible a Extranuero, green border $3.00

Tejusa, S.A., Barcelona (1955)

TE170-30-10, ND, 1 bearer sh. (par 1,000 P), Moreta, 12-1/4" x 9", blue border $3.00

Sociedad Anónima Textil Igualadina, Barcelona (1957)

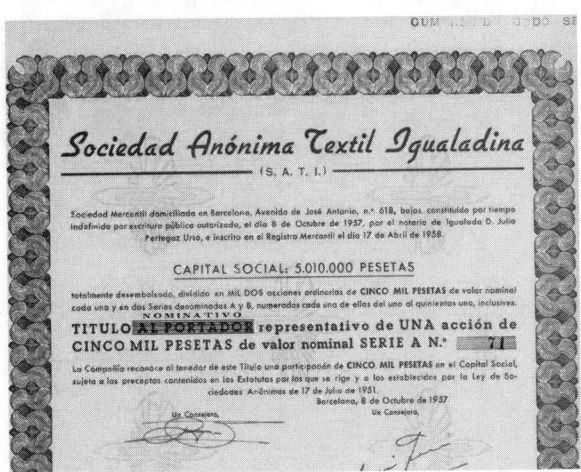

TE290-10-10, 1957, 1 sh. (par 5,000 P), w/o imprint, 12-1/4" x 11", blue border $3.00

The value of a stock certificate depends on:
- rarity
- the issuer
- signatures
- quality of engraving
- overall appearance
- condition
- date of issue

Union Espanola de Explosivos S.A., Madrid (1896)

*UN180-50-10, 1969, v, 500 peseta bearer sh. w. coupons, Editorial Vasca Miriam S.A. Bilbao, 13" x 8-1/4", brown on green $4.00

Vapores Industriales S.A., Tarrasa

*VA240-40-10, 1945, 1,000 Peseta bearer sh., green $4.00

Vinos Gasificados Blanxart S.A., San Sadurni de Noya

VI180-20-10, 1916, v, 500 P sh., 12" x 9-1/4", brown $11.00

> **It is generally assumed that only 5% of certificates survive to reach collectors.**

Viuda de José Tolrá, S.A., Castellar del Vallés (1975)

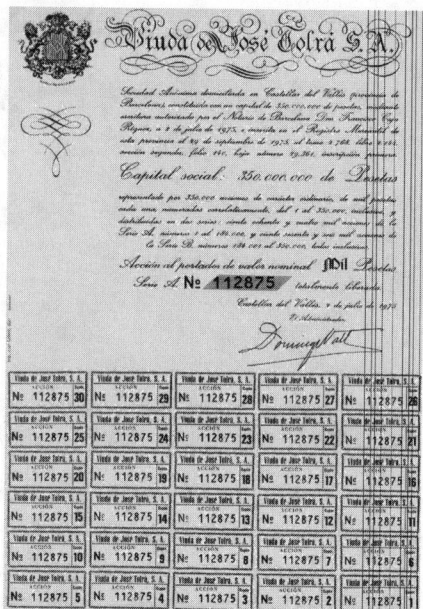

*VI340-10-10, 1975, v, 1 bearer sh. (par 1,000 P), Imp. Joan Sallent, Sucr. Sabadell; 8-1/4" x 11-3/4", black on white $4.00

Sweden

AB Kreuger & Toll, Stockholm

*KR140-30-10, 1928, 500 Kr. 3% debenture, wine red $15.00

Nordiska Textilaktiebolaget

*N40-20-10, 1919, 100 Kr. sh. w. coupons, blue
..................................$6.00

Saab-Scania

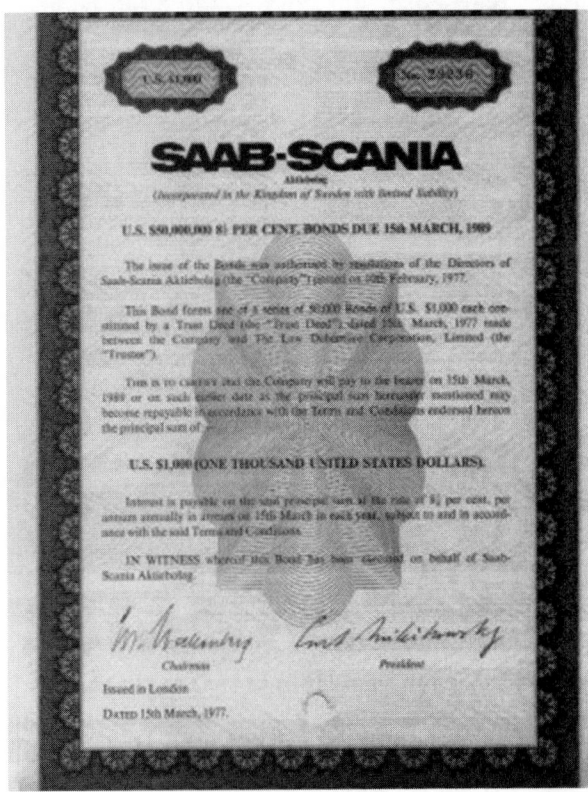

*SA320-50-10, 1977, $1,000 bond........$25.00

Svenska Kullager-Fabriken AG, SKF

*SV50-30-10, 1918, v, 10 sh. (par 100 Kronor),
black on pink $10.00

Kingdom of Sweden

*SV70-90-10, 1984, v, $62,000 series A zero
coupon bond, due 1990, brown $7.00

Switzerland

Brienz-Rothhornbahn-Gesellschaft, Bern

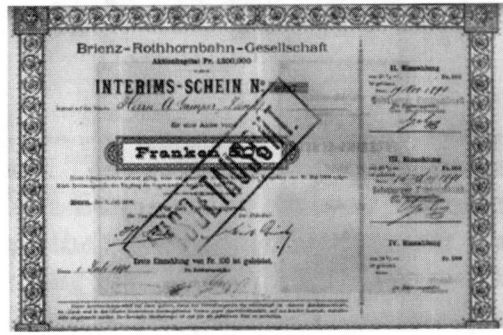

*BR150-20-10, 1890, 500 F interim sh.,
brown-beige $13.00

Crossair AG, Basel

*CR330-20-10, ND, v, 250 F sh., blue and pink
...................................$10.00

Curling-Club Küsnacht ZH, Küsnacht

*CU260-20-10, 1962, 500 F bearer sh., red-orange
...................................$3.00

Eisenbahngesellschaft Oensingen-Balstahl

*EI370-40-10, 1919, 500 F 5% bond, blue-green
border $19.00

Société Générale des Condensateurs Électriques S.A., Fribourg

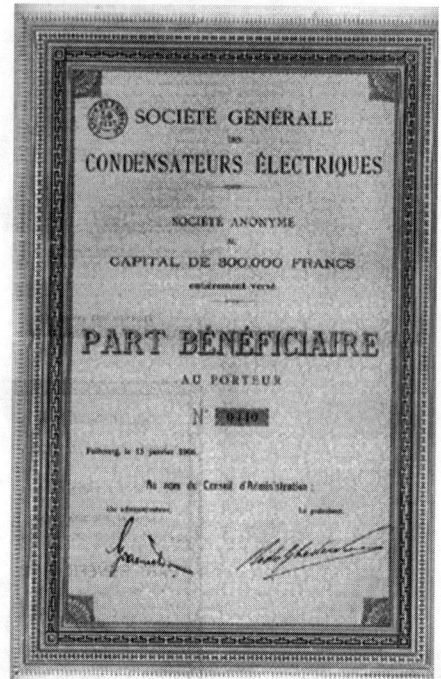

*GE270-20-10, 1906, bearer sh., blue on brown
...................................$3.00

Grand Casino de Chamonix-Mont Blanc

*GR80-30-10, 1923, v, 100 F bearer stock, blue
border $12.00

Kuntstoff-Presswerk AG Birmensdorf/ Zürich

*KU230-40-10, 1936, 100 F share, brown . . .$3.00

Luftseilbahn Erlenbach I.S. -Stockhorn AG, Erlenbach I.S.

*LU150-40-10, 1963, v, 500 F bearer sh., dark grey
. . . .$5.00

Montreux-Berner Oberland Bahn, Montreux

MO270-20-10, 1944, 100 F bearer sh. w. coupons, blue $10.00

Mystery Park AG

Based on Erich von Däniken's writings.

*MY190-20-10, 200x, v, 10 F bearer sh., blue
. . . .$19.00

Naphthagruben "Minerva", Lucerne

*NA240-30-10, 1923, 1,000 F bearer sh., brown
. . . .$5.00

Pilatus-Barn-Geselschaft Alpnach, Alpnach

*PI190-30-10, 1936, v, 100 F preferred bearer sh., green $7.00

Skilift AG Alpenrose Bumbach-Lochseite

*SK180-20-10, 1975, u/u 500 Fr. share certificate, blue $6.00

Skilift Rüschegg AG

*SK220-30-10, 1979, 100 Fr. share cert. w. coupons, green $3.00

Swissair

SW180-40-10, 1987-1993, v, 3% bond option certificate, pink and grey $25.00

S.A. de Transport Aerien Geneve, SATA, Geneva

*TR90-20-10, 1974, v, 100 F share, blue and light blue. $5.00

Verband Schweizeischer Eisenbahn-Vorarbeiter

VE270-30-10, 1917, v, 5 F, grey $4.00

T

Tunisia

Société Civile Immobilière Domaine Wood, Ras Tabia

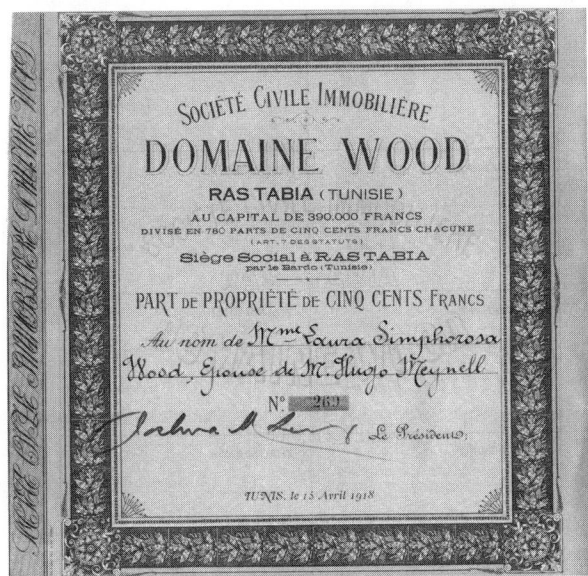

*IM100-20-10, 1918, 500 F bearer property claim w. coupons, Lith. A. Beau Fils & Cie. Tunis; 8-1/2" x 8-3/4", blue border $9.00

S.A. des Mines de Plomb & de Zinc du Djebel Oudiba (Tunisie), Tunis

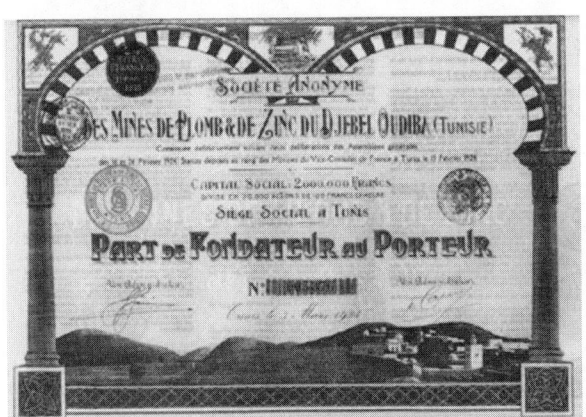

*MI140-10-10, 1924, founder's bearer stock, blue $13.00

Turkey

Chemins de Fer Orient

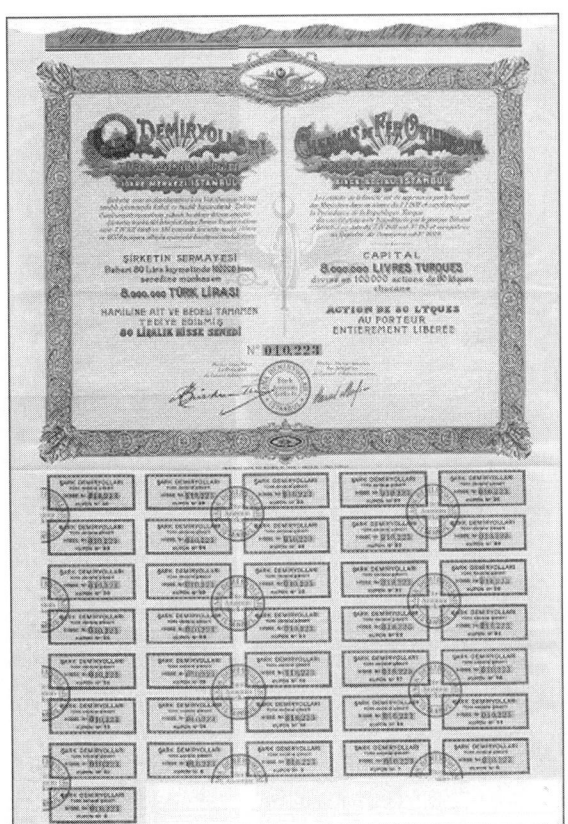

*CH90-30-10, 1936, v, 80 Lire bearer stock w. coupons, green $15.00

Conseil de la Dette Publique Répartie de l'Ancien Empire Ottoman

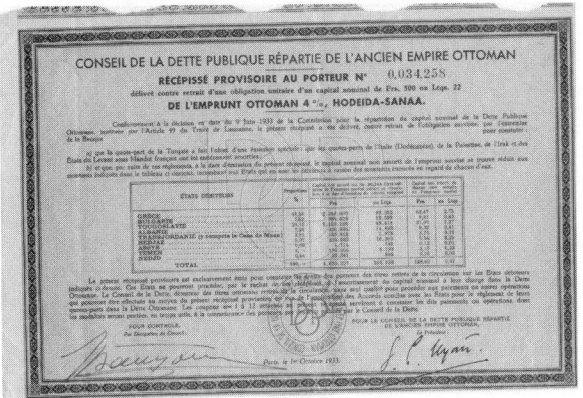

*CO180-30-10, 1933, 500 Franc 4% bearer bond, French text, Imprimerie Spéciale de Banque Paris, 10-3/4" x 6-3/4", brown $6.00

Compagnie Eaux de Constantinople S.A.

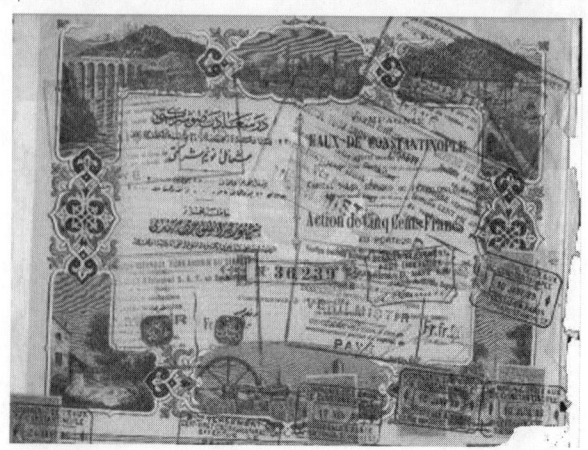

EA220-20-10, 1884, 500 F bearer share, text in
Turkish and French, blue **$7.00**

S.A. des Mines de Balia-Karaidin

MI240-20-10, 1922, v, 100 F=£4=LTQS 4.40
bearer share w. coupons, text in French-Arabic,
Viellamard Imp., 12-1/2" x 9", brown **$6.00**

U

Ukraine

Diakom-Ukraina
One of the many pyramid schemes where investors
lost all of their money.
DI30-20-10, 1993, 10,000 Karbo., unissued
certificate $4.00

Uruguay

Compania Aeronautica Uruguaya S.A., Montevideo

*AE30-20-10, 1936, v, 5 bearer sh. (par 100 Pesos),
green border $8.00

S.A. Molinera y Panificadora del Uruguay, Montevideo
Bread maker.

*MO140-20-10, 1930, v, bearer sh. (par 5 Peso
gold), brown border on green..........$7.00

This catalog has listings in an alphabetical
format. The reason is simple: Companies
diversify as they grow. For example, the
Canadian Pacific Railway company
recently split into five companies. They
represent the railway, hotels, shipping, airline, and petroleum interests of the company. During World War II, the Singer
sewing machine company made guns and
other defense-related equipment, so where
should we list it? It's far easier to use a
strict alphabetical order, rather than to
confuse the reader with topical classifications.

Y

Yugoslavia

Principality of Serbia

*80-30-10, 1881, v, 100 Franc bond, red **$6.00**

Royal Serbian Government Loan

*120-20-10, 1888, v, 10 gold Francs (Dinars) prime loan, text in German-Serbian-French, brown
. . . .**$8.00**

*120-40-10, 1895, v, 500 Franc 4% bond, text in French-Serbian-German, blue **$12.00**

Kingdom of Yugoslavia

*190-30-10, 1931, v, 1,000 F 7% stabilization gold loan, text in Serbian and French, brown. .**$12.00**

*190-40-10, 1933, v, 1,000 Franc 5% loan w. coupons, text in French, French revenue imprint of 1934, Markarnica, 13" x 13", maroon border $9.00

Pucka Štediona i Zalozni Zavod Dionicarsko Društvo u Osijeku

Serbian bank.

*PU50-20-10, 1923, v, 100 Dinar bearer share, text in Latin and Cyrillic characters, blue $9.00

Serbian-American Bank

SE80-20-10, 1922, v, 1000 Dinar bearer stock, grey-blue.........................$25.00

Pre-WWI we had Serbia, then post WWI emerged Yugoslavia. Recently we saw the split into Serbia, Maledonia, Croatia, Bosnia, Slovenia, Kosovo and Montenegro. For the sake of simplicity, all of these are listed under Yugoslavia.

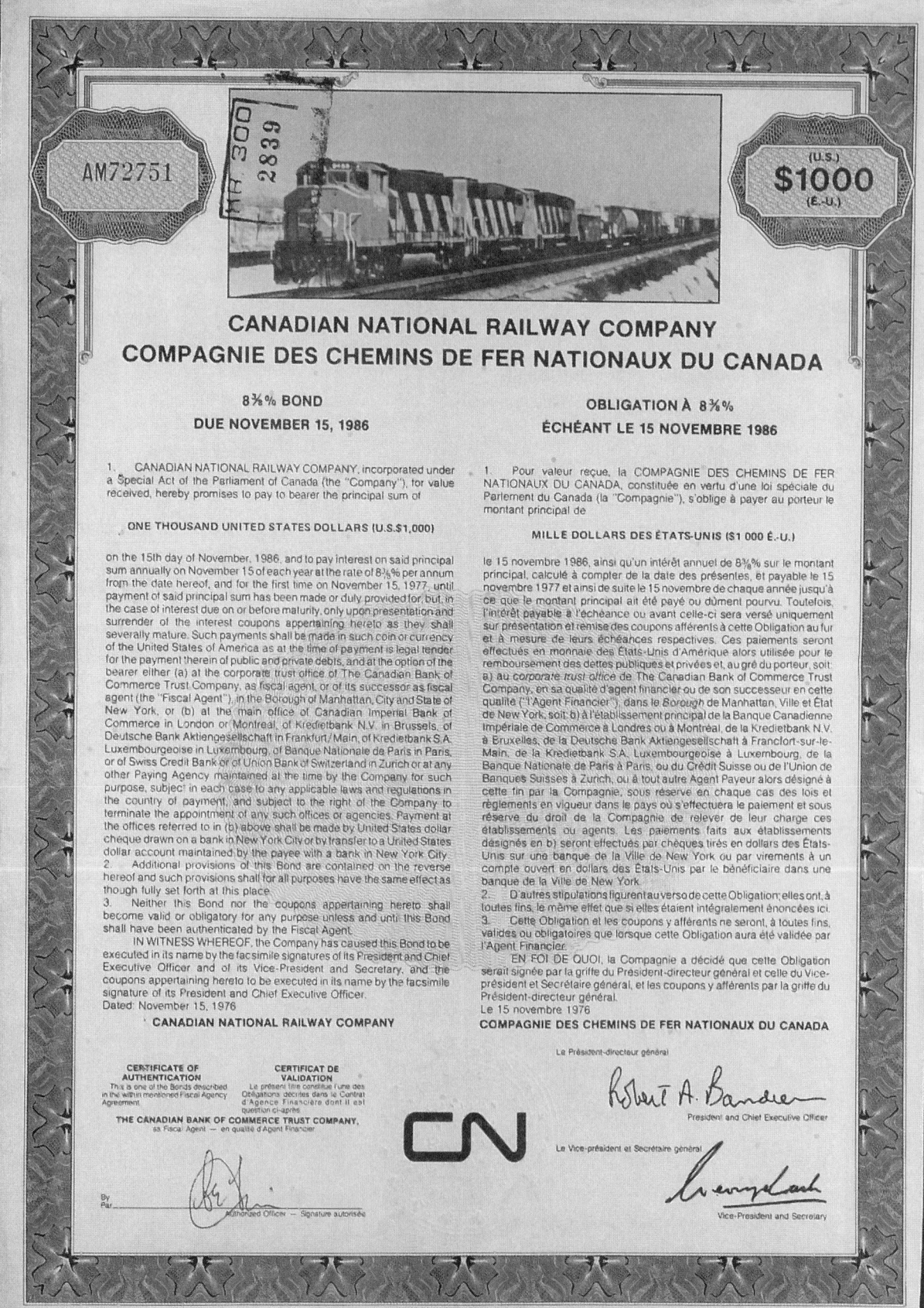

Canadian National Railway Company 8-3/8%, ten year $1000 (U.S. currency) bond dated November 15, 1976. Printed in the duo official languages of English and French.

OBLIGATION À 8¾% ÉCHÉANT LE 15 NOVEMBRE 1986

(suite)

Back of Canadian National Railway Company Bond on preceeding page. Modern bonds, like their very early predecessors, did not have redemption coupons.

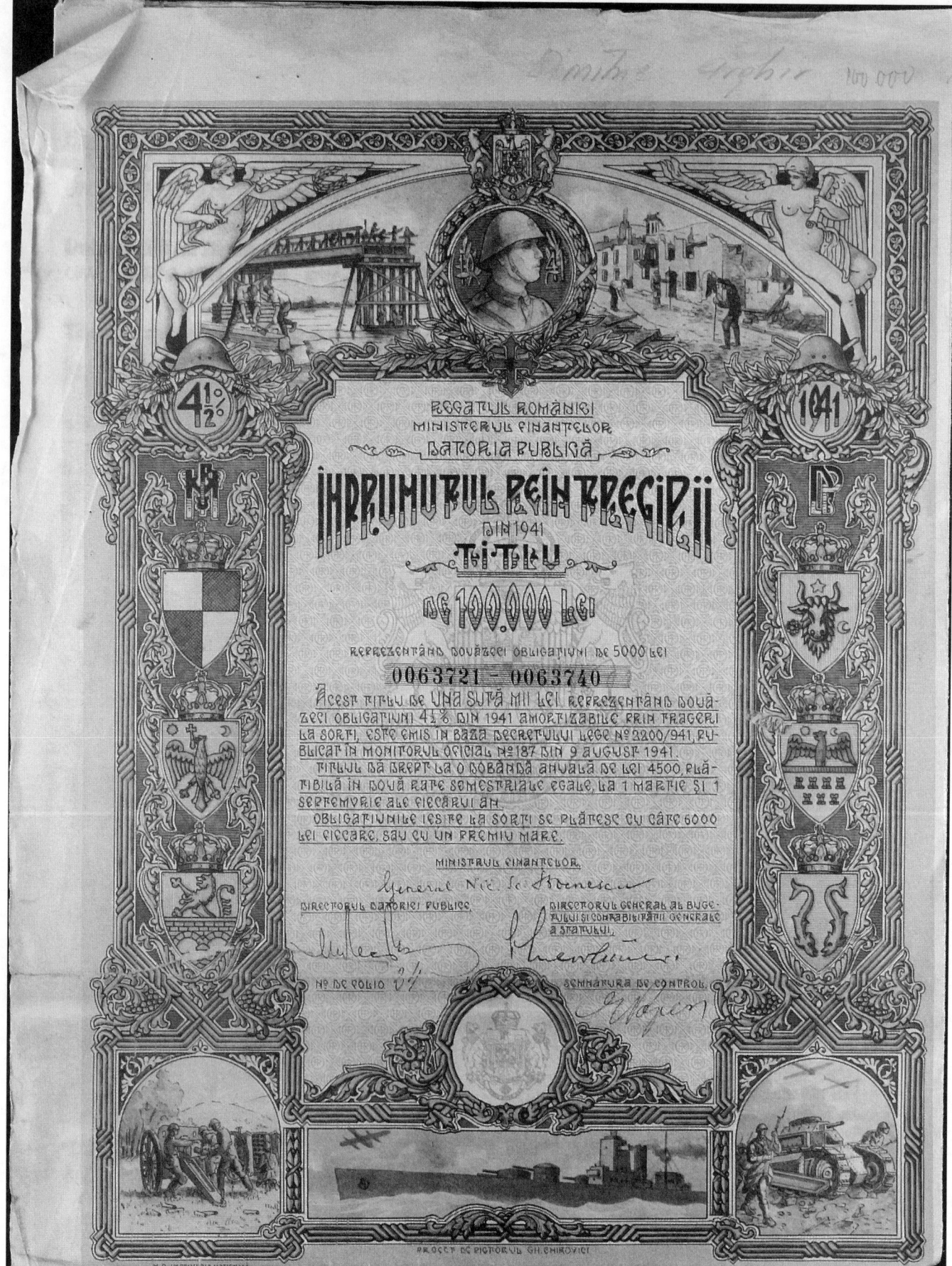

The Public Debt of Romania. Loan for the endowment of the army, dated 1941, 4-1/2%, LEI 100,000.

Redemption coupons of the Romanian LEI 100,000 bond on page 646.

Schatzanweisung des Deutschen Reich. This is a 3-1/2% interest bearing national bond, issued on June 10, 1941. The Nazi German National Bonds were easily distinguished from other bonds of the era by the distinct Nazi Eagle in the underprint.

Nazi German bond redemption coupons of 17 Reichsmark - 50 Pfennig.

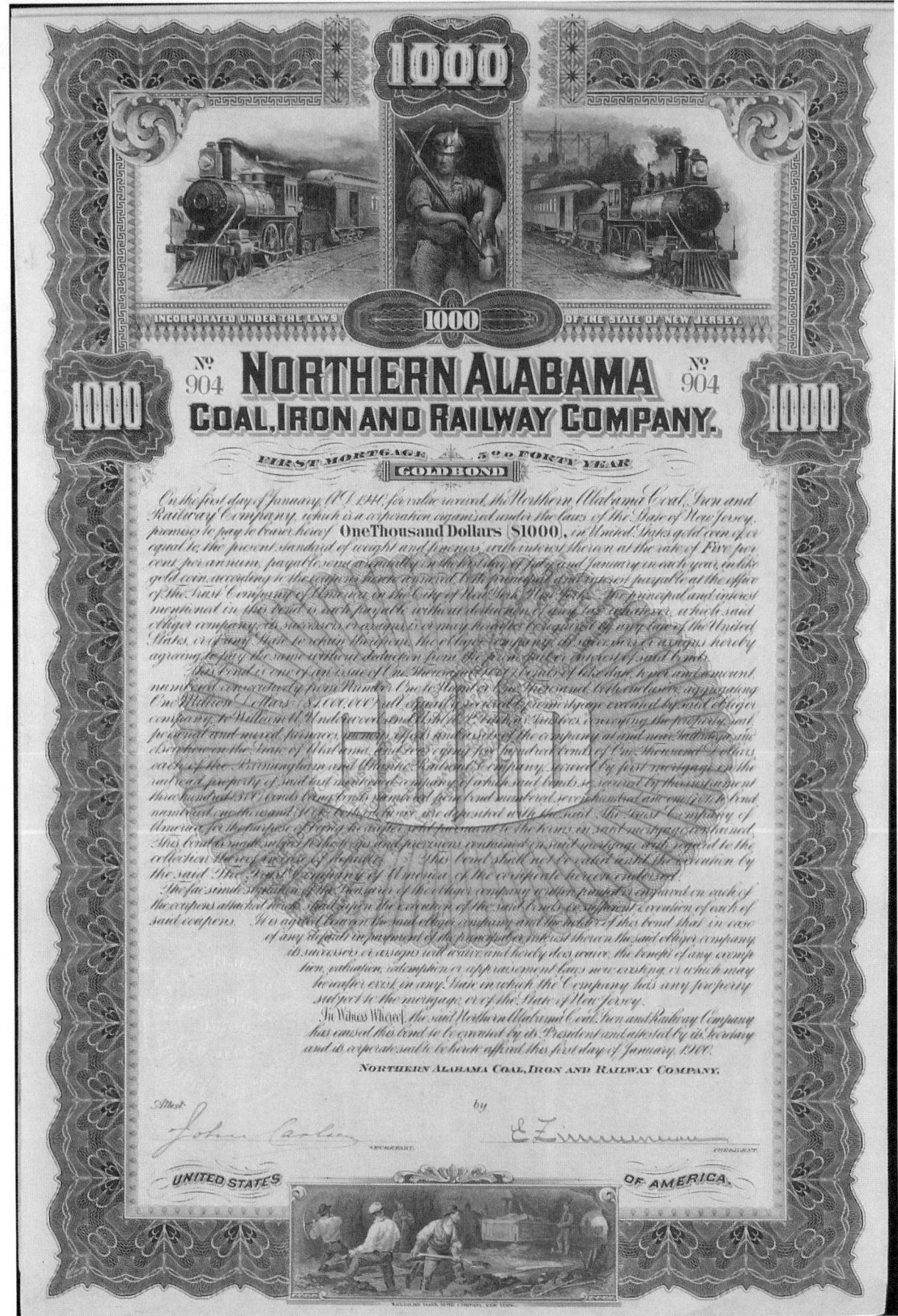

Northern Alabama Coal, Iron and Railway Company. $1000 5% Gold Bond issued on January 1, 1940 in the state of New Jersey.

Redemption coupons for $25.00 of the Northern Alabama Coal, Iron, and Railway Company. $1000 5% Gold Bond.

Index of US Stocks and Bonds

B

C

M

The Moraine Mining Company (IL par $10), 230

Morning Glory Mines, Inc. (par $1), 230

Morris Canal and Banking Company of 1844, 230

The Morris and Essex Railroad Company (NJ), 231

Philip Morris Incorporated (VA), 231

The Mortgage Finance Company of Baltimore, 231

Moulton Mining Company (MT territory par $5), 231

Mount Olive Coal Company (IL par $100), 231

Mount Olive Consolidated Coal-Coke Co. (IL, par $100), 232

Mount Whipple Gold Mining Company (AZ Territory), 232

Mountain City Copper Company (UT), 232

Mull Distributing Corporation (NY par $100), 232

Murray Creek Mining Company, Re-organized (CA 1896), 232

N

Napa and Sonoma Wine Company (1872 par $100), 233

Narragansett Pier Railroad Company, 233

The Nash Motors Company (MD no par), 233

Nashua Corporation (DE par $1), 233

Nashville, Chattanooga and St. Louis Railway Company (par $25), 233

Nashville Electronics, Inc. (TN par $0.10), 233

The Nassau Electric Railroad Company (NY par $100), 233

Natal Day Mining and Milling Company, Ltd. (ID par $1), 233

National Airlines, Incorporated (FL), 233

National Alfalfa Dehydrating & Milling Co. (DE 1946, par $3), 234

National Aviation Corporation, 234

The National Bank of Huntsville (AL par $100), 234

The National Bank of Wilmington and Brandywine, 234

The National Company (PA par $50), 235

National Consolidated Wire and Cable Company (ME par $100), 235

National Copper Company (ID par $1), 235

National Copper Mining Co. Ltd. (ID par $1), 235

National Fuel Gas Company (NJ), 235

National Liberty Insurance Company of America (NY par $2), 235

The National Marine Bank of Baltimore (par $30), 235

National Match Company, 236

National Metals Company (par $1), 236

National Mining Company, 236

The National Oil Refining and Manufacturing Company (AZ territory), 236

The National Onyx Mining, Milling and Improvement Company of Mexico (NJ par $500), 236

National Steel Corporation (DE 1929), 236

National Tea Co. (IL no par), 237

National Tunnel & Mines Company, 237

National Union Bank of Boston (MA 1865, par $100), 237

The National Water Works Company of New York (NY par $100), 237

Needham, Harper & Steers, Inc., 237

Needham Piano and Organ Company, 237

The Neighborhood Corporation (MD 1919, par $50), 238

Nekoosa-Edwards Paper Company (WI), 238

The Nellie Mining Company (AZ par $1), 238

The Nelson Mining Company (MT par 10¢), 238

Nevada Belmont Copper Mines Company (NV 1909, par $1), 238

Nevada Goldfield Reduction Company of Nevada (NV), 238

Nevada and Mountain Lakes Ice Co., 238

Nevada Power Company (NV par $1), 238

Nevada Quicksilver Mines, Incorporated (NV 1927 par $1), 238

New Bedford Acceptance Corporation of New Bedford, Massachusetts (MA), 239

New Bedford, Martha's Vineyard and Nantucket Steamboat Company, 239

City of New Britain, CT, 239

O

P

Quinby Oil Corporation (DE), 297
Quincy Mining Company (MI par $25), 297
Quincy Turn-Verein (par $10), 297

R

Racine Hardware Manufacturing Company
(WI par $100), 298
Radio Corporation of America (no par), 298
Radium Mothene Manufacturing Company
(WA par $1), 298
Railroad Electric Safety Appliance Company
(ME par $25), 298
The Ramie Company of America (par $50), 298
Range States Oil Company, Inc.
(NE par $0.10), 298
Raritan River Railroad Company, 298
The Rawhide Box Company (DE par $1), 298
Rawhide Coalition Mines Company (par $1), 299
The Raycraft Realty Company (NV), 299-300
Reading Company (PA no par), 299
Reading Fair Company, 300
Red Bird Mining Company
(WA 1924, par $0.10), 300
Red Hill Florence Mining Company
(NV 1916, par $0.10), 300
Red Hill Mining Company (AZ par $1), 300
The Red Hook Building Company
(NY par $1), 300
The Red Mountain Railroad, Mining & Smelting
Co. (AZ par $1), 300
Reiter-Foster Oil Corporation
(DE 1924, par $0.50), 301
The Reliable Mining Co. (WI par $1), 301
The Reliance Electric and Engineering Company
(OH), 301
Remington Rand Corporation, 301
Remington Rand Inc. (DE par $1), 301
Remsen Realty Company (NY par $100), 301
The Renhan Realty Corp. (no par), 301
Reo Motor Car Company (MI par $10), 301
Reorganized Kewanas Mining Company (NV),
301
Reorganized Pioneer Mines Company
(NV 10¢), 302
Republic Bank (PA 1987, par $5), 302

Republic Golden Gate Mining Company
(WA par 5¢), 302
Republic Insurance Company of Chicago, 302
Republican Valley & Kansas Railroad Company
(NE), 302
Research Investing Corporation
(NJ 1959, par $1), 302
Retzloff Chemical Company (par $10), 302
The Revine Gold Mining Company
(CO par $1), 302
Rheolite Company (WI par $25.00), 302
The Rhinelander Iron Mining Company (par
$25), 303
Richfield Oil Corporation (DE), 303
Richmond and Danville Railroad Company, 303
The Rico Mining Company (CO par $10), 303
Rifle Development Co. (CO par $500), 303
Ringling Bros.-Barnum & Bailey Combined
Shows, Inc., 303
Rio Grande Auto Sales (CO par $100), 304
Rio Grande Valley Gas Company
(TX 1946, par $1), 304
River Brand Rice Mills, Inc. (DE par $3.50), 304
The River-City Press, Inc., 304
The Riverside Iron and Coal Company of
Scranton (PA par $50), 304
Riviana Foods Inc. (DE par $3.50), 304
RJR Holdings Corp. (DE 1988), 304
Road-Runner Auto Company, 304
Roan Antelope Copper Mines Limited, 304
Roanoke Mining Company (ID), 305
Roberts Development Company (MO), 305
Rochester City and Brighton Railroad Company
(par $100), 305
Rochester Gas and Electric Corporation (NY
1904), 305
Rochester and Genesee Valley Railroad (NY
1854 par $100), 305
The Rock Island Company (par $100), 305
Rock Island and Peoria Railway Company, 305
Rocket Jet Engineering Corp. (CA 1951), 305
Rockwell-Poor Company (NY par $100), 306
Rockwell-Standard Corporation, 306
Rollins International, Inc., 306
Rome, Watertown and Ogdensburgh
Rail Road Company (NY), 306

T

Tacoma Boatbuilding Co., 345

Tallulah Falls Railway Company (GA), 345

Tamarack and Chesapeak Mining Company (par $1), 345

Tecopa Consolidated Mining Company (par $1), 345

Tehama Crusade Placers Ltd. (NV), 345

Telepost Company, 345

Tenabo Mining and Smelting Company (NV), 345

Tenneco Corporation, 345

Tennessee Brewing Company (par $100), 345

Tennessee Northern Railway Company (TN par $100), 346

Tennessee Valley Authority (USA), 346

Terminal Elevator Company (AL par $100), 346

Terre-Haute and Richmond Rail-Road Company (IN par $50), 346

The Terry Steam Turbine Company (CT par $5), 346

Texaco Inc. (DE), 347

Republic of Texas, 347

Texas Eagle Oil and Refining Company (DE), 347

Texas Hydro-Electric Corporation, 347

The Texas and Pacific Railway Company (par $100), 347

Texas Southern Oil & Gas Company (TX 1954, par $0.25), 348

Texas Star Flour Mills (TX par $100), 348

Thayer Oil and Gas Co. of Indiana (DE par $1), 348

Thiokol Chemical Corporation (DE 1930, par $1), 348

Third National Bank (TN), 348

Thompson Brothers Lumber Company (TX par $100), 348

J.M. Thompson Lumber Company (TX par $100), 348

Thompson & Tucker Lumber Company (TX par $500), 348

Thomson Divide Mining Company, 348

Three Rivers Development Co. (MT par $1), 349

Thunder Cave Corporation (UT), 349

Thwaites Furniture Company (MI), 349

Tigerton Canning Company (WI par $100), 349

The Times Investment Company, Times Printing Company of Seattle (WA), 350

Timlow Builders, Inc. (PA no par), 350

The Tioga National Bank and Trust Company, 350

Tobacco Products Corporation (VA 1912, no par), 350

Tobacco Shares Group Securities Inc., 351

Toledo and Ohio Central Railway Company (OH par $100), 351

Toman, Inc. (IN no par), 351

Tombstone Mill and Mining Company (CT), 351

Tonopah "76" Consolidated Mining Company (NV par $1), 351

Tonopah Divide Mining Company (NV 1912 par $1), 351

Tonopah Gold, Silver, Copper, Water & Milling Co. (SD par $1), 351

Tonopah and Goldfield Railroad Company (NV par $100), 351

Tonopah Mining Company of Nevada (DE par $1), 352

Tonopah Wall Street Mining Company (AZ territory 1905), 352

Tonopah Western Consolidated Mining Company, 352

Topper Corporation (DE), 352

Toulumme Copper Mining Company (AZ par $1), 352

Tractor Supply Co. (IL), 352

Trail Mines, Inc. (CO), 352

Trans World Airlines, Inc., 352-353

Transamerica Financial Corporation (DE), 353

Trans-Beacon Corporation (DE 1933 par $1), 353

Transcoastal Industries Corp. (NJ 1949, par $1), 353

Transocean Gulf Oil Company (DE), 353-354

Transierra Gold Mining Company (CA), 354

Transtates Petroleum Inc. (NY), 354

George A. Treadwell Mining Company (WV par $10), 354

The Tri-Bullion Smelting and Development Company, 354

The Tronton Rail Road Company (par $50), 354

Tropical Shells, Inc. (FL no par), 355

U

X

Y

Z

Countries Index

D

E

F

G

H

I

N

S

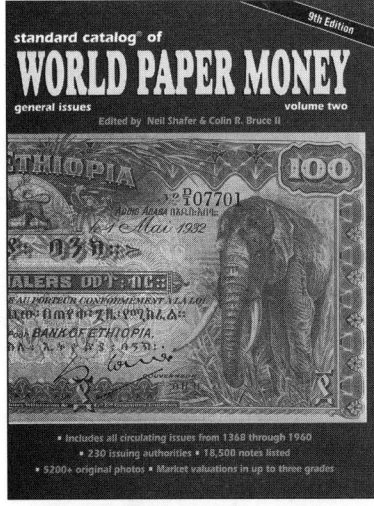

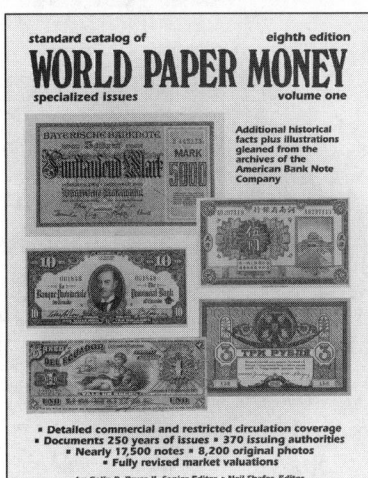
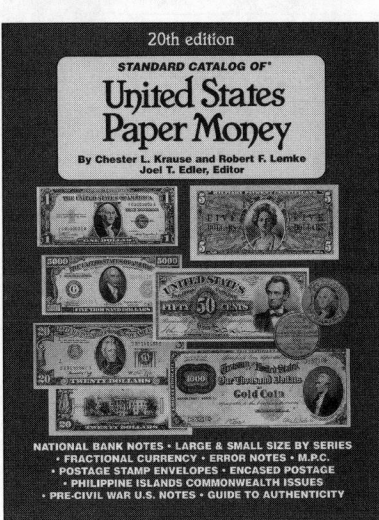

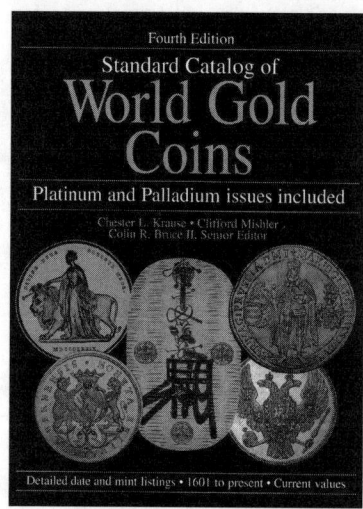